*Second Edition*

# THE GREEKS

## HISTORY, CULTURE, AND SOCIETY

## Ian Morris
*Stanford University*

## Barry B. Powell
*University of Wisconsin-Madison*

**Prentice Hall**
Boston   Columbus   Indianapolis   New York   San Francisco
Upper Saddle River   Amsterdam   Cape Town   Dubai   London   Madrid
Milan   Munich   Paris   Montreal   Toronto   Delhi   Mexico City   Sao Paulo
Sydney   Hong Kong   Seoul   Singapore   Taipei   Tokyo

**Editorial Director:** Leah Jewell
**Executive Editor:** Charles Cavaliere
**Editorial Assistant:** Lauren Aylward
**Marketing Director:** Brandy Dawson
**Marketing Assistant:** Ashley Fallon
**Production Manager:** Wanda Rockwell
**Creative Director:** Jayne Conte
**Cover Designer:** Margaret Kenselaar
**Cover Image:** Kore from the Athenian Acropolis, c. 490 B.C.
  Painted Umestone. Acropolis Museum, Athens
**Manager, Visual Research:** Beth Brenzel
**Manager, Rights and Permissions:** Zina Arabia
**Image Permission Coordinator:** Joanne Dipple
**Manager, Cover Visual Research & Permissions:** Karen Sanatar
**Full-Service Project Management:** Integra

**About the Cover:** The Euthydikos Korê, called "the sulky korê, from the Athenian Acropolis. Inscription on the base reads, "Euthydikos, son of Thaliarchos, dedicated me." Marble, c. 490 BC. (Acropolis Museum, Athens, Greece)

This book was set in 10/12 Palatino

Credits and acknowledgments borrowed from other sources and reproduced, with permission, in this textbook appear in page numbers 547–548.

Copyright © 2010 Pearson Education, Inc., publishing as Prentice Hall, 1 Lake St., Upper Saddle River, NJ 07458. All rights reserved. Manufactured in the United States of America. This publication is protected by Copyright, and permission should be obtained from the publisher prior to any prohibited reproduction, storage in a retrieval system, or transmission in any form or by any means, electronic, mechanical, photocopying, recording, or likewise. To obtain permission(s) to use material from this work, please submit a written request to Pearson Education, Inc., Permissions Department, 1 Lake St., Upper Saddle River, NJ 07458

**Library of Congress Cataloging-in-Publication Data**
Morris, Ian,
  The Greeks : history, culture, and society/Ian Morris, Barry B. Powell. —2nd ed.
    p. cm.
Includes bibliographical references and index.
ISBN-13: 978-0-205-69734-2 (alk. paper)
ISBN-10: 0-205-69734-8
  1. Greece—History—To 146 B.C.   I. Powell, Barry B.   II. Title.

DF214.M69 2010
938—dc22

                                            2009018082

10 9 8 7

**Prentice Hall**
is an imprint of

www.pearsonhighered.com     ISBN 13: 978-0-20-569734-2
                            ISBN 10:     0-20-569734-8

# CONTENTS

Maps   x

Preface   xiii

About the Authors   xvi

**Chapter 1   A Small, Far-Off Land   1**
Historical Sketch   1
Why Study the Greeks?   6
Who Were the Greeks?   7
The Structure of This Book: History, Culture, and Society   10
*Key Terms   11   •   Further Reading   11*

**Chapter 2   Country and People   12**
Greek Geography, Climate, and Agriculture   12
Demography   16
Migration   17
Health and Disease   18
Nutrition   22
Economic Growth in Ancient Greece   25
*Key Terms   26   •   Further Reading   27*

**Chapter 3   The Greeks at Home   28**
Gender Relationships: Ideals and Realities   28
Sexuality   34
Adults and Children   37
*Key Terms   40   •   Further Reading   40*

**Chapter 4   The Greeks Before History, 12,000–1200 B.C.   41**
The End of the Last Ice Age, 13,000–9,500 B.C.   41
The Origins of Agriculture, 9,500–5000 B.C.   42
Greeks and Indo-Europeans   44
Neolithic Society and Economy, 5000–3000 B.C.   45
The Early Bronze Age, 3000–2300 B.C.   46
The Middle Bronze Age, 2300–1800 B.C.   49
The Age of Minoan Palaces, 2000–1600 B.C.   50
The Rise of Mycenaean Greece, 1750–1500 B.C.   59

The End of Minoan Civilization, 1600–1400 B.C.  62

Mycenaean Greece: Archaeology, Linear B, and Homer  63

The End of the Bronze Age, circa 1200 B.C.  67

*Key Terms*  70  •  *Further Reading*  71

**Chapter 5    The Dark Age, 1200–800 B.C.  72**

The Collapse of the Old States  72

Life Among the Ruins  74

Dark Age "Heroes"  75

Art and Trade in the Dark Age  77

The Eighth-Century B.C. Renaissance: Economy  78

The Eighth-Century B.C. Renaissance: Society  80

The Eighth-Century Renaissance: Culture  86

Conclusion  91

*Key Terms*  92  •  *Further Reading*  92

**Chapter 6    Homer  93**

The Homeric Question  93

Milman Parry and Oral Poetry  96

The Oral Poet in Homer  99

Heinrich Schliemann and the Trojan War  100

The Tragic *Iliad*  101

Homer and the Invention of Plot  108

The Comic *Odyssey*  109

Odysseus and Homer  117

*Key Terms*  118  •  *Further Reading*  118

**Chapter 7    Religion and Myth  119**

Definitions of Religion and Myth  119

Hesiod's Myth of the Origin of the Gods  121

Greek Religion in History  124

Forms of Greek Religious Practice  125

Hesiod's Myth of Sacrifice  131

Gods and Other Mysterious Beings  132

Chthonic Religion  139

The Ungrateful Dead and the Laying of the Ghost  140

Ecstatic and Mystical Religion  143

Conclusion  147

*Key Terms*  148  •  *Further Reading*  149

**Chapter 8    Archaic Greece, 800–480 B.C.: Economy, Society, Politics    150**
Government by Oligarchy    150
Elite Culture    158
The Tyrants    167
The Structure of Archaic States    169
Conclusion    172
*Key Terms    172    •    Further Reading    173*

**Chapter 9    The Archaic Cultural Revolution, 700–480 B.C.    174**
Natural Philosophy in Miletus    175
Pythagoras: Philosophy and Social Science in the West    177
Hecataeus, Herodotus, and *Historiê*    179
Lyric poets    180
Material Culture    183
Art and Thought in Sixth-Century Greece    196
*Key Terms    197    •    Further Reading    197*

**Chapter 10    A Tale of Two Archaic Cities: Sparta and Athens, 700–480 B.C.    198**
Sparta    199
Spartiates, *Perioikoi*, and Helots    199
Plutarch's Sparta    202
Spartan Government    208
Athens    209
The Seventh-Century Crisis    209
Solon    211
Pisistratus and the Consequences of Solon's Reforms    214
Dêmokratia    219
Athens Submits to Persia    222
*Key Terms    224    •    Further Reading    224*

**Chapter 11    Persia and the Greeks, 550–490 B.C.    225**
Empires of the Ancient Near East    225
Lydia    229
Cyrus and the Rise of Persia, 559–530 B.C.    230
Cambyses and Darius, 530–521 B.C.    237
Persia's Northwest Frontier and the Ionian Revolt, 521–494 B.C.    242
The Battle of Marathon, 490 B.C.    247
*Key Terms    252    •    Further Reading    252*

**Chapter 12**  **The Great War, 480–479 B.C.  253**

Storm Clouds in the West  254

Storm Clouds in the East  257

The Storm Breaks in the West: The Battle of Himera, 480 B.C.  258

The Storm Breaks in the East: The Battle of Thermopylae, 480 B.C.  260

The Fall of Athens  263

The Battle of Salamis  264

The End of the Storm: Battles of Plataea and Mycale, 479 B.C.  267

Conclusion  271

*Key Terms*  272  •  *Further Reading*  267

**Chapter 13**  **Democracy and Empire: Athens and Syracuse, 479–431 B.C.  273**

The Expansion of the Syracusan State, 479–461 B.C.  274

The Western Democracies, 461–433 B.C.  276

Economic Growth in Western Greece, 479–433 B.C.  277

Cimon and the Creation of the Athenian Empire, 478–461 B.C.  278

The First Peloponnesian War, 460–446 B.C.  282

Pericles and the Consolidation of Athenian Power, 446–433 B.C.  284

Economic Growth in the Aegean  285

The Edge of the Abyss, 433–431 B.C.  290

*Key Terms*  292  •  *Further Reading*  292

**Chapter 14**  **Art and Thought in the Fifth Century B.C.  293**

Philosophy  294

Material Culture  299

*Key Terms*  315  •  *Further Reading*  316

**Chapter 15**  **Fifth-Century Drama  317**

Tragedy  317

The City Dionysia  322

The Theater of Dionysus  323

Narrative Structure  324

Character and Other Dimensions of Tragedy  327

Tragic Plots  329

Conclusion  331

The Origins of Comedy  331

The Plots of Old Comedy  332

The Structures of Old Comedy  333

Conclusion  335

*Key Terms*  336  •  *Further Reading*  336

**Chapter 16   The Peloponnesian War and Its Aftermath, 431–399 B.C.   337**

The Archidamian War, 431–421 B.C.   338

The Peace of Nicias and the Sicilian Expedition, 421–413 B.C.   347

Sicily and the Carthaginian War, 412–404 B.C.   356

The Ionian War, 412–404 B.C.   358

Aftermath, 404–399 B.C.   364

Conclusion   367

*Key Terms*   367   •   *Further Reading*   367


**Chapter 17   The Greeks between Persia and Carthage, 399–360 B.C.   369**

Sparta's Empire, 404–360 B.C.   370

Economy, Society, and War   374

Sparta's Collapse, 371 B.C.   377

Anarchy in the Aegean, 371–360 B.C.   378

Carthage and Syracuse, 404–360 B.C.   379

The Golden Age of Syracuse, 393–367 B.C.   383

Anarchy in the West, 367–345 B.C.   383

Conclusion   384

*Key Terms*   385   •   *Further Reading*   385


**Chapter 18   Greek Culture in the Fourth Century B.C.   386**

Material Culture   386

Plato   395

Aristotle   400

Conclusion   404

*Key Terms*   404   •   *Further Reading*   404


**Chapter 19   The Warlords of Macedon I: Philip II and Alexander the King   406**

Macedonia before Philip II   407

Philip's Struggle for Survival, 359–357 B.C.   410

Philip Consolidates His Position, 357–352 B.C.   411

Philip Seeks a Greek Peace, 352–346 B.C.   412

The Struggle for a Greek Peace, 346–338 B.C.   414

Alexander the King   418

The Conquest of Persia, 334–330 B.C.   420

*Key Terms*   429   •   *Further Reading*   429

**Chapter 20    The Warlords of Macedon II: Alexander the God    430**

The Fall of the Great King Darius, 331–330 B.C.    430

Alexander in the East, 330–324 B.C.    433

War in India, 327–326 B.C.    436

The Long March Home, 326–324 B.C.    438

The Last Days, 324–323 B.C.    441

Conclusion    443

*Key Terms    444  •  Further Reading    444*

**Chapter 21    The Greek Kingdoms in the Hellenistic Century,
                323–220 B.C.    445**

The Wars of the Successors, 323–301 B.C.    446

The Hellenistic World after Ipsus    452

The Seleucid Empire    452

Ptolemaic Egypt    457

The Antigonids: Macedonia    461

Conclusion    463

*Key Terms    463  •  Further Reading    463*

**Chapter 22    The Greek *Poleis* in the Hellenistic Century,
                323–220 B.C.    464**

Impoverishment and Depopulation in Mainland Greece    464

Athens in Decline    467

Sparta's Counterrevolution    467

The Western Greeks: Agathocles of Syracuse (361–289/8 B.C.)    471

Pyrrhus of Epirus    473

Hellenistic Society: The Weakening of Egalitarianism    476

Conclusion    479

*Key Terms    480  •  Further Reading    480*

**Chapter 23    Hellenistic Culture, 323–30 B.C.    481**

Hellenistic Historians    481

Poetry    483

Material Culture    486

Hellenistic Philosophy    495

Medicine    499

Quantitative Science in the Hellenistic Age    502

Conclusion    505

*Key Terms    506  •  Further Reading    506*

**Chapter 24    The Coming of Rome, 220–30 B.C.    507**

The Rise of Rome, 753–280 B.C.    507

Rome, Carthage, and the Western Greeks, 280–200 B.C.    510

Rome Breaks the Hellenistic Empires, 200–167 B.C.    515

Consequences of the Wars: The Greeks    518

Consequences of the Wars: The Romans    520

Rome's Military Revolution    523

The Agony of the Aegean, 99–70 B.C.    524

Pompey's Greek Settlement, 70–62 B.C.    529

The End of Hellenistic Egypt, 61–30 B.C.    531

Aftermath    538

*Key Terms    539    •    Further Reading    539*

**Chapter 25    Conclusion    541**

The Bronze Age (ca. 3000–1200 B.C.; Chapter 4)    541

The Dark Age (ca. 1200–700 B.C.; Chapter 5)    541

The Archaic Period (ca. 700–500 B.C.; Chapters 6–10)    542

The Classical Period (ca. 500–350 B.C.; Chapters 11–18)    542

The Macedonian Takeover (ca. 350–323 B.C.; Chapters 19–21)    543

The Hellenistic Period (ca. 323–30 B.C.; Chapters 22–24)    543

Conclusion    544

*Pronunciation Guide    545*

*Credits    547*

*Index    549*

# MAPS

## CHAPTER 1

MAP 1.1 The Ottoman Empire   2
MAP 1.2 Greek colonies   4
MAP 1.3 Modern Greece and the Balkans   8
MAP 1.4 Distribution of Greek ethnic groups during the Classical Period   10

## CHAPTER 4

MAP 4.1 The maximum extent of the ice sheet   42
MAP 4.2 The Fertile Crescent   43
MAP 4.3 Branches of the Indo-European family   44
MAP 4.4 Sites in Greece mentioned in Chapter 4   47
MAP 4.5 Map of Crete showing where ruins of Minoan palaces
        have been found   51

## CHAPTER 5

MAP 5.1 East Mediterranean areas mentioned in Chapter 5   73
MAP 5.2 Greek sites mentioned in Chapter 5   74
MAP 5.3 Phoenician trade routes in the Mediterranean   77

## CHAPTER 8

MAP 8.1 Sites mentioned in Chapter 8   152
MAP 8.2 The inter-city aristocracy; origins of the suitors for Agariste's hand   165

## CHAPTER 9

MAP 9.1 Sites mentioned in Chapter 9   175

## CHAPTER 10

MAP 10.1 Regions and sites mentioned in Chapter 10   200
MAP 10.2 Origins of fifty-four Athenian slaves   215
MAP 10.3 Complicated political landscape created by
         Cleisthenes' reforms   220

## CHAPTER 11

MAP 11.1 The Assyrian and Lydian Empires   226
MAP 11.2 The Persian Empire   231
MAP 11.3 The Persian invasions of 493 and 490 B.C.   247

## CHAPTER 12

**MAP 12.1**  West Mediterranean sites mentioned in Chapter 12    **255**
**MAP 12.2**  The Aegean campaign of 480 B.C.    **261**
**MAP 12.3**  The campaign of 479 B.C.    **268**


## CHAPTER 13

**MAP 13.1**  Western Mediterranean sites mentioned in the chapter    **275**
**MAP 13.2**  Sites in Aegean Greece mentioned in Chapter 13    **279**
**MAP 13.3**  Cities in the Athenian alliance, 449 B.C.    **280**
**MAP 13.4**  Theaters of war where Athenians of the Erechtheid tribe died    **283**
**MAP 13.5**  Sources of Athenian imports    **287**


## CHAPTER 14

**MAP 14.1**  Sites mentioned in Chapter 14    **294**


## CHAPTER 16

**MAP 16.1**  The Archidamian War and Peace of Nicias: Aegean sites mentioned
in Chapter 16    **337**
**MAP 16.2**  Sites in Sicily mentioned in Chapter 16    **341**
**MAP 16.3**  Map of the Pylos campaign, 425 B.C.    **342**
**MAP 16.4**  The first phase of the siege of Syracuse    **352**
**MAP 16.5**  The second phase of the Siege of Syracuse    **354**
**MAP 16.6**  The Ionian War and sites mentioned in Chapter 16    **359**
**MAP 16.7**  The Aegospotamoi campaign    **363**


## CHAPTER 17

**MAP 17.1**  The March of the 10,000    **371**
**MAP 17.2**  Aegean sites mentioned in Chapter 17    **372**
**MAP 17.3**  Sites in western Greece mentioned in Chapter 17    **379**


## CHAPTER 18

**MAP 18.1**  Sites mentioned in Chapter 18    **387**


## CHAPTER 19

**MAP 19.1**  Sites in northern Greece and Macedonia mentioned in Chapter 19    **408**
**MAP 19.2**  Aegean sites mentioned in Chapter 19    **411**
**MAP 19.3**  Alexander's invasion of the Persian Empire    **421**

# CHAPTER 21

**MAP 21.1** Main kingdoms and locations from the Wars of the Successors  **447**
**MAP 21.2** The Hellenistic world, 300 B.C.  **453**
**MAP 21.3** Third-century B.C. sites mentioned in Chapter 21  **455**

# CHAPTER 22

**MAP 22.1** The federal leagues of the third century B.C.  **466**
**MAP 22.2** Sites in the western Mediterranean mentioned in Chapter 22  **472**
**MAP 22.3** Pyrrhus' campaigns in Italy and Sicily  **479**

# CHAPTER 23

**MAP 23.1** Sites mentioned in Chapter 23  **483**

# CHAPTER 24

**MAP 24.1** Sites in Italy mentioned in Chapter 24  **508**
**MAP 24.2** Sites in the east Mediterranean mentioned in Chapter 24  **525**

# PREFACE

In this book we try to see ancient Greece as a whole: not just a narrative of events or an overview of culture, but history and culture taken together. From ancient Greece comes the modern conviction that through open discussion and the exercise of reason a society of free citizens can solve the problems that challenge it. In one period of Greek history, a society just so governed produced timeless masterpieces of literature, art, and rational thought at the same time that it waged terrible wars and committed countless cruelties. If we understand the past, we can live better in the present, but the past is hard to understand.

We have organized the material chronologically, beginning at the end of the last Ice Age. We take the story through the palaces of Mycenaean Greece and the depressed centuries of the Dark Age to the birth of city-states in the Archaic Period. We describe the triumphs of the city-states in the Classical Period and their subjection to larger kingdoms in the Hellenistic Period, after Alexander the Great conquered the Persian Empire, and finally their conquest by Rome. Of course Greek history continued after the Roman conquest, and continues today, but that is a story we unfortunately cannot tell here. Within these limits, we describe processes of social change and cultural achievements along with political events.

Two groups of imaginary readers were looking over our shoulders as we wrote. One was our students: For them we provide the names, dates, and details that you need to grasp Greek history, while avoiding technical jargon. Many of the names in this book will be unfamiliar. To assist with pronunciation, we provide an English pronunciation guide the first time each difficult name appears. The pronunciation guides are repeated in the index, which also functions as a glossary. We also use **bold** letters to highlight the most important names, places, and concepts. We repeat these names in a list of important terms at the end of each chapter, with page numbers of where the term first appears. We leave less important names in ordinary type, though we often give pronunciations for those as well.

Our second group of imaginary readers is the experts on ancient Greece. They can be tough critics. An expert's comment is always, "Yes, but. . . . " There are countless places in a book like this where experts will rightly point out that the evidence is ambiguous, the translation of key words debated, or that there are exceptions to our generalizations. They are quite right to worry about complexities and scholarly debates, but in the end, we have told the story in our own way. We hope that even our professional colleagues may find new ways of thinking about old problems—or, at least, will enjoy the read.

Our account differs in significant ways from the many excellent overviews of Greek history that already exist. First, we make special efforts to see the Greeks as part of a larger Mediterranean world. Older accounts tend to focus on the Aegean Sea, ignoring the Greeks of Sicily and southern Italy. We try instead to show how thoroughly linked developments were in eastern and western Greece. Most previous accounts also present non-Greek peoples like the Persians, Carthaginians, and natives of the west Mediterranean as cardboard characters, coming into the narrative only to defeat the Greeks or be defeated by them. We try to make clear their own motivations and their contributions to the larger story.

Second, we have rejected the prejudice that the only things worth knowing about Greece ended with the Peloponnesian War in 404 B.C., the death of Socrates in 399 B.C., or the battle of Chaeronea in 338 B.C. The final three centuries B.C. are vitally important in the story of the Greeks. The luxuries of Hellenistic Alexandria and the irresistible progress of Roman armies across the east Mediterranean are as much a part of this tale as the insights of Pericles and the beauty of the Parthenon.

Third, because so much of antiquity is apprehended through the eye, we include abundant maps and photographs of landscapes, objects, and buildings. Archaeologists' discoveries have changed the ways we understand ancient Greece, and we emphasize material culture throughout. When the name of a place appears on a map, we so indicate by printing the name in the text in SMALL CAPS.

As often as possible, we let the Greeks speak for themselves by including generous quotations from ancient authors. No supplements to this book are necessary to understand who the Greeks were and what they accomplished, but more extended readings from Homer, the historians, the tragedians, and the lyric poets would certainly complement the text. We make suggestions on further reading in modern scholarship as well as in the ancient sources at the end of each chapter.

In the first edition we made use mostly of translations from commercial sources, but for this edition we have prepared our own translations from the original sources. We do our best to strike a balance between contemporary usage and the sometimes exaggerated demands of the original mostly Greek texts.

*Ian Morris*

*Willard Professor of Classics*
*and Professor of History*
*Stanford University*
*imorris@stanford.edu*

*Barry B. Powell*

*Halls-Bascom Professor of Classics Emeritus*
*University of Wisconsin-Madison*
*bbpowell@wisc.edu*

# ACKNOWLEDGMENTS

We are grateful to the many colleagues and students who helped in writing the first edition of this book, particularly to Eric Cline (The George Washington University) and Carol Thomas (University of Washington), who read the entire manuscript and improved it with their advice. For the second edition, we have received many detailed and very useful reports from adopters of the first edition and other critics: Ben Akrigg, University of Toronto; Benjamin Garstad, Grant MacEwan College; Pericles Georges, Lake Forest College; John Kroll, University of Texas at Austin; David Leitao, San Francisco State University; Wilfred E. Major, Louisiana State University; D. Brendan Nagle, University of Southern California; Frances Pownall, University of Alberta; Christine Renaud, Carthage College; and Kathryn A. Simonsen, Memorial University of New Foundland. We are grateful for their labors and have done our best to incorporate their many insights—many thanks! We hope that future adopters will continue to share with us their own wisdom and advice. We also thank Charles Cavaliere, our editor at Pearson, for his patience and guidance, and the other hardworking staff at Pearson.

# ABOUT THE AUTHORS

**Ian Morris** is the Jean and Rebecca Willard Professor of Classics and Professor of History at Stanford University, where he teaches large lecture courses on ancient empires and Greek history. He founded and has served as director of the Stanford Archaeology Center and directed a major archaeological excavation in Sicily. He has published ten books on ancient history and archaeology. The latest of these, *Why the West Rules . . . For Now*, will appear in 2010. He has lectured at universities across America and Europe and appeared on television on the History Channel, Discovery Channel, and A&E Channel.

**Barry B. Powell** is the Halls-Bascom Professor of Classics Emeritus at the University of Wisconsin-Madison, where in his long career he has been well known as a teacher of large lecture classes in ancient civilization and myth and for seminars on Homer. He has lectured in many countries and is the author of the best-selling *Classical Myth* (6th edition, 2008), widely used in college courses. He is best known as the author of *Homer and the Origin of the Greek Alphabet* (1991), which argues that the Greek alphabet was invented in order to record the poems of Homer. With Ian Morris he published the internationally admired *A New Companion to Homer* (1997). The second edition of his popular introductory text *Homer* appeared in 2007, and he has written numerous other books, including a mock-epic, *The War at Troy: A True History* (2006). He appeared on the History Channel special *Troy: The True Story* (2005). His study *Writing: Theory and History of the Technology of Civilization* (2009) establishes a scientific terminology for studying the history of writing.

# CHRONOLOGICAL CHART

| | |
|---|---|
| 10,000 B.C. | **NEOLITHIC PERIOD** ("new stone age") begins in the Near East with the development of agriculture and sedentary communities |
| 4000 B.C. | Sumerian cuneiform writing is developed, c. 3400 |
| | Egyptian hieroglyphic writing, Pharaonic civilization emerge, c. 3100 |
| 3000 B.C. | **EARLY BRONZE AGE** begins in Greece with introduction of bronze metallurgy, c. 3000–2000 |
| | Sumerian cities flourish in Mesopotamia, c. 2800–2340 |
| | Minoan civilization flourishes in Crete, c. 2500–1200 |
| | Akkadian Empire in Mesopotamia, c. 2334–2220 |
| | Sumerian revival, c. 2200–2000 |
| 2000 B.C. | **MIDDLE BRONZE AGE** begins with the destruction of communities across the Greek mainland, c. 2000–1600 |
| | Old Babylonian Empire in Mesopotamia, c. 1900–1550 |
| | **LATE BRONZE AGE** (or **MYCENAEAN AGE**) begins, c. 1600 |
| | Hittite Empire rules in Anatolia, c. 1700–1200 |
| 1500 B.C. | Phoenician syllabic writing appears, c. 1500 |
| | Most likely date for a Trojan War, c. 1250–1200 |
| | **DARK** (or **IRON**) **AGE** begins with destruction of Mycenaean cities in Greece, c. 1200–1100 |
| 1000 B.C. | Greek colonies are settled in Asia Minor, c. 950–900 |
| | Greek colonies in Sicily and southern Italy, c. 800–600 |
| | **ARCHAIC PERIOD** begins with invention of Greek alphabet, c. 800 |
| | *Iliad* and the *Odyssey*, attributed to Homer, are written down, c. 800–750 |
| | Olympic games begin, 776 |
| | Rome, allegedly, is founded, 753 |
| | Hesiod's *Theogony* is written down, c. 750–700 |
| | *Homeric Hymns*, c. 700–500 |
| | Cyclic poets, c. 650–500 |
| | Age of Tyrants, c. 650–500 |
| | Cyrus the Great of Persia, c. 590–530 |
| | Xenophanes, c. 570–460 |
| | Pindar, 518–438 |
| | Simonides, late sixth to early fifth century |
| | Alleged date of the expulsion of the Etruscan dynasty at Rome and foundation of the Roman Republic, 510 |
| 500 B.C. | Bacchylides, early fifth century |
| | Persians invade Aegean Greece; battle of Marathon, 490 |
| | Carthage invades Sicily; Greek victory at Himera, 480 |

Persians invade Aegean Greece again; destruction of Athens;
Greek victories at Salamis and Plataea, 480–479
**CLASSICAL PERIOD** begins with end of Persian Wars, 480
Aeschylus, 525–456
Sophocles, 496–406
Herodotus, c. 484–420
Euripides, 480–406
Roman *Twelve Tables* are committed to writing, 451
Socrates, 469–399
Peloponnesian War, 431–404
Thucydides, c. 460–400
Biblical book of *Genesis* reaches present form, c. 400

400 B.C.
Plato, 427–437
Hippocrates, c. 400
Aristotle, 384–322
The Gauls sack the city of Rome, 394 or 390
Philip II of Macedon, Alexander's father, conquers Greece,
ending local rule, 338–337
Alexander the Great conquers the Persian Empire, 336–323
**HELLENISTIC PERIOD** begins with death of Alexander, 323

300 B.C.
Callimachus, c. 305–240
Apollonius of Rhodes, third century

200 B.C.
Three Punic Wars are waged between Rome and Carthage,
264–241, 218–201, 146
Plautus, Roman playwright, dies, c. 180
**ROMAN PERIOD** begins with Roman invasions of Greece,
200–194, 168, 146
Roman civil wars, Marius-Sulla, Caesar-Pompey,
Augustus-Antony, are waged, 88–31
Vergil, 70–19
Livy, 57 B.C.–17 A.D.
Julius Caesar rules as dictator, 46–44
Augustus defeats Antony and Cleopatra at battle of Actium, 31,
and annexes Egypt, 30
Augustus Caesar reigns, 27 B.C.–14 A.D.

100 A.D.
Plutarch, c. 46–120 A.D.

## CHAPTER 1

# A Small, Far-Off Land

Fair Greece! sad relic of departed worth!
Immortal, though no more! though fallen, great!

LORD BYRON
*Childe Harold's Pilgrimage*
*(1812–18), canto 2, stanza 73*

Byron was just twenty-five when he wrote *Childe Harold's Pilgrimage*. He was handsome and dashing, a wealthy lord in the most powerful nation on earth, and already one of England's most famous poets. The world was at his feet. Yet within a decade, he turned his back on it all. He sailed to Greece to join its uprising against the mighty Turkish OTTOMAN EMPIRE (Map 1.1).

Lord Byron died in 1824, hundreds of miles from home and family, in a terrible siege at a place called MISSOLONGHI in central Greece (Map 1.3). Why did Byron feel so strongly about Greece that he gave his life for its freedom? Why did thousands of others flock to join him? Why, in our own time, do millions travel to see the ruins that dot Greece's landscape? And why do people spend so much time studying Greek history, culture, and society? In this book, we try to answer these questions.

## HISTORICAL SKETCH

In the half-millennium 700 to 200 B.C.,[1] the Greeks engaged in a remarkable experiment. They built societies that were communities of equal citizens who systematically applied their reason to explaining the world. In the process, they created masterpieces of literature

---

[1] In place of the traditional B.C. ("before Christ") and A.D. (Latin *"anno domini,"* in the year of the lord), one sometimes finds B.C.E. ("before the common era") and C.E. ("common era"). Because the systems are conventional (Jesus was probably born in 7 B.C.), we have preferred the traditional usage.

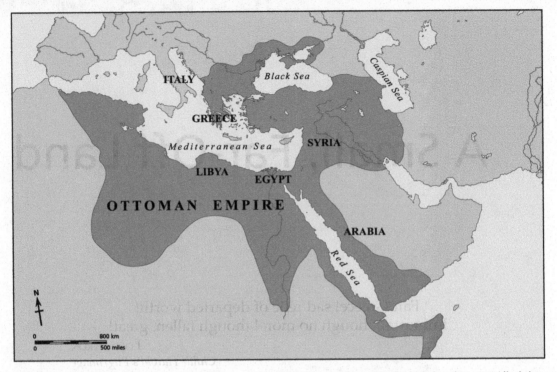

**MAP 1.1**   The Ottoman Empire. Between A.D. 1300 and 1919, the Ottoman Turkish Empire controlled the eastern and southern territories of the old Roman Empire. Though hated by some, the Ottomans were gifted administrators under whose sway Islamic culture produced some of its finest achievements.

and art. Democracy, philosophy, history writing, and drama began in ancient Greece, and the Greeks developed science, mathematics, and representational art in previously unimagined directions.

Two hundred years ago, Byron died for an idea, a vision of the ancient Greek spirit. His vision was idealized; he and his contemporaries saw in Greek art and literature timeless truths that laid bare the meaning of life. In 1820, on the eve of the Greek uprising against the Turks, his fellow poet John Keats (1795–1821) thought he had grasped the world's ultimate truths by simply gazing at painted Greek vases (Figure 1.1).

O Attic° shape! Fair attitude! With brede
Of marble men and maidens overwrought,
With forest branches and the trodden weed;
Thou, silent form, dost tease us out of thought
As doth eternity: Cold Pastoral!°
When old age shall this generation waste,
Thou shalt remain, in midst of other woe
Than ours, a friend to man, to whom thou say'st,
"Beauty is truth, truth beauty,—that is all
Ye know on earth, and all ye need to know."

Keats, "Ode on a Grecian Urn" (1820), stanza 5

°*Attic:* From Attica, the countryside around Athens. °*Cold Pastoral:* a scene set in a countryside that shall never change (hence cold, not living)

**FIGURE 1.1** No single Greek vase lay behind Keats's poem; he drew inspiration from seeing hundreds of pots in English museums before his death in Rome at the age of just twenty-six. This pot is the kind he had in mind, an Athenian red-figured (because the figures are red colored) amphora ("two-handled" vase), ca. 450 B.C.

The poet saw deeply, but thanks to 200 years of scholarship, we now see more deeply still. For Byron and Keats, ancient Greece was a simple and pure world of love and truth. Today we know much more about the Greeks. Theirs was an astonishing culture, but no utopia. The achievements of some Greeks rested on the backbreaking labor of others, often slaves from overseas. Their democracies excluded women. They fought endless wars and committed terrible acts of violence. Yet far from making us turn from the Greeks in revulsion, these discoveries make them more fascinating still. The Greeks lived in a harsh and real world, where they struggled with the same basic problems about freedom, equality, and justice that we face. Their difficulties show us that there are no simple answers.

Let us take the story back five thousand years, to a time when great **Bronze Age** civilizations (see Chronological Chart preceding this chapter for this and other historical terms) had arisen in **Mesopotamia** ("the land between the rivers," what is now Iraq) and Egypt.

The Mesopotamian kings claimed that they had special relationships with the gods and that unless they interceded, the gods would not smile on humans. The kings of Egypt went further, claiming that they themselves *were* gods. By 2000 B.C., somewhat similar societies formed in Greece. Their palaces flourished until 1200 B.C., but then were burned along with cities all over the east Mediterranean. We still do not know why this destruction occurred, but its consequences were momentous. In Mesopotamia and Egypt, the old order of godlike kings revived, but in Greece that way of doing things was over (if it had ever existed). From about 1200 until 800 B.C., writing disappeared from Greece; the country's population shrank and was isolated from the wider world. The present book focuses on the Greek societies that emerged from this **Dark Age** in the eighth century B.C., creating a new Greek world that had little in common with the Bronze Age.

This new world had several radical features. First, most Greeks now organized themselves in small city-states called *poleis* (this is the plural form; the singular is *polis*), not in kingdoms. Second, as population grew in the eighth century, some Greeks sailed off and established new communities around the shores of the MEDITERRANEAN (see Map 1.2). Third, Greeks came to see their city-states as communities of equal, free males, the basis for and origin of the concept of citizenship. Fourth, they refused to believe that the gods gave any individual or narrow elite a divine right to rule.

These developments presented the Greeks with problems and opportunities absent in other ancient societies. If the gods had not put sacred kings on earth to tell mortals what to do, just what *was* the relationship between mortals and the divine? Most Greeks thought that the gods were powerful and wise, that the world was full of spirits and ghosts, and that a few oracles and priests could give access to the supernatural. This access was open to challenge, however, and oracles and priests could not use it to dominate others. How, then, could mortals really know what was true?

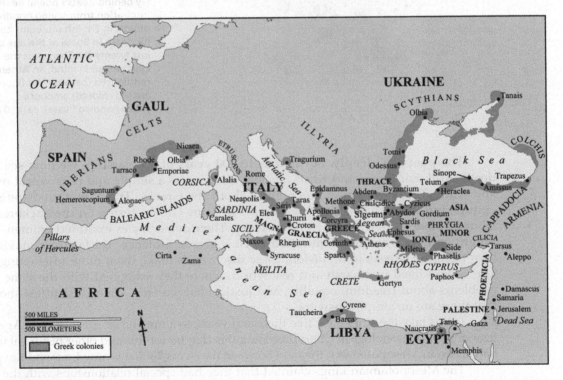

**MAP 1.2** Greek colonies.

These conditions created a fundamental conflict that we call **the Greek problem**, a set of conditions with which Greek thinkers struggled. Without God or gods to rule and to reveal the truth, many Greeks concluded that human reason was the only guide to truth. If no king had special access to truth, then all males must be roughly equally well qualified to discuss it, and the only source of good decisions must be the whole male community. (All Greek states made firm divisions between males and females: When Greeks used expressions like "everyone," "the community," or "the people," they normally meant all freeborn adult males.) By 500 B.C., the theory of equal qualification led to the world's first democracies (democracy comes from the Greek word **dêmokratia** [dē-mo-kra-tē-a], meaning "power of the people"), in which all male citizens debated and voted on the major issues.

Other Greeks drew different conclusions from the Greek problem. Some thought that elites should rule; the richest men, with the most respected family connections, could be trained in the skillful exercise of reason on behalf of the whole community. The conflict between mass and elite—democracy and experts—was a driving force in Greek history and one that remains familiar today. What is the place of intellectuals in a democracy? How should wealth be distributed? What do equality and freedom mean?

But while these philosophical debates raged, the Greeks still had to live in the real world. Like us, they had a growing population and conflicting demands on their resources. Leading men in every *polis* competed for power and wealth, and the rich as a group were often at loggerheads with the poor. Neighboring *poleis* fought for land and other resources, sometimes polarizing into great power blocs. The Greeks as a whole fought with powers such as Persia, a mighty empire in western Asia, and Carthage, a powerful trading city in what is now Tunisia. Different *poleis* found different solutions to the problem of working out a civil society independent of rule by gods and their agents, but always did so against the material realities of the southern Balkan Peninsula. Sparta developed a militaristic society, suppressing debate in the interests of security. Athens turned toward democracy and pluralism, glorying in open expression. Syracuse in Sicily alternated between Athenian-style creativity and rule by brutal tyrants.

These diverse responses to the Greek problem produced two results. First, there was constant intercity warfare, as different *poleis* promoted their own interests and their own visions of the good society. In the fifth century B.C., it looked as if Athens might defeat all comers, unite Greece, create a nation-state, and become its capital city. But after Sparta defeated Athens in 404 B.C., the wars only intensified, becoming increasingly expensive and destructive.

The second consequence of living with the Greek problem was more positive. Thinkers needed to explain not only how the universe worked independent of divine whim, but also why there was such variety in it. As early as the sixth century B.C., Greek intellectuals in Ionia on the west coast of Asia Minor (modern Turkey; see map on the inside front cover) developed rational models of the mechanics of the cosmos, accepting that the gods created the universe but assuming that the physical world continued to work because natural forces acted on each other. Their questions initiated Greek science and philosophy. In the fourth century B.C., they led to the epoch-making work of Plato and Aristotle, and in the third century B.C., to the mathematical discoveries of the Sicilian engineer Archimedes (ar-ki-mēd-ēz). Other thinkers extended logical, rational analysis, asking why Greek *poleis* were so different from each other and why Greece as a whole was so different from the Persian Empire and from other foreign peoples. This questioning gave us the writings of

Herodotus and Thucydides, and the origins of history, anthropology, and political science. At the same time, poets and artists struggled to define man's relationship to the gods. At the end of the Dark Age, during the eighth century B.C., Homer sang his *Iliad* and *Odyssey*, set in ancient days when men and gods walked together, and Hesiod (hē-sē-od) related the gods' own history. In the fifth century B.C., the great tragedians Aeschylus (ē-ski-lus), Sophocles (**sof**-o-klēz), and Euripides (ū-**rip**-i-dēz) retold Greek legends to explore profound moral problems, the sculptor Phidias (**fid**-i-as) gave visual expression to new ideas of man's place in the cosmos, and Athens built the Parthenon, one of the world's aesthetic masterpieces.

The upheavals, triumphs, and tragedies of the Greeks in the **Archaic Period** (seventh and sixth centuries B.C.) and **Classical Period** (fifth and fourth centuries B.C.) were driven by the Greek problem—If we cannot rely on the gods to tell us what is true, how do we know what to do? Sudden and unexpected changes began to make the problem irrelevant in the late fourth century B.C. A new king named Philip modernized and centralized Macedon, a large but loosely organized kingdom on the edge of the world of the *poleis*, and used its wealth and manpower to defeat the Greek cities. Conquering Greece was merely a sideshow to Philip, though, who planned to overthrow Persia itself. After his murder in 336 B.C., his dynamic son Alexander did just this.

Philip's and Alexander's conquests seemed superhuman. Both kings certainly saw their own triumphs as godlike, and in 324 B.C., Alexander ordered the *poleis* to worship him as a divinity. The great Greek experiment in founding society on reason was evolving into new forms. In many ways, the third century B.C. was the Greeks' golden age (a description often reserved for fifth-century Athens). The Greeks were more numerous and richer than ever. Their cities spread as far as Afghanistan. Their culture triumphed from the borders of India to the Atlantic, and their scientists and engineers made amazing breakthroughs. Such successes seemed to prove that the Greeks had answered old questions about where truth came from, but in the **Hellenistic Period** (from Alexander's death in 323 B.C. to Cleopatra's death in 30 B.C.) the Greeks had to wonder: How should we live together with the peoples we have conquered? And, as Roman armies cut a bloody path around the Mediterranean after 200 B.C., how should we live in a world with just one superpower?

## WHY STUDY THE GREEKS?

These problems interest people today because we share many of them with the ancient Greeks. Around A.D. 1500, at the end of the European Middle Ages, kings in Europe claimed that they ruled through divine right (as had the kings of ancient Mesopotamia), supported by a church that monopolized truth (as the temples guaranteed Mesopotamian kings' power). During the eighteenth-century European Enlightenment, however, philosophers and scientists challenged such beliefs. Like archaic and classical Greeks, they again asked how humans could know the truth and govern themselves well if they could not rely on divinely justified kings and all-knowing priests to tell them what to do. They came to much the same conclusion as the Greeks: Only through the exercise of reason, unhindered by respect for custom and tradition, can you find your way forward.

The American and French revolutions elevated constitutions—written by mortal men—ahead of sacred books. The revolutionaries held, as so many Greeks had believed before, that a state was a community of equal (male) citizens, founded on reason, aiming at the pursuit of happiness. In the nineteenth century, the right of free, equal citizens to rule themselves—in short, democracy—became a burning social question all over Europe, and, just as in ancient Greece, wide-ranging debates sprang up that revolutionized philosophy, science, history writing, literature, and art. People asked once again how they could make sense of the world through reason and found that the Greeks had already asked these questions a long time ago and had offered compelling answers. The spread of democracy in the twentieth century made the Greek experience to be of global interest, and in the twenty-first century, we find that the Hellenistic Greeks had anticipated two millennia ago our own need to build and live within complex, diverse societies.

The Greeks do not provide a blueprint for how to live, and we learn as much from their failures as from their successes. For example, they recognized that the freedom and equality of male citizens were logically incompatible with the subjection of slaves and women, but they saw no reason to change anything. Between A.D. 1861 and 1865, by contrast, 675,000 Americans died or were maimed fighting one another, largely to decide whether freedom included the right to hold slaves. The Greeks might have recognized America's problem, but its solution would have astonished them.

We might say, then, that the Greeks are *good to think with*. They conducted astonishing experiments in freedom, equality, and rationality that match our own efforts to build a rational and just society.

## WHO WERE THE GREEKS?

But who were these people, "the Greeks"? For about two hundred years—since Byron's time—the world has divided itself into nation-states. The theory behind nation-states is simple. Everyone belongs to an ethnic group defined by shared language, culture, and descent from common ancestors. Each group—Germans, Americans, Japanese, and so on—should govern its own destiny by forming a self-determining territorial state. The boundaries of the ethnic nation and the political state should coincide so that we find the Germans in Germany, the French in France, the Chinese in China, and so on.

In practice, though, things are not so simple. At the start of the third millennium A.D., the world is a complex ethnic patchwork. For example, while the largest concentration of Greek-speakers on the planet is in the city of Athens, the second largest is in Melbourne, Australia. You can get as authentic a Greek meal in Chicago as anywhere in the nation-state of Greece. Some Greek citizens feel strongly that the population of southern ALBANIA is ethnically Greek and should be part of the Greek state (Map 1.3). Other Greeks feel that Greece's frontiers enclose too many ethnic Albanians, who should be made to go away, even if they hold Greek citizenship.

Defining a "people," then, is never easy, but the one-people-one-state equation has dominated modern history. From it came the Holocaust and "ethnic cleansing." The Kurds' longing for a state to go with their ethnicity has destabilized the Middle East since World War I and continues to do so. Ethnic pride has been a major force in turning Afghanistan and Iraq into slaughterhouses and the Balkans into a simmering stew of violent hatred. Faith in the nation-state based on ethnic identity is one of the most powerful forces of modern times.

If we ask what a people was in antiquity, we see that much has changed. The concept of the nation-state simply did not exist in ancient Greece. Greek-speakers, who called themselves **Hellenes** (strangely, the word *Greek* comes from the name the Romans gave them), lived in cities scattered from Spain to UKRAINE (see Map 1.2). They agreed that their

**MAP 1.3** Modern Greece and the Balkans.

ancestral home, **Hellas,** lay around the Aegean Sea (roughly the area of the modern Greek nation-state plus the west coast of modern Turkey). Yet a Greek from Sicily felt just as Greek as one from Athens.

The notion that all ethnic Greeks should be politically unified had little appeal. The biggest *poleis,* Athens and Sparta, had territories of just 1,000 square miles, while the tiny island of Kea, covering barely one-tenth that area, was divided into three independent *poleis.* Greekness had nothing to do with belonging to a particular political unit.

So what was Greekness? Most modern nations define ethnic identity in terms of common ancestors, language, and culture. Such beliefs are sometimes patently false, and within any nation people may often choose among competing and contradictory stories to suit the needs of the moment. The Athenian Thucydides (thu-**sid**-i-dēz), writing around 400 B.C., described similar behavior in Greece:

> As far as I can see, Hellas never did anything in concert before the Trojan War, or was even known as Hellas. No such appellation existed before the time of

Deucalion, the son of Hellên,° but people went by their tribal names, in particular the name "Pelasgian." Then when the sons of Hellên gained power in Phthiotis,° and they entered into alliance with other *poleis*, one by one through this association they began to be known as "Hellenes." But it took a long time before they all took on that name. Homer is the best evidence. Although he lived long after the Trojan War, never does he give them a single name, but reserves "Hellenes" for the followers of Achilles, who came from Phthiotis and were the original Hellenes. Otherwise he uses the names "Danaans" and "Argives" and "Achaeans." Nor does he use the word *barbaroi*,° no doubt because the Hellenes had not yet been set off from the rest of the world by means of a single appellation.

Thucydides 1.2–3

°*Hêllen* (**hel**-ēn): In myth, the male ancestor of all the Hellenes (i.e., the Greeks), who gave his name to Hellas (Greece). °*Phthiotis* (thī-ō-tis): An area in central Greece. °*barbaroi*: Greeks called foreigners *barbaroi*, the root of the word "barbarian," because they thought foreign languages sounded like people saying "bar-bar-bar."

Thucydides applied his reason to the text of Homer to draw conclusions about the past: in Homer's day, the Greeks were not a single people. Just a few lines before introducing this model, he had explained that the Athenians claimed a different ancestry from other Greeks. They alone, they said, were *autochthonous* ("born from the soil"): they had always lived in Athens. Yet we know that other Athenians believed that their ancestors had at some time invaded their territory from outside, cohabiting with and then expelling people called the **Pelasgians** ("peoples of the sea"). There were competing stories and only a limited sense of Greekness. Most of the time, ancient Greeks identified primarily with the *polis* they lived in. If you stopped them as they went about their business and asked who they were, they would have said Syracusan, Athenian, Spartan, and so on, but not Hellene.

Sometimes, usually during serious wars, groups of *poleis* would recognize a larger identity forged from a common interest. When Athens and Sparta began the terrible Peloponnesian War in 431 B.C., those who considered themselves **Ionians** (descendants of Ion, a legendary ancestor) generally sided with Athens, while those who called themselves **Dorians** supported Sparta (Map 1.4) (the Dorians claimed descent from Heracles (**her**-a-klēz; = Hercules), who, according to myth, had conquered much of Greece in the distant past).

Occasionally, people could put aside regional and kinship identities to unite as Hellenes. Whether or not Hellên really existed, he became a potent symbol at such moments. In a great crisis in 480 B.C., when Persia invaded Greece and Carthage invaded Sicily, many Greeks ignored their local myths and united around a legendary common heritage as the sons of Hellên. Herodotus (her-**o**-do-tus), writing probably at Athens around 420 B.C. and describing a critical moment in the war with Persia, spoke of

our common Greekness, tied to a single language and based on shrines and sacrifices we hold in common and customs that come from a like upbringing.

Herodotus 8.144

Blood, language, religion, and customs are the foundations of modern nation-states. Greeks often felt distinct from peoples around them who did not speak their language or live like them, and wars with Persia and Carthage highlighted these distinctions. But they never translated this sense of Greekness into political unity, and after 300 B.C., the distinction

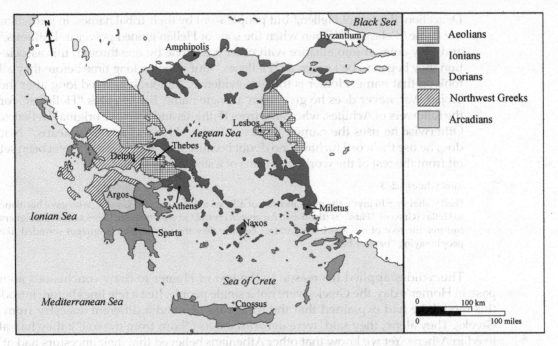

**MAP 1.4**   Distribution of Greek ethnic groups during the Classical Period. The groups were the Aeolians, Ionians, Dorians, Northwest Greeks, and Arcadians, and each group shared a dialect.

between Greek and foreigner partly broke down. Thousands emigrated from Greece to the Near East (now called the Middle East) and Egypt, though few learned the languages of the peoples they settled among. By contrast, native-born Egyptians, Syrians, and others learned Greek, took Greek names, spoke and wrote in Greek, wore Greek clothes, and acted in Greek ways. Who was to say, or know, after a few generations had passed, that one family was more "Greek" than another? By the time Rome conquered the eastern Mediterranean in the second and first centuries B.C., Greekness was widely diffused and was taking on new meanings.

## THE STRUCTURE OF THIS BOOK: HISTORY, CULTURE, AND SOCIETY

In the next twenty-four chapters, we tell the Greeks' story. The subtitle of our book—*History, Culture, and Society*—sums up our method. First, our format is narrative history, focusing on the half-millennium 700 to 200 B.C. Only by seeing individuals, events, and intellectual discovery in context can we understand them. Second, in the course of our narrative history, we emphasize Greek culture, which makes this small, far-off land so important. We describe literature, art, philosophy, and beliefs and place them in their historical context. Third, as our narrative unfolds, we explain Greek culture by looking at the larger Greek society, the institutions and economics of each period along with the Greeks' endless wars and their clashes with other powers. Out of these many conflicts— between rich and poor; free and slave; male and female; Athenians and Spartans; and Greeks, Persians, Carthaginians, Macedonians, and Romans—a remarkable culture grew, triumphed, and disintegrated.

## Key Terms

| | | |
|---|---|---|
| Attic, 2 | *dêmokratia*, 5 | Hellas, 8 |
| Bronze Age, 3 | Archaic Period, 6 | *autochthonous*, 9 |
| Mesopotamia, 3 | Classical Period, 6 | Pelasgians, 9 |
| Dark Age, 4 | Hellenistic Period, 6 | Ionians, 9 |
| *polis*, 4 | Hellenes, 7 | Dorians, 9 |
| the Greek problem, 5 | | |

## Further Reading

### BYRON AND THE GREEKS

St. Clair, Roger, *That Greece Might Still Be Free* (London, 1972). Vivid account of the Greek War of Independence and the Romantics who joined it. A great read.

### GENERAL REVIEWS OF GREEK HISTORY

*The Cambridge Ancient History*, 2nd ed., vol. III–VII (Cambridge, UK, 1982–94). Massive compendium of facts, focusing on political narrative history, but with some economic, social, and cultural coverage. Not an easy read, but it is the basic resource for serious scholars.

Camp, John, and Elizabeth Fisher, *The World of the Ancient Greeks* (London, 2002). Brief text by two archaeologists, with beautiful illustrations.

Cartledge, Paul, ed., *The Cambridge Illustrated History of Greek Civilization* (Cambridge, UK, 1998). Essays on various aspects of Greek culture by nine leading specialists, with excellent illustrations. It does not give a continuous narrative of Greek history, but, like Sparkes's book (see below), makes a useful supplement to the other works in this list.

Freeman, Charles, *The Greek Achievement* (London, 1999). Readable survey by a journalist-turned historian.

Pomeroy, Sarah, Stanley Burstein, Walter Donlan, and Jennifer Roberts, *Ancient Greece: A Political, Social, and Cultural History,* 2nd ed. (New York, 2007). Excellent survey concentrating on political history, but taking a serious look at social trends too.

Sparkes, Brian, ed., *Greek Civilization* (Oxford, 1998). A collection of nineteen essays on the Greeks, including a useful section of four essays taking the story from the end of the Roman Empire through the twentieth century A.D.

### ETHNICITY

Hall, Jonathan, *Hellenicity: Between Ethnicity and Culture* (Chicago, 2002). Sophisticated discussion of the evolution of Greek ethnicity.

Malkin, Irad, ed., *Ancient Perceptions of Greek Ethnicity* (Cambridge, MA, 2001). Wide-ranging essays on how the Greeks perceived themselves in antiquity.

## CHAPTER 2

# Country and People

What was it like to live in ancient Greece? In this chapter, we look at the basic rhythms of Greek life: geography, diet, health, and standards of living. In the next chapter, we describe the family, the basic building block of Greek society in ancient Greece. These two chapters provide the foundations for making sense of Greek history and culture.

In ancient times, economic changes generally happened too slowly for people to perceive them. Yet by the end of the period covered in this book, most Greeks lived longer, ate better, were sick less often, inhabited finer houses, and had more opportunities than their ancestors 500 years earlier. Life in Hellenistic times was still nasty, poor, brutish, and short by modern standards, but Greeks of this era were better off than those of the Dark Age.

## GREEK GEOGRAPHY, CLIMATE, AND AGRICULTURE

Plato, the Athenian philosopher of the fourth century B.C., described the Greeks as living like "frogs around a pond." Ninety percent of Greeks lived within a day's walk of the Mediterranean Sea. That was where the best farmland was, and people living inland were effectively cut off from the greater world. According to a Roman inscription set up in A.D. 301, it cost less to move a load of grain by ship the 1,000 miles from one end of the Mediterranean to the other than it did to pile it on wagons and drag it 75 miles inland, true to the old saying, "The land divides, the sea unites." The sea was the lifeblood of Greek civilization.

Nearly all Greeks, whether they lived in ATHENS, SICILY, or SPAIN (see maps on inside covers, front and back), knew much the same climate and geography, what we now call a "Mediterranean" environment. The Greek homeland around the Aegean Sea was a world of small coastal plains, cut up by hills and often backed by forbidding mountains (Figure 2.1). The plains were heavily cultivated, while scrub and brush covered the hills (Figure 2.2). Some mountains were homes to pine forests; others were bare and hostile. In the 320s B.C., after

**FIGURE 2.1**   Snow-capped summer peaks in the rugged Pindus range, which runs like a backbone down the center of Greece, dividing the land into small plains usually open to the sea. In the center is a small church.

Alexander's conquests, Greeks also settled in Egypt and Mesopotamia, where they encountered the great Nile, Tigris, and Euphrates rivers. Here farming depended on harnessing rivers through irrigation, but in the north Mediterranean, farmers relied on rainfall to water their crops.

**FIGURE 2.2**   The rich Thessalian plain spreads before Mount Olympus, the highest mountain in Greece. Beyond Olympus lies Macedonia.

Consequently, to most Greeks, nothing mattered more than rain. Greek writers' comments about the weather, combined with evidence like tree rings from fragments of ancient wood and waterlogged pollen from ancient plants preserved in lakebeds, suggest that the Mediterranean climate of 2500 years ago was quite like that of today. The hot, dry summers that draw modern tourists to Greek beaches were lazy days for ancient farmers. In July and August, it hardly ever rains, and temperatures reach 90°F. **Hesiod**, a poet who probably lived around 700 B.C., tells us in his strange poem of agricultural and moral advice called the **Works and Days** that

> When the thistle blooms and the loud cicada
> sitting in the tree its shrill dense song pours forth
> from beneath its wings in the exhausting summertime,
> then the goats are fat and the wine is best.
> The women are lustful but the men are weak,
> when Sirius drains dry the head and the knees
> and the skin is parched from the heat. Then I
> enjoy a shady rock and Byblos wine,°
> a cake of cheese and the milk of drained goats,
> the flesh of a heifer grazed in the woods, that
> never calved, and of first-born kids. Let us drink
> shining wine, seated in shade, my heart fat with food.

Hesiod, *Works and Days*, 582–93

°*Byblos wine*: Byblos was a trading city in Phoenicia (modern Lebanon); this is special, imported wine.

The cool, wet winters were the busy season. It can snow in December and January (but rarely does) in the Greek plains, and the mountains can get blizzards. Hesiod describes Lenaion, the Greek month equivalent to our late January and early February:

> Then the creatures of the wood, horned and
> unhorned alike, painfully chattering, flee
> through dense brush, caring only to find
> thick undergrowth as a shelter, or a hollow cave.
> Then like a man three-legged with a staff, whose back
> is ruined, making his way with face to the ground,
> like him they wander, to escape the white snow.
>        Then put on, as I urge you, a protection
> for your flesh, a soft cloak and a shirt covering
> your body. On a thin warp weave your thick weft.
> Put that on so that your hair does not shiver, raised up
> and bristling all over your body. Lace on
> your feet boots made from a slaughtered
> ox, close fitting, lined with thick wool.
> And when the cold time comes, stitch together the skins
> of newborn kids with the sinew of an ox, so that
> you make for yourself an escape from the rain.
> On your head put a cap of felt, specially shaped,

to keep your ears dry. The dawn is chill when Boreas°
comes on . . . Finish your work ahead of him
and get back home so that dark cloud from heaven
will not engulf you and drench your skin and clothes.
Be careful: this is the worst month of all.

Hesiod, *Works and Days*, 529–57

°*Boreas:* The north wind personified.

On average, Athens gets just 8 to 24 inches of rain a year, while the mountains of
Arcadia, less than one hundred miles to the southwest but towering to 3,000 feet, get five
times as much. But the rain in the plain is not just low; it is also unpredictable. Farmers
who sowed their fields with wheat would see their crop fail on average one year in four:
that is, when they harvested their grain, they recovered less than they had used as seed.
Barley is hardier and failed only one year in 20, so although Athenians preferred wheat
bread to hard barley, most of them made do with gnawing on barley loaves.

The small plains were the prime grain-growing areas, but the thinner soil on the
hills supported olives and vines. One of the pleasures of traveling in Greece today is
stumbling across hidden upland valleys and flourishing farms. But on the whole, the
mountains supported few crops and were used most by herdsmen leading flocks of sheep
and goats between high summer pastures and lowland winter grazing. Goats provided
milk, cheese, meat, and cloth from their hair; sheep provided meat and wool. The few
cattle, so expensive to feed, were used to pull plows and, occasionally, for meat.

The Mediterranean environment made Greek civilization possible but also set limits on
what could be done. Greeks liked to talk about how poor they were. At the end of the fourth
century B.C., the Athenian comic poet Menander described one character by saying

Poor guy, such a life! That's your real Attic farmer. He works hard the stony soil
that grows thyme and sage, harvesting a lot of pain and no profit.

Menander, *The Grumpy Old Man*, 604–6

Hesiod, who lived 400 years before Menander, also warns that only constant struggle
and backbreaking labor could yield a living:

The gods keep hidden from humans the means of life.
Otherwise you might easily work for a single day
and store up enough for a year without more labor.
Then you'd hang up your rudder over the fireplace
and put up your oxen and your laboring mules . . .
    So remember always my words, noble Perses,°
until Hunger shall hate you and Demeter,° with lovely
garlands, reverend, shall fill your granary with food.
For Hunger loves a lazy man. Both gods
and men hate a man who lives an idle life,

Hesiod, *Works and Days*, 42–46, 298–311

°*Perses:* Hesiod's brother, to whom he addresses the poem.    °*Demeter:* The goddess of grain.

like the stingless drones who eat the labor of bees,
eating without working. Be sure to organize
your labor rightly, so that your barns be filled
at harvest time. From labor your flocks grow to many
and wealth ensues. The gods love a man who works.
There's no shame in work, but in idleness.

## DEMOGRAPHY

When we want to know the facts of life in modern societies—life expectancy, health, population—we consult government records, but such documents did not exist in ancient times, and the educated Greeks who produced the surviving literary texts were not much concerned with such matters. They wrote tragedies, philosophy, and legal speeches, not statistical reports. Nonetheless, by combining the brief literary references to daily life that do survive with archaeology and by comparisons with other premodern societies, we can sketch a credible picture of ancient Greek **demography**.

Demography is the study of the biological aspects of human societies: their size, distribution, growth, rates of birth and death, marriage, and disease. Demographers have shown how a tremendous change began in all these aspects of life in western Europe in the eighteenth century A.D. and spread from there to most of the world. Before then, mortality and fertility rates were high and life expectancy at birth was low, but in the eighteenth-century "demographic transition" mortality sharply declined. For a while, this made population grow rapidly; then people restricted their fertility through late marriage and contraception, creating the quasi-equilibrium familiar today, with low fertility rates, low mortality, and high life expectancy at birth (over eighty in the United States). In premodern societies, about one-third of all babies born alive died before their first birthday. Barely half survived to five years. Those who made it through early childhood could expect to live into their thirties, but fewer than one in six people reached sixty, and just one in twenty made it to seventy.

These statistics broadly apply to ancient Greece, judging from the evidence of ancient skeletons. The fourth-century B.C. philosopher Aristotle observed that "most [deaths] occur before the child is a week old." Cemeteries include depressing numbers of infants and young children, often buried inside broken clay jars that served as makeshift coffins. In some periods, the very young were buried so casually that we recover few traces at all. Perhaps people dealt with death on this scale by trivializing it to reduce the emotional costs of seeing their young children die. Plutarch (**plū**-tark), a Greek writing in the Roman Empire around A.D. 100, suggests as much:

> We do not bring drink-offerings to dead infants, nor do we do what is customary for the dead. For they took no part in this world or in the things of this world. Nor do we pay respect to their graves or build monuments for them or lay out their bodies or sit by the body. By custom we do not mourn those of such an age.

Plutarch, *Moralia* 612A

In our own times, the death of a newborn baby can be a catastrophe, causing terrible psychological scars. In ancient Greece, it was just part of life. Every family experienced it, over and over again. High mortality demanded high fertility. To keep population stable in a society with high infant mortality, women had to average four or five live births. Given that some women did not marry, and that in some marriages one or both partners were infertile, many women must have had seven or more live births. But most ancient Greek women died in their mid-to-late thirties, after a childbearing life of just eighteen to twenty years: bearing and rearing children utterly dominated their lives.

While child mortality was common in ancient Greece, the death of adolescents and young adults from natural causes was not. The Greeks called those who died in these years *aôroi*, "the untimely ones," and bitterly mourned their loss. Their ghosts were powerful, and curse tablets—magic spells usually scratched on lumps of lead—were sometimes buried with them or dropped into wells, to give greater energy to the curse. A young man's death in battle was celebrated as glorious and honorable, but for disease or accident to carry off a young man or woman was simply unfair.

Ancient Greek skeletons suggest that most adults died in their thirties or early forties. Only a few reached their sixties, but we might hesitate to think of these as fortunate. Severe arthritis tormented many. Some Greek poets said they wanted to live into old age, but stressed that they wanted *healthy* old age. Some despaired and prayed to die before they got old. Yet the most famous ancient Greeks generally reached the age of seventy—the philosophers Socrates and Plato, the dramatists Sophocles and Euripides, and perhaps Aeschylus and Aristophanes (ar-is-**tof**-a-nēz). The historians Herodotus and Thucydides, the philosopher Aristotle, the statesman Pericles, and the sculptor Phidias all lived past sixty. Perhaps only those lucky enough, and wealthy enough, to live a long time in good health could establish reputations and rise to the top ranks of achievement.

But the facts of demography are not static. There was an upward trend in adult life expectancy across the Stone and Bronze ages, a decline during the Dark Age, and then a peak in classical and Hellenistic times. By 300 B.C., adults typically lived four or five years longer than did those 500 years earlier. If adult women live through more of their fertile years, there is potential for population growth, and this is just what happened. Combining evidence from inscriptions, excavations, and archaeological surveys, we can estimate that population increased about tenfold between 900 and 300 B.C. Around 900 B.C., there were probably no more than half a million Greeks, concentrated mainly around the western shores of the Aegean. By 300 B.C., six million people called themselves Greeks, lining the coasts of the Mediterranean from Spain to Syria, with some living far up the Nile and in the mountains of Afghanistan.

What caused these long-term changes? We review three possible explanations: migration, disease, and nutrition.

## MIGRATION

Population might have grown so much because people moved into the Greek homelands from outside, but that does not seem to be the case. The main form of migration into Greece was forced migration. beginning by the sixth century B.C., some *poleis* imported non-Greek slaves into Greece. Most slaves came from the northern Balkans and Asia Minor (modern Turkey). Athens was the largest purchaser, and at the height of this practice, in the fourth century B.C., it probably had 50 to 80,000 slaves. Some were born in Greece in captivity, but most were newly imported in each generation. If we add in all the other Greek states that imported slaves, our best guess (it can be no more than that) is that 2,500 to 3,000 slaves were imported into Greece per year in the fourth century. This represents 1 to 2.5 percent of the total population of Greece: a lot of people, but nowhere near enough to account for the population growth. In fact, the main patterns of migration involved Greeks moving *out* from their old homelands. Between about 750 and 650 B.C., Greek colonization in the west Mediterranean probably involved some 30,000 adult males (assuming that single men went, finding brides among the natives), or about 2 to 3 percent of the adult males in the Aegean; and between about 330 and 250 B.C., another 100,000 to 200,000 males emigrated to newly conquered Egypt and the Near East, often as soldiers of fortune.

These were important movements of people, both inward and outward, but they account for only a small part of the changes in populations during this period. To know why population grew, we must examine other factors.

## HEALTH AND DISEASE

The ancient texts tell us that terrible epidemics raged through Greece. The historian of the Peloponnesian War, the Athenian **Thucydides** (ca. 460–400 B.C.), described a plague that broke out in Athens in 430 B.C. while Spartan armies besieged the city. It killed Pericles, Athens' great leader. Thucydides himself caught it, but survived. His description shows his exceptional powers of observation, which he shared with Greek medical writers:

> The plague first broke out among the Athenians, although earlier there were reports of plague on Lemnos° and in other places, but there was no record of those incidents being so virulent or causing so many deaths as in Athens. At first the doctors were of no use in treating the disease, knowing nothing about it, but themselves died more swiftly than others because of their contact with the sick. No other human art was of any use. The more the afflicted attended the shrines or consulted the oracles, the more useless it all became. In the end they avoided such measures, overcome by suffering.
>
> The disease first began, so they say, in Ethiopia in upper Egypt,° then spread to Egypt and to Libya and most of the lands of the Great King of Persia. The plague fell suddenly upon the city of the Athenians, first striking the inhabitants of Piraeus,° who believed that the Peloponnesians [the Spartans] had poisoned the reservoirs. There were no wells there at that time. But later the sickness came into the upper city° and by this time the deaths had greatly increased in number.
>
> Others, both with medical training and without, will no doubt have views about the origins of the disease, and about what causes were capable of producing such extraordinary transformations. I will myself simply describe what it was like, what were its symptoms, so that if it should come again it will not go unrecognized. I myself had the disease and I saw others suffering from it.
>
> That year, as is generally agreed, there were few other diseases of any kind, but if one had been sick, that person was sure to fall to the plague. But those who were in perfect health also, for no clear reason, suddenly caught the disease.
>
> At first came hot flashes in the head and the eyes turned red and burned. The throat and tongue bled, and the breath smelled odd and repulsive.

°*Lemnos:* An island in the Aegean.    °*upper Egypt:* Up the Nile, that is, in southern Egypt.    °*Piraeus:* The harbor of Athens, about seven miles from the city.    °*upper city:* Athens, the city proper.

Next came sneezing and a hoarse voice, and the pain settled in the chest, accompanied by hard coughing. Then it attacked the stomach, leading to vomiting of every kind of bile for which medicine has discovered a name. The pain was enormous. For most there followed an empty retching, together with violent spasms that usually stopped after this phase of the disease, although in some case it continued much longer.

The skin was not hot to the touch, or livid, but fiery red and discolored, blooming with small pustules and ulcers. Within burned such heat that the afflicted could not bear to wear even the lightest clothes but went entirely naked. Sweetest of all would be to throw oneself into cold water, and many of the neglected sick did just that, falling into the public cisterns, consumed by unquenchable thirst. But it made no difference whether they drank little or much.

Their inability to rest or to sleep was a constant torment.

In the period when the disease was at its height, the body, so far from wasting away, showed surprising powers of resistance to all the agony, so that there was still some strength left on the seventh or eighth day when death came from the internal fever, in most cases. If the patient survived this critical period, then the disease descended into the bowels, producing a violent ulceration and uncontrollable diarrhea. Most later died as a result of the weakness caused in this way.

First settling in the head, the disease went on to affect every part of the body in turn, and even when one escaped its worst effects, it still left traces, fastening upon the extremities of the body, the genitals, fingers, and toes, and many who recovered lost the use of these members. Some went blind. Some, when they first began to get better, suffered from a total loss of memory, not knowing who they were and unable to recognize even their friends.

Words are of little use when one tries to give a general picture of the disease. As for the sufferings of individuals, they seemed almost beyond the capacity of human nature to endure. . . .

Such were the general features of the disease, although I have omitted the many variations of it that afflicted this or that person. At the time of the plague the ordinary array of diseases did not appear, and if they did, ended in the plague. Some died from neglect, others, even though cared for diligently. There was no such thing as a remedy to be applied generally, for what helped one, harmed another. Nor did it matter whether one was in excellent condition or poor; each alike succumbed to the disease, and attentive care was of no value. Worst of all was the despair into which they fell when realizing they had caught the plague. Seized by hopelessness, they lost all power to resist.

Those who attended the sick died in the greatest numbers, one catching the disease from the other. They died like sheep. More than anything this fact deepened the disaster, because when from fear of death no one would nurse another, everyone died alone. Whole households disappeared for want of a nurse. If on the other hand one did attend the sick, then they perished too, and especially those who acted from motives of moral responsibility. From shame they were unsparing of themselves in caring for their friends, when even the members of the household, broken by the evil fallen upon them, had given up performing the laments for the dead.

Those to take greatest pity on the dead and the sick were those who had recovered from the disease. They knew what was coming, and had themselves no fear, because no one ever caught the disease twice, at least fatally. Not only did these people receive the congratulations of others, but in the high elation of the moment entertained the vain hope that now they would never die of any other disease sometime in the future.

Thucydides 2.47–51

Thucydides adds a telling note:

Adding to the calamity was the arrival at this time of an influx of refugees into the city,° and they suffered most of all. Having no place to live, but huddled in stifling huts in the height of summer, they died like flies. The corpses of the dead were piled in heaps, and the half-dead careened down the streets and gathered at the fountains in their lust for water.

Thucydides 2.52

°*into the city:* Because of the Spartan invasion.

This plague was so severe because Athens was under siege. People were crammed into unsanitary conditions, and disease spread unchecked. In 1995, digging for a new subway stop in Athens, archaeologists discovered a mass burial of about 90 skeletons, all in a jumble, apparently victims of this plague. Study of their dental DNA suggests they died of typhoid fever, spread by fecal contamination, which was certainly abundant in the crowded city. Diseases, however, undergo rapid evolutionary change, and it is likely that the plague that Thucydides describes, the inspiration through the ages for many literary elaborations, has long ceased to exist.

Most of the time, the main factors limiting life spans were not such spectacular epidemics but everyday sicknesses that are no longer major threats in the developed world. By our standards, the Greek system for the disposal of waste was primitive and unhealthy. There were, of course, no flush toilets, and within the city human waste was first deposited in pots in the house or courtyard and then emptied into a pit near the house. When the pit filled, the contents could be sold to entrepreneurs who gathered the waste, then resold it as fertilizer. The dirty streets were in any event polluted by urine and animal and human waste, devoured by wandering pigs (the pig's taste for human excrement may stand behind prohibitions on eating swine).

Public health was almost nonexistent. There was little control over drinking water, through which disease can be easily spread. Thucydides describes how plague victims threw themselves into public water tanks. This was exceptional behavior, but every day people with running sores, diarrhea, and other infectious complaints polluted each other's drinking water. As if this were not enough, tuberculosis and malaria, whose ancient forms resembled modern ones, were common and deadly, and even minor injuries could turn septic and prove fatal. Wealth and status did not necessarily help: In Egypt, the ancient world's richest land, the pharaoh Tutankhamen (ca. 1341–1323 B.C.) seems to have died from an injury to his leg. Young children were particularly at risk, which explains the high infant mortality. Women often died in childbirth from infection and complications. Skeletons suggest that ancient Greeks spent much of their time feeling unwell, infested with internal parasites, their joints painful from heavy labor, and their teeth worn down from eating coarse foods (although with little sugar in their diet, they had few cavities).

These conditions explain why Greeks died so much younger than modern-day people, but not why their numbers grew so quickly after 800 B.C. The reason seems to be that although their health seems terrible to us, it was quite good when measured by ancient standards. The Greeks' relatively advanced medical skills may have been relevant. The most famous Greek doctor was **Hippocrates** (hip-**pok**-ra-tēz), who lived in the late fifth century B.C. He is a shadowy figure, but probably came from the island of Cos (cōs) in the southwest Aegean, where there was a kind of hospital in classical and Hellenistic times and a great temple to the healing god Asclepius. Hippocrates is said to have written the famous Hippocratic Oath that physicians take even to this day:

> I swear by Apollo the healer, and by Asclepius°, and by *Hygieia* [Health] and all powers that heal, and I call as witness all the gods and goddesses that I might keep this oath and promise as best that I can . . .
>
> I will use my power to help the sick as best I can in accordance with my judgment. I will never harm or wrong any man by my knowledge.
>
> I will never give a fatal drink to anyone if they ask, nor ever suggest such a thing. I will not enable a woman to secure an abortion.
>
> I will be chaste and reverential in my life and in my art.
>
> I will not perform surgery even on patients suffering from [kidney] stones. I will leave such procedure to those who practice that craft.
>
> When I go into a house, I do so in order to help the sick, never to do harm or injury. I will not misuse my status in order to indulge in sexual behavior with the bodies of women or men, free or slave.
>
> If I see or I hear something not to be divulged, in the course of my profession or in private, I will not reveal it. I will tell no one.
>
> Therefore if I observe this oath and do not violate it, may I be prosperous in my life and in my profession, so earning a good reputation among men for all time. If I violate this oath, may my lot be the opposite.
>
> Hippocrates, *The Oath*
>
> °*Asclepius:* The god of medicine.

Hippocrates was the greatest Greek physician, but he had many competitors. (We discuss Greek medicine further in Chapter 23, "Hellenistic Culture, 323–30 B.C.") The kings of Persia would use only Greek doctors and gave them huge gifts. The top doctors were among the richest men in Greece. Around 530 B.C., the ruler of a Greek island paid a doctor one hundred *minai* for his services—what a skilled laborer would earn in forty years!

Greek doctors excelled at diagnosis and prognosis, categorizing illnesses and predicting their course and outcome. But they were less skilled in diagnosing the causes of diseases and worse still at actually treating them. They lacked microscopes, which transformed the treatment of disease in modern times. Their knowledge of the body was crude, and they had little interest in dissection. Hippocrates summed it up by saying, "Life is short. Art is long. Opportunity is brief. Experiment is dangerous. Judgment is difficult." Aristotle—living a hundred years after Hippocrates—conceded that "the internal parts of the body, especially those belonging to humans, are unknown."

If you survived childhood in ancient Greece, you would probably make it through your twenties and thirties unless you suffered an injury or a particularly virulent infection came your way. After forty, your chances steadily declined. If you were rich, a doctor might stave off some threats. If you were poor, you were on your own.

## NUTRITION

Resistance to disease depends on health, and health depends on diet. Most ancient Greeks ate simply. Barley bread was their basic food. Poets called humans "bread-eating mortals"; meat was a luxury, and Greeks rarely ate it except at public sacrifices. There is roughly a ten-to-one conversion ratio between grains and animals, meaning that every calorie you get from eating beef costs ten calories in grains to produce (there is a further ten-to-one conversion ratio between herbivores like cows and carnivores like lions, which is one reason why people do not raise lions for meat!). In Greece, animals were raised more for muscle power than for meat, except at religious sacrifices, which required the slaughter of animals (Figure 2.3). Sheep and goats were the principal sacrificial victims, as they were the most common domestic animals, along with pigs, although there were regional specialties. In Boeotia (bē-ō-sha) in central Greece, giant eels were popular for sacrifices.

Homeric heroes scorned fish as a food, and in one episode in the *Odyssey* (12.327–35) men choose death over eating fish. But in classical times, fish were a delicacy. In comedy,

**FIGURE 2.3** At the sacrificial altar. A line of five women and one man, perhaps dancing, approaches an altar on which a fire burns. The man is nude, apparently an artistic convention, while the women and the priest are clothed. The priest is about to cook the meat of the sacrificial victim in the fire, from the outside of a black-figured Athenian wine-mixing bowl (*krater*), ca. 540 B.C.

the standard way to portray someone as decadent was to have him eat lots of fish. Small frylike sardines and sprats were cheap, and no doubt people living on the coast ate plenty of them. The best that people living inland could hope for was salted fish, while bigger fish like tuna, mackerel, and sturgeon were rare and expensive for everyone. The most important supplements to cereals were olives and wine (Figure 2.4). Bread, olives, and wine made up what historians call the **Mediterranean triad**, the core of the Greek diets from the third millennium B.C. until the twenty-first century A.D. So far, archaeologists have found little evidence of significant changes in the types of grains, olives, and vines grown throughout the first millennium B.C.

The typical diet was monotonous and protein-poor, but healthy and sometimes tasty. There was no sweetener except honey, and salt was hard to come by. Salt was used as a currency in the postclassical world, and provided the origin of our word "*salary.*" Garlic, onions, grapes, goat cheese, and some kinds of sausage were common. Rich Greeks spiced up their bread with sauces and dips and, by the late fifth century B.C., developed a varied cuisine. In the fourth century B.C., a Sicilian chef not only won an international reputation but wrote a mock epic poem about a culinary tour of the Mediterranean.

**FIGURE 2.4** Olive harvest; on a black-figured *amphora* ("jar with two handles") by the Antimenes painter, ca. 520 B.C. Three men knock olives from trees, while a fourth puts olives into a basket.

Historians of modern economies have found a strong correlation between the quality of children's nutrition and their height as adults. Modern historians generally study abundant records of army recruitment or factory hiring giving individuals' heights. No such documents exist from ancient Greece, but we can calculate heights from excavated skeletons. Ancient Greeks were short: in the classical period, men typically stood about five feet, six inches, and women five feet, two inches. Back in the Dark Age, Greeks had been shorter still—the average man by an inch and a half, and the average woman by two inches. Nutrition clearly improved between about 900 and 300 B.C., and sources of food became more reliable, so children went hungry less often. Compared to modern Mediterranean populations, classical Greeks were quite well nourished. As recently as 1949, recruits into the Cypriot army were shorter than Greek men of the fifth and fourth centuries B.C.

Part of the explanation for Greek population growth lies, therefore, in nutrition. As they moved from the Dark Age to classical times, Greeks ate better, lived longer, and multiplied. Life in the fourth century B.C. was hard, but it was better than life in the ninth century B.C.

## Standards of Living

A major element in the material quality of life—perhaps the most important, after food itself—is shelter. In the Dark Age, houses were simple. Most were one-room structures, with the back end often curved in a shape called apsidal, saving the builders from having to construct corners. All activities—cooking, eating, and sleeping—went on either in the one main room or in the open air. The walls were too thin to support a second floor. Six hundred years later, the basic components—mud-brick walls on stone foundations—were the same, but now houses had tile roofs and internal courtyards, shady in summer and sheltered from the rain in winter (Figure 2.5). They had functionally distinct rooms: cooking went on in one, eating in another, drinking in another still. Many had paved floors, simple drains sometimes used as a latrine (but chamber pots remained standard), and staircases to a second floor. The roofed part of the ground level covered some 2,400 square feet in typical houses, about the norm for contemporary American housing and five times the area of the typical Dark Age house. Depending on how much of the upstairs part was roofed, it may have been twice this size, a commodious and pleasant house by any standards.

As well as living longer and eating better, classical Greeks also had richer and more varied domestic goods than Dark Age Greeks. Greece had increased significantly in wealth: a fourth-century house must have cost five to ten times as much as one built in the tenth century.

The public amenities of Greek cities also improved drastically. By the sixth century B.C., major centers like Athens and Syracuse had underground pipes bringing drinking water to the downtown areas, and even quite small cities had fountain houses. Magnificent temples, beautiful statues, and strong fortifications were found all over Greece. In the tenth century B.C., Athens had an urban population under 2,000; in the fifth century, the population reached 40,000. In the fourth century B.C., Syracuse was twice that size. What caused these improvements in the material bases of life in Greece?

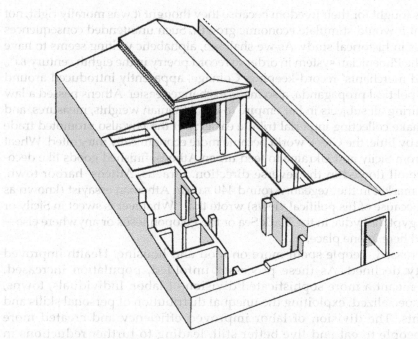

**FIGURE 2.5**  Reconstruction of
a house, ca. 350 B.C.

## ECONOMIC GROWTH IN ANCIENT GREECE

The last 250 years have witnessed a revolution in human life. Eighteenth-century Europeans learned to harness the power of fossil fuels, beginning with steam produced by burning coal. As this technology spread, inventors made increasingly radical breakthroughs. We nowadays take it for granted that technology drives economic growth, but this was not so in ancient Greece. In the Classical and Hellenistic periods, the basic technologies—plows and manure in agriculture, ships and carts in transport, bronze armor and iron weapons in war—had been around for centuries. There were steady, small improvements, but not until the third century B.C. did scientists in the Greek city of Alexandria in Egypt make inventions that could really improve production (see Chapter 23, "Hellenistic Culture, 323–30 B.C."). The economic growth that took place between the Dark Age and the Classical Period depended on changes in the way society was organized, not on new technologies.

Such changes were not the result of conscious economic planning. Even the great Aristotle had only the vaguest understanding of economics. Rather, while pursuing other goals, Greeks accidentally set free forces of growth that most other ancient societies had kept in check. One of the most important of these was the increasing personal freedom of the Greek citizen. In the Classical Period, ordinary citizens had better legal protection than members of most ancient civilizations. It was difficult (though not impossible) for wealthy neighbors or agents of the state to defraud them, seize their property, or sell them into slavery. Shielded to some extent from arbitrary plunder, they had more incentive to invest effort and resources into farming or to add to their income through trading and craft.

Ancient Greeks fought for their freedom because they thought it was morally right, not because they thought it would stimulate economic growth. Such unintended consequences are important themes in historical study. As we shall see, alphabetic writing seems to have been adapted from the Phoenician system in order to record poetry in the eighth century B.C., but it also simplified merchants' record-keeping. Coinage, apparently introduced around 600 B.C. as a form of political propaganda, also made exchanges easier. Athens passed a law around 425 B.C. requiring all subjects in her empire to use Athenian weights, measures, and coins, no doubt to make collecting imperial tribute easier; but the law also promoted trade between cities. Little by little, the Greek world became more economically integrated. Wheat and barley moved from Sicily and Ukraine to feed urban Athens; finished goods like decorated pots and olive oil flowed in the reverse direction. Piraeus, Athens' harbor town, became the greatest market in the Aegean. Around 440 B.C. an Athenian essayist (known as "the Old Oligarch" because of his political views) wrote that "Whatever is sweet in Sicily or in Italy, in Cyprus, Egypt, or Lydia, in the Black Sea or the Peloponnesus or anywhere else— all these are gathered here in one place."

As wealth increased, people spent more on food and housing. Health improved and early mortality declined. As these processes unfolded, population increased. Growing numbers meant a more sophisticated division of labor. Individuals, towns, and whole regions specialized, exploiting the unequal distribution of personal skills and natural endowments. The division of labor improved efficiency and created more wealth, allowing people to eat and live better still, leading to further reductions in mortality, which stimulated more population growth . . . and so on, in a self-reinforcing cycle. By our best guess, classical Greeks on average consumed 50 percent more wealth than their Dark Age predecessors.

Without this economic growth, the cultural achievements that fill this book could not have happened. But let us close this chapter by stressing two facts. First, although conditions were better for the typical Greek in the fourth century B.C. than they were in the tenth century B.C., life was still hard by our own standards. Even in the best of times, Greeks were stunted and malnourished compared to people in modern developed countries. Economic growth reached a ceiling, slowed, and finally stopped. You can go only so far by reorganizing institutions. Without technological advances, there are limits to growth. The Greeks reached these limits and never went further.

Second, Greek economic growth was linked to slavery. Only a minority of the population of Greece were slaves, but they played an essential role. People who could afford slaves could add labor to enterprises when they needed it and then dispose of unprofitable workers. Some wealthy people bought gangs of slaves and rented them to entrepreneurs for difficult and dangerous work like mining. Classical Greek civilization could not have existed without slavery, which gave an elite group the freedom to fashion a remarkable civilization. We ourselves use labor-saving machines to create comparable leisure, leaving us free to abominate slavery. How, then, should we evaluate the Greek achievement, given the different material circumstances in which they lived?

## Key Terms

| | | |
|---|---|---|
| Hesiod, 14 | demography, 16 | Hippocrates, 21 |
| Works and Days, 14 | Thucydides, 18 | Mediterranean triad, 23 |

# Further Reading

## PHYSICAL WORLD, DEMOGRAPHY, NUTRITION, AND ECONOMIC GROWTH

Walter Scheidel, Ian Morris, and Richard Saller, eds., *The Cambridge Economic History of the Greco-Roman World* (Cambridge, UK, 2007). Collection of essays by leading experts on every aspect of ancient economic history.

Garnsey, Peter, *Food and Society in Classical Antiquity* (Cambridge, UK, 1999). Excellent summary of food, nutrition, and health.

Hansen, Mogens H., *The Shotgun Method: The Demography of the Ancient Greek-State Culture* (New York, 2006). Good estimates of ancient Greek population sizes.

## DAILY LIFE

Garland, Robert, *Daily Life of the Ancient Greeks* (Westport, CT, 1998). Excellent survey of all aspects of everyday life. The best introduction to many of the topics in this chapter.

## HEALTH AND DISEASE

Grmek, Mirko, *Diseases in the Ancient Greek World* (Baltimore, 1989). A detailed introduction.

## ANCIENT TEXTS

Hesiod, *Works and Days*. In *Hesiod and Theognis*, tr. Dorothea Wender (Harmondsworth, UK, 1973). Agricultural poem.

Hippocrates, *Airs, Waters, Places*. In *Hippocratic Writings*, ed. G. E. R. Lloyd (New York, 1978). Account of climate and disease, probably written around 400 B.C.

Thucydides, *The Peloponnesian War*, tr. Rex Warner (Harmondsworth, UK, 1954).

## CHAPTER 3

# The Greeks at Home

If land was the economic foundation of ancient Greece, the *oikos*, "house/family" (the root of the word "*economic*") was its social foundation. The *oikos* was broader than our concept of family because it included slaves, close relations, and the house and its contents, but the basic *oikos* was still a monogamous union of man and woman to produce and rear legitimate children. We therefore begin with Greek relationships between the sexes. As always, our information has an Athenian bias, because of the preeminence of Athenian literature, and is largely from the Archaic and Classical Periods.

## GENDER RELATIONSHIPS: IDEALS AND REALITIES

Throughout Greek history, virtually all the men who wrote our texts agreed on a few points about marriage. Men should wed around the age of thirty; women, as teenagers. Brides should be virgins (although widows or divorcees could remarry); no man would marry a young woman who was not a virgin, what Greeks called a "broken vessel." A marriage (Figure 3.1) was contracted between a groom and the parents of his bride-to-be, who gave their daughter a dowry to help set up a new household. A wife was expected to obey her husband and not act independently, except within the *oikos*, where she was responsible for preparing food, rearing children, and producing cloth. Laws varied from *polis* to *polis*, but usually women owned little or no real estate, the basic economic resource. In most cities, laws limited women to trivial financial transactions and denied them access to the legal system, an all-male preserve. Some ancient authors took it for granted that husbands would beat disobedient wives. Although no source actually describes a beating, the swashbuckling Alcibiades (ca. 450–04 B.C.) is reputed to have assaulted his wife before a magistrate when she attempted to divorce him (he picked her up and carried her through the marketplace; she died suspiciously soon after: Plutarch, *Life of Alcibiades*, 8).

Of course, all our sources are texts produced by men for men. Scrappy evidence suggests that some women found ways around the laws on property and used men to get access to the courts. Scholars have assiduously examined the few dozen lines that survive

**FIGURE 3.1** A woman, named as Thalea, prepares for her wedding on a red-figured *pyxis,* a clay box for keeping trinkets, ca. 440 B.C. A servant (off photo to the right) offers the bride a chest, perhaps containing toiletries, while another (also named) approaches from behind to tie her hair with a ribbon. A third servant stands on the far left. Notice the bronze mirror on the wall, indicating an interior setting.

of the extraordinary, almost unique, female poet **Sappho**, who lived around 600 B.C., hoping to detect evidence for a female viewpoint on gender, but little can be said except that the tone of her poetry is similar to that of her male contemporaries. In the pitiful fragments that survive (a newly discovered fragment was published in 2005), we find that Sappho celebrates love and marriage as a woman's primary concerns (Figure 3.2). She addressed some poems to other women, suggesting to readers since Roman times (but never to Greeks) that she celebrated homoerotic love: hence the term *lesbian*, because Sappho lived on the island of Lesbos. However, her voice is never personal. she wrote poems to be memorized and performed by others at weddings, virtually the only time in a respectable woman's life when female sexuality could be publicly celebrated without shame. The men may have made the rules, but the respectable women—mothers, grand-mothers, aunts—enforced them.

Our male sources often represent women as an evil influence, virtually a separate species. Such **misogyny** ("hatred for women") is an important theme in Greek culture. Hesiod justified it with a story of how Zeus, ruler of the gods, created the dreaded race of females to punish men for having accepted the theft of fire from heaven (Figure 3.3). Zeus says

> "I'll give to men an evil thing
> in which each, in his heart, will delight, loving the evil."
>     So he spoke. The father of men and gods
> laughed, and he ordered Hephaestus° quickly to mix

°*Hephaestus:* The lame, ugly god of craftsmen (better known today by his Roman name Vulcan).

**FIGURE 3.2** Sappho, as imagined on the side of an amphora (two-handled jar) by a red-figure painted around 440 B.C., perhaps 150 years after her lifetime. The figure labeled "Sappho" sits on a folding chair and studies a papyrus with a poetic text (we cannot read it). A woman standing before her offers the lyre that accompanied many forms of Greek poetry.

earth with water, and within to place human
speech and strength, with a face like a deathless goddess,
the lovely beauty of a young girl. Athena°
would teach her to weave fine cloth, and upon her head
would Aphrodite° pour out golden charm
and wretched desire and limb-devouring care.
Zeus ordered Hermes° the messenger, the killer of Argus,
to place within her the mind of a female dog
and a deceitful heart. He spoke, the gods obeyed.
        The lame god,° obeying the will of Zeus,
molded earth into the likeness of a modest young girl,
and the gray-eyed goddess Athena gave her a belt
and clothes, and the goddess Graces and divine Seduction
placed golden necklaces upon her flesh. The Seasons,

°*Athena:* The virgin goddess of war and handicrafts, who sprang fully formed from Zeus's head.
°*Aphrodite:* The beautiful goddess of sexual attraction (Roman Venus).   °*Hermes:* Messenger of the gods, and god of trickery, trade, and travel (Roman Mercury); Argus was a monster with a hundred eyes that Hermes killed.   °*lame god:* Hephaestus.

**FIGURE 3.3** Epimetheus, brother of Prometheus, takes Pandora's hand as she rises from the earth; on a red-figured Athenian *krater* (wine-mixing vase), ca. 450 B.C. On the far left, Zeus oversees his plan to punish man by inventing woman. The messenger god Hermes carries his wand and wears a magic cap and shoes.

whose hair is beautiful, crowned her with spring flowers.
But within her heart the messenger of the gods placed
a deceitful nature, and he named her Pandora° because
all who dwelled on Olympus had given her something,
a sorrow to wheat-devouring men. And when the father
accomplished his steep, ruinous device he sent
the clever slayer of Argus, the messenger of the gods,
to bring the gift to Epimetheus,° who forgot
the warning of his brother Prometheus not
to accept a gift from Olympian Zeus, but to send
it back, so that evil not befall the race of mortals.
He took the gift and knew too late the evil
he had.
     Once the tribes of humans lived
free from evil, free from hard labor
and awful disease that brings the death-spirits;

°*Pandora:* "all-gifted."  °*Epimetheus . . . Prometheus:* Epimetheus (epē-mē-thŭs), a mortal whose name means "afterthought," was the stupid brother of the wily Prometheus (pro-mē-th s, "forethought"). Prometheus stole fire from heaven in a fennel stalk and gave it to humans; for this crime Pandora was punishment. Epimetheus married Pandora and all humans descend from their union.

> in misery mortals quickly grow old. The woman
> took off the heavy lid with her hands and scattered
> pains and evils among men. Only Hope remained
> in the hard-walled home, beneath the lid of the jar,°
> and did not fly outside before she clapped down
> the lid. But ten thousand miseries wander among humans.
> The earth is full of evil, and so is the sea.
> Diseases visit by day and uninvited come by
> night, bringing evils to mortals in silence, for Zeus
> who is wise removed their voice. There is no way
> to flee the mind of Zeus.

Hesiod, *Works and Days* 57–105

°*jar:* Apparently a gift from Zeus. A medieval mistranslation led to the phrase "Pandora's box."

Hesiod makes women's inferiority and dangerous intentions part of Zeus' cosmic plan to punish wicked mortals, who must previously have lived in an all-male paradise (he does not explain how they reproduced). The plan embodied the first female, the lovely but deceitful and lustful ("a female dog") Pandora, whose name, Hesiod says, means "all-gifted" because many gods endowed her with gifts (her name really means "giver-of-all," perhaps in origin a spirit of the bountiful earth). Later Greek writers offered more nuanced interpretations. The most interesting work was written soon after 400 B.C. by **Xenophon** (**zen**-o-fon), an Athenian aristocrat and professional soldier, as part of a longer story describing a fictional conversation between the wise Athenian Socrates and a man named Ischomachus (is-**kom**-a-kus; Figure 3.4 supports Xenophon's observations):

"But I [Socrates] would also gladly ask you this question, whether you yourself trained your wife in proper behavior, or whether her father and mother had already trained her in what it takes to run a household?"

"But Socrates, how could she have known anything? She came to me when she was fifteen years old. Up until then she had carefully been kept from seeing, hearing, or saying anything. Don't you think I should be pleased if she came knowing only how to turn wool into cloth, and how to divide the wool-spinning among the slaves? In fact," he said, "she came with excellent training of her appetite, which seems to me the most important thing for both husband and wife!"

"So then you yourself, Ischomachus, trained her in what she needs to know to manage the house? . . . What first did you teach her? Tell me. I would much rather hear this than a description of some exceptional athletic event, or of a wonderful horse race."

Ischomachus answered, "Well, as soon as she seemed manageable, when I had tamed her down enough so that she was in a position to carry on a conversation, I asked, 'My dear, I wonder if you have yet understood why I took you and why your parents gave you to me? You know as well as I that it would not have been hard to find someone else with whom to share our bed. But I for my own part was interested in who would be best to govern my household and to bear my children, and your parents had the same interest. They preferred me to all others, and I preferred you. If the gods grant us children, then will we take counsel about how best to raise them up. Such will be our common advantage, to have the best possible

**FIGURE 3.4** Women drawing water from a well house; on an Attic black-figured vase, ca. 530 B.C. One woman fills her amphora, while two others, jugs balanced on their heads, gossip. A third woman faces the other way. Drawing water was a regular chore for the household women.

allies and helpmates in our old age. And for now we share in a common household. I place all that I earn in a common pool, and you have done the same with the dowry you have brought. It is not important who has put in the most quantitatively, because we know that whoever is the greater partner deserves the most credit.'

"My wife answered in the following way, Socrates: 'How can I help you? What can I do? It is all up to you. My mother told me that it was my role to act in a responsible fashion.'

"'By Zeus, that is what my father said to me!' I said. 'It is just as much the husband's obligation as the wife's to behave responsibly, and to increase the wealth of the household in accordance with moral and legal behavior.'

"'But what,' said my wife, 'do you think that I can do to increase our wealth?'

"'Why,' I said, 'you must do what the gods made you capable of doing, and what custom approves. This, in my opinion, is the best possible behavior.'

"'And what are these things?' my wife asked.

"'Matters of no small importance, unless the tasks in the hive over which the queen bee presides are of small moment! For it seems to me that the gods have very prudently ordered the union of what we call male and female that they might form a partnership of the utmost mutual benefit. First of all, the union brings about offspring, which guarantees the furtherance of all species. Second, offspring provides support for parents in their old age, at least among humans. Third, humans do not live in the open air like beasts, but obviously require a roof over their heads. Of course, it will be necessary to work outdoors in order to provide things to put in the shelter. Such outdoor activities are plowing, sowing, growing, and herding flocks, which will provide the necessities for life. Once they have been brought inside it will be necessary to care for them and to do what must be done in the house. The raising of young children will require shelter too, as does the making of bread from grain and the weaving of cloth from wool. Because both indoor and outdoor tasks require work and attention, the god, as I see it, made woman's nature suitable for the indoor jobs and tasks, and man's nature suitable for the outdoor ones. For he made the body and soul of man better able to withstand cold and heat and travel and military expeditions. For this reason he imposed on him the outdoor tasks. Because he made the woman's body less capable of such endurance, it seems to me, the god assigned to her the indoor work. Because he had created in the woman and imposed on her the task of nourishing the newborn, he gave her greater affection for babes than he gave to the man. And because he imposed on the woman the job of protecting the stores, and realizing that for that purpose fear is an advantage, the god gave her a larger share of fear than he gave to the man.'"

Xenophon, *Oeconomicus* 7.4–20

Unlike Hesiod, Xenophon does not represent woman as man's punishment, but does believe that the gods made men superior to women: tougher, more disciplined, and more suited to an outdoor life. Yet marriage is a partnership. The husband is in control, but he and his wife must work together. A virtuous husband can educate his wife so that her contribution to the household becomes equal to his own. Socrates is so impressed by the description that he interjects, "Good heavens, Ischomachus! On your evidence, your wife has a mind as good as a man's!"

Another Athenian writer, Andocides (an-**dos**-i-dēz) (fourth century B.C.), gives a different account of Ischomachus' wife and tells us her name, Chrysilla. In Xenophon's version, she happily stays home, trying to live up to the standards that Ischomachus expects. In Andocides' version, she begins an affair with a man named Callias, who marries Ischomachus' daughter while sleeping with Chrysilla, his own mother-in-law, at the same time! Chrysilla then moves in with Callias, her lover, and his wife, her daughter. The distraught daughter attempts suicide before leaving Callias, who throws out Chrysilla, now pregnant with his child. Later, Callias takes Chrysilla back and adopts their son, and they all live together (though perhaps not too happily). Perhaps Xenophon idealized Chrysilla to exemplify what he (and many Athenian men) thought marriage *ought* to be like.

## SEXUALITY

Ischomachus says that he chose his wife because she was the best person to share his home and children. A wife's success was judged largely by her ability to produce sons. After all, a stable population required the average woman to have four or five live births, as we have seen; during periods of population growth, as in the fifth century, the average was seven to eight. Marriage followed swiftly on menarche, pregnancy swiftly on that. Most women remained pregnant or nursing for their entire married lives.

Male writers often refer to sexual activity in marriage as "work," the work of producing heirs, using the image of a farmer sowing seed in a field. Sex outside marriage was available to men in various forms, but was unacceptable for women. Many men owned slaves, and sexual relations between masters and slaves (female and male) were commonplace, but adultery with a free woman was dangerous. The woman's guardian—her father, husband, brother, or son—could, and sometimes did, kill the adulterer (though he usually spared the adulteress). Most *poleis* took steps to prevent retaliation from turning into blood-feuds by imposing heavy fines on adulterers. In Athens, for example, the fine for adultery was twice that for rape, apparently because a rapist committed a one-time assault, while a seducer turned a woman's mind against her *oikos*, inflicting a permanent scar on another man's property and reputation. Worse still, a seduced wife might pass off the adulterer's son as a legitimate heir, thereby stealing the entire household.

Prostitutes were an easier source of sexual pleasure for the male, and there were many of them in major *poleis* like Athens and Corinth. Greeks divided prostitutes into two categories: *hetairai*, or "courtesans," and *pornai*, or "whores" (root of *porn*ography, "whore-writing"). The famous Pericles kept a courtesan named **Aspasia;** she bore him a child and he kissed her in full view of his fellow citizens. She conversed with the day's leading intellectuals, and Plato joked that she wrote some of Pericles' speeches. A few courtesans made fortunes from their trade, but most sex-workers were *pornai* (singular form, *pornê*), often slaves who led unglamorous lives (Figure 3.5).

Comic writers in fifth-century Athens make prostitution sound fun-filled, but we occasionally glimpse the other side. The fourth-century Athenian speechwriter Andocides tells of a slave girl who slept with her master. He got tired of her and decided to sell her to

**FIGURE 3.5**   An aging *pornê* masturbates a client; from a red-figured Athenian *kylix*, ca. 510 B.C.

a brothel. The slave was so terrified that she poisoned him and, accidentally, a visiting friend too. When her plot was discovered, she was tortured and executed.

We know little about Greek brothels. A possible brothel of around 400 B.C. has been found in Athens, but its identification remains controversial. It is not obvious what archaeologists could find to prove that an ancient building was used for commercial sex, although in Roman Pompeii (destroyed A.D. 79) sexual scenes decorated brothel walls. The Athenian building had a maze of small rooms, and finds include many images of Aphrodite, the sex-goddess, and ornaments from Asia Minor and the northern Balkans, the source of many slaves in Greece. Other finds suggest that the building was an inn and a center for weaving—other sides of brothel life, according to literary sources.

Greek men also had sexual relations with boys and, occasionally, with men of their own age. In modern times, male homosexuality is sometimes coyly called "Greek love," but same-sex relationships among the Greeks were different from homosexual behavior in modern times. In its usual (and usually respectable) form, a mature male was the sexually active partner (the *erastês*, or "lover"), while a prepubescent passive partner (the *eromenos*, or "beloved") received the erect penis of the *erastês* between his thighs (so-called intercrural intercourse). Such **pederasty** ("boy-love") grew out of the social environment of the Greek symposium, or "drinking party," where prepubescent males served wine and learned about adult male behavior. In general, however, it was shameful to remain an *eromenos* after sexual maturity. The fifth-century B.C. comic poet Aristophanes savagely ridiculed men who put themselves in the position of a woman, that is, were the recipients in anal intercourse with other males. Nonetheless, in the fourth century B.C., an elite band of Theban warriors reportedly consisted of pairs of lovers, and the mature Alexander the Great, according to tradition, maintained sexual relations with a boyhood friend named Hephaestion.

In many *poleis* the adult *erastês* introduced his younger *eromenos* to the ways of polite society, establishing social contacts for help later in life (Figure 3.6). If the *eromenos* were

**FIGURE 3.6** Pederastic scene; from an Attic red-figured *kylix*, ca. 500 B.C. An older *erastês* kisses a younger *eromenos*. At left is a caged hare, a standard gift in pederastic relationships and often shown on vases. In the upper right are a strigil and sponge evoking the gymnasium where pederastic relationships flourished.

wealthy, talented, from a famous family, or particularly handsome, he would reflect back honor onto his *erastês*. Some Greek writers, notably Plato, thought that the relationship should remain chaste (hence the expression "Platonic love"), focusing on intellectual development; others thought it should be explicitly sexual but come to an end when the *eromenos* reached puberty and the first traces of a beard appeared. Spartan pederasty, expected of all males as a form of moral training, was closely tied to Spartan military training and, reportedly, often without overt sexual expression, just as Plato recommended.

We know a fair amount, then, about male sexual life, but our sources, written by men, say little about female sexual life. Athenian law required that women convicted of adultery be divorced, whether their husbands wanted it or not. The adulteress was disgraced and sent back to her parents, if they still lived. She was also forbidden to attend public religious festivals, the equivalent of males being banned from political life. With little chance of finding a new husband, an adulterous woman could not be saved from disgrace and poverty.

Occasionally, comic writers joked about free women having sex with male slaves, and comedies and vase-painting made great play out of women finding pleasure in dildoes. Many erotic illustrations survive—only Japanese art has shown the same concern with sex and pornography. The illustrations suggest that the Greeks were not prudish about sex, but they were meant for men's eyes alone in the sometimes licentious environment of the symposium. True, in art men are usually shown naked, unlike in any earlier society, but such conventions do not appeal to a prurient interest. They are trained toward an eye for athletic excellence. In contrast, until the fourth century B.C., respectable women in art are portrayed clothed, for it was shameful to see a woman's body. Some men felt that respectable women should be veiled in public. Parents were anxious for the safety of their children's bodies, and strict rules prohibited seduction within the gymnasium, where men and boys were naked and females forbidden. Greek erotic art probably represents general Greek attitudes toward sexuality no better than contemporary pornography represents modern attitudes.

## ADULTS AND CHILDREN

According to Euripides, one of the great tragedians of fifth-century B.C. Athens, children were the center of life. "Both the best of mortals and those who are nobodies love children. They differ in material things. Some have property and some do not; but the whole race is child-loving" (*Heracles Insane*, 633–6). Typically, married couples were surrounded by small children for most of their lives together.

Different *poleis* imposed different educations and customs on their citizens. Sparta, especially, was distinct. We will discuss Spartan customs in detail in Chapter 10, "A Tale of Two Archaic Cities: Sparta and Athens, 700–480 B.C." We know far more about Athens than other *poleis*, but we can perhaps generalize about "Greek customs" from our study of Athenian customs.

The burden of child-rearing fell on the mother. Xenophon explains:

> The man works to provide his partner in the begetting of children, and the children themselves, with everything he thinks will benefit them in life, and he is always looking out for a way to increase his support. The woman, by contrast, conceives the children and bears the burden, weighed down, her life endangered, giving off food from her own body, and when with great suffering she has borne the child and given birth to it, she nourishes and cares for it, although

the child has done her no good and does not even know who his benefactor is. He cannot even communicate what he wants, but she, guessing what he needs and would enjoy, attempts to supply these things. She labors long, enduring hardship night and day, and never knows if she will receive any gratitude.

Xenophon, *Memorabilia* 2.2.5

Birth and the first few days of life were hazardous for children and mothers. There were no hospitals, let alone epidurals (a local anesthetic) or Caesarian sections, but midwives no doubt had plenty of experience and the folk wisdom that comes from experience. All the same, Euripides, in his tragedy the *Medea*, has the heroine proclaim that she would rather stand three times behind a shield in battle than give birth once.

In theory, fathers had the right to decide whether to keep newborn babies or to expose them to die. Our information is poor, but apparently girls were exposed more than boys. Unwanted babies were left in well-known spots that slave traders would check, and the babies would either die of exposure or be sold into a lifetime of servitude. Many prostitutes began life in this way. The famous myth of Oedipus begins with his being exposed to die as an accursed child.

Wanted babies who survived their first few days underwent rituals that brought them into the community in a formal way. The most important was the *amphidromia,* or "running around." Holding the baby in his arms, the father walked around the hearth, presenting the baby to **Hestia** (**hes**-ti-a), goddess of the hearth (her name means simply "hearth"). The *amphidromia* established the child's legitimacy and its future status as a citizen. Friends and neighbors brought gifts of octopus and cuttlefish. The parents hung an olive branch outside the front door if the child was a boy, and a tuft of wool if a girl. Whatever the sex, they smeared the walls with black tar to turn away hostile spirits attracted by the bloody fluids that attend childbirth.

Many parents named the child at this fifth-day festival, but those who could afford to hold a second party delayed naming until the *dekatê,* the "tenth day," when women danced and honey cakes were passed around. Unlike in most modern societies, Greeks gave children only one name, used in conjunction with the father's name—for example, "Pericles, son of Xanthippos." The firstborn son of a family often took the name of his father's father; other sons commonly took variants on their father's name. As in our own world, names went in and out of fashion.

Greek medicine was superior to others in the ancient world but riddled nonetheless with superstition. For example, Galen, a famous second-century A.D. doctor (see Chapter 23, "Hellenistic Culture, 323–30 B.C."), advised against giving babies protein-rich colostrum, the premilk fluid which comes from a mother's breast before the milk itself and prevents infection. Families that could afford it gave their children to wet nurses, although mothers' milk is best. Swaddling (close wrapping to prevent movement) was common, although it can deform bones if the babies are malnourished. Doctors recommended weaning at dangerously early or strangely late ages, hardly ever at appropriate ones. Microscopic analysis of teeth shows that most Greek children experienced periods of malnutrition.

Whatever the medical disadvantages, intense bonds might develop between a child and its wet nurse. A wet nurse in a play by Aeschylus says:

My own Orestes, he wore me out.
I raised him, taking him from his mother.
Oh, the many and troublesome tasks

when he cried out to me in the night
waking me up, fruitless though I endured them . . .
For you must nurse the senseless thing
like a dumb beast the best you can,
what else can you do? While still in diapers,
a babe has no speech at all, whether it is hungry,
or thirsty, or wants to make water.
The young insides of children go on their own way.
Often I could tell, but just as often I was deceived
and had to wash the child's linen, as much laundry-maid as nurse.
Performing these twin duties, I raised up Orestes
for his father. And now to learn, cursed that I am . . .
that he is dead!

Aeschylus, *Libation Bearers* 749–63

Boys and girls were reared together until they were somewhere between five and seven years, spending most of their time with their mothers. They helped around the house. Ball games were popular, although the best balls available were simply inflated pigs' bladders. They were not very round but could be improved by heating in the embers of a fire. There were board games too, and games with dice and the squarish-shaped knuckle-bones of pigs (*astragaloi*), which adults used for gambling.

Death or divorce often ended marriages while children were still young. Men typically died in their forties, ten to fifteen years after they married. Their widows either moved back in with their birth family or remarried, leading to all kinds of legal complications. Far more children were orphans than in our world. Wealthy orphans had guardians to look after their estates, which could lead to acrimony and, when the child matured, years of lawsuits. Poor orphans relied on relatives, although if the father had been killed in war, they might get community support. For most orphans, life was very hard. In the cities, they easily fell into the underworld of prostitutes and thieves.

Around the age of seven, boys and girls with parents to support them began to be segregated. Most boys now spent more time in the fields (with their fathers if they were lucky), and girls learned the weaving and housekeeping skills they would need as wives. In wealthy families, boys (and a few girls) received formal schooling in the alphabet, concentrating on memorizing poetry (especially Homer) and performing it to the accompaniment of a lyre (Greek *mousikê*, meaning "the art of the Muse"). An educated man was expected to have some skill in these areas, but not too much. Even in Athens, where literacy was most widespread by far, probably only one male in ten could read. Most professionals in primary education were slaves, and no one wanted to be skilled enough to be mistaken for a slave.

Educated slave chaperones accompanied wealthy schoolchildren at all times and helped the children with their studies. These slaves and the schoolmasters spent a lot of time just keeping their pupils under control. Physical punishment was common, although aristocratic boys were not always happy being slapped around by slaves. There are stories of pupils attacking their teachers. in myth, the hero Heracles killed his music teacher by using his lyre as a club, then was acquitted on grounds of self-defense!

With the onset of puberty around fourteen, this kind of schooling ended. There was nothing like what we think of as higher education. By the late fifth century B.C., wealthy young men could attach themselves to intellectuals, sometimes following them around and listening to them talk, at other times hiring them for a fee, but few did this.

In many city-states, boys spent at least a couple of years between their fourteenth and eighteenth birthdays in formal military training under the supervision of mature men. This training involved garrison duty and experience sleeping in the rough, as if on campaign. Such behavior was highly developed in Sparta (see Chapter 10).

Greek literature is full of stories of conflict between fathers and rebellious teenage sons, and an Athenian legal speech by the orator Demosthenes (dem-**os**-then-**ēz**) describes juvenile delinquents calling themselves "the hard-ons" going around at night attacking older citizens. The comic poet Aristophanes refers to the "father-beaters" as if they were a familiar category of irreverent sons. Like most premodern societies, *poleis* had no police, but depended on fathers and other older kin to control wild male teenagers. Girls, by contrast, were normally married at this age and were under the control of a husband (and the husband's mother).

Technically, boys became adults and were admitted to the ranks of the citizen warriors at age eighteen. Fewer than half would have a living father by then; some would have already been masters of their own affairs for some time.

## Key Terms

| | | |
|---|---|---|
| *oikos, 28* | Xenophon, *32* | *amphidromia, 38* |
| Sappho, *28* | Aspasia, *35* | Hestia, *38* |
| misogyny, *29* | pederasty, *36* | |

## Further Reading

Dover, Kenneth, *Greek Homosexuality* (Cambridge, MA, 1978). The book that made scholarly study of this field respectable. A classic.

Garland, Robert, *Daily Life of the Ancient Greeks* (Westport, CT, 1998). Excellent survey of all aspects of everyday life. The best introduction to many of the topics in this chapter.

Golden, Mark, *Children and Childhood in Classical Athens* (Baltimore, 1990). Much the best survey of the evidence.

Halperin, David, Jack Winkler, and Froma Zeitlin, eds., *Before Sexuality* (Princeton, NJ, 1990). Important collection of essays on different aspects of sexuality in Greece.

Hubbard, Thomas, *Homosexuality in Greece and Rome: A Sourcebook of Basic Documents* (Berkeley, 2003). Collects Greek and Latin texts that inform us about same-sex activities.

———, ed., *Greek Love Reconsidered* (New York, 2000). Four scholars reconstruct Greeks' attitudes toward pederasty and their evolution.

Patterson, Cynthia, *The Family in Greek History* (Cambridge, MA, 1998). Good survey.

### ANCIENT TEXTS

Aeschylus, *The Oresteia*, tr. Robert Fagles (New York, 1984). Aeschylus' trilogy on the House of Atreus.

Hesiod, *Works and Days* and *Theogony*. In *Hesiod and Theognis*, tr. Dorothea Wender (Harmondsworth, UK, 1973). The basic poetic accounts of the origins of mortals and immortals.

Plato, *The Symposium*, tr. W. Hamilton (Harmondsworth, UK, 1951). Entertaining account of a drinking party and sexual mores in early fourth-century B.C. Athens.

Xenophon, *Conversations of Socrates*, ed. Hugh Treddenick and Robin Waterfield (New York, 1990). Some of the best sources about daily life and values in Athens, early fourth century B.C.

## CHAPTER 4

# The Greeks Before History, 12,000–1200 B.C.

In Chapter 2, "Country and People," and Chapter 3, "The Greeks at Home," we described some of the foundations of classical Greek life: the environment, demography, standards of living, and the family. But conditions of life in Greece were always changing. Now we will start tracing such changes, beginning with the long centuries that scholars call "prehistoric": times for which we have no written information, for which archaeology is our major source of evidence. Let us travel back some 15,000 years.

## THE END OF THE LAST ICE AGE, 13,000–9500 B.C.

Climate has a history. In the last 150 years, human activity has raised the average temperature on earth. But natural climatic changes are also well attested in the geological record. Shifts in the earth's axis and sunspot activity have caused several ice ages in the last two million years. A drop in average temperature of just 8°F would leave one-third of the world covered by ice all year round. The most recent Ice Age began about 35,000 years ago, ending just 13,000 years ago; but after a thousand years of warmth, a "mini Ice Age" followed, and not until about 9500 B.C. did a warm, stable climate set in (Map 4.1).

Greece stayed warmer than the rest of Europe, but at the coldest point, around 18,000 B.C., its winters were longer and colder than anything classical Greeks had to complain about. The average winter temperature in Athens around 15,000 B.C. was roughly 30°F. Today, it is closer to 50°F.

The earliest evidence of humans in Greece dates back 200,000 years, but fully modern humans (*Homo sapiens sapiens*) only entered 35,000 years ago. The population was tiny. Finds from caves suggest that people lived in bands of fifteen to twenty-five members. The few edible wild plants were available only in summer, so the tiny population was constantly moving, following herds of animals that migrated into the mountains in summer and came

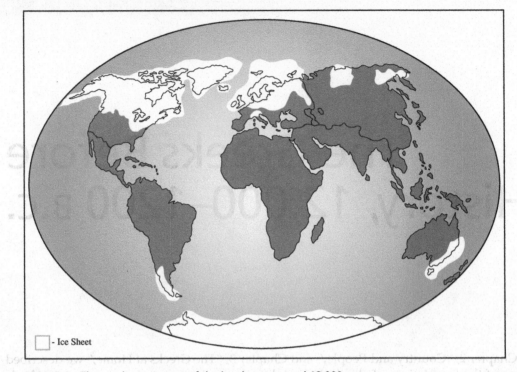

**MAP 4.1**   The maximum extent of the ice sheet, around 18,000 B.C.

down onto the plains in winter. Each band needed a huge territory to feed itself, and the whole of Greece probably supported only a few thousand people.

## THE ORIGINS OF AGRICULTURE, 9500–5000 B.C.

By 9500 B.C., temperatures settled close to modern levels. The wet mixed woodlands of Ice Age Greece gave way to the sparse and dry vegetation that we described in Chapter 2, and in the **Fertile Crescent** in the Near East, changes that were to transform Greek life were underway (Map 4.2).

As temperatures rose in the hill country that is now northern IRAQ and eastern TURKEY, an area that gets low but reliable rainfall (ten to twelve inches each year), wild grains were evolving. Some had large seeds that could be crushed into porridge and bread. People gathering these grains could support larger populations per square mile than was possible in the Ice Age. Bands got larger and split into more bands until once again they pressed against the limits their territories could support. Dwellers in the northern foothills of the mountains that bound the Fertile Crescent began selectively breeding wild grasses to produce better strains, creating the first genetically modified crops. In this revolutionary period, they also experimented with animal husbandry, taming cattle, sheep, pigs, and goats.

Such profound changes in food supply required equally profound changes in ways of life. Instead of moving around to collect whatever seeds and berries were available seasonally, dwellers in the Fertile Crescent settled in permanent villages, planting, weeding,

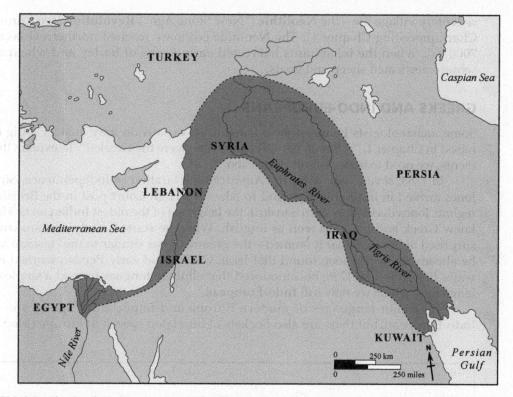

**MAP 4.2**  The Fertile Crescent: A band of well-watered land stretching from the Persian Gulf in the east (modern Kuwait and southern Iraq), northwest along the Tigris–Euphrates rivers (modern Iraq, Syria, and southeastern Turkey), then down the Mediterranean coast (modern Lebanon and Israel) to Egypt.

and harvesting crops. Agriculture was more work than gathering and hunting, but by offering higher and more dependable returns, it created an inexorable pressure to modernize: with hungry children to feed, who could resist settled agriculture? Population grew steadily in the settled communities until farmers vastly outnumbered the small bands that followed the old ways. When farmers wanted the thinly populated territory of food-gatherers—land that was empty most of the year as its occupants moved around collecting different resources—there was little that the gatherers could do.

As settled populations grew and lived cheek-by-jowl with new strains of domesticated animals, amid evil conditions of sanitation, new and deadly viruses emerged. Epidemic diseases come from animals, and gradually the settled farmers living with their animals acquired immunity to diseases that were devastating when introduced into smaller hunter–gatherer bands. The choices were clear: One could continue to live as a hunter-gatherer and perish of disease or starvation; settle down and join the farmers; or move away from them. Native Americans faced similar choices when faced by European colonists, inheritors of an economic revolution by then 12,000 years old.

By 7000 B.C., villages in Syria had hundreds of inhabitants, and by 6000 B.C., a settlement in Turkey called Çatalhöyük (cha-tal-**hu**-yū k) had perhaps 5,000 residents. The entire population of Ice Age Greece might have fitted into this one town. We call this complex of changes—the domestication of crops and animals and the shift toward sedentary village life—the **Neolithic** ("New Stone Age") **Revolution** (see Chronological Chart, preceding Chapter 1). The Neolithic economy reached northern Greece around 7000 B.C., when the inhabitants harvested early forms of barley and wheat and kept semidomesticated sheep and goats.

## GREEKS AND INDO-EUROPEANS

Some archaeologists believe that this neolithic expansion may answer a big question raised in Chapter 1, "A Small, Far-Off Land: Who were the Greeks?" To explain their arguments, we need to make a short digression.

In 1783, seven years after the American Declaration of Independence, Sir William Jones arrived in India from England to take up a High Court post in the British colonial regime. Jones decided to learn Sanskrit, the language of the oldest Indian texts. He already knew Greek and Latin, as well as English. When he started studying Sanskrit, he was surprised at how familiar it seemed—the grammar was similar to the classical languages he already knew. He soon found that Irish, Gothic, and early Persian worked in similar ways. In a lecture in 1786, he announced that all these tongues formed a single family of languages, which we now call **Indo-European**.

The major languages of modern Europe and important languages in Asia are Indo-European, but there are also pockets of unrelated speech in Europe (Map 4.3), and

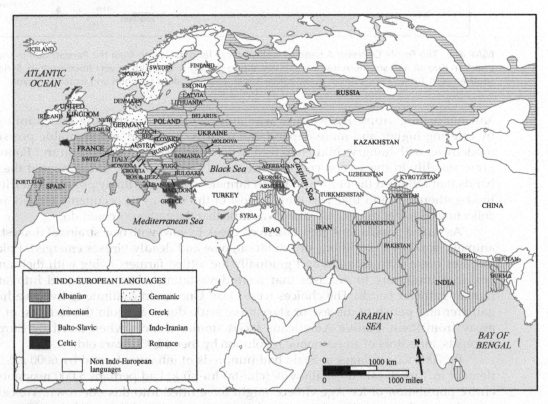

**MAP 4.3** Branches of the Indo-European family.

every country, including Greece, has non-Indo-European place-names. The simplest explanation is that at some time in prehistory, one group spoke a **proto-Indo-European** language, a single language that was somehow ancestor to all later Indo-European languages, and that group migrated across Europe and south Asia, displacing or replacing earlier inhabitants and their languages.

For 150 years, archaeologists have tried to discover when this language dispersal began and where the proto-Indo-Europeans came from. But while the pottery, stone tools, houses, and burials that archaeologists dig up *may* be related to ethnicity and language, they do not *have* to be. The spread of a new pot shape *might* indicate a migration, but there are other explanations too.

Some archaeologists argue that the first farmers, living in what is now eastern Turkey, spoke proto-Indo-European and spread Indo-European languages across the Old World as they took over new land, and there is plenty of archaeological evidence that new peoples, carriers of the Neolithic Revolution, moved into Greece in the seventh millennium B.C. But other archaeologists think that proto-Indo-Europeans dispersed much later, around 2000 B.C. Recent research on DNA from prehistoric skeletons suggests that both theories contain some truth, but arguments continue to rage.

Whatever the answer, though, origins are only part of the Greeks' story. The languages of the first farmers in Greece bore little resemblance to the language of Sophocles and Plato spoken 6,000 years later. The most important question is: How did society develop across this period?

## NEOLITHIC SOCIETY AND ECONOMY, 5000–3000 B.C.

If people could manage by gathering wild foods, probably they would, working harder (breeding crops, herding animals) only when necessary. A major innovation was the invention of the plow, which allowed farmers to turn the soil of larger areas than they could with handheld hoes or digging sticks. The drawback of plows was that farmers needed oxen to pull them. The oxen needed their own food, which meant plowing even more land and working harder still. But as population grew, the new technology spread. There are signs that plows were in use in the Danube valley around 4500 B.C., in Poland and in England by 3500 B.C., and in Spain before 3000 B.C. The evidence for plows in Greece is ambiguous, but they were probably common by 3000 B.C.

At first domesticated cattle seem to have been raised for their meat. Farmers who raise cattle for meat kill them young, but animal bones from excavations show that after 3500 B.C., around the time of the introduction of the plow, Greek farmers started keeping their animals longer. Archaeologists call this change the **secondary products revolution**, a shift toward raising animals as much for traction, milk, and wool as for meat.

The plow allowed larger-scale grain cultivation. In Greece, the Mediterranean triad of grain, olives, and grapes that we described in Chapter 2 was in place by 3000 B.C. This robust diet increased caloric output, improved health, and supported population growth. It also made agriculture more labor-intensive. People were working *much* harder by 2500 B.C. than hunter-gatherers had around 6500 B.C. Progress had costs as well as benefits.

Archaeologists interpret mute artifacts by drawing analogies with living societies at the same technological level. In modern times, hunter-gatherer societies are communal: there is little private property (because there is not much to own) and little hierarchy.

Farming societies, on the other hand, come to recognize private property, including land; the family is a core institution; and gender, age, and class distinctions become pronounced.

Plow technology marks a critical threshold because a good piece of land suddenly becomes valuable. People want to keep particular fields and pass them on to their children. Defining legitimate heirs becomes important. Unlike in simpler economic systems, men start to worry about female premarital virginity, because they want to be sure that the children who will inherit the land come from the husband and not someone else.

As a family with good land marries its children to those of an equally advantaged family, the best land is concentrated in the hands of a few, creating permanent inequalities of wealth. When some end up with no land at all, the only way for them to live is by working rich families' fields. Not only do some eat better than others, but some must toil all their lives, while others live in leisure. Hunter-gatherers wander an empty landscape. If band members argue, some can leave and gather berries elsewhere. A world based on farming cannot work like this. Farmers need seed, labor, animals, and a place to store food to see them through until the next harvest. They need organization. A village provides this, but the villagers must find ways to live together.

Anthropologists find that hunter–gatherer bands of a dozen or so people deal with most problems through face-to-face discussion. But once populations reach a couple of hundred, some individuals start to wield more influence than others. In villages of 1,000 people, permanent chiefs appear. This seems to have happened at some sites in Greece by 4500 B.C., when chiefs' houses appear, bigger than anyone else's.

By 3000 B.C., some people—probably these chiefs—were mobilizing food surpluses to support craftsmen. We find pots as early as 6000 B.C., but around 3000 B.C. come rapid advances.

## THE EARLY BRONZE AGE, 3000–2300 B.C.

In the **Early Bronze Age** craftsmen learned to mix copper with tin or arsenic to produce bronze, far harder than copper; from this metal the period takes its name (see Chronological Chart preceding Chapter 1). Yet most bronze and gold relics from this early period come from just a few graves. In the early third millennium B.C., the elite separated itself from the masses and obtained power and wealth.

The Early Bronze Age also saw advances in architecture. From bigger-than-usual Neolithic houses, we move to monumental buildings. At LERNA (Map 4.4), the **House of Tiles**, built around 2500 B.C., measured eighty by forty feet. Named for the clay roof tiles that covered it, the house contained storerooms and had a second floor. Some clay sealings were found within the building, small clay lumps made by impressing a hardstone seal with a carved design into clay, usually to seal documents or stores of food; perhaps the House of Tiles was an administrative center. It had plastered walls decorated with rectangular panels. There were wooden doors and stairs, and accurately laid-out corners. We have found the ruins of similar buildings from this period at Troy in Asia Minor and on the island of Crete; and at TIRYNS, near Lerna, there is a strange round building ninety feet across with mudbrick walls five feet thick.

When inequalities in wealth arise within communities, inequalities between communities always follow. Military tensions are reflected in a high wall studded with towers

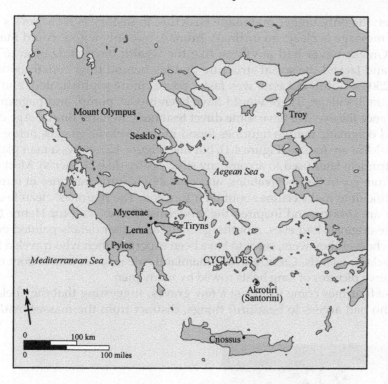

**MAP 4.4**  Sites in Greece mentioned in this chapter.

that protected the House of Tiles, and coastal sites were regularly fortified. There was wealth to be taken, and there were those ready to use violence to take it.

## Culture in the Early Bronze Age

Harder work, inequality, war—if these were the fruits of civilization, why bother? Perhaps ambitious and clever men forced others to work for them and held communities together through violence. But naked force never works for long. It is too difficult to compel everyone to obey. Rulers must persuade the ruled that they are better off despite the inequalities. Greece was close to the old, splendid civilizations of the Near East. Perhaps contact with eastern Mediterranean rulers helped Aegean rulers secure their power. As with the adoption of farming, carrying on with simple ways of life might be unsafe if you lived within striking range of societies with fortifications, metal weapons, and armies.

In Mesopotamia, early rulers owed much of their power to their claim of a close relationship with divine beings. In Egypt, the kings in a sense *were* gods. Mighty religious structures such as ziggurats (Mesopotamian tall-stepped mountains with temples on top) and pyramids (tombs for the pharaoh) benefited everyone by pleasing the gods, but also provided proof of the power and magnificent wealth of society's leaders. The rulers' special relationship with the gods justified building great monuments, and their ability to build great monuments proved this special relationship to be true. Such circular logic underlies the building of the immense Great Pyramid of Khufu (**ku**-fu) in Egypt around 2400 B.C., the tallest building in the world for 3,800 years. Its volume is

6,500,000 cubic feet; the only bigger manmade structure in history is New York's Fresh Kills landfill! The message is clear: no ordinary human, but only a god, could manifest such power. The Greeks never had anything like the wealth or organization to build such monuments and lacked the social structure that lay behind their construction.

Even so, by 2500 B.C., life in Lerna was faster paced, more sophisticated, and more exciting than in a small village. There would have been music, pomp, and pageant, and architecture to entrance the eye. We have some direct testimony to Early Bronze Age culture in the beautiful and enigmatic marble figurines found in the Cycladic islands, hence called **Cycladic figurines**. Most are female (Figure 4.1), but one (Figure 4.2) shows a man playing a lyre, a stringed instrument later used to accompany sung poetry (like Homer's). Most examples do not come from controlled excavations, and probably half the figurines in museums are fakes, so it is difficult to make claims about their function. The figurines' clean lines and abstract symmetry are striking and inspired the modernist British sculptor Henry Moore (1898–1986), but the originals had eyes, mouths, genitals, and other details painted on. The Cycladic peoples, whoever they were, seem to have been expert seamen who traveled to and fro between the Cycladic islands, Crete, and the mainland (see map on inside front cover). Some artifacts preserve pictures of long boats rowed by many men.

Many of these figurines come from just a few graves, suggesting that they belonged to a social elite who had access to beautiful things, distinct from the masses. Although

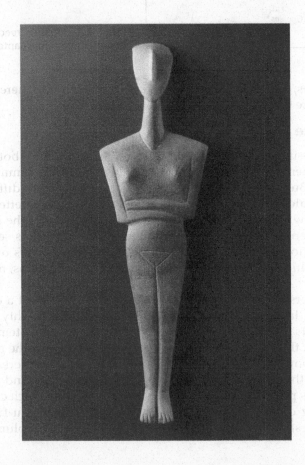

**FIGURE 4.1** Cycladic marble female figurine, ca. 3000–2500 B.C. Note the incised pubic area and the stylized presentation of the female form, leading some to believe that they are fertility idols.

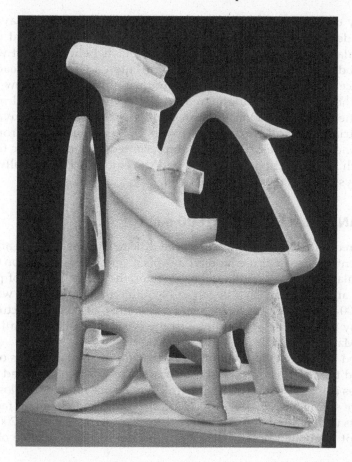

**FIGURE 4.2** Cycladic marble figurine of a man playing a lyre, ca. 3200–2200 B.C., from the Cycladic island of Keros, Greece, suggesting that sung poetry was part of Cretan life.

Greek culture might have seemed primitive to visiting Egyptians, civilization was changing the Greeks' way of life.

## THE MIDDLE BRONZE AGE, 2300–1800 B.C.

Around 2300 B.C., the House of Tiles burned to the ground, along with most major sites in mainland Greece. By 2200 B.C., figurines had disappeared from graves in the Cyclades, and by 2000 B.C., settlement had contracted to just a few sites. None had monumental buildings, and long-distance trade virtually stopped.

Something important happened around 2300 B.C., derailing social complexity on the mainland and in the Cycladic islands, but not, as we shall see, on Crete. The sophisticated mainland and island elites of the Early Bronze Age disappeared. For the next 500 years, from 2300 to 1800 B.C., people lived simpler, village-level lives. We do not know much about this period, which we call the **Middle Bronze Age**, a dark age obscure to modern scholars and characterized by social regression.

One explanation is that newcomers invaded Greece around 2300 B.C., with perhaps a second wave entering around 2000 B.C. The pottery, bronzes, houses, and graves we find after 2300 B.C. are different from those before, and violent conquest would explain the fiery end of Lerna and other sites. There were also upheavals in Anatolia, and some evidence pointing to a period of much drier weather that might have caused large population movements. Some archaeologists believe that it was at this time, and not around 6000 B.C., that Indo-Europeans entered Greece. Instead of a gradual wave of advance by farmers, made up of countless shifts of just a few miles spread over centuries, they envisage a single great invasion from a homeland maybe in Ukraine, north of the Black Sea. One version of this theory sees the invading Indo-Europeans as "patriarchal" and warlike destroyers of a gentler "Old European" civilization focused on mother-goddesses, perhaps represented by the Cycladic female figurines. However, such interpretations go far beyond the evidence. What really happened is shrouded in mystery and may well remain so.

## THE AGE OF MINOAN PALACES, 2000–1600 B.C.

The Middle Bronze Age recession on the mainland meant little to Cretans. If it had affected them too, the development of Greek culture would have been very different. But on Crete, separated from the mainland by seventy-five miles of water, the centralization of power and development of art and ceremony that began in Neolithic times continued without interruption. Around 2000 B.C., people at Cnossus and a few other sites built structures so large, and with so many similarities to buildings in the Near East, that we call them palaces (Figure 4.3 and Map 4.5).

These sites remained in use for centuries, and the foundations and basements of later phases severely damaged the remains of the earliest phases. Cnossus probably had third-millennium B.C. structures just as grand as those at Lerna and Tiryns, but they are lost. The first palaces had massive storage capacities, spacious courtyards, and elaborate façades. Europe's first experiments with writing took place here. The oldest writing, around 2000 B.C., is an undeciphered script of about 135 symbols often representing recognizable objects,

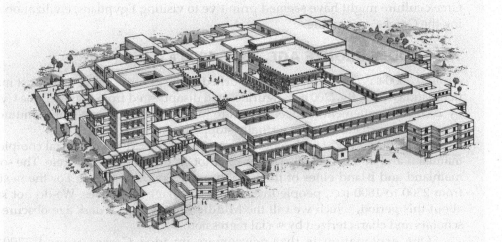

**FIGURE 4.3** Reconstruction of the palace at Cnossus as it may have appeared around 1500 B.C., comprising hundreds of rooms and covering several acres.

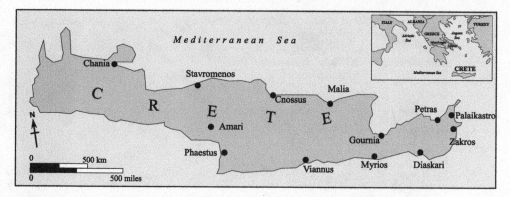

**MAP 4.5**   Map of Crete showing where ruins of Minoan palaces have been found.

mostly found on hard stone seals to be impressed on clay. We cannot read the script or even say what language it encoded (though we doubt it was Greek).

Another development coincides with the first palaces. Some Cretans started climbing mountains and building altars there, where they offered pottery and figurines to the gods. Some figurines they threw into chasms, perhaps to send them to the underworld; others they hung in shrines, particularly models of human limbs, perhaps in gratitude for healing (as seen even today in rural Greek churches). Some peak sanctuaries had elaborate and expensive architecture. Again, religion and ceremony aided the concentration of power.

One of the great problems in studying the Bronze Age is how to interpret the stories that Greeks wrote about it a thousand years later, that is, during the Classical Period. Most Greeks thought that Crete was once ruled by a great king named **Minos**, after whom we sometimes call the Bronze Age civilization on Crete **Minoan**. These stories provide details that archaeology never could; according to the most famous tale, Minos once failed to sacrifice a special bull to the god Poseidon, and the angry god caused Minos' wife (herself the daughter of the Sun) to fall in love with that very bull. She hid inside a wooden cow, which the bull mounted, and from their strange union came the half-man, half-bull, man-eating **Minotaur** ("bull of Minos"). Minos then built a maze called the Labyrinth and kept the Minotaur in it.

Archaeologists sometimes suggest that stories about the Labyrinth were attempts to make sense of the mazelike ruins of the palace at Cnossus, and that the mythical Minotaur began in distorted memories of a bull-leaping game played in the Cretan palaces (Figure 4.4). Some also think that the story of the Cretan queen's intercourse with a bull represents a religious ritual in which a queen pretended to (or really did) have intercourse with a bull.

Comparing legends and archaeological finds reveals the difficulty of understanding the past and raises a problem of method in historical study. Sometimes we have written sources of information produced by people actually present during the period described. These we call **primary sources**. Every reliable historical account must rest on written primary sources. At other times, we have only documents produced by people who were not present, either because they lived somewhere else or just happened not to be there that day, or because, like ourselves, they lived much later. Thucydides, the famous Athenian historian active around 400 B.C., wrote about king Minos but had no access to Minoan

**FIGURE 4.4** Bull-jumping fresco from Cnossus, ca. 1500 B.C., height including border about 25 inches. A red-painted figure balances on the back of a galloping bull, evidently somersaulting into the arms of a white-painted figure, while another white-painted figure, preparing to somersault, grips the bull's horns. The white figures seem to be female, while the red figure is male, following an artistic convention borrowed from Egypt and current throughout antiquity.

primary sources. Lacking such sources, he had to concede that "I have found it impossible, because of the remoteness in time, to acquire a really precise knowledge of the distant past or even of the history preceding our own period" (Thucydides 1.1).

We call written texts that are not primary sources **secondary sources**. Whenever we look at a secondary source, we must ask how the author knew anything about the subject. Did the author have access to primary sources? If not, then to a secondary source that itself drew on primary sources? Unless the answer to one of these questions is yes, there is no reason to believe anything a secondary source says.

The myths about Minos are entertaining, but they are secondary sources, and archaeological discoveries must remain the major source of information about Bronze Age Crete. After a century of research, beginning with the pioneer archaeologist Arthur Evans, who started digging at Cnossus in 1899, we have real information about the Cretan economy and way of life. The world of Cnossus' rulers was sophisticated and glamorous. Their craftsmen made elegant eggshell-thin vases (Figure 4.5) and painted geometric designs and marine motifs on the palace walls. The elite wore delicate gold jewelry, and tombs show that even common folk had bronze ornaments. After 1800 B.C., typical Minoan houses became much larger and were well built. Standards of living were (by ancient standards) quite high.

By 1800 B.C., the palaces were in direct communication with the Near East, mainly through the great trading city of Ugarit in north Syria. Minoan palaces look quite like Near Eastern ones, and an eighteenth-century B.C. clay tablet from the great Bronze Age city of Mari on the Euphrates River in Syria may be the first written reference to the Aegean. The tablet notes that the king of Ugarit had sent weapons, cloth, sandals, and pots from "Kaptara" as a gift to the king of Mari. Kaptara was probably Crete. Another tablet from

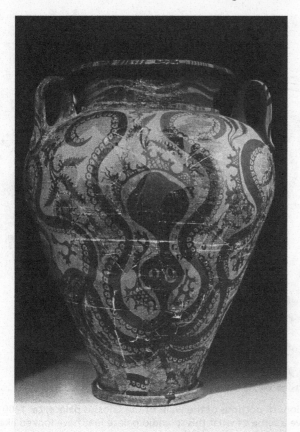

**FIGURE 4.5**   "Octopus vase," an amphora from Palaikastro, Crete, ca. 1500 B.C., height 11 inches. Marine motifs were common in Minoan art and reflect their intimacy with the sea and control over it.

Mari records that some of the gifts sent to Mari from Kaptara by way of Ugarit, including a pair of sandals, were sent on to the famous king Hammurabi of Babylon, who created one of the world's oldest law codes in the eighteenth century B.C.

The Cretans were minor players in Near Eastern diplomacy, but for the Minoan elite, these contacts were crucial. Their agents must have brought home tin, without which there would be no bronze, and exotic objects from the distant, rich kingdoms. Cretan leaders basked in luxury in their palaces. Other Cretans, or the leaders themselves, communed with gods on mountaintops, but dramatic events around 1750 B.C., in the Middle Bronze Age, undid some of this work. Some archaeologists think that devastating earthquakes struck (several fault lines run through Crete), others, that an internecine war destroyed the palace at Cnossus at this time, after which the reorganized Cnossians defeated everyone else to fashion a single Minoan state. We do not know what happened, but the palaces were quickly rebuilt on an even grander scale than before.

This **Second Palace Period** is the best-known phase of Minoan history. The palace at Cnossus covered an area the size of two football fields. To enter, visitors crossed a wide courtyard to reach an elaborate two-story façade (Figure 4.6). We may be sure that the palace made a strong impression on Cretan peasants and on traders from the rude villages of mainland Greece; surely the beings who lived in such houses seemed closer to the gods than mere mortals.

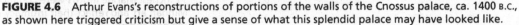

**FIGURE 4.6**   Arthur Evans's reconstructions of portions of the walls of the Cnossus palace, ca. 1400 B.C., as shown here triggered criticism but give a sense of what this splendid palace may have looked like.

The grand entrance to the palace led to a twisting, winding corridor that abruptly let out into a paved courtyard, 150 feet long and 75 feet wide, surrounded by towering blank walls. This too seems designed to astonish visitors. Tucked away in one corner was the throne room itself, where a high stone chair was flanked by wall paintings of griffins, a Near Eastern motif (Figure 4.7).

The most remarkable parts of the palace would have been closed to visitors. There were bathrooms with a drainage system holding flowing water to flush away human waste, the oldest attested example in the world. There were anterooms and storerooms, waiting rooms and dressing rooms, airy light wells and dark crypts, and vaulting staircases and subterranean vaults (Figure 4.8). Walls, floors, and even ceilings were painted in dazzling colors, often with beautiful naturalistic scenes of dolphins, birds, monkeys, fish, octopuses, and rulers in elaborate costumes (Figure 4.9).

Beneath all this gaiety, though, lay the palace's economic realities. Everywhere there were narrow chambers packed with pots and stone bins for storage. Each palace held vast quantities of grain, oil, and wine, as well as metals, wood, and materials of war. The rulers kept track of it with a new writing system that we call **Linear A** (Figure 4.10)—"linear" because the signs are made up of lines, and "A" to distinguish it from a later linear system (Linear B). We do not have enough samples to decipher the script, but most tablets seem to be economic accounts.

**FIGURE 4.7**  An alabaster throne with scalloped backrest and incised patterns sits on a dais between benches lining the walls of the Throne Room at Cnossus in Crete, ca. 1400 B.C. On either side of the throne are reconstructed frescoes of griffins in fields of lotuses, symbols of royal power.

The Minoan palaces, like those of the Near East, were **redistributive centers**, and Linear A allowed the rulers to run a centralized **command economy**. In theory, it worked like this: if one valley was well suited for wheat, that was all it grew; if a hillside was placed just right for olives, it was given over to them. (In practice, however, command economies do not work so neatly: it is difficult to tell people what to grow.) The harvested crops were brought to the palace, where they were recorded. Bureaucrats kept accounts in Linear A, skimmed off what the rulers needed, and sent back to each village a selection of goods that the rulers deemed necessary for the local people. The palaces did not control the entire economy, of course, and there would have been local systems of barter and rural markets. But from 2000 through 1400 B.C. or later—hundreds of years—the Cretans ran a wealthy and complex command economy without the use of coinage, which was not invented until 600 B.C.

Remarkably, no fortifications have been found at Cretan sites, unlike the well-protected dwellings of the Greek Mycenaeans on the mainland. Evidently, the Minoans faced no credible threats; the historian Thucydides in the fifth century B.C. described their power as a **thalassocracy**, "kingdom of the sea," and his explanation remains plausible. Nor did they fear internal attack, suggesting that the various Minoan palaces scattered around Crete belonged to a single state, run from Cnossus.

The eighteenth and seventeenth centuries B.C. were the high point of Minoan civilization. Typical houses were well made, covering 2,000–3,000 square feet. Mainland Greek houses did not equal these dimensions until the fourth century B.C. The aristocracy lived

**FIGURE 4.8** Reconstruction of a well in the central palace, allowing sunlight into the lower stories, supported by typical Minoan columns thicker at the top than at the bottom. Notice in the corridor reconstructed paintings of "figure-eight" shields made of a wicker frame covered in oxhide, also found in mainland art, and the rosettes surrounding the door, typical Minoan motifs.

**FIGURE 4.9** Arthur Evans's reconstruction of the dolphin fresco over the "queen's apartments" in a lower floor of the palace (some archaeologists think the fresco could have fallen from the floor above). Dolphins swim amidst tuna in a scene rich in nature, fantasy, and movement, making Minoan art some of the most delightful to survive from the Bronze Age. A typical frieze of rosettes bounds the bottom of the picture.

**FIGURE 4.10**   Linear A signs on a potsherd from Palaikastro, ca. 1500 B.C. These signs seem to designate a commodity of some kind, but Linear A remains undeciphered.

even better: the hilltops of Crete were dotted with villas, often decorated with wall paintings like those in the palaces, and filled with precious objects. Minoans had more contacts than ever with the East. Egyptian paintings show men called Keftiu—almost certainly Cretans—bearing gifts, and Minoan-style wall paintings, one even depicting bull-leaping, are known from Egypt, Syria, and Israel.

The Cretan Middle Bronze Age was truly an international age. The Minoans thrust their culture into the Aegean. **Akrotiri** on the Cycladic island of Santorini, miraculously preserved when buried in volcanic ash in 1628 B.C., is a Minoan Pompeii, giving us unique insights into daily life. Its people had time to flee with their valuables, but their ruined houses stand two floors high (Figures 4.11 and 4.12). Archaeologists have found so much Minoan pottery at Akrotiri and some other Cycladic sites that we must conclude that these sites were Cretan trading posts or colonies.

Was this a Minoan empire, then? Later Greek writers thought so, especially Thucydides:

> As far as we know, Minos was the first to establish a navy and to take control of most of the Hellenic Sea.° He ruled the Cycladic islands and first settled most of them by driving out the Carians° and placing his sons in as governors. No doubt he rid the seas of pirates as best he was able, and their profits became his.

Thucydides 1.4

°*Hellenic Sea:* The Aegean Sea.    °*Carians:* Caria was an area in southwest Anatolia (modern Turkey). For some reason, Thucydides thought that the Carians were the original settlers of the Cyclades.

But without primary sources, Thucydides could not be certain of the distant past, and archaeology helps less when we move from economic and cultural facts to political ones. Linear A tablets have turned up at Akrotiri and other Cycladic sites. They may be evidence for colonial administration, but perhaps independent bureaucracies copied Minoan methods.

**FIGURE 4.11** Partially excavated house at Akrotiri on the island of Santorini (ancient Thera). The walls are mud brick, set between beams resistant to earthquake. Storage jars still stand where they stood when the island volcano blew up in 1628 B.C., burying the town in ash (some have thought this catastrophe stands behind the legend of Atlantis).

**FIGURE 4.12** Fresco in a house at Akrotiri shows boats rowing into a harbor backed by multistoried houses, agreeing with Thucydides' description of the Minoan Crete as a thalassocracy. From the windows and rooftops, the inhabitants watch the fleet's return.

## THE RISE OF MYCENAEAN GREECE, 1750–1500 B.C.

Between 1750 and 1700 B.C., as Minoan power reached its height, something strange was happening in the mainland town of **Mycenae.** People carved into the rock a large stone-lined circle, , seventy-five feet across. what we now call Grave Circle B. Over the next century and a half, they buried thirty-five people in shafts dug within this circle. The richest burial was marked by two gravestones, one of them carved, and held four adults, one of them a man six feet tall, a giant in 1700 B.C. Chemical analysis of his bones suggests that he ate a lot of meat and some fish. The fill of the shaft contained some forty pots. Accompanying the dead were fourteen bronze weapons, a bronze vase, two gold cups, gold attachments sewn onto the clothes of the dead, a silver-coated wooden box, an extraordinary death mask made of electrum (a naturally occurring mix of gold and silver), and many lesser treasures. Mainland Greece had never before witnessed such wealth and artistry, even in the heyday of the House of Tiles.

Wealthy, warlike rulers had taken control of Mycenae. They may have grown rich trading with Minoan Crete or have won their power leading resistance to Crete. Whatever the source of their wealth, around 1650 B.C., while Grave Circle B was still in use, the Mycenaeans built a second monument, **Grave Circle A**, 150 yards uphill (Figure 4.13). Heinrich Schliemann, Troy's original excavator, sank his first trench directly into these graves in 1876. It remains one of the most amazing archaeological discoveries ever made.

**FIGURE 4.13**   Grave Circle A, ca. 1600–1400 B.C., discovered by Heinrich Schliemann in 1876. Within the grave circle are 37 vertical shafts that contained 19 skeletons, male and female, and an immense quantity of gold artifacts and beautiful weapons, one of the greatest archaeological treasures ever found. Limestone slabs decorated with martial themes marked the individual graves. The Mycenaeans built a protective circle around the graves and later enclosed the whole complex within the city.

**FIGURE 4.14** Mycenaean gold death mask. When Heinrich Schliemann saw this mask, with its noble features, beard, and mustache, he reportedly wired the king of Greece that he had "gazed upon the face of Agamemnon" (in fact, the graves are four centuries too early to have held Agamemnon's body, and Schliemann may never have said that).

The six shaft graves in Grave Circle A were stuffed with gold, jewels, silver, bronze, and pottery. The five gold death masks found here (Figure 4.14) still freeze visitors to the spot in front of their case in the National Museum in Athens. There are so many other precious objects that the museum cannot find room to display them all. The workmanship is astounding, from inlaid dagger-blades (Figure 4.15) to carved gems so tiny that the naked

**FIGURE 4.15** Dagger from Mycenae Grave Circle A, seventeenth century B.C. Bronze inlaid with gold, iron, and electrum, length about 9 inches. Warriors carrying shields, some in the Minoan figure-eight style, attack lions.

eye can scarcely make them out. Many of these objects are Minoan, or inspired by Minoan art, but martial themes of combat and war are now common, unlike the peaceful marine and festival themes of Minoan art. At the very height of the power of the Cretan palaces, a rival dynasty, representing itself in death as violent and aggressive, had appeared on the mainland and, evidently, taken control of it.

We call the civilization of the **Late Bronze Age** on the mainland **Mycenaean** (mī-sen-ē-an) after this site, but similar developments were underway elsewhere. On the coast of Messenia, seventy-five miles to the southwest, a large town had grown up at **Pylos** by 1600 B.C., and for several generations its wealthy nobility buried their dead in vaulted stone chambers called **tholos tombs**, which resemble underground stone beehives. In the sixteenth century B.C., the rich lords of Mycenae built similar tombs, though much larger. All were looted long ago, but their original wealth must have been very great.

There were palaces on the Greek mainland by 1500 B.C., which used a writing system called **Linear B**, derived from Minoan Linear A. Large caches of clay tablets inscribed in Linear B (Figure 4.16) have been found. In 1952, the British architect Michael Ventris deciphered Linear B and showed, to everyone's surprise, that it encoded an early form of Greek. Ventris was not a professional classicist but enjoyed code-breaking as a hobby. Linear B was not an alphabet like our own, where each sign stands for a single sound, but a **syllabary** of eighty or so signs, where each sign stands for a syllable

**FIGURE 4.16** Linear B tablets from Cnossus. Linear B reads from left to right, scratched along horizontal lines. The tablets record economic accounts, mostly lists of commodities from a single year, and survived because they were fired when the palace of Cnossus burned, probably around 1400 B.C.

(e.g., *ba, be, bi, bo, bu*), so the distance between what someone says and what the writing tells you can be very great. Mostly the tablets record names as part of a system of economic accounting. No literature of any kind survives. A single complete sentence survives from the many thousands of tablets. The Mycenaeans adapted Minoan Linear A writing, which recorded an unknown language, certainly not Greek, into Linear B, which recorded an early form of Greek, to aid them in running and recording their own redistributive economy.

All over Greece, new men had seized power, probably brutal warlords, but connoisseurs of the best Minoan art, who understood the value of bureaucracy. Linear B tablets call the kings *wanakes* (singular, *wanax*). The tablets tell us little about these kings, because their intended audience—other scribes—already knew who the *wanakes* were. But the architecture of Minoan and Mycenaean palaces and the art on their walls suggests that, as in the Near East, the *wanakes* may have persuaded their subjects to believe that they were closer to the gods than others. The *wanakes* divided Greece into several kingdoms; from the Pylos tablets we know that the one based there covered 800 square miles.

Around 1600 B.C., Mycenaean civilization was still in the shadow of the Minoans, but by 1400 B.C., Linear B was in use at Cnossus. Mycenaean Greeks now sat in the throne room of the greatest Cretan palace. How did this come to pass?

## THE END OF MINOAN CIVILIZATION, 1600–1400 B.C.

The volcanic eruption that destroyed Akrotiri may have played a part in the decline of Minoan civilization, but we cannot be sure of the details. The delightful ring-shaped island of Santorini, southernmost of the Cyclades and today a favorite for tourists, was once a solid circle of land with a small volcanic mountain at its center. But in 1628 B.C. (judging from tree rings in California bristlecone pines, which correlate with high acidity in ice cores from Greenland), the volcano blew up the middle of the island, one of the greatest eruptions discovered in the whole geological record.

The prevailing winds would have carried the worst of the ash cloud east, dumping it into the sea, but some of the red-hot dust blew south. The Cretans must have lived through days of darkness when death fell from the skies, fires raged out of control, and tidal waves thrust inland. A layer of ash twenty feet thick buried Akrotiri. The Minoan palaces survived this disaster, but it must have weakened them. Some have connected this geological event with the legend of Atlantis, first heard of in the philosopher Plato, but the connection cannot be proven.

Then, around 1450 B.C., the Minoan palaces did burn, perhaps by enemy action. Only Cnossus, and perhaps Chania in the west, survived. Minoan material culture disappeared from the Cyclades, now replaced by Mycenaean finds. Perhaps the eruption of 1628 B.C. shook Minoan strength, then internal wars or uprisings, or further natural disasters, gave the mainland Mycenaean Greeks an opening. They occupied Cnossus, leaving the other palaces in ruins. Then Cnossus itself was burned around 1400 B.C., preserving our earliest large horde of Linear B tablets and proving that Greek-speakers by then ruled in this palace. Gradually, the fine townhouses of the eighteenth and seventeenth centuries B.C. decayed, and standards of living declined. The ancient Minoan social order was gone forever.

**FIGURE 4.17** Victorian visitors at the Lion Gate at Mycenae, constructed around 1250 B.C. The sculpture is the oldest architectural sculpture in Greece and may be an emblem of royal power. It shows lionesses (probably) flanking a pillar. The king as "lion" is an old Near Eastern motif, as is the arrangement of two animals on either side of a central image.

## MYCENAEAN GREECE: ARCHAEOLOGY, LINEAR B, AND HOMER

By the mid-second millennium B.C., then, Mycenaean Greeks dominated the Aegean. Their palaces looked different from the non-Greek Minoan ones: they were on hilltops and heavily fortified. Crete produced nothing like the famous Lion Gate at Mycenae (Figure 4.17).

Minoan palaces were designed around a central courtyard, but Mycenaean palaces focused on the **megaron**, a rectangular building with a porch on the front and a round hearth in the middle (Figure 4.18). Mycenaeans painted their palace walls, as did Minoans, but enjoyed warlike as well as pastoral scenes. The main similarities between Minoan and Mycenaean palaces were the prominence of storerooms and written records.

In addition to their physical ruins, we have two potential sources of information about the Mycenaean palaces. The first is the Linear B tablets. They were temporary records scratched onto damp clay, evidently meant to be transferred later to another medium—perhaps papyrus from Egypt—that has not survived. Once the data had been transferred, the tablets would be moistened, scraped clean, and reused. But when the palaces were destroyed around 1200 B.C., the fires that raged through them accidentally preserved the tablets in use at that moment, baking them hard like pottery. The tablets tell us only about transactions that took place just before the palaces were destroyed.

Most tablets are dull economic records. A typical example reads "21 spinning-women, 25 girls, 4 boys; 1 *ta*" (no one knows what *ta* means; we show such unknown words in italics). What is the record for? What has happened? Another records "20 woolen

**FIGURE 4.18** Reconstruction of the throne room at Pylos. In the center is a great circular hearth beneath an opening in the roof supported by four pillars. Frescoes decorate the walls (after a painting by Piet de Jong).

cloaks that are to be well boiled," as if every minutia of palace property and personnel needed to be tracked. We can learn a lot from these texts. For example, Table 4.1 shows the number of animals recorded on Linear B tablets from Cnossus.

Even from our random sample of records, we witness an impressive palace economy, a complex organization run by dozens of officials whose names and titles fill the tablets. Beneath the *wanax* at the top was a finely graded social hierarchy in which everyone had a place. A tablet from Pylos lists "16 fire-kindlers, 10 *meridumate*, 3 *mikate*, 4 riggers, 5 armorers; Xanthos. 23 fire-kindlers, 6 *meridamate*, 5 riggers, 6 *mikata*, 3 armorers, 3 bakers. 4 *porudamate*. For Pallas, Purkolos, Axotas, Priameias, Eniausios, Ptejori, Qotawo, Anthas, Theopompos." Although we do not understand the meaning of many of these words, we can see that professions were carefully distinguished and the name of every professional was recorded. The tablets suggest that in Mycenaean society everyone owed obligations to superiors, while claiming certain goods or services from those below them. The bureaucracies at the center tried to keep everything under control, for their own advantage and the betterment of the community.

A second potential source of information about the Mycenaeans is Homer, the great epic poet of the eighth century B.C. The 28,000 verses of his *Iliad* and *Odyssey* tell of a Greek war against the city of Troy. The leading Greek cities in Homer's account were major

**TABLE 4.1**  Total number of sheep, goats, pigs, oxen, and stags recorded in the Linear B tablets excavated at Cnossus. The tablets do not explain what the palace administration was doing with the animals.

|  | Male | Female | Unclear sex | Total |
|---|---|---|---|---|
| **Sheep** | 8,217 | 1,554 | 386 | 10,157 |
| **Goats** | 1,004 | 771 | 50 | 1,825 |
| **Pigs** | 57 | 234 | 249 | 540 |
| **Oxen** | 0 | 0 | 8 | 8 |
| **Stags** | 0 | 0 | 16 | 16 |

centers in the Bronze Age, according to archaeological investigation, and Agamemnon, the Greek commander, came from Mycenae. Although there is no consciousness of historical time in the epics, they seem to be set in what we call the Mycenaean period. But Homer lived 400 years after the end of the Mycenaean palaces. He is very much a secondary source. Writing of any kind disappeared from Greece between 1200 and about 800 B.C., so we know that Homer had no primary accounts from the Bronze Age. How *could* he know anything about the Bronze Age?

Homer tells us his sources in the following passage, when he prepares to list the Achaeans (the Greeks) who fought at Troy:

> Sing to me now, you Muses who live on Olympus,
> for you are divine, you are there, you know all, but we hear
> only rumor and know nothing. Who were the leaders
> of the Danaans° and their captains? I could never tell
> their number or names, not if I had ten tongues
> and ten mouths and a voice unbroken, and my heart
> were bronze, if the Muses who live on Olympus, daughters
> of shield-bearing Zeus, did not remind me—I will tell
> the ships' commanders and all the ships they led.

Homer, *Iliad* 2.484–92

°*Danaans*: Another name for the Greeks.

Homer knows about the past because goddesses, the Muses (see Chapter 6, "Homer"), tell him about it! In Chapter 6, we have more to say about how Homer composed his epics, but for the moment we simply note that most historians think Homer knew little about the Bronze Age, in spite of his claim to divine guidance. Bits and pieces of information (like the names of famous people and settlements) were passed down by word of mouth, true, but Homer tells us more about what eighth-century B.C. poets thought the Mycenaean world *ought* to have been like than about actual Mycenaean life. Homer spoke to an eighth-century audience and drew on experiences from his own times, embellished by exaggeration (heroes are stronger, braver, and better-looking than men today) and by fantasy (talking rivers and horses, personal appearances by gods).

When we compare the poems with archaeological evidence, we quickly see how different Homer's world is from that of the Mycenaeans. For example, at one point

Telemachus (tel-**em**-a-kus), son of the great hero Odysseus, wants to sail off to find news of his father, missing for twenty years. Homer describes his preparations:

> Telemachus went down to his father's high-roofed storeroom,
> broad, where lay gold and bronze and cloth in chests
> and scented oil, jars of old sweet wine
> having a divine unmixed substance within,
> lined up all in a row along the wall,
> in case Odysseus should return home, after
> his agony. The two doors, tightly fitted,
> were shut, and a woman housekeeper both night and day
> watched over it, who guarded all in wisdom
> of mind, Eurycleia, the daughter of Ops, Pisenor's son.
> Straightaway she drew off wine into jars,
> and poured in barley from well-stitched bags. Back
> to the hall went Telemachus and mixed with the suitors.
> Bright-eyed Pallas,° the goddess, thought of one
> more thing. In the likeness of Telemachus, she went throughout
> the city, and standing beside each man she spoke,
> and urged them at night to gather at the swift ship.
> She asked Noemon the illustrious son of Noemon
> to lend her a ship. He gladly agreed.

*Homer, Odyssey 2.337–47, 379–87*
°*Pallas:* Another name for the goddess Athena, who helps Telemachus prepare the trip.

But Bronze Age palaces were not like this. They had dozens of storerooms, not just one. The economic nerve center in Homer's vision of Odysseus' palace is a big room with double doors, guarded by an old lady. There is no bustling bureaucracy, no rows of underground storage bins. When Telemachus gets his supplies, it sounds as if the king's palace does not even own a ship but must borrow one from a neighbor! The *Iliad* and *Odyssey* were myths that eighth-century Greeks told themselves to explain, at least in part, the physical ruins surviving from the past, visible in many places, such as the great Lion Gate at Mycenae. The Homeric poems are important sources for under-standing eighth-century Greek culture, but not for making sense of the Mycenaean world.

The archaeological record and the Linear B tablets tell us that Mycenaean society was more warlike than Minoan and wealth was less widely diffused. The Mycenaean *wanakes* were great rulers, whose civilization spread north to the slopes of Mt. Olympus. Mycenaean pottery has been found in Sicily and Sardinia, and Bronze Age shipwrecks show that Mycenaean Greece was involved in far-flung commercial networks. Ships moved all kinds of goods, from food to bronze ingots to writing tablets. For kings, soldiers, and traders (but not for ordinary village-dwellers) this was a big, cosmopolitan, international world. State archives of the Hittite Empire in central Anatolia complain about a western kingdom called **Ahhiyawa**, probably a mispronunciation of **Achaea** (a-**kē**-a), one of the three names that Homer would later use for the Greeks. In the thirteenth century B.C., Hittite kings wrote to the rulers of Ahhiyawa as equals, complaining bitterly of the differences between them. The Mycenaeans were important players on an international stage.

## THE END OF THE BRONZE AGE, CIRCA 1200 B.C.

A visitor from another planet around 1300 B.C. might have predicted that palatial civilization would continue expanding north and west. The Mycenaeans and Hittites were stronger than ever, and trade routes pulsed with life. But in the thirteenth century, Mycenaean metalworkers started using raw materials more sparingly, and Linear B tablets suggest shortfalls in tax collection. Fortifications at major sites expanded, and populations drifted from vulnerable villages to the security of defended settlements. Then, between 1225 and 1175 B.C., fires gutted the palaces all over Greece. This seems to have been the time of the Trojan War, if there was a Trojan War, and stories about the sack of Troy may go back to this catastrophic period. Over the next few centuries, dust blew over the ruins, which were slowly buried, then forgotten until the 1870s, when archaeologists exposed their secrets.

What happened? Thucydides says that:

> after the Trojan War Hellas was in a state of turmoil, with the constant shifting of populations so that the peaceful conditions required for growth did not exist. That the return from Troy took so long was itself responsible for much change. Most *poleis* were disturbed by civil strife, and when a party was exiled, they founded new cities.
>
> Thucydides 1.12

Thucydides believed that the ten-year siege of Troy destabilized Greece, adding that "many years passed by and many difficulties were encountered before Hellas could enjoy any peace or stability, and before the period of shifting populations ended." Homer and Thucydides both treat the Trojan War as important, but when we scrutinize Thucydides' account (a secondary source, written around 400 B.C.), we find that his main source of information was Homer (another secondary source!). Homer believed that the Muses inspired him, and Thucydides copied Homer.

The Linear B tablets are our only primary sources for life in the Mycenaean world, written in the dying moments of the palaces, but a long text from Pylos describing a religious ceremony may tell us something about the destructions. The scribe began on one side of the tablet, scratched through what he had written, then turned the tablet over, dashed off a few lines, then went back to the original (erased) side, adding more writing, before the text trails off unfinished:

> PYLOS: perform an action at the shrine of Poseidon and . . . the town, and bring the gifts and bring those to carry them. One gold cup, two women . . .
> PYLOS: perform an action at the shrines of the Dove-Goddess and of Iphimedeia and of Diwja, and bring the gifts and bring those to carry them. To the Dove-Goddess: one gold bowl, one woman. To Iphimedeia: one gold bowl. To Diwja: one gold bowl, one woman. To Hermes: one gold cup, one man.
> PYLOS: perform an action at the shrine of Zeus, and bring the gifts and bring those to carry them. To Zeus: one gold bowl, one man. To Drimios, the priest of Zeus: one gold bowl, one man (?).

> In the month of Plowistos: PYLOS: perform an action at the place
> Pakijane, and bring the gifts and bring those to carry them. To the Mistress: one
> gold cup, one woman. To Mnasa: one gold bowl, one woman. To Posidaeia: one
> gold cup, one woman. To the three-times-hero: one gold cup. To the Lord of the
> House: one gold cup.
>
> Pylos tablet Tn 316

In later Greek mythology, Poseidon was god of the sea, and this tablet shows that he, Hermes, Zeus, and Hera were already the objects of cult in the Bronze Age (though we do not know how beliefs about these gods might have later changed). The other divinities mentioned in this tablet were not worshiped in later periods. The offerings of *people* to gods may describe human sacrifice in response to a great crisis, perhaps the very one that destroyed the palace.

Another tablet from Pylos (which contains the only complete sentence to survive) may also refer to an impending disaster that called for extreme measures:

> As follows, the watchers are guarding the coastal area.
> Command of Maleus at Owitono:
> Ampelitawon, Orestas, Etewas, Kokkion.
> 50 *suweowijo* men of Owitono at Oichalia.
> Command of Nedwatas: Echmedes,
> Amphieta, and the *marateu*, Taniko.
> 20 Kyparissian *kekide* men at Aruwote,
> 10 Kyparissian *kekide* men at Aithalewes,
> and with them the follower Kerkios.
> Aeriqhoitas, Elaphos, Rimene.
> 30 men from Oichalia to Owitono,
> and 20 *kekide* men from Apuka,
> and with them the follower Aikota.
>
> Pylos tablet An 657

Some specialists see this tablet as describing a last-ditch defense of the coast against invaders; others suggest that these 130 men were just a routine force.

The ruins of the palaces give more hints. Sometimes huge walls collapsed or were bent at strange angles, houses had fallen off foundations, and bodies were found under rubble, suggesting that earthquakes were involved. The destructions of the Greek palaces seem to have been spread between 1225 and 1175 B.C., though, so there cannot have been a single giant earthquake; but there could have been what geophysicists call an "earthquake storm," spread over many years. Battered by repeated collapses, each causing fires, did the Mycenaean ruling class lose control?

On the other hand, the Greek disasters were not just local. Ugarit, the greatest emporium on the Mediterranean coast of modern Syria, was also destroyed around 1200 B.C., never to rise again, and the Hittite Empire collapsed at the same time. Of the great ancient kingdoms, only Egypt survived. An inscription at Karnak, the Egyptian capital 400 miles south of modern Cairo, says that in 1209 B.C. Pharaoh Merneptah defeated an invasion of Libyans and their allies, that is, peoples from the western deserts. In his slightly later funerary temple, Pharaoh Ramses III put up another inscription, saying that in 1176 B.C. he fought a coalition of invaders that had wiped out precisely those Asian sites that archaeology reveals were destroyed at this time:

Year 8 under the majesty of Ramses III . . . The foreign countries made a conspiracy in their islands [the Cyclades?]. All at once the lands were removed and scattered in the fray. No land could stand before their arms, from Hatti kingdom of the Hittites [in central Anatolia], Kodê [Cilicia in southern Anatolia], Carchemish [on the Euphrates River], Arzawa [probably in southern Anatolia], and Alashiya [Cyprus], being cut off at one time. A camp was set up in one place in Amor [probably in Syria]. They desolated its people, and its land was like that which has never come into being. They were coming forward toward Egypt, while the flame was prepared before them. Their confederation was the Peleset [probably the Philistines, who were Mycenaean Greeks], Tjeker [?], Shekelesh [perhaps Sicilians], Denyen [probably the same as Danaans, a word Homer used to mean Greeks], and Weshmesh [?] lands united. They laid their hands upon the lands as far as the circuit of the earth, their hearts confident and trusting: "Our plans will succeed!"

Now the heart of this god [Ramses III], the Lord of the Gods, was prepared and ready to ensnare them like birds. . . . I organized my frontier at Djahi [in the Nile delta] prepared before them: princes, commanders of garrisons, and *maryanu* [important military leaders]. I had the river-mouths prepared like a strong wall, with warships, galleys, and coasters, fully equipped, for they were manned completely from bow to stern with valiant warriors carrying their weapons. The troops consisted of every picked man of Egypt. They were like the lions roaring upon the mountain tops. The chariotry consisted of runners, of picked men, of every good and capable chariot-warrior. The horses were quivering in every part of their bodies, prepared to crush the foreign countries under their hoofs. . . .

Those who reached my frontier, their seed is not, their heart and their soul are finished forever and ever. Those who came forward together on the sea, the full flame was in front of them at the river-mouths, while a stockade of lances surrounded them on the shore. They were dragged in, enclosed, and prostrated on the beach, killed, and made into heaps from tail to head. Their ships and their goods were as if fallen into the water.

I have made the lands turn back from even mentioning Egypt, for when they pronounce my name in their land, then they are burned up . . . I have taken away their land, their frontiers being added to mine. Their princes and their tribes are mine with praise, for I am on the ways of the plans of the All-Lord, my august, divine father, the Lord of the Gods [that is, Amon, god of the state at this time].

Funerary text of Ramses III, Medinet Habu (J. A. Wilson, ANET, modified)

Historians call these invaders the **Sea Peoples**. They were probably involved in the destructions in Greece too; the Pylos tablet describing naval defenses may allude to them. The Sea Peoples included the Peleset, probably the **Philistines**, well known from the Hebrew Bible (hence the geographical term "Palestine"). Philistines settled five towns in what is now the Gaza Strip and southern Israel after Ramses III defeated them. Some of their towns have been excavated. the finds are almost identical to those from Greece in the twelfth century B.C.: "Philistine" pottery is indistinguishable from "Mycenaean" pottery. The Philistines were evidently Mycenaean Greek refugees, perhaps from Crete or Cyprus. Merneptah's inscription of 1209 B.C. also names a group that might have been "Akaiwasha" (the only partly phonetic Egyptian writing does not encode vowel sounds), rather like the Ahhiyawa in the Hittite texts. Other Egyptian texts also mention the Shardana, perhaps men from Sardinia. It looks like the years around 1200 B.C. were ones of extreme disruption, and the Greeks were as much its agents as its victims.

Later authors say that the Dorians, to whom all Dorian Greeks (see Chapter 1) traced their ancestry, entered Greece after the Trojan War, though archaeological research has not been able to verify the "Dorian Invasion." Still, such a movement may have been linked to the depredations of the Sea Peoples. Migrations may have coincided with ferocious earthquakes and possibly other natural disasters. Faced with economic collapse and starvation, bands of Mycenaean Greeks may have joined a broader tide of displaced peoples, as irresistible as any modern refugee movement. As one kingdom after another crumbled before them, the tide became a flood that engulfed Near Eastern civilization, until Ramses III stopped it in 1176 B.C.

We would like to know what impelled the Sea Peoples to move and why their attacks overwhelmed well-fortified positions. All we can say for sure is that a wave of violence swept across the Aegean and passed into the Near East ca. 1200 B.C., ruining all in its wake. In Greece, without the palaces, the *wanakes* had no function. Without the *wanakes* and their bureaucrats, Linear B writing disappeared. The artistic works favored by the kings ceased to exist. Population plummeted. By 1000 B.C., most traces of Mycenaean civilization had disappeared from the old centers of power. An age of darkness descended on Greece.

## Key Terms

| | | |
|---|---|---|
| Fertile Crescent, 42 | Minoan, 51 | Mycenaean, 61 |
| Neolithic Revolution, 44 | Minotaur, 51 | Pylos, 61 |
| Indo-European, 44 | primary sources, 51 | tholos tombs, 61 |
| proto-Indo-European, 45 | secondary sources, 52 | Linear B, 61 |
| secondary products | Second Palace Period, 53 | syllabary, 61 |
| revolution, 45 | Linear A, 54 | *wanakes*, 62 |
| Early Bronze Age, 46 | redistributive center, 55 | megaron, 63 |
| Lerna, 46 | command economy, 55 | Ahhiyawa, 66 |
| House of Tiles, 46 | thalassocracy, 55 | Achaea, 66 |
| Cycladic figurines, 48 | Akrotiri, 57 | Sea Peoples, 69 |
| Middle Bronze Age, 49 | Mycenae, 59 | Philistines, 69 |
| Cnossus, 50 | Grave Circle A, 59 | |
| Minos, 51 | Late Bronze Age, 61 | |

# Further Reading

### NEOLITHIC AND EARLY BRONZE AGE GREECE

Broodbank, Cyprian, *An Island Archaeology of the Early Cyclades* (Cambridge, UK, 2000). Reviews social developments in the islands in the fourth and third millennia.

Diamond, Jared, *Guns, Germs, and Steel: The Fates of Human Societies* (New York, 1997). Pulitzer prize-winning essay on the evolution of society and how the Neolithic revolution in the Near East set the framework for subsequent human history.

Mithen, Steve, *After the Ice: A Global Human History, 20,000–5000 B.C.* (Cambridge, MA, 2004). Fascinating review of humanity's responses to the end of the Ice Age.

Renfrew, Colin, *Archaeology and Language: The Puzzle of Indo-European Origins* (London, 1987). Archaeological arguments that Indo-European languages were spread by Neolithic farmers before 6000 B.C.

### MINOAN CRETE

Doumas, Christos, *The Wall Paintings of Thera* (Athens, 1992). Well-illustrated study of the wall paintings from Akrotiri on Santorini.

Hägg, Robin, and Nanno Marinatos, eds., *The Function of the Minoan Palaces* (Stockholm, 1987). Papers on the archaeology and art history of the Minoan palaces.

### MYCENAEAN GREECE

Cullen, Tracey, ed., *Aegean Prehistory: A Review* (Boston, 2001). Up-to-date review of discoveries in the Neolithic and Bronze Age Aegean.

Dickinson, Oliver, *The Aegean Bronze Age* (Cambridge, UK, 1994). Accurate survey of the evidence, although the organization sometimes makes it difficult to use.

Drews, Robert, *The End of the Bronze Age* (Princeton, NJ, 1993). Survey of theories explaining the fall of the palaces around 1200 B.C.

van de Microop, Marc, *A History of the Ancient Near East*, 2nd ed. (Oxford, 2007). Excellent brief summary of Near Eastern history.

### THE AEGEAN AND THE NEAR EAST

Chadwick, J., *The Decipherment of Linear B*, 2nd ed. (Cambridge, UK, 1970). Exciting tale of the decipherment by one of the principals.

Cline, Eric, and Diane Harris-Cline, eds., *The Aegean and the Orient in the Second Millennium* (Liège, 1998). Proceedings of a conference on Bronze Age Greek connections with the Near East.

Kuhrt, Amélie, *The Ancient Near East, ca. 3000–330 B.C.*, 2 vols. (New York, 1995). Volume 1 has an excellent survey of the period down to 1200 B.C. The standard work.

Pritchard, J. B., ed., *Ancient Near Eastern Texts Relating to the Old Testament*, 3rd ed. (Princeton, 1969-ANET). Standard collection of texts.

## CHAPTER 5

# The Dark Age, 1200–800 B.C.

To Greeks of the Classical Period, the Bronze Age was another world, its ruins dotting the landscape, and stories about the heroes who lived in them surviving only on the lips of singers. Only modern research has made possible any real understanding about what happened after the great disasters, and even now the five centuries that follow 1200 B.C. offer more mysteries than certainties.

## THE COLLAPSE OF THE OLD STATES

At the end of the Bronze Age, the whole of the east Mediterranean was in crisis. In central Anatolia, the collapse of the Hittites opened the gates to invaders who overran the country-side. But urban civilization survived, and by 1100 B.C. powerful new kingdoms—PHRYGIA (**fri**-ja) in the west and URARTU (ur-**ar**-tu) in the east—emerged (Map 5.1).

Both had wealthy and, by the late Iron Age in Urartu, literate courts, although few texts survive. Along the southeastern fringe of the old Hittite empire, in northern Syria, tiny "neo-Hittite" kingdoms formed (these are the Hittites mentioned in the Bible). In ASSYRIA, a major Bronze Age state on the upper Tigris River in what is now northern Iraq, the royal family dissolved into murderous, feuding factions in the twelfth century B.C. A strong-man finally killed all his rivals and reunited the territory, but when he died in 1076 B.C., the kingdom fell into anarchy. Its king lists break off, and we hear no more about Assyria until almost 900 B.C., when it returns with a vengeance. Population movements convulsed the Near East through the twelfth and eleventh centuries B.C. The Sea Peoples were part of a larger pattern. Semitic-speaking pastoralists (sheep herders, goat herders) called Aramaeans (ar-a-**mē**-anz), also known from the Bible, had for centuries gone back and forth between the Syrian desert and the settled plains. They exploited Assyria's decline to settle in DAMASCUS (once called Aram), which became one of antiquity's greatest cities.

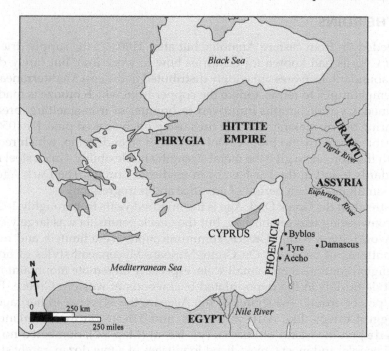

Black Sea

HITTITE
EMPIRE

PHRYGIA

URARTU

Tigris River

ASSYRIA

Euphrates River

CYPRUS

PHOENICIA

• Byblos
• Tyre      • Damascus
• Accho

Mediterranean Sea

N

0    250 km
0         250 miles

EGYPT   Nile River

**MAP 5.1** East
Mediterranean areas
mentioned in this chapter.

Despite Ramses III's victory over the Sea Peoples, Egypt lost its empire in the
Levant in the eleventh century B.C. We can get a sense of the changes by comparing two
texts. One, written by a petty prince on the coast of Palestine to the pharaoh around
1350 B.C., begins: "To the king, my lord, the sun god from heaven: Thus Zatatna, prince
of ACCHO [modern Akko], your servant, the servant of the king, and the dirt under his
two feet, the ground which he treads . . . seven times, seven times I fall, both prone and
supine!" In the second text, written soon after 1100 B.C., that is, 250 years later, the
pharaoh sent an agent on a diplomatic mission to BYBLOS (**bib**-los) in Phoenicia
(present-day Lebanon). The prince of Byblos told him bluntly: "As for me—me also—
I am not your servant! I am not the servant of him who sent you either!" The pharaoh's
agent clearly had no power over him. As its empire slipped away, Egypt broke up into
smaller kingdoms, sometimes ruled by invaders from the western deserts or the distant
southern Sudan.

Everywhere in the twelfth and eleventh centuries B.C. were movements of population
over the ancient world, the fall of states, the murder of untold thousands, the burning of
cities, and economic chaos. The old established states in Egypt and Mesopotamia and Syria
fared better than Anatolia, while the Greek states fell hardest and most completely and took
the longest to recover. They began with less and ended with less still. By 1000 B.C., the
population of Greece may have been one-third what it was in 1300 B.C. After 1100 B.C., if
there was a shortage of food in one area, there was no one to relieve it by bringing in food
from another area. Agriculture declined and monumental stone architecture disappeared,
as did writing. There were migrations into and out of Greece. Long-distance trade faded
away and became a thing of the past.

## LIFE AMONG THE RUINS

Bronze-makers needed tin from eastern Anatolia, but after 1100 B.C. the supply dried up. The inhabitants of Cyprus had known for centuries how to work iron, but rarely did so when bronze was abundant. Iron ores are widely distributed in the east Mediterranean but require very hot temperatures to refine, unlike the copper from which bronze is made. As the tin trade declined, Cypriote smiths improved techniques of iron-smelting, breaking down the iron-bearing ore by making very hot fires using pitch-soaked pine. By 1050 B.C., iron was a serviceable alternative to bronze. Only later did steel develop, which requires mixing carbon with the iron ore to give the metal strength and flexibility. Greek steel never achieved the standards found in the Far East or in medieval Europe. The Dark Age was also the Iron Age, simultaneously a period of advance and retrogression.

The darkest stretch of the Greek Dark Age is the hundred years from roughly 1025 B.C. through 925 B.C. Ironworking was established, but the Greek peninsula was largely cut off from the outside world. Even within Greece, communications were limited, and regions developed local patterns of behavior. On Crete, Minoan–Mycenaean styles of houses, burials, art, and religion continued on a small scale, especially on remote mountaintops, as did Mycenaean-style burials in the depopulated backwoods of western Greece. But in the old centers of power around the shores of the Aegean, the Mycenaean heritage was forgotten. The biggest towns, like ATHENS, ARGOS, and THEBES on the mainland and LEFKANDI (lef-kan-dē) on the island of EUBOEA (yū-bē-a) (Map 5.2), numbered no more than 1,000 or 2,000 people, and most Greeks lived in villages of a few dozen, rarely staying in one location for more than a generation or two.

In this shrunken world, cut off from the Mediterranean and daily reminded of how far it had fallen by a landscape full of Mycenaean ruins, a new society took shape at the

**MAP 5.2**  Greek sites mentioned in this chapter.

end of the eleventh century B.C. We know it only from archaeology, and there is little of that—just a few graves and the foundations of flimsy houses. Some social distinctions, at least, survived. Most villages had one or two well-off families who claimed the best land and flocks, while their neighbors scraped by as dependents. In bigger towns like Athens, there may have been something like an aristocracy.

The Linear B tablets mentioned a local official called a *qasireu* (ka-**si**-re-u), and in Homer's eighth-century B.C. poetry, the leading man in each community is called a *basileus* (ba-**sil**-us), a later form of the Mycenaean *qasireu* and often translated "king." Perhaps after the collapse of the upper social levels of Mycenaean society, the *qasireu* was the most elevated rank that still meant something in Greek society. These village head-men, descendants of an ancient Mycenaean elite, evolved into a minor nobility, the *basileis* (plural, ba-**sil**-ē s).

## DARK AGE "HEROES"

The leaders of Dark Age communities represented themselves in their funerals as a homogeneous group. There is little variation in their simple graves or their plain, one-room houses. Religious behavior has left few traces. People continued visiting Bronze Age sacred places, but set up no temples or altars and left few offerings at shrines.

There were, however, some exceptions. In 1981, archaeologists made a remarkable discovery at Lefkandi on the long island of Euboea that runs along the east coast of mainland Greece. They found the remains of a large building, dating around 1000–950 B.C., unlike any other found anywhere in Greece at this time. Its plan is typical of Dark Age houses, but at 150 feet long, the structure is five times as big as a normal house (although it would have fit easily into the central courtyard of the Minoan palace at Cnossus). Under its floor were two burials: the cremation of a man in a decorated bronze urn, a 200-year-old heirloom from Cyprus, along with iron weapons; and the inhumation (i.e., burial without burning) of a woman adorned with gold jewelry (Figure 5.1). In an age when gold grave goods are almost unheard of, hers were remarkable. She wore a Babylonian gold chest piece that was already a thousand years old, an heirloom. Next to her was an iron knife with an ivory handle. Inhumation is rare at Lefkandi, and she may have been a human sacrifice at the man's funeral. In a second shaft were four horses. A huge pot stood over the graves, and soon after the funeral, the large house was deliberately filled with earth and converted into a giant mound.

This extraordinary site stands out from all other Dark Age finds. Later Greek literature perhaps explains it. The texts are full of stories about the *heroes*, men born from the sexual union of gods and mortals. Greece once was peopled by a race of heroes. According to Hesiod, who probably lived around 700 B.C., the gods created five successive races on earth: of gold, silver, bronze, heroes, and iron. He tells us that after the gods destroyed the bronze race,

> Zeus son of Cronus made another race, a fourth
> upon the thick-clodded earth, more just, more good,
> a divine race of heroes, called demigods,
> the race before our own on the bountiful land.
> Evil war and dread battle destroyed some of them
> beneath the seven-gated walls of Cadmus' Thebes,

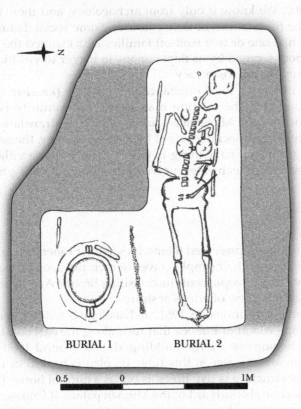

BURIAL 1                    BURIAL 2

0.5            0                          1M

**FIGURE 5.1** The burials in the floor of the large house at Lefkandi. Burial 1 is the male cremation in a bronze urn; Burial 2 is the female inhumation.

fighting on account of the flocks of Oedipus,
and the others died beneath Troy, having crossed in their
ships the sea's broad bosom for fair-haired
Helen's sake. But still others Zeus the father
stood apart from death's finality and gave
them means to live and houses at the bounds of the world.
There they live, free of care, on the Islands of the Blest,
those lucky heroes, beside the shores of deep-roiling Ocean.

Hesiod, *Works and Days*, 157–71

The war of the Greek heroes against Troy was central in Greek myth and provides the setting for Homer's *Iliad* and *Odyssey* (see Chapter 6, "Homer"). Greeks seem to have placed the heroes and the Trojan War in the days of the Mycenaean palaces. In Greek, the word *heros* is used of Homer's great fighters, alive on the windy plain of Troy, but in later Greek it always refers to someone who is dead. The Greeks extended the usage of the word to apply not just to the fighters in the olden days, but to the eminent dead of their own day, recognized in various ways by glorious death in battle, by successfully founding a colony, by a great athletic victory, or sometimes for no reason except that an oracle said that some man deserved "heroic" honors.

The Greek countryside was dotted with tombs and shrines of the dead who were important. A man would be cremated and his ashes placed in a bronze urn, accompanied by weapons and perhaps his horses, just as in the large house at Lefkandi. His grave was marked by a mound and sometimes a huge gravestone and offerings were left at it. The burial at Lefkandi is the earliest known example of someone accorded such "heroic" honors at death and the most splendid throughout the entire Dark Age. Who was this man, and is any memory of him preserved in Greek myth? We would like to know; but we never will.

## ART AND TRADE IN THE DARK AGE

New artistic styles emerged. Around 1025 B.C., potters, whose work we know best because of fired clay's durability, developed a highly abstract style called **Protogeometric**, "first Geometric," because it preceded the more linear Geometric style that appeared around 900 B.C. Protogeometric pottery is characterized by concentric circles and semicircles drawn by means of a multiple compass that produces several parallel lines at the same time. Figures of humans and animals, which sometimes appeared on Mycenaean ware, now virtually disappear. The new style was simple, plain, and austere, but the results could be pleasing. Weavers probably used similar designs, but only scraps survive. Bronze workers made large but delicate pins to fasten clothes, but few other forms of Dark Age art come down to us.

Developments in the east Mediterranean were about to change conditions in remote and provincial Greece. Phoenicia had been a major trading center before 1200 B.C. and was reviving. The Bible notes that King Solomon of Israel (ca. 950 B.C.) and a King Hiram of Tyre, a major Phoenician port city, allied to trade with the land of Ophir (perhaps in the Red Sea) and Tarshish, probably in southern Spain. Before 900 B.C., Near Eastern objects already reappear in Greece (particularly in graves at Lefkandi on Euboea, Athens on the mainland, and Cnossus on Crete), probably brought by Phoenicians, and Greek pottery is found at TYRE (Map 5.1), up the coast in Syria, and even inland around the Sea of Galilee. The Greeks were drawn into an expanding economic system with its center in Phoenicia on the coast of the Levant, present-day Lebanon (Map 5.3). A handful of adventurers had a disproportionate influence. Exotic objects not seen in Greece for centuries became again

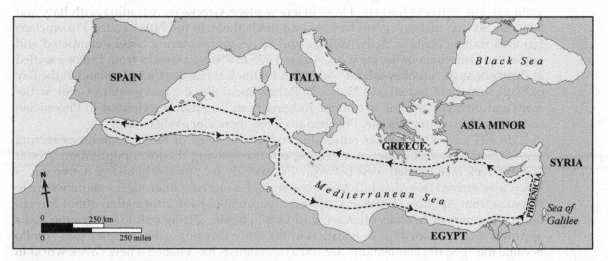

**MAP 5.3**  Phoenician trade routes in the Mediterranean.

available. In a few places, Greeks began for the first time since the Late Bronze Age to make valuable gifts to the gods, particularly at **OLYMPIA** in the wooded, virtually uninhabited backcountry of the western Peloponnesus, later site of the Olympic Games. Many of the earliest bronzes at Olympia were made in ARGOS, across the rugged mountains of ARCADIA (see Map 5.2). By making pilgrimages to distant Olympia, across such tough terrain, wealthy Argives displayed both piety and affluence.

The pace of life quickened in the ninth century B.C. as towns grew, new forms of riches appeared, and foreign faces, speech, and customs again became familiar in some ports. There were experiments in art, housing, burial, and the worship of gods, but nothing to prepare for the explosion of innovation that would come in the eighth century B.C. At this point a Greek Renaissance brought the Dark Age to an end.

## THE EIGHTH-CENTURY RENAISSANCE: ECONOMY

From Iran to Spain, population grew rapidly in the eighth century B.C. Evidence from polar ice cores, sediments on the beds of lakes and bogs, and pollen surviving from ancient plants shows that after 800 B.C. average temperatures fell a few degrees, and winter rains increased. This was harmful to people who lived in cold climates but made farming easier in the hot, dry Mediterranean Basin. Crop yields probably rose, and mortality declined. In this slightly more favorable environment, population doubled in eighth-century B.C. Greece. Most Dark Age Greeks had just a few dozen neighbors in their tiny villages, but by 700 B.C. villages of a hundred were common. Towns like Athens and Argos grew to 5,000 residents. This brought many advantages, but having twice as many mouths to feed from the same area of land meant disaster unless property could be redistributed or output increased. If those who had adequate property resisted change, conflict was inevitable.

Land hunger led to more intensive use of resources—getting more food from the same land by working harder—by manuring the fields and plowing and weeding more often. Hesiod took such labors for granted. "Pile work on work, and still more work," he said. When possible, people brought new land into cultivation by using land previously considered marginal, but only more hard work could make the rocky soil yield a living. Better to find good land in a new place. Greeks were trading with Italy and SICILY by 800 B.C. and saw good harbors and fields there. In the 740s B.C., the Phoenicians founded trading posts in Sicily, Tunisia, and Spain, and seafaring Greeks competed and associated with them in the far west. Around 775 to 750 B.C., Greeks from Euboea settled at **PITHEKOUSSAI** ("monkey-island," so called for unclear reasons), a little island in the Bay of Naples (modern Ischia) (see Map 5.2). Pithekoussai was the first western Greek settlement and probably a home to traders. Judging from the short inscriptions in Phoenician script on pottery from this site, Phoenicians lived there alongside Greeks.

In 734 B.C., other Greeks emigrated to the east coast of Sicily, sometimes seizing unoccupied land and sometimes driving off or enslaving the local population. About 30,000 Greek men headed west between 750 and 650 B.C., probably taking native wives when they arrived (see Map 1.2). Many communities received information about where to colonize from Apollo's shrine at Delphi, a clearinghouse for information about foreign lands. Founders of colonies often went to Delphi before setting out, to receive the god's approval and sponsorship. In addition to his other functions, the complex god Apollo became the "god of colonization." By 700 B.C., colonists had created a new Greek world in Sicily and southern Italy. In the *Odyssey*, a poem about sailing these dangerous seas,

Homer describes how land-hungry Greeks might have felt seeing resources apparently wasted by those who did not exploit them intensively:

> There is a level island that stretches across
> the harbor, not close to the shore of the Cyclops'° island,
> not far out, wooded. Wild goats without number
> roam there. The footfall of men does not drive them away
> nor do hunters go there as they stalk the peaks of mountains
> panting mightily. The island is not held by flocks,
> nor is it plowed, but unsown, unharvested, it knows
> not the hand of man, but nourishes only the bleating
> goats. Nor do the Cyclops have ships with red-painted prows, nor do
> shipwrights live among them to make for them
> well-benched ships, that might accomplish every thing,
> carrying them to the cities of men, as men
> travel often across the sea to others. Such artisans,
> too, would make this place nice to live. It's not bad
> in any way and would bear every kind of crop
> in season. The sea-meadows run well-irrigated, gentle,
> along the shores of the sea. Your vines would never
> give out. There is level land, where you would forever reap
> deep crops in season, so rich is the soil beneath.
> There's a harbor good for mooring, no need of a cable,
> nor for anchors, nor to tie up the prow. There
> you can bring your ship ashore and wait until
> your men again feel the urge to travel and the
> winds blow fair

Homer, *Odyssey* 9.116–41

°*Cyclops:* A one-eyed giant.

We call the overseas Greek settlements "colonies," but they were actually independent *poleis,* not satellites of their mother-cities, with whom they sometimes had acrimonious differences and to whom they did not necessarily owe loyalty: The great Peloponnesian War of 431–404 B.C. would be triggered by a dispute between a mother-city and her colony. Some colonies grew larger and richer than the Aegean *poleis* from which they came. The territory they seized doubled the amount of good land under Greek control, and they chose sites with fine harbors, like the island Homer describes. At first, the position of the Greek colonies was precarious. Some sites failed and had to relocate; some disappeared altogether (like Roanoke in sixteenth-century A.D. America). Those that survived flourished in the second generation. The houses are bigger, and temples appear. More settlers kept coming, and some colonies, like Syracuse in Sicily, sent out subcolonies of their own. The new settlements spread Greeks all round the Mediterranean and the cold northern Black Sea.

Greeks could also extend production in this time of burgeoning population by stealing their neighbors' land. There were several wars for land in the late eighth century B.C. The most famous was Sparta's invasion of **MESSENIA**. Messenia is a territory that lies west of Sparta across a high mountain range (Map 5.2). After a long struggle, the Spartans annexed Messenia, enslaved its population, and divided its land among themselves.

The Messenians now worked the land for Spartans, handing over most of the produce. The reduction of Messenia to servitude was an extreme response to population growth and made Sparta peculiar among the Greek city-states (see Chapter 10, "A Tale of Two Archaic Cities: Sparta and Athens, 700–480 B.C."), but many Greek states used force on a smaller scale to take control of disputed border zones.

Another response to growing population was *more efficient organization*. The Minoans and Mycenaeans had refined their organization by inventing a form of writing and imitating the bureaucratic structure of literate Near Eastern economies. Making use of written records, they told some people what to grow to get the most out of their land, and they set up others in workshops. The palaces moved goods between the occupational groups, raising efficiency through the division of labor. What the palaces accomplished through centralization, eighth-century B.C. Greeks did through markets. In this way, archaic-classical Greece differed profoundly from Bronze Age Greece. In the eighth century B.C., no one was telling anyone what to grow, make, or trade, except in enslaved communities like Messenia. Free Greeks acted on their own authority and were governed, as we would say, by the forces of the marketplace. The results were more efficient than in the Bronze Age. The population grew and lived better. These responses to growing population had social costs, however; some of them high.

## THE EIGHTH-CENTURY B.C. RENAISSANCE: SOCIETY

To exploit their land more intensively, Greeks needed to increase the amounts of labor and capital (in the form of animals, manure, irrigation ditches, better plows, etc.) that they put into each field. Rich people with a lot of land wanted poorer people to work it, while the poor wished to have enough land to employ their own labor effectively. If the rich could concentrate all land in their own hands, the poor would have to work for them; if the land could be distributed equally, the poor could support themselves.

Some of the colonies in Sicily may have conducted a kind of social experiment, giving each man equal land and equal rights, but patterns of burials suggest that egalitarian ideals were in any event gaining ground everywhere in the eighth century B.C. During the Dark Age, the elite received more formal burials than the poor, but after 750 B.C., most people began receiving equal treatment at death. As social power shifted from rich to poor, the divisions that would plague archaic Greece took shape as did struggles between those who thought that a small aristocracy should control land, labor, and the conduct of war and those who thought that all the men in a *polis* had an equal voice in such matters.

Extending the land under cultivation brought in more food but called for still more labor, while occupying someone else's land required force and the qualities that make force effective. Political boundaries, the divisions between territories, became more important and better defined. Competition for land made Greeks more aware of belonging to particular groups, such as the Athenians or the Corinthians, and in the new forms of organized violence, ever more was at stake. There were important advances in arms and armor. Around 700 B.C. we begin to find fine bronze armor, the first seen since Mycenaean times (Figure 5.2), and fortifications proliferated and became stronger.

Warfare favors centralized power: Someone has to muster fighters, design strategy, and see that orders are obeyed. In this new atmosphere, rudimentary state institutions appeared, directing communal policies and monopolizing the use of violence. In some cases, the growing importance of war allowed Dark Age chiefs to become kings who made key decisions. Was Greece returning to Bronze Age monarchy?

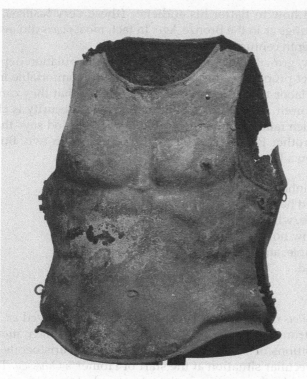

**FIGURE 5.2**  Breastplate (*cuirass*), ca. 650 B.C., from a burial. The bronze is artistically modeled to the man's pectoral and abdominal muscles.

We learn a good deal about these emerging strong-men from Homer and Hesiod, who call them *basileis*. The poets thought that the *basileis'* authority came in part from their closeness to the gods. To Homer, Odysseus was "godlike," and many heroes who fought at Troy were born from the union of gods with humans. Some of the most powerful men in the eighth century B.C. may have claimed to be sacred rulers, and Hesiod says that *basileis* in his own day (around 700 B.C.) enjoyed the divine favor of the Muses, who gave them eloquence and the power that comes with it:

> Whomever of the *basileis* the daughters of great Zeus
> wish to honor, upon his tongue, as they watch him
> being born, they pour sweet dew and his words
> flow like honey from his mouth. All people look
> to him as he passes rules in accordance with straight
> judgments, and through his easy speech skillfully
> stops even a great quarrel. The *basileis*
> are wise in this, that when the public suffers
> harm, they set things right with ease, persuading
> by means of gentle words. When he comes into
> the assembly, they woo him with honeyed reverence,
> like a god. He stands out above the crowd.
> Such is the power of the Muses' holy gift to man.
>
> Hesiod, *Theogony* 80–93

Hesiod no doubt understood how to flatter his audience (these very *basileis*), but the *basileis* never became mighty kings as in the Bronze Age. In fact, most *poleis* did away with kingship altogether in the seventh century B.C.

In an agricultural society, growth that can support a larger population depends on rulers strong enough to protect property rights so that people feel comfortable investing time and resources into their labor and property, but not so strong that they can simply help themselves to anyone's profit. The *basileis'* inability to provide security is clear in a story that Hesiod tells, and such failures undermined the *basileis*. Hesiod says that when his father died, he and his brother Perses divided their inheritance in two. But Perses bribed the *basileis* to award him a larger share:

> We already divided our inheritance, but you seized
> more than your share and held it, greatly praising
> the gift-devouring *basileis*, who like to take on a case
> like this. Fools! They know not that half
> can be more than the whole, and that great profit
> lies in a poor man's bread.

Hesiod, *Works and Days* 37–41

The weakness of the *basileis* meant that Greek state-formation followed an unusual path. Institutions became stronger and more efficient, but the ordinary men in the community resisted the ambitions of would-be kings and haughty aristocrats. A good illustration comes from the peculiar situation at the start of Homer's *Odyssey*. The great hero Odysseus had been a good *basileus* on Ithaca, the tale runs, but the gods caused him to disappear for ten years on his way home after spending the previous ten years at Troy. For twenty years, Ithaca lived without a *basileus*. Most Ithacans presumed Odysseus dead and got on with their lives. But a crowd of aristocratic suitors descended on Odysseus' house, vying for the hand of the beautiful Penelope, his supposed widow. They devoured his stored wealth and slept with his maidservants until, in the twentieth year of Odysseus' absence, Odysseus' grown son Telemachus (tel-**em**-a-kus) decides to get rid of the aristocratic suitors:

> At once he ordered the clear-voiced heralds to summon
> to the assembly the Achaeans with their long hair.
> The heralds shouted out, and the Achaeans quickly
> gathered. And when they were gathered together and crowded
> the meeting ground, Telemachus entered the place
> of assembly, and in his hand he held a bronze spear.
> He was not alone; two swift hounds accompanied him.
> Athena cast a wondrous charm about him.
> Everyone looked at him as he entered. He sat
> down in his father's seat, and the elders made way.
> Then to them the hero Aegyptius began to speak,
> who was bent with age and knew many things . . .
>      "Hear me, men of Ithaca, what I have to say.
> Never have we held an assembly or met in session
> since godlike Odysseus sailed in his hollow ships.

Who now has summoned us in this way? one of the
youngsters? or one of the old-timers? or has someone
announced some army that is coming, someone who can
describe it clearly because he first learned of it
himself? or will he speak of some other matter
of public concern and address us?

Homer, *Odyssey* 2.6–16, 25–32

Homer took it for granted that men from important families, like Telemachus, were
the center of attention in politics. Odysseus even had his own seat in the assembly.
Aegyptius says there has been no assembly since Odysseus left for Troy twenty years
before, so we might assume that Odysseus had dominated Ithacan politics; on the other
hand, Aegyptius has no idea which Ithacan called this meeting, so clearly other men
besides a *basileus* could call assemblies. Aegyptius thinks of "the Ithacans" as a group
responsible for communal well-being.

Telemachus stands up and explains that it was he who summoned the assembly. He
describes the suitors' outrages:

" . . . Thronging our house day after day
they party on and on. They drink the shining wine
as if there was no tomorrow. Everything wasted.
No longer is there a man such as Odysseus was,
who might expel this curse from my household.
Surely I could not accomplish it. I would only appear
ridiculous and knowing nothing of power.
If I did have the power, I would do something about this.
Their deeds are intolerable! It's no pretty sight,
what they've done to my house! You should
take shame, all of you, and be mortified in the eyes
of all those who live around us. Fear the anger of the gods,
or seeing these evils they will whirl against you!
I beg you in the name of Zeus on Olympus,
and Themis too, who dissolves and gathers assemblies—
Stop! my friends, and leave me alone to be worn
away in sorrow, if ever my father, the excellent
Odysseus, ever did harm with evil intent
to the well-greaved Achaeans—now, I suppose, you repay
it by the harm you do to me, with evil
intent, encouraging these men. It would be better for me
if you consumed my wealth and my cattle. At least
if you ate them, one day there would be recompense."

Homer, *Odyssey* 2.55–76

In Ithaca, state institutions are weak. There is no police. Because there is no third
party to enforce justice, and Telemachus lacks the strength to fight the suitors himself,
he appeals to the community's moral sense. They should be embarrassed to allow such

goings-on in Ithaca and be concerned that the gods will punish them. Telemachus marvels that the Ithacans tolerate such behavior and pretends to wonder whether Odysseus had done them some wrong to justify their inaction. Telemachus presents himself as the champion of justice and advocates the community's right to judge even the mightiest among them, including the young, rich, arrogant suitors.

One of the suitors stands up and replies that none of it is their fault. Telemachus should send his mother back to her father, and the suitors would then approach him about a remarriage. Telemachus denounces the scheme, and Zeus sends an omen: two eagles fight in the sky above. An old man says this means that Odysseus will return and punish the suitors. Unlike in the highly civilized Assyria or Egypt, there are no professional omen-interpreters in this society. Eurymachus, a suitor, speaks up:

> "Hey old man, why don't you go home and prophesy
> to your kids? In case they might suffer something
> or other in times to come. I'm a better prophet
> than you are. There are birds aplenty soaring through the rays
> of the sun, but not all are signs from another world.
> Odysseus, come on, died in some far place,
> and you should have died with him. You wouldn't rant
> your prophecies then, nor would you be stirring up
> this angry young man, thinking you might get
> some gift from him. Now I prophesy to you,
> and what I say shall come to pass. If you,
> so filled with wisdom, so knowing of life, with your fancy
> words stir up this young man to run riot, he will
> be first to pay. Nor will he be able to do
> a thing about it. As for you, we'll slap on a fine
> that won't be fun to pay. You'll wish you'd never
> been born."
>
> Homer, *Odyssey* 2.178–93

Unlike Telemachus, Eurymachus is full of threats and shows contempt for the gods in saying that the sign means nothing. Another Ithacan, Mentor, sadly observes:

> "Hear me, men of Ithaca, what I have to say.
> Let no scepter-bearing basileus willingly be kind
> and gentle, knowing how one should act, but let
> him be always hard and the doer of evil things!
> As it is, no one remembers godlike Odysseus
> from all the people he ruled, how gentle, how like
> a father he was.
>     I don't begrudge the well-born
> suitors if they want to commit acts of violence in the perversity
> of their minds: They lay their heads on the line
> when with violence they consume the house of Odysseus,
> whom they think will never return. But I
> hold it against you as you sit there, every man

in silence, and you refuse to speak and to end the suitors'
outrage, who are few in number, while there are many of you."
        Leocritus, son of Euenor, answered.
"Mentor! You fool! Crazed, mad! What do you mean,
urging us to lay off? It's a rough game to fight
against more men than yourself, over a meal!
Even if Odysseus the Ithacan himself should come
home and rage in his heart to expel the suitors
who dine in his house, I don't think his wife would take
much pleasure in him. No, however much she wanted to.
No, here, on the spot, he'd meet an ugly death,
if he fought against our multitude. What you say
is gibberish . . . Enough of that! Now go to your homes
—each one of you!"
        So he broke up the assembly in a jiffy,
and everyone went home to his house. But the suitors returned
to the house of godlike Odysseus.

Homer, *Odyssey* 2.229–59

Mentor thinks the community should stop the rich and impious suitors, but the
Ithacans do nothing, and one of the suitors abruptly dismisses them. Homer took it for
granted that Ithaca should have a *basileus*, but also assumed that the *basileus* must act justly
and that Ithaca's men would decide what counted as just behavior. The assembly could in
theory denounce the elite, but they hold back. Institutions are weak and the suitors are
ready to resist anyone who attacks them. Although the suitors retain control, battle lines are
drawn between the mass of Ithacans, including virtuous leaders who stand for decency,
and self-interested aristocrats out for selfish gain. In his description of the events in Ithaca,
Homer probably reflects similar divisions in his own society of the eighth century B.C.

The same social divisions appear in Hesiod's poem, *Works and Days,* although
Hesiod offers a very different perspective. He presents himself as a hardworking farmer
dispensing advice on how to live a good life. We earlier quoted his criticism of the *basileis*
for taking bribes, after which he continues:

O Perses, listen to justice, avoid arrogance.
Arrogance is evil for a common man, and even
the noble cannot easily bear it, but is weighed down
by it and slides into senseless behavior. Better
by far is that other road, that leads towards justice.
Justice wins out over arrogance in the end.
The fool learns this through suffering. For Oath runs
more swiftly than crooked judgments. When Justice
is dragged from the way, driven out by gift-eating men,
who judge with crooked judgments, there is a rushing
noise; then she returns to the city and the houses of people,
draped in a mist, bringing evil to humans, who drove
her out and did not judge straightly.

Hesiod, *Works and Days* 213–24

Hesiod denounces the *basileis* of his small village of Ascra (not far from Thebes) for their injustice. They ignored *dikê* (dē-kā), "justice," and their impiety caused the gods to abandon mankind. Hesiod champions the moderate, middling farmer, like himself, who has a clear sense of right and wrong, and pursues wealth fairly:

> For if a man gains great
> wealth through force of hands, or lies and steals,
> as often happens when greed deceives the mind
> of man, and shamelessness overtakes shame,
> then the gods blot him out and diminish his house
> and soon his wealth is gone.

Hesiod, *Works and Days* 320–25

Around the same time the prophets of the Hebrew Bible denounced the kings of Israel and Judah for similar injustices, also predicting that God would bring punishment for their failure to behave justly. Comparable sentiments turn up much earlier in Egyptian and Mesopotamian literature. But Homer and Hesiod differ from the Near Eastern authors. Whereas the Hebrew prophets Amos and Isaiah believed that they should point out the rulers' faults, and Egyptian texts expected the pharaoh to correct injustice, Greek authors believed that ordinary men themselves had the right to correct injustice. It was up to the *community* of farmers to determine what was good and proper and to resist the wicked *basileis*. From such extraordinary attitudes was to grow the male-citizen democracy of fifth-century B.C. Athens.

## THE EIGHTH-CENTURY B.C. RENAISSANCE: CULTURE

Eighth-century B.C. social conflicts were intimately tied to cultural developments. Since 3000 B.C., Near Eastern kings alone mediated between this world and the gods. Kingship came from heaven. But the Greeks now separated religion from social power.

When Dark Age Greeks prayed to the gods, they met at a special place, killed an animal in the god's honor, poured drink offerings (libations), roasted most parts of the animal on a fire, and ate. Around 750 B.C., they began to build stone altars for the fire and to offer gifts at shrines. The Olympic Games were founded near this time, traditionally in 776 B.C., though we cannot verify the date. At the games, when warfare was suspended, Greek athletes from different towns competed. The earliest athletes came from near Olympia, but by the sixth-century B.C. competitors were coming from all over the Greek world. Their gifts to the shrine of Zeus were rich and by 700 B.C. included objects of bronze, silver, and gold.

During those same years, Greeks started building temples—houses for the gods' images. Temples were at first modest, though bigger and better built than the houses around them. Larger towns, like Eretria (e-**re**-tri-a) on the island of Euboea, built "hundred-foot" temples called *hekatompeda* in Greek, and soon after 700 B.C., Corinth and Argos built *hekatompeda* completely from stone. Seventh-century B.C. temples dwarfed all contemporary buildings. They were the biggest expenditures in capital, labor, and ambition since the Mycenaean palaces.

Dark Age ritual meals evolved into elaborate sacrifices and feasts with impressive dedications to the gods. After battles, winners might offer one-tenth of their plunder to a god, and great sanctuaries like Olympia, Delphi, and Delos filled up with such offerings. Periodically, the priests cleaned up the sanctuaries, digging big pits and burying the old but hallowed offerings. At many sanctuaries, archaeologists cannot put a trowel into the earth without turning up eighth- and seventh-century B.C. offerings. The increasingly self-conscious *poleis* marked out areas for the gods, communal sanctuaries that embodied local identity and pride. Most *poleis* set up two major sanctuaries, one in the heart of the main town and one on a frontier that helped define the community against its neighbors, solidifying its claim to the land.

At the same time that spending on religious architecture increased, rich grave goods declined. After 700 B.C., anyone who wanted to show off his wealth did so not by a huge grave mound or buried suits of armor, which would glorify the family alone, but by making gifts to the gods at public shrines, which benefited the whole community. Private displays of wealth also declined. Shortly before 700 B.C., a few people built houses as big as modern American houses, sometimes covering 2,500 square feet and even having a second floor. After 700 B.C., such mansions virtually disappeared until the fourth century B.C.

In some places, people now started leaving offerings near Bronze Age tombs, perhaps to honor the long-dead race of heroes. As well as redefining their relationships with the gods, eighth-century B.C. Greeks were rethinking their relationships with their ancestors. Another change, the revival of representative art in the **Late Geometric style** of vase painting (roughly 750–700 B.C.), may be connected with this development. After a long hiatus since the end of the Bronze Age, during which few figures are found in Greek art, Late Geometric paintings show humans in battles and at funerals (Figure 5.3). It is hard to tell whether the scenes evoke the long-lost race of heroes or contemporary practices, or a mixture of both. Many of the well-known Greek myths seem to have been invented in this period, perhaps stimulated by the influx of images from Near Eastern art on objects made of cloth (now all lost) and on metal objects like armor and bowls.

The greatest cultural innovation by far was the invention of the **Greek alphabet**. As we have seen, Linear B syllabic writing, which recorded Greek, disappeared completely after 1200 B.C. Around 800 B.C., an unknown Greek or Near Easterner invented a new script based on an earlier Semitic script used in the Levant from at least 1000 B.C. Sometimes called the Phoenician alphabet, the script on which the Greek alphabet was based was really an odd syllabary in which each sign stands for a consonant plus an implied vowel, to be provided by the native speaker. (To distinguish the Phoenician writing from the Greek alphabetic writing, some scholars call Phoenician writing a *consonantal script*.) The Phoenician syllabary did not, however, belong to the Phoenicians alone, but was one of a family of closely related writings called **West Semitic writing** used all over the Levant, including Syria, Phoenicia, and Palestine. Possible forerunners to this family of writings, which includes Hebrew writing, have recently been found in southern Egypt, dating as early as 1800 B.C.

It takes a lot of skill and experience to read something written in a West Semitic script. West Semitic writing was revolutionary because it needed just twenty-two signs and because of a unique method of learning by memorizing a fixed sequence of names and signs, an ancient ancestor of our "ABC song." The consonantal value of a sign (but no vocalic values) was encoded in the name of the sign as the first sound of the name. We still say, in a somewhat similar fashion, "A is for apple, B is for brave, C is for

**FIGURE 5.3** The earliest figured art since Mycenaean times shows funerals and battles. On the top panel on this large Late Geometric vase from Athens, called a *krater* ("mixing bowl," for wine), ca. 750 B.C., a body is laid out on a bier. On either side of the bier, mourners tear their hair. In a panel below, warriors ride in chariots.

cat, . . . " Because no vocalic values are encoded, you cannot pronounce West Semitic script (including Hebrew) unless you speak the language. By stark contrast, anyone can pronounce a document in the Greek alphabet, even if he or she has no idea of what is being said. The Greek alphabet was the first technology that preserved the approximate sound of speech.

Many scholars assume that Phoenicians developed their script for traders' record-keeping, but there is no direct evidence for this. The Phoenicians did not even have a system of numbering until much later, when they borrowed one from the Greeks. Rather, the West Semitic writing seems to have been used to record political activity, family histories, prayers to the gods, and rules of behavior. Surviving West Semitic texts (including early forms of the Bible) were probably dictated rather than composed silently in the modern manner; for this reason, West Semitic writing paid exclusive attention to sound, ignoring the many nonphonetic aids to communication that earlier Mesopotamian cuneiform and Egyptian hieroglyphic writings employed. Small portions of the Hebrew Bible may date back as far as 1000 B.C. Although most parts of the Bible were written much later, some as late ca. 200 B.C., the documents it contains probably reflect the range of records and literature kept in this widespread family of West Semitic writings during the Dark Age, from which only the Hebrew scriptures have survived.

Archaeologists on Crete have found objects with Phoenician inscriptions from as early as 900 B.C.; but not until after 800 B.C., in the midst of all the upheavals described previously, did someone adapt these symbols to suit the sounds of Greek speech, poetic speech in particular (Table 5.1).

The adapter of the Phoenician script, the inventor of the Greek alphabet, no doubt lived in a bilingual community (perhaps the cosmopolitan island of Euboea). The adapter divided the Phoenician syllabic signs into two categories: one to represent vowels (in Greek, literally "things sounded") and the other to represent the sounds that go with vowels, or consonants ("things that sound along with something else"), and added a few new signs to the end of the series. The adapter's radical invention was not so much the introduction of vowel signs, which had existed in earlier writings, including Linear B, as his invention of the spelling rule that a sign from one group, the "vowels," must always accompany signs from the second group, the "consonants." Where a Phoenician would write, "Th mn sng t m, Ms, vrstl/n hs mn ws, w wndrd fll fr ftr h/hd sckd th scrd ctdl f Try," the Greek alphabet could now write something like "The man sing to me, O Muse, versatile/in his many ways, who wandered full far after he/had sacked the sacred citadel of Troy"—the first few lines of Homer's *Odyssey*. In practical terms, the Greek alphabet was the first system of writing that you can pronounce, once you have learned the rules, whether or not you know the underlying language. It could be used to record any language at all and since its invention has become, in its Roman variation, the most widely used script in the world by far, recording hundreds of languages from Turkish to Chinese (in the so-called Pinyin script).

Why did the adapter go to the trouble of inventing a script with two kinds of signs and the rule that they must always work together? We can be confident that it was not to record lists of "woolen cloaks to be well boiled," like the Mycenaean record-keepers, nor to create a writing system capable of recording every human language. One can record poetry in consonantal, syllabic, or even hieroglyphic scripts, and Near Easterners and Egyptians had done so for 2,000 years, but the Greek language, especially Greek poetry, uses complex clusters of vowels that cannot be represented by such systems. A great deal of evidence leads us to believe that, whatever Phoenician writing was used for, the earliest Greek alphabetic writing was used to preserve poetic texts. Although surprising, the fact explains a great deal about the special importance that poetry held in Greek society, far and beyond the influence it had held in earlier literate civilizations. Poets were to the Greeks as prophets were to the Hebrews, or priests to the Egyptians, defining culture and its values. Homer appears to have lived at the time of the invention of the Greek alphabet, and his poems are probably the first texts ever recorded in this revolutionary system (Figure 5.4).

The alphabet gave Greeks the means to record the words of the greatest poets, and from this time on, literary evidence (almost all in the form of poetry until about 450 B.C.) survives in increasing quantities. The invention of the Greek alphabet and the recording of the Homeric poems separate Greek prehistory, the Dark Age, from Greek history, the Archaic and Classical Ages.

**TABLE 5.1**    The Phoenician and Greek writing systems. The Greek alphabet used the *waw* sign in two places: for the *digamma*, which had the sound of English *w*, and for one of the five new signs, the vowel *u*. Later, the Greeks dropped the *digamma*, but it has come down to us through the Latin alphabet (the Western form of the Greek alphabet) as the letter *F*. *San* was an alternate sign for the *s* sound and was soon dropped, as was *qoppa*, similar to *k*, but it survives as our letter *q* (used only before the letter *u*).

| Phoenician Symbol (ca. 700 B.C.) | Semitic Name | Approximate Semitic Sound | Greek Symbol (ca. 700 B.C.) | Modern Greek Symbol | Greek Name |
|---|---|---|---|---|---|
| | 'aleph | glottal stop (catch in voice) | | A | alpha |
| | beth | b | | B | beta |
| | gimel | g in glory | | Γ | gamma |
| | daleth | d | | Δ | delta |
| | he | h | | E | epsilon |
| | waw | w | | --- | wau, digamma |
| | zayin | z | | Z | zeta |
| | heth | "strong" h | | H | eta |
| | teth | "strong" t | | Θ | theta |
| | yod | y in yellow | | I | iota |
| | kaph | k | | K | kappa |
| | lamed | l | | Λ | lambda |
| | mem | m | | M | mu |
| | nun | n | | N | nu |
| | samekh | s | | Ξ | xi |
| | 'ayin | pharyngeal consonant (gagging sound) | | O | omicron |
| | pe | p | | Π | pi |
| | tsadhe | ts | | --- | san |
| | qoph | "rough" k | | --- | qoppa |
| | resh | r | | P | rho |
| | shin | sh | | Σ | sigma |
| | taw | t | | T | tau |
| | waw | w | | Υ | upsilon |
| | | f | | Φ | phi |
| | | x | | X | chi |
| | | c | | Ψ | psi |
| | | | | Ω | omega |

HOSNUNORXESTONPANTONATALOTATAPAIZEITOTODEK{M}M{N?}N
Whoever of all the dancers now dances most gracefully . . .

**FIGURE 5.4**  The Dipylon Oinochoe, with transcription (by Barry B. Powell) of one of the oldest Greek alphabetic inscriptions inscribed near its shoulder, found in Athens, ca. 740 B.C. The inscription, reading from right to left, is a perfect hexameter, Homer's meter, plus a few puzzling signs at the end. The alphabet was used to record Greek verse from the beginning.

## CONCLUSION

Down to 1200 B.C., Greek society was not so different from the rest of the East Mediterranean. The Neolithic revolution had spread from the Near East to Greece by 6000 B.C.; the secondary products revolution arrived by 3000 B.C., and complex societies emerged soon after. The mainland societies collapsed around 2300 B.C., but by 2000 B.C., large palaces appeared on Crete, using Linear A writing to run complex bureaucracies. In the eighteenth and seventeenth centuries B.C., Minoan society was rich and sophisticated, with ordinary people enjoying high living standards, and Minoan-type institutions spread through the Cyclades. By 1700 B.C., warlike societies gained great wealth on the mainland and at some point took over Crete. They too fell victim to unexplained disasters around 1200 B.C., and all the Mycenaean centers on the mainland were burned.

Great kings and palaces revived in western Asia in the tenth century B.C., but not in Greece. Although there are hints of recovery in the ninth century B.C., the Greek Dark Age continued until the eighth century B.C., and the city-states that then emerged were very different from Near Eastern societies. The *poleis* had a sense of community—so strong that would-be rulers could not claim that the gods had singled them out. In this inventive period appeared new forms of religious, artistic, and poetic expression. New *poleis* around the

Mediterranean and Black Sea revolutionized the Greek economy and provided scope for social experiments. In place of the centralized, redistributive economies of the Bronze Age, eighth-century B.C. Greeks relied on individuals to exchange goods as they thought best.

Around 700 B.C., the *poleis* were small, poor, and weak by Near Eastern standards. They were internally divided by feuds within the aristocracy and by feuds between the aristocrats and the masses. They were also divided among themselves, as city-states competed for resources. In the next two chapters, we examine two of the cultural pillars that supported the new framework: the Homeric epics and Greek religion.

## Key Terms

Assyria, 72

Lefkandi, 74

Euboea, 74

*basileus*, 75

Protogeometric, 77

Olympia, 78

Pithekoussai, 78

Messenia, 79

*dikê*, 86

*hekatompeda*, 86

Late Geometric style, 87

Greek alphabet, 87

West Semitic writing, 87

## Further Reading

### THE DARK AGE

Dickinson, Oliver. *The Aegean from Bronze Age to Iron Age* (London, 2007). Survey of the archaeological evidence. Not always as straightforward as Snodgrass' classic *Dark Age of Greece*, but more up-to-date.

Popham, Mervyn, Evi Touloupa, and L. Hugh Sackett, "The hero of Lefkandi," *Antiquity* 56 (1982): 169–74. Brief excavation report on the tenth-century B.C. finds at Lefkandi.

Snodgrass, Anthony, *The Dark Age of Greece* (Edinburgh, UK, 1971; reissued 2001). Now out of date on recent finds, but still the best archaeological survey of the Dark Age.

Whitley, James, *The Archaeology of Ancient Greece* (Cambridge, UK, 2001). Chapters 5 to 10 are an excellent recent overview of Dark Age and archaic archaeology.

### THE EIGHTH CENTURY B.C.

Boardman, John, *The Greeks Overseas*, rev. ed. (London, 1999). The best introduction to the archaeological evidence for Greek colonies.

Burkert, Walter, *The Orientalizing Revolution* (Cambridge, MA, 1992; German original 1984). Stimulating study of literary and archaeological evidence for Greek contacts with the Near East in the eighth and seventh centuries.

de Polignac, François, *Cults, Territory, and the Origins of the Greek City-State* (Chicago, 1995). Original analysis of the significance of religious changes in the eighth century.

Edwards, Anthony. *Hesiod's Ascra* (Berkeley, 2004). Excellent sociological study of Hesiod's *Works and Days*.

Hurwit, Jeffery, *The Art and Culture of Early Greece* (Ithaca, NY, 1985). Excellent analysis of vase painting and poetry.

Morris, Ian, and Barry B. Powell, eds., *A New Companion to Homer* (Leiden, 1997). The essays in part IV discuss Homeric history and archaeology.

Powell, Barry B., *Homer and the Origin of the Greek Alphabet* (Cambridge, UK, 1991). Argues that alphabetic writing was invented specifically to record Homer's poetry.

———, *Writing and the Origins of Greek Literature* (Cambridge, UK, 2003). Describes the new possibilities that the alphabet offered and the relationship between art and song.

Snodgrass, Anthony, *Archaic Greece* (Berkeley, 1981). Outstanding combination of archaeological and textual evidence.

———, *Archaeology and the Emergence of Greece* (Edinburgh, 2006). Collection of important essays by the leading authority on the archaeology of Dark Age Greece.

## CHAPTER 6

# Homer

We quoted Homer several times in Chapter 4, "The Greeks before History, 12,000–1200 B.C.," and Chapter 5, "The Dark Age, 1200–800 B.C." Homer is the first known European poet and of such importance to the Greeks that we need to pause our narrative to look more closely at the controversies that have surrounded him, and the stories that he told, which in so many ways shaped Greek thought and culture.

In trying to discover the truth about the past we must be able to evaluate our written sources to derive information from them. But the origin and meaning of written sources can be highly obscure, and never more so than the poems of Homer. The questions raised in efforts to evaluate Homer's poems are models for questions applied to other ancient written documents.

Homer became the basis for Greek education (Figure 6.1) and is still widely read in high school and college classes. He is also our best source for knowing what the Greeks were thinking in the eighth century B.C. as they fought each other and sailed across dangerous seas to found new *poleis* in alien lands. Who was Homer? When did he live? How were his works written down? What are his poems about? He seems to come from the void, a flare suddenly lighting up the Dark Age, illuminating a new world. Such problems constitute the **Homeric Question**, a central issue in humanistic study for the past 200 years.

## THE HOMERIC QUESTION

The oldest surviving texts of the *Iliad* and the *Odyssey* date back to around A.D. 1100, separated from the poet by nearly 2,000 years. Scholars produced them in the late Roman capital of Byzantium, present-day Istanbul. Pieces, but only pieces, of *ancient* texts of Homer survive from the dry sands of Egypt, where Homer was read and loved by Greek-speakers who settled the Nile Valley after the conquest of Alexander the Great in 333 B.C. Some papyrus fragments date back to the third century B.C. More papyrus fragments of Homer survive than of any other poet, and twice as many fragments of the *Iliad* as of the *Odyssey*. The papyrus fragments sometimes have extra lines not found in our texts, but on the whole they are remarkably similar.

**FIGURE 6.1**   A boy recites a memorized epic poem to his schoolmaster, who checks his work against a text, on an Athenian red-figured drinking cup (*kylix*), ca. 480 B.C. Behind the schoolmaster, a second pupil practices the lyre, which accompanied songs.

We know almost nothing about Homeric texts earlier than these papyri. We have no primary sources for Homer's life, for where he lived or when, although traditions reaching back to the fifth century B.C. said that he was born on the coast of Asia Minor or just off it on the island of Chios. Scholarly books today often describe Homer as an Ionian, someone from Asia Minor, but in fact we have no direct knowledge.

## Friedrich August Wolf

Even in the ancient world, intellectuals noticed that nothing certain was known about Homer. He was an enigma, a complete mystery. But the modern form of the Homeric Question was cast in A.D. 1795 with the publication of a famous book, *Prolegomena ad Homerum* ("Introduction to Homer"), written in Latin by a German scholar, **Friedrich August Wolf**. Wolf was deeply influenced by revolutionary analyses then being applied to the Bible. Scholars asked, Where did the Bible come from? How old is it, and who wrote it? Are the events it reports historical? The name of God is given in different forms in the first five books of the Hebrew Bible (called the *Pentateuch*, "five rolls"), and scholars showed that Genesis, for example, consists of four strands, recognizable and to some extent separable from one another. Thus we can explain such inconsistencies as that woman was created twice, on the seventh day as man's peer and again from the rib of Adam. Hebrew scholars, working in exile in Babylon in the sixth century B.C., had evidently combined once independent written accounts to fashion something like the Bible that has come down to us, according to modern biblical scholarship.

Homer, too, contains strange inconsistencies. For example, in book 9 of the *Iliad*, the Achaean commanders send a contingent to the angry Achilles to beg him to return to the war, which they are losing. As representatives, they select Odysseus, famous for his persuasive speech; Ajax, one of the greatest warriors; and Phoenix, Achilles' tutor. Two heralds will go along. Then, a few lines later, Homer informs us that "the two of them walked along the loud-resounding sea . . . " although there were five (or three, if you don't count the heralds). In another passage, a warrior is killed, then turns up again fighting on the windy plain.

Such difficulties, of which there are many, looked rather like those facing scholars who studied the Bible. Wolf emphasized that writing was unknown to the Homeric warriors. Only once does Homer mention writing and then in a garbled fashion, as if he did not quite understand what it was. If Homer lived in a world without writing, Wolf asked, how could he have *written* his poems?

## The "Pisistratean Recension"

Various authors, beginning with Plato (or someone imitating him) in the fourth century B.C., connected the Athenian tyrant Pisistratus (pī-**sis**-tra-tus, ca. 590?–527 B.C.; see Chapter 10, "A Tale of Two Archaic Cities: Sparta and Athens, 700–480 B.C.") to the performance and perhaps the shape of the Homeric poems. Plato (or someone imitating him: *Hipparchus* 228 B) speaks of a kind of performer called a **rhapsode** whom Pisistratus required to "take up where the other left off." Rhapsode probably means "staff-singer," because he held a staff as he declaimed (Figure 6.2). Rhapsodes were sometimes professional reciters who memorized the Homeric texts and presented them at the Athenian festival of the Great Panathenaea ("all-Athenian") held every four years. Pisistratus used this festival to further his cultural program and enhance his political stature.

The illiteracy of Homer's world, combined with traditions that something happened to the *Iliad* and the *Odyssey* in sixth-century B.C. Athens, led Wolf to conclude that the Homeric poems were the product of editorial activity in Pisistratus' time, similar to that which had produced the early books of the Bible while the leaders of the Jews were held captive in Babylon. Scholars call Wolf's explanation the "theory of the Pisistratean Recension." Giving support to the theory is a remark by the Roman orator Cicero, in the first century B.C.—700 years after Homer—that Pisistratus assembled the books of Homer, previously scattered, to fashion the text we now have.

Once, Wolf thought, there must have been separate songs that someone combined to make up our poems. There was no Homer, any more than Moses "wrote" the first five books of the Bible (in which Moses' death is described). "Homer," a name that could conceivably mean "he who fits things together," is just a name applied to texts "fitted together" by unknown editors, according to this manner of thinking. Wolf had evidence on his side, together with a modern critical method that has borne rich fruit in biblical studies, where all scholars now accept that the "Books of Moses" are redactions by unknown editors, probably in the sixth century B.C., at least 200 years after Homer. Most serious scholars accepted Wolf's conclusions and tried to identify where in the texts one original song ended and the next began. Such scholars were called Analysts (from the Greek word for "dissolvers"). They divided the poems into "early" and "late" portions. Objections by the great German writer Wolfgang von Goethe (1749–1832) and others that a single poetic mind stood behind the texts, in spite of all the fancy arguments, were

**FIGURE 6.2**  Rhapsode delivering an epic poem, on an Athenian red-figured amphora (two-handled water jar), ca. 470 B.C. A partial line of poetry comes from his mouth, "That once in Tiryns. . . . "

dismissed as the fantasies of romantic amateurs. But despite their scientific methods, Analysts disagreed on how to divide the poems into the parts that Wolf's theory required. In their long and heated disagreements, they failed to solve the mystery of the Homeric poems.

## MILMAN PARRY AND ORAL POETRY

The terms of the Homeric Question changed through the work of the Californian **Milman Parry** (1902–35), a scholar of Greek who died at the age of thirty-four of self-inflicted gunshot wounds in a hotel room in Los Angeles (perhaps a suicide). As an undergraduate, Parry noticed an inexplicable fact about the style of Homeric verse. Each line contains six units, each of which contains the three beats *long-short-short* or the two beats *long-long,* a meter called **dactylic hexameter** ("dactylic" means fingerlike, because the finger has one long joint and two short joints, and "hexameter" means having six divisions). Every sixth unit, which ends a "line," is always a *long-long.* An example in English is the first line of Henry Wadsworth Longfellow's poem *Evangeline* (1893), "This is the forest primeval. The murmuring pines and the hemlocks . . . " Within this highly stylized rhythmical pattern appear numerous fixed phrases attached to names—for example, "swift-footed Achilles" or "Hector of the shining helm." These fixed phrases are a distinctive feature of Homer's style, even in many English translations. Parry was first in nearly 3,000 years of study to realize that the different descriptive epithets (e.g., "swift-footed") are not used to clarify the dramatic situation—what is happening in the story—but vary simply according to *where* in the poetic line the phrase appears.

For example, Odysseus is called "godlike" when the poet needs to fill out the last five beats of the line, "much-knowing" to fill out the last seven beats, "much-suffering god-like" to fill out the last nine beats, and "descended-from-the-gods" to fill the first seven beats of the line. Similar epithet systems exist for other heroes and the gods. Rarely are there alternative epithets, but only a single one for each position in the line. Such a system of linguistic formulas was not explicable according to the familiar rules of poetic composition, nor to Homer's imitators in later Greek and Latin literature, nor to modern English classes. The formula became the defining feature of oral poetry and a major discovery in the history of literary criticism.

Parry speculated that nonliterate poets used formulas to compose without writing. With a graduate student named Albert Lord, he traveled to Serbia, northwest of Greece, where oral singers still flourished. They were called *guslari* because they accompanied their songs by bowing a one-stringed instrument called a *gusle* (Figure 6.3). Parry and

**FIGURE 6.3** Avdo Mejedovich, Milman Parry's best singer, bowing his one-string *gusle* in 1935.

Lord befriended several *guslari*, questioned them about their lives, and took down their lyrics in writing and by means of a device for recording songs on aluminum wire, powered by the battery of a Model T Ford. The *guslari*, who were illiterate, turned out to have learned to compose metrical song by prolonged exposure, an apprenticeship, to older singers. We might compare the metrical speech that the *guslari* learned in this way to a special kind of language in which a recurring rhythm is a part of the "grammar," a structural component essential to communication but invisible without literate analysis.

Because they could not read and write, *guslari* did not think in terms of separate words when they sang. They used the same Serbo-Croatian word for not only the word "word," but also for "phrase," "sentence," "line," "episode," and even a whole "song." Being illiterate, they did not know what a "word" was. They insisted that they could reproduce exactly a song, a "word," sung by another *guslar*, even after one hearing. This claim really meant that they could follow the same sequence of events, or themes, not the same exact words, as we think of them. The *guslari*, like Homer, composed metrically, although the concept of "line," which depends on writing, was unknown to them. Like Homer, they often made up their lines from fixed phrases and repeated whole lines: One in eight lines in Homer is repeated somewhere.

Milman Parry argued from analysis of Homeric style that Homer's poetry was not the product of poetic composition as we know it, then provided an ethnographic analogy based on original fieldwork. Homer, he suggested, must have been like the Yugoslav *guslari*.

Parry's early death and World War II delayed the spread of his theories, but in the 1950s and 1960s, Albert B. Lord's publications made them the standard approach to understanding Homeric poetry. Parry and Lord discovered that in oral poetry there is considerable forgiveness for inconsistency, the sort of details that so troubled the Analysts, because a live audience does not notice or care about inconsistencies and of course there is no text against which the poem can be checked. Various type-scenes reappear in oral poetry, for example, arming scenes, when warriors prepare to fight; assembly scenes, when men gather to discuss issues and make decisions; and feasting scenes. These type-scenes enabled poets to compose quickly at the level of the story, as the formulas enabled them to compose at the level of the "line," essential to entertain restless audiences.

Above all, Parry discovered that there is no such thing as a *fixed text*. Every time a poet sings "the same song," it is different, because nothing has been memorized. Composing oral poetry has more in common with playing in a rock band than with composing poetry in writing. The oral poet hears someone else's song and remembers its basic plot and themes, which are often highly stylized, just as a guitarist in a band picks up chord sequences for the verses and choruses of a song, which are also often highly stylized, by hearing them a couple of times. The oral poet would know certain useful formulas by heart and use them at convenient points in the "line," just as the guitarist knows standard licks and inserts them as fillers to keep a solo going or to liven up the song. Above all, the oral poet and the improvising musician both know how to put well-known phrases together in new ways and to create new phrases. Some poets and some musicians are hacks, recycling what everyone else does. A few are creative geniuses, inventing powerful new expressions and giving new meanings to classic ones. Such was Homer.

The poet composes as he goes (virtually all Greek oral poets were men), in a special language. Each time he sings a tale, he normally observes the same sequence of themes, but the words are different. In performance, the oral poet must constantly respond to the demands of the audience, who can be attentive or distracted, amused or bored. The average length of an oral poem is about 700 lines, equivalent to a couple of hours of performance. The *Iliad* is around 16,000 lines long!

Only writing can preserve the words of an oral poem, but it does not preserve emphasis, intonation, musical accompaniment, gesture, or the many other subtle communicative features of an oral poet's performance. Again, we might compare oral poetry with rock music. We think of a track recorded in a studio as somehow canonical, but seeing a good band perform live is an entirely different, and richer, experience. Writing creates from oral song something new and something different, a *text*, a material object marked with signs that can be made to deliver up an approximation of human speech, a single aspect of oral song. You can never speak of an oral poem as being passed down from one singer to another *verbatim*, word for word, because oral poems are composed afresh every time they are sung. Verbatim repetition of a poem depends on a text and cannot exist without it. Therefore the poems of Homer are unique recordings of special performances never heard in just this form either before or after the moment that they were transformed from oral delivery into written texts.

## THE ORAL POET IN HOMER

The Greeks called oral poets *aoidoi*, "singers" (*aoidos* is the singular form, origin of the word "ode"). Homer himself, in the curiously self-conscious *Odyssey*, describes two *aoidoi*. One, named Phemius (fē-mi-us, meaning "famous"), is forced to entertain the suitors besieging Odysseus' palace. In the following passage, Athena, disguised as a seafaring merchant, has come to Odysseus' palace on Ithaca to advise Telemachus, Odysseus' son, who is eager to show the stranger hospitality:

> In came the proud suitors. They sat down
> in a row on the stools and chairs. The heralds poured
> water over their hands. Maids brought bread
> heaped in baskets and boys filed their bowls with wine.
> They put forth their hands to the good things before them.
> But when the suitors had set aside their desire
> for food and drink, they turned their minds to other
> things, song and dance, for they are the best
> part of the feast. A herald placed a lyre, a beautiful one,
> in the hands of Phemius, who was forced to sing for the suitors.
> He strummed the lyre and prepared to sing a lovely song.

Homer, *Odyssey* 1.144–55

The suitors' affection for good food, good cheer, and good song no doubt reflects real tastes of Homer's eighth-century B.C. contemporaries, although of course these men in particular are morally corrupt and will pay a terrible price for their crimes. The portrait of the singer in their midst must reflect real custom too. In this way a literary text serves as a source for historical understanding.

## HEINRICH SCHLIEMANN AND THE TROJAN WAR

We noted earlier that most historians think that Homer tells us more about society in his own day than about Mycenaean times, when the Trojan War is supposed to have taken place. Of course oral poets of the eighth century B.C. had no access to primary sources from hundreds of years earlier. Homer could have known about Bronze Age society only if oral poets had preserved details of institutions and culture intact for centuries, but that is unlikely.

People often ask, was there really a Trojan War? Even if Homer knew little about Mycenaean society, could the story of the war itself be based on a real conflict? Scarcely has any historical question been examined more intensely, using the full armament of modern linguistics, literary studies, historical method, and archaeology. The comparative evidence remains ambiguous. Twentieth-century A.D. Serbian *guslari* often sang about the battle of Kosovo, a real battle between Christians and Turks in A.D. 1389, but they got every detail wrong, including who won the war. The *Song of Roland*, a famous French epic composed around A.D. 1100, focused on the real battle of Roncesvalles, fought in A.D. 776 That poem too (there are several versions) got the details, and even the armies involved, badly wrong. Oral tradition distorts information about the past.

By the 1860s, Analyst scholars had convinced academics that "Homer" was an amalgam of different poets and that the Trojan War was just a fiction, but a German named **Heinrich Schliemann** was not so sure. Schliemann read Homer as a boy, was star-struck by the stories, made a fortune in business, became an American citizen, retired early, and set out to prove to the professors that the Trojan War was not just a fiction. A local British resident had already dug some pits on a hill called Hissarlik (Turkish for "fortress") in northwest Turkey, but he found mostly Roman remains. From reading Homer, Schliemann convinced himself that Hissarlik was the site of ancient Troy and in 1870 descended on the site with an army of workers. He was a reckless archaeologist by modern standards, and sometimes dishonest in reporting his finds, but he took from the ground phenomenal Bronze Age treasures. At Troy, he found great walls surrounding a citadel on a promontory overlooking the Scamander plain and the Hellespont, just as Homer had described. So, Schliemann and many others concluded, the Trojan War was real after all.

A consummate showman, Schliemann sent home photographs of his young Greek wife decked out in what he claimed was the very jewelry of Helen of Troy (Figure 6.4). Stolen from Berlin in World War II by Russian troops and feared lost, the jewelry reemerged in a museum in St. Petersburg in the 1990s. Archaeology was such a new science that no one really knew what Schliemann was finding. We now know that a city at Hissarlik was in fact violently destroyed (whether by war or earthquake) around 1200 B.C., just when ancient scholars liked to think that Troy fell (without records, they were only guessing). Hittite tablets, written in a Mesopotamian cuneiform script but in a Hittite language, refer to a place called Wilusa, which may be the equivalent of Ilion, the Greek name for Troy. Another Hittite text refers to someone named Alexander, a Greek name and in Homer a second name for Paris, who in the Greek story ran away with Helen and so began the war. Were Greeks living in Troy in the Late Bronze Age? Earlier, we referred to Hittite complaints about the Ahhiyawa, perhaps the land of the "Achaeans," and other parallels have been drawn between names found in Hittite accounts and names in the Greek tradition. New excavations in the 1990s recovered a single piece of writing at Troy, a bronze seal with parts of two names inscribed in a native Hittite script. They also found a ditch around the city, and perhaps a wall, though controversy rages over these claims; eminent professors have actually come to blows over them!

**FIGURE 6.4**   Heinrich Schliemann with Sophia Schliemann, who wears the "gold of Troy," an elaborate gold diadem and necklace. Taken from Berlin by Russian troops in 1945, the gold was thought lost until rediscovered recently in a museum in St. Petersburg. The jewelry dates to the Early Bronze Age, ca. 2500 B.C., much too early for Helen of Troy!

Possibly there was a great siege at Troy; there had to be some reason why stories clustered around this particular city. But Homer's account may have little—if anything—to do with any actual war, and even if it does preserve ancient facts, we can never know this. His poems succeeded because they entertained and inspired a vividly Greek sense of moral behavior and a Greek vision of the world as a stage for moral conflict. They were the basis for classical education, and educated men, and occasionally women, took these poems very seriously.

## THE TRAGIC *ILIAD*

What kind of stories are the Homeric poems, which have exacted so profound an influence? The *Iliad* takes place over a period of fifty-three days in the tenth year of the Trojan War, but only five days pass between Books 2 and 22 (out of 24 books). Although the epic is vast and sprawling, its focus, even in time, is tight. The first word in the poem is *anger*, announcing a story about the consuming, self-destructive effects of this terrible all-too-familiar human emotion:

> The anger sing, O goddess, of Achilles, son
> of Peleus, the destructive anger, which caused ten
> thousand pains to the Achaeans, and sent many fine
> souls to the death god, the souls of heroes,

and their bodies it made prey for dogs and for all the birds.
It was Zeus' plan. Begin from the time when they stood apart
in anger, Agamemnon king of men and godlike Achilles.

Homer, *Iliad* 1.1–6

Everyone feels anger, but the emotion is especially familiar to men who live by the sword. Anger can be a life-preserving force on the field of battle, enhancing courage in combat, but within a group, and to the individual, anger brings destruction. Such is the topic of Homer's poem. An offended Achilles knew he was right, and so did his companions. The outcome of his justified sense of grievance was the death of his best friend, Patroclus, and the certitude of Achilles' own imminent death. Homer's study in anger must have fascinated his original audiences, who were warriors too.

## Timê and Geras

To become angry about what is wrong, you need strong convictions about what is right. Moral systems can be ranged along a spectrum from **shame cultures** to **guilt cultures**. Heroic societies, such as Homer describes, are generally shame cultures. Shame comes from falling short of an ideal pattern of social conduct. If your companions think ill of you, you have "lost face." If the loss is serious enough, you may feel that your life has lost meaning. American troops fighting the Japanese in the South Pacific during World War II learned to their sorrow how tenacious a warrior who prefers death to dishonor can be. Guilt, on the other hand, is the consequence of transgression against internalized norms, often understood as the laws of God. The sanctions of shame are external, something physical, tangible, material, like medals or trophies. The sanctions of guilt, by contrast, are internal—feelings of remorse when the individual has behaved wrongly.

In the shame-culture of Homer's *Iliad*, a man's standing before others was called *timê* (tē-mâ), translated as "honor, respect" or "value, price." Every warrior strove for *timê*. The external, tangible sign of *timê* was *geras* (**ger**-as) or "prize," ordinarily a material object, something tangible. A man could not have *timê* without *geras*: One implied the other.

The poem opens abruptly when a prophet of Apollo named Chrysês (**krī**-sēz) comes to the Greek camp and begs for the return of his daughter Chryseïs (kri-**sē**-is, "daughter of Chrysês"), whom the Greeks had captured in a raid. As we noted earlier, Homer does not call the besiegers of Troy "Greeks," but "Achaeans" (perhaps the Mycenaeans called themselves this), Danaäns (descendants of Danaüs, a tribal name), or "Argives" (men from Argos, the plain on which stood the Bronze Age city of Mycenae). The assembled Greeks urge that the girl be returned to avoid conflict with the dangerous prophet. But Agamemnon, the principal *basileus* in an assembly of many *basileis*, had won the girl as his concubine in a division of the spoils. She was his *geras*, and to lose her would be to lose *timê*, hence all reason to strive for achievement in life:

Then all the Achaeans shouted assent, that they
should respect the praying-man and accept his shining penalty tokens.
But Agamemnon, son of Atreus, did not agree. He rudely
sent him away, and he lay a powerful word [mythos]
upon him: "Don't let me catch you hanging around

the hollow ships, either now or returning later.
If so, your praying staff wrapped in fillets
will do no good. The girl I shall not release.
Old age shall first overtake her in my house,
in Argos, far from her native land, going back
and forth before her loom and servicing my bed.
So get out, do not bother me, if you want to get out alive."

Homer, *Iliad* 1.22–32

Homer describes his characters by such formulaic epithets as "shining," "swift-footed,"
or "of thick arms" but never gives detailed information about a person's inner nature. Rather,
he shows people in action, revealing who they are by how they speak and what they do. Fully
one-half of Homer's poetry is in direct speech, people speaking and often arguing with one
another. In this instance Agamemnon's refusal to accept ransom from the priest protected his
*timê* but endangered the entire expedition, because the priest was in a position to harm them
all. Chrysês prays to Apollo, who as the god of plague in fact now kills the Achaeans in large
numbers.

A much-alarmed Achilles, one of the many *basileis* who with his followers make up
the Greek army, speaks before a second assembly and urges that they consult a prophet
and seek a solution to the plague. Agamemnon is unhappy with this proposal because
prophets always oppose him, but he nonetheless allows the prophet Calchas (**kal**-kas) to
speak. Just as Agamemnon feared, Calchas declares that the plague has come from
Agamemnon's refusal to surrender his *geras*, the daughter of Chrysês, to her father, a
priest of the plague god Apollo.

The stage is set for the eruption of Achilles' anger. Surely Agamemnon is caught in
a double bind of his own making. If he gives up the girl, he loses *timê*. If he refuses, he
loses *timê* anyway for not caring about the expedition's well-being. Blustering, desperate
really, he announces that he will take someone else's *geras* to replace the one he is losing,
for it would be unseemly for him, the head *basileus* and leader of the expedition, to be
without *timê*:

His black brains filled with wrath and his eyes like flashing fire.
With a dangerous glance he first spoke to Calchas. "O prophet
of evil, not once have you spoken something pleasant
to me. You only care to prophesy misfortune,
you've never prophesied something fine and seen
it come to pass. And now, prophesying before
the Danaans, you say that the reason far-darting Apollo
destroys them is that I refused the penalty tokens
in exchange for the daughter of Chrysês, whom I very much wish
to take home. In fact I prefer the girl to my own wife
Clytemnestra. She's as fine in beauty and figure and as clever
in mind and as skilled. Nonetheless I am willing to give
her up, if that's for the best. I would rather see
the army safe than perish. But you will have
to get me another *geras*, for I can't be the only one

to be without a *geras*. That would not be right.
I think you all see that my *geras* is going elsewhere."
    Achilles swift of feet, like a god, answered him.
"O glorious son of Atreus, most greedy of all
to possess things, how shall the courageous Acheans give you
a *geras*? We do not see a common store laid up of many
things. All that we've carried away from the towns,
these things are given, and it's hardly right that the army
give back what they've already received. Look—for now
you give back the girl to the god, and we Achaeans will pay
you back threefold or fourfold, if Zeus ever grant
that we sack the well-walled city of Troy."

Homer, *Iliad* 1.103–29

Achilles' political power is less than Agamemnon's, because he rules fewer people, yet he should have more (or at least as much) *timê* because of his achievements in battle. We saw that Homeric Ithaca was a stateless society, where people had to rely on their own and their family's strength to get things done. Similarly, the Achaean army has little of what we would call military discipline. Achilles does not shrink from telling his supposed superior how he should approach the most important issue in a warrior's life, the achievement of *timê*.

## Achilles' Anger

Enraged at Achilles' words, Agamemnon threatens to take Achilles' own *geras*, or that of another warrior. His intolerable behavior deeply offends Achilles. The hotheaded fighter draws his sword, thinking to cut down the commander in public view. The whole expedition will collapse in failure. A great crisis has come about, described in lightning pace in the first few hundred lines of Homer's *Iliad*, one of the great openings in the history of literature.

    Only a god's intervention can prevent the inevitable. Athena comes from heaven and seizes Achilles by the hair, holding him back, but only Achilles can see her. She promises that, if he restrains himself, he will in the future receive three times the *timê* he has now. Flushed with anger, but hearing the goddess, Achilles puts back his sword. He says what many have thought when in a struggle with an unjust superior, words that will bring death to many men:

Looking beneath his brows, Achilles spoke
to him. "Yes, clothed in shame, greedy
for gain, how will you persuade anyone to go
with an eager heart on a journey, or engage men
in brutal combat? Not for anything the Trojans did
to me have I come to fight—they are blameless as far
as I am concerned. They never drove off my cattle
or horses, nor did they come to rich-glebed Phthia,°
the nurse of men, and plunder the harvest. For shadowy
mountains and echoing sea stand between us.

°Phthia (thī-a): Achilles' homeland in southern Thessaly (central Greece)

No, we followed you, to do you pleasure,
you who have no shame, seeking to win
*timê* for you and for Menelaüs from the Trojans,
dog-faced man! Surely you take no interest
in any of this. And now you threaten personally
to take away my own *geras* that I struggled
much to obtain, and the sons of the Achaeans gave
her to me. It seems I never get a *geras*
equal to your own when the Achaeans sack a well-peopled
town of the Trojans, though my own hands accomplish most
in grievous war. But when apportionment comes, your *geras*
is always much greater than mine, which is small though precious.
With it I go to my ships, worn out with fighting.
Now I return to Phthia. It's better to go back
with my beaked ships than to remain here without honor [*atimos*],
piling up riches and wealth for you."

Homer, *Iliad* 1.148–71

But Achilles does not go home. Instead, he prays to his divine mother, Thetis, and asks that she intercede with Zeus to turn the battle against the Greeks. They will be sorry that they allowed Agamemnon to bully him! Agamemnon's men come to Achilles' hut and they take his *geras*, the girl named Briseïs, just as Agamemnon threatened. Achilles does not resist. He sulks, waiting for the death of his so-called friends, the Achaean warriors, to begin.

## The Embassy and Achilles' Crisis

Homer takes the opportunity of Achilles' absence from the action to give considerable background about the war, including a list of all the ships with their commanders' names and how many men traveled on each. After much fighting, the battle goes against the Greeks, thanks to Zeus, who responded to Achilles' mother Thetis' request.

Desperate at the military situation, Agamemnon calls an assembly. He and the other war-leaders resolve to persuade Achilles to return to the fight, or surely they will all die. Fast-talking Odysseus, hard-fighting Ajax, and elderly Phoenix, Achilles' boyhood tutor, form an embassy to beg Achilles to return. Agamemnon offers Achilles *geras* aplenty, including the hand of his own daughter in marriage once they return to Greece, if Achilles will give over his anger and come back to the war (now Achilles will be his son-in-law!). Here is the moment promised by Athena when she restrained Achilles from violence against Agamemnon—three times the *timê* that he had before.

To everyone's astonishment, Achilles contemptuously rejects the embassy's offer:

"He wouldn't dare to meet me face to face,
dog that he is. I don't think we are going to make
plans together or accomplish something. He deceived me!
He offended me. I don't think he will trick me again with his words.
He's done enough. He can go to hell. Zeus the counselor
has taken his brains. Hateful are his gifts to me, not worth
a hair. Not if he gave me ten times as much

as all he has, or twenty times as much—and even
if he should get a lot more—even as much
as is stored in Orchomenus,° or in Egyptian
Thebes,° where houses contain the greatest amount
of wealth, where there are a hundred gates to the city,
and each so broad that two-hundred men in horse drawn
chariots could pass through each—not if he gave me
as much as there are sands of the sea, or dust
in the air, not even then would he persuade me,
that Agamemnon, until he pays in full
the price of his soul-stinging disrespect!"

Homer, *Iliad* 9.372–87

°Orchomenus: A city near Thebes, where important Bronze Age ruins have been found.    °Thebes:
Not the Greek polis of that name, but a magnificent city in Egypt, capital of that country during the
New Kingdom (ca. 1650–1150 B.C.). Egyptian Thebes is four hundred miles south of Cairo.

Phoenix, Achilles' childhood tutor, offers other arguments for returning to the battle,
concerned that through stubbornness Achilles will lose his *timê* altogether. Achilles will
have none of it:

Phoinix, dear old man, a favorite of Zeus,
I have no need of this *timê*. I get
my *timê* from Zeus, I think. I'll always have it
so long as I remain beside the beaked
ships, so long as there is breath in my lungs
and life in my limbs.

Homer, *Iliad* 9.607–10

Achilles' companions are astonished at his refusal. Agamemnon offered him great
wealth and the honor that comes with it. But in the crisis of values that is Homer's central
concern (and one that must have reverberated with Homer's contemporaries), Achilles rejects
the system on which the heroic culture was built. He has internalized his sense of value: It
doesn't matter what men think of him, because he receives his *timê* from Zeus. Achilles makes
his own personal island of guilt culture in the midst of a shame culture sea.

As a crisis of values, his position is curiously modern. After refusing to accept
Agamemnon's offer, Achilles henceforth lives in his own private world, ill attached to
his companions. In his isolation he is the type of the tragic hero, its model and origin,
progressively isolated until utterly alone in the face of an impending death.

## The Deaths of Patroclus and Hector

As the Trojans attack ever more boldly, Achilles' companion (believed in later tradition,
but not in Homer, to be his lover) Patroclus upbraids his friend for his indifference to the
suffering of their companions. He begs Achilles to let him sally forth and break the Trojan
attack. Achilles reluctantly agrees and lends Patroclus his armor. At first, Patroclus kills
many, then comes up under the walls of Troy. Hector, the greatest of the Trojan princes,
kills him and strips his armor.

When Achilles learns of Patroclus' death, which he himself caused by refusing Agamemnon's offer, he falls into paroxysms of grief and then rage against Patroclus' killer, Hector. He attacks the Trojan forces single-handedly. In a surreal passage he even fights the River Scamander, whose waters he chokes with corpses. He corners Hector under the walls of Troy and kills him. Hector's mother and father, Hecuba and Priam, look on from the walls above. Achilles binds Hector's corpse to his chariot and drags it to his camp.

## The Ransom of Hector and the End of Achilles' Anger

Achilles accepts Agamemnon's gifts after the death of Patroclus, but with little interest. Although he has transferred his anger from Agamemnon to Hector, even after Hector's death Achilles burns with hate. Every day, he drags the body behind his chariot, punishing the flesh of the man who killed his friend. If only he himself had returned to the fight, Patroclus would still be alive.

In a scene charged with overtones of a descent into the land of the dead, old King Priam loads a cart with ransom and, protected by Hermes (guide of the souls to the other world), travels at night across the plain into Achilles' camp. To the astonishment of the great Achilles, King Priam appears suddenly at his hut. Achilles ought to kill him as the father of the man who killed his friend, but he sees in the pathetic king, who has lost so many of his sons, the image of his own father, who according to the prophecy of Achilles' imminent death will soon lose his only son, himself:

> Unseen by anyone great Priam slipped inside
> and coming close to the hands of Achilles he took
> hold of his knees and kissed his hands, the terrible
> man-killing hands that had murdered his many sons.
> As when in thoughtless act a man kills another
> man in his own country, then flees to the country
> of others, and he comes to the house of a wealthy man,
> and all who see him wonder—in just this way
> Achilles wondered at Priam, as noble as a god.
> The other wondered too, and they looked at one
> another. Priam spoke in supplication:
> "Remember your own father, O Achilles like a god,
> who just like me is on the threshold of old age.
> No doubt those around him treat him badly, and there is
> no one to ward away ruin and evil. But so long
> as you are alive, he rejoices hearing this, and he hopes
> every day that he will see his own son returning from Troy.
> But I am most ill-fated, who bore the best
> sons in broad Troy. I tell you not one is left.
> There were fifty when the sons of the Achaeans came.
> Nineteen were of a single womb, other women
> of the palace bore the rest. The rage of Ares
> loosened their limbs, though they were many, but the one
> who remained, who protected the city and those within it,
> him you have just now killed as he fought for his country,

> Hector. On his account I now come to the ships
> of the Achaeans, begging for him, and bringing boundless
> penalty-tokens. So have shame before the gods,
> Achilles, take pity on me, remembering your own
> father. Truly I am more pitiable than he, for I
> have suffered what no man before ever did, when I placed
> my hand on the face of the man that killed my son."
>
> So he spoke, and he raised in Achilles the desire
> to weep for his father. Taking Priam's hand gently,
> he put him from him. The two of them remembered
> their dead. The one groveling at Achilles' feet
> remembered man-killing Hector, but Achilles thought
> of his own father, and of Patroclus, and the sound
> of their moaning went through the hut.
>
> Homer, *Iliad* 24.477–642

Achilles persuades Priam to eat with him, and each man admires the other. Achilles accepts the ransom and puts Hector on the wagon to be carried back to Troy. The poem ends with the burial of horse-taming Hector. Achilles is still alive. The city still stands.

Thus Achilles abandons anger against his companions and against his most bitter enemies. In the eighth century B.C., Homer's Achilles rejected a system of values based on *geras* and *timê* by which others lived. Even in classical times, 300 years later, Greeks judged a man by his ability "to help his friends and harm his enemies." In a precocious moral vision, Homer shows us Achilles finding a common humanity in both King Priam and his own father, united by the terrible suffering that human life brings.

## HOMER AND THE INVENTION OF PLOT

Although Homer's poems are the oldest surviving examples of Western literature, there is little in Homer that cannot be anticipated in earlier literatures in the Near East, except the transcendence of plot. In Near Eastern literature, events are strung together one after the other as beads on a string. Homer is the first poet who worked with a recognizably modern plot. Aristotle, writing in the fourth century B.C. and a careful student of Homer, was the first to notice that a plot has three parts: beginning, middle, and end. In an essay on poetry called the *Poetics*, he says:

> A whole is what has a beginning, a middle, and an end. A beginning is something that does not of necessity follow from something else, but after it some state or event does happen by natural result. The ending is the opposite because it follows inevitably, or, for the most part is the natural result of some-thing that precedes it, but after it comes nothing else. A middle follows something, and something follows it. Well-constructed plots [*muthoi*] do not just begin anywhere, or end anywhere, but must follow the principles that I have described.
>
> Aristotle, *Poetics* 1450b

Literature gives the impression of being like life, but it is not like life. Literature has its own rules, and the sort of literature Aristotle describes has a plot, a Homeric invention. In modern terminology we may say that a plot begins with the *setup*. In the setup we learn who the main character is and what his or her *dramatic need* is, what he or she wants to possess, have, achieve, or accomplish. Characters in plotted literature are defined by their dramatic need. In the *Iliad*, Achilles is the main character, and his dramatic need is to satisfy his anger, first against Agamemnon, then against Hector. The setup also establishes the *dramatic context*, the backdrop against which the main character functions, in this case the troubled camp of the Achaeans in the tenth year of a siege of Troy.

Then something happens to change the direction of the story, to begin the middle of the plot that Aristotle describes. The middle is ordinarily the largest segment. In the parlance of the plotting of a modern feature film, this middle is introduced by a **plot-point**, when something happens and the direction of the story changes. In a feature film, which is normally 120 minutes long, the first plot-point always occurs around the thirtieth minute. In the *Iliad*, the first plot-point comes early, when Achilles withdraws from the fighting and prays to his mother for revenge against the Achaeans. The action for the middle portion is now set and the real story begins, the working-out of Achilles' anger.

Conflict dominates the middle of a plot, presenting the main character in contention with forces opposing the fulfillment of his or her dramatic need. In the modern feature film, the middle is twice as long as the beginning (setup) and has its own plot-point, or midpoint, which binds together the two halves of the middle (it comes around the sixtieth minute, when the movie is halfway through). In the *Iliad*, the midpoint comes when the Achaeans, devastated by Hector, send an embassy to Achilles to beg him to return to the fighting. The embassy is a kind of bridge between the fighting before and the fighting after, but the basic situation remains unchanged. Achilles refuses the embassy, which allows a further working-out of his prayers for revenge—more fighting, more death, and more suffering by his former friends.

The middle portion of a plot, like the beginning, ends with a plot-point, an event that again turns the story in a different direction, toward the resolution of conflict. In the *Iliad*, Patroclus' death accomplishes this, the second plot-point. In the ending Achilles kills Hector, hoping to satisfy his anger, and in the final scene he does abandon it. Along with Hector's body he gives up the anger that caused him and those around him "ten thousand pains." The first word in the poem is *anger*, and the last scene shows how, through an intuition of the unity of all human experience, Achilles gave up his anger and resolves the plot.

## THE COMIC *ODYSSEY*

The remarkable *Odyssey* too has a tripartite plot, but moves more in spirals than in a straight line. Whereas the *Iliad* describes a man at odds with his society, a man apart, the *Odyssey*, whose first word in Greek is *man* (not *human* but specifically *male*), describes a man who journeys far, suffers much, then returns to his proper place in society. The *Odyssey*'s pattern of renewal and reintegration into society is opposite to the *Iliad*'s pattern of progressive alienation. Whereas the *Iliad* is tragic, the *Odyssey* is comic, according to an old way of understanding these poems. In everyday speech, we use *comic* to mean humorous, but when literary critics say *comic*, they mean a story that ends in harmony and acceptance. Humor, of which there is a good deal in the *Iliad*, is not comedy, and there is little humor in the *Odyssey*. Because nothing expresses social integration better than a wedding, comedies—for example, those of Shakespeare—often end in weddings. So does the *Odyssey*, in a mock re-wedding between Odysseus and Penelope.

Whereas Achilles' concern in the *Iliad* is to win *timê* at all costs, in the *Odyssey* the hero strives to return home and to his former position there, at all costs. Whereas Achilles meets obstacles with violence, threatening to kill his own commander, then cutting down the greatest Trojan, Odysseus also overcomes obstacles, but through intelligence, trickery, and disguise. In the first line of the poem, he is the man "versatile in his ways," who can approach a problem from different angles. Elsewhere, Homer uses an epithet for Odysseus that means "wily," "clever," or "devious." Achilles abhors such qualities and says so in the speech he gives to the embassy. In these respects, the *Iliad* and the *Odyssey* are utterly different, yet they complement one another in a striking fashion: No episode described in the *Iliad* is repeated in the *Odyssey*, which provides considerable information about the Trojan War omitted in the *Iliad*, including the story of the Trojan Horse, the funeral of Achilles, and the return of Menelaüs and Helen to Sparta. For this reason perhaps the only thing that virtually all Homeric scholars agree on is that the *Odyssey* was composed *after* the *Iliad*, and by a man who knew the *Iliad* intimately. Since there were no libraries or a reading public in the eighth century B.C., this man must have been Homer himself.

## The Quest for Truth

The story of the man who wandered is not original to the Greeks. In the Mesopotamian *Epic of Gilgamesh*, already 2,000 years old when Homer was born, the hero Gilgamesh wandered far from his home through the Mountains of Mashu to the place of the sun, then across demonic waters, seeking a way to escape mortality. Even the opening words of the Gilgamesh epic are similar to those of the *Odyssey*:

> Of him who found out all things, I will tell the land,
> of him who experienced everything, I will teach the whole.
> He searched lands everywhere.
> He who experienced the whole gained complete wisdom.
> He found out what was secret and uncovered what was hidden.
> He brought back a tale of times before the Flood.
> He had journeyed far and wide, weary and at last resigned.

*Gilgamesh*, SBv 1 (tr. by S. Dalley)

Gilgamesh was a seeker of truth about the meaning of mortality. In the *Odyssey*, less explicitly, the hero is a seeker too:

> The man sing to me, O Muse, versatile
> in his ways, who wandered full far after he
> had sacked the sacred citadel of Troy. He saw
> the cities of many men and learned their minds,
> but suffered greatly in his heart on the high seas,
> trying to save his life and to bring his companions
> home. Even so he could not save them, though he tried.
> They perished through their own folly, the fools! for they ate

the cattle of Helios Hyperion,° who took away
from them the day of their homecoming. Of these things,
start where you please, tell us goddess, daughter of Zeus!

Homer, *Odyssey* 1.1–10

°*Helios Hyperion:* The sun.

In fact Odysseus seemingly learns nothing in his journeys. Yet the poem is a paradigm for truth-seeking, of wandering in search of knowledge, even though the hero knows no more when he ends than when he began.

## The *Odyssey* and History

Homer may have inherited the story of the wanderer from the much older ancient Near East, but his tale is massively colored by Greek life of the eighth century B.C. The colonial movement that we described in Chapter 5 was particularly important. Around 775 B.C., Greeks founded Pithekoussai ("monkey-island") in the Bay of Naples, a settlement of perhaps 5,000 occupants, a large number in so remote a place. And between 730 and 650 B.C., probably another 30,000 Greeks settled in Sicily and Italy. Taking an open boat from Greece to Italy was a stupendous adventure. It is not surprising that monsters and magical creatures lurked beyond the waves that fill the *Odyssey* (Figure 6.5).

The Greeks who settled in the west went there not for adventure, but for profit, a motive reflected in the first book of the *Odyssey*, when Athena comes to the palace in Ithaca disguised as a sailor named Mentês (**men**-tēz):

"I shall tell you these things straight out—I am Mentês,
son of wise Anchialus, and I rule over the oar-loving
Taphians. I have arrived on ship with my companions,
traveling over the wine-dark sea to visit men
of foreign speech, to Temêsê° to get copper,

°*Temêsê:* Unknown, but perhaps in southern Italy.

**FIGURE 6.5** Warship on the inside lip of an Athenian black-figured drinking cup (*kylix*), ca. 520–15 B.C. While more advanced than ships used in the eighth-century B.C., it is still an open boat with rowers on either side, a single mast and sail, and a short deck for the helmsman, who steers with an oar. The ship would appear to sail on the "wine-dark sea" of the actual wine that filled the cup.

and I carry a cargo of shining iron. My ship
lies there beside the fields, away from the city
in the bay of Rheithron, under woody Neion.°

Homer, *Odyssey*, 1.179–86

°Rheitron and Neion: Perhaps Rheitron is one of the modern harbors on Ithaca; a mountain there is still called Neion (maybe because of the *Odyssey*).

The tiny island of Ithaca, where Odysseus' palace was sited, lay directly on the coasting route from Greece to Italy. Early Greek explorers headed down the narrow channel between Ithaca and the nearby island of Cephallenia, stopped in the Ithacan harbor on the southern side of the island, and then veered north to the island of Corcyra (kor-sī-ra—called Corfu in English). The Corinthians founded a colony on Corcyra in 733 B.C., a sort of halfway house between the familiar world of Greece and "barbarian" lands beyond. Already, in the fifth century B.C., Thucydides thought Corcyra was Homer's island Phaeacia, where Odysseus stops before reaching home and where he tells famous stories of his adventures.

Outward-bound sailors from Corcyra crossed open water to the heel of Italy (as early as 800 B.C., Greeeks were trading with the natives of this region), then headed south along the Italian coast before turning north through the dangerous Strait of Messina, from an early time thought to be Homer's Scylla and Charybdis (Figure 6.6).

Thence they sailed northward along the coast to the Bay of Naples, where Greeks mixed with Phoenician seafarers and came into early contact with the mysterious Etruscans north of Rome. It would be no surprise if Homer himself had made this journey:

**FIGURE 6.6** The Strait of Messina, crossed by modern ferries, from the modern town of Messina on the Sicilian side. Beyond the strait you can see on the right of the photo the tip of the toe of the boot of Italy, near where stood the ancient Greek colony of Rhegium (modern Reggio). Dangerous currents in the Strait have long been thought to be the real-world model for Homer's Scylla and Charybdis. Early Greek colonists crossed these straits to travel north to the first Greek colony in the Bay of Naples.

He shows a good familiarity with the island of Ithaca (with some perplexities), which he seems to have known firsthand.

## The Odyssey and Folktale

As a trickster, Odysseus has parallels in folklore throughout the world. We can view the poem as a kind of folktale. Following a common pattern, the hero, reduced to the lowest social class, a beggar in his own household, overcomes enormous odds (over one hundred suitors oppose him) to become king and marry the queen. The *Odyssey*'s inner meaning, however, is a story about a man who went to the other world and returned reborn, also a folktale motif. There are strong folktale components too in Odysseus' famous adventures in which the trickster hero's greatest enemy is Death, whom he meets repeatedly in many guises—as ogre, monster, temptress, witch, and the all-engulfing flood of the sea. Females constantly threaten or aid him. The poem is a study in female types, positive and negative. Although the general setting is the same heroic world as in the *Iliad*, and many of the same heroes appear, Homer directs his focus on the everyday world of Ithaca populated by beggars, slaves, serving girls, and loutish aristocrats.

Folktales contain folksy morals about how one should act, and they appeal to the universal instinct that the wicked must be punished or destroyed. Early in the poem, Homer announces this theme in declaring that Odysseus' companions "perished through their own folly." Often in folktales, a violated prohibition leads to destruction. The companions perished because "they devoured the cattle of Helios Hyperion," which they were told not to do.

The poem's preoccupation with right, wrong, and punishment is clear in Zeus' announcement near the beginning of the poem. Poseidon has gone to banquet with the blameless Ethiopians (somewhere in the misty south) while Zeus sits with the other gods in the halls of Olympus and reflects on the fate of Aegisthus (ē-**gis**-thus), a cousin of Agamemnon, who committed adultery with Agamemnon's wife, Clytemnestra, then helped her to murder Agamemnon when he returned from the war. Later, Orestes, the son of Agamemnon and Clytemnestra, grown to manhood, killed Aegisthus and his own mother to avenge his father's death:

> Among them the father of gods and men was first
> to speak. In his breast he thought of noble Aegisthus,
> whom far-famed Orestes killed, the son of Agamemnon.
> Thinking about him he spoke among the deathless ones
> and said, "Whoa! mortals are too ready to blame
> the gods. From us, they say, comes all evil, when really
> it's through their own folly they suffer, even more than is necessary.
> Take Aegisthus—he had no need to bed the wife
> of Agamemnon,° and Orestes killed him when he returned
> home, although he knew the sheer destruction to come,
> because we told him in advance, sending Hermes,
> the far-sighted Argeiphontes,° so that he should not kill
> because we told him in advance, sending Hermes,
> the husband and he should not bed the wife. For 'from
> Orestes will come vengeance for the son of Atreus,° when he comes

°wife of Agamemnon: Clytemnestra.   °Argeïphontes (ar-jē-i-fon-tēz): "Argus-killer," an epithet of Hermes: Argus was a mythical monster.   °son of Atreus: Agamemnon.

to maturity and longs for his own land.' So spoke
Hermes, but he did not persuade the mind of Aegisthus,
although he wanted to help. And now he's paid the price."

Homer, *Odyssey* 1.29–43

Zeus' observation is common in later Greek literature: Mortals are responsible for their own actions and should not blame the gods when things go wrong. We find no such speculations in the *Iliad*, where men die every day simply because Fate has so decreed or because they are warriors, but not because of some evil they have done. What evil did Hector ever commit? This strong moral stance, a feature of folktale, underlies the *Odyssey*'s grand narrative of the destruction of the suitors. Odysseus' bloodthirsty slaughter of over one hundred men may shock some, but the suitors should not have behaved as they did and they cannot expect better. The suitors were fools who violated Odysseus' property rights. They got what they deserved.

## Telemachus, Son of Odysseus

After Zeus pronounces his view that men make their own fates, Athena rises in the divine assembly and objects that Odysseus, a righteous man, has been imprisoned for seven years on the island of the beautiful **Calypso** ("concealer") in the navel of the sea. Zeus agrees to send Hermes to set him free.

Homer shifts the narrative to Ithaca. Telemachus is under siege by the rowdy suitors, who want to marry his mother and become the new *basileus*. The disguised Athena urges Telemachus to leave his father's house and go into the world to learn his father's fate. He should take a boat to the town of Pylos on the mainland coast where King Nestor, who fought side by side with Odysseus at Troy, rules. Perhaps, although it is ten years after the war, he might know something. In his travels Telemachus in fact learns nothing about his father's whereabouts, but by being thrown against the world he himself becomes a man, fit to stand at his father's side and to inherit his father's house and power.

## The Adventures of Odysseus

At first we learn about the situation on Ithaca and the personalities involved, including the absent Odysseus, about whom everyone speaks (the *setup*). Then Homer changes scene and switches his story to Odysseus, who prepares to escape from the remote island of Calypso (*plot-point one*). Odysseus builds a raft and sails away, but his enemy Poseidon—the sea—spots him and stirs up a great storm. The raft breaks up and for three days Odysseus swims through the rugged seas, then comes ashore on the island of **Phaeacia**, where a King Alcinoüs ("powerful of mind") rules. The virgin princess Nausicaä ("ship-girl") meets him on the shore and takes him to the palace.

For many days, no one asks the dark stranger who he is. At a banquet, the man of mystery asks the *aoidos* to sing the song of the Trojan Horse, a trick that Odysseus himself designed. Overcome with emotion when hearing the song, Odysseus weeps. "Why are you weeping?" the king asks. "Because I," he replies, "am Odysseus." There are more than twenty of these recognition scenes in the *Odyssey*, a common device in folklore; there are no recognition scenes in the *Iliad*.

To the Phaeacians, who sit spellbound at the banquet, Odysseus recounts his wanderings, some of the most famous stories in the world. Nevertheless, they take up only one-sixth of the whole *Odyssey*. Odysseus' journeys are presented in patterns of three: first two short tales and then a long one.

After leaving Troy, he and his men, with twenty boats, came to the land of the Thracians, northwest of Troy, but in a raid lost many men. They depart, but a storm drives them to the land of the **Lotus Eaters**. The Lotus is a drug; if you eat it, you forget your purpose, to go home again. Odysseus comes next to the land of the giant one-eyed **Cyclops**, where he is imprisoned in a black cave sealed by a huge stone and his men eaten alive. He tricks the giant by saying his name is Nobody. He gets the giant drunk and puts out his one eye with a stake. The Cyclops cries out to his neighbors that "Nobody" is harming him, so his neighbors tell him to go back to sleep. By another trick Odysseus escapes from the cave (Figure 6.7).

After a nearly successful journey home, courtesy of the Wind King, and a brief but deadly adventure with more cannibal-giants, Odysseus comes to the island of **Circê**, "hawk." Only his own boat still survives of the apparently twenty that set sail from Troy. The witch Circê changes his men to pigs, but when Odysseus defeats her with help from the god Hermes, Circê releases his companions from the spell. Odysseus and his men spend a pleasant year on the island, when at last his followers remind him of his purpose, to reach home. Circê informs Odysseus that first he must cross the river Ocean, which surrounds the world, and consult the spirit of the dead prophet Tiresias (tī-rē-si-as) to learn what awaits him. Odysseus sails away and puts ashore in a misty land. He fills a pit

**FIGURE 6.7** Odysseus, oddly painted in white (usually white means "female"), leads his men in plunging a stake into Polyphemus' eye; on a large amphora (two-handled jar) from Eleusis, ca. 670 B.C., one of the earliest certain illustrations of a Greek myth (see also Chapter 9, "The Archaic Cultural Revolution, 700–480 B.C.," Figure 9.10). The cup that Polyphemus holds refers to the detail in the story that Odysseus made him drunk before blinding him.

**FIGURE 6.8** Odysseus and the Sirens on an Athenian red-figured amphora, ca. 450 B.C. Odysseus, bound to the mast, hears the Sirens' song while his men, their ears plugged with wax, row past the island. Note the apotropaic ("turning away" evil) eye on the prow of the ship.

with lamb's blood and speaks with the ghosts who gather around the pit, including the ghosts of Tiresias and Agamemnon. The ghost of the murdered Agamemnon praises Odysseus' faithful wife Penelope, so unlike his own homicidal wife, then warns Odysseus that, women being what they are, he too should be careful about returning home!

Traveling on, they pass the island of the **Sirens**, whose song, promising knowledge, no man can resist. Odysseus stuffs the ears of his men with wax but is himself lashed to the mast so that he cannot give into the Sirens' temptation: He alone hears the song and survives (Figure 6.8).

Now he must pass between the monster Scylla and the whirlpool Charybdis. The monster eats five men, but the rest escape and come to the island of Helios Hyperion, the Sun. Circê warned him not to eat the Sun's cattle that grazed there, but Odysseus' hungry men disobey. Even in the prologue, this incident is given as the archetype for the immoral behavior of men doomed to a bad end, the folklore motif of the violated prohibition.

When they sail away from the island of the Sun, Zeus blasts their boat to punish the men's impiety. Odysseus alone escapes, clinging to the rudder. He is swept into the whirlpool Charybdis and is nearly destroyed. At last he comes to the island of Calypso, where the poem began. Unlike the *Iliad*, which advances in a straight line, the *Odyssey* can move in spirals, repeatedly turning back on itself as characters recall things that happened before, just as in many modern films.

## Important Themes in the Adventures of Odysseus

The adventures of Odysseus are folktales of independent origin that Homer adapted for his epic poem. Odysseus' first enemy is the sea and its god Poseidon. The vast sea, the water from which life emerges, is the negation of life; being lost on it is like death. When Odysseus comes ashore in Phaeacia after Poseidon destroys his raft, he is naked like a babe. He takes refuge in a dark cave of bushes, like a womb. The young girl Nausicaä, with marriage on her mind, rouses him from sleep, and he appears naked before her. Later, he says that she "gave him life." The symbolism of rebirth, as elsewhere in the *Odyssey*, governs the narrative here. The *Iliad*, by contrast, never tells its story through action that has symbolic meaning.

As the sea obliterates all, so does Sleep (the brother of Death) or narcosis (the lotus) stand between Odysseus and his return. He falls asleep just offshore from Ithaca after leaving the Wind King. He is asleep on the island of Helios while his men devour the sacred cattle. He is put ashore on Ithaca wrapped in a deep sleep.

The adventures, like much folktale, preserve the child's vision of a world eating itself, in which eating and being eaten are the central experiences of life. The Cyclops and Laestrygonians eat Odysseus' men, and Circê's pigs, once men, are as edible as any swine, although Homer does not say so. Scylla eats five of his men. In proper Greek society of Homer's day, one was obliged to receive a wandering stranger of the proper social class with courtesy and food, a custom called **xenia,** "treatment of a stranger." The Cyclops inverts the customs of *xenia.* Instead of offering his guest a meal, he makes a meal of them! Just so did the suitors violate *xenia* and take meals for themselves from another's store, without permission. Folktales are filled with monsters, and we find our share in the *Odyssey*, but also the seductive wiles of death-dealing females hold back the male from his goal. In the everyday world, Clytemnestra, who murdered her husband Agamemnon, stands for the treacherous deadly woman. In the strange world of Odysseus' wandering, Circê, with her beauty, wishes to lure Odysseus into bed where she can "unman" him. The Sirens are irresistible with the beauty of their song (like the beauty of Homer's own song), and only a trick allows him to escape. The monstrous Scylla is female.

On the other side are the "good females." Nausicaä, the virgin princess, finds him by the shore, and the queen of the Phaeacians, her mother, is eager to help him return to Ithaca. In the divine world, Athena favors Odysseus. In the everyday world, Penelope is the beneficent female, staving off the lustful suitors and staying alive in the midst of conspiracy. Men want to sleep with her, as Aegisthus slept with Clytemnestra, and she too has a teenage son. Unlike Clytemnestra, she avoids the temptations of adultery and murder and welcomes back her husband into the marriage bed.

## ODYSSEUS AND HOMER

After Odysseus returns to Ithaca (*plot-point two*), we observe the working-out of the revenge of the *basileus*, the resolution of conflict brewing since the beginning of the poem. Fully half of the *Odyssey*, the scenes on Ithaca, is devoted to the third part of Aristotle's tripartite plot structure. No modern audience schooled in cinema would tolerate so leisurely an ending, though Homer enlivens his story by many false tales, secret penetration into the house, and mass murder of the young men. There are repeated scenes of recognition as Odysseus strips off his lying exterior, like the layers of an onion, to reveal himself at last as the son of Laertes, the true king and true husband of the queen. First, he reveals himself to a faithful swineherd in a remote part of the island (Odysseus is master of his property); then he reveals himself to his son Telemachus, returned from abroad (Odysseus is father to his son). He comes to the palace, where the dog Argus recognizes him (Odysseus, the noble sportsman). In the palace, the nurse recognizes him from a scar on his leg as she bathes his feet (Odysseus is master of the house). The suitors recognize him when he strings a powerful bow, his own, by which act Penelope declared she would choose her next husband. With this very bow he begins the massacre (Odysseus is again *basileus* of Ithaca). Witnessing the corpses of the suitors, Penelope gratefully asks the nurse to bring out the master's bed for Odysseus to sleep in. The request is a trick. "That's impossible,"

Odysseus protests, "I myself built it around an olive tree growing in the ground." Thus Odysseus proves to Penelope that he is her true husband, and they retire to bed. The poem ends with an artistically unsatisfying recognition with his father and a contrived brief skirmish with the relatives of the dead suitors, interrupted by a thunderbolt from Zeus. Order is in any event restored to the *oikos* and to the world, a comic vision of optimism and affirmation. The *Odyssey*'s resounding comic triumph of right over wrong relieves the bleak uncertainty of the tragic *Iliad*. The *Odyssey*, not the *Iliad*, is the model for the ubiquitous plots of modern cinema, which need an "up" ending to be successful.

## Key Terms

| | | |
|---|---|---|
| Homeric Question, *93* | Heinrich Schliemann, *100* | Phaeacia, *114* |
| Friedrich August Wolf, *94* | shame culture, *102* | Lotus Eaters, *115* |
| rhapsode, *95* | guilt culture, *102* | Cyclops, *115* |
| Milman Parry, *96* | *timê, 102* | Circê, *115* |
| dactylic hexameter, *96* | *geras, 102* | Sirens, *116* |
| *guslari, 97* | plot-point, *109* | *xenia, 117* |
| *aoidoi, 99* | Calypso, *114* | |

## Further Reading

Dougherty, C., *The Raft of Odysseus* (New York, 2000). Close reading of the *Odyssey* and the adventures in the west.

Edwards, M., *Homer: Poet of the Iliad* (Baltimore, 1988). The clearest single book on the *Iliad*. Most helpful in its book-by-book commentary and its extensive bibliography.

Latacz, Joachim, *Troy and Homer* (Oxford, 2004). Exciting up-to-date review of new finds at Troy and their relationship to Homer.

Malkin, I., *The Returns of Odysseus* (Berkeley, 1998). Superior study of the *Odyssey*, colonization, and the place of Ithaca.

Morris, I., and Powell, B., eds., *A New Companion to Homer* (Leiden, 1997). Scholarly essays on every aspect of modern Homeric scholarship.

Murnaghan, S., *Disguise and Recognition in the Odyssey* (Princeton, NJ, 1987). Good treatment of this topic.

Powell, B. B., *Homer*, 2nd ed. (Oxford, 2007). Concise, up-to-date synthesis of scholarship,

with account of origins and analysis of both poems. The most widely read single book on Homer.

Strauss, Barry, *The Trojan War* (New York, 2007). Excellent account of Homer's war story and the historical realities.

Tracy, S. V., *The Story of the Odyssey* (Princeton, NJ, 1990). Synopsis of the complex story.

### ANCIENT TEXTS

Homer, *The Iliad,* tr. Robert Fagles (New York, 1990). Good verse translation.

Homer, *The Odyssey,* tr. Robert Fagles (New York, 1996). Companion to his translation of the *Iliad*.

*Myths from Mesopotamia: Creation, the Flood, Gilgamesh and Others*, tr. S. Dalley, 2nd ed. (Oxford, 2000). Contains the classic Near Eastern epic *Gilgamesh*, dating back to the third millennium B.C.

## CHAPTER 7

# Religion and Myth

In Chapter 1, "A Small, Far-Off Land," we suggested that understanding religion is fundamental to making sense of the Greeks. Unlike most other ancient societies, Greeks generally refused to believe that anyone had privileged access to the supernatural, giving them the right to rule human society. The "Greek problem" that this created, of how people could know what to do without divine direction, plays a large part in the story in this book.

Classical Greek religion seems to have taken shape largely in the eighth century B.C. It was not codified in a book, like the Hebrew and Christian Bibles or the Islamic Koran; rather, the Greeks told stories that we call *myths* that had no sacred status. *Myth* comes from the Greek word *mythos*, but to the Greeks *mythos* had a broad meaning, suggested in earlier reading selections where we have translated *mythos* as "thoughts" (of Zeus) and "command" (of Agamemnon). It could also mean just a *saying* and, by the fifth century B.C., it could mean *plot*. Nor did the Greeks have a word with quite the same meaning as our *religion*. Like most societies, they normally did not think of religion as a category separable from daily life itself. Discussing Greek religion and myths, then, means seeking realities that the Greeks themselves will not easily have recognized. We will nonetheless accept these modern categories but must be clear about what we take these words to mean.

## DEFINITIONS OF RELIGION AND MYTH

Religion and myth are both forms of symbolic thought, chiefly expressed through speech, but also through visual art, music, and dance. The Romans explained their word *religio*, root of the word *religion*, in three different ways: first, as coming from *re-ligo*, "to bind someone back so they cannot do something," that is to establish a taboo (Latin *obligatio*, the word "obligation," is from the same root, as are *ligament* and *ligature*); second, as coming from *re-lego*, "repeat" a magical formula over and over so that it is effective; or third, as coming from *re-linquo*, "to leave alone," to treat in a special way. We are no more sure than they about the word's derivation, but in actual usage Latin *religio* variously designates an external force, an internal emotion, a cult practice, or a taboo. It never refers to the combination of beliefs, rituals, and canons of moral behavior that the word "religion" implies for us.

The Christian and Muslim notions of religion grew out of the efforts of these respective traditions to define themselves against each other and against Judaism. Every religion is different, but we might think of each as *a set of practices based on belief in supernatural beings*. Unlike political conviction, which also motivates action, religious belief implies acceptance of the reality of nonhuman, usually invisible beings. Normally, these beings know what we do, judge us, are powerful, and can harm or help us.

People in most cultures hold notions like these, but the modern view that specific *beliefs*—accepting something unprovable as a basis for action—are the core of religion grew from the early Christian church's need to decide which of the many divergent interpretations of the historical life, puzzling teachings, and disputed mission of Jesus were true. Some argued, for example, that Jesus was divine and therefore did not die on the cross, and a long, bitter, and divisive conflict raged over whether Jesus had a single divine nature (called Monophysitism) or a dual nature, both human and divine. The Nicene Creed of the fourth century A.D., versions of which are still recited in Christian churches, was written in Greek but called a "creed" from its Latin translation, which begins *credo*, "I believe." The creed was a definitive statement of what was true, or orthodox (from a Greek word meaning "right-seeming"), about Jesus' nature, mission, and teachings, rejecting other interpretations as heterodox ("wrong-seeming") or heretical ("choice" of the wrong interpretation). The Nicene Creed announced that God the Son was coeternal with God the Father, opposing influential theories that the son was inferior to the father (called Arianism, after Arius, a priest of Alexandria ca. A.D. 250–336).

Just as our thoughts about religion would have puzzled ancient Greeks, so would our isolation of myth as a topic for discussion. The Greek *mythos* appears commonly in works of the poets, starting with Homer, but never with the modern meaning of "a fanciful tale to explain, justify, or amuse, involving gods or other supernatural beings." This meaning of myth goes back to the eighteenth-century European Enlightenment and to an influential collection of stories, *The Origin of Fables*, published in French in 1724 by Bernard Fontenelle. Still, in the fifth century B.C., intellectuals had begun to distinguish what we call *history*, the rational search for truth about the past, from *myth*, a story without rational claims to the truth. The Athenian Thucydides, writing around 400 B.C., was the first author we know of to describe false stories as "mythical" (*mythôdes*, "like a *mythos*"):

> In inquiring about the facts of what happened in the war I did not judge it best to record the first thing I came upon, nor to reconstruct from probability what happened, but in many cases I was there myself or I learned of events from others who were there, asking them about each thing with a close attention to detail. Still, it was difficult to discover the truth, because eye-witnesses would give different account of the same events, either from partisanship or a faulty memory. As for those who hear this account, the lack of a mythlike element *mythôdes* will for some decrease their pleasure, but it will be enough for me if those find my words useful who wish to know the truth about the past, and hence what is likely to come in the future thanks to the durability of human nature.

Thucydides 1.22

In dismissing the *mythôdes*, the "mythlike," Thucydides seems to criticize Herodotus' *History*, which appeared just a few years earlier and contained many fanciful tales. Early Christian theologians, thinking about the meaning of Jesus' life and death, were Thucydides' intellectual heirs: They too sought to know truth by understanding the past. So do we still, when scholars agonize over what is true and not true in, say, the story of the Trojan War. Myths may contain historical elements but are not concerned with the truth about the past as such.

Whereas religion is a set of practices based on belief in invisible nonhumans, *myth is a story*, sometimes about such beings, but sometimes not. A long search for the essence of myth has proved fruitless. For our purposes, we may think of myth as a story that matters within a community, which is told and retold for that reason. The story of Oedipus, who killed his father and married his mother, is a good example. Homer mentions these details as if they were everyday knowledge.

One common approach divides myths into three categories. First are **divine myths**, stories in which gods are important, creating the universe and establishing its rules. Such stories explain where the world came from. Second are **legends** (or sagas), stories about heroes and the human past, analogous to our history. Third is **folktale**, similar to our novels and feature films; such stories are recognized as fictional, though they may contain moral advice. These distinctions are useful, although myths have a way of slipping in and out of the categories to which we assign them.

Because both myth and religion can be concerned with the external forces that surround and influence us, they are easily confused. Gods and goddesses are prominent in myths, endowed with personality and will. The confusion is worsened because myth and religion may focus on similar problems: how to understand through intellect and express through language otherwise incomprehensible phenomena.

Myths too can be central to religious practice. The Egyptians told a myth about how Osiris died but came back to life through the magic of Isis. By referring to this story in hieroglyphic writing and placing the writing next to the mummy, the Egyptian priest helped the individual to share a similar destiny. The Greeks told a story about the madness that befell Pentheus, king of Thebes, when he denied the power of Dionysus, the god of wine and revelry: Such is the experience of all who refuse the god's revivifying power, the story seems to say. Although religion is not itself myth, but practice, the two can intertwine inextricably.

## HESIOD'S MYTH OF THE ORIGIN OF THE GODS

Religion tries to establish good relations with invisible powers and provide insurance against misfortune, but before philosophy, only myths explained why religion was necessary at all, why things are the way they are. Such is the overall purpose in Hesiod's poem, the *Theogony*, created probably around 700 B.C. Its opening lines raise the question of truth and falsity in myth. The Muses gave Hesiod the gift of song, but not everything the Muses sing is true, Hesiod says. Near the very beginning of Greek literature appears the notion that poetry can be "just a myth":

It was they [the muses] who taught Hesiod beautiful song [*aoidê*],
while he cared for his sheep beneath jagged Mount Helicon.
These are the first words that the goddesses spoke to me [that is, Hesiod],
the Muses who live on Olympus, the daughters of Zeus
who carries the aegis.° "Miserable shepherds, nothing
but reproach, stomachs merely, we know how to tell

°*aegis*: A magical goat-skin shield.

> lies that resemble the truth, but we also know
> how, when it takes our fancy, to speak the truth."
> So said the well-spoken daughters of great Zeus.
> Then as a staff they plucked a bow of blooming
> laurel, a wonderful staff, and they breathed into me
> deathless song, that I might sing that
> which shall come to pass and that which was.
> And they urged me to sing of the race of the blessed ones,
> who never die, but to sing first and last
> always of them.
>
> Hesiod, *Theogony* 22–34

Hesiod distinguishes between true and false stories because he wishes to emphasize how his own story is true, inspired by the gods. In his story, his *mythos*, Hesiod will declare the greatness of Zeus by describing how Zeus came to power and established the customs that make up the world as we know it:

> "Greetings, daughters of Zeus, give us a pleasant
> song. For you sing always of the holy race
> of the deathless ones . . . Tell me of these things,
> O Muses whose home is on Olympus, from
> the beginning, and tell me in order of each thing
> that came into being."
>
> Hesiod, *Theogony* 108–15

At the beginning, according to Hesiod's influential account, which the Muses inspired, appeared three beings. First was **Chaos**, which means "gap" or "chasm," as if something had yawned, as if one thing had become two. Out came **Gaea** (jē-a), Earth, something to stand on. Tartarus, the darkness that is always down in the earth, also sprang from Chaos. **Eros**, the force of sexual desire, that restless, irresistible energy that drives all living things and creates new living things, came from Chaos as well.

Gaea begot her own consort **Uranus** (yu-ran-us), Sky, to form the first clear duality: Up and Down, Above and Below. Gaea/Earth made the mountains, the glades of nymphs, and then gave rise to Pontus/Sea. Male Sky is above, and female Earth is below. Pontus/Sea is wet, and male too, like semen, and lies hard against the Earth, embracing her. Hesiod's metaphors are explicitly sexual because the world is like we are. Only through sexual union, and the generations from it, can the world grow and change. The race of the gods is like the race of human rulers who are begotten, who beget others, who struggle, triumph, and fade away. The gods are within the world; they do not stand outside it.

The first duality, Gaea/Earth and Uranus/Sky, united in primal sexual embrace. From their union came a host of creatures of obscure nature and meaning, the race of **Titans**. Most Titans had no cult in Greek religion; they were entirely mythical beings. Two of them, **Cronus** and Rhea (rē-a), are critical to Hesiod's story. Uranus/Sky was a bad father:

> All those who came forth from Earth [*Gaea*] and Sky [*Uranus*], the most
> dread of all children, hated their father from
> the beginning. For he did not allow them to come out into

the light, but as each was born, he hid them away
in a cranny of Earth, and Sky took delight in his wicked
deed. Huge Earth moaned within,
being stretched to the limit. Then she devised an evil,
tricky device. Straightway making a kind
of gray iron, she fashioned a huge sickle
and she showed it to her children. Making bold
she spoke, grieving in her heart, "O children of mine
and of a reckless father, if you will let me persuade you,
we can take revenge upon your father
for his wicked outrage. It was he first
who undertook shameful deeds." So she
spoke, and they were all afraid, and not one
of them dared to speak. Then great wily Cronus
took heart, and he answered his prudent mother:
"Mother, I will undertake to accomplish this deed,
for I have no use for our cursed father: It was he
first who undertook shameful deeds." So he spoke.
Huge Earth took great joy in heart. She hid
him in ambush. She placed in his hands the sharp-toothed
sickle. She explained to him the whole plan. Great Sky
came, dragging night behind, longing for
Earth's love, and he embraced her and stretched out upon
her completely, when from the place of ambush his son
seized him with his left hand, while with his right he held
the huge sickle, long, sharp-toothed, and he cut off
the genitals of his father with a swoosh, and he threw them behind
him to be borne away. And they were not flung
from his hand in vain.

Hesiod, *Theogony* 154–82

On the surface, Hesiod's cosmic tale is about family dissension, so often the essence
of Greek myth, but the tale of domestic abuse cloaks a description of creation as separation
embodied in the name *Chaos*, "gap" or "chasm." Hesiod's myth attempts, we might say, to
explain by means of ordinary categories of thought what is otherwise inexplicable.

Uranus/Sky and Gaea/Earth begot children, but the children could not come forth
because Sky would not let them emerge from Earth's womb, as if Sky and Earth were
locked in constant sexual embrace. Uranus/Sky's fault was sexual in nature, which both
Gaea/Earth and Cronus called "shameful things." One of the original three beings was
Eros, sexual attraction. Unless this cosmic attraction could be broken, female and male
would forever be bound in sexual union, and there could be no world. When Cronus severed his father's genitals, which joined Uranus/Sky to Gaea/Earth, Uranus rose upward,
where he has been ever since. First there was one thing: Uranus and Gaea, masculine and
feminine locked in eternal embrace. Now there were two separate beings and a proper
space between them wherein change can take place. But the beginning of the world in
bloody castration of father by son will bring a legacy of danger, suspicion, terror, and hate.
The ground was watered with Cronus' blood, and from it grew the **Furies** (or *Erinyes*),
the angry persecuting spirits, especially of murdered members of one's own family; the

Giants ("earth-born ones"), a blood-thirsty race who would one day oppose Zeus and his relatives; and the spirits of the trees which cover the earth, because only blood in the ground, as from sacrifice, could bring life to the mighty trees.

Most terrible of all was Aphrodite, "born from the foam" (Greek *aphros* = "foam") that gathered around the severed organs of Uranus when they fell into the sea. It is a ghastly image. The foam that gathered around the severed genitals is like the foam that gathers around the genitals of a man in human intercourse, but these organs have been sliced away. Such was Aphrodite: ferocious sexual attraction that arises from gore and brings bloody disaster in its wake. The danger of sexual attraction and of woman, who uses sexual attraction as a weapon against the male, is a central theme in Greek myth and in Greek culture.

The awful crime of Cronus, working with his mother against his father, bred more crimes, as Hesiod goes on to tell. Cronus proved to be as wicked a father as Uranus before him. Uranus pushed his children back into Gaea (as if stuffing up the womb with his penis), but Cronus was a cannibal and swallowed his children whole. The wife is a husband's undoing: Gaea conspired with her son Cronus to overthrow her husband Uranus; now Rhea, Cronus' sister/wife, destroyed the power of her husband too. She saved her last child, Zeus, from being eaten by Cronus by wrapping a rock in swaddling clothes and giving it to Cronus to swallow. Stupid Cronus fell for the trick, while Zeus, his life spared, was raised in secret on the island of Crete, hidden in a cave.

When Zeus grew up, he deposed Cronus and became king himself, although Hesiod does not tell us how. His power threatened repeatedly, Zeus defeated his mighty enemies and, unlike his father and grandfather, established a permanent disposition over the world we live in now. All praise to great Zeus, father of gods and men! Hesiod ends his poem.

Myth is a story that explains not only how things came to be, but why things are the way they are. Hesiod's complex story, of which we have examined a portion, explains the origin and role of the great forces that make up the world.

## GREEK RELIGION IN HISTORY

Hesiod describes how Zeus came to power by overthrowing his father, who had previously overthrown his father. It is a story and does not require action. Greek religion was very different from myth and mostly independent of it, although stories were sometimes told in explanation of religious practice. Greek religion was **polytheistic**, "having many gods," and **anthropomorphic**, "imagining gods in the form of humans." The powers that surround us have their own wills and psychology, mysterious and unpredictable but similar to our own. Greek religion was a typical form of religion, found in other ancient cultures, but you have to know something about the history of religion to understand how it worked.

All humans have religion, even those who deny it. Through their illusions, humans have attached their religious fear to every conceivable kind of person, place, or thing, hoping by the stone of amazing color, the brilliant orb in the sky, the eerie spirit from beyond, or the amazing man, to be saved from the forces that relentlessly punish them.

There are two broad categories of religion: **evolutionary** and **revealed**. An evolutionary religion embraces the totality of things feared by a social group at any one time and has no specific origin. Evolutionary religions are always polytheistic, like Greek religion, though not necessarily anthropomorphic. Evolutionary religions evolve from humans' constant changing response to the hostile world around them. Although such religions impose moral behavior, they have no teaching as such. Ancient Greek religion was an evolutionary religion.

The famous Egyptian religion was another evolutionary religion, a bewildering chaos of fetishes (objects with power), magic, symbols, gods, and powers, all of which coexisted without complaint. There were books of spells and rituals, but no sacred book, and few myths. Greek religion was different from Egyptian, but shared these same general qualities.

Revealed religions, by contrast, have founders, men with special relations to the divine. The oldest revealed religion was that of the strange Egyptian pharaoh Akhenaten ("servant of the Aten," c. 1360–1345 B.C.), who claimed a special relationship with Aten, the one God. Akhenaten outlawed the evolutionary and polytheistic religion that had long guided Egypt and guaranteed personal happiness after death. Similarly, Yahweh was revealed to Moses, who founded the religion of Israel (although the race descends from Abraham). Saint Paul and the Apostles founded Christianity on the basis of the life of Jesus. Zoroaster founded a religion in Iran, and Sakyamuni founded Buddhism (if it is a religion and not a philosophy). Revealed religions are monotheistic, or close to it (Christianity is monotheistic, but admits three divine persons in one). No prophet ever came down from the mountains to announce to suffering humanity: "There are many gods!" Revealed religions are tied to written documents—the "books of Moses," the Koran, the New Testament. Revealed religions can appear independently of writing (e.g., the religion of the Paiute prophet Wovoka from Nevada in the late nineteenth century A.D.), but they do not last. The closest the Greeks came to revealed religion was the movement called Orphism, which had books, teachings, and an alleged founder (see the Section "Ecstatic and Mystical Religion," later in this chapter), but Orphism was restricted to a philosophic elite and was more what we would consider a cult.

Greek evolutionary religion embraced powers and fears of all kinds. As we have seen, its gods were within the world, which they did not create. These powers—gods, nymphs, and other spirits—did not die (ordinarily), but they were born. The Greek gods had favorite humans and intervened in human affairs but did not live within the human heart. They were powerful, but their power had limits. All gods, including Zeus, were subject to **Fate** (Latin *fatum*, "that which has been spoken"), the way things must be.

## FORMS OF GREEK RELIGIOUS PRACTICE

All religions, evolutionary and revealed, share common practices, although different religions emphasize different practices. Let us examine the most important religious practices to form a context for understanding Greek religion.

### Magic

Our relation to the stupendous powers that govern every facet of life demands more than feeling and speculation. **Magic** forces such powers to do what we wish. Some scholars distinguish magic from religion, but the two are hard to disentangle. We might think of magical effects as dependent on magicians, who force gods to their will, whereas in religion, the gods act on their own will. Magic appears in Greek literature and in Greek society but was less important in Greece than in many other evolutionary religions. The educated elites who wrote Greek literature generally felt that magic was beneath them, but some Greeks did practice magic, and they left behind evidence of their spells and incantations.

Magic can work by imitation of the desired effect. If I wish to harm you, I make a wax doll and stick pins into it. Some Greeks did just this, then buried the dolls with criminals' corpses to increase the doll's power to do harm. Archaeologists have found such dolls in graves. In another form of magic, the magician may do on a small scale what is meant to happen on a large; sprinkling from a bucket of water will bring rain, and at one Attic festival, water was sprinkled during a prayer for rain. A third form of magic works by symbolism, assuming that the name of a thing and the thing itself are the same: Thus the police supposedly shout, "Stop in the name of the law!" as they chase criminals down dark alleys. Cursing or blessing by name is a further example. By invoking the gods' names, we can compel them to obey our will; a body of Greek hymns survives whose purpose was to attract the gods' attention by naming them and telling stories about them. The biblical commandment against taking God's name in vain works similarly, and in Judaism the written name of God is never pronounced because of its power. Magic is perhaps closer to primitive science with invalid axioms than to what we think of as religion, but it leaves its traces in all cults and many myths.

## Persuasion

Magic might force invisible powers to obey one's will, but in dealing with very great powers, persuasion and propitiation by sacrifice can be preferable. Because the powers are like ourselves, we can persuade them to follow this or that course. We too are liable to flattery, bribery, and shame. The story of Chrysês in the first book of Homer's *Iliad* (see Chapter 6, "Homer") is a good example. This priest persuaded Apollo to punish the Achaeans when Agamemnon refused to release Chrysês' daughter and then sent him away:

> So he spoke, and the frightened old man believed his command [*mythos*].
> He walked in silence along the shore of the much-resounding
> sea. When he had got a good distance away, the old man
> prayed to King Apollo, whom well-tressed Leto
> bore. "Hear me O Silver-Bow, you who dwell
> in Chrysê and holy Cilla, you whose might
> rules over Tenedos, plague-god Smintheus—if ever
> I've nicely roofed a shrine for you, or burned
> fat thigh-bones of bulls of goats in your honor,
> then answer my prayer: May your weapons take revenge
> on the Danaans for my suffering!" Thus he spoke
> in prayer, and Apollo heard him, and he came down
> from the peaks of high Olympus storming in his heart,
> carrying his bow around his shoulders and his quiver
> sealed at both ends. And his arrows clanged against
> his shoulders as he raged, as he sped along. He was
> like night. He took up position apart from the ships
> and he loosed an arrow. Terrible was the clang of the silver
> bow. First he struck the mules and the swift hounds,
> but then his showering arrows struck the bodies
> of men. Ever burned thick the pyres of the dead.
>
> Homer, *Iliad* 1.33–52

Chrysês uses the magic of names to insure the god's attention: He does not call just any Apollo, but the well-known one who rules over the villages Chrysê (**krī-sē**) and Cilla (**sil**-la), locations unknown to us. This Apollo rules Tenedos (**ten**-e-dos) too, an island near

**FIGURE 7.1**  The archer god Apollo and his sister Artemis kill the children of Niobê, who bragged of having more children than Leto, Apollo and Artemis' mother. The children fall, three boys and a girl, pierced by arrows. Athenian red-figured pot, c. 450 B.C.

the Trojan plain. He is Smintheus, meaning "of the mice," apparently because Apollo can bring plague or drive it away. Such local names pin down Apollo in the welter of the world, much as we dial a phone number. They get the god's attention and alert him to the need to destroy the Achaeans, who have offended his priest.

Chrysês then explains why he deserves this favor. He has, first, built a roof over Apollo's special place; and, second, he has burned animal parts on Apollo's altar. Apollo therefore owes Chrysês something for his services, and Chrysês is calling in his marker. Apollo is persuaded and does as Chrysês asks.

Homer's description shows how closely related and easily confused are myth, religion, and magic. These lines are the earliest information we receive about Apollo, one of the most celebrated of ancient gods. What do we learn about Apollo? He is a bowman and carries a quiver on his shoulder. He comes like the night, swift and dark, a killer. First, animals die, then humans—such is his power. That is what Chrysês wanted, what he prayed for, why he sacrificed at Apollo's shrine and roofed it, a religious act. Yet Chrysês is like a magician who creates his own effects through Apollo's agency; priests are dangerous and should not be meddled with. These special details are, however, part of a myth, the story of the Trojan War. From this passage derive subsequent representations of Apollo shown with a bow and arrows (Figure 7.1).

Homer gives a mythical description of what his audience would understand as plague, when animals and humans die mysteriously, as often happens on military campaigns. The cause was a magician allied with a god who had shrines throughout Greece (Figure 7.2).

## Sacrifice

Later in the *Iliad*, when the suffering Achaeans agree to return Chrysês' daughter so he will release them from disease, they restore relations with Apollo through **sacrifice**—the killing of an animal or offering of fruits and plants, the most visible expression of

**FIGURE 7.2** The shrine of Apollo at Delphi, one of the major Greek sacred sites. The oracle of Apollo at Delphi is important in many Greek myths (e.g., Oedipus the king, who killed his father and married his mother). Visible in the center-left are columns from the god's temple; above, center-right, is the open-air theater from which a path led up the hill to an athletic stadium. Beyond the mountain in the background lies the Gulf of Corinth.

religion in the ancient world. Sacrifice was what you did in Greek religion (Figure 7.3). The psychology of sacrifice is summed up in the Latin saying, *do ut des,* "I give that you might give." The Achaeans gave to Apollo so Apollo might allow them to live:

> They threw out the anchors, they tied up the prows. The men
> leaped to the shore of the sea. They brought out the sacrifice
> for far-shooting Apollo. Chryseïs ["daughter of Chrysê"] got out of the deep-sea
> ship. Leading her up to the altar, clever
> Odysseus placed her in the hands of her father, and he
> spoke to him: "Chrysês, Agamemnon king of men
> has sent me to return her to you and to perform holy sacrifice
> to Apollo on behalf of the Danaans, that we might appease
> the god, who sends wretched suffering upon the Argives."
> So speaking he placed her in his hands, and the priest

**FIGURE 7.3** The sacrifice of Polyxena, a daughter of King Priam of Troy, over the grave of Achilles. A figure labeled Neoptolemus (Achilles' son) cuts the virgin princess' throat as if she were an animal, spilling the blood into the flame. Human sacrifice was extremely rare in classical Greece.

received her with joy in his heart. The Achaeans then arranged
the cattle in a row around the well-built altar. They washed
their hands and took up the barley to be scattered. On their
behalf Chrysês prayed mightily, raising his hands:
"Hear me, O god of the silver bow, who hovers
around Chrysê and holy Cilla and rules over Tenedos
with power. Yes, you heard me before when I prayed,
and you showed me honor, and you punished well the Achaeans.
Even so once again fulfill my prayer:
Put an end to the terrible plague upon the Danaans."
So he spoke in prayer, and Phoebus Apollo
heard him. When they had prayed and scattered the barley,
and raised up the heads of the victims and cut their throats
and skinned them out, then they cut out the thigh bones
and wrapped them in fat in a double layer, and on top
of them they placed pieces of raw flesh. The old man
burned them on a cleft-stick, and he poured out shining wine.
The young men near him held five-tined forks in their hands.
And when they had burned the thigh bones and tasted the innards,
they cut up the rest and stuck pieces on spits, and they cooked
them well and pulled them off the fire. And when
their work was done, the feast was ready, they ate.
No man's hunger lacked a share in the banquet. And when

they put aside the desire for drink and food,
young men topped off the mixing bowls with wine,
and tipping the gods from each cup, they filled each man's
cup. And so all day long they celebrated the god
with song, singing a hymn of praise, flattering
the god who shoots from afar. He delighted to hear them.

Homer, *Iliad* 1.436–74

We can supplement Homer's description with other reports. First, the cattle that made up an important sacrifice were grouped around the altar in a circle, a formation of magical power. Cattle were valuable, and their bequest to the god made a powerful impression. The officiants then purified themselves. Somebody brought a bowl of water ("they washed their hands"). Purification was religiously important because humans are constantly threatened by defilement from their own waste and from the fluids of intercourse and childbirth. Women were especially liable to impurity and dangerous to religious practice. Defecation, urination, intercourse, childbirth, menstruation, and death (which produces its own repulsive fluids) were strictly forbidden in religious precincts, in ancient Greece and elsewhere. The barley grains sprinkled on the animals performed the same magical purificatory function as the water, being a rain of the fruitful, life-bearing seed. The grain purified the animal and separated it from the everyday world. The Latin word *sacer* means "separated from everyday human usage," made over to a divinity, from which comes the words *sacred*, *consecrate*, *sacrifice*, *sacrament*, *sanctify*, and *saint*.

The animal's death would bring life to the men: *do ut des*, "I give that you might give." The sacrificial knife, we learn from other descriptions, lurked in the seed-filled basket from which the grain is scattered, awaiting the priest's hand. As the men sprinkled the grain, they told the god what they wished in return. The men drew back the head so the animal looked up, assenting to the shedding of its blood and stretching its throat taut (Figure 7.4). Priests in Greek religion (and most other ancient religions) were butchers, skilled in killing, skinning, and dismembering animals.

The animal was skinned and the thigh bones cut out and wrapped in juicy fat in a sort of sandwich. Pieces of meat from all parts of the animal were sprinkled over the fat (as Homer describes). The meat-sprinkled fat-sandwich represented the entire animal, whose good parts the hungry men ate, while the god received the undesirable fat and inedible bones. Chrysês burned this fat-sandwich on a spit and doused it with wine.

Meanwhile, someone roasted the entrails. The rest of the animal was sliced and roasted on forks. Many Greeks ate meat only at sacrifices, an important source of protein in the otherwise meager diet. The excitement of killing a large animal; the prayers; the splash and stink of blood as it gushed out of the animal's throat into the flames of the altar (or was first caught in a bowl); the thick and redolent smoke from the burning blood, bones, and fat; and the scent of roasting meat—such was the essence of Greek religion from the Bronze Age until Saint Paul promulgated the voluntary self-sacrifice of Jesus, which obviated the need for the further killing of animals and humans. The Greek calendar was largely a cycle of festivals to this or that divinity, when people would taste sacrificed meat. Public sacrifices brought the community together, affirmed values, and added protein to the diet. The average Greek experienced religion in this and in no other way.

**FIGURE 7.4**  A bull led to sacrifice in the Athenian Panathenaic procession, illustrated on the Parthenon, 440s –430s B.C. The bull rears its head, presenting its throat, a good omen. Marble, carved under the supervision of Phidias.

## HESIOD'S MYTH OF SACRIFICE

Hesiod tells a myth explaining why, in Greek sacrifice, humans received the good parts and gods got the worst:

> At the time that the gods and the humans who die settled
> accounts at Meconê,° Prometheus, in good cheer, took
> a great ox and carved it up and placed it before Zeus,
> to trick his mind. The meat, the innards, and the fat
> he put in a hide and covered them with the stomach
> of the ox. But the white bones, as a trick, he covered
> with shining fat, and set them down as an offering.
> The father of gods and men said to him:
> "Oh son of Iapetus,° most excellent of kings, Wow,
> you've divided the portions [moirai°] in a prejudiced manner." Thus spoke
> Zeus in sarcasm, whose counsels never perish,
> but Prometheus, of wily mind, smiled faintly,
> and not forgetting his deceitful plan said:
> "Why Zeus, most glorious and greatest of gods who will live
> forever, take whichever portion you want,
> whichever your best judgment advises you."

°*Iapetus*: A Titan, father of Prometheus.    °*moirai*: In Greek myth the Moerae are the "Fates," one's portion in life.    °*Meconê* [me-kō-nē]: Sicyon, in the north Peloponnesus.

> So he spoke, holding the trick within
> his mind, and Zeus whose counsels never perish
> saw and understood the trick. But he meditated evil
> in his heart for the race of humans who die and he determined
> to bring this about. Thus with both his hands he took
> up the white fat. And anger came into his heart,
> and rage overcame when he saw the white bones of the cow,
> a trick! And that's why the tribes of humans who dwell
> on the earth burn white bones for the gods on the sacrificial altars.
>
> Hesiod, *Theogony* 543–58

Hesiod's myth is a good example of a story that explains the cause (Greek *aition*) of something—in this case, the division of the animal in sacrifice—called an **etiological myth**. Hesiod's *Theogony* ("begetting of the gods") is itself an etiological tale explaining how Zeus came to rule the world. Myth often explains, telling us why things are as they are; religion, the killing and eating of animals, is practice, a mode of action.

The conditions for sacrifice, which brings all good things to men, are now established. The basic facts of human life are tied to sacrifice. Sacrifice brings us to the world of the gods and guarantees us its benefits.

## GODS AND OTHER MYSTERIOUS BEINGS

Many scholars distinguish two broad categories of Greek religious practice. The first was directed toward the **Olympians**, gods who in poetic fancy lived on lofty Mount Olympus between Macedonia and Thessaly, Greece's highest mountain (9,573 feet; see Figure 2.2). The second was **chthonic cult** ("of the earth," where the dead are buried), directed toward ghosts, underworld spirits, and various halfway supernatural beings like the heroes. Both forms of religion served similar ends, however, and in practice they overlapped, but for the sake of discussion we treat them separately here.

### Greek Polytheism

The Greek word for god is *theos* (root of *theo*logy, "study of god"), possibly from the same root, meaning "bright," that gives us the name *Zeus* and the Latin *Ju*-piter and *deus* (root of *deity*). *Theoi* (the plural of *theos*) are the "shining ones," perhaps because they occasionally appear to humans as luminous beings. Whereas ghosts are the departed breath of the living, gods have very diverse origins and natures.

We get some inkling of how complex is the category "gods" by looking again at Hesiod's *Theogony*, our most important early source of information about Greek religion. In the following passage, we *italicize* each god (or group of gods) that Hesiod mentions:

> Let us begin with song of the Heliconian **Muses**,
> who dwell on Mount Helicon, high and mystical,
> and dance with delicate feet round the violet-dark spring
> and the altar of the mighty **son of Cronus**.° They bathe
> their tender flesh in the waters of Permessus or of Hippocrene ("spring of
>    the horse")
>
> °*son of Cronus*: Zeus.

or of mystical Olmius and they dance their beautiful dances,
lovely, on the peaks of Helicon. They pound with their feet.
Setting out from there, hidden by thick mist, they travel
through the night. They raise their gorgeous voices, singing
of Zeus who carries the aegis and of reverend **Hera**
of Argos, whose sandals are golden, and the daughter of aegis-bearing
Zeus, gray-eyed **Athena** and Phoebus **Apollo**
and arrow-shooting **Artemis** and Poseidon who holds the earth
and shakes it, and imposing **Thetis** and **Aphrodite**
who looks with glancing eye and **Hebê** whose crown
is golden and beautiful **Dionê** and **Leto** and **Iapetus**
and wily Cronus and Eos and great **Helius** and bright **Selenê**
and **Gaea** and great **Oceanus** and dark **Night** and the sacred race
of all those deathless ones who live forever.
For you once taught Hesiod beautiful song (aoidê)
as he herded his flocks beneath mystic Helicon.

Hesiod, *Theogony* 1–23

The Greeks called the **Muses** gods, *theoi*, or referred to a single god, the Muse (Figure 7.5). The Muse(s) personified the mysterious force that enabled *aoidoi* ("singers") to strum a lyre and tell an entrancing story in metrical song. We attribute similar abilities to inspiration, the "taking in of a spirit." The Muses favored some people and did not favor others, but the actual power to sing was never personal. Greeks never "expressed themselves" in their poetry as do modern poets.

The Muses perhaps were gods who worked from without to create effects in people's lives, but they originated largely as a manner of speaking about artistic power. They are a good example of the power of poetry to mold religious expression in early Greece. Highly local, they did not live in the sky or far away, but on Mount Helicon above the tiny village of Ascra in southern Boeotia, where Hesiod lived some time in the eighth century B.C. Like young girls from Hesiod's village, the Muses bathed in an obscure stream called Permessus. No one outside a radius of a few miles could have heard of these places, or of

**FIGURE 7.5** The poet Musaeus (mu-sē-us) on the left and a Muse on an Attic red-figured amphora. Musaeus, a legendary poet ("man of the Muse") wears a laurel wreath and a cloak. His name is inscribed above him. His right hand rests on a lyre with a tortoiseshell sounding box, to accompany his songs. Hesiod tells us the names of nine Muses; the one shown here is labeled Terpsichorê (terp-**sik**-o-rē, "delighter in dance"), usually thought of as the inspirer of lyric poetry and dance; c. 450–420 B.C.

Hippocrene (**hip**-o-krēn, "spring of the horse"), probably a spring on Mount Helicon. The altar of Zeus around which they dance has never been identified.

Hesiod, therefore, begins his hymn to the universal Zeus with a hymn to the very local Muses, who themselves sing a hymn to Zeus and a long list of other gods, our earliest such list in Greek (except for some names on Linear B tablets). We now examine these gods briefly and individually. Some recur countless times in the culture of the ancient Greeks, while others may be unfamiliar.

## The Olympians

"Gray-eyed Athena," "Phoebus Apollo," and "arrow-shooting Artemis" in Hesiod's list belong, with Hera and Zeus, to what became a canon of the twelve greatest gods, formalized by the early fifth century B.C. The canon may lie behind an altar "To the Twelve Gods" set up in Athens. The twelve Olympian gods, sculpted on the Parthenon frieze (part of which is shown in Figure 7.6), are listed here:

| | |
|---|---|
| Zeus | Artemis |
| Poseidon | Apollo |
| Demeter | Athena |
| Hera | Hermes |
| Ares | Dionysus |
| Aphrodite | Hephaestus |

**FIGURE 7.6** Gods on the Parthenon frieze. At center, the beardless youthful Dionysus (or Apollo) turns to speak to Poseidon (at left), while Demeter (at right) watches the procession. Marble, c. 440s–430s B.C.

Of these twelve gods, Hesiod's list does not include Demeter, Ares, Hermes, Dionysus, or Hephaestus—the gods of grain, war, travel, wine, and metalworking. Hesiod talks about these gods in other contexts but does not seem to know a canonical list.

## Zeus and Hera

Head of the Olympians is aegis-bearing **Zeus**. *Aegis* means "goatskin" and refers to a magical implement, perhaps a shield, which Zeus carried, perhaps symbolizing the thundercloud (but in art, Athena is far more likely to carry it). The undiscovered altar around which the Muses dance in Zeus' honor, according to Hesiod's account, was no doubt on the peak of Helicon, for such altars "on high places" were the abode of weather gods all over the Mediterranean, hated by the Hebrew prophets because of their power and influence. Their shrines were often on mountaintops because storms gather there. The storm god had many names: Hadad in Syria, Marduk in Babylon, Teshub among the Hittites, but always, like Zeus, he was the great power of the sky felt in storms that consume the earth with rain and blast trees and rocks (Figure 7.7a, Figure 7.7b).

To Zeus, Hesiod joins "reverend **Hera** of Argos, whose sandals are golden," a great goddess in her own right and already mentioned in Linear B tablets. She had an important sanctuary near Argos, to which Hesiod refers. She, like the Muses, had a local origin, but her power spread far and wide. As the bull symbolized Zeus, Hera was the cow, the female principle of fruitfulness. In Greek religion, she protected marriage.

Ancient goddesses were always defined by their relationship to fertility and reproduction (as were women in society), unlike the male gods, whose duties were not unified by a common thread (nor were those of men in society). In religion, Hera was an important goddess who received magnificent temples and rich sacrifices, but in Homeric myth, she is a nagging, snooping wife, always opposing the designs of her portentous and philandering husband Zeus. In the following passage, Hera complains to Zeus for scheming with another goddess behind her back to help the Trojans, whom Hera loathes:

> "Who now of all the gods, has been conspiring with you?
> You so love to go apart from me
> and to make your secret decisions. You never want
> to tell me what you're up to—not one single
> word!" The father of men and gods answered her:
> "Hera, don't hope always to know my plans [**muthoi**].
> My plans will be rough for you, although you are
> my wife! Whatever is right for you to hear,
> you will hear, and before any other god or human.
> But that which I wish to keep hidden from all the gods,
> don't ask me about it or go snooping around!"
> Then cow-eyed reverend Hera answered: "Why most
> dread son of Cronus, what on earth have you said?
> I don't think that in the past I've pried
> overmuch or snooped around. Go ahead and plot away
> to your heart's content . . . " And cloud-gathering Zeus answered:
> "You drive me crazy! You're always guessing my thoughts
> and nothing I do escapes you. Nonetheless

(a)

(b)

**FIGURE 7.7** (a) The Hittite storm-god Tarkhunzas carries an ax in one hand and a trident, emblem of the thunderbolt, in the other. Similar figures of storm-gods appear in the art of the Near East from the third millennium B.C. until late antiquity. (b) Zeus carries a similar forklike device, but pronged at either end: it is the thunderbolt, his special weapon. Tarkhunzas: basalt orthostat from Zinjirli (in Turkey), c. 900 B.C.; height 51 inches. Zeus: Attic red-figured amphora, 460s B.C., height, 12 inches.

you can do nothing about it. I will only
hate you more. And that will be more shivery for you!
If it is as you say, then that must be the way
I want it. So shut your mouth and take your seat,
and obey my command [*muthos*], unless all the gods on Olympus
coming to your aid won't be of the slightest use
when I lay my resistless hands upon you!"

Homer, *Iliad* 1.549–67

## Athena, Apollo, and Artemis

Athena, Apollo, and Artemis are magnificent gods in Greek religion and myth. In religion, **Athena** protected Athens and several other cities. She encouraged arts, especially women's weaving, even as Athens was preeminent in artistic production. In myth, Athena favored the Achaeans in the Trojan War and protected Odysseus on his journey home (Figure 7.8). In Greek vase painting she often stands beside a hero, such as Perseus or Theseus.

**Apollo** was a complex god. Artists represented him as a beardless young aristocrat (Figure 7.6). He was the archer-god, but (unlike his sister Artemis) never hunted. He favored the Trojans and guided the arrow, fired by Paris, that killed Achilles. Apollo

**FIGURE 7.8** Athena stands between Odysseus, on the left, and princess Nausicaä and a friend, on the right. Her spear pointed downward, she looks toward her protégé. She wears the war helmet and the snaky-edged aegis around her neck. Odysseus has just emerged naked from the bushes and surprised the girls, washing clothes by the sea.

embodied aristocratic values and the power possessed by men of knowledge, like his priest Chrysês in the *Iliad*. His connections with the inner world made him the god of prophecy. As the divine aristocrat, Apollo brought success to those who sang and played lyres at elite drinking parties (artists often show him holding a lyre). The seventh-century B.C. *Homeric Hymn to Apollo* celebrates his singing:

> I want to mention Apollo who shoots from afar,
> at whose entrance in the house of Zeus everyone trembles.
> All spring from their seats as he comes close, stringing
> his bow. Leto alone remains seated beside Zeus
> who delights in the thunderbolt, and it is she who loosens his bow
> and closes his quiver, who takes from his mighty shoulders
> with her own hands his bow and hangs it up
> on a golden peg on her father's column. She leads
> him to his seat. The father offers him nectar
> in a golden cup and offers a toast
> to his son. Then all the other gods take
> their seats as mistress Leto rejoices, for she
> has born a powerful son who carries the bow . . .
> Everywhere, Phoebus, singing is your domain,
> on the mainland that nurtures heifers, and on the islands.

*Homeric Hymn to Apollo* 1–13

Arrow-shooting **Artemis** received temples all over the Greek world, far more than Hera. She helped animals, particularly wild ones, to reproduce. Though a goddess of fertility, she was paradoxically a virgin, because, more than others, virgins are poised to reproduce. In myth, the virgin Artemis was Apollo's twin sister, though no one has explained why. Hesiod also mentions their mother, Leto.

Artemis appears in many myths about hunting. Often, she is offended in some way and sends horrific retribution, like the Calydonian boar, which ravaged the countryside when a king forgot to sacrifice to her at his wedding. She appreciates human sacrifice: Agamemnon sacrificed his daughter Iphigenia to Artemis so that favorable winds would carry the fleet to Troy.

## Other Gods

Hesiod's "Poseidon, who holds the earth and shakes it," and "Aphrodite who looks with glancing eye" belong to the later canonical list of the twelve Olympian gods. **Poseidon** was the earthquake god and lord of the Aegean Sea. In religion, he received the prayers of sailors and those who lived through the earthquakes that plagued the eastern Mediterranean. In myth he persecuted Odysseus, whose enemy was indeed the sea, foreign lands, and death. Hesiod associates **Aphrodite's** name with *aphros*, "foam," but it appears to be a corruption of Astartê, a Near Eastern goddess of sex and war. By 900 B.C., Astartê was established on Cyprus, brought there by Phoenicians. Hence, Cyprus was called Aphrodite's home, and she was often called the Cyprian.

Hesiod's "Hebê whose crown is golden and beautiful Dionê and Leto" are scarcely known outside a few stories. Thetis is the mother of Achilles. Hebê is "Youth," a straightforward personification (Heracles married her on Olympus after he became immortal), and Dionê is a feminine form of Zeus, perhaps his original consort in an earlier stage of Greek religion before being displaced by Hera. The Muses close their list with three personifications of nature, Dawn (Eos), Sun (Helius), and Moon (Selenê); with the almost unknown Iapetus (probably the same as Japheth in the Bible, a son of Noah) and wily Cronus (father of Zeus); then three primordial beings, Earth (Gaea), the encircling waters (great Oceanus), and dark Night.

In organizing our earliest testament to Greek polytheism, Hesiod worked backward from the present world order, where Zeus and Hera reign together with their brothers, sisters, and children, toward an earlier era, when gods less personalized and unfamiliar to contemporary Greek religion were in power. In the Muses' hymn, Hesiod carries us back to the beginnings of things in earth, water, and darkness.

## CHTHONIC RELIGION

Cultism is what people do in religious contexts. However, a religious cult is not always directed toward anthropomorphic gods with a psychology more or less like ours yet with far greater power. There are also personal, hidden, envious, and dangerous ghosts and spirits. Nearly all ancient (and many modern) peoples believed in ghosts and spirits, and much of what we think of as religion belongs to ancient ghost-cult.

### The Breath-Soul

Greek *psychê* (sī-kē, pl. *psychai*), poorly translated as "soul," literally means "breath" (as do Latin *anima* and Hebrew *ruach*, also translated as "soul"). Spirit- and ghost-cult derives from the belief that when people die, they are not gone but transformed. The obvious fact about a dead body is that it no longer breathes. The *psychê* has escaped. Death is the departure of the insubstantial breath-soul from the body.

The breath-soul, denied the pleasures of life and mindful of hurts received, is invisible and very dangerous. To avoid the ghost's displeasure, it is important to demonstrate anguish at its departure by wearing dark, unattractive clothing that hides our sexual natures (a source of pleasure). The living should either deny themselves food (which brings pleasure) or invite the ghost to a special feast in its honor. It is good to abuse your body in other ways, by biting off a finger (Agamemnon's son Orestes did this after killing his mother Clytemnestra) or cutting your hair, and it is always good to destroy property of the deceased; one should not benefit from another person's death. Among their many functions, grave-offerings might prevent the dangerous ghost's displeasure over someone having taken its property.

### Odysseus and the *Psychai*

Homer's *Odyssey* is informative about Greek conceptions of ghosts and the mechanics of appealing to them. When Odysseus and his men wanted to leave the beautiful witch Circê's island after a year, she told them how to cross the river Ocean (one of the gods Hesiod mentions) to consult the *psychê* of the famous prophet Tiresias:

> When our boat reached that point we drove
> out the sheep, then went along the shore of Ocean
> until we came to the place that Circê described.
> Here Perimedes and Eurylochus° held the victims

°*Perimedes* and *Eurylochus*: Companions to Odysseus.

fast, while I drew my sharp sword from beside my thigh
and with it dug a pit the width and depth
of a forearm, and around it I poured out offerings to all
the dead, first of honey mixed with milk,
then of sweet wine, and third of water. On top
I sprinkled white barley. I vowed again and again
to the strengthless heads of the dead that when I returned
to Ithaca I would kill a barren heifer,
the best of all, in my halls, and that I would load
a pyre with treasures, and to Tiresias alone, apart,
I would kill a jet-black ram, that stands out from all
my flocks. When I had summoned the tribes of the dead by prayers
and incantations, taking the sheep I cut
their throats over the pit, and the black blood ran in.
The psychai of the dead gathered up from Erebus°—
brides and unmarried youths and old men of wide
experience and foolish young girls first finding sorrow,
many wounded from bronze, and warriors still wearing their blooded
armor. Most of them ranged before the pit,
this side and that, making an eerie moan,
and chill fear took hold on me. Then,
encouraging, I told my men to flay the sheep
dead from the merciless bronze, and to burn their bodies,
and to cry out to the gods, and to mighty Hades and dread
Persephonê. Myself, drawing my sharp sword from beside
my thigh, I sat down, and I did not allow the strengthless
heads of the dead to come closer to the blood, before
I should speak to Tiresias.

Homer, *Odyssey* 11.20–50

°*Erebus*: "Darkness," the underworld.

The *psychai* are thin, faint versions of their human selves. They have lost the vitality that blood, coursing through veins, gives to the living. Hence it is important, in sacrifice at tombs, to pour the blood of animals onto the grave, as Odysseus pours blood into a pit at the edge of the River Ocean (Figure 7.9). Wine, milk, honey, and water, the fluids of life, are excellent too. Beginning in the eighth century B.C., Greeks made offerings at ancient tombs, or to unknown heroes, or sometimes just "to the hero." Chthonic cults existed side by side with cults of the Olympian gods, and Greeks did not distinguish them strongly. After all, some of the Olympian gods may have begun as ghosts, and the psychology of sacrifice in appealing to invisible powers was uniform in Greek religion.

## THE UNGRATEFUL DEAD AND THE LAYING OF THE GHOST

Although evanescent, ghosts are not innocuous and may persecute the living who have wronged them. A good example of ghost-persecution appears in the *Oresteia*, a group of three plays by Aeschylus, performed in Athens in 458 B.C. In the first play, *Agamemnon*, Clytemnestra, the queen of Argos, murders her husband, Agamemnon, when he returns victorious from Troy. The second play, the *Libation Bearers*, is set many years later.

**FIGURE 7.9** Odysseus and the ghost of Elpenor, who fell from a roof and broke his neck as the expedition departed. The figures are labeled. The unburied Elpenor's *psychê* emerges, its legs hidden from the knees down, raising his left arm against a crag. Odysseus sits beside the fleece of a sacrificed sheep, his sword ready to deflect the ghosts as he gazes sorrowfully into Elpenor's eyes. Attic red-figured jar, c. 440 B.C.

Clytemnestra has had a terrible dream: To appease Agamemnon's ghost, she sends a group of slaves to pour libations (drink offerings, a form of sacrifice) over his grave. But only the murder of Clytemnestra herself, blood for blood, will satisfy this ghost.

Ghosts, especially ghosts of the murdered, send bad dreams, but they may also appear to friends in dreams. Nearly universal in human societies is the ghost-dream, when a person recently dead appears to a relative or friend with exceptional, even terrifying vividness. In the *Iliad*, Achilles has avenged the death of his friend Patroclus by killing Hector, and that night Patroclus' *psychê* appears to him:

> The son of Peleus lay down near the much-resounding sea,
> groaning deeply, amidst his many Myrmidons,°
> but in open ground, where the waves rolled against
> the land. Sleep took him, releasing all pain,
> dissolving sorrow from his breast, poured out
> upon him. His wonderful limbs were tired from pursuing
> Hector up against the walls of windy Troy.
> Then came to him the *psychê* of wretched Patroclus,
> seeming exactly like him in height and his fine eyes

Homer, *Iliad* 23.59–76

°*Myrmidons*: Followers of Achilles.

> the same and the sound of his voice. And his clothes were just
> the same as the ones he wore. He stood over Achilles'
> head and spoke to him: "You sleep, but you have forgotten me,
> Achilles. When I was alive you cared for me,
> but not now that I am dead. Bury me so that
> I may quickly pass the gates of Hades.
> The *psychai*, the shades of the breathless dead, keep me
> away, nor shall they allow me ever to mix
> with them beyond the river, but I shall wander
> helpless before the high-towered house of Hades.
> But give me your hand. I beg you with my tears.
> Never shall I return from the house of Hades,
> once you have given me to the fire."

The ghost of Patroclus begs to be released from this world, where it still wanders: Only a proper burial can "lay the ghost." For some reason, water divides the land of the dead from the land of the living, a symbol central to the meaning of the *Odyssey*, and Patroclus needs to cross it. Then Patroclus will be gone. The obligation to lay the ghost ordinarily falls on the family, but Achilles serves this role for Patroclus because they are in a foreign land. After all, the family is first to receive an unhappy ghost's complaint, like Clytemnestra. The family's need to lay the ghost is the basis for Sophocles' celebrated tragedy *Antigonê* (441 B.C.), in which the king forbids the burial of a treacherous prince, bringing catastrophe down on everyone. The purposes of Greek religion were collective, not for the well-being of individuals. The penalty for leaving the ghost to wander will be visited on the entire family, or even the whole world.

## Miasma

We saw earlier how Chrysês, through magic, invoked Apollo and brought disease to the Achaeans. The wandering or vengeful ghost, too, may stand behind every sort of misfortune. The ghost brings **miasma** (mī-*az*-ma) "stench," often translated as "blood-pollution," and anyone coming in contact with a murderer is liable to persecution as well. Such is the basis of the most famous story from antiquity, told in Sophocles' tragedy *Oedipus the King* (429 B.C.). A priest appears before Oedipus, powerful king of Thebes, to announce that plague has broken out in the *polis*:

> O Oedipus, king of my land,
> you see us of different ages sitting
> before your altars. Some are not strong enough
> to take wing, and others are heavy
> with age. I am a priest of Zeus,
> these children are chosen from among
> the young. In marketplace sit others,
> their heads crowned with suppliant wreathes,
> and others sit before the double doors
> of Pallas° or before the shrine of
> Ismenus° where the god gives oracles
> by gazing at embers. For the polis, as you
> yourself can see, for long already rocks

°*Pallas*: Athena.    °*Ismenus*: That is, Apollo, who had an oracular shrine near the spring Ismenus in Thebes.

and pitches and cannot lift its prow
from the depths and the bloody surf.
Blighted are the fruitful plants on the earth,
blighted the herds that feed in the fields,
and the sterile childless women.
Among us is a fire-bearing god,
who strikes and spares not the polis,
hateful plague, emptying the house
of Cadmus,° and black Death grows
rich with agony and tears.

Sophocles, *Oedipus the King* 14–30

°*house of Cadmus*: The royal house of Thebes, descended from the legendary Cadmus.

The cause of the plague, we soon learn from an oracle, is the unavenged murder of King Laius, who preceded Oedipus on the throne, killed mysteriously at a crossroads. The ghost is abroad and wants blood. As Sophocles' story unfolds, we learn that Oedipus himself killed Laius and that Laius was Oedipus' own father, although he did not know it. Worse still, Oedipus has married the widowed queen, his own mother, who hangs herself in horror when she learns the truth. Appalled at his deeds, Oedipus blinds himself with pins taken from his dead wife/mother's gown. Murder would be simple were it not for the ghost's malevolence!

## ECSTATIC AND MYSTICAL RELIGION

In Olympian and chthonic religion, the worshipper makes sacrifice, sings hymns, and says prayers to obtain what is desired. The ordinary devotee watches, content to follow the commands relayed. His or her share in worship is the proper performance of ritual. But in another kind of Greek cult, worshippers sought direct communion with deities, or even complete loss of self in the divine.

### The Eleusinian Mysteries

Many people who know nothing about Greek religion have heard of the **Eleusinian mysteries**. The very word *mystery* comes directly from descriptions of what happened at a temple to Demeter and Persephonê in the small town of Eleusis, five miles west of Athens. A *mystês* was a "person with closed eyes," required of those initiated into the rites of the temple. The mysteries functioned for over 1000 years, but no one ever described what happened in them. To do so was punishable by death.

We do know that every year a magnificent procession went from Athens through the countryside to the temple. Ordinarily, a Greek temple was the god's house, containing its image. Sacrifice took place outside the temple, on an altar facing east. At Eleusis, by contrast, celebrants went into a unique rectangular building supported by a forest of columns (Figure 7.10). According to a late commentator, during the ceremony a flash of light, perhaps from a fire, came from a stone hut in the building's center. All Greeks—men, women, and slaves—were eligible for initiation into the mysteries, which promised a happier life in the afterworld.

The *Hymn to Demeter* (attributed to Homer, though actually composed two centuries after his time) tells the myth of the founding of the cult at Eleusis. Hades, god of death, requested permission from his brother Zeus to marry his niece **Persephonê**, daughter of **Demeter**. Zeus agreed. While Peresphonê was playing by the seashore with her friends, Hades appeared from the earth in his chariot, seized the girl, and carried her to the underworld.

**FIGURE 7.10** Ruins of the temple at Eleusis. Behind the figure are seats for initiates and in front of the figure are the foundations of the small building from which emanated a flash of light. The large hall was nearly square, with seven rows of columns supporting the roof. Fifth century B.C.

Demeter, goddess of wheat-growing, searched everywhere for her daughter. She came to Eleusis disguised as an old woman and became nurse to the king and queen's child. At night, she placed the child on the flame of the hearth to burn away its mortal parts. One night, the queen saw them and cried out. Demeter revealed herself to the terrified queen and demanded that a temple be built on that spot.

Meanwhile, fertility had disappeared from the earth. Alarmed, Zeus arranged that Persephonê could return to the upper world, but only on condition that she had eaten nothing in the House of Hades. In fact, she had eaten one pomegranate seed, which Hades gave her. Therefore, she could spend only two-thirds of the year above ground with her mother, the other third below it with her lawful husband Hades, king of the dead.

The myth, similar to very ancient Near Eastern stories about fertility, explains how the cult at Eleusis was founded, but tells us little about the rituals there. The myth promises new life in Persephonê's return to the upper world but cautions that death is necessary. Demeter and Persephonê were called the Two Ladies, or just The Goddesses. They were two aspects of a single force, one making for life, the other for death.

## The Orphics

As the cult at Eleusis claimed Demeter as its founder, the **Orphics**, the "followers of Orpheus," claimed the legendary Orpheus. According to myth, Orpheus was the greatest of singers, whose song even entranced nature. His bride Eurydice died on his wedding day, bitten by a serpent. Orpheus descended to the underworld, charming the ghosts and the spirits there and winning back Eurydice, on condition that he did not look back at her until they reached the upper world. He failed and so lost his beloved forever (Figure 7.11).

**FIGURE 7.11** Orpheus plays among the Thracians, who listen entranced. After losing his wife a second time, he wandered in Thrace associating only with men and, according to some accounts, invented homosexuality. In anger at his behavior, Dionysus' followers tore him to bits. Attic red-figured vase, c. 440 B.C.

Whereas the Eleusinian mysteries were open to all, including slaves, the Orphics were a small, self-contained group, probably all male. Because Orpheus had gone to the underworld and returned, his followers claimed special knowledge about human destiny, our relation to the divine, and life after death. More philosophy than religion, Orphism taught that a spark of God dwells in every human. Only through a pure life—abstaining from sex, certain foods, and especially abstaining from the bloody sacrifice that stained the altars of heroes and gods—could initiates achieve knowledge of the divine self locked in the tomb of flesh.

The Orphics were a countercultural movement, interpreting reality differently from most contemporaries. They never were many, but they deeply influenced Plato, who in turn influenced the early Christian church fathers. Plato wrote as follows about the body and soul:

It seems to me that this too [the derivation of the word *sôma*, "body"] can be explained in several ways, if you change the spelling slightly, even very slightly. Some say that it is the "tomb" [*sêma*] of the soul, in which the soul is buried for the time being . . . It seems that the followers of Orpheus make the most of this word [*sôma*], as being the place where the soul pays the price for its misdeeds, so that the body is like an enclosure in which the soul is kept [*sôzetai*], like a prison. For that is what the body is, as its name shows, an enclosure for the soul until it has paid whatever penalties it owes.

Plato, *Cratylus* 400c

Hence the Orphic expression *sôma sêma,* "the body is a tomb." Such thoughts were widely discussed in the fifth century B.C. and lie behind modern notions of the soul trapped "in this mortal coil." Before Plato's refinement of Orphic and Pythagorean thought, the soul was the miserable and insubstantial *psychê;* after Plato, some philosophers saw the soul as a transcendent, eternal spark, more real than our bodies or this world. But these were always minority views.

## The Cult of Dionysus

The Olympians lived far away in the sky or on a mountain, while ghosts lived beneath the ground, near their human bones. **Dionysus,** by contrast, lived within the yellow sap of the vine, the spirits of red wine, fructifying white semen, and nourishing white milk. You know Dionysus when he comes, when you are a sprig sprouting from the tree of life.

In the cult of Dionysus, also called **Bacchus,** followers tore apart wild animals and ate them raw: they behaved like animals, which they had become (Figure 7.12). Intoxicated, they left the human, moral realm. Dionysus, as the life-force, was not human and had no interest in human affairs. Women were believed to be especially susceptible to his power. Abandoning responsibilities to husband and family, **Bacchae** ("the female followers of Bacchus") followed the god, wandering in bands through wild places. The Greeks called their secret ceremonies *orgia,* origin of the word "orgy." Drunkenness and sexual license awakened the god's power within.

Myths said Dionysus was snatched from the ashes of his mother Semelê's (sem-e-lē) womb, destroyed when Zeus appeared to her in his full glory. Jealous Hera had tricked Semelê into asking Zeus for this favor. Raised by nymphs, the young Dionysus wandered

**FIGURE 7.12** Dionysus in ecstasy. The god wears ivy in his hair and a leopard skin around his shoulders as he tears a deer in half. Followers of the god ate animals raw, and sometimes still alive, to imbibe the life-force; in myth they ate human infants. Attic red-figured vase, c. 450 B.C.

afar and then returned to Greece. Many rejected him and his cult of ecstatic identification with transhuman forces. They might as well have denied the tides of the sea or the hurricane, and those who denied him paid in horrible ways for their failure to understand.

The most famous myth of resistance to Dionysus is in Euripides' tragedy, the *Bacchae* (403 B.C.), in which the foolish Pentheus, king of Thebes, rejects the god, goes mad, and is torn to pieces by Bacchae as he tries to watch their rituals. In the play, the chorus celebrates the god's power:

> Who's on the street? Who?
> Let him get out of the way and go inside.
> Let his speech be pure!
> Let him speak favorable things!
> I shall sing of Dionysus according
> to eternal custom.
> Blessed is he who is favored by the god,
> knowing the divine initiation,
> who brings blessings to his life
> and sanctifies his soul,
> dancing like a raging one
> in the mountains,
> with holy purifications,
> revering the rituals
> of great Mother Cybelê,°
> stretching forth his thyrsus,°
> crowned with ivy,
> adoring Dionysus.

Euripides, *Bacchae* 68–82

°*Cybelê*: A mother goddess in Phrygia with whom Dionysus was closely associated.   °*thyrsus*: A phallic staff entwined with ivy.

Unlike the Olympians, Dionysus and the celebrant became one. Scant wonder that early Christians adopted Dionysiac imagery on tombs to celebrate the promise of renewed life offered by their own religion.

## CONCLUSION

Greek religion had much in common with other ancient polytheistic religions, like those of the Egyptians and the Mesopotamians, but differed from Jewish revealed religion, which depended on written documents held to reflect God's will directly. The Greeks wanted to persuade the Olympian gods and to satisfy with sacrifice the host of other spirits and ghosts that filled the world. We get one version of Greek religion when we read Homer or examine the Parthenon, where gods and goddesses behave as personalities, and quite another from documents like the following calendar of sacrifices, where the gods are bare names in a list, set alongside obscure spirits and powers of the local landscape:

> In Boedromion [September/October] festival of the Proerosia: for Zeus Polieus ["Zeus of the City"] a choice sheep; women acclaiming the god, a piglet bought

for holocaust sacrifice;° for the worshipper the priest will provide dinner; for Cephalus [an Athenian hero] a choice sheep; for Procris [an Athenian heroine], an offering-tray; for Thorikos [personification of a county], a choice sheep; for the Heroines of Thorikos, an offering-tray; at Sounion [near Athens] for Poseidon, a choice lamb; for Apollo, a choice goat; for Kourotrophos ["Nourisher of the Young"] a choice female piglet; for Demeter, a full-grown victim; for Zeus Herkeios ["Protector of the fence" around the house], a full-grown victim; for Kourotrophos, a piglet; at the salt-marsh for Poseidon, a full-grown victim; for Apollo, a piglet.

G. Daux, "Le Calendrier de Thorikos au Musée J.-P. Getty," *Antiquité classique* 52 (1983) 122; quoted in Zaidman/Pantel, 82

°*holocaust sacrifice:* When the entire victim was burned.

The calendar stipulates sacrifices for but a single deme (roughly a village; there were 140 in Attica) for a single month. It says nothing about where the sacrifices will take place or who will pay for them, because everyone knew. Such was the everyday reality of Greek religion.

The Greeks introduced two unusual elements to their otherwise rather conventional polytheism. The first was exuberant storytelling, outstanding for its inventiveness and continuing appeal. These myths deeply influenced the Greeks, who loved them, learned them by heart, and imitated them in art. Religion is something one does as well as believes; the Greeks prayed, then killed animals and ate them. Myths are stories; first one thing happened, then another. Because the actors in Greek stories were sometimes the recipients of religious sacrifice, Greek myth and religion intermingle in a bewitching (and exasperating) way.

The Greeks' second innovation, which we emphasize often in this book, was to separate religious from social power. The gods, heroes, spirits, and ghosts were important and (so the Greeks believed) intervened regularly in human affairs. However, no one could use special access to the supernatural to justify power in this world, as did the kings of the ancient Near East. As we shall see in the next chapter, this strange separation had serious consequences for Greek society.

## Key Terms

| | | |
|---|---|---|
| *mythos*, 121 | evolutionary religion, 126 | Poseidon, 140 |
| divine myths, 122 | revealed religion, 126 | Aphrodite, 140 |
| legends, 122 | magic, 126 | *psychê*, 140 |
| folktale, 122 | sacrifice, 129 | miasma, 144 |
| Chaos, 123 | etiological myth, 133 | Eleusinian mysteries, 145 |
| Gaea, 123 | Olympians, 133 | Demeter, 145 |
| Eros, 123 | chthonic cult, 133 | Persephonê, 145 |
| Uranus, 123 | Muses, 134 | Orphics, 145 |
| Titans, 123 | Zeus, 135 | Dionysus, 148 |
| Cronus, 124 | Hera, 136 | Bacchus, 148 |
| Furies, 125 | Athena, 138 | Bacchae, 148 |
| polytheistic, 125 | Apollo, 138 | |
| anthropomorphic, 125 | Artemis, 140 | |

# Further Reading

## RELIGION

Burkert, W., *Structure and History in Greek Mythology and Ritual* (Berkeley, 1979). Astute analysis of problems in the study of myth, with dissection of structuralist theories.

————, *Greek Religion* (German original, 1977; Oxford, 1985). The standard, one-volume history, useful for reference.

Buxton, R., *Oxford Readings on Greek Religion* (Oxford, 2001). Collection of important papers on Greek religion, mostly from the 1980s and 1990s.

Connelly, Joan, *Portrait of a Priestess: Women and Ritual in Ancient Greece* (Princeton, 2007). Valuable new study of a major topic.

Dodds, E. R., *The Greeks and the Irrational* (Berkeley, 1959). How the Greeks interpreted the irrational in their own experience. A pioneering work.

Easterling, P. E., and J. V. Muir, eds., *Greek Religion and Society* (Cambridge, UK, 1985). Chapters by leading British scholars on aspects of Greek religion.

Garland, R., *The Greek Way of Death* (Ithaca, NY, 1985). Greek attitudes and practices concerning death and the dead.

Guthrie, W. K. C., *The Greeks and Their Gods* (London, 1950). Dated but useful survey of the Olympians.

Johnston, Sarah Iles, *Restless Dead: Encounters between the Living and the Dead in Ancient Greece* (Berkeley, 1999). Superior study of ghost-cult.

Mikalson, J., *Athenian Popular Religion* (Chapel Hill, NC, 1983). How the person in the street understood religion.

Parker, R., *Athenian Religion: A History* (Oxford, 1996). Scholarly treatment of religion in our best-known city-state.

Zaidman, L. B., and P. S. Pantel, *Religion in the Ancient Greek City*, tr. P. Cartledge (Cambridge, UK, 1992). Accessible summary of the major issues.

## MYTH

Edmunds, L., ed., *Approaches to Greek Myth* (Baltimore, 1990). Useful essays on the interpretation of myth, with most schools of thought represented.

Kirk, G. S., *Myth: Its Meaning and Function in Ancient and Other Cultures* (Berkeley, 1970). Good on schools of interpretation.

Powell, B. B., *Classical Myth*, 6th ed. (Upper Saddle River, NJ, 2008). Review of all the Greek and Roman myths, with interpretation and historical background and many illustrations.

Veyne, P., *Did the Greeks Believe in Their Myths?* (French original, 1983; Chicago, 1988). Complex essay on the nature of belief.

West, M. L., *Hesiod: Theogony* (Oxford, 1966). Standard edition of the Greek text, with invaluable notes and introduction.

## ECSTATIC AND MYSTERY RELIGION

Burkert, Walter, *Ancient Mystery Cults* (Cambridge, MA, 1987). With sections on the Orphics and the Eleusinian mysteries.

Mylonas, G. E., *Eleusis and the Eleusinian Mysteries* (Princeton, 1961). Best book on the topic by the excavator of the site.

## ANCIENT TEXTS

Aeschylus, *The Oresteia*, tr. Robert Fagles (Harmondsworth, UK, 1966). Three tragedies performed at Athens in 458 B.C., including *The Libation Bearers*.

Hesiod, *Theogony*. In *Hesiod and Theognis*, tr. Dorothea Wender (Harmondsworth, UK, 1973). The basic poetic account of the origins of the gods, composed c. 700 B.C.

Sophocles, *The Theban Plays*, tr. E. F. Watling (Harmondsworth, UK, 1947). Three tragedies about the legendary royal family of Thebes, including *Oedipus the King*.

## CHAPTER 8

# Archaic Greece, 800–480 B.C.: Economy, Society, Politics

In Chapter 6, "Homer," and Chapter 7, "Religion and Myth," we discussed the twin props of early Greek culture, Homer and religion. In this chapter, we examine how the *poleis* developed between the upheavals of the eighth century B.C. and the great wars of 480 B.C., a period historians call Archaic Greece. The patterns of Greek life that we described earlier crystallized in this era: Living standards rose, equal male citizenship became the core principle of social organization, beliefs were systematized, and an intellectual revolution began. These were years of intense and sometimes violent conflict, both between *poleis*, for control of larger regions, and within *poleis*, where individuals and factions among the rich struggled for power, while the poor struggled against them. This chapter and the next provide a broad sketch of historical and intellectual developments in this age, although there were many local differences.

## GOVERNMENT BY OLIGARCHY

The Bronze Age Greeks had great kings, the *wanakes*. Weaker kings, *basileis*, replaced *wanakes* in the Dark Age. By the eighth century B.C., Homer and Hesiod took *basileis* for granted and even called them "dear to the gods," but they also thought that *basileis* had to conform to community values. On Ithaca, Odysseus and Telemachus had to show that they were stronger than the other noblemen, who might also claim the title *basileus*. The *basileus* often seems to be merely the leading man among a group of feuding chiefs. In the *polis* of the seventh century B.C., the *basileis* lost their power to **oligarchies**, meaning "rule of the few."

An oligarchy could be a handful of men or a council of hundreds. Rule by oligarchy sets Archaic *poleis* apart from Greece's neighbors in western Asia, where typical states were monarchies ("rule by one man"). Rich men in Greek *poleis* liked to call themselves **agathoi**, meaning "the good people," and to call the poor **kakoi**, "the bad people," but despite the divisive language, Greek oligarchs were in fact not greatly elevated above ordinary citizens. The balance of power between *agathoi* and *kakoi* varied through time and between one *polis* and another, but in general, poor, lowborn Greeks were more assertive than poor, lowborn Egyptians or Syrians, where state institutions and class divisions were very old and highly developed. Across the seventh and sixth centuries B.C., more and more power came into the poorer citizens' hands. Even around 700 B.C., at the beginning of the Archaic Period, the rich could face stern criticism. In Chapter 5, "The Dark Age, 1200–800 B.C.," we saw how Hesiod abused his local *basileis* when they defrauded him, calling them "eaters of bribes" and "fools." He assumed there should be social hierarchy, but he also claimed the right to judge the *basileis'* performance on the basis of a traditional morality. When they violated such laws, only ruin could follow:

> When gift-eating men pass judgments with crooked counsel,
> and Justice is dragged from the road, there is a rushing sound.
> Justice, wrapped in a mist, pursues the polis,
> weeping, and the places of the people, bringing evil
> to the humans who have driven her out and who do not live
> the straight life . . . Often the whole city suffers because
> of one evil man, who sins and meditates arrogant
> acts. Upon them the son of Cronus [Zeus] sends pain
> from heaven, starvation and disease. And the people die.
> Nor do the women bear children, but the households come
> to nothing through the designs of Olympian Zeus. At other times
> the son of Cronus will destroy their broad army or tear down
> their walls or sink their ships on the sea. O you *basileis*,
> take heed of this punishment. The deathless gods are near
> to humans and take account of those who harm
> others by crooked counsel and take no heed
> of the vengeance of the gods.
>
> Hesiod, *Works and Days* 220–24, 240–51

As the Archaic Period wore on, ordinary citizens increasingly challenged the right of any man, no matter how rich or talented, to make decisions for the entire community. For example, a poorly preserved inscription dating around 550 B.C. from the island of CHIOS (see Map 8.1) mentions a *basileus*, who clearly has significant functions, but then refers to a People's Council, which has major powers of hearing appeals and inflicting fines. The inscription says little else about this council or its tasks. But by about 525 B.C., we hear about the **dêmos**, "the people," as a whole making important decisions in several *poleis*.

The three main reasons why the archaic Greek *agathoi* had relatively little power in the face of the *kakoi* were economic, military, and ideological. Let us review each in turn.

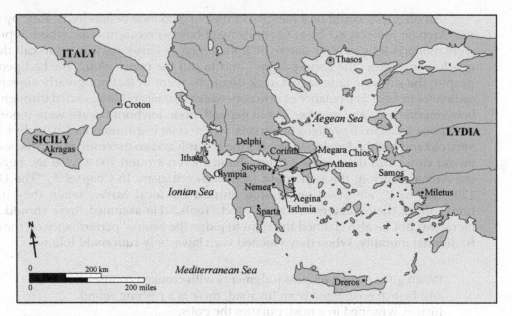

**MAP 8.1** Sites mentioned in this chapter.

## Wealth

Land and labor were the bases of wealth within Greece. If a man had plenty of land and enough workers, he could produce more agricultural goods than his family needed, then exchange the surplus for goods that the family desired but could not or would not produce themselves. Such exchanges might be over short distances, giving food to black-smiths or carpenters in return for specialized products, or might involve shipping produce across the Mediterranean in search of profitable outlets. Herodotus tells the story of a merchant blown off course by severe winds around 600 B.C. Arriving on the Atlantic coast of Spain, he found eager buyers at windfall profits for the exotic Greek goods he carried.

Of course, opportunities for amassing wealth varied according to local conditions. For example, the island of THASOS was suited for growing wine grapes. Families that planted more vines than they needed for domestic consumption could ship their surplus to places less favored for viticulture or could sell their grapes to specialist traders. By 600 B.C., large pots called amphoras ("two-handled vessels") used to ship wine and olive oil turn up far from their centers of manufacture. Most *poleis* had iron ore in their territory, but many lacked good timber or building stone. Only a lucky few, like Athens and Thasos, had silver. The need to move goods and materials offered opportunities to those who could sail ships and stomach the risks that came with trade across the high seas.

We can get a rough idea of how rich Archaic aristocrats were. At the end of the Archaic Period, in 480 B.C., an Athenian named Kleinias equipped a warship at his own expense. This meant paying to build the ship, fit out the rigging, and support 180–200 men for a campaign of three to six months. In Athenian money, this cost between five and eight silver **talents**, a very large sum (enough to feed a village of 250–400 people for a year).

Herodotus, who told the story, regarded the outlay as spectacular, but he also knew that Kleinias was not the richest man in Archaic Greece. Probably dozens of Greeks in Sicily could have outspent him. Sicily had better rainfall than Athens and more arable land. The ruling class of AKRAGAS in Sicily grew rich from selling olive oil and wine to Carthage, the great Phoenician trading colony on the north coast of Africa in what is now Tunisia. Between 550 and 450 B.C., they built the most spectacular series of temples ever raised by Greeks (Figure 8.1).

Yet the richest Sicilian Greeks remained poor by comparison, for example, with even minor nobility in the Persian Empire. Herodotus says that in the same year that Kleinias so impressed the Athenians by paying for a warship from his own pocket, the richest private individual in the Persian Empire offered to give the Persian king 18,000 silver talents—well over a million pounds of silver! The Persian king rewarded his favorites by giving them vast estates and the revenues of entire cities, dwarfing what was possible in Greece.

In Greece there were no great mansions or imposing tombs. By 600 B.C., most new houses had three or four rooms around a small courtyard. Most tombs were individual burials without elaborate markers and with just a few pots as grave goods. The only real wealth found in archaeological investigations comes from sanctuaries. However, some Greek temples were awe-inspiring (see Chapter 9, "The Archaic Cultural Revolution, 700–480 B.C."), and offerings to the gods included small amounts of gold and silver jewelry and larger amounts of bronze armor, vessels, and ornaments. Most *poleis* had one or two grand sanctuaries with stone temples that received the finest offerings and dozens of

**FIGURE 8.1** Temple ruins at Akragas in Sicily, sixth century B.C. The Akragantines built seven enormous temples along a ridge. Today, many Greek temples in Sicily are better preserved than those in the Aegean.

smaller shrines where local people dedicated pottery. The relatively narrow gap between the rich and the poor in Archaic Greece is an important reason why Greek aristocrats were weaker than in the developed societies of the East.

## War

The second reason why Archaic Greek aristocrats were relatively weak was military. The Greeks developed a peculiar way to fight, devastatingly effective in the right conditions but leaving little scope for aristocrats as heroic leaders. Tyrtaeus (tir-tē-us), a seventh-century B.C. poet from Sparta, described Greek tactics:

> Let each man take his stand, biting his lips,
> his legs set firmly apart, covering his thighs
> and legs beneath with his broad shield, and his chest
> and shoulders too. Let him brandish his powerful spear
> in his right hand, let him toss the crest of his helm
> above his head. Let him learn to fight by doing
> mighty deeds and not stand, shield in hand,
> apart from the missiles. Let him close with the enemy
> and with his long spear, or brandishing his sword, let him wound
> and take down the enemy. Placing his toe against the enemy's toe,
> and shield against shield, crest against crest, helm
> against helm, chest against chest, let him fight the enemy,
> holding tight the hilt of his sword or his long spear.

Tyrtaeus fragment 11, lines 21–34

The mainstay of Archaic Greek armies was the heavy infantryman, or **hoplite** (hop-līt, from *hoplon*, "shield"). He normally wore fifty to seventy pounds of bronze armor—greaves on his shins, a solid breastplate, an enclosed helmet with horsehair crest, and a wooden shield faced with metal—and carried a spear six to eight feet long (Figure 8.2). Infantrymen in most countries surrounding Greece, by contrast, carried small shields made of wicker or leather: Holding a single handle in the middle of such a shield, soldiers could manipulate it to parry blows but could not stop strong spear thrusts.

The hoplite's very different round shield, about three feet across, was made of hard-wood covered in bronze and could block all but the fiercest blows. It weighed about sixteen pounds, and short, poorly nourished ancient Greeks could not have held it up by a single, central handle for long. It therefore had two handles: one on the rim, gripped by the hand, and the second a broad strap in the center through which the forearm passed (Figure 8.3).

Holding the shield this way created a new problem; it covered only the left side of the fighter's body. Hoplites therefore massed shoulder-to-shoulder in a **phalanx**, a dense formation six- or eight-ranks deep, so that each hoplite shielded the right (unprotected) side of the man standing to his left. Only the man on the far right of each line remained exposed, a position of great military honor. So long as the hoplite phalanx maintained formation, it presented the enemy with an unbroken wall of bronze shields many ranks deep and a forest of deadly spear tips, an overwhelming and catastrophic force, as the Persians were to learn.

**FIGURE 8.2** Bronze statuette of a hoplite; from Corinth, ca. 500 B.C., height 8 inches.

**FIGURE 8.3** Warriors clash to the music of a flute player on a Protocorinthian wine jug, the "Chigi Vase," ca. 650 B.C. Height 4 inches. Scholars disagree about whether a hoplite phalanx is represented here, but notice the round shield with central strap and rim strap on the central figures.

To maintain formation, a phalanx had to move slowly and deliberately and tended to creep crablike to the right as each man sought to stay well protected by the shield of his neighbor. Unlike Egyptian or Persian infantry, fighters trained together regularly, but even so, the phalanx could lose order on broken ground, leaving the hoplites vulnerable to lightly armed but more maneuverable troops who would skirt their flanks. Herodotus has a Persian general make fun of hoplite warfare, saying:

> From what I hear the Hellenes are accustomed to go to war with little reflection, in wrong-headedness and folly. When they declare war against one another, they seek out the most suitable ground, where it is most level, and go there to fight. The result is that even the victors suffer heavy losses. As for the losers— they are destroyed completely.
>
> Herodotus 7.9

Hoplites almost never stormed fortifications or fought in hills but met on carefully selected flat ground, as if war were a sporting event, which to some extent it was. The two phalanxes advanced deliberately to within 200 yards of each other, raised a chant, and then waited to see if the enemy lost his nerve. Homer describes men waiting to launch an ambush from hiding, but his words probably apply just as well to the tense moments before a hoplite battle:

> The skin of the coward is constantly changing. Nor is
> the spirit in his breast stayed so that he remains
> steadfast, but he keeps changing from one knee to the other,
> and he shifts his weight from foot to foot, and his great heart
> in his chest pounds and his teeth chatter, dreading death.
>
> Homer, *Iliad* 13.279–83

If neither phalanx lost its nerve, they advanced again, now running, but still trying to keep order. They charged the last few yards, smashing head-on, the front ranks shoved forward by the mass of men behind, lunging with their spears just before the bloody collision. Most spear points would skid off the protective bronze, but some bit home over or under the wall of shields, finding exposed throats and groins. Bronze clashed on bronze. Spears shattered into splinters, or their points were driven into the enemy's heavy armor. A hoplite battle was a gigantic, deadly scrimmage. When their spears fell useless in the crush of bodies, the men at the front drew short swords and hacked away, kicking, choking, and punching. The fighters could not see or hear much inside their closed helmets. Their bodies ran with sweat as they fought for their lives, dependent on the men on either side, in front and behind, their blood rising in an orgy of killing.

There was no way to direct this kind of fighting. Only discipline, strength, and courage counted. The initial spear-thrust before the actual collision opened gaps in both front lines into which the leading hoplites pushed. If they kept their heads and their order, they could widen these breaches, pushing over the fallen bodies, deeper into the opposing mass. After a few moments or many minutes, one side would start to give way. The men in the front ranks, packed together, could not run away. Decisive panics would begin in the rear as men in the fifth or sixth rank suddenly confronted a murderous, raging enemy.

In an instant, the phalanx could dissolve into a hysterical mob as men broke from the back and fled. Any who stood their ground were bowled over by the weight of the surging and now victorious enemy. The battle was over and the slaughter began, as the Spartan poet Tyrtaeus explains:

> Those who dare to stand shoulder to shoulder and to go
> straight to the hand-to-hand against the foremost
> of the enemy, of these do fewer fall. Also
> they protect the army behind them. The fighting
> mettle of men who give into fear loses all
> value. No man could ever tell in words
> the evil things that befall a man who has behaved
> shamefully. It is a pleasant act, to spear a man
> in the back as he runs away in the heat of battle.
> It is a shameful thing to see a man lying dead
> in the dust with a wound from the point of a spear in his back.
>
> Tyrtaeus, fragment 11.11–20

In this final phase, the rear ranks of the victorious phalanx leaped past their exhausted colleagues, stabbing at exposed backs as their shattered foes threw away their heavy shields and ran for their lives. According to an old saying, a Spartan mother handed her son his shield before campaign, telling him to come back "with this, or upon it"—victorious or a corpse.

Some historians think this style of warfare evolved gradually across the ninth, eighth, and seventh centuries B.C., whereas others suggest that it emerged suddenly with the invention of hoplite armor around 650 B.C., abruptly making an older, aristocratic style of war obsolete. In any event, the new tactics depended on rising standards of living, because each hoplite bought his own expensive armor. By about 600 B.C., probably a quarter or a third of the citizens of a typical *polis* could afford their own armor. In the eighth century B.C., the few wealthy men with bronze armor had significant advantages over poorer fighters, but in the seventh and sixth centuries, they lost these advantages. In the phalanx, aristocrats and better-off smallholders fought and died side by side as a team. Archaic Greek aristocrats could not define themselves against the mass of citizens in either economic or military terms. If Greek aristocrats had been rich enough to equip an effective cavalry, they might have become an elite of military virtuosos, like Japanese samurai or medieval European knights. Or, if they had armed bands of hoplites at their own expense, they might have dominated Archaic warfare. But they could not afford it and they could not claim that the community depended on them for survival.

## Ideology

The most important reason for the relative weakness of Archaic Greek aristocrats, however, was ideological. No ruling class, no matter how rich or how necessary in war, can maintain power by coercion alone. Even totalitarian regimes prefer propaganda to compulsion because the costs of forcing everyone to do what they are told, all the time, are just too high. As we saw in Chapter 4, "The Greeks before History, 12,000–1200 B.C.," in the Bronze Age Near Eastern rulers justified their power by claiming special ties to the gods, but in Archaic

Greece such claims were not persuasive. The poet Sappho, writing around 600 B.C., imagined herself and her friends communing with the gods, sharing golden cups brimming with wine, and dining at the same glittering tables: She and other poets claimed to be equals to deities and the great kings of the East. But for every Greek poet who asserted special connections to the gods, another rejected such pretensions. Eastern luxury and divine honors were both unattainable and undesirable. In the Near East and Egypt, normally only a few religious specialists, drawn from powerful families, could perform sacrifices. In Greece, by contrast, anyone could do so. When Herodotus visited Persia, he was amazed to discover that no sacrifices could take place unless a religious professional called a Magus presided.

Economics, war, and ideology reinforced each other. Had Greek aristocrats been as rich as the rulers of Babylon, they might have convinced ordinary citizens of their close relationship with divinity, through displays of pomp and glory. Or had a warrior elite been able to slice through enemy phalanxes, they might have seemed godlike. Conversely, if an elite had controlled access to the gods, they might have been able to establish claims to more resources, and perhaps few would have dared to stand against them in battle.

Although the richest men did dominate politics during the Archaic Period, their grip was weak. Some did claim the right to rule because they were godlike, but most *agathoi* claimed merely to have superior moral qualities, moderation, and wisdom. They claimed to deserve privilege, including control of political decisions, because their talents exemplified a middle way in life. By 500 B.C., ordinary citizens in several *poleis* had rolled back even this limited elite domination of politics and moved toward male democracy, although aristocrats tried to maintain cultural forms that set them apart from the masses. In the next section, we examine the most important of these.

## ELITE CULTURE

### Drinking

The upper-class authors of the surviving literature rarely refer to public bars, but curse tablets—magical curses usually written on lead and dropped in a well or buried with a corpse—make it sound as if there was one on every corner. For example:

> I bind Callias the barman and his wife Thraitta, and the bar of the bald man, and Anthemion's bar near [the lead tablet is damaged here, and we cannot read this word . . . ] and Philo the barman. Of all these I bind their soul, their trade, their hands and feet, their bars . . . and also the barman Agathon, servant of Sosimenes . . . I bind Mania the barmaid at the spring, and the bar of Aristander of Eleusis.
>
> Cited in Davidson, *Courtesans and Fishcakes*, p. 55

All kinds of people (free and slave, male and female, rich and poor, young and old) frequented bars, though we know little about them. Patrons could buy wine in bulk to take home or in smaller measures to drink on the premises. Some bars were probably very pleasant. The one excavated building likely to have been a bar, from fourth-century B.C. Athens, was spacious and contained fragments of wine amphoras from all over Greece. Even the highbrow philosopher Plato mentions one fourth-century barman's skill.

But *agathoi* preferred private parties called symposia (sim-**pōz**-i-a, "drinking together"; singular form, **symposium**). A normal party included nine men. The host sent out invitations on wax tablets. The conventional starting time was after sunset, and the party could continue till dawn. The partygoers gathered in a room called an *andrôn* ("men's room") in a house or sometimes rented a room (often from a sanctuary). The symposiasts lay on couches placed against the walls around a central altar (a custom copied from the Near East) and ate dinner from tables set up by each couch. Then the drinking began.

The symposium had elaborate rules. The party chose a toastmaster by rolling dice. The toastmaster made two key decisions: what ratio of wine to water to use and how many cups each guest should drink. Greeks thought that drinking neat (unmixed) wine drove men mad, and given the length of a symposium and the variable quality of wines, mixing one or two parts of water to each part of wine was no doubt sensible. The rule about how many cups to drink was meant to keep all the guests roughly equally inebriated. The toastmaster then announced a libation, an offering to the gods, by pouring a small amount of wine onto the ground. Every act of drinking—even solitary drinking under a shady tree in the heat of summer, according to Hesiod—began with a libation.

There could be entertainers, including musicians, dancers, acrobats, and clowns. Cities even passed laws about what entertainers should be paid and how long their shifts should be. In intimate settings, an aristocrat could impress his friends by singing popular poetry that he had memorized. Earlier we saw examples of sexual behavior in the Greek symposium, and written sources confirm that sexual activity was common, whether between guests and prostitutes or between male drinkers and younger boys who served wine (Figure 8.4).

**FIGURE 8.4**   The symposium ("drinking party"). On an early-fifth-century B.C. Athenian vase, a naked *hetaira* entertains the male diners on a double flute. On the far right, a diner plays a game called *kottabos*. The drinker twirls a large, shallow drinking cup called a *kylix* on his forefinger, then flings the dregs of the wine (once the skin of the grape) across the room to knock down a small statuette, usually of a satyr. The diner to his left reaches for the *hetaira*, while on the far left two elderly men are deep in their cups; one holds two *kylikes*.

If the symposium lasted all night, the participants could become very drunk. According to one Athenian comic poet,

> The first cup is to health, the second to love and pleasure, the third to sleep, the fourth to violence, the fifth to uproar, the sixth to drunken revel, the seventh to black eyes, the eighth to the lawyer, the ninth to bile, and the tenth to madness and throwing chairs around.
>
> Euboulos (cited in Garland, *Daily Life*, p. 101)

Parties could end with the revelers wandering the streets, starting fights, and generally raising hell. Yet symposium culture was part of aristocratic identity, and severe stigma attached to those who did not know how to act at symposia, and to those who did not drink in symposia at all. A poet named **Theognis** (thē-**og**-nis), who probably lived in MEGARA (between Athens and Corinth) in the sixth century B.C., describes how to be a good toastmaster in a poem that was itself probably composed for the symposium:

> Don't hold someone back among us who wants to leave,
>    but don't force out the other fellow who wants
> to stay. Don't rouse the chap who has fallen into sweet sleep,
>    drunk from the wine as we dined, nor urge
> the man who's awake to take a nap. For nothing
>    is pleasant that comes from compulsion. Stand
> beside the man who wants a drink and give him one.
>    We can't have a party every night.
> As for myself, I drink in moderation, and never
>    long for soothing sleep before I
> return home. I make clear that wine is the finest beverage
>    a man can drink. I'm no teetotaler,
> but I don't drink too much either. When somebody drinks
>    more than a moderate amount, then he loses
> control over his tongue and over his thoughts. He rambles
>    like a fool, an embarrassment to his sober friends.
> He's ashamed of nothing when he is drunk. Though of good
>    sense when sober, now he's a fool.
> So because of these things, do not drink more than you ought,
>    but quietly stand up and go before you get drunk.
> Don't let your belly master you as if you were a common
>    day-laborer. And if you'd stay, then don't drink.
> You are always babbling this foolish word "Pour!" No wonder
>    you're drunk! Here's a toast to a friend . . . here's a drink
> on a bet . . . here's an offering to the gods and . . . because I have cup
>    in hand, why not? The one who wins
> a drinking bout is the one who drinks and still speaks sense.
>    You who hang around the mixing- bowl,
> try to speak sensibly, keeping yourselves from animosity.
>    Let your remarks be general, relating
> to no one particular. Then you will have a fine symposium.

Theognis 467–96

The man who could not hold his liquor in a symposium was no better than a laborer, the antithesis of the aristocrat. Theognis was terrified that lower-class behavior, the manners of the *kakoi*, was infecting the ranks of those who set themselves apart by their cultivated moderation. As Theognis saw it, the world was going wrong because the *kakoi*, men who lacked good birth, manners, and taste, were taking over. Everything was now for sale, he complained to his young boyfriend Kyrnos:

> Let me tell you, Kyrnos, because I like you, what I
>     myself, when a lad, learned from the *agathoi*.
> First: Take no honor, prize, or cash for doing
>     a base or unjust deed. Second:
> Have nothing to do with the *kakoi*, but always
>     associate with the *agathoi*.
> Drink with them, eat with them, sit with them, court them, for their
>     strength is great. From noble men
> you'll learn noble things. If you mix with the *kakoi*,
>     you'll ruin your innate nobility. Remembering this,
> stay with the *agathoi*, and you will see
>     how I gave you good advice.
>
> Theognis 27–38

A proper aristocrat conversed intelligently about politics, love, the gods, and other elevated topics and did not act like a buffoon. Theognis was eager to suggest that his rivals lacked character and dignity.

Of course, anyone could claim that when he drank at home with friends they were having a "symposium." Perhaps this is why rules proliferated, so that men like Theognis could set themselves above not only poor laborers but also hard drinkers who lacked moderation. In the fifth and fourth centuries B.C., Athenians often suspected that symposia were hotbeds of aristocratic plotting against democracy—and with good reason.

## Athletics

Another principal way some Archaic Greeks tried to set themselves above others was through athletics. Many societies have some kind of sports, but Archaic Greeks developed them in unusual ways. Watching athletics was entertaining and taking part was exhilarating, but Archaic Greek athletics also had important social functions. They defined who the Greeks were to themselves. Only Greeks could enter the greatest athletic competition, the games held at **Olympia** every fourth year. Hence the judges were forced to make decisions about what it meant to be "Greek." Athletics also defined a class of special Greek men. Only those with wealth and leisure could spend enough time in training to stand a chance in the top games. Finally, athletics created a hierarchy within this class of gifted athletes: Only a few could win.

Athletics were important in Homer's vision of the heroic age, but in Homer athletic activity was informal. The funeral of the hero Patroclus in the *Iliad* has events of boxing; wrestling; archery; javelin-throwing; and foot, horse, and chariot races so contentious that the competitors almost come to blows. On his long journey home from Troy, Odysseus is entertained after dinner on the island of Phaeacia with similar games, and when he declines to take part, one of the locals insults him, saying he is not of the proper social class. When Odysseus finally reaches home, he is pressed into an impromptu boxing match while disguised as a beggar.

Archaic aristocrats formalized the rules of athletics. A fourth-century B.C. scholar calculated that proper competitions began at Olympia in 776 B.C., a date that came to be widely used as a fixed point from which other events could be dated. At first, competitors came from near Olympia, but by 600 B.C., there were entrants from all over Greece. During the games, a sacred truce suspended all warfare. The Greeks took this custom so seriously that in 480 B.C., as a Persian army pushed its way into central Greece, several *poleis* refused to fight until the Olympic truce was over. In the sixth century B.C., other **panhellenic** ("all-Greek") **games** sprang up at DELPHI (where Apollo had his shrine), ISTHMIA (near Corinth), and NEMEA (near the ruins of Bronze Age Mycenae), making a circuit, with at least one major festival every summer. Most cities had their own official games, and there were huge numbers of informal competitions.

Any Greek man could enter an athletic contest, and there were even a few events for unmarried girls (although women were not allowed near the Olympic games). We do not know what proportion of Archaic Greeks trained for athletics, but **gymnasia** ("naked places," so called because Greek men exercised naked) were common, and standards were very high. The story of Arrachion (told by one Philostratus, who lived in the third century A.D.), who won the *pankration* ("all-in wrestling") at Olympia in 564 B.C., illustrates how far competitors would go (Figure 8.5). The only rules in the *pankration* were no biting and no gouging of the eyes (Spartans thought these rules too restrictive and allowed everything except strangulation). The story runs that Arrachion's opponent caught him in a brutal hold, wrapping his legs around Arrachion's waist and crushing him while

**FIGURE 8.5** Two naked athletes fight the *pankration* from a red-figured Athenian pot, ca. 450 B.C.

choking him with his hands. Arrachion started losing consciousness but managed to grab one of his opponent's toes. He wrenched the toe out of its socket and twisted it around. Arrachion was suffocating, but the agony of a dislocated toe proved too much for the opponent, who raised his hand in submission. The judges rushed over to award Arrachion the victory, only to find that he had died in his moment of triumph. The spectators were astonished at his bravery and determination. He became a folk hero, honored by paintings and statues still on display a thousand years later.

Another sixth-century athlete, Milo from CROTON in Italy, won the olive crown for wrestling six times at Olympia, six times at Delphi, ten times at Isthmia, and nine times at Nemea. Milo was famous for eating vast quantities of meat. According to Pausanias, a Roman tourist of the second century A.D. who saw Milo's statue at Olympia 700 years after his death, Milo could snap a cord tied round his head simply by holding his breath to make the veins on his head bulge. And no man was strong enough even to bend back Milo's little finger.

Arrachion and Milo were exceptional, but they had many rivals. Serious athletes spent hours every day at the gymnasium with professional coaches, and even ordinary men dropped in regularly. The fascination with athletics turned gymnasia into social centers where older men talked in the shade and philosophers wrangled. A cult of the male body developed around these naked exercises, reflected in the common representation of males in art as being nude, even while performing everyday activities. Not surprisingly, pederasty was closely linked to athletic training:

Happy the lover who works out at the gym, then goes
home to sleep all day with a beautiful boy.

Theognis lines 1,335–6

According to legend, athletes competed naked (an alarming prospect for wrestlers and pankratists) because a man once lost an Olympic footrace when his loincloth fell off and he tripped. Whatever the truth, nakedness allowed men to assess each other's bodies, and many Greeks, though short and unhealthy by our standards, were in peak physical condition. Some people's admiration went to extraordinary lengths. After training, athletes rubbed themselves down with olive oil, then scraped off the mixture of oil, sweat, and dirt. Some believed that this residue contained the athlete's inner strength. Some even ate it, to share this almost godlike power. Women adored athletic victors, as the early-fifth-century B.C. poet **Pindar** (ca. 522–438 B.C.) reports about one Telesicrates, winner of the race in armor at Delphi in 474 B.C.:

For often at the seasonal festival of Pallas°
the maidens have watched you in silence
as you won at the games,
and each wished that you could be her husband,
or a dear son, O Telesicrates—
or they watched in the games at Olympia,
or the games of deep-bosomed Earth,°
even in all the games of your country.

Pindar, *Pythian Ode* 9.97–103

°*Pallas*: At Athens, at the Panathenaic games.   °*deep-bosomed Earth*: At Delphi, where Earth was said to have been worshiped before Apollo came.

*Poleis* voted public honors for athletic champions, including free meals, pensions, and statues. The oracle at Delphi even ordered that some athletes should receive cult honors as *heroes* after their deaths. By 500 B.C., professional poets, including Pindar, specialized in victory hymns, charging enormous sums to immortalize athletes' fame. These victory odes tell us a lot about the values aristocrats linked to athletic prowess. The odes were publicly performed to music, with large choruses dancing intricate steps, and enjoyed by popular audiences. In one ode, Pindar contrasts the winner of the wrestling contest at Delphi to his defeated rivals:

> Now four times you have come down from above
> on bodies beneath you, wishing them ill,
> to whom no similar glad homecoming was adjudged
> in the Pythian games,° nor does sweet laughter
> surround them as they meet their mothers,
> raising delight. Instead they cower
> in the back streets away from their enemies,
> bitten by disaster.

Pindar, *Pythian Ode* 8.81–87

°*Pythian games*: The games at Delphi.

Pindar and other professional ode-writers offered a service to those who could afford it. They celebrated the great athletes' claims to godlike qualities, but they also recognized that these claims aroused hostility and suspicion, and explained to audiences that the entire city could take pride in its aristocrats' athletic triumphs. Victors were among the most famous men of their age. Their glory often earned them a special voice in the city, although they could face criticism for arrogance.

## Intermarriage

The Archaic elite also tried to mark itself off through selective breeding. Theognis was horrified that the *agathoi*, the elite of culture and taste (he and his friends), was being degraded by the boorish behavior of the *kakoi* and that money now mattered more than a good bloodline:

> We want a good ass, and well bred horses, O Kyrnos,
>     for quality is in the breeding. But when
> a man of good birth goes out to marry, he'll pick
>     a girl from the *kakoi*, if she's
> got a lot of money. Nor will a well-born girl
>     turn down a kakos, if she wants riches
> rather than to marry an *agathos*. Money rules all!
>     Nobles marry *kakoi* and *kakoi*
> marry the *agathoi*. Money has ruined the race.

Theognis 183–90

Aristocrats throughout the ages have tried to restrict marriage to those they think meet their own standards of breeding, and the following passage from Herodotus, set in the 560s B.C., shows how expectations about refinement, athletic prowess, bloodlines, and marriage flowed together:

> Cleisthenes [klī-sthen-ē-z],° the son of Aristonymos, grandson of Myron and great-grandson of Andreas, had a daughter whose name was Agaristê [ag-a-ris-tē]. He wished to search out the noblest of the Hellenes to marry her to. When he won the four-horse race at the Olympic games, Cleisthenes announced that whoever of the Hellenes thought himself worthy to be his son-in-law should appear on the sixtieth day or earlier at SICYON (see Map 8.2), because he wished to marry his daughter within one year of the sixtieth day. And so all the Hellenes who thought highly of themselves and of their lineage gathered there as suitors. Cleisthenes had made a race-track and a wrestling-ring expressly for this purpose.
>
> From Sybaris in Italy came Smindyrides, the son of Hippocrates, the softest and most delicate man in all Sybaris at this time, and from Siris, also in Italy, came the son of Damasos, son of the Amyris nicknamed the wise. These men came from Italy. Then there was Amphimnestos, son of Epistrophos, from Epidamnus on the Ionian Gulf. From Aetolia came Males, brother of Titormos, the strongest man in Greece, who had gone to live in the remotest part of Aetolia to escape other human beings. From the Peloponnesus came Leokedes, son of Pheidon the tyrant of Argos . . . Next was Amiantos, the son of Lycurgus, from Trapezos in Arcadia, and Laphanes, an Azanian from the city of Paios, son of the Euphorion who entertained Castor and Pollux under his own roof, as the story goes in Arcadia, and ever thereafter was host to anyone who came to his

°*Cleisthenes:* Sole ruler, or tyrant, of the small *polis* of Sicyon near Corinth.

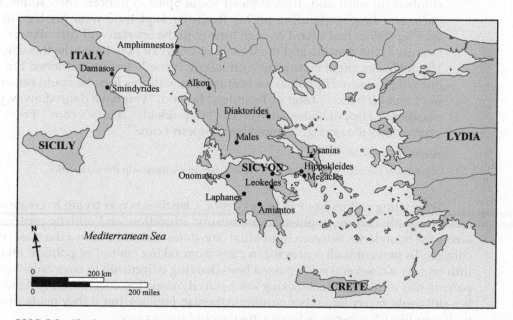

**MAP 8.2**   The intercity aristocracy: origins of the suitors for Agaristê's hand.

house. From Elis came Onomastos, son of Agaios. From Athens came Megacles, son of the Alcmeon who visited Croesus, and another man, Hippokleides, son of Tisander, richest and most handsome of all the Athenians. From Eretria, at this time at the height of its prosperity, came Lysanias. He was the only man to come from Eretria. From Krannon in Thessaly came Diaktorides, one of the Skopadai. From the Molossians came Alkon.

Those were the suitors who came. Arriving at the appointed day, Cleisthenes first asked them about their parentage and their clan; then, keeping them there a full year, he attempted to discover their worth as men, their character and education and disposition, going to each one individually but also speaking to them altogether. Those who were young he would take to the gymnasium, but the most important thing was how they acted at table. For the whole time they were there, he acted in this manner and he entertained them magnificently.

For some reason the two candidates from Athens impressed him the most, and of these Hippokleides, son of Tisander, not only because of his manly qualities but because some generations back he was related to the Cypselids of Corinth.°

Finally the day came that was set for deciding about the marriage, and Cleisthenes was obliged to make his choice. Sacrificing a hundred oxen, he feasted both the suitors and all the citizens of Sicyon. After they had eaten, the suitors entered in a singing-contest and in public speaking. Hippokleides surpassed the others in these events, and as the drink flowed he asked the flute player to play him a tune, and when he did so Hippokleides danced. Whereas perhaps in his own eyes he danced very well, Cleisthenes, looking on, now began to have doubts about the whole business. After a short pause Hippokleides asked that a table be brought in. When the table came in, he climbed up on it and, first, danced some Spartan dances, then some Attic ones, and finally, standing on his head, he kept time with his legs in the air. Cleisthenes had a hard enough time with the Spartan and Attic dances, and because of the dancing and the shameless behavior now hated the thought that Hippokleides might become his son-in-law. Nonetheless he restrained himself, but when he saw Hippokleides beating time with his legs, he could no longer hold himself back. "O son of Tisander," he said, "you have danced away your marriage." Hippokleides answered, "Hippokleides doesn't care!" From this event comes the saying, "Hippokleides doesn't care!"

Herodotus 6.126–30

°*Cypselids of Corinth:* Another family of tyrants, whom we discuss in the next section.

By inviting suitors from all over Greece, Cleisthenes was trying to create an aristocracy of wealth, culture, sophistication, beauty, education, and athletic prowess that cut across the boundaries between individual city-states and stood above the mass of ordinary citizens. To prevent such a noncitizen class from taking control of political affairs, in the fifth century B.C. several *poleis* passed laws denying citizenship to boys only one of whose parents was a citizen, thus blocking inter-*polis* dynastic loyalties. Wealthy Athenian families still could marry into other wealthy Athenian families, but if they made marriage ties with men like Cleisthenes of Sicyon, they would pay a price.

Symposia, athletics, and intermarriage did open gaps between aristocrats and the nonaristocrats, but these gaps were narrow, far weaker than the immense chasm between rulers and ruled in the Near East.

## THE TYRANTS

Aristocrats channeled much of their rivalry into athletics, but such activities were always sideshows compared to the real struggle for political power. We described in Chapter 5 how increasing competition between communities in the eighth century B.C. encouraged ever-better organization and the creation of centralized institutions, and as the city-state increased in power, the benefits from controlling public offices increased.

The story of Agamemnon and Achilles in the *Iliad* suggests that from early on Greeks were aware of how damaging feuds between aristocrats could be. Some of the oldest surviving public inscriptions deal with preventing the pursuit of power from descending into violent conflict. A difficult inscription from Dreros on Crete, our very earliest Greek legal document, dating between 650 and 600 B.C., gives the following rules:

> May the gods be kind. This has been decided by the *polis*: When a man has been *kosmos*, for ten years that same man shall not be *kosmos*. If he should become *kosmos*, whatever judgments he gives, he himself shall owe double, and he shall be useless as long as he lives, and what he does as *kosmos* shall be nothing. The swearers to this shall be the *kosmos*, the *dêmioi*, and the Twenty of the City.

> R. Meiggs and D. Lewis, *Greek Historical Inscriptions* (Oxford 1969), no. 2.

The *kosmos* seems to be the top official in seventh-century B.C. Dreros, and other officials—the *dêmioi*, "men of the people," and the Twenty of the City—agree to restrict everyone to a single term as *kosmos* each decade. The agreement is the kind of law we ourselves are familiar with. It commits people to agreed limits. If one prominent man tries to hold on to power, the others will not cooperate. So long as everyone plays by the rules, no one can seize power. Most early Greek laws take this form, being more about procedure than substance.

Most aristocrats did play by the rules, but a few were ruthless enough and strong enough to ignore what others thought. Setting themselves up as sole rulers, scorning agreements, these strong men were called *tyrannoi* (singular, *tyrannos*), from which the word **"tyrant"** derives.

One way to become a tyrant, in a world largely lacking standing armies or police, was to gather an armed force and bully other aristocrats into cooperating. It helped to have popular support, so aspiring tyrants often claimed to be defending the interests of ordinary citizens against other aristocrats. Such a situation led to *stasis*, the Greek word for "civil discord." Theognis, as always, sees the matter through the eyes of the old aristocracy:

> The *agathoi* have never ruined a polis, O Kyrnos, but when
>  the *kakoi* resort to violence, and they ruin the *dêmos*,
> and give judgments in favor of the unjust to earn bribes and gain power,
>  know that the polis will soon be shaken, even though

now it's in peace. When the *kakoi* undertake such crimes,
    then public evils follow. From this
comes *stasis*, and bloody civil war, and rule by tyrants.
    May such never befall our polis!

Theognis 43–52

Ruthless men found ingenious ways to raise armed forces. Several faked attacks on themselves and so persuaded their colleagues to authorize bodyguards, who then staged a coup. Others hired mercenaries. In one story, the aristocratic council running Akragas wanted to build a new temple. Following standard procedure, it raised funds and then offered them to whoever would build the temple to its specifications for the lowest cost. The winner of the auction took Akragas' money, used it to hire mercenaries, and seized the city. Yet another method was to marry into the family of a tyrant who ruled another *polis* and then get him to back a coup.

Thucydides tells of a failed coup in Athens in 632 B.C.:

In former times there was an Athenian named Cylon [kī-lon], an Olympian victor, of good birth and himself an able man. He married the daughter of Theagenes from Megara, at that time tyrant of Megara. When Cylon inquired of the Delphic oracle, the oracle told him to seize the Acropolis during the "greatest festival of Zeus." Getting some troops from Theagenes and enlisting his own friends, when the time came for the Olympic games Cylon seized the Acropolis with the intention of becoming tyrant. He thought that the games must be the "greatest festival of Zeus," and that the fact that he had won at those games would be to his advantage. But whether the oracle meant a festival of Zeus in Attica or someplace else as being "the greatest," Cylon did not know and the oracle did not say . . . When the Athenians heard what had happened, they all came in force from the countryside to resist Cylon's plans, and they besieged them on the Acropolis . . . Those besieged with Cylon suffered terribly from hunger and thirst. Cylon and his brother escaped, but the others, being in dire straits and some even dying of hunger, sat down as suppliants before the altar on the Acropolis. Those set to guard over them, when they saw they were dying, persuaded them to leave their position before the altar on the condition that no harm would come to them. Then they took them out and put them to death.

Thucydides 1.126

Yet even if Cylon had succeeded, his problems would only have been beginning. It was one thing to gather an armed gang and proclaim oneself sole ruler (no one ever called himself "tyrant," a term of abuse); it was another to maintain this position. Herodotus tells how Periander, tyrant of Corinth, sent an ambassador to Thrasyboulos, tyrant of Miletus, asking him how to maintain power:

Thrasyboulos led the ambassador from Periander out of the city. They entered a field of wheat and all the while that Thrasyboulos questioned the ambassador why he had come from Corinth, he cut off the tops of the tallest ears of wheat and threw the cut pieces away. He kept this up until he had destroyed the best and heaviest of the crop of wheat. In this way he went through the field, then sent the messenger away without a word. When he got back to Corinth, Periander was eager to learn what Thrasyboulos had said. "Nothing, and I am amazed that you would send me to a man obviously crazed and destructive of his own property—" and he described what Thrasyboulos had done. Periander at once understood that Thrasyboulos was directing him to destroy all those in the city who were in some way outstanding, and from this moment his behavior toward his citizens became harsh.

Herodotus 5.92

Alternatively, instead of killing the top men, tyrants could cut deals with them by giving them government offices and sharing control of the state. Whatever course they chose, though, tyrants needed a delicate mixture of diplomacy and brutality, and most tyrannies fell after one or two generations. The men who founded them were ruthless, bold, and talented, but few of their sons and grandsons were so skillful. Power went to their heads. Our sources emphasize sexual scandals: Tyrants forced themselves on the wives, daughters, and sons of prominent men, who formed alliances against them and sooner or later expelled or destroyed them.

Thucydides summed up the impact of tyranny on Greece:

All the tyrants who ruled in Greek *poleis* looked only to their own interests, wishing only to protect themselves and to increase the wealth of their households. For this reason they governed their *poleis* always with an eye to maximum security. Hence they never accomplished anything important, and they never went beyond local interests. The tyrants in Sicily, however, did rise to great power.

Thucydides 1.17

After 500 B.C., tyranny largely disappeared from Aegean Greece. Sparta opposed tyrants on principle, sometimes sending armies to help dissidents overthrow them. Feuding aristocrats learned to handle disputes without creating opportunities for someone to seize power. Athens even created an institution called **ostracism**, a kind of annual unpopularity contest in which the citizens exiled for ten years any man who looked like he might make himself tyrant (see Chapter 10, "A Tale of Two Archaic Cities: Sparta and Athens, 700–480 B.C.").

Thucydides singles out Sicily as the exception to his rule that tyrants performed no great deeds. Tyrants appeared in Sicily around 580 B.C. and were most common between about 490 and 465 B.C., just as they were disappearing in the Aegean. They returned in force around 400 B.C. We have noted several times in this chapter that the Sicilian *poleis* had many economic and sociological differences from the Aegean world, and we have more to say about Sicilian tyrants in later chapters.

## THE STRUCTURE OF ARCHAIC STATES

If Archaic Greek aristocrats were relatively weak as a social class, so too were the institutions of the states they controlled. We are used to states with huge bureaucracies that control unimaginable finances. Modern governments have agencies to oversee employment, welfare, education, the arts, transportation, and so on and are usually one of the biggest employers in a country. Before the twentieth century A.D., however, states had far fewer offices and concentrated on a handful of tasks. Oligarchs and tyrants took responsibility only for war and religion and for finding the money to pay for them.

## Defending the State

If an enemy threatened the *polis*, officials called up the army. This meant sending out word that the hoplites should assemble on a certain day. In the fifth century B.C., the state might pay for food and hired men to carry the soldiers' armor, but probably did not do so in Archaic times. Normally, a war was settled by a single battle. Campaigns were usually fought in the summer, the agricultural off-season, and were over in a week or two. Both sides needed to settle the matter and get home before the autumn planting. Costs were minimal. Armies lived off the land, and the side that won often made a profit. At the very least, the winners could sell bronze armor taken from the enemy who died in the battle. If they captured any towns, there would be loot.

Because all soldiers were amateurs, there were no peacetime standing armies and no need for states to borrow money or drain their treasuries to pay for long campaigns. Navies were tiny before the 480s B.C. The biggest state expense was fortifications, but even these were simple, and many cities had none. War was cheap for the state. Hoplites had to give up their time to train to keep order in the madness of battle, but the individual citizens bore the cost.

## Religion

Religion could be more expensive than war. Before about 750 B.C., Greeks did not build temples or give the gods elaborate gifts. In the eighth and seventh centuries B.C., by contrast, hundreds of temples were built and millions of objects dedicated, but private individuals again bore most costs. State officials were involved mainly in building very large temples and putting on communal festivals. By 700 B.C., some communities had one or more of the temples called *hekatompeda*, "hundred-footers," as focuses for worshiping a patron divinity. In the seventh century B.C., rich states started building these from stone, with tiled roofs, and in the sixth century, lavish sculpture became common. Tyrants particularly liked advertising their power by building temples, and some Sicilian cities built great avenues of temples.

A big stone temple cost far more than a hoplite war, but the expense could be spread out over long periods. The construction of the enormous temple of Olympian Zeus at Athens (Figure 24.12 in Chapter 24, "The Coming of Rome, 220–30 B.C.") was begun around 530 B.C., but only finished 650 years later, by a Roman emperor! Temple-building was correlated with successful wars, with plunder covering many of the costs.

Festivals could also be expensive. We know little about everyday Archaic religion, but in Classical times groups of local worthies administered village festivals, raising money for sacrificing animals, chiefly goats and sheep. Many citizens ate beef only when the state put funds into a larger festival. The state recouped some costs by selling the animals' hides to leather tanners, but a good calendar of state festivals would cost more each year than warfare.

## Welfare and Infrastructure

Two obvious categories of modern state spending that were largely missing in Archaic Greece are welfare and spending for infrastructure like roads and bridges—things that make society function smoothly. Families took care of their sick and elderly and educated their young. If you had no family, you had no chance in life but would die young or become a wandering beggar. The closest thing to state intervention in employment was the redistribution of land and the loans that some tyrants made to farmers, driven by fear that landless men were potential revolutionaries. Poor citizens constantly demanded redistribution of land and sometimes states obliged. Some of the tyrants' public building projects created jobs for the unemployed men who had drifted into the cities from bankrupt farms, and getting rid of such potential troublemakers was one purpose of overseas colonies.

Although the state generally took little interest in infrastructure, around 600 B.C. Corinth's tyrant built a stone dragway across the four miles of the Isthmus of Corinth so that ships could avoid sailing hundreds of miles around the Peloponnesus (and so that Corinth could tax traders using the road). Around 530 B.C., an engineer named Eupalinos dug a mile-long tunnel, eight feet wide and eight feet high, through a mountain to bring fresh water into the town of SAMOS (see Map 8.1), and by 500 B.C. simple clay pipes did the same thing for several cities. But such projects were exceptions. The roads in Greece were bad, and only few cities (Corinth and Samos among them) invested in good harbors.

The one way in which Greek states did intervene energetically in economic behavior was by minting coins (Figure 8.6). Just before 600 B.C., the non-Greek kingdom of Lydia in Asia Minor began issuing uniform pieces of electrum (a naturally occurring mixture of gold and silver) stamped with a symbol to guarantee their weight, and between 600 and 570 B.C. various Greek *poleis* followed suit. The earliest Greek coins were for such large denominations that they could hardly have had much financial use, and some historians suggest that they were made to advertise state authority or perhaps to simplify state pay to mercenary soldiers for long periods of service. Such motivations seem as much political as economic, but well before 500 B.C. the economic advantages of having tokens with guaranteed metal content had become obvious, and Greek cities were issuing small copper and bronze coins for everyday use.

**FIGURE 8.6** Two sides of a coin from the island of Aegina in the bay off Athens, ca. 560 B.C. These coins were known as "turtles" from the design shown on the left. On the right is a deep punch mark, perhaps to show that the coin was made of the same metal all the way through.

## Finance

In 2008, federal government outlays in the United States were almost one-third of the gross domestic product. In Britain, the figure was 40 percent; in Sweden, 59 percent. We have no figures from Archaic Greece, but government spending probably never exceeded 1 or 2 percent of the gross domestic product. The state got nearly all its money from publicly owned property, indirect taxes (i.e., harbor dues, customs and excise, market fees, as distinct from direct taxes on land or income), and "gifts." Condemned criminals often forfeited their property to the community, and such revenues met many military and religious expenses. Minerals normally belonged to the community, and some of the profits of mining went to the public treasury. Further, a tithe (10 percent) of plunder from wars was given to the gods and could be used to defray religious costs.

Much revenue came from imports and exports, with traders paying fees to use harbors and markets. In maritime cities like Corinth, such taxes probably brought in the bulk of state income. Inland communities did less well, but people always needed to exchange things and could be made to pay for the protection that states gave to commerce. When there was a crisis, the richer citizens might be asked to contribute a percentage of their wealth to the community to pay for war or to finish a temple. Some burdens, like paying for parts of festivals, might be farmed out to rich citizens, who could win public respect by funding them. The rich needed a stable state and the gods' goodwill, so they were often willing to pay.

In the last 50 years, modern Western states have typically collected 33 to 50 percent of their tax revenue from income taxes. Archaic *poleis*, by contrast, brought in nothing from this source—or from inheritance taxes, land taxes, or poll taxes. A few tyrants imposed such direct taxes, but they were bitterly resisted as invasions of the citizens' freedom, tantamount to slavery. Indirect taxes encourage smuggling, but they met the *poleis'* modest financial needs better than direct taxes because they only required a small bureaucracy. Direct taxes were difficult to assess and collect. In following this path, *poleis* were like many pre-twentieth-century states.

## CONCLUSION

In some ways, Archaic Greece was much like other ancient societies: Its economic base was agricultural, it was hierarchical, gender distinctions were strong, and it was polytheistic. But in other important ways it was unusual, or even unique. The structures of hierarchy were weak. There were few kings or powerful priesthoods. There was no scribal class serving the interests of the state. The ruling aristocrats held power because they controlled political institutions, not because of great wealth, military supremacy, kinship with the gods, or a monopoly on literacy. A distinctive civilization was emerging.

---

## Key Terms

oligarchy, *150*
agathoi, *151*
kakoi, *151*
dêmos, *151*
talents, *152*
hoplite, *154*

phalanx, *154*
symposium, *159*
andrôn, *159*
Theognis, *160*
Olympia, *161*
Panhellenic games, *162*

gymnasia, *162*
pankration, *162*
Pindar, *163*
tyrant, *167*
ostracism, *169*

## Further Reading

Davidson, James, *Courtesans and Fishcakes: The Consuming Passions of Classical Athens* (New York, 1997). Lively study of popular culture.

Fisher, Nick, and Hans van Wees, eds., *Archaic Greece* (London, 1998). Collection of essays on every aspect of archaic Greece.

Forrest, W. G., *The Emergence of Greek Democracy* (London, 1966). Now somewhat dated, but still one of the most readable accounts of archaic Greece.

Garland, Robert, *Daily Life of the Ancient Greeks* (New York, 1998). The best review of the topic.

Hall, Jonathan, *A History of the Archaic Greek World ca. 1200-479 BCE.* (Malden, MA, 2007). Good introductory account of the period.

Hanson, Victor, *The Western Way of War* (New York, 1989). Superb treatment of hoplite warfare from the soldier's point of view. A classic.

McGlew, James, *Tyranny and Political Culture in Ancient Greece* (Ithaca, NY, 1993). A study of how archaic tyrants presented themselves.

Miller, Stephen, *Arete: Greek Sports from Ancient Sources* (Berkeley, 1991). Useful collection of ancient texts about athletics.

Murray, Oswyn, *Early Greece*, 2nd ed. (Stanford, 1993). Thorough overview of Archaic Greek civilization.

————, ed., *Sympotica* (Oxford, 1990). Collection of essays about every aspect of the symposium.

Osborne, Robin, *Greece in the Making* (London, 1996). A general survey of archaic Greece. Strong on archaeological evidence.

Pleket, Harry, and Moses Finley, *The Olympic Games: The First Thousand Years* (London, 1976). Well-illustrated introduction to ancient Greek athletics from the perspective of the greatest festival.

Raaflaub, Kurt, and Hans van Wees, eds., *The Blackwell Companion to Archaic Greece* (Oxford, 2009). Up-to-date essays by leading experts on all aspects of Archaic Greek history.

Snodgrass, Anthony, *Archaic Greece* (Berkeley, 1981). Outstanding essay on the development of Greek society, focusing on archaeological evidence.

van Wees, Hans, *Greek Warfare* (London, 2004). Excellent overview.

### ANCIENT TEXTS

The Poems of Theognis. In *Hesiod and Theognis*, tr. Dorothea Wender (Harmondsworth, UK, 1973). Critical view of sixth-century B.C. society, full of information on the symposium.

Pindar, *The Odes*, tr. Maurice Bowra (Harmondsworth, UK, 1969). Readable translations of these famously difficult poems, written ca. 500–460 B.C., praising athletic victors.

Herodotus, *The Histories*, rev. ed., tr. Aubrey de Selincourt (Harmondsworth, UK, 1996). Written around 420 B.C., but full of stories about Archaic Greece.

## CHAPTER 9

# The Archaic Cultural Revolution, 800–480 B.C.

The Archaic *poleis* were small, open societies. Their weak oligarchs never established good claims to religious authority; ordinary people could, and did, criticize them. Debate was tolerated. In most *poleis*, aristocrats made political decisions through discussion in councils, and during the sixth century B.C. these councils expanded to include more citizens.

The Archaic *poleis* were open in another sense: Some of their members traveled far and wide, bringing home new ideas from overseas. In the sixth century B.C., something remarkable came from the combination of these forms of openness. For centuries, learned men in EGYPT and BABYLON (Map 9.1) had thought about the world, compiled data, and developed analytical techniques. Sometime before 3000 B.C., someone in Egypt, needing to predict the annual floods of the Nile, established a 365-day calendar, today only slightly improved. In the second millennium B.C., Babylonian thinkers created a base-60 numerical system that we still use in the minutes of an hour and the degrees of a compass. Superior decimal systems emerged in first-millennium-B.C. Mesopotamia, although 2,000 years passed before Arabs imported from India the crucial concept of zero and standardized the simple symbols 1, 2, and 3 that the whole world now uses. Using their base-60 system, the Mesopotamians developed algebra, solved quadratic equations, and drew up logarithmic tables. By 1600 B.C., they had recorded observations on the movements of the planet Venus in mathematical language. Before 500 B.C., they had systematically applied mathematical theory to observing the stars. Both Egyptians and Babylonians developed geometry to high levels, calculating the areas and volumes of different shapes and surveying field boundaries accurately. The famous Egyptian pyramids are eloquent testimony to their ability to translate mathematical calculations accurately into material realities. Rulers of the Assyrian Empire were patrons of learning and compiled collections of Babylonian scholarship, but when their empire collapsed in 612 B.C., Babylonian scholars scattered far and wide. Some of them, apparently, came to the eastern shores of the Aegean Sea.

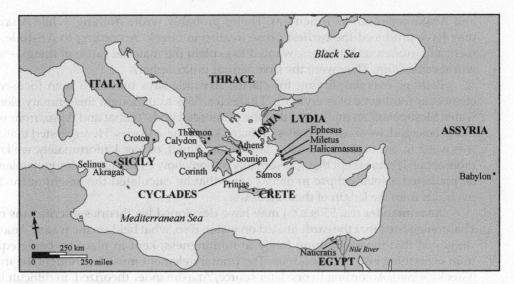

**MAP 9.1**  Locations mentioned in this chapter.

## NATURAL PHILOSOPHY IN MILETUS

Early in the first millennium B.C., Greeks had settled in what is now western Turkey, emigrating through Athens (according to a common story) to escape the problems of Dark Age mainland Greece. These Greeks, who claimed to be descendants of a man named Ion, called the area they settled IONIA. Along this coast, and above all in MILETUS (mī-lē-tus), ancient Mesopotamian learning and new Greek institutions fused in the sixth century B.C. in what we now call the **Ionian Enlightenment**. Scholars use the word "enlightenment" deliberately to evoke comparison with the European Enlightenment of the eighteenth century A.D., which saw enormous advances in scientific thought, the substitution of naturalistic explanations for religious ones, and the application of rational, scientific criticism to all spheres of life. In Miletus, such principles were articulated for the first time.

Milesian thinkers responded to Mesopotamian learning in three important ways. First, they asked different questions, not so much about *how* things worked, but *why*. It was interesting to know how planets moved around the skies, but *why* did they do so? Second, rather than adding to Babylonian wisdom, they removed something: the gods. It was not good enough to say, "The planets move like this because the gods want them to." The Milesians first articulated the theory that "natural causes," independent of the will of this or that god, govern events in nature: Science depends on this theory. Third, they systematized knowledge. Traditional thought had compartmentalized the world. The royal scholars of Assyria, split up into separate offices within the bureaucracy, could hold incompatible theories; but in a small city like Miletus, where the town's old men gathered to talk every day in the main square (*agora*), theories that explained one part of the natural world needed to be consistent with those that explained another.

Little survives of the writings of the Milesian thinkers, and we rely mostly on what later Greek scholars, particularly Aristotle (384–322 B.C.), said about them. Aristotle tells us that there were three major thinkers: Thales (**thā-lē**z), Anaximander (an-ax-i-**man**-der), and Anaximenes (an-ax-**i**-men-ēz). Thales probably wrote nothing, while Anaximander may have produced the earliest prose treatise in Greek. According to Aristotle, all three men, and numerous followers, wanted to explain the material cause of things—where the world came from. They were the first natural philosophers.

Perhaps oversimplifying for clarity, Aristotle says that each man focused on one element as the source of everything. **Thales** (ca. 580s B.C.) thought this primary element was water. Mesopotamian myth held that the primordial gods Tiamat and Apsu, from whom the world emerged, were water. Thales probably knew these stories. He suggested that all matter was water in one of three different states: solid, liquid, or gas. Unfortunately, we know little more about Thales except that (presumably by somehow drawing on Mesopotamian records) he predicted a solar eclipse in 585 B.C. and that he calculated the height of the Egyptian pyramids from the length of their shadows.

**Anaximander** (ca. 550s B.C.) may have developed his theories as criticisms of Thales. Thales suggested that the earth floated on water; if so, what held up the water? Anaximander suggested that the earth hung freely in nothingness, kept in place by being equidistant from everything else in the cosmos. The primary element must, he thought, be the Infinite (Greek *apeiron*). According to one later source, Anaximander theorized, in difficult language, how matter was created from the Infinite:

> He [Anaximander] says that that which is productive from the Infinite (*apeiron*) of hot and cold was separated off at the coming-to-be of this world, and that a kind of sphere of flame from this [the "hot"] was formed around the air surrounding the earth [the "cold"], like bark round a tree. When this [the "hot"] was broken off and shut off in certain circles, the sun and the moon and the stars were formed.
>
> Pseudo-Plutarch, *Stromata* 2 (trs. Kirk, Raven, and Schofield, modified)

Thales had suggested that everything came from water; Anaximander asked how water could turn into other things, such as its opposite, fire. Various sources suggest that Anaximander thought the Infinite had no qualities except boundlessness, but within the Infinite four qualities were in competition: hot, cold, wet, and dry. Change comes from this competition as first one quality, then another, becomes ascendant. As opposites spin off simultaneously from the Infinite, water puts out fire, then the fiery sun dries up water. All change is cyclical, reflecting changes in the ascendancy of one quality over another—thus we move through spring, summer, autumn, and winter. The Infinite is in constant motion, a sort of wiggling, and because of this wiggling motion, opposite qualities can congeal, producing sun and stars, which are hot and dry, and earth, which is wet and cold. The cosmos came into being through the Infinite's inbuilt tendency to wiggle. Life emerged from the warm slime, because the hot and wet make life. The earliest creatures, Anaximander claimed, were fish, and humans evolved from them.

Some of Anaximander's explanations have startling parallels to modern theory. Relying on reason, logical inference, and a sprinkling of evidence, Anaximander rejected earlier stories of how the gods made the universe, instead focusing on how the one original substance (the Infinite) became many and how the many things changed into other things. No agent is responsible for the movement of the Infinite, because motion is somehow a quality inherent in it. Not only was matter formed out of the Infinite, but the Infinite has generated worlds beyond number. Anaximander would have welcomed modern descriptions of the universe.

Using astronomical observations, Anaximander offered the first mechanical theory of the cosmos. The earth, he said, is shaped like a column drum, three times as wide as it is deep, suspended at the center of the Infinite. Around it are three rotating rings of fire shrouded by mists, but the mists have small gaps though which we glimpse the fire. The smallest ring is nine times the diameter of the earth, and we call the flecks of fire that we see through its numerous gaps "stars." The second ring, eighteen times the earth's diameter, has one gap, which we call the "moon." The third, twenty-seven times the earth's diameter, also has one gap, which humans call the "sun." Spatial relationships were crucial to Anaximander, who produced the first known map of the world.

His fellow Milesian **Anaximenes** (ca. 520s B.C.) took over much of Anaximander's thought but found other explanations for how substances turned into new substances. He defined the Infinite more precisely, now as air. Through eternally ongoing processes of rarefaction and condensation, he theorized, air condenses into liquid water, and liquid water condenses into solid ice. Heat reverses these processes, turning ice to water to air to fire; so too all matter will return to air. The very soul of a man is a rarefied form of air, taken from the essence of the universe. The Greek word for soul, *psychê*, means "breath," as we have seen.

To Aristotle, living some 200 years after Anaximenes, these theories seemed childish. Selecting water or air as the primary substance was arbitrary, and no Milesian integrated theory with observation very well, let alone developed experimental methods. We might call their attempts to explain change in nature by means of natural forces semiscientific rather than fully scientific, but they were still an advance on either Babylonian or Egyptian analyses. Anaximenes' processes of rarefaction and condensation required no divine intervention. Milesian models, too, were generalized, seeking to explain all of nature, not just bits of it. All theories were necessarily interrelated and were open to rational criticism.

The Ionian Enlightenment did not mean that suddenly every Greek sat down to argue about the Infinite. Few could have understood such obscure arguments, any more than most of us today grasp theoretical astrophysics. Anaximenes' principles of condensation and rarefaction seem almost common sense when compared to string theory, which posits multiple universes and countless invisible dimensions. But by 500 B.C., such speculations created a model for rational inquiry into the causes and nature of change that spread to other fields of inquiry.

## PYTHAGORAS: PHILOSOPHY AND SOCIAL SCIENCE IN THE WEST

The Ionian Enlightenment began in Miletus, but other thinkers in Ionia shared in it. One was **Pythagoras** from the island of SAMOS, near Miletus. Many legends grew up around him, so it is hard to say what he really taught, but he seems to have pushed Milesian thought in three directions: toward mathematics, mysticism, and politics.

Pythagoras fled his native Samos in 531 B.C. to escape from its tyrant. He settled in CROTON, a Greek city in southern Italy. Pythagoras emphasized both the differences and the connection between gods and mortals. The human soul, he said, was a spark of divinity. Through transmigration (reincarnation), the same spark dwelled within a sequence of fleshly containers, animal as well as human. Pythagoreans, therefore, never ate meat for fear of consuming a spark of the divine. Every human's job, Pythagoras said, was to turn away from the material dross enclosing the divine spark within us and, through moral purity and ascetic practice, to free the spark to rejoin its source in the divine infinite.

Pythagoras was the first to call the universe the *kosmos*, meaning "ordered whole." He saw the individual as a *kosmos* in miniature. The individual's goal was to attain in miniature the same order that governed the universe, and mathematics was the way to comprehend that order. The Greeks used letters to express numbers, which made arithmetic difficult, but Pythagoras, or his followers, made remarkable advances in geometrical thought about space and proportion. He discovered how to express the intervals of musical harmony as relations between the numbers one, two, three, and four. The octave, for instance, is a two-to-one ratio: If you pluck an open string on a guitar, then stop it at the halfway point (12 frets up), the two notes are harmonious in the relation of the octave. If you stop the string so that the lengths of its two parts stand in a ratio of three to two, the note you get is a fifth, also harmonious with the unstopped string. These relationships are the building blocks of musical harmony. They are not subjective but inherent in the *kosmos* itself. Musicians do not need to know the math behind what sounds good, but the mathematical basis nonetheless exists, independent of human judgment. Pythagoras had exposed the structure of reality. Mathematics proves that the world is an ordered *kosmos*. Pythagoras and his followers made further discoveries, allegedly including the famous Pythagorean theorem that everyone learns in school (Mesopotamians and Egyptians also understood this theorem): In a right-angled triangle, the square of the longest side is equal to the sum of the squares of the other two sides. Mathematics uncovers how reality works, and Pythagoreans believed they were unlocking the universe's secrets.

Pythagoras saw two principles at work in the *kosmos*: the Unlimited, which was shapeless and bad, and the Limiting, as when a musical string limited by exact intervals produces ordered harmonies, which is good. Followers could attain perfection by replacing disharmony (unlimited intervals) in their own lives with harmony, achieving union with the *kosmos* and allowing the divine spark to rejoin the infinite. One (unity = the point), two (duality = the line), three (trinity = unity + duality, the plane), and four (quadrinity = the solid) add up to ten, the number of perfection in the *kosmos*, the universe, and in the microcosm, the individual. Ten is the number of perfect harmony.

Such mystical theories sound less concrete than the Milesians' speculations about matter, but whereas the Milesians cared about substance and how it changed—what the universe was made of and how one thing became another—Pythagoras cared about structure, the ordering of things. Number was the key to structure at every level, from the *kosmos* to the individual, including the level of politics.

The openness of Greek society allowed thinkers to develop systematic methods of analysis. Pythagoras (or his followers) seized Croton in Italy and several other cities, reorganizing society in a utopian effort to make it conform to their mathematical theories. We know little about details, but for a while Pythagorean aristocrats were the most powerful men in western Greece. Eventually, Pythagoras' utopias failed, generating bitter civil wars. But the application of scientific abstractions to society as well as to nature had come to stay, with enormous consequences.

## HECATAEUS, HERODOTUS, AND *HISTORIÊ*

By 500 B.C., other schools of thought were developing in the Greek cities under Persian rule in Ionia and in the independent cities of southern Italy and Sicily. Some of them fused Milesian semiscience with Pythagoras' application of reason to human society. Hecataeus (hek-a-tē-us), also from Miletus, was an important innovator. He was active around 500 B.C., but only fragments of his writings survive. He was steeped in Enlightenment speculation and improved on Anaximander's map of the world. He wrote two important prose works. One was a systematic account of the peoples around the Mediterranean basin, combining geography, ethnography, and politics. The second analyzed genealogies. Even in Greece, a few aristocrats still claimed to have gods as ancestors and told stories to prove it. Hecataeus provided rational explanations for these stories. While not denying the gods' existence, Hecataeus underlined their separation from humankind, increasing the need for rational accounts of human behavior. A later writer preserves the memorable opening of his study of genealogies: "Hecataeus of Miletus speaks thus. I write these things as they seem to me to be true. For the tales of the Greeks are many, and, it seems to me, laughable."

Hecataeus seems to have pioneered a new genre of inquiry into the causes of human events, but his successor **Herodotus**' account of the Persian invasions of Greece was the first systematic attempt to explain human events in human terms. Herodotus was born around 484 B.C., as Archaic times ended, and although he seems to have lived and worked in Athens, he hailed from HALICARNASSUS, thirty miles south of Miletus. Just as Anaximander wrote in response to Thales, and Anaximenes to Anaximander, Herodotus replied to Hecataeus, whom Herodotus mentions eighteen times, usually to correct him. Herodotus opened his great *Histories* by explaining that

> This is the presentation of the *historiê* ["inquiry"] of Herodotus of Halicarnassus so that the events of the human past might not disappear with the passage of time, and that great and marvelous deeds, some displayed by the Greeks and some by barbarians,° may not be without glory. I also want to explain what was the reason that the two peoples fought with each other.
>
> Herodotus 1.1
>
> °*barbarians*: As noted earlier, Greeks called all non-Greeks barbarians.

In Greek, *historiê* meant "inquiry," but now the word "history" means a rational, orderly investigation into human events. We use it to describe the study of the past, but for Herodotus *historiê* included the present too.

Herodotus' book is not history as most of us think of it. He wished to preserve the memory of men's great deeds, much like Homer in the *Iliad*. Like Homer, Herodotus made up speeches at vital moments in the story, even when he could not possibly have known what was said or whether anything was said at all, as one occasion when he imagines a conversation between the Persian king and queen in their bed! In its purpose, length, ambition, and all-embracing curiosity about the world and the things in it, Herodotus' *historiê* resembles Homer's epic. If putting a fictional speech in a character's mouth was the way to get a point across, so be it.

The presence of the gods further distinguishes Herodotus' text from modern historical writing, as when Herodotus cheerfully tells us that the gods toppled mountains onto the Persians. Like other Ionian Enlightenment thinkers, he accepted the reality of the gods. Thales had famously remarked that the world was full of gods. But like Thales and his successors, Herodotus assumed that causes and effects nonetheless normally lay in the human realm, amenable to systematic analysis. After opening his book with the sentence quoted above, he relates various semimythical explanations for the origin of the conflict between Persia and Greece put forward by "learned men," ending with the Trojan War. He then adds a remarkable paragraph:

> That's what the Persians and Phoenicians say [about the mythical origins of the Persian wars]. I am not going to get into whether things really happened in this way, or in some other, but I will stick to what I myself know about who first injured the Greeks. Having made this clear, I shall proceed to the beginning of my narrative.
>
> Herodotus 1.5

Herodotus leaps forward from the mythical Trojan War to the sixth century B.C., where he can rely on his own knowledge to make statements of fact. He believes in the gods and gives them their due when reasonable, but no Muses tell him what happened, as they had informed Homer. He traveled extensively and, like an investigative reporter, asked his own questions, weighed what he saw and heard, and explained events as he understood them. Truly, Herodotus was the father of history in the sense that he was the first to investigate systematically the human causes of human events.

## LYRIC POETRY

At the same time as conversations were taking place about what the world is made of, and how things change within it, poets were developing highly varied new styles, which scholars loosely lump together as "lyric poetry." Only fragments of a once huge corpus survive, as quotations in later grammarians and as chance finds on old pieces of papyrus reused as mummy wrappings in Egypt. We know the names of about one hundred poets from the seventh through fifth centuries B.C., who lived all over the Greek world.

The Greek alphabet was initially used to take down epic verse by dictation. The possessors of this technology were the male Greek *agathoi*, whose social life was based in the symposium, its drink and song, and its political and sexual adventure. They were never a scribal class, as was required with the difficult technologies of writing used in the Near East, but simply aristocrats with a taste for poetry. Within 100 or 150 years after learning the rules of alphabetic writing, so they could reperform Homer and other epic poets, the *agathoi* began creating new kinds of poetic expression *in writing*, unknown in the oral past. Most of these poems are really song lyrics. This poetry embodied previously unknown, often complex rhythmic patterns, and invented new words that did not exist in spoken Greek. In *choral lyric*, meant to be danced and sung by groups of boys or girls (*choros* = "dance"), the rhythms behind the words matched the dance steps in ways we cannot now determine. In songs sung by one person to the accompaniment of a lyre (hence *lyric* poetry), the rhythms reflected, also in unknown ways, the musical accompaniment. Greek lyric has often been taken to reflect the "rise of the individual" or "the invention of personal emotions" because of the strong, even violent, feelings expressed, but we must remember that such poems were never read in a room by a private person, but rather experienced, usually at the symposium, rather as we experience popular music.

The earliest and most celebrated lyric poet was **Archilochus**, who lived in the seventh century B.C. A nearly complete poem, poorly understood but apparently a comic description of a sexual adventure, surfaced in the 1970s on a mummy-papyrus, but otherwise we have mostly short quotations in other writers. Archilochus was a fighter, and proud of it:

> I long for a fight with you just as a thirsty man wants a drink.
>
> fragment 69 Diehl (125 West)

In his claim

> I am a servant of King Enyalios,°
> knowing the lovely gift of the Muses
>
> fragment 1 Diehl (1 West)
> °*Enyalios*: Ares.

he encodes the *agathoi*'s combination of martial dedication with love of poetry. Yet, though *agathos*, he is unafraid to mock pretension:

> I don't like a tall general, nor one in braids
> or proud with his curls, or shaved beneath the chin—
> he should be small, and bowlegged around the knees,
> going boldly ahead on his feet, full of heart.
>
> fragment 60 Diehl (114 West)

Living in a cynical time, the singer is no Achilles; he values his life more than honor. In one of his most famous poems Archilochus boasts that

> Some Thracian° rejoices in my shield, which beside a bush
> I abandoned, unwilling, a very nice shield in fact.
> Still, I saved my skin. What do I care about that shield?
> To hell with it! I'll get another one, just as good.
>
> fragment 6 Diehl (5 West)
> °*Thracian*: A non-Greek tribesman from the Balkans.

Archilochus has no desire to stand at the top, where the wind is strong, but praises the middle way, a central Greek ideal:

> The affairs of Gyges° are of no interest to me,
> nor has envy ever grasped me, nor do I desire
> the deeds of the gods, and I do not want to be a great tyrant.
> All this is far from my eyes . . .

fragment 22 Diehl (19 West)

°*Gyges*: A king of Lydia famous for his wealth.

And he well understands the symposium, with its opportunities for drink and sex:

> She gulped it down to the tune of the flute, as a Thracian
> or a Phrygian gulps his beer, bent over and worked from the rear . . .

fragment 28 Diehl (42 West)

The poems of Archilochus and many other lyric poets were created to be memorized and performed in the all-male symposium, but the famous Sappho, who lived on the island of Lesbos around 600 B.C. seems to have written mostly for weddings. This kind of poem, called an *epithalamium*, "the song sung outside the bedroom," uniquely allowed celebration of a respectable young woman's sexual desirability. Only one of Sappho's poems survives complete, but we have fragments of others. In one she compares a bride to Helen, the most famous bride (and adulteress!) of Greek legend:

> Some say that the most beautiful thing
> on the black earth is a troop of horsemen,
> others say it is a band of soldiers, others still
> a host of ships. But I say it is whatever one loves.
> It is easy to make anyone understand this.
> Helen, the most beautiful of mortals,
> abandoned her most noble husband and,
> sailing, went far away to Troy.
>
> She thought no more of her child or her dear parents . . .
> [only a few letters remain from several lines] . . . reminds me of Anactoria, who
> is not here,
>
> whose lovely, shining footfall, and the dark flash
> of her face I would rather see
> than the chariots of the Lydians, or the mail-clad spearmen struggling on a
> dusty field . . .

Lobel-Page fragment 16

What is the most beautiful thing on earth? Not wealth, horses, ships, or men in armor, but whatever one loves, Sappho answers—a sentiment appropriate to a wedding. We cannot say who Anactoria was; perhaps she was the bride who had not yet appeared when the song was sung. It is easy to see how in Roman times, and later, Sappho was understood to celebrate homoeroticism between women, but the Greeks never understood her in this way.

Little Greek lyric poetry survives because in the second century A.D., when literary texts were being transferred from papyrus rolls to codices (i.e., books with pages and spines), almost no one could understand its obscure dialects and vocabulary, and its social setting was completely alien. Hence, few of the poems were copied and almost the entire corpus was lost. In the tiny bits that survive, we peek into an aristocratic realm of political posturing, erotic fantasies, celebrations of drunkenness, and the ideals of friendship and loyalty, another fruit of the extraordinary cultural flowering throughout Greek-speaking lands at this time.

## MATERIAL CULTURE

The same furious energy that drove speculation about physical and social realities and inspired new forms of poetic performance also drove a revolution in Greek material culture. Immigrant craftsmen were as important for introducing new art styles as eastern intellectuals were for introducing new forms of thought, but in art as in philosophy, transplanting Near Eastern traditions into the unusual sociology of the *poleis* encouraged developments in unprecedented directions.

## Sculpture

Near Eastern and Egyptian kings had used stone sculpture to glorify themselves since the Bronze Age. Early Greek travelers must have seen examples, but Greek *basileis* had neither the wealth nor the power to make such symbolism useful. The most lavish Greek sculptures from the impoverished Dark Age are little bronze figures of humans and animals, a few inches tall, dedicated at sanctuaries (particularly Olympia). The first experiments with stone carving took place on the island of Crete, where Near Eastern influence had always been strong. Early examples are rough heads and scenes in low relief on limestone blocks on Cretan tombs from around 700 B.C., strongly recalling Assyrian art. As states spent more money on public sanctuaries, they borrowed Near Eastern techniques (and perhaps hired Near Eastern craftsmen) to represent divinities in more elaborate ways. In early shrines, a simple plank of wood or block of stone may have represented the deity, and when Greek carvers started making freestanding limestone statues of gods around 650 B.C., they retained a slablike appearance. A statue known as "the Auxerre goddess" (once kept in a museum in Auxerre, France; Figure 9.1) is a good example. Virtually two-dimensional, the figure stands in a frontal pose with feet together, left hand at the side, right hand held to the chest. She wears a short cape over a straight-sided, belted tunic from which her bare feet emerge. Her hair is arranged in thick ridges, terminating in corkscrew curls over her brow. The skirt is lightly incised (and originally painted) with rectangular designs. The Near Eastern features, stiff posture, and Egyptian-like wig for hair characterize the **daedalic (dē-da-lik) style**, named after the legendary craftsman Daedalus, who built a labyrinth maze for King Minos in which to imprison the Minotaur, only to have Minos imprison him and his son Icarus in it. It is an odd term, because if Daedalus existed, he would have lived during the Bronze Age, a thousand years before the statues we call "daedalic." All the same, art historians use *daedalic* to mean early Greek art, with primitive features.

**FIGURE 9.1** The Auxerre *korê* ("maiden"), a daedalic statue, ca. 640–630 B.C. It is named after the French town Auxerre, where it used to be displayed, but was almost certainly made in Crete. Height 26 inches.

The daedalic style evolved rapidly as Cretan temples grew more elaborate in the late seventh century B.C. Near Eastern visitors to Crete around 620 or 610 B.C. would have found familiar-looking sculptures used in strange ways, on temples and occasionally in cemeteries, but never on palaces, as in the Near East. Egyptian styles soon influenced Greek sculpture as innovation shifted from Crete to the Cycladic islands and the mainland. Around 670 B.C., the ruler of Egypt had ordered all Greek merchants in his country to operate out of a single port, at NAUCRATIS in the Nile Delta (the site has been excavated), an event of immediate importance to Greek culture. Various mainland, island, and Ionian *poleis* set up trading posts there. By 600 B.C., Naucratis was the major conduit for the transfer of styles and technique from Egypt to Greece.

For 2,000 years, Egyptian craftsmen had carved statues to a standard format. They took a block of stone, often limestone, marked it out in squares on the flat faces of the stone according to a pattern book, then worked inward, as in the statue of Prince Ranefer ("Ra is beautiful"), of about 2300 B.C., shown in Figure 9.2. Ranefer's hands are clenched at his sides, holding an unknown object, and his left foot is slightly advanced. He wears a kilt

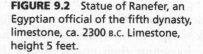

**FIGURE 9.2**  Statue of Ranefer, an Egyptian official of the fifth dynasty, limestone, ca. 2300 B.C. Limestone, height 5 feet.

and stares fixedly into space. In the sixth century B.C., nearly 2,000 years later, Egyptian statues still looked similar, and in fact changed little until the Romans conquered Egypt another 500 years later. Such artistic conservatism depended on the statues' magical purpose as substitute bodies for the *ka*, or "vital essence," of the deceased in case the mummy was destroyed.

Greek carvers borrowed Egyptian techniques to produce new types of statue, which archaeologists call *kouroi* ("young men"; singular, ***kouros***) and *korai* ("young women"; singular, ***korê***). The similarities between Figures 9.2 and 9.3 are striking. Both have straight arms with clenched fists and an unnatural pose, with the left leg slightly advanced, both feet flat on the ground, and the body directly over the upright right leg (the pose would be possible only for people whose left legs were longer than their right). Unlike the Egyptian statue, however, supported by a flat upright slab at the back, the Greek statue is

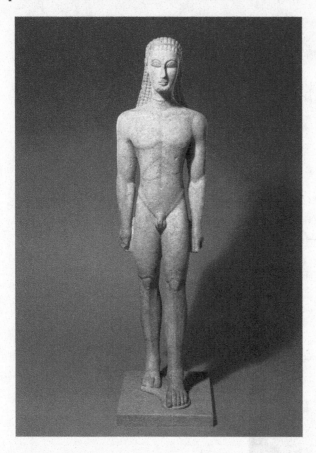

**FIGURE 9.3** The "New York" *kouros*, supposedly from Attica, ca. 600 B.C. Height 6 feet.

freestanding. It is also naked, as Egyptian statues never were. Early Greek female statues, by contrast, were always clothed.

Egyptian sculpture changed little in 3,000 years, but in Greece styles changed by the decade. Because they did not serve religious hierarchies like their Egyptian counterparts, Greek sculptors were free to experiment, softening the unnatural musculature of the *kouroi*, loosening their poses, raising their right heels from the ground, and introducing contemporary hairstyles, as in the fine example of about 480 B.C. shown in Figure 9.4. The sculptor has moved very far from his Egyptian prototypes. He observed the human body rather than working from sketchbooks. The anatomy has been modulated and made more naturalistic, as has the face. The muscles of the abdomen approximate real musculature. The statue seems alive, swelling with a vitality rarely found in Egyptian statues. Traces of paint remain on the hair, and pubic hair would also have been painted on. The right leg is forward. The sculptor reached out to create in stone an idealized naked Greek youth.

The female *korê*, "young girl," corresponded to the male *kouros*. The *korê* was always fully clothed. An extraordinary series of these charming statues was found on the Athenian Acropolis in pits where the Athenians swept debris after Persians sacked the city in 480 B.C. Figure 9.5, carved about 530 B.C., is called the Peplos *Korê* from the woolen dress (*peplos*) she wears. Like the *kouroi*, she has an "archaic smile," a fixed grin

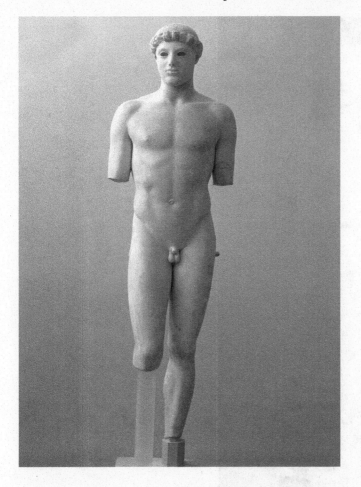

**FIGURE 9.4** The Kritios boy, found on the Acropolis in Athens, ca. 480 B.C., apparently the creation of a sculptor named Kritios. Marble, height 3 feet, 10 inches.

found on most sixth-century statuary: Its meaning is unknown. Long braided locks, painted red, fall on either side of her breasts, outlined by the *peplos*, which ends just above her belted waist. Her drapery is complex and naturalistic, and her face thoughtful. Unlike the *kouroi*, the *korai* stand with feet side by side. In this statue, the sculptor has boldly freed the figure from the block of stone by attaching an extended left arm (now missing).

As with natural philosophy, transplanting Near Eastern and Egyptian practices to a very different social setting gave Greeks the freedom to innovate. Sculpture was expensive; only the rich could hire carvers and pay to move large blocks of stone. In Assyria, such spending was the preserve of kings and nobles, but in Greece there were few kings and no grand palaces. A few nobles put *kouroi* and *korai* over their graves (like Figure 9.3), but most were placed in sanctuaries (e.g., Figures 9.4 and 9.5). Greek sculptors took their basic techniques from Egypt and Syria, but because they made up new rules for the use of statues, did not feel bound by conventions. Cycladic and Athenian masons innovated by using hard marble, abundant in both areas, rather than soft limestone, as was common in Egypt. The driving question in Archaic Greek culture—what is humanity if we are separated from the gods?—may have encouraged

**FIGURE 9.5** The Peplos *Korê;* from Athens, ca. 530 B.C. Marble, height 48 inches.

sculptors to think about what made the human body what it is. They faced similar issues as the philosophers, but gave answers in stone, not words.

## Architecture

Sociological changes drove architectural innovations too. The most important was the separation of religious and secular space around 700 B.C. As we noted in Chapter 5, "The Dark Age, 1200–800 B.C.," the gods may have been worshiped in chiefs' houses in the Dark Age. Presumably, the chiefs' special ties to gods are reflected in Hesiod's sense that Zeus gave special favor to good *basileis*. After 700 B.C., *basileis* disappeared, and as egalitarian ideals developed, the worship of the gods was largely separated from the homes of mortals.

Some of the earliest sanctuaries consisted of a simple altar under the open sky, where animals were killed, cooked, and eaten. By 750 B.C., communities began adding buildings for the god's image near the altar. The earliest temples, like Dark Age houses, had one curved end. Already by 700 B.C., some were a hundred feet long. Early in the seventh century B.C., craftsmen learned to make clay roof tiles, and temple-builders replaced thatch with this superior material. The heavy tiles required strong walls, now often built entirely from carefully cut stone blocks with columns bearing the weight. The building was divided into a long main room (*cella*), where the cult statue stood, and a short back porch (*opisthodomos*, "back-house"), unconnected to the cella, where civic treasure was stored, with a row of columns down the middle. Still more columns (a *colonnade*) surrounded the building and the entire structure was built on a platform (*stylobate*).

These temples required much wood and stone and were enormously expensive by Greek standards, but the communities that sponsored them took civic pride in their construction. Seventh-century B.C. architects often used huge blocks of stone, much bigger than in later times, despite having only simple cranes, as if they rejoiced in the difficulty of the task they set themselves, to honor the gods and celebrate the community. The new building styles gave opportunities for elaboration in decorating the upper part of the temple with painted plaques and molded faces.

By 600 B.C., distinct canons of temple building had evolved, familiar to us today, called the **Doric** and **Ionic orders** after the two principal Greek ethnic divisions (Figure 9.6). A third order, the Corinthian, with elaborate capitals of acanthus leaves, was added later (Chapter 18, "Greek Culture in the Fourth Century B.C.").

Regardless of what order a builder worked with, temples had three parts. At the top was the *entablature* ("superimposed board"), consisting of a pitched, tiled roof, a decorated

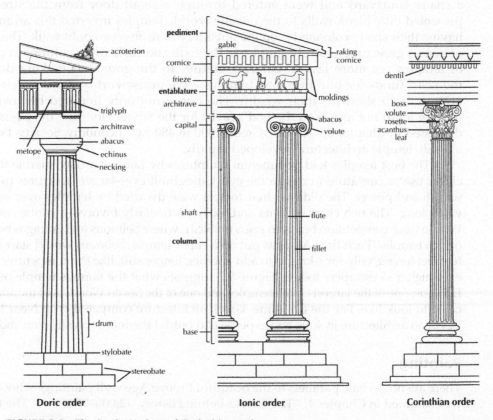

**FIGURE 9.6**  The Doric, Ionic, and Corinthian orders.

frieze beneath it, and a plain support of stone blocks called the *architrave* (**ar**-ki-trāv, "chief beam"). At the front and back of the temple, the triangular areas under the roof (the end gables), called **pediments**, often had sculpture.

The second architectural element was the columns, where the main difference between the orders lay. All types of columns tapered toward the top, but Doric columns had no bases, were less fluted than Ionic, and had a plain top (what architects call the capital). A Doric capital was called an *echinus*, which means "sea urchin," because its cushion shape reminded Greeks of that creature so common on their beaches. Ionic columns had fancier capitals, with curved volutes ("rolls"), and Corinthian columns had the fanciest capitals of all. The third element was the temple's base. The columns stood on a *stylobate* (**stī**-lō-bāt, "column-walk"), which stood on a series of progressively larger slabs forming steps, and finally on a leveling course.

The Doric and Ionic orders had only a loose connection to Dorians and Ionians as ethnic groups. Greeks thought that the Doric order was more "masculine," and it was generally preferred on the mainland and on Sicily in both Ionian and Dorian cities. The more elegant or "feminine" Ionic order was preferred in Greek cities on the coast of Asia Minor. The earliest Corinthian column is from the mid-fifth century B.C., but Corinthian columns were never common until the Roman Period.

Temple design grew out of Dark Age house design, but no one could confuse sixth-century temples with private houses, which followed their own line of development. By about 550 B.C., most new houses had half a dozen rooms grouped around a shady courtyard and were entered through a small door from the street. Houses presented only blank walls to the outside world. Temples inverted this arrangement by having their shady colonnades on the outside, where anyone could walk. The decoration of houses grew progressively simpler in the sixth and early fifth centuries B.C., while that of temples got more lavish. Offering statues to the gods and making donations to the *polis'* funds for building new temples were praiseworthy ways for sixth-century aristocrats to show off their wealth. The donor not only honored his own name by making a gift but also won the god's favor for the whole city (like the Olympic victors discussed in Chapter 8, "Archaic Greece, 800 to 480 B.C.: Economy, Society, Politics"). As a result, temple architecture developed rapidly.

The best temples had pedimental sculptures by famous artists, marble façades, and clever use of curvature to charm the eye. Cities built ever-larger structures to show their wealth and power. The old hundred-footers were dwarfed by temples over one hundred yards long. The rich cities of Ionia and Sicily particularly favored gigantic constructions. We can trace competition between *poleis* on Sicily, where Selinous and Akragas built avenues of rich temples. Each time Akragas put up a super-temple, Selinous would start a new one a few feet longer, only for Akragas to add another, longer still, like the competitive building of ever-higher skyscrapers today. Figure 9.7 suggests what the famous temple of Artemis of Ephesus, one of the largest Greek temples and one of the Seven Wonders of the ancient world, came to look like. For the first time, Greek architecture competed with Near Eastern and Egyptian architecture in scale and expense and outdid them in sophistication and beauty.

## Painting

There are no Archaic parallels to the beautiful Bronze Age wall paintings whose fragments we examined in Chapter 4, "The Greeks before History, 12,000–1200 B.C." The fact that we

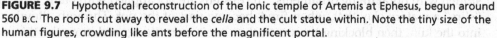

**FIGURE 9.7** Hypothetical reconstruction of the Ionic temple of Artemis at Ephesus, begun around 560 B.C. The roof is cut away to reveal the *cella* and the cult statue within. Note the tiny size of the human figures, crowding like ants before the magnificent portal.

lack archaeological contexts like the Santorini eruption partly explains this, but it also seems that wall painting was less important in Archaic Greece than in the Bronze Age, in accordance with the unostentatious lifestyle of Greek aristocrats.

Remains of painted pottery, however, are superabundant. Several million examples survive, mostly decorated with simple bands or solid blocks of black paint. Starting around 750 B.C., a few had figured scenes. Near Eastern influence then became so strong that we speak of an **orientalizing phase** in Greek art, lasting through the seventh century B.C. Corinth was one of the main trading cities in archaic Greece and, not surprisingly, under the aggressive tyrant dynasty of the Cypselids, was also the main center for orientalizing vase painting. A painting style called Protocorinthian flourished between about 725 and 625 B.C. The finest examples are miniatures (Figure 9.8; see also Figure 8.3). Unlike the Late Geometric figures in Figure 5.3, the warriors here are flowing and energetic, in multicolored paint. The craftsmanship is extraordinary, the figures less than an inch tall. Corinthian workshops produced millions of such vessels to hold the scented oils that athletes used in the gymnasium. Greeks associated perfume with the luxurious East, which made orientalizing decoration appropriate for its containers.

By 625 B.C., Corinthian painting settled down into the **Ripe Corinthian** style, favoring a dense texture of detail of Eastern inspiration (ca. 625–550 B.C.; Figure 9.9). The effect is rich, like tapestry: band after band of repetitive animals, every square inch of background

**FIGURE 9.8**  A Protocorinthian aryballos (a-ri-**bal**-os), or perfume flask, ca. 650 B.C. This vase was painted by the same artist who painted the "Chigi vase." It is less than 3 inches tall.

stuffed with floral filling ornaments. The designs are not applied with paint, but with a thin "slip," a watery clay that, when fired, became part of the pot. Through allowing oxygen into the kiln, then blocking the vents, then again permitting oxidation, the thin slip turns a dark color, while the natural color of the clay shows through. After firing, the potter used a sharp tool to scratch detail within the black figures and ornaments, often adding red or white highlights in actual paint.

Athens, by contrast, developed a wild seventh-century style known as **Protoattic** (Figure 9.10). Protoattic painters put their best work on large vessels. Figure 9.10 shows one of the most extraordinary. On the neck (also shown in Figure 6.6 in Chapter 6, "Homer"), Odysseus blinds the Cyclops. On the shoulder, a lion attacks a boar, and on the belly are Gorgons, mythical female creatures whose gaze turns a viewer to stone. Unlike the disciplined Protocorinthian vases, this scene has random filling ornaments floating in the background. The drawing is loose and sketchy. The rigid Athenian Late Geometric style had dissolved into a kind of chaos. In its day, Corinthian work was much more successful, being sold and imitated all over the Mediterranean, but the future lay with Athenian painters.

In the early sixth century B.C., Athenian painters wedded the inventiveness of Protoattic with the order and precision of Corinthian in an extraordinary new **black-figured** style. Athenian painters continued to portray mythical characters, but learned from and then surpassed the Corinthians' neatness and tight composition. One of the most famous ancient pots, the François vase (Figure 9.11), shows in the main scene, on the shoulder, the marriage of Achilles' parents; on the neck are the funeral games of Achilles' friend Patroclus; and on the lip, the killing of a giant boar that, according to legend, terrorized the town of Calydon in the generation before the Trojan War. Beneath the main scene is

**FIGURE 9.9**   Corinthian *olpê* (wine jug), ca. 600 B.C. Height 18 inches.

a procession of Dionysus, the god of wine, and below that a frieze of winged monsters called griffins. Even the foot has a figured scene, of a mythical battle between pygmies and cranes. The pot has 200 figures, dozens of them with names painted in. Among the names we can read *KLEITIAS EGRAPSE*, "Kleitias painted it," and *ERGOTIMOS EPOIESE*, "Ergotimos made it" (although we do not know whether "made it" means that Ergotimos physically threw the pot or owned the workshop). Animal scenes were now relegated to providing subsidiary ornament, as the human form became the vase painter's main subject.

Pottery was cheap compared to sculpture, but by 550 B.C. a few Athenian painters raised the medium to the status of a serious art (Figure 9.12). Exekias was perhaps the greatest of these artists. Figure 9.12 shows his representation of a powerful moment from the Trojan War story. After Achilles was killed, all the Greek heroes wanted his armor. The great hero Ajax lost his mind with rage when the other Greeks refused to award it to him. Blind with fury, he attacked them, but when his wits returned, he found that he had actually slaughtered a flock of sheep, not the other Greeks, who now stood laughing at him. Dishonored, he planted his sword in the ground and threw himself on it. This became a popular subject for black-figure painters, but whereas most showed Ajax impaled on his

**FIGURE 9.10** The Eleusis vase, a famous Protoattic amphora, ca. 675 B.C., found at Eleusis near Athens, where it had been used as a baby coffin. (Figure 6.6 shows a detail from the neck.) Height 4 feet, 9 inches.

sword, kicking and squirting blood, Exekias filled the scene with impending tragedy. The great but flawed hero smoothes the earth around his deadly sword, his brow furrowed in concentration. A solitary palm to the left, indicating the outdoor setting, and the carefully stacked arms to the right, evoking the armor that drove Ajax to this end, frame the majestic central figure. Ajax's own eyeless helmet appears to watch with chilling disinterest. Only a great artist could achieve such a harrowing effect in such a simple medium.

Top Athenian craftsmen competed to sell their wares and innovated constantly. Black figure worked by painting the figures in slip, then firing the pot so that the background preserved the color of the reddish clay while the painted slip oxidized black. In a new **red-figured** style, invented around 530 B.C., painters simply reversed the procedure, painting the background with slip and leaving the figures in the color of the pot. By using slips of different density, they could add subtler details than incision allowed. At first, red figure was perhaps a novelty style; some of the earliest examples show the same scene in black figure on one side and in red figure on the other. But within a few years, ca. 520 B.C., the best painters switched to red figure. In Figure 9.13, the painter realizes the full potential of the technique, using different lines, shading, drapery, and nudity to superimpose a satyr, a fawn, and the messenger-god Hermes—a complex design impossible in black figure. It lacks the profundity of Exekias' best work but is a delightful, virtuoso scene.

**FIGURE 9.11** The François vase, a black-figured Athenian krater of about 570 B.C., named after the man who discovered it in the nineteenth century. Kleitias and Ergotimos signed the vase and covered it with mythological details. Kleitias painted in the names of dozens of characters. Height 2 feet, 2 inches.

**FIGURE 9.12** The suicide of Ajax on an Athenian black-figured amphora by Exekias, ca. 540 B.C. Height of scene, 10 inches.

**FIGURE 9.13** Red-figured scene of Hermes, a satyr, and a fawn on an Athenian amphora, by the Berlin Painter ca. 480 B.C. Height of scene, 10 inches.

## ART AND THOUGHT IN SIXTH-CENTURY GREECE

From Ionia to Sicily, Greeks of the sixth century B.C. began remarkable explorations of the human condition. The Milesian natural scientists worked in such a rarefied intellectual environment that only a few Greeks understood them, while sculptors created art that - thousands saw and appreciated. Philosophers commanded written expression while vase painters were artisans, worrying about getting the best clay and keeping kilns firing at the right temperature. These painters came from all over Greece, and even beyond. A leading painter at Athens in the 550s B.C. signed his work Lydos, "the Lydian," while a workshop owner in the 480s signed his vases as Brygos, "the Brygian." Lydia was a kingdom in western Asia Minor, and the Brygians were a Thracian people, living in modern Bulgaria. Both regions supplied many slaves to Greece (see Map 10.2 in Chapter 10, "A Tale of Two Archaic Cities: Sparta and Athens, 700–480 B.C."), and it is quite likely that Brygos and Lydos came to Athens as slaves.

In eastern kingdoms, representational art circulated in royal and other elite contexts, adorning palaces or temples to which few were admitted. Archaic *poleis*, by contrast, were cities of images open to all: Thought-provoking sculpture, architecture, and paintings were everywhere. Pythagoras put his theories into action in politics, and Herodotus perhaps gave public readings. The weak hierarchy of the Archaic *poleis* created an unusually open society. The ancient learning and art of Mesopotamia and Egypt were transformed. In Ionia, new knowledge created the first natural philosophy and semiscientific analyses of society. By 500 B.C., Greek society looked different from its neighbors, and Greek culture was winning admirers from Persia to the Strait of Gibraltar.

## Key Terms

Ionia, *175*

Miletus, *175*

Ionian Enlightenment, *175*

Thales, *176*

Anaximander, *176*

Anaximenes, *177*

Pythagoras, *177*

Herodotus, *179*

*historiê*, *179*

Archilochus, *181*

daedalic style, *183*

Naucratis, *184*

*kouros*, *185*

*korê*, *185*

*cella*, *189*

Doric order, *189*

Ionic order, *189*

pediments, *190*

orientalizing phase, *191*

Ripe Corinthian, *192*

Protoattic, *192*

black-figure, *193*

red-figure, *195*

## Further Reading

### PHILOSOPHY

Barnes, Jonathan, *The Presocratic Philosophers*, 2 vols. (London, 1979). Barnes relies on modern analytic philosophy to discuss ancient philosophers.

Furley, David, *The Greek Cosmologists: The Formation of the Atomic Theory and Its Earliest Critics*, vol. 1 (Cambridge, UK, 1989). Sophisticated analysis of Milesian philosophy.

Guthrie, W. K. C., *The Greek Philosophers: From Thales to Aristotle* (London, 1950). Superb short review by a leading scholar.

Lloyd, G. E. R., *Demystifying Mentalities* (Cambridge, UK, 1990). One of the best studies of the relationships between philosophy and other forms of thought in archaic Greece.

——, *Early Greek Science: Thales to Aristotle* (London, 1970). Very clear brief survey.

### HISTORIOGRAPHY

Harrison, Thomas, *Divinity and History: The Religion of Herodotus* (Oxford, 2000). Outstanding reassessment of the place of religion in Herodotus' history-writing.

Luraghi, Nino, ed., *The Historian's Craft in the Age of Herodotus* (Oxford, 2001). Wide-ranging essays on how Herodotus composed his *History*.

Thomas, Rosalind, *Herodotus in Context* (Cambridge, UK, 2000). Analysis of Herodotus' achievements against their contemporary intellectual background.

### ART

Hurwit, Jeffrey M., *The Art and Culture of Early Greece, 1100–480 B.C.* (Ithaca, NY, 1985). Excellent interpretive study of painting, poetry, sculpture, and architecture in Dark Age and archaic Greece.

Moon, Warren G., ed., *Ancient Greek Art and Iconography* (Madison, WI, 1983). Essays on Greek painting.

Osborne, Robin, *Archaic and Classical Greek Art* (Cambridge, UK, 1998). Imaginative interpretation of Greek art.

Pedley, John Griffiths, *Greek Art and Archaeology*, 2nd ed. (New York, 1998). Standard introductory textbook, well illustrated.

Rasmussen, Tom, and Nigel Spivey, eds., *Looking at Greek Vases* (Cambridge, UK, 1991). Essays by experts, covering different ways of approaching painted pottery.

Stewart, Andrew F., *Greek Sculpture: An Exploration*, 2 vols. (New Haven, CT, 1990). Comprehensive analysis of Greek sculpture, with very thorough illustrations.

### ANCIENT TEXTS

Kirk, G. S., J. E. Raven, and M. Schofield, eds., *The Presocratic Philosophers*, 2nd ed. (Cambridge, UK, 1983). The Greek text and good translations and explanations for all the sixth-century B.C. philosophers.

Miller, Andrew, *Greek Lyric* (Indianapolis, 1996). Good translations of a selection of archaic poetry.

# A Tale of Two Archaic Cities: Sparta and Athens, 700–480 B.C.

In Chapter 8, "Archaic Greece, 800–480 B.C.: Economy, Society, Politics," and Chapter 9, "The Archaic Cultural Revolution: 700–480 B.C.," we reviewed developments across Archaic Greece as a whole, but in fact, no two *poleis* followed exactly the same path. In this chapter we look in detail at the two best-documented *poleis*, Sparta and Athens. These cities dominated the Classical Aegean, but they were among the most unusual Archaic *poleis*.

Like all *poleis*, Sparta and Athens faced conflicts within their ruling elites, between these elites and the masses, and between the community as a whole and neighboring states. Both responded by creating internally egalitarian male citizen communities but in very different ways. In Sparta, state-owned serfs called **helots** worked the land while citizens followed a life-long program of military training in centralized institutions. Athens, on the other hand, encouraged markets and democratic practice; monogamous families were the core institution of Athenian society. While Spartan men were occupied within military institutions, Spartan women developed parallel all-female groups. Athenians, by contrast, drew boundaries within the household, headed by the senior male. Spartans and Athenians both defined citizenship in ethnic terms, but whereas Spartans saw themselves as a conquering race ruling over indigenous helots, most Athenians believed they had always lived in their own land. Whereas Spartans used helots as dependent labor, Athenians turned to non-Greek chattel slaves imported from overseas and privately owned. Sparta and Athens were equally "Greek," but their different ways of being Greek, each with its own institutions, were to tear the Aegean world apart in the fifth century B.C.

## SPARTA

### The Spartan Mirage

Ancient historians usually complain about not having enough evidence, but with Sparta we almost seem to have too much. Greeks and Romans loved writing about Sparta and created an idealized but unrealistic version of it that historians call the **Spartan mirage**. The mirage was a vision of stability, hierarchy, and order in which all knew their place. Greeks regularly contrasted Sparta with Athens, the archetype of undiscipline, freedom, and disorder. Some Greeks (like some moderns) hated the image of Spartan authoritarianism; others loved it. But the stereotype of Sparta was not its reality, which the Spartans themselves deliberately concealed.

The Spartan mirage begins with the story of **Lycurgus** (lī-**kur**-gus), who is said to have created perfect laws for Sparta. He made all Spartan men equal, regulated their lives, and forged the ultimate fighting machine, according to the legend. Around A.D. 100, the learned Greek Plutarch wrote an admiring biography of Lycurgus, but even he conceded that:

> Concerning Lycurgus the lawgiver there is nothing at all that is not disputed: birth, travels, death, and above all what he accomplished as a lawgiver and statesman. Least of all do historians agree about when he lived.
>
> Plutarch, *Life of Lycurgus* 1

We do not know how much in the stories that Plutarch and others tell is true and how much is fiction, but there is certainly a lot of the latter. Writing 800 years after the supposed career of Lycurgus, Plutarch reports on events for which there were no contemporary written records and around which generations of speculation swirled. For much of his information Plutarch depended on the Athenian Xenophon, writing in the fourth century B.C., who actually lived in Sparta. But Xenophon too is separated by generations from the much earlier days when the seeds of Spartan power were sown.

## SPARTIATES, *PERIOIKOI*, AND HELOTS

Archaeology reveals that Sparta was a major Bronze Age center. In later stories, Helen came from Sparta; she ran off with Paris and thus began the Trojan War (see Chapter 6, "Homer"). Sparta was destroyed by fire around 1200 B.C., and LACONIA—the region around Sparta—declined (see Map 10.1). There are few Dark Age sites in Laconia, and only around 900 B.C. did new settlements appear.

The Spartans spoke the dialect of Greek called **Dorian**, which to an Athenian would have sounded weird but roughly intelligible. According to legend, the Dorians were a distinct people who invaded southern Greece in the twelfth century B.C. soon after the fall of Troy (see Map 1.4 in Chapter 1, "A Small, Far-Off Land"). Archaeologists have argued for a century over whether this Dorian invasion can be verified in the material record, but have reached no agreement. So far as Archaic and Classical history is concerned, though, the important thing is that Spartans *believed* that they descended from conquering Dorians and believed that this descent gave them the right to dominate the defeated indigenous peoples.

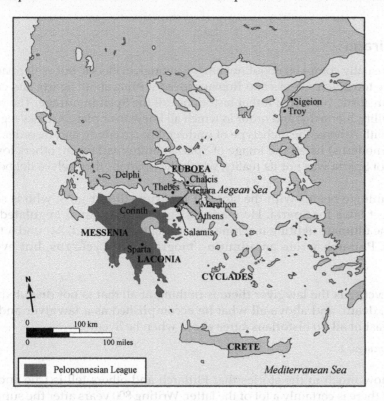

**MAP 10.1** Regions and sites mentioned in this chapter. The darker area represents the sixth-century Peloponnesian League.

Probably in the ninth century B.C., the Dorian Spartans conquered LACONIA and reduced its population to dependence (Figure 10.1). The luckier Laconians were called *perioikoi* (peri-oi-koi), meaning "dwellers-around." They lived in dozens of independent villages, paid tribute to Sparta, and served in the Spartan army but did not contribute to decisions about when and where Sparta went to war. Less fortunate Laconians became helots, state-owned slaves. The full Spartan citizens (called **Spartiates**), 5,000 in number, divided up the land, and the helots worked it for them. The seventh-century Spartiate warrior-poet Tyrtaeus said helots were "like donkeys exhausted under great loads: under painful necessity to bring their masters fully half of the fruit their plowed land produced" (West, 6).

Like the *perioikoi*, helots had their own villages and could marry, but were subject to many disabilities. Plutarch called helotage "the cruelest and most lawless system," and other ancient writers agreed. Helots were sometimes made to wear ridiculous outfits, paraded drunk in public, and whipped. Every year, Spartan officials declared ritual war against them, removing religious pollution for killing a helot, in effect making murder legal. To make the relationship brutally clear, Plutarch explains:

> The overseers of the young would from time to time send out the most intelligent of the young men, dispersed into the countryside in different directions. All they had were daggers and bare provisions, but nothing else. When day came, they scattered into obscure and out of the way places where they hid

**FIGURE 10.1** The mountain road from Sparta southeast to Kalamata, a typical landscape in southern Greece.

themselves and remained silent. At night they came out into the highways and killed every helot they could find. Often they would walk through the fields and kill anyone who seemed unusually strong or powerful.

Plutarch, *Life of Lycurgus* 28

This extreme system, aimed at terrorizing the helots into obedience (they probably outnumbered Spartiates at least five to one), only partly succeeded. The helots and *perioikoi* naturally hated the Spartiates. Xenophon said that they "showed clearly enough, if there was ever any mention of the Spartiates, they would be glad to eat them, even raw" (*Hellenica* 3.3.6). The helots rebelled whenever they got a chance, and the Spartiates' fear of uprisings shaped every aspect of their society.

In the eighth century B.C., population growth increased pressure on resources. Feuds within the elite, struggles between rich and poor, and wars between communities escalated. Some Greeks sent out colonies, but the Spartans' earlier success in conquering Laconia perhaps convinced them that war was the answer to their own problems. Between 740 and 720 B.C., Sparta overran the large, fertile territory of **MESSENIA** to the west of the Spartan valley of Lacedaemon, across high mountains (Figure 10.2). They

**FIGURE 10.2** The wooded slopes of Mt. Taygetos, elevation 6,000 feet. The valley of Lacedaemon lies at the bottom of the slope and the plains of Messenia, which the Spartans conquered in the eighth century B.C., on the other side of the mountains.

reduced its population to the status of helots, probably doubling the land and labor under Spartan control.

Occupied Messenian land and labor made the Spartiates relatively rich. The great challenge was how to distribute the spoils of war. Some Spartans were shut out from the profits, and an excluded group called the *Partheniai*, which means "born of virgins," planned a coup in 706. Their name may mean that they were not considered full citizens and were therefore denied a share of the plunder. Whatever the details, when the plot was discovered, the entire group was exiled. Shifting from conquest to colonization, the *Partheniai* sailed to southern Italy and founded Sparta's only colony there, Taras (modern Taranto). New wars of expansion after 700 B.C. met with only limited success and demands grew for a redistribution of land. A Spartan king was assassinated and around 650 B.C. the Messenians rose up, to be crushed with unrelenting savagery. Tyrtaeus' military poems (quoted in Chapter 8) were composed against the background of that war.

## PLUTARCH'S SPARTA

The Spartiates responded to the complex problems of maintaining peace among their citizens while suppressing the helots by becoming full-time warriors. They believed that Lycurgus designed this system, but modern historians doubt it, suggesting instead that the system took shape gradually, perhaps beginning in the ninth century when Sparta conquered Laconia, or in the late eighth, during the first Messenian War. Spartan society was certainly militarized by the late seventh century B.C., after the second Messenian War.

The Spartan war machine and the society built to support it reached its highest form in the sixth and fifth centuries B.C., then declined in the fourth, as we shall see.

For the details of Spartan society, by far the most influential account is found in Plutarch's *Life of Lycurgus* and it deserves to be quoted at length:

An extraordinary and revolutionary action by Lycurgus was the redistribution of the land. For there was great inequality in this regard, and the city was filled with the indigent and the helpless. Wealth had become entirely concentrated in the hands of the few. He wished to drive out violence, and envy, and crime, and luxury, and those diseases still older and greater that afflict a city, wealth and poverty. To do so he persuaded his fellow citizens to group all properties together into a common lot and to redistribute them anew. All would live together as equals, sustained by equal access to the necessities of life, pursuing preeminence through excellence alone. They would proceed on the principle that there was no difference between one man and the next, except that established by blame for shameful behavior and praise for good behavior.

Acting as he had promised, Lycurgus divided the remainder of Laconia into 30,000 lots and distributed them to the *perioikoi*. As parcels for the Spartiates, he divided the land within the city of Sparta into 9,000 lots . . . There is a story that when somewhat later Lycurgus was returning from a trip and passing through the countryside, which had recently been harvested, and when he saw the heaps of grain standing in row after row all exactly the same, he smiled and said to those standing near, "Why all Laconia looks like an estate that recently has been divided equally among many brothers."

He also undertook to divide up movable property in order to remove every trace of inequality, but when he experienced resistance to direct expropriation, he tried another tack and through political means attempted to restrain their greed. First he withdrew all gold and silver currency and ordered that money would now be made of iron. Then to a great mass and weight of it he assigned a small value, so that if you had ten *minas*° worth, you would need a large storeroom and a yoke of oxen to move it. When this currency took hold, whole classes of crime disappeared from Lacedaemon. For who was going to take someone's money, or bribe someone with it, or rob it, or plunder it, when it could not be hidden and no one wanted it anyway? You couldn't even cut it up for something else, for, according to the story, Lycurgus doused the surface of the red-hot iron with vinegar, which took away its use for anything else, once it became brittle and hard to work . . .

In order to continue his campaign against luxury and the desire to obtain wealth, he instigated his third and finest political reform, the institution of the common mess. Now they would all dine together and eat the same common and specified sauces and cereals. No one would eat at home, lying at table on expensive couches, fattened up by servants and cooks as if they were voracious animals kept in a dark place, destroying their character along with their bodies indulged in every fancy and surfeit, which requires long naps, warm baths, abundant leisure, and practically speaking constant nursing . . .

°*ten minas:* Enough money to feed a family of four at a basic level for three years. Plutarch's point is that while you could put ten *minas* in coins in your pocket, in Sparta this much money would be unmanageable.

The boys too went to the messes, which served for them as a school for self-discipline. There they heard political discussions and witnessed instructive models for living as a free man. They became accustomed to make fun and to jest without becoming indecent, and not to be offended when they were themselves the butt of a joke. This seemed to be an especially Spartan trait, to put up with a joke. But if you got tired of it, you could ask the man to stop and he would . . .

Of all their dishes they most value black broth such that the older men have no interest in meat, but leave that to the young men. They themselves have only black broth poured out for their meals . . .

After drinking modestly they go home without a torch. They are not allowed to use a light on any of their journeys so that they might grow accustomed to the darkness and learn to travel at night cheerfully and without fear. So, that is the way they organized their messes . . .

Concerning education, which Lycurgus considered to be the most important task of the lawgiver, he started out right from the beginning, with marriage and childbirth . . . To women he paid the greatest attention. He hardened their bodies through running, wrestling, and throwing the discus and the javelin so that the young, taking root in the wombs of powerful bodies, might be strong and develop better. The women themselves, endowed with strength, would in this way more successfully and easily bear the pangs of childbirth.

He took away prudery and delicacy and effeminacy of every kind and accustomed the young girls, as much as the boys, to parade in the nude and at certain festivals to dance and sing, even while the young men were present . . . There was nothing shameful about the girls' nudity. They were modest and there was not a hint of immorality. Instead it encouraged a customary simplicity and a desire for physical fitness. It encouraged the females to highmindedness, because they too had access to excellence and ambition. Thus they were led to speak and think as Gorgo, wife of Leonidas, is said to have done. A woman, evidently a foreigner, said to her, "Only Spartan women rule over men." And Gorgo replied, "Yes, because we are the only ones who give birth to men!"

This behavior was conducive to marriage—I mean the appearance of the girls in the nude during processions and during athletic contests while the boys looked on, drawn not by intellectual interests, but by sexual desire (as Plato says) (Figure 10.3). Furthermore, Lycurgus placed a social stigma on men who would not marry. They were forbidden to watch the games in the nude. In the winter they were compelled to march in a circle around the agora stark naked, singing a song against themselves to the effect that they were justly punished because they did not obey the laws. And they were deprived of the honor and attention that young men customarily show to older men. For this reason no one complained about what was said to Dercyllidas, although he was a famous general. When he came up, a young man refused to yield his seat, saying, "You never bore a son who would one day yield his seat to me."

They captured women for marriage, not when they were small and undeveloped, but when they were in their prime and fully ripened. Once a woman had been taken, a "bride's maid," as she was called, took possession of her, cut her hair to the scalp, dressed her in a man's cloak and sandals, then lay her down on a mattress in a dark room. The groom—not drunk, hence sexually potent, sober as always—first had dinner in the mess, then slipped into the

**FIGURE 10.3** Running girl, bronze, ca. 520–500 B.C., found in Serbia but probably made in Sparta. She is not naked like the girls in Plutarch's account but bares one breast, and both knees are exposed. Height about 4 inches.

room, loosened her belt, and carried her to a bed. Then after a short while he departed, fully composed, to sleep in his usual place with the other young men. And so it went, the groom spending his days with his age-mates, sleeping with them at night, visiting his wife in secret, and taking every precaution, ashamed and afraid that someone in her house might recognize him.

In the meanwhile his bride thinks of every device and conspires with her husband, that they might meet unobserved, when possible. They act in this way not for a short time, but for so long that sometimes a woman might give birth before her husband has ever seen her by day. Meeting in such a way was an exercise in self-restraint and self-control. Hence their bodies were ripe for reproduction and ever fresh for making love, ready for intercourse, not worn out and dulled by constant sexual relations. Always there remained a little spark of desire and affection between the couple.

Having arranged such conditions of modesty and order within marriage, Lycurgus cast out empty and womanish jealousy. While ruling out wanton and worthless behavior, he established that it was a good thing for worthy men to share in the begetting of children, laughing to scorn those who thought that there can never be a sharing in such matters, and who avenge any such behavior through murder and war. If an elderly man with a young wife found a well-bred young man who suited his fancy, he might well allow him to impregnate his wife with his noble seed, then adopt the child who came from the union. Likewise a worthy man who admired a woman with fine children, whose behavior was modest and respectable, might persuade her husband to allow him to sleep with her. In her fruitful soil he would plant noble children of fine breeding, linked to noble ancestors by blood and family . . .

The father did not determine whether or not the child was to be reared, but he carried it in his arms to a place called the *leschê*, where sat the eldest men of his tribe.° They examined the infant and if they found it to be well-formed and strong, they ordered that it be reared, and they assigned to it one of the nine thousand lots. If, however, the child was puny and ill-formed, they sent it to a place called "place of rejection," a steep spot by Taygetos,° thinking that a child not equipped from the beginning with good health and strength was useless to live, both to itself and to the state . . .

Lycurgus would not allow that the children of Spartiates be turned over to purchased or rented tutors, nor was a father allowed to rear his child as he pleased. Instead, when a child reached the age of seven, Lycurgus took him and enrolled him in a troop where through sharing a common discipline and nurture the children learned to play together and to study together. He appointed as leader of the troop the boy who stood out for intelligence and who was bravest in fighting. All kept their eyes on him, and when he gave orders, they obeyed, and when he punished someone, they submitted. Thus education became a practice in obedience. The older men would observe the boys as they exercised, and would set them on to battles and quarrels so that they accurately could determine the quality of each, and whether they were daring, and whether they would stand their ground in a fight.

They learned letters as much as they needed to. The rest of their education was directed to teaching them how to obey orders and to endure hardships and to win in war. For this reason as they grew older they intensified their physical training, clipping their hair short, going barefoot, and exercising naked. When they were twelve years old, they no longer wore a tunic; they received but a single cloak for a whole year. Their flesh was hard and unused to warm baths and ointments. Only on a few days a year did they experience such delights. They slept together divided into troops and companies on mattresses that they made by breaking off with their hands the tops of reeds that grew along the Eurotas—no knives allowed . . .

At this age young men of good birth began to court them as lovers. The older men, too, paid close attention and came frequently to the gymnasia, being present when the boys were fighting or joking with one another. This was no idle interest because the men felt that, in some way, they too were the fathers, tutors, and commanders of the boys. For this reason on many occasions, and in any place, there was someone to chastise and admonish the boy who went astray . . .

°*eldest men of his tribe: Poleis* divided their citizens into kinship groups called *phylai,* which historians translate as "tribes." Dorian cities had three tribes, and Ionian cities four.   °*steep spot by Mount Taygetus:* Excavations in the 1970s located this gorge, and bones of infants were found there.

"Eirens" was the name given to boys when they were two years beyond the boys' class . . . The Eiren, being a boy twenty years old, commands his subordinates in their mock battles and, indoors, uses them as servants for his meals. He orders the larger boys to gather wood and the smaller boys to gather vegetables. They steal what they bring, some sneaking into gardens, others creeping slyly and cautiously into the men's messes. If he is caught, the boy receives lashes from the whip as a clumsy, unskilled thief. They also steal what food they can, learning to be adept in pouncing on those who were asleep or keeping careless watch. If he were caught, he was whipped and given no food. Their meals are meager in order that, to avoid hunger, they are driven to daring and cunning . . .

They take their stealing so seriously that there is a story about a boy who stole a young fox and hid it under his cloak, then allowed the fox to devour his entrails with its claws and feet so that he died rather than reveal his theft. By no means is this story incredible, judging from the Spartan young men today. I have seen many of them dying under the lash at the altar of Artemis Orthia° . . .

A boy's lover shared in the boy's honor or disgrace. There is a story about a boy who let forth an unseemly cry while fighting, so the magistrates fined the lover! Sexual relations of this sort were so esteemed that even unmarried girls would have love affairs with respectable women. Yet there was no rivalry. If two men loved the same boy, that served as a basis for friendship as they eagerly together pursued efforts to perfect the character of the one they loved.

They taught the boys to speak in a style that mixed the piquant with grace and condensed broad observations in a few words. Lycurgus, as we reported, made iron money to be worth little, although its weight was great. He did the opposite for the currency of speech. He developed a way for reexpressing a wide range of thoughts in a few, concise words. As he saw it, boys who were accustomed to remain silent would give sentientious and well-trained answers. Just as the seed of a man who engages constantly in intercourse is fruitless and sterile, so intemperate and constant babbling is vapid and mindless.

Plutarch, *Life of Lycurgus* 8–19

°*Artemis Orthia:* A local cult, where violent initiations were performed.

Plutarch deeply admired Sparta, yet his account can horrify modern readers. He makes Sparta sound like a place where brutalized, half-starved, illiterate child molesters bullied the weak, stole, and repressed all common decency. Did husbands really allow other men to sleep with their wives in order to breed better warriors? Or for the first year or two of marriage pretend they were not married? Possibly Spartan customs recognized several different kinds of unions, and Plutarch, writing centuries later, misunderstood and combined them into one peculiar kind of marriage. Plutarch, of course, placed these curious customs in the distant past, claiming always that Lycurgus wanted the Spartans to do this or that, but modern times had corrupted his sacred institutions.

Xenophon, writing about Sparta 500 years before Plutarch but still long after Lycurgus, also thought that the Spartans' ancestral ways were disappearing. Already in the fifth century B.C. some Spartans were rich enough to win Olympic chariot races, the pinnacle of glory for the wealthy. Yet while the story that Lycurgus suppressed wealth and inequality cannot be literally true, it did define the Spartans to themselves. Dedication to "the good old days" reminded Spartiates of what being a Spartan meant and explained away inequalities as recent aberrations.

We should not believe every word in Plutarch, but Archaic Sparta was certainly different from most *poleis*, and we can draw some general conclusions from Plutarch's account. The Spartan claim that luxury, wealth, and debt were recent departures from an older equality encouraged martial valor in a state that was a band of brothers. Boys grew up in single-sex paramilitary institutions; girls grew up at home, with few men around. Pederasty flourished, and women may have had more license than elsewhere, in the conviction that such behavior would produce stronger sons. To make sure their sons grew up brave, tough, and disciplined, Spartans undermined the nuclear family, the basis of society elsewhere in Greece. Every *polis* wanted effective warriors, but no other was willing to pay so high a price.

## SPARTAN GOVERNMENT

Sparta had an unusual political system, with four main political institutions: the kings, the Council of Elders, the Council of Ephors ("overseers"), and the Assembly. By 700 B.C., most *poleis* discarded kings, but Sparta, always different, had two. Two families, the Agiads and the Eurypontids, each provided a king, possibly a relic of some compromise in Sparta's early history. The kings had authority in war and were the highest religious officers. The two rulers, often in disagreement, had equal standing and in Archaic times led the army jointly, until one king left the other king in the lurch in a war against Athens in 506 B.C. After that a new law decreed that only one king could be with the army at a time.

The two kings also served with twenty-eight other members on the **Council of Elders**. The five Ephors (see below) presided over the Council, which settled all serious lawsuits and determined what questions to put before an Assembly consisting of all Spartiate males. Because Sparta had no written laws, the power of the Council of Elders went beyond that of modern judges and juries combined. The Assembly also elected the Elders. When there was a vacancy, all men over sixty (when they ceased to be eligible for military service) paraded before the Spartiates, and whoever got the loudest shout was chosen.

Being made an Elder was the greatest honor in Sparta. Only about 5 percent of the population lived until their sixtieth birthday, meaning that roughly one out of every ten men still alive in their sixties would attain the rank of Elder. Very few Elders lived to serve on the Council for more than ten years, whereas a king who came to the throne as a youth could serve for forty years or more. The kings' influence on the Council waxed and waned.

Each year the Assembly also elected by acclamation the five **Ephors**. Ephors served for one year and could not be reelected. They supervised the kings and Elders, with authority to impeach or depose them if they broke the (unwritten) laws. Two Ephors always accompanied the kings on campaign and could even arrest the king if he fell short in his military obligations. The Ephors also supervised Assembly meetings. They held formidable but mostly negative powers. At the end of a year in office, each Ephor had to submit to a judicial review by the new Ephors. Ephors had to be very careful about whom they offended while in office. Curiously, we do not seem to know the name of a single Ephor, suggesting that it was not an office that served as the basis for a political career.

The **Assembly** included all Spartiate men aged over thirty and met outdoors at each full moon. The Elders made proposals and the citizens of the Assembly shouted approval or disapproval, with little discussion.

The Spartans prided themselves on their balanced constitution, in which different institutions exercised checks and balances on each other. The kings controlled war and religion;

the Elders controlled law; and the Ephors ensured fair play. In theory, the citizens of the Assembly made the final decisions, although as early as the seventh century B.C., a law was added that allowed the kings and Elders simply to adjourn the Assembly and proceed without its approval if they felt that the citizens of the Assembly were making "a crooked choice."

Political power was in the hands of a tiny elite. The Spartiates made up less than 5 percent of the population of Laconia, and the effective decision-makers were barely 1 percent of the Spartiates. Because each institution within this political elite depended on the others, drastic change was difficult, and the Spartan constitution was fairly stable from the seventh or sixth until the third century B.C. The absence of a hierarchy of offices, however, combined with Spartan deference to authority, meant that charismatic individuals could play the system and gain great power. Kings who did well in war and diplomacy extended their influence into civil society; when the kings were weak, enterprising Ephors or Elders did the reverse. Backroom deals, favoritism, and betrayal were common. When Sparta had strong leaders, the system worked well, but when leadership was weak, it worked poorly. Because of the habit of deferring to authority, indecision was easier than action. Sparta relied on oracles when its leaders could not decide, and other *poleis* bribed oracles to mislead Spartans.

Yet Sparta never had a tyrant, avoided serious civil unrest for half a millennium, and for generations remained undefeated in battle. For much of this period, Sparta was the greatest military power in Greece. No wonder people inquire into the secret of its success.

Sparta's leaders had continued the policy of annexation that worked in Messenia, but after setbacks around 560 B.C., they abandoned it. Thereafter, they worked with oligarchies in other cities, offering them military support against popular uprisings, would-be tyrants within their own ranks, and rivals in other *poleis*. In return, the cities joined a Spartan alliance that modern historians call the **Peloponnesian League** (see Map 10.1). The allies swore "to have the same friends and enemies, and to follow the Spartans wherever they lead." They did not pay tribute and could not be forced to go to war. The League was bicameral, with the Spartan Assembly voting first, then the allies as a group having the right of veto. Even if the allied assembly agreed on war, individual allies could still reject Spartan plans. The League was basically defensive, of limited effectiveness, and rarely acted north of the Isthmus of Corinth. Nevertheless, by 500 B.C., the combination of the Spartiates' ferocity and the numbers of allied hoplites meant that no Greek state dared challenge Sparta directly. As we shall see in Chapter 11, "Persia and the Greeks, 550–490 B.C.," and Chapter 12, "The Great War, 480–479 B.C.," even the greatest foreign powers did so at their own very grave risk.

## ATHENS

Archaic Athens faced many of the same problems as Sparta, but responded differently. The result, a *polis* based on equal male citizenship, was similar in both cases. But Athenians and Spartans each defined *citizens* and *equal* in their own way. The two cities were as different as was possible within ancient Greece.

## THE SEVENTH-CENTURY CRISIS

As population grew in the eighth century B.C., both Athens and Sparta had more mouths to feed. Whereas Sparta had a tradition of military expansion, Athens did not. Its neighbors were more populous, richer, and better organized than Messenia. They were not ripe for conquest. Nor did Athens follow the example of its neighbors and send colonies to Sicily, although no one knows why. Population growth put great pressure on farmers. In the precarious ancient economy, drought, a run of bad harvests, poor planning, or simple bad luck could force a farmer to seek help. As Hesiod (ca. 700 B.C.) explains, the first step for failing farmers was to ask relatives, friends, and neighbors for help:

> Measure well when you borrow from a neighbor, then
> pay him back as much, or more if you can.
> Thus when again in need, you will have a friend.

Hesiod, *Works and Days* 349–51

But what if you could not pay back what you had borrowed?

> Give to him who gives, and don't give to him
> who does not. One gives to the generous, one gives not
> to the stingy. Give is a good girl, Grab is a bad one,
> the giver of death . . .
> Don't ever go with your children and wife, grieving
> in heart, to beg food from the neighbors who really don't care.
> You might succeed two times or three, but if
> you bother them again, you will get nothing. Your many words
> will be useless, your argument will fail.

Hesiod, *Works and Days* 354–56, 399–403

Hesiod assumes that borrowers and lenders alike were farmers living close to the margin. Rather than going to an equally poor neighbor, a failing farmer might approach someone richer, who could demand the borrower's land, or even his person, as security. If the borrower failed in his obligations, the lender could take his land or make him a debt-slave. This is what happened in seventh-century Attica, according to an important document ascribed to Aristotle (fourth century B.C.):

> In other respects the political organization of the Athenians was oligarchic, and the poor were enslaved by the rich, themselves, and their children, and their wives. They were called "dependents" and "sixth-parters" because that's how much they paid in order to work the fields of the rich. "All the earth belonged to the few," as the saying went, and if they did not pay the rents, they became liable to seizure, both themselves and their children. All loans were made on the security of the person up to the time of Solon. He first stood for the interests of the *dêmos*. For most citizens slavery was the most difficult and bitter fact of the way the Athenians conducted themselves, although they suffered in other respects. You might say that the poor had no share in anything.

Aristotle, *Constitution of Athens* 2

The concentration of wealth in the hands of the rich generated resistance. In Sparta, as we saw, there was a failed coup in 706 B.C., but the Spartiates maintained cohesion and reorganized society around their triumphant hoplite army. In Athens, by contrast, the ruling elite, called the *Eupatridai* (yu-pa-**trē**-dī, "well-born ones"), basically fell apart. They were widely resented because of their wealth and their control of politics. In 632 B.C., a young Olympic victor named Cylon (**kī**-lon) launched a coup, helped by his father-in-law, the tyrant of Athens' enemy Megara down the coast (we quoted Thucydides' account of this incident in Chapter 8). When Cylon failed, the Athenians massacred his followers, despite having promised them safe passage. The recriminations that followed deepened divisions within the Athenian aristocracy, and the Athenian Assembly laid a curse on the important **Alcmaeonid** (alk-mē -o-nid) family for its part in murdering the suppliants—with unexpected repercussions to follow a whole century later.

In 621 B.C., a man named Dracon (**drā** -kō n) was empowered to set up a new law code (famous for prescribing death for virtually every crime, hence the word *"draconian"*), but the code did not reduce tensions. This divided society was poorly suited for providing patriotic soldiers, and Athens lost wars with several neighbors over the next twenty years. Megara seized the large island of Salamis off Athens' harbor, worsening Athens' land shortage and exacerbating conflicts at home. The *Eupatridai* were in such disarray that rather than planning reconquest of the island, they passed a law condemning to death anyone who mentioned the loss. As Johnny-come-latelies to Greek colonization, the Athenians finally sent a colony to the north Aegean, but in 607 B.C. it was defeated and ignominiously thrown out. In the seventh century B.C., there were few signs of Athens' future greatness.

## SOLON

Athens had lost territory; its aristocracy was racked by feuds; and class warfare was breaking out. Alarmed, in 594 B.C. the *Eupatridai* chose **Solon** (sō-lon), one of their own number, to work out a compromise with the rebellious poor. Solon produced a new law code as comprehensive as that which the Spartans attributed to Lycurgus. Solon, however, certainly existed. Some 300 lines of his poetry survive in quotations by later authors and the wooden boards recording his laws could still be seen on the Acropolis in the fifth century B.C. In the fourth century B.C., lawyers liked to claim that any laws favoring their clients had been passed by Solon, to make them sound more weighty, but in spite of the legends the main outlines of his reforms are clear enough.

Solon, like the Spartans, saw the ideal society as a band of brothers. The Spartans made their system work by stealing their neighbors' land, turning the former owners into serfs, and breaking down family structures to support the warrior brotherhood. No such options were available to Solon, who reorganized the existing economy and society by redefining property rights.

He began with Athenians' ownership of their own bodies. From now on, no one could own another freeborn Athenian. All current debt-bondsmen were freed; those sold into slavery abroad were brought home; no loan could ever again be secured on someone's person; and all outstanding debts were canceled. He then redistributed land, although we are not sure how. In one poem, he appeals to "the mighty mother of the Olympian gods, dark Earth, whose boundary stones fixed in many places I once removed; enslaved before, she is now free." But in another poem he says, "It gives me no pleasure to act with the violence of tyranny or to share the country's rich land equally between *kakoi* and *esthloi*" (*esthloi* is another word for *agathoi,* "the good people"). Probably he did not redistribute the land into equal-sized plots, as Lycurgus was thought to have done at Sparta, but returned to its original owners land that had been used as security on bad loans. We know that there were still big landowners in the later sixth century, but also a broad class of peasant freeholders. Solon also defended the right of childless landowners to sell, give, or will their land to whomever they wished, regardless of what their relatives thought. Plutarch, who wrote a *Life of Solon* as well as of Lycurgus, recognized that "the effect of this law was to make every man's possessions truly his own."

Athenians called Solon's reforms the *seisasachtheia* (sās-ak-**thē** -a), or "shaking-off-of-burdens." But there were still too many people and not enough land, and just ending debt-bondage could easily have made things worse: If the poor could not borrow on the security of their persons, the rich had less reason to lend in bad years. But Solon also promoted a sounder economic base. He banned the export of grain from Attica. Bad harvests can turn into famines if rich landowners can get a better price for their wheat abroad, so Solon required them to sell all grain at home. Much Athenian soil was not good for growing cereals, but was excellent for olives and vines: Solon encouraged these crops. He clarified weights and measures to simplify exchange, required fathers to teach their sons a trade, and established incentives for craftsmen to come to Athens.

Archaeological finds reflect increased prosperity after Solon. Sculpture and pot painting reached new heights of excellence in early sixth-century Athens. Athenian clay vessels for olive oil, called "SOS amphoras" after the designs on their necks, are widespread around the Mediterranean, and after 550 B.C. Athenian fine pottery turns up everywhere from Spain to Syria. Athens expanded her silver mining, exporting silver coin and importing more and more food (Figure 10.4). Athens not only survived the crisis but flourished.

Solon overhauled the political system by dividing all citizens into four census classes based on wealth:

1. The *pentakosiomedimnoi*, "five-hundred-measures men," whose land yielded over 500 *medimnoi* (a unit of measure) of produce each year. They could hold all political offices in the state.
2. The *hippeis*, "horsemen," who produced 300 to 499 *medimnoi*. They could hold all offices except treasurer.
3. The *zeugitai*, "yokemen" (probably meaning they had enough land to need a team of oxen), producing 200 to 299 *medimnoi*. A *zeugitês* could hold lower political offices but could not serve as treasurer or as archon (ar-kon), "leader."
4. The *thêtes*, or "poor," producing less than 200 *medimnoi*. They could not hold political offices but attended the Assembly and served as jurors.

**FIGURE 10.4** Two sides of an Athenian silver coin, ca. 525–500 B.C. On the left is the goddess Athena in her trademark helmet; on the right are other symbols of Athens—an olive branch, an owl, and three Greek letters spelling "Athe," in abbreviation for Athens. These coins, known as *owls*, are found all over the Mediterranean and attest to Athens' export of silver to pay for imports (particularly food and slaves).

Nearly all Athenians were *thêtes*. A *medimnos* consisted of about seventy-five pounds of barley or ninety pounds of wheat, so the requirements for belonging to the upper classes were high. A typical peasant farm in classical Attica was about five hectares (one hectare is about two and a half acres), but to qualify as a *zeugitês*, a man would need ten to twenty hectares, and as a *pentakosiomedimnos*, at least twenty-five to fifty hectares. Although the top property class was poor by Near Eastern standards, probably only one in ten Athenians qualified.

Nine **archons** were elected each year from the top two classes. One served as chief archon, with extensive powers. A man could be archon only once, but after his year in office he became a life-member of the council known as the **Areopagus** (a-rē-op-a-gus, "stake of Ares"), named after the hill beneath the west end of the Athenian Acropolis where the council met (the Acropolis was the fortified hill that dominates Athens, where the Parthenon stands to this day). This upper-class body tried major lawsuits, especially murder, and had general judicial oversight.

As a balance against the power of the Areopagus, Solon created juries manned by citizens of all classes to hear appeals. He allowed any Athenian, regardless of census class, to bring suit against anyone else before these juries. According to Aristotle, Solon deliberately worded the laws vaguely so the juries completely controlled legal interpretation (his most democratic reform, Aristotle thought).

The Assembly, apparently open to all citizens who wanted to attend meetings, probably decided war and peace and elected the archons, and perhaps dealt with other major decisions. In Sparta the citizen assembly simply shouted yes or no to proposals made by the Elders, and if the Elders did not like the assembly's response, they could overrule it. Solon apparently wanted to give the poor more power and designed a **Council of 400**, men chosen from the four traditional Athenian "tribes" (*phylai*), based on kinship, one hundred men from each tribe (but *thêtes* could not be members). This Council drew up the agenda for Assembly meetings; and since whoever controls the agenda always controls the meeting, this act gave even citizens of modest means a voice in politics.

Solon wanted to strike a balance between the rich and the poor and to restrain elite feuding. He advised the rich:

You, making quiet the strong heart in your breast,
you who have driven to the summit of satiety
in your possession of good things—set your mind on the middle way.
For we shall not be persuaded, nor will
everything go just your way . . .
For I gave to the *dêmos* as much reward as is fitting,
neither taking away from their honor nor adding.
As for those who had power and were admired for great wealth,
I was careful that nothing improper happened
to them. I took my stand, spreading out my strong
shield over both parties, and not
allowing either side to take unjust advantage.

Solon fragments 4c, 5 (West)

Solon departed most strongly from the Spartans in seeing the ideal community as an agglomeration of independent households, with the male heads of the households coming together in ritual, war, and politics to constitute a brotherhood. Solon had no interest in Spartan-type public dining messes, but worked to strengthen the nuclear family and the authority of its male head. Plutarch says that Solon limited dowries to reduce fortune-hunting men marrying for money. He insisted on the sexual basis of honest marriage, decreeing that "an heiress' husband should have intercourse with her at least three times a month. Even if they have no children, this is a mark of honor and affection that a man owes to a chaste wife. It removes many of the frustrations that arise in such cases and prevents their differences from bringing about a complete estrangement" (Plutarch, *Solon* 23). Solon also regulated women's behavior and travel, restricting them to the domestic sphere under male control. Unlike the Spartiates, Athenian men combined the roles of husband, father, farmer, warrior, trader, and citizen. They would support themselves through their own enterprise, not through the labors of state-owned slaves.

## PISISTRATUS AND THE CONSEQUENCES OF SOLON'S REFORMS

At first Solon's reforms appeared as ineffectual as Dracon's reforms from thirty years earlier, and in 590 B.C. and again in 586 B.C elite conflicts grew so severe that no archons were appointed. A certain Damasias, elected archon in 582 B.C, refused to step down in 581, probably seeking a tyranny, and had to be forced out. In the 570s B.C, three factions formed, known as the parties of the Plain, Shore, and Hill, combining regional and class solidarities to support individual aristocrats. Aristotle says, "In general, there was a kind of sickness that characterized their relationships with one another. Some saw the origin and cause of their troubles to be the cancellation of debts, 'for that brought us poverty.' Others were upset with how things were simply because of the great change, others because of mutual envy" (Aristotle, *Constitution of Athens* 13.3).

Solon's cancellation of debts must have thrown the upper class into chaos, giving windfall profits to some and ruining others. Many lost land they thought their own, and most lost their ability to coerce labor. There was little reason to have a large estate if there was no one to farm it. A normal family can effectively work only a few acres—nowhere near enough to qualify as *zeugitai*, let alone as *pentakosiomedimnoi*. Solon's poetry gives the impression that few *Eupatridai* cared to spend all day in the hot sun behind a heavy plow. They might hire workers, but they would need to make enough profit from selling produce to pay competitive wages. With a large, landless population the cost of labor is low, but by returning land to the poor Solon effectively increased the price of labor. People preferred working their own land to being wage earners. To compound the problem, the times when large landowners needed labor most—the seasons of sowing and harvesting—were the same times that small farmers also needed labor.

The Athenian aristocracy solved their problem in the early sixth century B.C. by importing foreign slaves. In the seventh century, it was cheaper to reduce the local poor to serfdom than to import and maintain slaves, but in the sixth century more slaves became available and in Athens slavery became structurally necessary to society. Cheap slaves came on the market from the BALKANS, UKRAINE, and ANATOLIA (Map 10.2). When Herodotus listed the customs of the Thracians (living in modern Bulgaria), he matter-of-factly said, "They carry on an export trade in their own children."

Slaves allowed rich Athenians to stay rich without having to drive the poor back into serfdom. Ironically, freedom and slavery depended on each other: The free Spartiates depended on enslaved helots and the free Athenians on imported slaves. By the fourth century B.C., probably one in four residents of Attica was a slave. Slaves could be found in

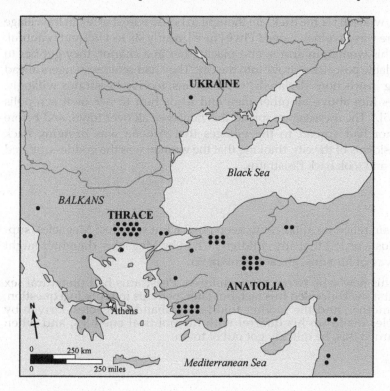

**MAP 10.2** Two groups of classical Athenian inscriptions tell us the origins of fifty-four Athenian slaves. Each dot on the map represents one of these slaves.

nearly every walk of life, particularly crafts, mining, and domestic service. Many pedagogues, teachers of the rich, were slaves. Even modestly wealthy households would own a slave.

In 561 B.C., a powerful aristocrat named **Pisistratus** (pī-**sis**-tra-tus) launched a bloodless coup and established a tyranny in Athens. Pisistratus had won popularity by recapturing the island of Salamis from Athens' rival Megara. Following a strategy for seizing power described in Chapter 8, he pretended to have been attacked by rivals so that the Assembly allowed him a small bodyguard armed with clubs for his protection. Like most *poleis*, Athens had no standing army or police. Pisistratus then simply announced that he and his clubmen were taking over. Nonetheless, Aristotle says, "he administered affairs more like a citizen than a tyrant," governing through political alliances more than the implied threat of his club bearers.

Sometimes the difference between being a tyrant and being the most influential oligarch was subtle. In 556 B.C. two Athenian rivals—Megacles (a suitor at the court of Cleisthenes; Chapter 8) and Lycurgus (not the same as the legendary Spartan of the same name)—pushed Pisistratus aside, but he remained in Athens and continued to play a role in politics. Soon after, Lycurgus pushed Megacles aside too, so in 551 B.C., Megacles made Pisistratus an offer: If Pisistratus would marry Megacles' daughter, Megacles would help him regain the tyranny. Herodotus tells a strange story about this incident:

> Pisistratus agreed to the terms proposed. Then, to bring about his return to power, they devised what to my mind was the silliest trick in history, especially in light of the fact that the Hellenic people have always been thought to be more clever than barbarian peoples and more removed from idle simplicity, and among the Hellenes

the Athenians, who fell for the trick, are thought to be the wisest of all. In the village of Paeania there was a woman named Phyê [ **fu**-ē ], nearly six feet tall and beautiful. Decking out this woman in armor, and placing her in a chariot, they got her to strike a formidable pose, then drove into the city. They had sent messengers ahead who following instructions declared: "O Athenians, receive Pisistratus willingly. Athena values him above all other men and leads him to her own acropolis [cf. Figure 10.5]." The messengers spread this nonsense all over town, and before long the rumor had spread to the villages that Athena was bringing back Pisistratus. Residents of the city, thinking that the woman was the goddess, offered prayers to her and took back Pisistratus.

Herodotus 1.60

Pisistratus again relied on alliances to keep power, but soon lost Megacles' support. Pisistratus worried that any children he had by Megacles' daughter might stand in the way of his sons, already grown. So:

Not wanting his new wife to have any children, Pisistratus had unnatural sex with her. At first she concealed this fact, but later, perhaps in reply to a question, she told her mother, and the mother told her husband Megacles. Driven by anger, Megacles made up his quarrel with his political enemies, and when Pisistratus learned this, he quickly got out of town.

Herodotus 1.61

**FIGURE 10.5** Chariot driven by Athena with Artemis as passenger. Artemis wears a decorated gown and holds a bow. Athena wears a cloak but no helmet or other attribute. Both figures are named. Archaic Athenian black-figured vase, signed by Sophilos, ca. 580 B.C.

In exile again, Pisistratus went over the situation with his two sons, Hippias and Hipparchus. He borrowed money and soldiers from rich men and tyrants in other cities and hired mercenaries. In 546 B.C., he and his men landed in Attica on the beach at Marathon (site of the famous battle against the Persians in 490 B.C.). Various malcontents joined him. For a while, the Athenians ignored him. Eventually they sent out an army, but it had little heart for a fight, and Pisistratus surprised it while the Athenian soldiers were eating lunch and napping. He persuaded them to go home but took their weapons.

Pisistratus had again triumphed, but this time his grip was tighter and Athenians later looked back on his reign as a golden age of peace and security. By the time Pisistratus died in 527 B.C., archaeology reveals that Athens was richer than in Solon's time: Its houses were better built, its public facilities had improved, and its petty industry and mining were vigorous. Athenian goods were widely exported. By the 520s B.C., Athenian "black glaze" drinking vessels were the most common traded wares around the whole Mediterranean. The city's growth to perhaps 25,000 people, many of them artisans, meant that Athenian farmers could now always find buyers for their produce, while the high value of Athenian manufactured goods meant that farmers from other *poleis*, or even outside Greece, could get a good enough price for their grain to make it worth shipping to Athens. Athenian farmers exchanged high-value olive oil for imported food. The painful conflicts of the seventh century slipped away under Pisisistratus' rule.

All the same, Pisistratus feared aristocratic plots. Rather than following Thrasyboulos' advice to kill the outstanding men in the city (Chapter 8), he made them part of the successful enterprise, allowing potential rivals to hold office and profit from the regime. He also elevated poorer citizens, listened to the Assembly, and followed the laws. He instituted new taxes, something everyone hated about tyrants, but from the revenue he provided loans to the farmers to develop their land. He constructed ambitious public buildings. Some of these, like fountain houses and drains, benefited everyone. He overhauled the legal system, creating local justices who reported directly to him. In reducing aristocratic power he strengthened the institutions of the centralized state.

When Pisistratus died in 527 B.C., his sons ruled as a junta, but the oldest of them, **Hippias**, wielded the real power. He and his brother **Hipparchus** continued to promote Athens as a cultural center, inviting great poets to their court. Pisistratus had himself instituted festivals, including a revised Panathenaea, and introduced public recitations of Homer's poems based on complete texts (see Chapter 6). Athens became a leading center for innovation in sculpture and painting. However, in 514 B.C., Hipparchus fell in love with a boy named **Harmodius**, who was in turn the beloved (*eromenos*) of the older **Aristogeiton** (a-ris-tō-jī-ton, the *erastês*). Harmodius rebuffed Hipparchus, who then used his influence to exclude Harmodius' sister from carrying a basket in the great Panathenaic festival, a massive insult to Harmodius' family. Harmodius and Aristogeiton decided to murder the tyrants, but the plot misfired. Hippias escaped; only Hipparchus died. Guards killed the boy Harmodius on the spot. They captured Aristogeiton and tortured him to death.

In the fifth century B.C., many misremembered the incident as a political act and thought that Harmodius and Aristogeiton had overthrown the tyrants (which they did not). Many honored them as champions of freedom, though their real motives were sex, anger, and revenge. Their descendants were exempted from taxes and had the right to dine at public expense. Popular songs celebrated Harmodius and Aristogeiton as Athens' saviors. A famous bronze statue, the first to be bought with public funds, was erected in the agora in 509 B.C. Later carried as plunder to Persia, Alexander the Great recaptured the statue and returned it to Athens (Figure 10.6).

**FIGURE 10.6** Harmodius and Aristogeiton. When Hippias fell in 510 B.C., the Athenians set up statues of Harmodius and Aristogeiton in the Agora. The Persians took the original group in 480 B.C. (Alexander the Great later returned it), so the Athenians set up new statues. These too are now lost, but this photograph shows a Roman copy, today in Naples. The clean-shaven Harmodius holds a sword in his upraised left hand while his bearded lover Aristogeiton extends a rock in his left hand, a protective cape draped over his arm.

Harmodius' and Aristogeiton's attack provoked a vicious crackdown. Hippias executed or exiled many noblemen and soon lost the support of leading families. He appealed to the curse laid on the Alcmaeonid family back in 632 B.C., because of their role in the Cylon affair, to get this powerful clan exiled. Exploiting Sparta's opposition to tyrants and faith in oracles, the Alcmaeonids responded by bribing the Delphic priests to give the same response to every Spartan who sought advice: "First free Athens." The Alcmaeonids also rebuilt the temple of Apollo at Delphi, recently damaged by fire, and paid for an expensive marble façade out of their own pockets. Sparta and Hippias had previously had good relations, but Sparta's attitude, Herodotus says, was "no matter—the commands of the god are more important than human ties."

An initial Spartan raid on Athens in 511 B.C. failed when Hippias' friends in Thessaly sent him 1,000 cavalry, who routed the Spartan hoplites. But the next year, Sparta's king

Cleomenes returned with a larger army and defeated the Thessalians. Many Athenians now joined the Spartans, and Hippias withdrew to the Acropolis. The Spartans captured Hippias' sons and released them in return for Hippias' pledge to go into permanent exile. The tyrants had fallen at last. Hippias fled to the distant court of Persia, soon to assist the greatest enemy that Classical Greece ever faced.

## DÊMOKRATIA

Having dismembered the Athenian tyranny, supposedly at the command of the Delphic oracle that was under the influence of the rival Athenian Alcmaeonid clan, the Spartan king Cleomenes promptly went home (510 B.C.) and Athens returned to the kind of chaotic aristocratic politicking that Pisistratus had suspended in 546 B.C. In these conditions, an Alcmaeonid named **Cleisthenes** (klī-sthen-ēz) emerged as a strongman in the state. Throughout Archaic times, aristocrats had mobilized ordinary citizens to overthrow their rivals, putting new oligarchs or a tyrant in their place, but after about 525 B.C. citizens insisted on taking parts of government for themselves. In this spirit, Cleisthenes ceded power to ordinary Athenians in return for their help.

Cleisthenes' first step was to break up the four old "tribes" (*phylai*), kinship groups that had been sources of aristocratic power (not the same as the four wealth classes that Solon established). Cleisthenes divided Attica into thirty units called *trittyes* ("thirtieths"). Modifying the regional groupings so important in politics since the 570s B.C., he formed ten new tribes by clustering the *trittyes* into ten groups, each consisting of three *trittyes*: one from the coastal area, one from the inland area, and one from the urban area (Map 10.3). Each *trittys* contained several villages or city neighborhoods, designated by the word *dêmos* ("people," but when used to describe one of Cleisthenes' units, historians translate it "deme"). Formerly, Athenian men were known by their personal name (they had only one) and their father's name (e.g., Hippias son of Pisistratus). From now on, they were known by their name and deme (e.g., Pericles of Cholargus).

Solon's Council of 400, which drew up the agenda for the Assembly, had one hundred men from each of the old four tribes. Cleisthenes replaced this body with a **Council of 500**, composed of fifty men selected by lot from each of the ten new tribes. Councilors had to be over thirty, served for a year, and could serve only twice in their lifetimes. This meant that almost every Athenian citizen would have to serve at some point in his life. Men were chosen by lot to serve as president of the Council of 500 for twenty-four hours. Roughly three out of every four citizens would fill this position at some point in their lives, and about one citizen in twelve would hold the position on a day when there was a meeting of the full Assembly. On that day a citizen of the lowest standing and social class could very well preside over thousands of his fellow citizens as they made life-and-death decisions about war and peace or the food supply.

Athenians eventually termed their radically egalitarian political system *dêmokratia*, "power of the people." The word "democracy" of course comes from this word. Athenian *dêmokratia* looks undemocratic today, because the *dêmos*, "people," excluded women, children, and slaves, but from the ancient Greek perspective it was a radical system. The men on the Council of 500 came from every walk of Athenian life, from peasants to politicians. Cleisthenes himself might sit in the Council next to a farmer who had never been more than a day's walk from his home, and both were expected to have something to say. The constitution *required* that all citizens be involved. Athenians wanted ordinary citizens to set the agenda.

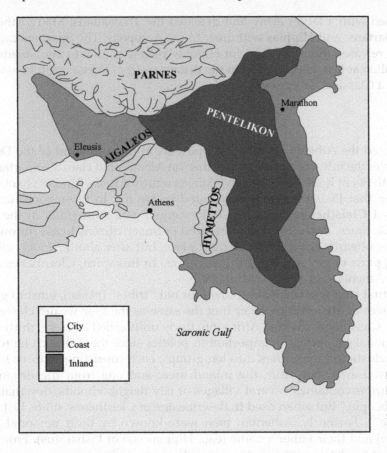

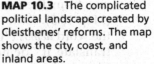

**MAP 10.3** The complicated political landscape created by Cleisthenes' reforms. The map shows the city, coast, and inland areas.

All citizens were free to come to the Assembly, discuss the issues, vote, and put decisions into action. Political power did not depend on winning elections once every four years, but on coming to the Assembly, speaking, and persuading people on the day of the vote. Politicians had to keep turning up at meetings of the Assembly; a single vote could wipe out years of work. Political leaders could attempt bribery and make secret deals, but after the citizens took over Athens' government, real power came from speaking well in the Assembly. If a man lost the people's support, they might fine, exile, or even execute him.

Athenians recognized the importance of individual leaders. In Chapter 8, we mentioned the remarkable annual unpopularity contest called **ostracism**, designed to prevent anyone from becoming *too* popular and (like Pisistratus) from using the Assembly as a stepping-stone to tyranny. Each year, the Athenians could vote to send one man away for ten years, a punishment in anticipation of a crime (but the ostracized man's property remained intact until he returned). First the Assembly voted on whether there should be an ostracism that year. If 6,000 citizens voted and the majority said yes, then each citizen took a fragment of broken pottery (an *ostrakon* in Greek, hence ostracism) and wrote a name on it. Those who could not write could buy prewritten potsherds (Figure 10.7). Whoever got the most votes had to leave town for ten years.

Athenians went to extraordinary lengths to minimize the political advantages that education, experience, or contacts gave some men. They wanted all men to be involved in making decisions that affected the group and even used complicated lottery machines to randomize participation. The Athenians would not have thought our political systems democratic. If rich people with years of experience in professional government, law, or business make the major decisions, these systems are oligarchies, not democracies, even if we vote every four years on which wealthy professionals govern us.

*Dêmokratia* developed Archaic traditions but also broke with them. The sense of community was strong in early Greece, where the *agathoi* never really distanced themselves from the *kakoi* and were always answerable to them. The Greeks rejected divine kingship and increasingly turned to public discussion to solve problems. Cleisthenes and democratic reformers in other *poleis* extended such principles. Formerly, aristocrats were answerable to the people, but claimed to act as guardians. In the late sixth century, the citizens began to doubt that aristocrats had any advantage in wisdom. Sometimes a rich man would have the best idea, sometimes a poor man. Because all citizens shared wisdom, the only sensible way to run a state was to make its institutions as open as possible.

Few Greek texts spell out this new vision explicitly, because most literate people (the aristocracy) were ambiguous about or even hostile toward democracy. The clearest statement comes in one of Plato's philosophical dialogues, probably written in the 390s B.C. In it the professional teacher Protagoras explains the logic of democracy to Socrates (who later challenges it). Protagoras cast his explanation as a myth, not an abstract argument. When the gods created the world, he said, they told Epimetheus ("Afterthought") to hand out attributes to the animals. To some he gave claws and teeth; to others, protective shells; to others still, speed. By the time he came to humans, he had given away all the available powers. But his

**FIGURE 10.7** An *ostrakon* with the names of the famous Themistocles, who led the Athenians to victory against Persia in 480 B.C., and the unknown Odeadeios. Over 200 *ostraka* inscribed "Themistocles" were found in a single deposit, evidently to be passed out to those who could not write.

brother Prometheus ("Forethought") stole fire and arts such as speech and house-building from the other gods and gave them to humans as their special gift:

> Thus provided for, men lived scattered about. There were no cities. They perished from wild animals because they were weaker in every way. Their technical skill was sufficient to keep them fed, but of little use in the war against the wild animals. For they lacked the arts of politics, of which war is a part. They sought to save themselves by gathering together and founding cities, but when they did so, they injured one another through the lack of political skills, with the result that they scattered once again and continued to perish. Zeus, fearing that the race might be wiped out utterly, sent Hermes to bring to humans a sense of respect and a respect for justice, so that the cites might be well ordered and the inhabitants bound by ties of friendship.
>
> "Shall I distribute these qualities as the other skills, so that, for example, one man knowing the arts of healing is able to care for many individuals, and so with the other experts? Shall I impart a sense of justice and respect in this way, or impart them to all?"
>
> "To all," said Zeus, "and may all have a share. You cannot have cities if only a few possess such qualities, as they do with the other arts. And set down this rule of mine, that if anyone is unable to incorporate the qualities of respect and justice, then he must be put to death as a plague to the city."
>
> Thus, and for this reason, O Socrates, the Athenians, and all other peoples, when they are discussing skill in building, or in any other craft, they think that only a few are able to offer advice. If someone outside the circle of experts wants to offer advice, they do not tolerate it—and rightly so, as it seems to me. But when they seek advice about political wisdom, which must always proceed according to the dictates of justice and moderation, rightly they listen to the opinion of every man. For they think that everyone must share in this kind of virtue, or else cities cannot exist. That, O Socrates, is the cause of this.

Plato, *Protagoras* 322B–3A

If Protagoras' logic holds, democracy is the only rational way to run a community. But to critics, democracy simply maximized the input of ignorant people. What right did Cleisthenes have to bring the rabble onto the political stage, to gain his own advantage? Isagoras, Cleisthenes' major rival in Athenian political circles, asked Sparta's king Cleomenes to return to Athens and set things straight. Cleisthenes fled in 508 B.C. as Cleomenes marched in with a small force and banished 700 families. Isagoras wanted to set up a ruling Council of 300 men to run Athens with himself at its head. He asked Cleomenes to disband the current Council responsible for setting the Assembly's agenda, but the city rose up in a mob. Cleomenes and Isagoras fled to the Acropolis and for two days crowds raged outside its gates. On the third day, Cleomenes and Isagoras quietly surrendered, selling out their friends in return for safe passage to Sparta.

## ATHENS SUBMITS TO PERSIA

The new democracy was saved from Spartan oligarchic interference, but there was no guarantee of its future. Sparta's enraged King Cleomenes roused the Peloponnesian League to attack Athens and contrary to Sparta's traditions of opposing tyranny planned to install Isagoras as tyrant. He arranged a triple attack in 506 B.C. with armies from Thebes and Chalcis invading at the same time as Sparta. Athens seemed doomed, until Sparta's Corinthian allies discovered the plan to make Isagoras tyrant. They would not fight for such a purpose. When Demaratus, co-king with Cleomenes, discovered why the Corinthians had withdrawn, he too marched home in disgust. Never again would the Spartans send two kings into the field at once. In the chaos, the other allies withdrew. The Athenians wheeled their army around, caught first the Thebans, then the Chalcidians, and destroyed them utterly.

Cleomenes abandoned his support for Isagoras, and the plan to make him tyrant, and invited to Sparta Hippias (last of the Pisistratids, whom Cleomenes had himself deposed in 510 B.C.), promising to restore him to power. In 505 B.C. Cleomenes mustered a second Peloponnesian army, but the Corinthians again refused to join and this coalition army too dissolved. The Thebans foolishly sought revenge for the previous year's defeat without Spartan help, only to be routed a second time. Athens' victory astonished Greece:

> The Athenians were going from strength to strength. It is clear that equality before the law is a vigorous quality not only in a single respect, but in all respects. For when the Athenians were ruled by tyrants, they were no stronger in war than any of their neighbors, but once they threw out the tyrants, they became the best fighters anywhere. These facts make clear that so long as they were held back, constrained by tyranny, they deliberately performed poorly, but when they became free every man was eager to do something for himself.
>
> Herodotus 5.78

Athens had come far since Solon's reforms a century earlier, but after expelling Cleomenes in 508, Herodotus tells us, the Athenians made a terrible blunder:

> After these things, the Athenians sent to bring back Cleisthenes and the 700 households exiled by Cleomenes. Realizing that they were at war with the Lacedemonians and with Cleomenes, they sent messengers to Sardis,° wishing to make an alliance with the Persians. When the messenger arrived at Sardis and explained what they wanted, Artaphernes the son of Hystaspes, governor of Sardis, asked who *were* these Athenians and where did they live, who sought to become allies of the Persians. When they told him, he put it to them straight: If they would give earth and water to King Darius, he would make an alliance with them. If they did not give it, they should depart. The envoys, acting on their own authority, said they would give it, because they wished to conclude the pact. Then they went away, but at home suffered severe censure for what they had done.
>
> Herodotus 5.73

°*Sardis:* The capital of Lydia in western Turkey, the westernmost province of the Persian Empire (see Chapter 11).

From fear of Sparta, Athens had voluntarily submitted to Persia, the greatest empire the world had ever seen. Giving earth and water acknowledged that the Persian god, Ahuramazda, was supreme being in the heavens, and that their king, Darius, was his embodiment on earth with a right to rule over it. Submission was final and permanent. Backing out was rebellion against the divine order, and Darius was bound by the laws of heaven to punish rebels of any kind. The facts that Persia did not help Athens in 506 or 505 B.C., and that the Spartan threat failed to materialize, were beside the point. The Athenians had no idea what they had gotten into, but they would soon find out.

## Key Terms

helots, *198*
Spartan mirage, *199*
Lycurgus, *199*
Laconia, *199*
Dorian, *199*
*perioikoi*, *200*
Spartiates, *200*
Messenia, *201*
Council of Elders, *208*

Ephors, *208*
Assembly, *209*
Peloponnesian
    League, *209*
Alcmaeonid, *211*
Solon, *211*
archons, *213*
Areopagus, *213*
Council of 400, *213*

Pisistratus, *215*
Hippias, *217*
Hipparchus, *217*
Harmodius, *217*
Aristogeiton, *217*
Cleisthenes, *219*
Council of 500, *219*
*dêmokratia*, *219*
ostracism, *220*

## Further Reading

### SPARTA

Cartledge, Paul, *The Spartans* (New York, 2002). Highly readable overview of Spartan history by the world's foremost authority.

Ducat, Jean, *Spartan Education: Youth and Society in the Classical Period* (Swansea, UK, 2006). New analysis of Sparta's unusual social system.

Finley, Moses, "Sparta and Spartan Society." In Moses Finley, *Economy and Society in Ancient Greece* (New York, 1981). This essay, first published in 1968, is the inspiration for most modern work on Sparta. It turned attention away from fanciful reconstructions of Spartan prehistory and toward concrete analysis of how institutions functioned.

Manfredi, Valerio Massimo, *The Spartan* (New York, 2001). A novel set in ancient Sparta. More accurate than most historical novels.

Pomeroy, Sarah, *Spartan Women* (Oxford, 2002). Straightforward and sensible account of a complex subject.

Powell, Anton, ed., *Classical Sparta: Techniques Behind Her Success* (London, 1989); Anton Powell and Steve Hodkinson, eds., *The Shadow of Sparta* (London, 1994) and *Sparta Beyond the Mirage* (London 2002); and Steve Hodkinson and Anton Powell, eds., *Sparta: New Perspectives* (London, 1999). Proceedings of four major conferences on different aspects of Spartan history.

Whitby, Michael, ed., *Sparta* (Edinburgh, 2002). Collection of classic articles spanning thirty-five years.

### ATHENS

Finley, Moses, *Ancient Slavery and Modern Ideology*, chapter 2 (London, 1980). Sparkling account of the Solonian crisis.

Gallant, Tom, *Risk and Survival in Ancient Greece* (Stanford, 1991). Models the life-cycle of Athenian farming families. Excellent use of modern comparative agricultural data.

Murray, Oswyn, *Early Greece*, 2nd ed. (Stanford, 1993). Excellent survey of the Archaic period.

Raaflaub, Kurt, Josiah Ober, and Robert W. Wallace, eds., *The Origins of Democracy in Ancient Greece* (Berkeley, 2007). Collection of essays on early Athens.

Shapiro, H. Alan, *Art and Cult under the Tyrants* (Mainz, Germany, 1989). Study of Pisistratus' use of religion, architecture, and propaganda.

### ANCIENT TEXTS

*Iambi et elegi Graeci ante Alexandrum cantati 2: Callinus. Mimnermus. Semonides. Solon. Tyrtaeus. Minora adespota*, ed. M. L. West, rev. ed. (Oxford, 1992).

Aristotle, *The Athenian Constitution*, tr. P. J. Rhodes (New York, 1984). The main narrative for sixth-century B.C. Athenian history. Written at Athens, 330s or 320s B.C.

Plato, *Protagoras and Meno*, tr. W. K. C. Guthrie (Harmondsworth, UK, 1957). Two influential dialogues, early fourth century B.C.

Plutarch, *Life of Lycurgus*, and Xenophon, *Spartan Society*. In *Plutarch on Sparta*, tr. Richard Talbert (New York, 1988). The most important sources for Spartan society. Plutarch wrote around A.D. 100; Xenophon, in the early fourth century B.C.

## CHAPTER 11

# Persia and the Greeks, 550–490 B.C.

Through conquest, colonization, trade, and internal reorganization, Archaic Greece adjusted to population growth. The Greeks learned to manage elite feuds, conflicts between rich and poor, and wars between states. By 500 B.C., the Greeks were richer, more stable, and more creative than ever before. But all these changes had happened in centuries when they faced no external threats, and that was about to change.

Expanding population, trade, and wealth across the whole Mediterranean basin made the interstate environment more competitive. As tax revenues grew, rulers spent more on war, forcing their neighbors to do the same. In the meanwhile, ruthless kings carved out empires in western Asia. In the 550s B.C., Lydia made the Ionian Greek cities pay tribute, and a decade later Sparta was drawn into Near Eastern affairs when Persia reached the Aegean. In the 510s B.C., Persian troops crossed the Hellespont into mainland Europe, and, as we have seen, Persia received Athens' formal submission in 506 B.C.. In 490, Persia attacked Athens. At the same time, the growing power of the Sicilian Greeks alarmed the nearby Phoenician city of Carthage in what is now Tunisia. In east and west alike, tensions erupted in the fateful year of 480 B.C., when Persia and Carthage both sent huge forces against the Greeks. The Greeks triumphed, but the effort of doing so changed their world forever.

## EMPIRES OF THE ANCIENT NEAR EAST

### Assyria

What did these foreign powers want, and why did they attack the Greeks? To answer these questions we must make a short detour back into Near Eastern history. In the tenth century B.C., while Greece was still home to small, shifting populations isolated from the larger world, a new empire arose in the Near East. In the 930s B.C., the **Assyrians**, an agricultural people

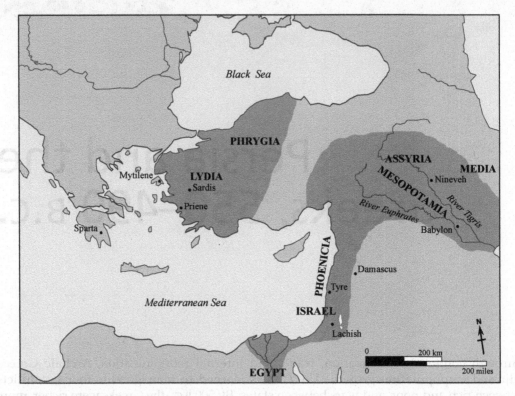

**MAP 11.1** The Assyrian and Lydian Empires.

who lived along the upper banks of the Tigris River in what today is northern Iraq (Map 11.1), began raiding their neighbors for plunder, and within 50 years these bandit-kings had reached the Mediterranean coast. They believed that their god **Ashur** ruled the heavens and required all humans to recognize this. The Assyrian aristocracy provided troops, and the kings rewarded them with plunder; the enriched nobles then provided more troops, who won more victories. Armed with formidable new siege engines (Figure 11.1) and supply systems that could feed vast forces, the war machine rolled on. Assyria installed friendly client-kings or put in Assyrian governors over the defeated peoples. Some rulers simply submitted to Assyria and paid tribute. They avoided devastation and might themselves join the Assyrian elite, receiving Assyrian support in local disputes (Figure 11.2).

But some peoples were more difficult to conquer. In 739 B.C., Assyria took Babylon, the greatest city in Mesopotamia, but it repeatedly rebelled. The little kingdoms of Israel and Judah also resisted fiercely; they believed their god Yahweh was even more jealous than Ashur and had sent Assyria to punish them for disobedience to the laws laid down by Moses. In response to their intransigence, Assyria depopulated Israel in 722 B.C. and brought in foreigners to settle the land. The transplanted foreigners became the Samaritans, objects of deepest hatred in times of the New Testament. In 689 B.C. the Assyrians burned Babylon to the ground.

The Assyrians reserved their greatest rage for vassals who submitted but then rebelled, because such people had broken their word to the great god Ashur. In the following inscription, King Ashurnasirpal II ("Ashur Is Guardian of the Sun") describes what he did to one group of rebels:

**FIGURE 11.1**   Assyrian siege warfare, depicted in Tiglath-Pileser III's palace at Nimrud, ca. 730 B.C. A wheeled siege engine, protected by hides and armed with rams, advances up a slope to break the city's walls. The fate of the city's inhabitants—impalement on stakes—is foreshadowed at the upper left. To the right, Assyrian bowmen stand behind wicker frames.

I built a pillar over against his city gate and I flayed all the chiefs who had revolted, and I covered the pillar with their skin. Some I walled up within the pillar, some I impaled upon the pillar on stakes, and others I bound to stakes round about the pillar. And I cut the limbs off the officers, the royal officers who had rebelled.

**FIGURE 11.2**   Jehu of Israel submitting to the Assyrians in 841 B.C., from the Black Obelisk of Shalmaneser III. In the only known depiction of an Israelite king, Jehu prostrates himself before Shalmaneser. Between Jehu and Shalmaneser, the god Ashur (depicted as a winged sun disk) and the goddess Ishtar (a star) hover. Jehu submitted in return for Assyrian protection against the king of Damascus. Black marble, height 5 feet.

Many captives from among them I burned with fire, and many I took as living captives. From some I cut off their noses, their ears, and their fingers, of many I put out the eyes. I made one pillar of the living and another of heads, and I bound their heads to tree trunks round about the city. Their young men and maidens I burned in the fire. Twenty men I captured alive and I walled them up in the wall of his palace. The rest of their warriors I consumed with thirst in the desert.

Ashurnasirpal II, 883–859 B.C. (D.D. Luckenbill, *Ancient Records of Assyria and Babylon*, Ancient Records Series 1, in Geoffrey T. Bull, *The City and the Sign: An Interpretation of the Book of Jonah*, London, 1970, 109–10)

The kings decorated their palaces with such inscriptions, describing violence in honor of Ashur, and with relief carvings showing the fate of conquered peoples (Figure 11.3). The Hebrew Bible records the terror inspired by the mighty Assyrians, who became a byword for irresistible might. The same Byron whose verses on Greece opened this book famously imagined what the Israelites saw:

The Assyrian came down like a wolf on the fold
And his cohorts were gleaming in purple and gold;
And the sheen of their spears was like stars on the sea,
When the blue wave rolls nightly on deep Galilee.

Lord Byron, *The Destruction of Sennacherib* (1815), stanza 1

**FIGURE 11.3** Assyrian relief showing refugees from Lachish in Judea (701 B.C.), in the palace of Sennacherib at Nineveh, Mesopotamia (Iraq). At the top exiles flee, carrying provisions; at the bottom Assyrian soldiers skin alive a rebel whose arms are pinned to the ground.

Assyria fed on war, and Assyrian demands transformed western Asia. To pay off the Assyrians, and to escape depredation, a group of people known as Phoenicians, seafarers who lived on the coast of modern Lebanon, intensified their trade in the west Mediterranean and founded overseas colonies in western Sicily, Sardinia, and—most importantly—at **Carthage** ("new city"), near modern Tunis. They brought metals, food, and slaves home from the west, exchanging them for such transportable manufactured objects as textiles, carved ivory, and perfumes. Phoenicia grew rich while buying protection from Assyria, and Carthage became the greatest city in the west Mediterranean.

When Assyria attacked Egypt in the 660s B.C., Egypt's king hired formidable Greek hoplites as mercenaries, but the Greeks never had to defend themselves directly against Assyria, because in 612 B.C. Babylonian rebels and a warrior people from the mountains of western Iran called the **Medes** (mēdz) burned to the ground Assyria's capital at Nineveh (near modern Mosul in Iraq). One consequence of the turbulence, mentioned in Chapter 9, "The Archaic Cultural Revolution, 700–480 B.C.," was the flight of Mesopotamian thinkers to Ionia on the west coast of Asia Minor; and now Ionia too was about to be drawn into the world of the Near Eastern empires.

## LYDIA

Few Greeks ever saw Nineveh, but PHRYGIA (Map 11.1), which lay about two hundred miles inland on an ancient road that led from the uplands of Anatolia west to the sea, was much closer to Greece. The Greeks told stories about Phrygia's **King Midas**, who turned everything he touched into gold, according to a famous story. Midas was a real man (Assyrians called him Mita) who reigned around 700 B.C. In the 1950s, American archaeologists excavated his intact tomb under a mound 150 feet high, discovering remarkable artifacts and Mita's body, from which forensic experts could even reconstruct his face.

**LYDIA**, whose capital lay further west on the same road, was only seventy-five miles from the Aegean Sea and nearer still to the coastal Greeks. Lydia's phenomenal wealth amazed the Greeks, who told legends about **Gyges** (gī-jēz), a usurper who seized Lydia's throne in the 680s B.C. According to Herodotus, Gyges was originally the king's bodyguard. The foolish king, obsessed by his wife's beauty, ordered Gyges to hide in a closet so that he would see her naked too, so that someone else would know what a lucky man the king was. Unfortunately, the wife spotted Gyges and calmly told him that to avenge her honor, either he or her husband must die. Soon, Gyges was the new king, married to his predecessor's widow. (Plato heard a different story [*Republic* 2.359a–2.360d], that Gyges was a shepherd who found a magic ring on a superhuman corpse. The ring made its wearer invisible. Using it, Gyges seduced the queen and, with her help, killed the king and took the throne.)

Gyges and his well-organized successors subdued the Ionian Greeks and made them pay him tribute. When one city refused around 590 B.C., Lydian engineers heaped a great mound against its walls. When the mound reached the top, troops poured into the city, massacring the Greeks. When archaeologists excavated the site in the 1950s, the huge siege mound was still there.

A triumphant Lydia drew Greece into an increasingly international world. One Greek courtesan made her way to Egypt, where she earned a fortune; Greek mercenaries sailed up the Nile and scratched their names on the legs of already ancient statues (vandalism then, but an important historical source now); and around 600 B.C. the poet Sappho's brother fought as a mercenary for Babylon.

In 560 B.C., a new king named **Croesus** (krē-sus) assumed Lydia's throne. It was him, not Gyges, whom Herodotus blamed for the subsequent clash of east and west:

> I know for a fact who was the first man to harm the Greeks. I will tell you about him and then proceed with the rest of my presentation . . .
>
> Croesus, a Lydian by race, son of Alyattes, ruler over all the peoples who lived west of the Halys river° . . . was the first foreigner, as far as we know, who through military conquest reduced some Greeks to the paying of tribute and forced others to be his allies. He conquered the Ionians and the Aeolians and the Dorians living in Asia, and he formed a pact of friendship with the Spartans. Before the rule of Croesus all the Greeks were free.
>
> Herodotus 1.5–6
> °*Halys River*: In central Anatolia.

Croesus took the coastal Greeks into his empire, taxed them, and installed client-tyrants to rule over them. Herodotus says he planned further conquests:

> In this way the Greeks in Asia were compelled to pay tribute. Croesus then turned his attention to the building of ships, that he might take possession of the islanders. When everything was set to begin building the ships, something happened to call the whole plan off. According to some it was a certain Bias of Priene,° or it was Pittacus from Mytilene° who, coming to Sardis,° said the following when Croesus asked about news from Greece: "O king, the islanders are raising a force of ten-thousand horse in order to attack you in Sardis." Croesus, thinking that he spoke the truth, exclaimed: "Well, I wish that some god would prod them to do just this, to attack the Lydians on horseback!" "O king," the man replied, "I think that you are eager to catch the islanders on horseback on the mainland, and rightly so. And what do you think that the islanders desire more, when they learned of your plans to attack them with ships, than to catch the Lydians at sea, that they might take revenge against you for enslaving the Greeks living on the mainland?"
>
> Croesus took such pleasure in the reply that, thinking it much to the point, he decided to give up the naval expedition. And so he made a pact of friendship with the Ionian islanders.
>
> Herodotus 1.27
> °*Priene* (prī-ē-nē): An Ionian Greek colony on the coast.   °*Mytilene* (mi-ti-lē-nē): The principal Greek city on the island of Lesbos, just off the Ionian coast. Later Greeks canonized a group of seven archaic wise men. Bias and Pittacus were two of them.   °*Sardis:* The capital of Lydia.

Croesus stopped his westward expansion; events further east were about to command his full attention.

## CYRUS AND THE RISE OF PERSIA, 559–530 B.C.

When Croesus inherited Lydia's throne in 560 B.C., Persia in southwest Iran was a minor client-state of Media. Forty years later, Persia ruled the greatest empire the world had yet seen, stretching from Egypt to Afghanistan (Map 11.2; Figure 11.4). Interactions with Persia would dominate Aegean history for the next two centuries.

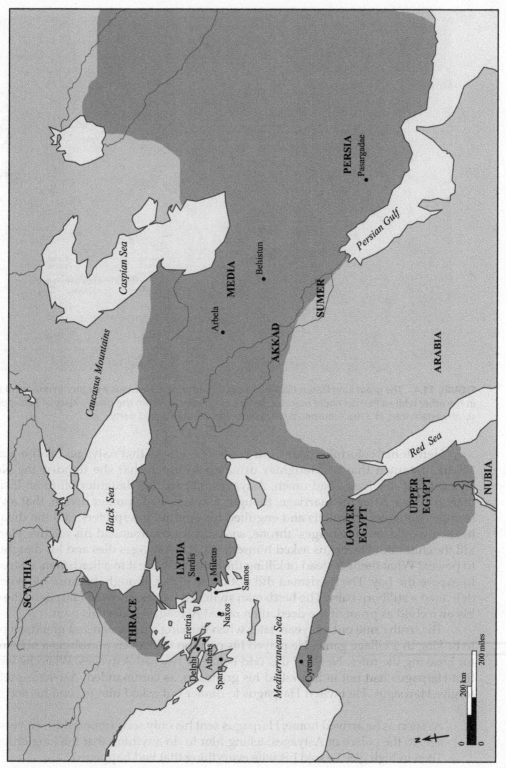

**MAP 11.2** The Persian Empire.

**FIGURE 11.4** The great king Darius (550–486 B.C.) sits enthroned. He holds a scepter in one hand and a lotus in the other while a Persian noble makes a gesture of obedience. From the great palace at Persepolis in southwestern Iran, in 330 B.C. burned by Alexander the Great in a wild party.

Herodotus' colorful account, our main source, says that Astyages (as-**tī**-a-jēz), king of Media, dreamed that his daughter urinated so much that she flooded the Near East. Warned that this was a bad omen, Astyages married his daughter off to an insignificant man in Persia. After the marriage, though, Astyages had another dream, that a vine grew from his daughter's genitals and engulfed his empire. Interpreters said the dream meant her son would seize Astyages' throne, so Astyages commanded his relative Harpagus to kill the child. But Harpagus asked himself, What if Astyages dies and his daughter comes to power? What then? Instead of killing the child, he gave it to a herdsman, instructing *him* to expose the boy. The herdsman did not do so either, though, because his wife had just delivered a stillborn baby. The herdsman switched babies, showed Harpagus the corpse of his own child as proof of the deed, then raised Astyages' son as his own.

The truth came out ten years later when the king's unrecognized grandson pretended to be king in a village game. He played his part too well, even punishing a nobleman's son for breaking the rules. News of this odd behavior reached Astyages. When he worked out that Harpagus had not in fact killed his grandson, as commanded, Astyages pretended to forgive Harpagus. He invited Harpagus to dinner but asked him to send his son over first:

> As soon as he arrived home, Harpagus sent his only son, around thirteen years of age, to the palace of Astyages, telling him to do anything that the king ordered. Then in high glee he told his wife everything that had happened.

When Harpagus' son arrived at the palace, Astyages had him butchered and cut up the body into pieces. Some he roasted, the other parts he boiled, and had the whole fixed up as a nice meal. The hour for dinner came. The guests arrived, including Harpagus, and before Astyages and all the others were set platters heaped high with mutton—except for Harpagus. Before him was placed the flesh of his own son, except for the head, hands, and feet, which were set aside on a platter covered by a lid.

When Harpagus appeared to have eaten as much as he wanted, Astyages asked him how he liked the meal. Harpagus said that he liked it very much, whereupon those whose job it was brought in the platter. Standing beside Harpagus' chair, Astyages told him to take off the lid and take whatever he pleased. Harpagus removed the cover and saw the remains of his son, but he did not show astonishment and kept control of himself. Astyages asked him if he knew what animal's flesh he had eaten. He said that he knew, and that whatever the king did was for the best. He spoke no more, but gathered the remaining pieces of flesh and took them home, planning, I suppose, to bury all of it together. And in this way was Harpagus punished.

Herodotus 1.119

Astyages now sent his grandson (renamed **Cyrus**) to live with his birth mother (Astyages' daughter). Cyrus grew up and became chief of the Persians. Harpagus, who had stayed on as Astyages' top assistant, burned for revenge and secretly urged Cyrus to revolt. When he did, Astyages foolishly sent Harpagus against him at the head of his army. Harpagus promptly joined the rebels, and in 550 B.C. Cyrus overthrew Astyages and took the empire, just as Astyages' dreams had predicted long before.

Such outlandish tales are typical of Herodotus. To him, the story illustrated a fundamental difference between the Greek *poleis* and the eastern empires. In a *polis*, no man stood so far above the other citizens that he could treat them so brutally, while the eastern rulers—Assyrian, Median, Lydian, or Persian—took such differences in status for granted. Greek belief that no man could be truly free under Persian rule was to have serious consequences when Persia attacked the Greeks.

When Cyrus actually came to power, he quickly overran the Medians' large empire on the Iranian plateau and in Mesopotamia. In 546 B.C., the very year that Pisistratus launched his third coup at Athens, Cyrus moved beyond Astyages' frontiers into Anatolia to threaten Croesus of Lydia. Seeing danger looming, Croesus asked two Greek oracles (one at Delphi) what to do, perhaps trusting them because they were outside his jurisdiction and not beholden to any political power:

Croesus provided an embassy of Lydians with gifts to the oracles and instructed them to ask whether Croesus should attack the Persians and if he ought to bring in an allied army. When they arrived to where they had been sent, the Lydians offered up the gifts, then inquired of the oracles, saying, "Croesus the king of the Lydians and other peoples, thinking that you are the only true oracles in the world, has brought these gifts worthy of your power to prophesize. And so he asks you whether he should launch a campaign against the Persians, and whether he ought to ally himself with another power." Such were the questions, and the replies of both oracles were the same: If he attacked the Persians, he would destroy a great empire. He should also try to find out who were the most capable of the Greeks, and he should bring them into an alliance.

When Croesus learned the answers the oracles had given, he was overjoyed, confident that that he would destroy the kingdom of Cyrus.

Herodotus 1.53–54

Croesus contracted an alliance with Sparta, hired mercenaries, and marched against Cyrus. After an indecisive battle late in 546 B.C., Croesus returned to Sardis, intending to expand his alliance in the following spring. Assuming that Cyrus would go into winter camp, as was normal for ancient armies, and wanting to save money, Croesus disbanded his mercenaries. But Cyrus followed Croesus and suddenly appeared before Sardis. In a panic, Croesus wrote to Sparta, asking for immediate assistance; but by the time the Spartans set sail, Sardis had already fallen.

Cyrus decided to burn Croesus alive. As Croesus sat on top of the pyre, waiting for the flames (Figure 11.5), he remembered the day, years before, when the wise

**FIGURE 11.5** Croesus on the funeral pyre; from an Athenian red-figured vase, ca. 490 B.C. Croesus, holding his kingly scepter, pours a libation while his servant lights the fire.

Athenian lawgiver Solon had visited him. "Consider no man happy until he is dead," Solon had advised, indifferent to Croesus' power and prosperity. Croesus thought him a fool, but now he understood what Solon meant. "O Solon, Solon!" he cried. Cyrus, who was enjoying the execution, wanted to know what Croesus meant by this outburst and ordered the pyre put out. But the flames had taken hold. Croesus wept and called on Apollo to save him—after all, Apollo's oracle at Delphi had advised him about destroying a great empire. Suddenly rain fell from the clear sky, extinguishing the fire.

Such fairytales of the reversal of fortune dominate Herodotus' stories about the eastern empires. Croesus, miraculously saved, now became Cyrus' closest adviser, and sent an angry embassy to Delphi to find out why (as he thought) the oracle had lied. Herodotus reports the Delphic priestess' reply:

> As far as the oracle was concerned, Croesus did not rightly criticize it. For the god had declared that he would destroy a great empire if he marched against the Persians. After an answer like that it would have been wise for him to have sent again to ask whether that was his own empire, or that of Cyrus. Because he did not understand what was said, nor did he ask a second time, it was pretty clear that the fault was his own . . .
>
> When Croesus heard the reply, he agreed that the fault was in truth his own and not the god's.

Herodotus 1.91

Some Ionian Greeks thought that Cyrus' destruction of Lydia might bring them freedom. They asked Sparta for help, but the Spartans sent only observers. Even this caused trouble:

> The most distinguished of those aboard the Spartan ship, a man by the name of Lacrines, was dispatched to Sardis to forbid Cyrus, on behalf of the Spartans, from doing any harm to the Greek cities. If he did, the Spartans would take action. When the herald reported this, Cyrus, according to the story, turned to some Greeks who happened to be with him, and asked, "Who *are* these Spartans? And how many of them are there, that they should send me such a command?" When he learned which men they were, and how many, he replied, "I've never been afraid of men like that, who have a special place in the middle of the city where they gather, swear fine oaths, and cheat one another. Such people, if I have anything to say about it, will not be regretting the troubles of the Ionians, but their own."

Herodotus 1.153

For now, Cyrus turned back to Mesopotamia to attack Babylon on the Euphrates, at this time the greatest city in the world. Two accounts of its fall in 539 B.C. survive. According to Herodotus, Cyrus defeated a Babylonian army then besieged the city. The Babylonians had large stores of food, so the innovative Cyrus dug a canal and drained the Euphrates into a nearby marsh. The Babylonians had not guarded the gates along the river, and tunnels normally filled with water now became dry passages for Cyrus' troops.

Herodotus adds that the city was so big that when the outskirts were captured the people in the center did not realize it. There was a festival going on, and they continued to dance and enjoy themselves until their doom was upon them. This account emphasizes the scale of Cyrus' power, enabling him to divert one of the world's great rivers to capture the world's biggest city.

The other account of Babylon's fall, the official Persian version that survives in an inscription on a clay cylinder (Figure 11.6), illustrates the very different role of religion in Persia from its place in Greece. In his own account, Cyrus says that there was no battle. Rather, Babylon's chief god Marduk *wanted* Cyrus to conquer the city in order to correct the Babylonians' improper conduct of their religion:

> Marduk, the great lord, a protector of his people, beheld with pleasure [Cyrus'] good deeds and his upright mind [and therefore] ordered him to march against his city Babylon. He made him set out on the road to Babylon, going at his side like a real friend. Without any battle, he made him enter Babylon, sparing Babylon any calamity. He delivered into [Cyrus'] hands

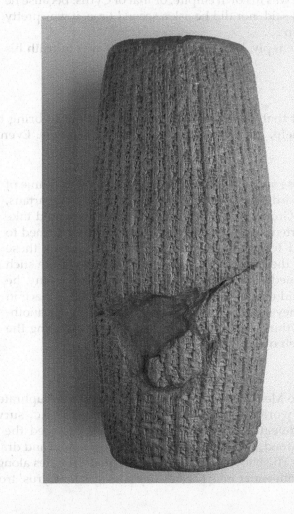

**FIGURE 11.6** The Cyrus Cylinder, discovered in Iraq in 1879. Inscribed in Akkadian cuneiform, the text tells of Cyrus' conquest of Babylon. Nine inches high, 538 B.C.

Nabonidus, the king who did not worship [Marduk]. All the inhabitants of Babylon as well as of the entire country of Sumer and Akkad,° princes and governors, bowed to [Cyrus] and kissed his feet, jubilant that he [had received] the kingship, and with shining faces

From the Cyrus Cylinder (*Ancient Near Eastern Texts Relating to the Old Testament*, ed. J. B. Pritchard, 3rd ed., Princeton 1969, 315–6).

°*Sumer and Akkad*: A formulaic phrase meaning simply "Mesopotamia."

The Assyrians had believed they had to subjugate others in order to make this world parallel Ashur's heavenly dominance. Cyrus followed a dualistic religion called **Zoroastrianism** (which still exists). Its early form is hard to reconstruct, but the prophet Zoroaster seems to have claimed that the universe was a battleground between the one uncreated creator **Ahuramazda** ("wise God"), the principle of light and goodness, and Ahriman ("the liar"), the force of darkness. Ahuramazda had chosen Cyrus' family, the **Achaemenids** (a-kē-men-idz), to lead the struggle in this world. Like the Assyrians, Zoroastrians accepted that other gods existed, but believed that they understood the supremacy and primacy of Ahuramazda. The Persians fought not only for conquest and its benefits, but to hasten Ahuramazda's victory over "the liar." Cyrus' Zoroastrianism followed a familiar practice in the royal propaganda of the ancient Near East, using subject peoples' beliefs to prove his right to rule over them. Similarly some Jews decided that Cyrus was the chosen one of Yahweh when in 539 B.C. he released the Jewish elders from captivity in Babylon (transported there in 586 B.C.) and allowed them to return to Jerusalem. Vast military resources and religious persuasion combined to fuel Cyrus' rapid conquests, making Near Eastern warfare completely different from the bloody but sportsman-like hoplite battles we described in Chapter 8, "Archaic Greece, 700–480 B.C.: Economy, Society, Politics."

## CAMBYSES AND DARIUS, 530–521 B.C.

The world had never seen a conqueror like Cyrus. He carried Ahuramazda's name to the Aegean Sea and the borders of Egypt then died in battle in Afghanistan in 530 B.C. fighting a nomadic warrior queen (Figure 11.7).

Cyrus' son **Cambyses** (kam-bī-sēz) continued the Achaemenid expansion, attacking Egypt in 525 B.C. The country fell quickly. Cambyses raced west to Cyrene, a Greek city in Libya, and south to Nubia (in what is now Sudan). He planned to go further, to attack Carthage and the Ethiopians, whom he called "the tallest and best-looking people in the world."

As with Cyrus' attack on Babylon, we have two versions of Cambyses' adventures in Egypt, both informative about Persian imperialism. First, we consider a long inscription set up between 520 and 510 B.C. by one Udjahorresne (u-ja-hor-es-nā), who had been an Egyptian general until 525 B.C.

The Great Chief of all foreign lands, Cambyses, came to Egypt, and the foreign peoples of every foreign land were with him. When he had conquered this land in its entirety, they established themselves in it, and he was Great Ruler of Egypt and Great Chief of All Foreign Lands.

His majesty assigned to me the office of Chief Physician. He made me live at his side as Companion and Administrator of the Palace.

**FIGURE 11.7** The Tomb of Cyrus, in Pasargadae, southwest Iran. Cyrus' embalmed body lay in a gold sarcophagus on a gold couch beside which stood a treasure-laden golden table, but the tomb was looted long ago. After the seventh-century A.D. Arab invasion, the empty mausoleum was known as the Tomb of the Mother of Solomon. Fifteen feet square, set on a stepped stone plinth.

I made a petition to the majesty of the King of Upper and Lower Egypt,° Cambyses, about all the foreigners who dwelled in the temple of Neith,° in order to have them expelled from it, so as to let the temple of Neith be in all its splendor as it had been before. His majesty commanded to expel all the foreigners [who] dwelled in the temple of Neith, to demolish all their houses and all their unclean things that were in this temple.

His majesty commanded to give divine offerings to Neith-the-Great, the mother of god, and to the great gods of Sais,° as it had been before. His majesty commanded [to perform] all their festivals and all their processions, as had been done before. His majesty did this because I had let his majesty know the greatness of Sais, that it is the city of all the gods, who dwell there on their seats forever.

°*King of Upper and Lower Egypt:* The traditional title of the pharaoh since the days of Narmer, the first pharaoh of all Egypt, around 3100 B.C.   °*Neith:* Early war goddess of the Delta whose attribute was two crossed arrows; perhaps the same as the Phoenician goddess Tanit and identified with Athena by the Greeks.   °*Sais:* A city in the central Egyptian delta where Neith had an ancient temple, and capital of Egypt after its liberation from Assyria in 664 B.C.

The one honored by the gods of Sais, the chief physician, Udjahorresne, he says:

The King of Upper and Lower Egypt, Cambyses, came to Sais. His majesty went in person to the temple of Neith. He made a great prostration before her majesty, as every king has done. He made a great offering of every good thing to Neith-the-Great, the mother of god, and to the great gods who are in Sais, as every beneficent king has done. His majesty did this because I had let his majesty know the greatness of her majesty Neith, that she is the mother of Ra° himself.

Statue Inscription of Udjahorresne 11–27 (M. Lichtheim, *Ancient Egyptian Literature III*, Berkeley 1980, 37–41)

°*Ra:* The sun god.

The inscription suggests that after conquering Egypt, Cambyses ruled as if nothing had changed, acting "as every king has done" and adopting traditional Egyptian royal titles like "King of Upper and Lower Egypt." As Cyrus had done at Babylon, Cambyses represented himself as defender of the gods. Udjahorresne accepted Cambyses' claim and changed sides, perhaps hoping that he could influence Cambyses to protect and enrich the temple of Neith, which Udjahorresne cared about deeply.

Persia needed men like Udjahorresne to run her empire. In return, local notables willing to change sides got Persian support against their own enemies, for example, the foreigners living in Neith's temple. Some collaborated; others resisted, particularly in Egypt and Babylon. These wealthy regions had a strong sense of ethnic identity and hovered constantly on the brink of rebellion. To control the Greeks, Persia would need similar collaborators.

Our second account comes from Herodotus. He heard about priests who had resisted Cambyses, not about collaborators like Udjahorresne. Herodotus says that Cambyses had always been strange but in Egypt went completely mad. Instead of the piety that Udjahorresne praises, Herodotus says that Cambyses insulted Egypt's gods and even stabbed a sacred bull, whose death presaged Cambyses' own doom. Both accounts contain some truth: Cambyses rewarded Egyptians who worked with him and punished those who did not, and different people apparently had different stories to tell. Herodotus says that Egypt's gods now pushed Cambyses into self-destruction. He married his own sister then killed her by kicking her when she was pregnant. He buried noblemen alive upside down. He misinterpreted a dream and concluded that his brother Smerdis back in Persia was plotting against him. When Cambyses had Smerdis murdered, the Magi, Persia's ritual experts, hatched a plot against him. In 522 B.C., one of the Magi—who, by an implausible coincidence, was also named Smerdis and looked just like Cambyses' murdered brother—impersonated the dead Smerdis, whose killing had been covered up, and raised a revolt. Cambyses jumped on his horse to return to Persia, but accidentally stabbed himself in the thigh in just the same spot that he had stabbed the sacred bull. As he traveled, the wound festered and he died.

Back in Persia, the false Smerdis reigned for seven months until a nobleman's daughter in the harem unmasked him. Royal ideology held that the Achaemenids were on earth to perfect the world for Ahuramazda, so a pretender undermined the whole cosmic order. Seven aristocrats overthrew the false Smerdis, then argued about who should replace him. They agreed to let a divine omen settle the matter: They would mount their horses on the outskirts of the city, and whoever's horse neighed first after the sun came up would have the throne. But one of the conspirators, **Darius** (da-rī-us), had hatched a plan with his groom Oebares (ē-bar-ēz):

> Oebares, when dark came, took from the stables the mare that Darius' stallion most liked to cover. He led her outside town and tied her up. Then he led out the stallion, round and round the mare, closer and closer, and at last he allowed him to cover her. At the crack of dawn the six men mounted their horses, as they had agreed. They rode through the suburb and when they came near where the mare had been tied up the night before, Darius' horse ran up and neighed. Just when the horse did this, there was lightning and thunder from a clear sky. That assured the result, as if a sign from heaven: The five other men leaped down from their horses and kissed the ground before the feet of Darius.
>
> That's one version of what happened, but according to another the Persians say that he rubbed the mare's genitals, then kept his hand covered inside his trousers. When the sun was rising and they were about to release the horses, he withdrew his hand and put it to the nostrils of Darius' horse. Smelling the mare, the horse snorted and neighed.
>
> Herodotus 3.85–87

These stories sound like gossip, but Herodotus' account of what happened next is partly confirmed by a huge inscription that Darius put up in the mountains separating Mesopotamia from Persia (Figure 11.8).

Set 340 feet above the ground, where only gods could see it, it was carved in three different languages and scripts, perhaps for the gods of different peoples. In it Darius justified his seizure of power, emphasizing his legitimacy, piety, and justice. Glossing over how he had really won the throne, he insisted he was a genuine Achaemenid, fighting Ahriman, the liar, to make the world perfect.

> I am Darius the Great King, King of Kings, King in Persia, King of countries, son of Hystaspes, grandson of Arsames, an Achaemenid.
>
> Says Darius the King: My father was Hystaspes; Hystaspes' father was Arsames; Arsames' father was Ariaramnes; Ariaramnes' father was Teispes; Teispes' father was Achaemenes.
>
> Says Darius the King: For this reason we are called Achaemenids. From long ago we have been noble. From long ago our family has been kings.
>
> Says Darius the King: eight of our family were kings before. I am the ninth. Nine in succession we have been kings.
>
> Says Darius the King: By the favor of Ahuramazda I am King; Ahuramazda bestowed the kingdom on me.

A list follows of pretenders to the throne whom Darius punished, in variations on the following theme:

> Says Darius the King: One man by name Tritantaechmes, a Sagartian—he became rebellious to me. Thus he said to the people, "I am king in Sagartia, of the family of Cyaxares."°

°*Cyaxares:* The father of Astyages of Media, who reigned 624–585 B.C., grandfather of Cyrus.

**FIGURE 11.8** The Behistun inscription, ca. 520 B.C. The huge billboard, 75 feet by 50 feet, records the struggles Darius faced in gaining the throne. Behistun lies 250 miles southwest of Tehran on the Silk Road from China to Babylon. The inscription is too high up the cliff to be read—except by Ahuramazda and other interested gods.

Thereupon I sent off a Persian and Median army; a Mede by name Takhmaspada, my subject—him I made chief of them. Thus I said to them, "Go forth. The hostile army that shall not call itself mine, that do you strike!" Thereupon Takhmaspada went off with the army. He joined battle with Tritantaechmes. Ahuramazda helped me. By the favor of Ahuramazda my army struck that rebellious army and took Tritantaechmes prisoner and led him to me. Afterwards I cut off both his nose and his ears and put out one eye. He was kept bound at my palace entrance, and all the people saw him. Afterward I impaled him at Arbela.

Darius, Behistun inscription 1.1–12; 3.78–91 (R. Kent, *Old Persian Grammar Texts, Lexicon*, New Haven 1953, DS of 22–58)

Cutting off noses, poking out eyes, impaling, crucifixion, and burying alive were standard tools of policy. Near Eastern kings were proud of their cruelty: It not only deterred other rebels but showed that the godlike "Great King" was free to act in any way he chose. It was wonderful to be terrible. In the citizen community of a Greek *polis*, however, where there were few distinctions in wealth or power, such behavior was unthinkable. When everyone was equally human, violently dishonoring others, even slaves, was *hybris*, "violence," a punishable crime. Herodotus rightly saw that the *poleis* were very different from Persia.

## PERSIA'S NORTHWEST FRONTIER AND THE IONIAN REVOLT, 521–494 B.C.

By 519 B.C. Darius had the empire under control. Cyrus and Cambyses had been great conquerors, but Darius saw the need for internal organization. The empire had thirty to thirty-five million inhabitants (perhaps ten times as many as all the Greeks combined). Darius set up local governors called **satraps** and made administration cheaper by shifting its costs onto them. Satraps were virtual kings within their provinces so long as they kept the peace, kept taxes flowing to Darius, and provided troops when asked. The empire was so big that it took months or years for Darius to raise troops to respond to threats or rebellions, and it was the satraps' job to deal quickly and cheaply with local problems. In return, they could of course enrich themselves.

Persia's northwest frontier had been quiet since Cyrus met Sparta's envoy in 545 B.C., but Darius had ambitions there. He developed Persia's first fleet and cut a forerunner to the Suez Canal, linking the Mediterranean and Red Seas. Herodotus says that

> Darius discovered the greater part of Asia.° He wanted to find out where the Indus River met the sea, the only river except for the Nile where crocodiles live. Therefore he sent a party of men whose words he trusted down the river. After this voyage Darius conquered India° and made frequent use of the Southern Ocean. °
>
> Herodotus 4.44
>
> °*Asia*: the Near East.   °*India*: That is, Pakistan.   °*Southern Ocean*: the Indian Ocean.

Around 521 B.C., even before he consolidated his rule, Darius seized the rich Greek island of Samos just off the coast of Asia Minor, near Miletus. Herodotus tells a famous story about how this happened. Polycrates, tyrant of Samos, was well known for his wealth and prosperity, but worried that his luck was bound to change. In the early 520s B.C., before Cambyses' conquest of Egypt, Polycrates wrote about his fear to his friend the pharaoh, who advised him to destroy the thing he loved most: By doing himself intentional harm, he would forestall future harm. Polycrates chose a gold ring and threw it into the sea. A huge fish swallowed the ring, only for one of Polycrates' subjects to catch the gorgeous fish and present it to the tyrant. When his servants cut up the fish for dinner, they found the ring and returned it to Polycrates, who knew then that he was doomed. Sure enough, in 523 B.C., the Persian satrap tricked him, captured him, and crucified him on a rock in the hot sun.

Step by step, Darius moved north and west. The Scythian nomads of Ukraine had long terrorized the Near East, and in 514 B.C. Darius launched a great punitive expedition against them. Darius pursued the Scythians for months but could not force them to give battle. As supplies grew scarce and he decided to withdraw, the Scythians went onto the offensive, cutting off his foraging parties. They rode up to Darius' only point of escape, a bridge over the River Danube, and tried to persuade the Ionian Greek subjects he had left as guards to abandon it. If Darius and his army were destroyed, the Scythians urged, the Greeks could rebel and be free.

The Greeks discussed this proposition. The Athenian Miltiades (mil-**tī**-a-dēz), who would later command the victorious troops at the battle of Marathon, happened to be with the Greek contingent and—perhaps because he was from the mainland and not the Ionian coast—favored the Scythian proposal. However, the pro-Persian tyrant of Miletus, **Histiaeus** (his-ti-**ē**-us), opposed it, pointing out that

> as things stood, each [Greek leader in Ionia] owed his position as tyrant to Darius. If Darius fell, he himself would not be able to maintain his power over the Milesians, nor would any other tyrant control their people. When left to their own devices, the cities would choose to live in a democracy rather than under a tyrant. Once Histiaeus had expressed his views, everyone agreed to it, whereas before they were inclined to support the Scythian proposal.
>
> Herodotus 4.137

As Histiaeus saw things, his position was like Udjahorresne's: It was better to be a tyrant under Persia than a regular citizen in a free *polis*.

To fool the Scythians, the Greeks demolished part of the bridge, but left enough intact that they could easily repair it. Darius raced to reach the bridge before the Scythians cut him off.

> The Persians . . . were barely able to find the crossing. They arrived at night and the discovery that the bridge was broken sent them into a panic that the Ionians had left them in the lurch. Now Darius had with him an Egyptian with the loudest of all voices. Darius stood this man on the bank of the Ister and ordered him to call out "Histiaeus of Miletus!" Histiaeus heard him at once and set his ships to ferrying the army over the river, and he joined the broken parts of the bridge. In this way the Persians escaped. The Scythians tried to find them, but failed. For these reasons the Scythians hold the Ionians, as free people, to be the most low-born and unmanly of all men and, considered as slaves, they are the most abject and subservient and most unlikely to run away, the Scythians say.
>
> Herodotus 4.140–42

Despite the close call, Darius' Scythian expedition did stop the Scythian raids. He was acutely aware of what he owed to Histiaeus and asked him what he would like as a reward. Histiaeus requested and received a small territory in a timber-rich area of the north Aegean.

Darius left an army in Europe to subdue the tribesmen in Thrace (roughly present-day Bulgaria) and the Greek cities along the north shore of the Aegean, and as a Persian general wound up his campaign in 512 B.C., he noticed Histiaeus' new territory. It struck him as a natural fortress, and he warned Darius that Histiaeus might be planning a revolt. Darius therefore made Histiaeus an offer he could not refuse: to give up his new territory and come and live with the king at the imperial court as an honored advisor. "Forget about Miletus and this new settlement of yours," Darius said, "come with me to Susa [a Persian capital]. All I have will be yours. You will eat at my table and be my counselor." Histiaeus was heartbroken about leaving Miletus but knew refusal meant death. He transferred rule over the city to his nephew Aristagoras (a-ris-**tag**-or-as) and began the long journey east.

The Persian empire was now firmly established in the Aegean, and Darius' satraps eagerly exploited opportunities to extend their power. Consequently, when Athenian envoys offered him earth and water in 506 B.C., hoping for Persian support against Sparta, Artaphernes, the satrap in Sardis, readily accepted. As the Persians saw it, the Athenians were now the great king's slaves and recognized Ahuramazda's primacy. Persia was swallowing the Greeks.

But in 499 B.C., the northwest frontier exploded. The troubles began in 500 B.C. when a democratic faction seized the wealthy Greek island of Naxos in the central Aegean. The democrats exiled the former oligarchs, who fled to Miletus; arriving there, they asked its new tyrant Aristagoras, the nephew of Histiaeus, to restore them. Aristagoras agreed and asked the satrap for troops to capture Naxos for the empire, saying he could repay the expenses from plunder. Artaphernes agreed, but after four months the siege failed. Aristagoras was now terrified. He could not repay the money Artaphernes had advanced him, and he would probably be executed—painfully—for his blunders.

On hearing the news, Histiaeus—Aristagoras' uncle and the former ruler of Miletus but now trapped in Darius' court—took a gamble:

> From these many causes of alarm Aristagoras had come to contemplate rebel-
> lion [against Persia]. Now at just this time there arrived from Susa the man with
> the tattooed head,° sent by Histiaeus, instructing him to revolt against the Great
> King. Histiaeus wished to communicate to Aristagoras that he should revolt,
> but knew no safe way to do so, because all the roads were watched. Therefore
> he shaved the head of his most trusted slave, pricked the message on the scalp,
> then waited until the hair grew back. As soon as it did, he sent him to Miletus,
> ordering that Aristagoras shave his head and have a good look. The message
> indicated, as I've explained, that he should revolt. Histiaeus did this because he
> was very unhappy living in Susa and he hoped that, if a revolt should break
> out, he would be sent down to the sea to take care of it. He reasoned that if
> Miletus did not revolt, he would never see it again.
>
> Herodotus 5.35
>
> °*man with the tattooed head:* Herodotus' phrasing makes it sound like this was a well-known story.

Aristagoras started talking to other Ionian cities about revolt. Ionia had flourished under Persian rule, but many Ionians still saw in Persia a repressive, old-fashioned tyranny. Feeling the winds of change, Aristagoras surrendered his tyrannical powers to the ordinary citizens and helped other Ionian cities overthrow their tyrants. Then he sailed to mainland Greece, hoping to spark a general Greek struggle against Persia. Sparta, who had warned Cyrus in 545 B.C. not to harm the Greek cities, declined to help, but Athens agreed to send twenty ships, even though she was a vassal state in Persian eyes. Nearby **Eretria**, on the island of Euboea, sent another five ships. As Herodotus observed, "These ships were the beginning of evils for Greeks and barbarians."

The Ionians marched inland, caught the satrap by surprise, and burned Sardis. The uprising then spread to Cyprus in the eastern Mediterranean, but gradually the local satraps organized their forces. The tide turned against the Greeks, and the Athenians, disillusioned at Ionian incompetence, returned home. Meanwhile Darius, impatient at his satraps' slow progress, began gathering a huge imperial army to deal with the situation. This was Histiaeus' chance: He persuaded Darius to send him back to the Aegean to help suppress the uprising.

By this point, in 497 B.C., some Ionians regretted their decision to rebel against Persia. Aristagoras, always attuned to the popular mood, fled Miletus to the property in the north Aegean that Histiaeus had originally received as his reward from Darius. Within a few months, he was killed by treachery. Histiaeus now defected from Persia, but Miletus did not want another tyrant and so drove him away from the city. After more adventures, Histiaeus became a sort of pirate king, working out of the Greek colony of Byzantium (modern Istanbul).

But the Persians were closing in. In 494 B.C., Darius ordered his forces against Miletus, the heart of the rebellion. The Ionians staked everything on the war at sea and elected the experienced sailor Dionysius from Phocaea, the northernmost Ionian city in Asia Minor, to organize the marine resistance.

Naval warfare, ancient as much as modern, required efficient organization. The ships, called **triremes** (trī-rēmz; Figure 11.9), had three banks of oars down each side. They were long, thin, and, without keels, unstable, but with trained crews could move quickly and were maneuverable. Each ship had archers and slingers plus marines to board enemy vessels, but their main weapon was a ram, a wooden spike sheathed in bronze on the prow just below the waterline. The basic tactic was to row full speed into an enemy ship, driving this ram through its hull. A curved beak above the ram prevented entanglement so the attacker could back away while water flooded through the hole into the enemy ship. To maneuver deftly and break the enemy's line required stamina and discipline. Disorganized sailors—like the Ionians, drawn from several independent *poleis*, with no clear command structure—were helpless against organized forces. Herodotus explains what happened:

> The Ionians turned themselves over to Dionysius. Every day he led the fleet in columns and taught them how to use their rowers to force a break in the opposite line. He placed armed soldiers on board and, after hard practice,

**FIGURE 11.9**   A modern reconstruction of a trireme, with a student crew.

he kept the ships at anchor for the rest of the day [instead of letting them beach their ships]. Thus all day long the Ionians received no rest. They put up with it for a week and did everything he said. But after that the Ionians began to grumble, being unused to such labor and worn out from working under the hot sun. "What god have we offended that we should be so ground down? We must have been out of our minds to place ourselves in the power of this jackass Phocaean, who has contributed a whole three ships to the fleet! He's got us all right—and he torments us with incurable affliction. Many of us have already fallen ill, and many others are to suffer the same. Anything would be better than these ills, and whatever slavery we are about to suffer [from the Persians] would be better than what we suffer now. Hey, let's refuse to obey any more orders."

They said things like that, and after this no one would do what he was told. Like an army they pitched tents on the island and lay about in the shade and would not board the ships or go on with their training . . .

The Samians, when they saw the inordinate lack of discipline among the Ionians, concluded that it was going to be impossible to overcome the Persian fleet.

Herodotus 6.12–13

When the Persians attacked, the Samians deserted and the Greek line broke up. Some crews fled; others fought heroically but were destroyed all the same. The Persians burned Miletus and its temples and deported the survivors 2,000 miles away to the Persian Gulf.

In spring 493 B.C., the army devastated the other Ionian cities (except for island Samos, rewarded for its treachery with survival). The adult men were massacred, the best looking boys castrated to be made eunuchs, the prettiest girls sent to the royal harem, and many others sold into slavery. But even though Darius committed acts of savage terror, he also listened to Ionian grievances. He obligingly replaced the hated tyrants with democracies, set up regional courts to suppress lawlessness, and commissioned a comprehensive land survey. Nonetheless, Ionia's cities, which had been among Greece's richest in the sixth century and had made original contributions to philosophy and poetry, never recovered from the devastation.

Histiaeus, whose machinations had inflicted so much suffering on Greeks and Persians alike, came to a bad end when the Persians caught up with him and his pirates:

Histiaeus, thinking the king would not punish him with death for his fault, devised the following measure to save his life. As he was running away, he was overtaken and captured by a Persian, who was about to spear him when Histiaeus cried out in Persian, "I am Histiaeus of Miletus!" If when he was captured alive he had been taken to King Darius, nothing would have come of it, as it seems to me; he would have pardoned him. But as it was, for this very reason, Artaphernes, the governor of Sardis, and Harpagus,° the man who captured him, did not want Histiaeus again to have such influence in

°*Harpagus:* A Persian general, not to be confused with the Harpagus who helped Cyrus to power in 559 B.C.

the Persian court. Therefore when he arrived at Sardis under arrest they first impaled him, then cut off his head and pickled it and sent the head to Darius in Susa. When Darius learned what had happened, he was angry with the perpetrators because they had not brought Histiaeus to him alive. He commanded that the head be cleansed and tended to, and that it be given a burial appropriate to a man who had been of great service both to himself and to all the Persians. Thus ends the story of Histiaeus.

Herodotus 6.29–30

## THE BATTLE OF MARATHON, 490 B.C.

The Ionian Revolt was a turning point for the Greeks. The Athenians had openly renounced their submission to Ahuramazda and to Persia and knew that Darius would punish them as he had the Ionians. When Phrynichus, a leading playwright, produced a tragedy called *The Sack of Miletus* (now lost), Herodotus (6.21) says that "the audience in the theater burst into tears. The author was fined a thousand drachmas for reminding them of their own troubles and they forbade anybody ever to stage the play again." A thousand drachmas was a huge sum of money, enough to support a family of four for five years.

In 492 B.C., Darius sent his son-in-law Mardonius along the north coast of the Aegean with a fleet (Map 11.3). Darius announced his intention to punish Athens and Eretria for supporting the revolt, but he in fact probably intended to subdue as many Greek towns as he

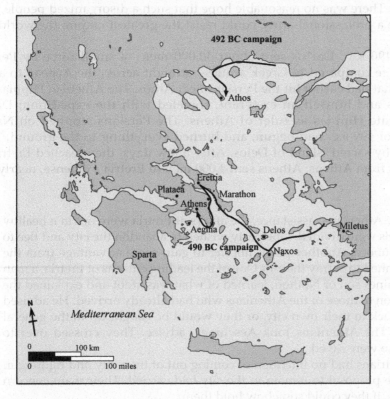

**MAP 11.3** The Persian invasions of 492, 490 B.C.

could. Everyone in Mardonius' path surrendered, but the admiral sailed into a terrific storm, and Herodotus (6.44) says that "around 300 ships were lost with over 20,000 men. The sea near Mount Athos is full of monsters, so that those sailors who were not dashed to pieces on the rocks were seized and devoured. Others, unable to swim, drowned; others still died of cold." Undeterred by the disaster,

> Darius made efforts to discover what were the Greeks' intentions, whether they were going to fight him or surrender and give up. Therefore he sent heralds up and down Greece, asking earth and water for the Great King. He sent heralds to Greece, and to the coastal towns already under tribute to the king he sent messengers requesting the provision of war ships and of ships able to transport cavalry. While these preparations were underway, the heralds on the mainland received what the king asked for from many of the towns, and from all the islanders whom they visited with their request.

Herodotus 6.48–49

Many *poleis* submitted. Some aristocrats preferred being tyrants under Persia to living in free democracies, and the oligarchs of Aegina (ē-jī-na) hoped for revenge on neighboring Athens, their traditional enemy. The Athenians, by contrast, executed Darius' heralds (against sacred custom), and the Spartans, telling the ambassadors that if they wanted earth and water they should get it themselves, pitched them headfirst down a well. Aegina and Athens went to war with each other even as the Persians closed in on them. There was no reasonable hope that such a disorganized people, who did not even have a professional army, could resist the greatest empire the world had ever seen.

In summer 490 B.C., Darius sent about 30,000 men—a small force by Persian standards, but huge compared to Greek armies—straight across the Aegean to avoid the sort of storm that had earlier hit the Persians near Athos. The Athenian Hippias, the son of Pisistratus and himself an ex-tyrant, traveled with the expedition; Darius planned to reinstate Hippias as ruler of Athens. The Persians stopped on Naxos, where the revolt of 499 B.C. had begun, and burned everything to the ground. They occupied the nearby sacred island of Delos. After a few days, they reached Eretria on Euboea, just miles from Athens. Athens sent 4,000 men to Eretria's defense, nearly half her hoplites, but

> in spite of the Athenians' assistance, the affairs at Eretria were not in a healthy state. Counsels were divided. One party wished to abandon the city and flee to the hills of Euboea. Another party, hoping to gain some advantage from the Persians, planned to betray the city. One of the leading citizens of Eretria, a man named Aeschines son of Nothon, learned of what was afoot and explained the whole situation to those of the Athenians who had already arrived. He advised them to go back to their own city, or they would be caught up in the general catastrophe. The Athenians took Aeschines' advice. They crossed over to Oropus and so were saved . . .
>
> The Eretrians had no intention of coming out of their city and fighting in the open. The proposal to remain in the city had carried. Their main concern was the walls, if they could somehow hold them.

The attack came and with power. For six days they fought, and many fell on either side. On the seventh day two leading citizens, Euphorbus son of Alcimachus and Philagrus son of Cyneas, betrayed the city to the Persians. They entered the city and stripped the temples bare, then burned them in revenge for the temples burned at Sardis. They enslaved the entire population, as Darius had directed.

Herodotus 6.100–101

Athens was next. The Persians sailed down the coast and soon after dawn on September 8th, 490 B.C., landed on the beach at **Marathon** northeast of Athens. There they organized their forces for an easy march inland.

Fire signals flashed across the dry hills of Attica to warn the Athenians, who convened the Assembly to discuss the crisis. The Athenians ran their army the way they ran their city, democratically. Each year they elected ten generals, who formed a committee that voted on tactics. The generals took turns chairing the committee for a day each, a recipe for indecision and disaster, but at this critical moment one of the ten, **Miltiades** (mil-tī-a-dēz), took charge. On his advice Athens' 9,000 hoplites grabbed whatever food they had and headed straight for Marathon. The generals meanwhile sent a runner named Pheidippides (fī-dip-i-dēz) to tell Sparta that the storm had broken:

Pheidippides reached Sparta on the day after he left Athens.° Appearing before the rulers of Sparta he said, "O men of Sparta, the Athenians ask you to help them and not to allow the most ancient city of the Hellênes to be enslaved by foreigners. For already Eretria has been enslaved and Greece is weaker by one fine city." So he delivered his message, and the Spartans were inclined to help the Athenians, but could not do so at once because they did not want to violate their laws. It was the ninth day of the month and they said they could not take the field until the full moon. So they waited for the full moon. In the meanwhile Hippias, son of Pisistratus, guided the Persians to the plain of Marathon.

Herodotus 6.106–7

°*Athens*: A phenomenal achievement; the distance is 149 miles. In 1983 a race was held over the same route, and the winner covered it in twenty-two hours.

Historians debate whether it was really respect for religion or a secret desire to see Athens humbled that held Sparta back. The Athenian generals had better luck with another runner, who went to the little city of Plataea on the border between Athens and the powerful Boeotian city of Thebes. The messenger reminded the Plataeans how Athens had saved them from a Theban attack thirty years before, and Plataea's full force of 1,000 hoplites raced grimly to join the Athenians at Marathon.

The men of Athens marched all night, reaching Marathon around dawn. To get from the beach to Athens, the Persians would have to pass through the low hills that the Athenians occupied. The Athenians quickly set up a strong position across the Persian line of march, and that night or the next morning the Plataeans joined them. The two armies waited. The Persians hoped that traitors would betray Athens, saving them a troublesome uphill attack, while the Athenians hoped that the Spartans would come. But then Pheidippides staggered back into Athens with the awful news: The Spartans would not come for another week.

The Athenian leadership split down the middle. Five of the ten generals, stunned by the size of the Persian force, urged a return to Athens to sit out a siege. Although the

Persian infantry was lightly armed, and no match for hoplites, these generals feared that Persia's cavalry and archers would destroy the Greek phalanx before matters came to hand-to-hand combat. The other five generals, led by the forceful Miltiades, feared that if they withdrew without fighting, the city would be betrayed to massacre, slavery, and death. An eleventh official, the archon known as the War Archon, accompanied the army and had a tie-breaking vote. The War Archon voted to fight.

The face-off lasted a week. Even those generals who supported Miltiades hesitated to take responsibility for the actual battle, so the Athenians sat tight until it was Miltiades' turn to chair the generals' committee again. Before dawn on September 17th, Miltiades mustered the Athenians and Plataeans. To keep from being outflanked, he extended their line in the dark until it covered nearly a mile, the same length as the Persian front:

> The disposition of the Athenian forces on the plain of Marathon had a certain result: Because they stretched out their line to be as long as the Persian line, the middle was reduced to but a few ranks, and here it was weakest. The two wings, however, were strong. Once their dispositions were made, and the sacrifices were of good omen, the word was given to move and the Athenians charged at a run against the enemy. The distance between them was not less than a mile. When the Persians saw the Athenians charging at them, they prepared to receive the line. They thought the Athenians quite insane, or seized by a suicidal madness, that being so few they should charge at a run, unsupported by cavalry or archers. Well, that's what they imagined! Then the Athenians hit them in a mass, and they fought in a way not to be forgotten. They were the first Greeks, as far as we know, ever to attack at a run, and the first who dared to look without flinching at Persian dress and the men who wore it. Before that time even the word 'Persian' struck fear in the heart of the Greeks.
>
> The fighting at Marathon went on for a good while. In the middle of the field, manned by Persians and Sakai,° the enemy had the upper hand. They broke the Greek line and were pursuing them inland away from the sea. Both Greek wings, however, one made up of Athenians, the other of Plataeans, were victorious. But they allowed the defeated enemy to escape, and combining the two wings into a single unit they attacked the foreigners who had broken through in the center. And the Athenians were again victorious. They pursued the fleeing Persians to the ships, cutting them down and calling for fire as they took hold of the ships. In the melee the War Archon was killed, fighting bravely, and of the generals Stesilaos the son of Thrasylaos fell. Cynegirus, the son of Euphorion,° had his hand cut off with an ax as he seized the prow of a ship, and so died. Many other well-known Athenians fell. In this fashion the Athenians seized seven ships. But the rest escaped, with the Persians aboard.

Herodotus 6.111–115

°*Sakai*: Scythians.   °*son of Euphorion*: Another son of Euphorion also fought at Marathon that day: the tragedian Aeschylus. On his epitaph, Aeschylus was prouder of being in this battle than of all his dramatic triumphs.

Herodotus (6.117) tells us that "in the battle of Marathon some 6,400 Persians were killed; the Athenian losses were 192." Probably, the Athenians did not know exactly how many Persians they killed: 6,400 is 192 divided by three then multiplied by one hundred—that is, the Athenians thought that for every three of them who fell, a hundred Persians died. But whatever its exact losses, most of the Persian army was clearly still intact, and as the ships carried the Persians safely off the beach, the Athenians saw a flash of light from the hills behind them: Someone was using a brightly polished shield as a mirror, catching the sun's rays to signal to the Persians. Traitors were evidently ready to betray the city. The Persian fleet hoped to reach Athens while the hoplites were still at Marathon, catch it undefended, and win the war despite losing the battle.

The Greek soldiers, bone-tired, immediately set off back to Athens, a grueling twenty-six-mile forced march through the mounting heat of the day. Herodotus does not tell the story, but later reports say that the Athenians sent a messenger racing back to Athens. "We have won," he gasped, as he staggered into the marketplace then dropped dead from exhaustion. The messenger's run inspired the modern marathon race when the Olympic Games were reinvented in 1896. (It takes a modern professional runner just over two hours to cover twenty-six miles.)

The Athenians in the city, heartened by the news, manned their defenses, put a watch on the gates, and waited. The Persians had to sail seventy miles, which would take nine or ten hours at top speed. The Athenians had to cross twenty-six miles of hills "as fast as their legs would carry them," according to Herodotus, requiring about the same time.

The Athenian hoplites approached the city as evening fell. They saw no flames or pall of smoke, no Persian ships darkening the bay. They took up position outside the city and readied for battle. The Persian fleet came into view. The Persians would now have to fight their way ashore again through the very men who had slaughtered their friends just hours before. The sailors rested on their oars, and the commanders debated. As darkness fell, the Persians sailed back to Asia.

Outnumbered, abandoned by Sparta, and surrounded by traitors, the Athenian amateurs had destroyed an attempted landing by a professional Persian army. Even the Spartans were impressed:

> After the full moon two thousand Spartans set out for Athens, being so eager to get there on time that they reached Attica on the third day° after leaving Sparta. Of course they arrived too late for the battle, but wishing to see the Persians they marched to Marathon to have a look at the bodies. Then, having praised the Athenians for their accomplishment, they went back home.

Herodotus 6.120

°*third day:* They covered fifty miles per day!

Marathon was *the* moment for Athens. Nearly seventy years later, when the comic poet Aristophanes wanted to express Athenians' pride in their city, his chorus (old men dressed as wasps to symbolize their ferocity) harked back to Marathon:

> We alone are the true men of Attica, born from the earth,
> a most manly race and of highest value to the city
> in time of war, when the Persian came, filling
> the city with smoke and setting fire to everything,
> desiring by force to eject us from our hives.
> Running forth, brandishing spear and shield, we fought them,

drunk with the bitter wine of anger, man against man,
biting our lips from rage. And you could not see
the sky from the thickness of the arrows. With the gods' help
we drove them back by evening. For the owl of omen°
had flown over the army before the battle.
Then we pursued them like the fishers of tuna, spearing them
in the pants, stinging their jaws and their eyes.
That's why by foreigners nothing is feared more than the Attic wasp.

Aristophanes, Wasps 1077–90

°Owl of omen: The owl was the symbol of Athena, the city's patron goddess.

Athens was saved—for now.

## Key Terms

Assyrians, 225

Carthage, 229

Medes, 229

King Midas, 229

Lydia, 229

Gyges, 229

Croesus, 230

Cyrus, 233

Zoroastrianism, 237

Ahuramazda, 237

Achaemenids, 237

Darius, 240

Cambyses, 237

*hybris*, 242

satraps, 242

Histiaeus, 243

Eretria, 244

triremes, 245

Marathon, 249

Miltiades, 249

## Further Reading

Boardman, John, N. G. L. Hammond, David Lewis, and Martin Ostwald, eds., *The Cambridge Ancient History IV: Persia, Greece, and the Western Mediterranean ca. 525 to 479 B.C.*, 2nd ed. (Cambridge, 1988). Encyclopedic survey of the Greek world, Persia, Italy, and Carthage, with excellent chapters.

Briant, Pierre, *From Cyrus to Alexander: A History of the Persian Empire* (Winona Lake, IN, 2002). Superb detailed history of the Persian Empire.

Burn, A. R., *Persia and the Greeks*, 2nd ed. (London, 1984). Very readable review of the Persian War, with an excellent appendix by David Lewis dealing with the evidence from the Persian side.

Kuhrt, Amélie, *The Ancient Near East* II (London, 1995). A masterly survey of Assyrian and Persian history. The best introduction.

Kuhrt, Amélie, *The Persian Empire* (New York 2007). Excellent up-to-date survey.

Morris, Ian, and Walter Scheidel, eds., *The Dynamics of Ancient Empires* (New York 2009). Contains fine introductory essays on the Assyrian and Persian empires.

Sancisi-Weerdenburg, Heleen, Amélie Kuhrt, and others, eds., *Achaemenid History Workshops*, 10 vols (Leiden, The Netherlands, 1987–1994). Series of major conferences covering all aspects of Persian history. Indispensable for serious research.

Vidal, Gore, *Creation* (New York, 1981). A novel set against the vast backdrop of the Persian Empire at the end of the sixth century B.C., ranging from Greece to China. Gripping and historically well informed.

Wiesehöfer, Josef, *Ancient Persia: From 550 B.C. to 650 A.D.* (New York, 1996). Fine brief survey of the three ancient Persian Empires, with focus on primary Persian sources. Fresh look at Persian history from its Near Eastern perspective.

### ANCIENT TEXTS

Herodotus, *The Histories*, tr. Aubrey de Selincourt, rev. ed. (New York, 1996). Books 1 through 6 narrate the rise of Persia to the battle of Marathon.

# The Great War, 480–479 B.C.

When Darius surveyed his vast empire in 490 B.C., Marathon looked like merely a minor setback in the grand scheme of things. Persia's casualties were lower than in the storm of 492 B.C., and the expedition had punished the sinful Eretria, as intended. Nonetheless, the defeat was a setback, and Darius needed to act swiftly to reassert his authority.

Herodotus describes the situation in the Persian court:

> When Darius the son of Hystaspes heard what had happened at Marathon, and being already before this extremely angry against the Athenians for their attack on Sardis, he now resolved to launch a still more terrible punishment, an invasion of Greece. He sent out messengers to all the cities under his control in a call to prepare for war, and this time they would need to provide far more than before in the way of troops, warships, horses, and transports. After these announcements were made, Asia was in a stir for three years as the most distinguished men were enrolled for the campaign and as preparations were made.

Herodotus 7.1

But luck was with Athens. First, Egypt rebelled, a dangerous crisis surpassing the situation in Greece. Then Darius died in 486 B.C. and Babylon rose up too. Darius' son **Xerxes** (zerk-sēz) suppressed both revolts but was inclined to leave the western frontier alone. However, some advisors urged him to renew the attack, particularly **Mardonius**, commander of the disastrous naval expedition in 492 B.C. Xerxes agreed, then changed his mind, but then (according to Herodotus, because of a frightening dream) decided to invade after all. But the Greeks had gained a vital breathing space.

253

## STORM CLOUDS IN THE WEST

It was now 483 B.C. Diodorus of Sicily, a historian living in the first century B.C., tells the following story:

> Xerxes, urged on by Mardonius, desired to drive all the Greeks from their homes. He sent messengers to the Carthaginians suggesting that they work together and form an alliance, he to attack the Greeks in Greece while they, after gathering a large armament, at the same time to attack the Greeks in Sicily and Italy. In accordance with this agreement, the Carthaginians gathered a large sum of money and hired mercenaries from Italy and also from France and Spain. In addition they enrolled citizens from Carthage itself and peoples living in the whole of Libya. After three years' preparations they had assembled a force of 300,000 infantry and 200 warships.
>
> Diodorus of Sicily 11.1

Herodotus does not mention this alliance, and it may be that Greeks later simply assumed that simultaneous attacks from Persia and Carthage *must* have been coordinated. Certainly both great powers were concerned about the Greeks. As we saw in Chapter 11, "Persia and the Greeks, 550–490 B.C.," Sparta and Persia exchanged sharp words in 545 B.C., and in 499 Athens backed the Ionian rebellion. In the West, the Greek cities were not only powerful, but very rich. Compared to the Aegean, Sicily had rather few *poleis*, but each had a large territory, good land, and reliable rainfall. Sicilian Greeks, like Sparta, could solve some social problems by conquering surrounding lands, and by 500 B.C. had taken the best coastal plains from the native Sicilian populations (Map 12.1).

They pushed some indigenous peoples into the inland hills and reduced others to serfdom. Sicilian merchants grew rich selling grain to Aegean Greece and wine to Carthage, and taxes on trade through their harbors paid for breathtaking temples at Selinus, Akragas (present-day Agrigento), and **Syracuse**, leaving some of the finest ruins to survive from all the ancient world. Perhaps because they were so rich, Sicilian aristocrats distanced themselves from the lower classes more than did Aegean nobles (though nowhere near as much as Egyptians or Persians). The forces that produced democracy in the Aegean were felt in Sicily, but the aristocrats' greater strength there led to violent civil wars, and around 500 B.C., when tyranny disappeared in the Aegean, some super-rich Sicilians exploited the constant unrest to install themselves as tyrants. Fifth-century Sicilian tyrants were stronger than their sixth-century Aegean predecessors because the states they ruled were more centralized and richer. With this wealth they hired mercenaries, reducing their need for support from citizen hoplites and enabling them to push still further inland at the natives' expense.

In western Sicily, relations between Greeks, natives, and Phoenicians were tense at the end of the sixth century (Table 12.1). The Phoenicians lived in three independent western Sicilian settlements at MOTYA, PANORMOS (present-day Palermo), and SOLOEIS. These trading centers enjoyed good relations with a native inland people called the Elymians but not always with the Greeks. Around 510 B.C., a Spartan adventurer—King Cleomenes' half-brother—tried to set up a colony near Motya. The Sicilian Phoenicians

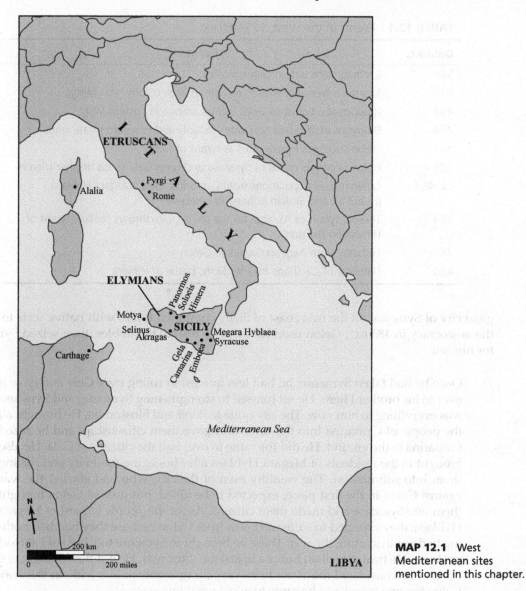

**MAP 12.1** West Mediterranean sites mentioned in this chapter.

allied with the Elymians to destroy the colony and kill its leader. Meanwhile, Greek pirates were hurting Phoenician trade. Back in 535 B.C., Carthage had crushed the pirates in a sea battle near Corsica, but by 500 B.C. the raids were worse than ever. The same Dionysius who had tried to organize the Ionian fleet in 494 B.C., and met with such resistance, had fled to Sicily after the disaster and become a pirate king himself, robbing only the Phoenicians, never the Greeks.

In the 490s B.C., the tyrant of the small city of **Gela** (jē-la) on the south coast of Sicily, instead of attacking the natives, attacked other Greeks. This tyrant, whose name was Hippocrates, quickly took over most of eastern Sicily, and when he died in 491 B.C., his former cavalry commander **Gelon** (jē-lon) took his place. When the poorer citizens of the

| **TABLE 12.1** Events in the West, 535–480 B.C. | |
|---|---|
| **Date B.C.** | **Event** |
| 535 | Carthaginians defeat Greek pirates |
| 510 | Spartan adventurer tries to establish Greek colony near Motya |
| 498 | Hippocrates, tyrant of Gela, creates empire in eastern Sicily |
| 494 | Dionysius of Phocaea emigrates to Sicily and becomes pirate leader |
| 491 | Gelon succeeds Hippocrates as tyrant of Gela |
| 485 | Gelon becomes tyrant of Syracuse and gives Gela to his brother Hieron |
| ca. 483 | Gelon moves populations from Camarina, Gela, Megara Hyblaea [hi-**blē**-a], and Sicilian Euboea to Syracuse |
| 483 | Theron, tyrant of Akragas (in the south), overthrows Terillus, tyrant of Himera (in the north) |
| 481 | Embassy from Aegean Greeks to Gelon |
| 480 | Hamilcar of Carthage invades Sicily; battle of Himera |

great city of Syracuse on the east coast of Sicily combined forces with native serfs to expel the aristocracy in 485 B.C., Gelon used his army to restore the nobles, then seized Syracuse for himself.

> Once he had taken Syracuse, he had less interest in ruling over Gela and gave it over to his brother Hiero. He set himself to strengthening Syracuse, and Syracuse was everything to him now. The city quite took off and blossomed. He brought all the people of Camarina into the town and gave them citizenship, and he razed Camarina to the ground. He did the same to over half the citizens of Gela. He also brought in the residents of Megara Hyblaea after besieging their city and forcing them into submission. The wealthy men of the city, who had started the war against Gelon in the first place, expected to be killed, but instead Gelon brought them into Syracuse and made them citizens. As for the people [*dêmos*] of Megara Hyblaea, they expected to suffer no harm from Gelon because they had had nothing to do with starting the war. These he brought to Syracuse too, but sold abroad as slaves. He treated Sicilian Euboea in just the same way. He did this in both cases because he considered the *dêmos* to be very disagreeable to live with. In this way Gelon became tyrant and he came to wield great influence.

Herodotus 7.156

Gelon acted more like an Assyrian or Persian king than a Greek leader, wiping out whole cities, moving populations around to build up his own city, and putting his brother in charge of Gela without reference to the citizens' wishes. Like an Achaemenid, he ran politics as a family business. He made marriage alliances with Theron, tyrant of Akragas, the second greatest city in Sicily. Between them, Gelon and Theron dominated eastern and central Sicily, and in 483 B.C. Theron ousted Terillus, the tyrant of Greek **Himera**, on the north coast of the island. This brought on a crisis, because Terillus had good relations with Carthage, and by replacing him Theron effectively shut Phoenician traders out of central Sicily.

We do not know much about how the Carthaginians interpreted events because although they may have kept historical records, virtually all their literature was lost when Rome destroyed this proud city in 146 B.C. (see Chapter 24, "The Coming of Rome, 220–30 B.C."). Our meager information about Carthage comes from hostile comments by Greek and Roman authors and from archaeological excavations since the 1970s. We can say this much, though. Carthage was run by an oligarchy, and its great harbor provided an ideal center for traders shipping goods between the east and west Mediterranean. As early as 508 B.C., Carthage made a treaty with Rome (then still a minor power) regulating access to markets in central Italy and negotiated similar deals with the more powerful cities of Etruria, north of Rome. So when Theron of Akragas deposed Carthage's ally Terillus of Himera in 483 B.C., Carthage could not allow an ambitious Greek tyrant to disrupt its highly profitable trading system. The Carthaginian oligarchs may not have wanted to conquer Sicily, but they had to respond. The Greeks needed to learn what their real place was in the world.

## STORM CLOUDS IN THE EAST

By 483 B.C., western and eastern Greeks knew that wars were imminent. It was time to put aside local squabbles and recognize their common Greekness. Cooperation was easier in Sicily than in the Aegean, because Sicily had fewer cities and the ruling families in Syracuse and Akragas, linked through marriage, dominated the island. Planning was a family affair. In the Aegean, by contrast, both Athens and Sparta claimed leadership. Their inability to cooperate in 490 B.C. inspired little confidence, and many cities had submitted to Darius without a murmur.

When Xerxes started gathering forces in 483 B.C., Sparta did nothing. An Athenian named **Themistocles** (the-**mis**-tō-klēz) saw the need to act, and chance intervened. There were rich veins of silver in Attica, which the state owned and leased to private entrepreneurs, taking a cut of the profits; and in 483 or 482 B.C. a silver strike at the mines at Laurium in southwest Attica brought the state a windfall of one hundred talents, an enormous sum. Like a modern government with a budget surplus, Athens needed to spend the money:

> The Athenians planned to share out the wealth by giving ten drachmas to each man. But Themistocles persuaded the Athenians to give up this plan and instead build 200 warships, to be used in the campaign against Aegina.° This war, at just that time, was to save Greece, for it forced the Athenians to become a naval power. In fact the ships were never used for the purpose for which they were built, but served Greece in her hour of need.
>
> Herodotus 7.144
>
> °*Aegina*: An island just outside the harbor of Athens.

While Themistocles worked behind the scenes to supervise the construction of the fleet, and other Greeks dithered, Xerxes finished his preparations. Herodotus says that Xerxes raised 5,283,200 men (not counting eunuchs, cooks, and prostitutes!). This cannot be true; five million troops would have been 20 percent of the entire empire. By Herodotus' reckoning the army required 4,000 tons of grain per day (400,000 tons for a three-month campaign), drank entire rivers dry, and cities went bankrupt providing it with a single dinner.

We do not know how large Xerxes' army really was, but most modern historians guess it was around 500,000, which would still make it the largest army the ancient world had ever seen. So large a force could not carry enough food and water to stay alive in Greece in summer, and Greece did not produce enough to support the Persian host. Ships would therefore be decisive, because only a fleet coasting along the shore could carry provisions for so immense an army. If the Greeks could disable Xerxes' fleet, his army would starve; that had to be the basis for Greek strategy.

Xerxes hoped to avoid fighting altogether by terrifying the Greeks into submission. Terror had worked before. He undertook massive engineering works, actually bridging the Hellespont with a bridge of rafts and cutting a canal through the Athos peninsula, where Mardonius' was wrecked twelve years earlier (remnants of this canal can still be seen). In October 481 B.C., Xerxes' envoys arrived in Greece. The Delphic oracle advised the Greeks to make terms, and several important *poleis* sent earth and water in submission. Only in November 481 B.C., when Xerxes had already reached Sardis in Lydia, did Sparta at last summon the Greeks to resist. Only thirty-one *poleis* responded.

Despite mutual hostilities, Athens accepted Spartan leadership. The allies sent an embassy to Gelon in Syracuse to seek his help. He offered 200 warships, 20,000 hoplites, 4,000 light infantry, 4,000 cavalry, and all the food the Greeks needed—but only on condition that he, Gelon, would be commander-in-chief. The Aegean Greeks balked, and Gelon withdrew:

> Gelon feared that the Greeks could not be successful against the Persian, but as tyrant of Sicily he could hardly travel to the Peloponnesus and place himself under the rule of the Spartans. Hence he chose a different course. As soon as he heard that Xerxes had crossed the Hellespont, he sent three small ships under the command of Cadmus, son of Scythes, from the island of Cos, to Delphi. With him he sent a great deal of money and many kind words and instructed him to await the outcome of the war. If the Persians won, he was to give the money to Xerxes together with earth and water from Gelon's dominions. If the Greeks won, he was to bring the money home.
>
> Herodotus 7.163

## THE STORM BREAKS IN THE WEST: THE BATTLE OF HIMERA, 480 B.C.

Hamilcar (ham-il-kar), the Carthaginian general, seems to have had modest aims in 480 B.C. Rather than destroying the Sicilian Greeks, he wanted to reopen the island for trade. He raised huge sums of money and hired a host of mercenaries. Violent storms sank many of his transport ships, but his reduced force nevertheless easily defeated a Greek army outside Himera on the north coast of Sicily and laid siege to the city. Theron of Akragas, on the south coast of the island, wrote to Gelon in Syracuse, asking him to come at once to Himera to forestall a Carthaginian victory. Gelon set off with 50,000 infantry and 5,000 cavalry.

Hamilcar had problems feeding his large army, and when Gelon reached Himera, Hamilcar's men had scattered to find food. Gelon's cavalry captured large numbers of them. The Greeks besieged in Himera had expected destruction at any moment, but Gelon's success revived their spirits. Gelon now sought a decisive battle. Diodorus of Sicily (first century B.C.) tells the story:

Gelon's native ingenuity was helped out by an accident in the following way. He had decided to burn the enemy fleet. While Hamilcar was preparing a magnificent sacrifice to Poseidon in the naval encampment, there arrived cavalrymen with a letter-carrier possessing documents from Selinus° [in the southwest of the island] saying that they would send their cavalry on the day agreed to. That was the very day on which Hamilcar planned the sacrifice.

Gelon therefore sent out cavalry of his own with instructions to skirt around the neighborhood and at daybreak to arrive at the camp, pretending to be the cavalry from Selinus. Once inside the wooden palisade, they were to kill Hamilcar and set fire to the ships. He also sent scouts into the overlooking hills. They were to watch the camp and when the cavalry got within the walls, to give the signal. For his own part Gelon drew up his army and waited for the signal from the scouts.

At the crack of dawn the cavalry rode up and the guards admitted them, thinking they were allies. Immediately they galloped to where Hamilcar was making the sacrifice and cut him down. They then set fire to the ships. When the scouts gave the signal, Gelon attacked the camp in full battle array.

At first the leaders of the Phoenician contingent formed up in battle line and met the Sicilians in vigorous hand-to-hand combat. The trumpets calling to battle sounded from either side and cries went up from both sides, one after the other, each striving to outdo the enemy in their volume of sound. Many died, and the battle went back and forth until suddenly the flames from the burning ships shot up high into the air and the word went out that the general was dead. The Greeks were emboldened, and their spirits raised high by the rumors going round and by the hope of victory. They fought ever harder against the barbarians, while the Carthaginians, dispirited and despairing of victory, turned and ran.

Gelon had ordered that no man be taken alive, and after great slaughter of those in flight no fewer than 150,000° men were killed. Those who escaped fled to a strong position and at first fought off their attackers, but the location had no water, and soon thirst forced them to surrender to the victors. Gelon had won an important victory through his abilities as a general, and his fame grew wide not just among the Sicilians, but in the whole world . . .

After the battle at Himera twenty longships escaped, which to serve his routine requirements Hamilcar had not pulled up on the beaches. While nearly everyone else was being killed or captured, these ships escaped unnoticed. They picked up many of those who were fleeing, became overloaded, and when they encountered a storm, sank, killing all on board.

Only a handful, traveling in a small boat, made it back to Carthage, where they delivered to the citizens a succinct report: "All who crossed to Sicily are dead."

Diodorus of Sicily 11.21–22, 24

°*Selinus:* A major Greek city in western Sicily, which generally pursued pro-Carthaginian policies.
°*150,000*: An impossible number—this would be fifteen times the size of the Athenian army at Marathon.

Gelon's victory at Himera made him the most influential man in Sicily. Hailed as the savior of the Greeks, his word was law. For Carthage, however, the campaign was a disaster. Terrified that Gelon would now invade North Africa, the Carthaginians offered a huge indemnity in return for which Gelon left Motya, Panormos, and Soloeis untroubled. Akragas also profited mightily by enslaving thousands of Carthaginian soldiers who had fled across the interior of Sicily. Diodorus noted, "There was such a multitude of captives that it looked as if the island had made the whole of Libya [i.e., North Africa] prisoner."

So ended Hamilcar's invasion. More than seventy years would pass before Carthage challenged the Greeks again.

## THE STORM BREAKS IN THE EAST: THE BATTLE OF THERMOPYLAE, 480 B.C.

Xerxes was more ambitious than Hamilcar: He wanted to conquer Greece totally. His strategy was simple—march directly to Athens; burn it; do the same to Sparta, forcing the Greeks either to fight (and lose) a decisive battle or to give up, paralyzed by fear. Judging from past experience, the Greek alliance would break up before Xerxes actually had to fight. It was a sound strategy and it was hard to see how it could fail.

The Greek strategy was equally simple: Make it fail. They could not hope to win an open battle, so they would defend one of the passes along the coast that Xerxes would have to cross in order to stay in contact with his fleet, which provisioned the army. Man-for-man, light-armed Persians were no match for Greek hoplites, but holding off Xerxes was not the same as defeating him. Persia had a huge fleet: If blocked at a pass, they could sail around it toward Athens and Sparta.

There were only three places where the Greeks might hold the Persians (Map 12.2). The first was the beautiful VALE OF TEMPE (**tem-pē**), between the towering mountains Olympus and Ossa at the northern border of THESSALY, whose cavalry the Greeks badly needed. Ten thousand hoplites and a hastily assembled fleet, including the 200 new Athenian triremes, rushed north toward Tempe, only to learn that there was a second way into Thessaly, and that if they took their stand at Tempe they would be outflanked. The Greeks therefore fell back south, leaving Thessaly undefended. The Thessalians surrendered to Xerxes.

The second natural defensive position was THERMOPYLAE (ther-**mop**-i-lē, "the hot gates") between Thessaly and the district of Locris, where seemingly impassable mountains came within a few yards of the sea. Thermopylae was a logical place to make a stand because it was north of Athens and the Greek fleet could block the narrow straits of Artemision just off the coast, separating the northern tip of the island of Euboea from the mainland. On the other hand, Xerxes might get there before the Greeks, or by sailing around the south end of the long island of EUBOEA, he might trap the Greek fleet at ARTEMISION and destroy it. The third option was to abandon central Greece altogether and withdraw to the Isthmus of Corinth. That meant giving up Athens, perhaps destroying the alliance. In any event, Xerxes could easily outflank the Isthmus and land his army wherever he liked in the Peloponnesus. Sparta nonetheless consistently favored this dangerous plan.

Furious arguments paralyzed the Greeks in the crucial spring of 480 B.C. as Xerxes' vast forces marched on inexorably. Unable to decide what to do, the Greeks sent some troops to Thermopylae, but only a tiny force of 300 Spartans led by King **Leonidas** with

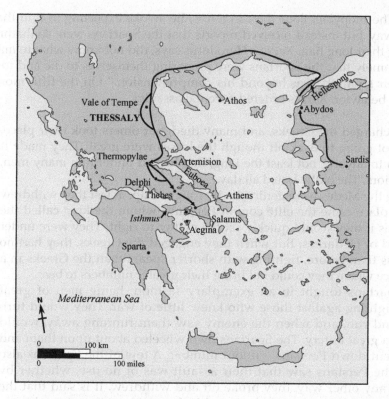

**MAP 12.2** The Aegean campaign of 480 B.C.

around 5,000 allies. Leonidas, convinced of the need to take a stand at Thermopylae, rushed to get there before the Persians. He repaired an old wall across the narrow pass while the entire Greek fleet took up a position nearby off Cape Artemision. The Greek fleet and army faced terrifying odds, yet the Spartans, true to their reputation, showed almost reckless bravery as they awaited the onslaught. A story circulated that the Persians would shoot so many arrows that they would block out the sun. "That's good," one Spartiate commented. "If the Persians hide the sun, we shall have our battle in the shade."

In this moment of crisis, the Greeks turned to their gods. An Athenian oracle recommended praying to Boreas, god of the north wind. As if in answer, a terrible storm hit the Persian fleet up the coast north of Thermopylae. Xerxes had so many ships that they had to ride at anchor eight rows deep, and when the fierce wind sprang up, it smashed 400 ships against the rocks. Thousands drowned. Nonetheless Persia's fleet pressed on, only to discover the Greeks blocking the straits at Artemision. They expected the Greeks to flee and leave Thermopylae exposed, and Eurybiades (yu-ri-bī-a-dēz), the Spartan commander of the allied fleet, was tempted to do just that—until, according to rumor, the Euboeans secretly gave the Athenian Themistocles thirty talents to persuade Eurybiades to fight at Artemision, thus protecting Euboea. The wily Themistocles gave five talents to Eurybiades, bribing him to stay and fight, then pocketed the difference, making a fortune while achieving his own military aims.

Greek sailors were probably as skilled as Xerxes' Phoenicians, but after a week, half the Athenian ships were damaged. The Persians kept up the pressure at Artemision and, as the Greeks had feared, sent a large naval force around the south end of Euboea to trap the Greeks in the channel. On land, Xerxes meanwhile advanced against the handful of hoplites holding Thermopylae. Four days in a row, he awoke expecting to find that the Greeks had run away, but instead received reports that the Spartans were sunbathing in the nude, combing their long hair. Xerxes, Herodotus says, did not know what to make of this: "The truth, namely that the Spartans were preparing themselves to die and to meet death with all their strength, was beyond his comprehension." On the fifth morning, astonished at their behavior, Xerxes ordered a frontal assault:

> The Medes° charged the Greeks, and many died, but others took their place. They were not going to back off though the losses were great. They made it plain enough to anyone, not least the king, that he had under him many men, but few warriors. The battle lasted all day.
>
> Because the Medes were getting badly roughed up, at last they withdrew and in their place came the elite core of Persians, whom the king called the Immortals,° as if they would quickly set the matter to right. They were under the command of Hydarnes. But when they engaged the Greeks, they had no better success than before, fighting with shorter spears than the Greeks in a confined space where they could not bring their greater numbers to bear.
>
> The Spartans fought in an exemplary fashion, being men of great experience fighting against those who knew little of war. They would turn their back and run, and when the enemy saw them running away, would charge with a great outcry. The Spartans then wheeled about upon them and in this way cut down Persians without number. A few of the Spartans also fell. When the Persians saw that their assault was of no use, whether by divisions or any other way, they broke off and withdrew. It is said that the king, who was watching the attacks from his throne, three times stood up in terror for his army.

Herodotus 7.210–12

°*Medes:* Although the Medes were a distinct people from the Persians, Greek writers used Medes as a synonym for Persians. To *medize* was to submit to Persian power. °*Immortals:* An elite force of 10,000 infantry.

The next day, Xerxes hurled still more men against the phalanx, and the slaughter continued. Leonidas rotated contingents in and out of line so that they never tired, while mounds of the Persian dead grew around them. Xerxes' best men were falling, and the fleet he sent south around Euboea had not returned. Unknown to him, it had run into yet another storm, losing hundreds more ships.

A Greek traitor named Ephialtes turned the tide. He told Xerxes of a path over the mountains, coming out behind the Spartans. That night, Hydarnes led the Immortals over the path, brushing aside the few defenders. A runner informed Leonidas that the pass was turned. Realizing that all was lost, Leonidas sent the allies away. But he and the 300 Spartans were under orders, and whatever happened, they would honor their word. Seven hundred men from the small town of Thespiae near Thebes also refused to leave; they joined the Spartans for the last stand.

> As the Persians under Xerxes advanced, the Greeks under Leonidas, as if going to their deaths, came out further than before into the wider part of the pass. In earlier days they had taken protection behind the wall, going out from it to

fight only in the narrow portion of the pass, but now they joined with the enemy in the wide part. The Persians died in great numbers. Behind the Persian fighters stood their commanders, urging them forward with the lash of the whip to fight in the hand-to-hand. Many fell from the cliffs into the sea and were drowned, and many others were trampled to death under foot. The number of the dead was beyond counting.

Knowing of their certain death because of the men skirting the mountain, the Spartans fought beyond measure, as if mad. By now the spears of most were shattered, so they fought the Persian with their swords. Leonidas fell at this time, fighting most bravely, and others of great worth with him, the best of the Spartiates. I learned their names. In fact I learned the names of all three hundred of the Spartans.

Many distinguished Persians fell too, including two brothers of Xerxes . . . The struggle between Greeks and Persians over the body of Leonidas was intense, until through their bravery the Greeks were able to drag it away, and four times they turned back the Persian attack.

So things stood until the Greeks learned that Ephialtes and the Persian troops were about to arrive. Then the contest changed. The Greeks withdrew again into the narrows and took up position in mass at the top of the small hill at the entrance to the pass. The stone lion dedicated to Leonidas stands there today. Here they continued to fight with their swords, which some still had, or with just their hands, and with their teeth. But the Persians showered them with missiles, coming at them from the front over the wall, or closing in from behind.

Herodotus 7.223–25

Over their bodies, the Greeks later set up a famous inscription:

Go, tell the Spartans, passerby
That here, obedient to their wishes, we lie.

## THE FALL OF ATHENS

The battered fleet escaped the trap set by the Persians off Cape Artemesion and withdrew to the narrows around the island of **Salamis** just off the harbor of Athens, while the Greek army withdrew back to the Isthmus. In 481 B.C. a Delphic oracle had advised Athens to "trust its wooden walls," which Themistocles and most other Athenians took to refer to the fleet; some, however, imagined that the "wooden walls" of the oracle meant they should barricade the Acropolis with wooden planks. The Persians sent fire arrows into this wooden wall, then climbed the almost impregnable rock by a back path. Still the Athenians held out:

When they saw them coming up onto the Acropolis some of the Athenians leapt to their death from the walls, while others took refuge within the temple. The first Persians on top attacked the doors, burst them open and killed all the suppliants inside. When every single one was dead, they stripped the temple bare and burned the entire Acropolis.

Herodotus 8.53

Athens was a smoldering ruin. The Spartan commander of the allied fleet, Eurybiades, now wanted to sail back to the Isthmus, join the land army, and there await the Persian attack. Themistocles, on the other hand, understood that the Greeks' only chance for victory was to provoke Xerxes into a naval battle: only if the Greeks destroyed the Persian fleet could they hope to hold the Isthmus. If they could lure Xerxes into the narrows around the island of Salamis, Themistocles reasoned, the Persian numbers would be neutralized, as they had been at Thermopylae. The stakes were high. Athens was already destroyed. If the fleet fought and won, the city might be rebuilt; if not, the city would remain in Persian hands forever.

Themistocles rounded on Eurybiades:

> "If you remain here," he cried, "you will by your act do the right thing. If not, you will destroy Greece. The outcome of this war depends on the fleet. Trust me. If you do not remain, we will pick up our belongings and sail to Siris in Italy, which has long been our possession and which, according to the oracles, we must one day inhabit. Once you have lost us as allies you will remember my words."
>
> Herodotus 8.62

Eurybiades relented, for the time being.

## THE BATTLE OF SALAMIS

There was no good reason for Xerxes to fight at Salamis. Victory there would end the war quickly, but if he just sailed to the Isthmus, the Greeks would have to follow, and he could meet them on his own terms. Herodotus says that Artemisia, the only woman commander in the war, gave Xerxes precisely this advice.

While Xerxes deliberated, the Greek generals criticized Eurybiades for agreeing to stay at Salamis. They demanded a second council. Seeing they were going to give up Salamis, Themistocles quickly sent a slave to Xerxes with this message:

> "The general of the Athenians has sent me in secret, without the knowledge of the other Greeks, because he favors your cause and looks forward to your success over the Greeks. He told me to report that the Greeks are afraid and are planning to slip away, and that now is the perfect moment to achieve your goals, if you do not allow them to slip away. They are completely at odds with one another and will not resist you. Rather, you will see them fighting at sea with each other, the pro-Persians on one side and the anti-Persians on the other."
>
> Herodotus 8.75

Xerxes took the bait and ordered his fleet forward, cutting off the Greeks' escape. There would be battle at Salamis. Themistocles had played his hand well: If the Greeks won, he would be the hero, but if Xerxes won, Themistocles could claim to be the author of his victory.

At dawn, the Persians rushed into the narrows. The 380 Greek ships were outnumbered two to one. Terrified, they backed water, but ran out of room. For a moment the line seemed about to break when one ship—no one could remember after the battle if it was from Athens or Aegina—lunged forward and rammed a Persian. The navies then fell on each other. Aeschylus, one of the greatest Athenian dramatists, fought in the Greek fleet that day, and eight years later, in his play *The Persians*, had a messenger describe events from the Persian side:

> Straightaway ship struck ship with brazen prows.
> A Greek ship began the attack.
> The high stern of a Phoenician bark collapsed
> One ship drove against the next.
> At first the strength of the Persian fleet held fast,
> but once most ships were gathered in the narrows,
> and they could not help one another,
> but were struck by brazen mouthed assaults,
> all our equipment was shattered.
> The Athenians ships, in a calculated way,
> rounded us in a circle and struck.
> The hollow ships were turned upside down.
> You could no more see the sea,
> overwhelmed by flotsam and blood.
> Dead bodies covered the beaches and rocks.
> Every ship tried to save himself in a wild retreat,
> whoever had survived from the Persian fleet.
> They struck them, severed their spines
> with the splinters of oars
> or the pieces of wrecked debris,
> as if they were tunnies or a net filled with fish.
> The moans of the dying mixed with wailing
> overcame the open sea until
> the eye of black night covered them over.
> Not if I had ten days could I list all the evils
> nor tell all that happened.
> Be sure of this: On no other one day
> did so great a number die.

Aeschylus, *The Persians*, 408–32

Herodotus gives an even-handed account:

> A large number of ships were destroyed in the battle of Salamis, the majority of them at the hands of the Athenian or Aeginetan ships. Because the Greeks were fighting in order and according to a plan, whereas the Persians had completely lost their formations and had no plan, something of the kind was bound to happen. Nonetheless the Persians fought well that day, far better than they had fought off Euboea. Every man did his best in fear of Xerxes, for each man thought that he was watching his own performance . . .

> There were Greek casualties, but few in number. Knowing how to swim, those Greeks who lost their ships, if they were not killed in the actual fighting, swam over to Salamis. But most of the enemy, not knowing how to swim, were drowned. The most were killed when the ships that first engaged in combat turned and ran. They only became entangled in their own ships drawn up in ranks behind them, pressing forward and hoping to accomplish something for the king.
>
> Herodotus 8.86, 89

The remnants of the Persian fleet scattered. The Greeks towed the disabled and captured ships to safety and waited for Xerxes to renew the battle, because even after losing hundreds of vessels, he outnumbered the Greeks. But the second attack never came. Xerxes feared that the Greek fleet would break out from Salamis and cut the bridges to Asia; the Greeks might even capture him. His general Mardonius, sure to be blamed for persuading Xerxes to invade Greece, volunteered to stay behind with the best soldiers while Xerxes retreated. The next night, the Persian fleet slipped away to protect the Hellespont bridges. Jubilant, the Greeks raced after them. Themistocles urged attacking the Hellespont, but Eurybiades let them go. Why repeat Xerxes' mistake, risking everything on an unnecessary battle against a desperate foe? The ever-resourceful Odysseus-like Themistocles sent a second message to Xerxes saying it was *his* idea to allow him to escape, in case he some day needed Xerxes to return the favor!

Xerxes left Mardonius in Thessaly with 300,000 men, according to Herodotus (most historians think the force was less than half that size). The king himself stayed a few days in Athens, then began the retreat. He Without a supporting fleet carrying supplies, the withdrawal became a rout:

> Xerxes reached the Hellespont in forty-five days, having scarcely any of his army with him. As the army marched, they lived off what they could take from the local inhabitants. If they could find no supplies, they ate the grass growing from the earth, or stripped the bark off trees, both domestic and wild, and ate that, or shook down the leaves and ate them. Driven by starvation, they left nothing behind. Plague and dysentery killed many on the road. The sick they left behind, turning them over to the cities along the way . . .
>
> Having passed through Thrace, the army reached the Hellespont. Boarding their ships (for winter weather had destroyed the bridge) they arrived at Abydos,° where there was far more food than they had been finding along the way. Eating overmuch, and drinking unfamiliar water, many died of the few who remained. At last the remnant reached Sardis in the company of Xerxes.
>
> Herodotus 8.115, 117

°*Abydos:* A city on the Asiatic side of the Hellespont.

The campaign was a disaster. Xerxes had poured out the empire's blood and gold; hundreds of thousands had died; the fleet was broken; and it was all for nothing.

## THE END OF THE STORM: BATTLES OF PLATAEA AND MYCALÊ, 479 B.C.

Herodotus, writing 60 years later, saw that after Salamis the war was as good as over:

> I now feel obliged to voice an opinion that will appear objectionable to most people; nonetheless, it seems to me to be true. If the Athenians in terror of the approaching event had abandoned their city, or if they had not abandoned it but awaited the Persian and gave him what he wanted, no one would have attempted to resist the king at sea. If no one opposed Xerxes at sea, it is easy to see what would have happened on land. No matter how many lines of fortifications they drove across the Isthmus of the Peloponnesus, the Spartans would have been betrayed by their allies: Not willingly, but having no choice in the face of Persian naval power. Once isolated, the Spartans would have performed marvelously, then died nobly. Either they would have suffered this, or seeing that all the other Greeks were going over to the Persian, they too would have reached an accord. In either case Greece would have fallen to the Persians. I certainly cannot see what use walls across the Isthmus would have done anyone, so long as Xerxes commanded the sea. If therefore one were to say that the Athenians were the saviors of Greece, he would not be mistaken. They held the balance—to whatever side they inclined, there would go the victory. Having chosen that Greece should remain free, she stirred up those Greek who had not already joined the Persians. It was Athens—after the gods—who drove back the Persian king.
>
> Herodotus 7.139

In autumn 480 B.C., though, this fact was far from clear. Mardonius still had a huge army in Thessaly, and for all the Greeks knew, Xerxes would return with a new fleet the next year. Mardonius hoped to exploit such fears and offered Athens generous terms to change sides. The Athenians gave an impassioned reply:

> "There is not so much gold in the world, nor land so fair, that we would take it in payment for going over to the Persian and enslaving Greece. There are many things preventing us from doing this, even if we wanted. First and greatest are the statues and temples of the gods that you burned and despoiled. It is our bound duty to take revenge for these acts as far as it is in our power to do so, not to clasp the hand of those who perpetrated these crimes. Then there is the Greek nation—bound together by a common tongue, common religious shrines, and ritual practice, and customs in general. It world hardly be right for Athenians to betray all this. Know this well, if you do not already know it, that so long as one Athenian remains alive, Athens will never make peace with Xerxes."
>
> Herodotus 8.144

Stirring words, but when spring came, Mardonius burned Athens again (Map 12.3). The Spartans continued fortifying the Isthmus, but otherwise did nothing. Athenian messengers begged Sparta to march north: Each day the Ephors said they would answer

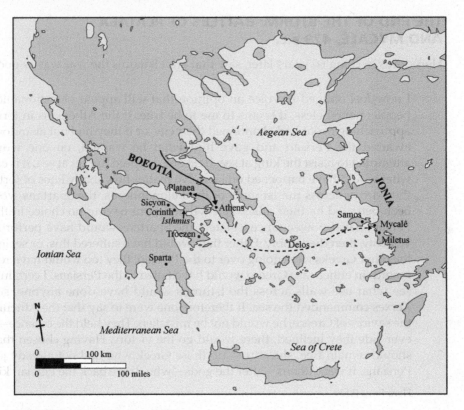

**MAP 12.3** The campaign of 479 B.C.

on the next day. After Salamis, the Isthmus was secure, so why should Spartans risk their lives for Athens? After two weeks, the Athenians reminded Sparta who had won security for the Isthmus. They delivered an ultimatum: despite their hatred of Xerxes, they would defect if the Spartans did not march north to assist them. The Spartans feigned shock at the Athenians' lack of faith. Just hours before, they announced, the Spartan army had at last set out under Pausanias (pow-sā-nē-as), regent for Leonidas' infant son, to seek out and destroy the Persian army.

When Mardonius heard that the Greek armies were marching north, he fell back to Boeotia, where the terrain was good for his cavalry. The Greeks took up position in the foothills near the village of **Plataea** in southern Boeotia, hoping that the rough ground would neutralize Mardonius' cavalry.

The Greeks had the largest army that the independent *poleis* ever assembled, consisting of 40,000 hoplites and 70,000 light troops, but (as always) few horsemen. Pausanias and Mardonius each wanted a decisive battle. When they consulted the omens, however, each received the same answer: If you defend, you win; if you attack, you lose.

Thus the armies faced each other for seven days. Every day the Persian cavalry rode out, hoping to lure the Greeks down from the hills, without success. The Greeks, however, were feeling the pressure. They had little food and less water in the barren foothills. On the eighth day, the Persians intercepted a huge Greek supply train of 500 mules. Two days later, Mardonius committed his cavalry more heavily, making it hard for the Greeks to reach their only water supply.

The Greek position was desperate. Pausanias ordered an overnight withdrawal to a point between two branches of a river, with plentiful water and protection from the Persian horsemen. But no one was really in charge of the overall operation. Some Greeks panicked and fell back all the way to Plataea and one Spartan commander refused to retreat at all. The Athenians waited to see what would happen. By dawn, Pausanias had persuaded everyone to move in the same direction, but a steep ridge now separated the main force of 5,000 Spartiates, 35,000 helots, and 1,500 Tegeans (Tegea was a town in the Peloponnesus) from the 8,000 Athenians, and the rest of the Greeks were nowhere to be seen.

Mardonius took his chance and closed on the Spartans while on the other side of the ridge Greek mercenaries fighting for Persia attacked their fellow Greeks, the Athenians. The Persians facing Pausanias set up a barricade of shields and loosed hails of arrows. Pausanias, still trying to obtain favorable omens, held his men back as he opened the entrails of one sheep after another. The impatient Tegeans rushed forward just at the moment that Pausanias got his good omen and ordered the Spartan attack:

At first the battle took place at the barricade of shields, but when these fell, the fight broke out in a fury and went on for a long time close by the temple of Demeter. The Persians would seize hold of the Spartan spears and break them. The Persians were not less in courage and strength than the Greeks, but they had no armor, lacked experience, and did not have the same skill as their opponents. They would come out one at a time or ten at a time, but whether there was more of them or fewer, they attacked the Spartiates and were destroyed. Where Mardonius chanced to be, riding atop his white charger and surrounded by his thousand elite Persian soldiers, there they attacked the enemy with greatest energy. So long as he remained alive, they held their own and defended their position and killed many of the Spartans. But after he was killed, and his personal bodyguard was killed, the finest of the Persian fighters, then the other Persians yielded, turned, and ran. Above all it was their lack of armor that undid them; for they fought as if naked against men clad with armor ( Figure 12.1).

**FIGURE 12.1** Greek warrior stabbing a Persian on a red-figured Athenian amphora, ca. 475 B.C. The Greek wears bronze armor, while the Persian has a leather suit and cap with long flaps.

The Persian force broke and fled to its fortified camp:

> When the Spartans came up to the camp, the fight for the wall grew stronger. So long as the Athenians were not there, the defenders held their ground against the Spartans, who were not trained in attacking defensive works. When the Athenians came up, the fighting became intense and lasted a long time. Finally through valor and hard fighting they made their way over the barricade and forced an opening. The Greeks poured through it . . .
>
> Once the wall was broken, the Persian ranks fell into complete disorder. They utterly forgot their military discipline, as tens of thousands of terrified soldiers were trapped in a small place. They were such easy picking for the Greeks that of the 300,000 who made up the army (not counting the 40,000 who escaped with Artabazus) not 3,000 survived.°
>
> Of the Spartans 91 were killed, 16 Tegeans, and 52 Athenians.

Herodotus 9.62–63, 70

°*3,000 survived*: Herodotus exaggerates the Persian losses, but they were surely heavy.

Supposedly on the very same day, another battle was fought on the Asian side of the Aegean, smaller than Plataea, but with consequences equally profound. Greeks from SAMOS had brought news to the Greek fleet (now at DELOS, center of the Cyclades) that all IONIA was ready to throw off Persian rule (see Map 12.3). All that the fleet needed to do was sail to Samos and defeat the few Persian ships there. They set sail, but the Persians, forewarned, retreated to a promontory on the coast near Samos called **Mycalê** (**mi**-ka-lē), beached their ships, and fortified an enclosure around them. The Greeks pursued, beached their ships, and disembarked. Shouting into the Persian camp, they invited the Persians' Ionian allies to defect. The Persians, not trusting the Ionians, sent most of them away and marched out alone to engage the Greeks.

The Greeks advanced in two columns. The Athenians arrived first:

> So long as the Persians kept up their line of shields, they defended themselves and by no means had the worst of it. But once the Athenians and their neighbors in line, wanting the credit to go to themselves and not to the Spartans, called out to one another and made a great effort, then everything changed. They burst through the line of shields and in a mass attacked the Persians. At first the Persians resisted, but after a short while they fled back into the fortification. The Athenians and men of Corinth, Sicyon, and Tegea, aligned in formation, attacked the wall. Once the wall was taken, the enemy lost all heart for fight, except for the Persians. These in small group continued to engage the Greeks as they came through the barricade . . .
>
> While the Persians were still fighting, the Spartans arrived with their comrades and shared in what remained of the fighting. Losses among the Greeks were considerable, especially among the Sicyonians, whose commander Perilaos was killed. The Samians were fighting on the Persian side, although they had been disarmed, and they saw right from the start that the battle was in doubt and did all they could to help the Greeks. When the other Ionians saw the Samians doing this, they followed their lead and deserted from the Persians and attacked them.

The Milesians had been ordered to watch the passes through the mountains, to keep them safe in case something happened like what did in fact happen. They were also appointed this task so that they would not try something in the midst of the Persian army. In fact they did just the opposite to what was ordered, leading the fleeing Persians by roundabout paths that brought them back to the fighting, and they themselves, as their most bitter enemies, set upon them and killed them. This was the second Ionian revolt.°

Herodotus 9.102–4

°*second Ionian revolt:* The first, of course, was in 499 B.C.

The hard-won victory at Mycalê eliminated the last viable Persian force in the Aegean Sea. The Ionians were free.

## CONCLUSION

Herodotus says that he wrote his *History* "so that human achievements may not be forgotten in time, and great and marvelous deeds—some displayed by Greeks, some by barbarians—may not be without their glory." He succeeded better than he could have imagined. 2,500 years later, Marathon, Thermopylae, and Salamis are three of the most famous names in the history of war. Leonidas' courage and Xerxes' *hybris* are not forgotten.

Herodotus, in his grand inquiry (Greek *historiê*), wanted to explain how and why the Greeks defeated the Persians. At one level, he told a highly moralistic story: Satiety (Greek *koros*) from too much wealth and power excited the envy (Greek *phthonos*) of the gods, who sent *atê*, "madness," so that men forgot their inherent limitations, committed violence (Greek *hybris*), and suffered retribution (Greek *nemesis*). Thus did Croesus, Polycrates, Cambyses, Darius, and Xerxes come to grief. But at another level, Herodotus emphasized very material factors: the hoplites' superior armor, the Spartans' discipline, the Athenians' determination, and Themistocles' unscrupulous genius. Against all odds, these forces broke the grandest army the world had ever seen.

Was the sacrifice worth it? The Greeks had preserved their freedom. Xerxes intended to destroy Athens and Sparta utterly; the war saved them. Yet only thirty-one *poleis* risked fighting Persia, and some of the greatest cities—Selinus in the west, Thebes in the east— actually helped the invaders. Persia and Carthage cared little what their subjects did so long as they paid their taxes. Ionia flourished for half a century under Persian rule, until the brutal destructions of 494 B.C. In return for taxes, Persia provided peace and freedom from random violence. Leading intellectuals worked in cities loyal to Persia, and the Persians allowed the Ionians to set up democracies in 493 B.C. Would it have made much difference to Greek culture if Persia had won at Marathon or Salamis, or Carthage at Himera? In the west, a Carthaginian victory might well have made little difference: Hamilcar aimed only at restoring the status quo. In the Aegean, so long as Persia continued its policy of leaving its subjects alone, a victorious Darius in 490 B.C. might have made equally little difference to the broader development of Greek culture. However, a victorious Xerxes in 480 B.C. would surely have prevented the explosion of intellectual and artistic achievement in Athens that we examine in the next chapter, an explosion in many ways dependent on the confidence, wealth, and power that victory in war gave to Athens.

In 479 B.C., Syracuse stood alone as the dominant power in Sicily, and Sparta and Athens stood together as triumphant but uneasy allies in the Aegean. Gelon needed only to extort concessions from Carthage; Sparta and Athens needed to defend Ionia against renewed Persian attacks, which everyone thought would come. Whatever the long-term consequences of Carthaginian and Persian victories might have been, in the short run, the Greek victories created a whole new set of problems.

## Key Terms

Xerxes, 253

Mardonius, 253

Syracuse, 254

Gela, 255

Gelon, 255

Himera, 256

Themistocles, 257

Hamilcar, 258

Thermopylae, 260

Leonidas, 260

Salamis, 263

Plataea, 263

Mycalê, 268

## Further Reading

In addition to the books listed in Chapter 11, the following are recommended:

Green, Peter, *The Greco-Persian Wars* (Berkeley 1996). Spellbinding account by a leading historian.

Harrison, Thomas, *The Emptiness of Asia* (London, 2000). Excellent treatment of the evidence of Aeschylus' play, *The Persians*.

Lancel, Serge, *Carthage* (Oxford, 1995). Review of the city's history by a prominent archaeologist.

Lazenby, J. F., *The Defense of Greece, 490–479 B.C.* (Warminster, UK, 1992). Excellent overview.

Strauss, Barry, *The Battle of Salamis* (New York, 2004). Lively account of the crucial battle, by a leading military historian.

### ANCIENT TEXTS

Aeschylus, *The Persians*. In *Prometheus Bound and Other Plays*, tr. Philip Vellacott (Harmondsworth, UK, 1961). Aeschylus' tragedy, written in Athens in 472 B.C., describing the battle of Salamis from the Persian perspective.

Diodorus of Sicily, *The History*, Book 11. In *The Library of History IV*, tr. C. H. Oldfather (Cambridge, MA: Loeb Classical Library, 1946). Parallel Greek and English texts. Writing in the first century B.C., Diodorus describes the war in Sicily in 480 B.C.

Herodotus, *The Histories*, tr. Aubrey de Selincourt, rev. ed. (New York, 1996). Books 7 through 9 describe the war of 480–479 B.C. Written at Athens, ca. 420 B.C.

## CHAPTER 13

# Democracy and Empire: Athens and Syracuse, 479–431 B.C.

As the summer cooled to autumn in 479 B.C., Greeks waited to see what would happen next. In the west, Gelon was becoming the greatest tyrant Greece had known, seemingly bent on creating a new kind of Greek state where many cities were ruled by a single king, somewhat like the Persian Empire. In the east, the war left Athens dominant at sea and Sparta on land. But Xerxes would surely seek revenge; could the alliance survive?

Aegean and western Greeks underwent similar experiences in the nearly fifty years from the battle of Plataea in 479 B.C. through the outbreak of the Peloponnesian War in 431 B.C. Syracuse and Athens both extended the power of their state institutions, finding new ways to raise money, fund warfare, and control the peoples around them. Both eastern and western Greece saw (by ancient standards) strong economic growth, and Athens and Syracuse became great cultural centers. But in the details, the two regions were quite different. Syracuse totally dominated Sicily. Athens, by contrast, built her power by leading an anti-Persian alliance, slowly taking over more functions within the alliance until she became virtually the capital city of a multi-city state. But Athens did not dominate old Greece, because Sparta remained a formidable and increasingly hostile rival. Athens and Syracuse also differed economically. Sicily prospered by exporting cereals; Athens, by importing them and selling silver and manufactured goods. The different bases of wealth were to have major repercussions. Although the Theban poet Pindar called Syracuse "the fairest Greek city," no one doubted that Athens was the wonder of the world—"the school of Greece," in the words of Thucydides. Although small by modern standards, with about 40,000 people living within just one square mile, Athens led an intellectual and aesthetic revolution without parallel. We are still very much under the influence of discoveries made at this time.

Historians sometimes call this exhilarating time a golden age, but it had a dark side too. Economic and political expansion fueled Athens' cultural triumphs and threatened Sparta. War drew in not just Athens and Sparta, but also Syracuse, Persia, and Carthage.

Let us first review political and economic developments in western Greece, then turn to the Aegean. Our coverage is necessarily uneven, because so much more evidence survives from Athens than from Syracuse.

## THE EXPANSION OF THE SYRACUSAN STATE, 479–461 B.C.

In Chapter 12, "The Great War, 480–479 B.C.," we left Gelon in his moment of triumph. Having defeated Carthage at Himera, he campaigned in the 470s B.C. to persuade Aegean Greeks that his victories were as great as theirs against Persia. He dedicated a golden tripod at Delphi to glorify his success: The stone base survives, inscribed "Gelon son of Deinomenes, the Syracusan, dedicated this to Apollo." It contrasted sharply with the Aegean Greeks' victory monument, another gold tripod whose bowl was supported by a bronze column in the form of a serpent. Part of the column survives today in Istanbul, standing in the open air, where it was transported in the fourth century A.D. (Figure 13.1).

Its pithy inscription reads: "These fought the war," followed by a list of 31 cities. While the Aegean cities fought as communities of citizens, Gelon *was* the state.

**FIGURE 13.1** The serpent monument erected in Delphi 479 B.C., now in the Hippodrome ("horse track") in Istanbul. Constantine the Great transported it from Delphi to then Byzantium in A.D. 324 and set it up in the central oval of the enclosed horse-racing arena. The column was manufactured with bronze taken from Persian armor. Intact until the seventeenth century, it once had three heads (one is in the Istanbul National Museum) and supported a golden bowl made of Persian gold. Three legs of a tripod, also of Persian gold, also supported the rim of the bowl. At the bottom, inscribed on the coils, are the names of the thirty-one Greek states who opposed the Persians, introduced by the words "These fought the war." The list does not always agree with that given in Herodotus.

Gelon died in 478 B.C., at the height of his glory. His spectacular funeral drew mourners from all over the Mediterranean. His brother **Hiero** (hī-er-ō), whom Gelon had left in charge of Gela in 485 B.C., now moved to Syracuse, handing Gela to another brother, Polyzalos (po-li-**zā**-los). Gelon and Hiero propelled Sicily toward a different political structure from the Aegean, with tyrant families ruling multi-city states, using relatives to govern smaller cities, and treating everyone as subjects. Both tyrants depopulated entire cities when it suited them, moving their people to Syracuse or selling them into slavery. They used mercenaries to fight their wars, turned them against the citizens if their power was threatened, and settled ex-mercenaries on the lands of cities they emptied. In a brutal world, they held the power.

Hiero maintained peace with Carthage, making no moves against the Phoenicians in Sicily, or even against SELINUS (Map 13.1), a rich Greek city that had sided with CARTHAGE in 480 B.C. However, Hiero did win a great sea battle against the Etruscans in 474 B.C. near CUMAE (**ku**-mē) in the Bay of Naples and resumed Gelon's glorification of Sicilian achievements. When his team won the chariot race at Delphi in 470 B.C., Hiero hired Pindar to commemorate it in typically complex verse, claiming that the battles of Himera and Cumae were equivalent to Plataea and Salamis, and that Gelon and Hiero too had saved Greece from slavery:

> Grant, I beg, o son of Cronus,°
> that the Phoenician and Tyrrhenian° war-cry
> remain quiet at home,

°*son of Cronus:* Zeus. °*Tyrrhenian:* Another name for Etruscan.

**MAP 13.1** Western Mediterranean sites mentioned in this chapter.

remembering the ship-groaning violence before Cumae
and what things they suffered, overwhelmed by the command of the Syracusans,
who cast down their youth from the swift-prowed ships in the sea,
dragging out Greece from grievous enslavement.
From Salamis I will win as pay the Athenians'° gratitude,
in Sparta from the battle before Cithaeron°
where the Medes who shoot with bent bows were beaten,
and beside the well-watered peak of Himera by singing a song for the sons of
Deinomenes,°
which they earned from their valor
when the hosts of the enemy gave way.

Pindar, *First Pythian Ode* 71–80

°*Athenians':* Pindar will win credit with the Athenians by celebrating in song the battle of
Salamis.°*Cithaeron:* This mountain stands behind Plataea, site of the great battle of 479 B.C. °*sons of
Deinomenes:* That is, Gelon and Hiero.

In the 470s B.C., Etruria, Carthage, the Sicilian Phoenicians, and even their long-time
native allies the Elymians in western Sicily declined before the growing power of
Syracuse. The tyrants had defeated their non-Greek enemies, but the two old problems of
elite feuds and class conflict came back to haunt them. Polyzalos, brother of the dead
Gelon and the living Hiero, chafed at being stuck in provincial Gela and persuaded
Theron of Akragas, Syracuse's most important ally, to join him in challenging his own
brother Hiero. When Theron died in 472 B.C., his son Thrasydaeus attacked Syracuse.
Hiero crushed Thrasydaeus so thoroughly that the citizens of Akragas expelled him and
set up a democracy. Thrasydaeus' former mercenaries, fearing they would not be paid,
then tried to seize Akragas. They lost the war but captured a smaller city and hung on for
years. Everything was going well for Hiero, but the Syracusans resented being ruled by a
tyrant. Thus, when he died in 467 B.C., they expelled his family and then fought a brutal
civil war against his former mercenaries.

As chaos spread and tyrants fell all over Sicily, the Greeks who had been forcibly
transferred from one city to another started returning home to wage civil war against
those (often ex-mercenaries) who had taken their land. Bloody wars raged from 466 to 461
B.C. between the "old" and "new" citizens. Finally, all the Sicilian cities signed a **Common
Resolution** in 461 B.C. Old citizens won the right of return and ex-mercenaries won partial
citizen rights. Syracuse's old network of alliances was broken, and, in theory, the Sicilian
*poleis* were once again free and equal.

## THE WESTERN DEMOCRACIES, 461–433 B.C.

The Common Resolution created large and diverse *poleis*, mixing old and new citizens,
former mercenaries, and naturalized natives. Many cities set up democracies as soon as
they were freed from tyranny, but their citizen communities remained less cohesive
than those in the Aegean, and aristocrats preserved greater power within the *polis*. At
Syracuse, a board of elected generals was particularly important and regularly opposed
the **demagogues** ("leaders of the people"), whose inclinations were democratic.
Violence broke out in 454 B.C. when officials condemned a demagogue for organizing a

bodyguard of poor citizens, and Syracuse introduced its own version of ostracism (called *petalismos* because names were written on *petaloi*, olive leaves, not *ostraka*, potsherds).

For nearly 300 years, the Sicilian Greeks had been taking over the best land, driving the natives off or reducing them to serfdom. Like all less-developed peoples on the fringes of empires, the natives could either submit or resist, normally by copying the aggressors' own institutions. Indigenous Sicilians did both. In western Sicily, the Elymians abandoned their villages and concentrated in the city of **Segesta**, which was to play a major role in Mediterranean politics in the fifth century B.C. In eastern Sicily, a charismatic native leader named Ducetius used war and persuasion to forge a league of native Sicels. They created a Sicel army, issued coins, and in 453 B.C. founded a new city at a spectacular holy site where sulfur springs had formed two giant craters.

The Common Resolution had created a power vacuum, and Ducetius tried, but failed, to exploit it. By the time the struggle ended, in 440 B.C., Syracuse had overrun the Sicel League and sold thousands of Sicels into slavery. Even without her tyrants, Syracuse remained the largest and richest Sicilian *polis*, fueled by taxes on the Sicels and harbor dues from booming trade. In 439 B.C., she expanded her army and navy and bullied or persuaded most Dorian-speaking Greeks in eastern Sicily to support her. By the decade's end Syracuse was threatening non-Dorian Greeks too.

These developments alarmed Athens. In 433 B.C., Athens formed a military alliance with the cities of Leontini (in eastern Sicily) and Rhegion (on the tip of the boot of Italy). Leontini, surrounded by Syracuse's renewed alliance, was under intense pressure; Rhegion, facing the Strait of Messina, had long been Syracuse's enemy. By this move, an aggressive Athens set eastern and western Greece on a collision course.

## ECONOMIC GROWTH IN WESTERN GREECE, 479–433 B.C.

Despite such political turmoil, the Greeks in Sicily and southern Italy flourished in the fifth century. Population boomed, probably doubling to reach perhaps a million Greeks living in the west. Syracuse, the largest city, had around 40,000 residents by 415 B.C. (as many as Athens), and Akragas and Selinus each had at least 20,000. Fifth-century houses were spacious, typically having four to eight rooms around a shady courtyard. Many had a second floor. As Diodorus (first century B.C.) reports:

> Once the tyranny of Syracuse was overthrown, and all the cities of Sicily set free, the whole island made great strides toward prosperity. They were at peace and inhabited a good and fertile land whose fruits were so abundant that soon they increased their estates, and they filled the land with slaves and domestic animals and all the benefits of wealth. For they were taking in enormous revenues and not spending anything on the usual wars.

Diodorus of Sicily 11.72

The wealth came largely from exporting produce grown on land taken from the natives. The Greeks worked the land intensively, often with slave labor, and sold grain, olives, and wine to the land-poor Aegean and to Carthage, receiving finished goods and silver in return. We know most about Akragas. Taxes on trade with Carthage paid for the most spectacular temple-building program in Greek history, and some landowners grew very rich. Diodorus says that when one of them won a victory in the games at Olympia in 412 B.C.,

> riding in a chariot he was led into the city in a parade that consisted of three hundred chariots, in addition to much else, each chariot drawn by two white horses, and all of them belonging to citizens of Akragas. In general, from earliest youth they led a life luxury, wearing exceedingly fine clothes and ornaments of gold, and having strigils° and wine-flasks made of silver and even gold.
>
> °*strigils:* Scrapers, usually made of iron or bronze. After exercising, athletes would oil themselves, then scrape off the oil, dirt, and sweat with a strigil.

One house was so grand that its wine cellar had

> 300 great casks cut out of the rock itself, each with a capacity of about 900 gallons. Beside them was a wine vat, plastered and with a capacity of 9,000 gallons, from which the wine flowed into the casks.

In amazement, Diodorus also noted that

> when Akragas was under siege [in 406 B.C.], they passed a decree bearing on the guards at their posts: They could have not more than one mattress, one cover, one sheepskin, and two pillows. Considering this was their most rigorous kind of bedding, you can imagine in what luxury they lived ordinarily.
>
> Diodorus of Sicily 13.81, 84

A complicated economic system was evolving. As urban centers developed in Sicily, standards of living and population rose everywhere. Even indigenous peoples shared in the new wealth.

## CIMON AND THE CREATION OF THE ATHENIAN EMPIRE, 478–461 B.C.

As the rejoicing died down after the battles of Plataea and Mycalê, the Spartans apparently imagined that conditions would return to the way they were before the war. They tried to persuade Athens not to build new city walls, saying that Athens could rely on Sparta's protection, but the crafty Themistocles kept the Spartans negotiating while the Athenians secretly finished new walls. Thwarted, Sparta turned to Ionia as a region over which to exercise power. Only a fleet could protect the Ionians from Persia, but although the Spartans were nominal commanders of the fleet, Athenian ships dominated. Sparta, therefore, proposed that the Ionians should relocate to mainland Greece, where they could live under Spartan protection. The result of defeating Persia would be the loss of their homes and their fertile land!

When the Ionians refused to migrate, Sparta tried to keep control of the allied fleet. Pausanias, the hero of Plataea, took charge in 478 B.C., drove the Persians from the island of Cyprus, then sailed back to capture Byzantium, guarding the entrance to the BLACK SEA (Map 13.2). But Pausanias' arrogance deeply offended the other Greeks. Reportedly he wrote to Xerxes, offering to betray Greece in return for Xerxes' daughter's hand and the

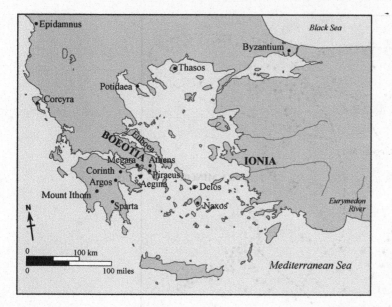

**MAP 13.2** Sites in Aegean Greece mentioned in this chapter.

position of satrap of Greece once it was part of the Persian Empire. The Ephors discovered his duplicity, removed him from his command, and sent out a replacement; but the Ionians refused to work with another Spartan. Consequently,

> The Spartans went back home and sent out no more commanders, fearing that by going abroad they were liable to corruption, which they saw as being the case with Pausanias. Furthermore, they wanted to withdraw from the Persian war and thought that the Athenians were perfectly capable of running things and, at that time, friendly to themselves. In this way the Athenians took over the leadership [of the fleet], and the allies went along with it through their hatred of Pausanias.

Thucydides 1.95–96

It was a bloodless coup. Athens' leading politicians—Themistocles, his rival Aristides (a-ris-tī-dēz), and a young man named **Cimon** (kē-mōn)—saw an opportunity to take control of an Aegean-wide alliance and use its navy to protect Athenian trade routes and to further Athenian interests generally. By 500 B.C., Attica's population (perhaps as many as 150,000 people) was more than Attica could feed from its own resources, even in a good agricultural year. Athens now depended on grain imports, especially from Ukraine and Crimea north of the Black Sea. Athens' need to secure her critical grain route became *the* strategic economic issue in fifth-century-B.C. Greece.

In 477 B.C. Athens and her allies met on the holy island of Delos, where Aristides presented a plan for waging war against Persia. A permanent fleet would cost far more than any *polis* could afford, he explained, so some cities (especially Athens) would provide ships and men, and the smaller ones could contribute money. His plan was fair: The small states bought cheap security and the big states received subsidies for their fleets. Dozens of cities accepted the proposal and the promise of responsible Athenian leadership (Map 13.3).

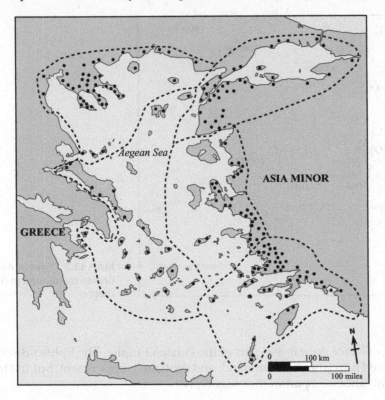

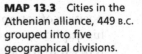

MAP 13.3 Cities in the Athenian alliance, 449 B.C. grouped into five geographical divisions.

The obvious choice for commander was Themistocles, victor of Salamis, but his fellow-citizens feared that he aimed at tyranny and did not trust him; he was exiled from Athens some time between 476 and 471 B.C. Meanwhile, Sparta's Ephors found Pausanias guilty of treason and starved him to death in a temple where he took refuge. The Ephors later alleged that Themistocles was also plotting with Persia, so the Athenians agreed to find him, wherever he might be, and kill him: Overly ambitious men were not to be tolerated in a democratic society. Hunted all across the Aegean, Themistocles took refuge with Artaxerxes I, who had succeeded Xerxes on the Persian throne. The king enriched and honored him.

The dashing young Cimon took command of the allied fleet and stormed the remaining Persian bases in the north Aegean. His strategy was to hound the Persians out of the Aegean and capture as much plunder as possible, while ensuring that no one enjoyed the Athenian fleet's protection without paying for it. Cimon attacked towns that refused to join the alliance, and when Naxos decided to withdraw from it in 476 B.C., Cimon compelled the island to keep paying:

Naxos was the first city to be enslaved in contravention of the terms of the alliance, and something similar happened to other cities as circumstances arose. Different causes led different cities to rebel, but mostly it was the failure to pay tribute or contribute ships or even to contribute anything at all. For the Athenians were sticklers for the exact terms being met and they made themselves unpopular by making harsh demands on those who were unaccustomed and unwilling to make such sacrifices. In other ways, too, the Athenians were no longer so popular as rulers. Although they did more than their fair share of the fighting, this only placed them in a position to prevent anyone from leaving the alliance. The allies themselves were to blame for this situation. Because of the reluctance of most of them to go on campaign and to leave their homes, they paid a certain sum of money instead of the ships they were supposed to contribute. On this account the Athenian navy grew strong at their expense, and when they revolted, they found themselves inadequately armed and inexperienced in war.

Thucydides 1.98–99

Athens was converting the allied cities into subjects. Diodorus says that some Spartans thought they had been fools to surrender naval command, and in 475 B.C. the Council of Elders discussed attacking Athens, but decided against it. In the meanwhile, Xerxes still planned revenge. In 469 B.C. he gathered 200 ships and an army at the Eurymedon River on the south coast of Asia Minor. Cimon engaged both forces on the same day and won shattering victories.

The battles at the Eurymedon River made many Greeks wonder whether they any longer needed the naval alliance—and they feared Athens' growing power. In 465 B.C., in a dispute with the wealthy island of Thasos in the northern Aegean over markets and mines, Athens sent in the allied fleet and began a siege. The Spartan Council now secretly voted to invade Attica in order to force the Athenians to withdraw, but just after the vote, a major earthquake hit Sparta, killing many Spartiates. The helots and some *perioikoi* rose up, this time in the fiercest revolt in Spartan history. Far from attacking Athens, Sparta now sought Athenian help against the helots!

Athens' mood had changed decisively since 479 B.C. The city was now the greatest naval power in the world, and rising politicians who insisted that Athens did not need Sparta had won the Assembly's confidence. Cimon, Athens' greatest general, vigorously opposed this view:

> When Athenians gained in power, they were annoyed at Cimon when they saw that he was strongly inclined to the Spartans. For he was always exalting the Spartans in comparison with them, especially if he was chiding them for something or urging them on. As Stesimbrotous° remarks, he liked to say, "But the Spartans don't act like that." In this way he awakened envy and hatred toward himself from the citizens.
>
> °*Stesimbrotus:* An author of the fifth century B.C.

When the Spartans asked for help in 464 B.C. after the earthquake,

> Ephialtes° opposed the plan, urging them not to go to their aid and restore the city of those opposed to their own interests, but to let the matter lie and to allow Sparta's haughtiness to be trodden under foot. Cimon, however, persuaded the people to place the advantage of Sparta over the increase of Athens and to send out a large force of hoplites to go forth and to assist them. Ion° preserves the very words by which he convinced them, saying that "they should not allow Greece to go lame or the city to be deprived of its yoke-mate."
>
> °*Ephialtes:* A rising politician (see below).   °*Ion:* A historian from the island of Chios who lived at this time.

Cimon helped Sparta push the rebellious helots back to rugged Mount Ithomê, where the war became a siege. Athens' siege of Thasos and Sparta's of Ithomê dragged on in parallel. Thasos fell in 463 B.C., but in 462 Sparta had to ask again for help:

> Again the Athenians came to their support, but Spartans were frightened by their boldness and enterprise and sent them away as being, alone of the allies, a band of conspirators. The Athenians returned home in a fury and openly vented their hostility on those sympathetic to Sparta. On a flimsy pretext they ostracized Cimon and exiled him for ten years.
>
> Plutarch, *Life of Cimon* 16–17

## THE FIRST PELOPONNESIAN WAR, 460–446 B.C.

As we saw in Chapter 10, "A Tale of Two Archaic Cities: Sparta and Athens, 700–800 B.C.," leaders in the Athenian Assembly had to persuade the Assembly to support their plans day-in, day-out, in constant debates. By 462 B.C. Cimon had lost touch with the city's mood, and his rivals, **Ephialtes** (ef-ē-al-tēz) and the young **Pericles** (per-i-klēz), turned the Assembly against him. In 461 B.C. Ephialtes convinced the Assembly to transfer crucial powers from the Council of the Areopagus, consisting of ex-archons who served for life, to the Assembly, thus undermining conservative leaders' power and broadening the democracy. Many historians date the flowering of the radical Athenian democracy to this moment. Passions ran deep, and when Ephialtes was murdered soon after the constitutional change, Athens teetered on the brink of civil war.

Domestic and foreign policy were tightly linked, and the radicalized Assembly turned against Sparta. Apparently, some Athenians believed that the only way to protect democracy was to break up the Peloponnesian League so that Sparta could no longer help reactionaries within Athens. Athens' hoplites could never defeat Sparta in the field, but by allying with disaffected members of the Peloponnesian League, Athenians hoped to encircle and split off Sparta's most important ally, Corinth. If Corinth went over to Athens' side, Sparta would be crippled. Athens' strategy led to the so-called First Peloponnesian War (460–446 B.C.), a kind of cold war fought mostly between Athens' allies and Sparta's allies. By 457 B.C., Argos, south of Corinth, and Megara, north of Corinth, had voluntarily joined Athens, and the island of Aegina and the cities of Boeotia northwest of Attica submitted too. The noose was tightening around Corinth.

Athens had not switched from anti-Persian to anti-Spartan policies; she pursued both at the same time. In 460 B.C., Egypt revolted from Persia. Egypt had vast wealth and supplies of grain, and Athens sent a huge force of 200 ships to help the Egyptian rebels. The struggle dragged on for six years, with Athens sending more and more ships. Despite her exertions in the cold war with Sparta and the hot war with Persia, Athens still found resources to build fortifications called the **Long Walls**, linking Athens and its harbor of Piraeus, about five-miles distant. Now no matter what the Spartans did on land, with its unstoppable access to the sea Athens could never be starved out.

In Chapter 10, we quoted Herodotus' comment that after Athens threw off tyranny in 508 B.C., freedom unleashed the citizens' strength and the city became a great power. The reforms around 461 B.C. triggered a second extraordinary outpouring of Athenian energy. A casualty list from 459 B.C. shows that Athenians were fighting all over the east Mediterranean that year ( Map 13.4). With Athens so heavily committed, the Corinthians

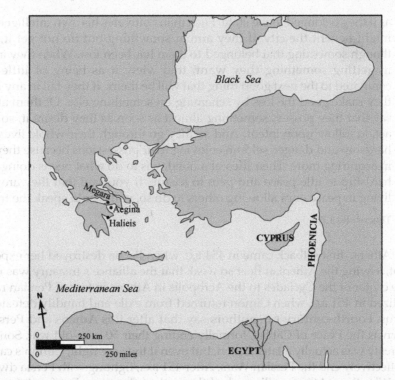

**MAP 13.4**   Theaters of war where Athenians of the Erechtheid tribe died fighting in 459 B.C. Some fell close to home (Halieis, Megara, Aegina); others died far away (Cyprus, Phoenicia, Egypt). The Erechtheids were just one of ten Athenian tribes (*phylai*); Athenian soldiers may have fought in other theaters that we do not know about.

raided Attica, only to be humiliatingly defeated by a band of Athenians too young or too old to be away with the army. According to Thucydides, a Corinthian speaking to the Spartans later contrasted Athenian energy with Spartan caution:

> You Spartans appear to have no understanding of what kind of people you are going to have to fight in the Athenians, who are completely different from you in so many ways. They are always willing to try something new, and no sooner do they perceive it than they have accomplished it. You like things to stay as they are. You have no original ideas, and when you undertake something, you quit before the job is done. They on the other hand show daring beyond what is warranted, take risks against their better judgment, and in the midst of difficulties are cheerful about the outcome. But you are unwilling to do what you are really able to do, do not trust your judgment even when it is sound, and think that you will never be rid of danger.
>
> Think of this too: They never hang back, while you can never get started. They travel abroad, while you stay at home. For they think that by going abroad they may acquire something, while you think that by staying home you might preserve what you already have. When they triumph over their enemies, they attack again; when they are defeated, they scarcely notice it. They use their bodies

as if they belonged to the state. Each man cultivates his own intelligence so that he might benefit the city. If they aim at something but do not get it, they feel as though something that belonged to them has been lost. When they are successful in getting something they want, they view it as being of little importance compared to the next good thing that will be theirs. If they fail in any undertaking, they make good the loss by scheming on something else. Of them alone can you say that they possess something almost as soon as they desire it, so swiftly does action follow upon intent. And so they go through their whole lives, working in hardship and danger, seldom enjoying their possessions because they are so busy in acquiring more. Their idea of a holiday is to do what needs doing. They prefer hardship to idle peace and pain to leisure. If you said that they are incapable of living in peace or of allowing others to do so, you would speak the truth.

Thucydides 1.70

Athens' first setback came in 454 B.C. when Persia destroyed her expeditionary force in Egypt, leaving the Athenian fleet so weak that the alliance's treasury was moved from Delos at the center of the Cyclades to the Acropolis in Athens in fear of Persian raids. The situation stabilized in 451 B.C. when Cimon returned from exile and handily defeated the Persians on Cyprus. Fourth-century B.C. authors say that after this Athens and Persia signed a treaty known as the Peace of Callias, formally ending their 50-year-old war. Some historians think this treaty was actually a later fiction; but even if they are right, Cimon's campaign in Cyprus did effectively end the Persian Wars. After 451 B.C., fighting with Persia dwindled to nothing.

Why then, Athens' allies asked themselves, keep paying for defense against a threat that no longer existed? Some Boeotian cities rebelled in 447 B.C. and defeated an Athenian force sent to force them back into submission. This made Athens looked weak, and the island of Euboea, vital to Athens' communications and a major source of grain, rose up in 446 B.C. Next, Megara turned on Athens, and Sparta prepared to invade Attica. Pericles, now the leading figure in the Athenian Assembly, moved quickly in this moment of crisis. He reconquered Euboea before Sparta intervened, and late in 446 B.C. negotiated a treaty with Sparta called the Thirty Years' Peace. Her great grab for power defeated, Athens renounced all claims to mainland Greece, apparently turning back the clock to the days when Sparta was the greatest Greek power.

## PERICLES AND THE CONSOLIDATION OF ATHENIAN POWER, 446–433 B.C.

In reality, Athens was doing no such thing. Pericles championed a subtle strategy: Avoid entanglements, hold on to the allied cities, keep collecting tribute, and continue centralizing power. Eventually, he reasoned, Athens would have the resources to overwhelm Sparta. Athens was becoming something like a capital city, reducing formerly independent *poleis* in the Aegean to provincial centers. The allies' tribute was effectively a tax paid for security. When there were revolts, Athens took over the cities' legal or financial administration, often sending out garrisons and officials or confiscating land and redistributing it to Athenian citizens. Athens made decisions on foreign policy without consulting the cities involved and insisted that everyone use Athenian weights, measures, and coinage. Major lawsuits were to be tried in the city of Athens, even if the crime had been committed abroad.

Pericles' successes made him the most powerful politician Athens had ever seen:

Pericles said that if they kept an even keel and maintained the fleet, and in time of war did not add to the empire, and watched over the safety of the city itself, that they would be victorious . . .
        Pericles, because of his position, and his intelligence, and his incorruptibility, was able to hold the people in check while they were still free. It was he who led them, not they who led him. Because he never attempted gain through inappropriate means, he was under no obligation to flatter them. His status was so high that he could even contradict them in anger. Certainly when he saw them going too far in a mood of overconfidence, he would explain to them the danger. And when he saw that they were discouraged for no good reason, he brought them back to their mood of courage. It was a democracy in name, but in reality it was rule by the first citizen.

Thucydides 2.65

Athens consistently followed his policies; her only major war between 446 and 431 B.C. was to crush a revolt on the island of Samos in 440 to 439 B.C.
        The steady expansion of Athenian state power was the most important development in Classical Greek history. Back in the eighth and seventh centuries B.C., Sparta had made herself more than a normal city-state by conquering Messenia, but in the sixth century her expansion stalled, and Sparta stabilized as the head of a Peloponnesian alliance. In the 480s B.C., the tyrants of Syracuse and Akragas had created multi-city states in Sicily, but these proved unstable and collapsed in the 460s B.C.. Now Athens was creating a new and uniquely powerful multi-city state.

## ECONOMIC GROWTH IN THE AEGEAN

Greek population throughout the Mediterranean probably doubled during the fifth century B.C., perhaps reaching five million in the 430s B.C. Paradoxically, more people meant more wealth for everyone, as the growth of Athenian power fueled rising standards of living.

### Trade

Most of the tribute that Athens took from other cities was spent on the fleet. Most ships were built in Piraeus, Athens' harbor, and most sailors were Athenians. Cash flowing into Athens ended up in the hands of oarsmen, riggers, and other state employees. Some of these men were part-time farmers, while others did no agriculture; but all bought food, and because Athenians had money to spend, foreign importers brought food to Piraeus. Because grain came in from Sicily, Egypt, and Ukraine, Athenian farmers could specialize in more profitable crops like olives, fruits, and legumes, selling them in urban markets and buying imported grain. Because Athens' markets flourished, artisans concentrated there, producing textiles, metalwork, pottery, and other goods that the grain traders could buy and carry back to sell in their home cities, making profits at both ends of their voyages. Athenian pottery made at this time is found virtually all over the Mediterranean.
        Most Greeks were still farmers, consuming at home most of the food they grew. But the increasing integration of regions through seaborne trade meant that each region could concentrate on the activities for which it was best suited. Economic growth was driven by

the big cities, whose citizens reaped the greatest benefits, but country people gained too. Even small villages now had well-built houses.

As Athenian purchasing power increased, the population of Attica soared to around 350,000, with 40,000 living in the city itself. The fleet suppressed piracy and guaranteed the trade routes. Around 440 B.C., an anonymous writer, known today as the **Old Oligarch** because of his hostility toward democracy, described the material benefits from naval power (see Map 13.5):

> If I must mention even minor matters, the Athenians have found out all manner of good cheer by mixing with all kinds of foreign peoples. Whatever is sweet in Sicily, or in Italy, or in Cyprus, or in Egypt, or in Pontus, or in the Peloponnesus—all these things are gathered together in one place through domination over the sea.
>
> *The Old Oligarch* 2.7

The Old Oligarch describes a cosmopolitan Athens, but even small cities had regular visitors from overseas. Many Greeks involved in trade chose to settle in *poleis* other than their own, hoping to be able to go home as rich men. Such men were called **metics** (from the Greek verb *metoikein*, "to live with"). Metics had to pay residence taxes and usually could not own real estate in their adopted community. Many were menial workers, but a few became wealthy. Aristotle spent much of his life as a metic in Athens, and metics and slaves (some of them women) ran the major banks in Athens (though rich citizens usually owned the banks).

## Slavery

We saw in Chapter 10 that Solon's ban on debt bondage made the use of foreign slaves a logical response to the need for cheap labor, and in the fifth century B.C., the slave trade boomed. By the 430s B.C., a quarter of the population of Attica, some 75,000 people, may have been slaves, imported mainly from the Balkans and Asia Minor (see Map 10.2). Large landowners often found it easier to buy or rent slaves than to hire free labor. Hundreds of small workshops in Athens each employed a handful of slaves each (Figure 13.2). Anyone who could afford it would have a slave or two as domestic servants (Figure 13.3), while up to 20,000 men at a time served out their days in the narrow, airless shafts and inhuman conditions of the Athenian silver mines.

Greek slavery was very different from pre-1865 American slavery. Most obviously, American slave owners justified their institution by claiming that all African Americans were inferior to all European Americans. Those enslaved by the Greeks were ordinarily not Greek, spoke different languages, and were considered to be inferior by nature, but the Greeks had no such clear ideology as the American slave owners. In the fourth century B.C., Aristotle proposed a theory of "natural slavery," holding that the gods had made all non-Greeks inferior to all Greeks and that non-Greeks therefore deserved to be enslaved, but the theory had many critics (see Chapter 18, "Greek Culture in the Fourth Century B.C."). Except in the mines, Greek slaves worked in small groups, often alongside their masters. Greece was unsuited to plantations with gangs of hundreds of laborers, like those on nineteenth-century American cotton and sugar plantations. Finally, whereas three-quarters of American slaves in 1850 were field hands, Greek slaves worked in virtually every occupation, and some were skilled workers and even teachers. Thucydides says that in 413 B.C., 20,000 skilled slaves—probably a quarter of the slave population—ran away from Athens.

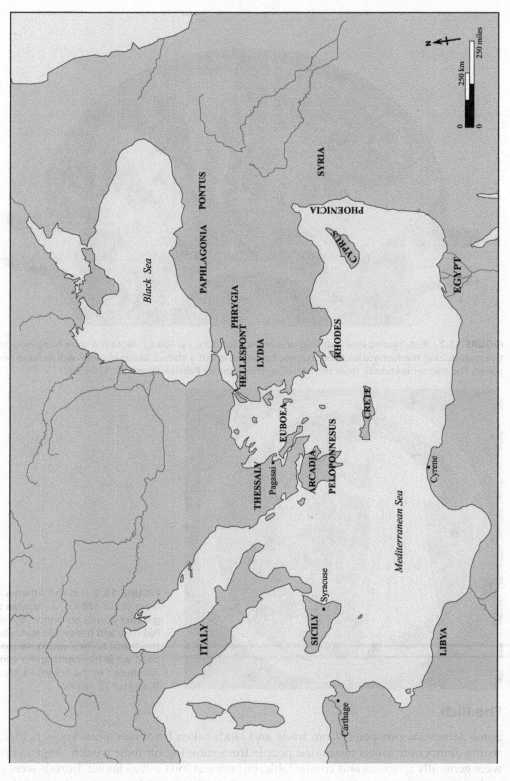

**MAP 13.5** Sources of Athenian imports mentioned by the Old Oligarch and Hermippus.

**FIGURE 13.2** Red-figured vase painting of a bronze foundry, ca. 480 B.C. Note the tools hanging above the men stoking the furnace and the sculptor hammering out a statue. Many workers would have been slaves. The painter is known, from this vessel, as the Foundry Painter. Diameter 12 inches.

**FIGURE 13.3** On this Athenian cup from about 480 B.C., a Thracian slave girl (her origins are shown by her red hair, and her servile status by its shortness) holds a young partygoer's head while he vomits up his wine. Attributed to the Brygos Painter. Diameter 12 inches.

## The Rich

Some Athenians prospered from trade and lands taken from rebellious subject cities, but strong democratic ideals restrained people from showing off their wealth. Aegean houses were generally spacious and comfortable, but none stands out as lavish. Burials were plain and uniform. Citizens erected few monuments to their own importance. Instead the rich performed *litourgiai*, "public services," paying for festivals, sacrifices, or rigging warships. Rich politicians curried favor with the people by spending more than they had to on these **liturgies**. For example,

> Cimon had the wealth of a tyrant. He performed the liturgies lavishly, and he supported many demesmen. Any man of Laciadae° could go to him every day to obtain his basic needs. And his lands were unfenced so that whoever wished could take the fruit he wanted.

Aristotle, *Constitution of Athens* 27

°*Laciadae:* Cimon's deme.

Not everyone applauded this system, though. According to the Old Oligarch,

> As far as the equipping of choruses or the fitting out of gymnasiums is con-cerned, or the outfitting of triremes, the poor know that the rich equip choruses while the *dêmos* dance in them, and that the rich fit out gymnasiums and outfit triremes, while the *dêmos* work out in the gyms and row on the triremes. The *dêmos* think it right that they receive money for singing and running and sailing on the triremes, because they take the money and the rich get poorer.

The Old Oligarch 1.13

Normally in ancient societies, those who had the wealth also controlled political office. In fifth-century Athens, however, the poor exercised enormous political power. As the Old Oligarch saw it, the poor controlled Athens because they rowed in the fleet. Because Athens' safety depended on them, they had a right to run the city through democratic institutions and even to export democracy to the subject cities. In Athens, the struggle for power was between the old aristocrats and the Athenian people *(dêmos)* as well as between Athens and her subjects. As the Old Oligarch explains,

> As for the constitution of the Athenians, I have no praise for their having adopted such a form of government. For they have chosen to make the poor superior to the rich. I do not praise them for this. Let me now explain how they maintain their customs, which they themselves have decided upon and which seem in error to the rest of the Greeks.
>
> Let me first point out that it is just that the poor and the *dêmos* have more power than the well-born and the rich, for this reason: The *dêmos* sail the ships and bring power to the city. Helmsmen, and stroke-callers, and ships' captains, and prow-men, and shipwrights—these are the men who bring power to the city much more than the hoplites and the well-born and the rich. Because that's the way things are, it seems right that everyone is allowed to participate in governance, both by lot and in elections and that any one of the citizens may say what he wishes . . .
>
> As for the allies, when the Athenians sail out to them, they indulge in mali-cious prosecutions and they hate the rich. They know full well that the ruled must hate the ruler, and that if the rich and wealthy are strong, the power of the Athenian *dêmos* will last but a short time. For this reason they show no respect to the rich, but take away their money and drive them out of town and kill them, and so enhance the power of the poor. But the rich Athenians do what they can to

protect the rich in the allied cities, knowing that it is good for themselves to preserve the better sort in the allied cities . . .

They are lacking in one thing. If as masters of the sea they inhabited an island, they could do any evil they pleased and suffer nothing for it, so long as they controlled the sea. Their country could not be ravaged nor attacked by the enemy. But as it is, the farmers and the rich fawn on the enemy more, while the *dêmos*, having nothing that the enemy will burn or cut down, live without fear and do not fawn on the enemy . . .

Because therefore they did not have the luck to inhabit an island from the beginning, here's what they do: They place all their wealth on the islands, trusting to their power over the sea, and they look the other way while Attica is cut to pieces, thinking that if they take pity on it they will suffer even greater losses . . .

The Athenians seem to me to make the wrong decision when in cities wracked by internal dissension they favor the party of the lower classes. They do this with forethought. For if they were to favor the upper classes, they would favor the party that does not see things as they do. In no city are the upper classes well disposed to the *dêmos*, but the lowest classes are always friendly to the *dêmos*. For similar people are like-minded with similar people. In this fashion the Athenians pursue policies friendly to their interests.

*The Old Oligarch* 1.1–2, 14; 2.14, 16; 3.10

Athens transferred power and property downward from the old elites to the masses, and inward from the subject cities to Athens. The democratization of social power unleashed tremendous energy and wealth, but fueled old hostilities within the elite and between rich and poor. In the 420s B.C., as we shall see, class hostilities combined with interstate conflict to turn murderous.

## THE EDGE OF THE ABYSS, 433–431 B.C.

Athens and Syracuse were exceptional places by the 430s B.C., bustling, prosperous, and powerful democracies in which philosophical, literary, and artistic breakthroughs were almost commonplace. Artists and scholars moved back and forth between them. If any society merits the term "golden age," it was surely that of Syracuse and above all Athens in the middle of the fifth century B.C. Crowds flocked to watch masterpieces of drama day by day, great buildings rose higher in both cities. With Pericles at the helm, the Athenian ship of state seemed on course. The city's walls were strong, the fleet ruled the seas, and peace reigned. But Sparta, a land-based power, feared maritime Athens, while Athens feared Syracuse, a rich, grain-exporting Dorian state with a navy.

In 435 B.C., Athens got involved in a complicated dispute between **Corcyra** (modern Corfu), a Corinthian colony on a large island off Greece's northwest coast (Map 13.2), and Corcyra's own colony **Epidamnus**, in what is now Albania. Epidamnus had grown wealthy, but bitter civil strife broke out between the old aristocrats and the ascendant pro-democratic group. The Epidamnians asked for assistance from their mother-city Corcyra, but when Corcyra turned them down they appealed to Corinth (the mother-city of their mother-city). The Corinthians were happy to help, offended by Corcyra's lack of respect. They sent new colonists to Epidamnus, but Corcyra, resenting Corinth's interference, besieged Epidamnus and captured it. Corinth now turned on Corcyra itself, and the worried Corcyraeans sought help from Athens. The Athenians debated at length, then decided that because Corcyra had its own large fleet and was a convenient base for potential action against Syracuse, they would make the alliance. They broke Pericles' rule of avoiding new entanglements, but the risk seemed worthwhile.

In 433 B.C. (as we saw) Athens also made treaties with Rhegion and Leontini (Map 13.1) to counterbalance Syracuse's revived power in eastern Sicily. In the same year, Athenian ships supporting Corcyra fought a naval battle with the Corinthian ships supporting Epidamnus, and in 432 B.C., a dispute broke out over yet another Corinthian colony, Potidaea in the north Aegean. Although Potidaea was a Corinthian colony, she was also an Athenian subject-city, and when Athens put her under siege, the Athenian forces trapped some Corinthian visitors inside.

The showdown at Potidaea added to Spartan anger at Athens, but the final straw was Athens' treatment of Sparta's little neighbor Megara. Ostensibly because the Megarians had trespassed on land belonging to the goddess Demeter, Athens banned Megarians from all harbors in cities that Athens controlled. Like many cities in the 430s B.C., Megara had a small territory and a large population, and therefore relied on trade to bring in food. Athens' embargo spelled hunger and desperation. The despair of the Megarians became a topic for laughter in Athenian comedy (see Chapter 15, "Fifth-Century Drama," for Aristophanes' jokes about Megarian hunger), but no one at Sparta was laughing.

The Spartans could not allow Megara to fall under Athenian control. Sparta put pressure on Pericles by invoking the curse passed on the aristocratic Athenian Alcmaeonid family after Cylon's failed coup nearly 200 years before (Chapter 10), demanding that the Alcmaeonids—including Pericles—should again be expelled from the city. Athens must also raise the siege of Potidaea, Sparta demanded, and above all Athenians must revoke the Megarian decree, if they wished to avoid war. According to Plutarch:

> It is not easy to see why the decree [against Megara] was passed in the first place, but all agree that it was because of Pericles that the decree was not revoked. Some say that it was from the highest motives, and with a thought for the best result, that Pericles set himself firmly against revoking the decree, thinking that the plan was set in motion to test his resolve and that to go along with it would have been a sign of weakness. But others think that he opposed the Spartans through arrogance and a desire to display his own power.

Plutarch, *Life of Pericles* 31

Some jokes in Aristophanes' comedies suggest that Pericles was protecting his foreign girlfriend Aspasia, two of whose call girls had been abducted by Megarians; others say that Pericles provoked war to divert attention from his efforts to protect his close friend, the great sculptor Phidias (see Chapter 14), under prosecution for embezzling. Although he had dominated Athenian politics for twenty years, Pericles' enemies had recently successfully prosecuted several of his friends (including Phidias, who died in prison). It is hard to know how seriously we should take Aristophanes' humor, but there is no doubt that the Spartans decided that unless they fought Athens now, the balance of power would tip further in Athens' favor. That was, no doubt, a correct assessment and is just how Thucydides understood the breakout of war in 431 B.C.:

> The Spartans took a vote and decided that the treaty had been dissolved. They voted for war not so much because they were persuaded by the allies as they feared the rising power of Athens, seeing that most of Greece already was subordinate to them.

Thucydides 1.88

## Key Terms

Hiero, *275*
Common Resolution, *276*
demagogues, *276*
Segesta, *277*
Cimon, *279*

Ephialtes, *282*
Pericles, *282*
Long Walls, *282*
Old Oligarch, *286*

metics, *286*
liturgies, *289*
Corcyra, *290*
Epidamnus, *290*

## Further Reading

Balot, Ryan, *Greek Political Thought* (Oxford, 2006). Excellent introduction to Classical Greek political theory.

Boedeker, Deborah, and Kurt Raaflaub, eds. *Democracy, Empire and the Arts in Fifth-Century Athens* (Cambridge, MA, 1998). Collection of essays by leading scholars.

Davies, John, *Democracy and Classical Greece*, 2nd ed. (New York, 1993). Good analysis of fifth-century geopolitics with a strong focus on the role of states other than Athens and Sparta.

Kagan, Donald, *The Outbreak of the Peloponnesian War* (New York, 1969). First volume of a four-book series, covering the period 478 to 431, from a master of political and military history.

Lanni, Adriaan, *Law and Justice in the Courts of Classical Athens* (Cambridge, UK, 2006). Study of some of the central institutions of Athenian democracy.

Low, Polly, *Interstate Relations in Classical Greece* (Cambridge, UK, 2007). Recent study of the dynamics of diplomacy and politics.

Meiggs, Russell, *The Athenian Empire* (Oxford, 1972). Careful analysis based heavily on inscriptions. Very good on details, though the main thesis is now partly outdated because of the redating of many of the inscriptions.

Morris, Ian, "The Greater Athenian state," in Ian Morris and Walter Scheidel, eds. *The Dynamics of Ancient Empires* (New York, 2009). A new look at Athenian, Syracusan, and Spartan power in the fifth century.

Ober, Josiah, *Democracy and Knowledge: Learning and Innovation in Classical Athens* (Princeton, 2008). Innovative study of how democratic forms of knowledge helped Athens succeed.

Powell, Anton, *Athens and Sparta* (London, 1989). Probably the best introductory survey of the period covered in this chapter.

Ste. Croix, Geoffrey de, *The Origins of the Peloponnesian War* (Ithaca, NY, 1972). Excellent study of Athenian–Spartan power politics, with a particularly good analysis of Sparta.

Scheidel, Walter, Ian Morris, and Richard Saller, eds. *The Cambridge Economic History of the Greco-Roman World* (Cambridge, UK, 2007). Chapters 12–14 cover Classical Greece.

van Alfen, Peter, ed. *Agoranomia: Studies in Money and Exchange Presented to John H. Kroll* (New York, 2006). Expert essays on Classical Greek coinage and economics.

### ANCIENT TEXTS

Diodorus of Sicily, *The History*, Books 11 and 12. In *The Library of History IV*, tr. C. H. Oldfather (Cambridge, MA: Loeb Classical Library, 1946). Parallel Greek and English texts describing Sicilian history, written in the first century B.C.

Plutarch, *Lives of Themistocles, Aristides, Cimon, and Pericles*. In *The Rise and Fall of Athens*, tr. Ian Scott-Kilvert (Harmondsworth, UK, 1960). Much important information on fifth-century Athens in biographies written around A.D. 100.

Strassler, Robert, ed., *The Landmark Thucydides* (New York, 1996). The abundant maps and excellent endnotes make it easy to follow Thucydides' account.

Thucydides, *The Peloponnesian War*, tr. Rex Warner (Harmondsworth, UK, 1954). Book 1 describes the years down to 431 B.C. Written at Athens in the late-fifth century B.C.

## CHAPTER 14

# Art and Thought in the Fifth Century B.C.

As late as the Persian Wars, a traveler who wanted to meet the leading Greek intellectuals and artists needed to visit dozens of *poleis,* from ELEA (el-ē-a) in southern Italy to EPHESUS (**ef**-e-sus) in Ionia. By the 430s B.C., though, our traveler could catch most of them with just two stops, at ATHENS and SYRACUSE. Athens became what Thucydides called "the school of Hellas." Everyone who was anyone spent time there. In the 430s B.C. about one Greek in fifteen lived in Attica, yet more than half the cultural figures whose names have survived were Athenian and more than half of those who were not Athenians nevertheless spent substantial parts of their careers in Athens. More inscriptions survive from Attica during the fifth century B.C. than from the rest of Greece combined, testifying to unusually high rates of literacy. Plato's philosophical dialogues give a sense of this extraordinary, cosmopolitan intellectual world, where Socrates could drop by a friend's house for dinner and run into leading artists and thinkers from all over Greece. One man wrote a comedy about how it felt to return to his hometown after making it big in Athens. Just as actors, artists, and musicians congregate in New York and Los Angeles in our times, so in fifth-century Greece all roads led to Athens and Syracuse.

Astounding achievements in philosophy, art, drama, and historical thought made the names of Athens' creative geniuses—Aeschylus, Aristophanes, Phidias, Socrates, Sophocles, Thucydides, and many others—familiar 2,500 years later. We devote two chapters to this remarkable cultural explosion, showing how Greeks, responding to particular problems, produced timeless cultural classics. In this chapter we examine how Syracuse and above all Athens displaced older centers of philosophy and art, and in the next we describe the invention of a whole new art form, drama.

## PHILOSOPHY

### Heraclitus and Anaxagoras, the Last Ionian Giants

The terrible Persian destructions in 494 B.C. ended Ionia's role as the center of Greek thought. **Heraclitus** (her-a-klī-tus) of Ephesus (Map 14.1), profound but inscrutable, was the last important thinker there. He grew up before his city's sack but did most of his work between 494 and about 475 B.C. He took issue with previous theories about the cosmos. More of his writings survive than those of the earlier Ionian philosophers (he deposited a book of them in the temple of Artemis in Ephesus), but his brief and cryptic sayings ("The path up and down is one and the same") can strain comprehension.

Heraclitus criticized his predecessors for focusing on sensory perceptions, arguing that "Eyes and ears are bad witnesses if the soul is without understanding," that is, we cannot learn the truth about the world through our senses. Truth, he argued, lies in the *logos*—"order," "word," or "reason," a philosophical term with a very long future before it: In the Christian gospel of John, an heir to Ionian thought, *logos* is equated with God. The unseen *logos* arranges that all things exist through conflict, which for Heraclitus was good.

To Heraclitus the world was like a bow. Strung taut and leaning against a wall, it seems static, but really the bow is a tension of opposites striving against each other, as becomes clear if the string snaps. When things appear to be at rest, opposing and conflicting forces are in balance.

"Everything flows," Heraclitus said in one of his most famous pronouncements. The world is change, so "you cannot step into the same river twice," because the water is constantly moving. So too, said Heraclitus, is all reality.

Because all is change, all that lives does so at the expense of something else: "Fire lives the death of air, and air of fire; water lives the death of earth, and earth the death of water." Heraclitus' notion of fire, air, water, and earth as basic qualities looks back to

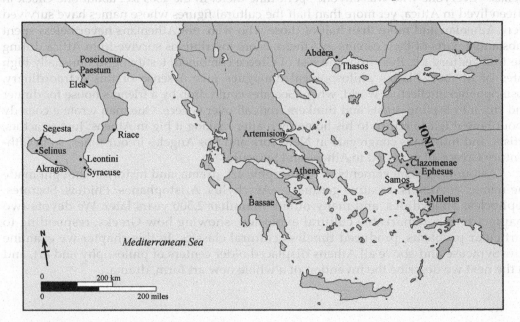

**MAP 14.1** Sites mentioned in this chapter.

Anaximander's four qualities, and like the Milesians before him, Heraclitus identified one element as the basis of everything. He called it *fire* (we might say "energy"). "The world," he wrote, "is an ever-living fire, kindled in some measures and going out in equal measures." For Heraclitus, fire, which he seems to identify with the *logos*, symbolizes the strife and never-ending flux of the world. Fire lives through consuming, and although it may look the same, its substance is ever-changing. Fire is like the *logos*, the divine intelligence that motivates the world.

Ionia's ruin in 494 B.C. dampened intellectual activity, but by the time of the Persian Wars, the debates begun in the sixth century had in any event run their course; Heraclitus disagreed with Pythagoras over the nature of the universe, but he had no way to resolve the disagreement. As intellectuals drifted toward Athens, they began to ask different questions. **Anaxagoras**, from CLAZOMENAE in Ionia, was a crucial transitional figure. Born around 500 B.C., he moved to Athens probably in 456 and befriended Pericles. He must have formulated many of his theories in Ionia but became famous only in Athens. Like some sixth-century B.C. Ionians, Anaxagoras asked "Where do things come from?" He began his only book by saying, "All things were together": Initially there was a unity, but the action of pure mind (*nous*) separated matter into the variety we now see. The separation was not complete so that everything contains a little bit of everything else. "As things were in the beginning," he wrote, "so now are they all together." The only pure force is *nous*, "mind" itself.

Anaxagoras' important contribution to scientific thought was to distinguish between matter, that which is moved, and mind, that which moves. In his own day, though, he was more famous for challenging conventional beliefs about the gods. As he saw it, the sun was not a god but rather a giant glowing rock. Even sophisticated Athenians were offended, and around 437 B.C. they exiled him for impiety. Not even Pericles could save Anaxagoras from democratic intolerance.

## Parmenides, Zeno

At the same time that Heraclitus and Anaxagoras were teaching, a distinct philosophical school grew up in southern Italy, where in the sixth century B.C. the great Pythagoras had emigrated from the island of SAMOS to establish a sacred community. One of its leading thinkers, **Parmenides** (par-**men**-i-dēz) of ELEA (south of Naples), agreed with Heraclitus that our senses mislead us, but where Heraclitus thought that they trick us into thinking that reality is stable, whereas in fact its essence is change, Parmenides thought that our senses trick us into thinking that reality consists of change, whereas in fact it never changes.

Parmenides arrived at his surprising conclusions by focusing on the ambiguity inherent in speech. He began from the Greek word "is" *(esti)*, which in Greek can also mean "exists." In English we might put his point this way: "What is" (in Greek *esti*, or what exists) is obviously not "what is not" *(ouk esti,* what does not exist), so if "what is" *(esti)* were to change into something else, it would become "what is not" *(ouk esti)*; in which case "what exists" *(esti)* would become "what does not exist" *(ouk esti)*—which of course is nonsense. Things either "exist" *(esti)* or they do not *(ouk esti)*, and there can be no in-between stages, which the concept of change requires. Therefore, motion cannot exist, since motion is a form of change. Space does not exist either, because space is that "which is not" and that "which is not" cannot be "that which is."

Parmenides exalted pure reason over dependence on the senses, laying the basis for future abstract thought that reaches conclusions independent of (and sometimes contrary to) external appearances (as in much of modern science). Parmenides' follower **Zeno** of Elea (ca. 490–430 B.C.) went still further with famous puzzles, the **paradoxes of Zeno**, "proving" that motion, and hence change, is illusory. Imagine, Zeno said, that Achilles, known for swiftness, wanted to overtake a tortoise, known for slowness. He could never do so, because first he would have to reach the point where the tortoise had started, by which time the tortoise would have moved on a short way. When Achilles reached the tortoise's second position, it would have moved on again, and so on, *ad infinitum*. Similarly, you cannot get from here to there because first you must get halfway there, then cross half that distance, then half of that, and so on forever, never reaching your goal. Certainly arrows appear to soar through the sky, but at any one moment the arrow is someplace on its arc, hence has no opportunity to get anyplace else. The arrow appears to move, but cannot. The logical errors in Zeno's paradoxes (which view space as a series of points) are not obvious and were not clarified until the seventeenth century A.D.

## The Pluralists Empedocles and Democritus

Parmenides and his followers rejected Ionian theories tracing the variety of the world back to one substance, because such a description required that one thing change into another. Yet their conclusion, that things in the world do not exist, sticks in the throat; it just cannot be true. Parmenides' immediate successors are called **pluralists** because they reasoned that if there is no one thing from which the many derive, then the world must be made of many things in the first place. The most important pluralists were Empedocles, Anaxagoras, and Democritus (de-**mok**-ri-tus).

The extraordinary **Empedocles** (em-**ped**-o-klēz; ca. 492–432 B.C.) lived in wealthy and famous AKRAGAS in south-central Sicily. Active in politics and an Olympic athlete, he behaved like a shaman, claiming that his knowledge worked wonders, controlled the winds, and even raised the dead. He explained his theories in highly complex poetry, engaging in a kind of international dialogue with Pythagoras and Parmenides.

Empedocles identified four original substances: earth, air, fire, and water. In this respect he echoed Anaximander but added that all things that are, are combinations of these four "roots." Bone, for example, is two parts earth, two parts water, and four parts fire. Motion is possible even without space, because things move like fishes through water, the water enclosing them and touching them at all times.

The Ionians thought that the single original substance moved by itself, as in the inherent wiggle of Anaximander's Infinite, but Empedocles (like Anaxagoras) saw the need for an external force to cause motion. This force was dual, Love and Strife, one joining the elements, the other breaking them apart. Yet these forces are inherent in the elements, not separate from them: Love is "equal in length and breadth to the world," Empedocles said.

Seeing no creative intelligence standing behind reality, Empedocles explained the complexity of the world's forms, and the suitability of such organisms as eyes and ears to their purpose, by saying that once, through chance encounter, there had been all sorts of unsuitable creatures and things (e.g., humans with cows' heads), but that only the fittest experiments survived—an extraordinary anticipation of modern evolutionary theory (although Empedocles, unlike Charles Darwin, offered neither evidence nor a coherent theory).

Such refined intellectual debates flourished in the far west, but Aegean thinkers followed them. **Democritus** of ABDERA in Thrace (460–380 B.C.) was a strange man who shunned fame (he visited Athens, but, he said, "no one knew me," so went home again and lived in a tiny room in his father's garden). He devised an **atomic theory**, of course without experimental evidence, in a form that changed little until the nineteenth century A.D. Instead of Empedocles' four changeless elements in constant recombination, he postulated a plethora of tiny "uncuttable" *(atomos)* things eternal in themselves, which recombined with other tiny things to form the phenomenal world. These tiny things were "atoms" because to isolate the very tiny things of which the world is made, one must keep slicing it until it cannot be sliced anymore. That last uncuttable thing is the *atom*.

The atoms are similar but have different sizes and shapes. Democritus denied Parmenides' argument about the nonexistence of space, saying, "*What is not* does exist, no less than *what is*." The atoms, floating in space like motes in a sunbeam, drift into contact, stick together, and form the things of the world, but why the atoms move at all, Democritus could not say.

Different qualities derive from the density and shape of the atoms. In soft things the atoms are far apart, with plenty of space between them, and in hard things they are compacted together. Sharp atoms taste "bitter," whereas smooth atoms taste "sweet." Colors depend on the shape of the atoms and how they reflect light, which itself is a stream of atoms. The soul is made of atoms too, the finest of all. At death they break up, and the soul dissolves into its constituent atoms. There could therefore be no question of an afterlife or of reincarnation, as Pythagoreans believed.

## Rhetoric, the Sophists, and Socrates

In this extraordinary intellectual environment, written texts allowed thinkers who lived in Ionia to argue with thinkers who lived in Sicily as if they were attached to an Internet. Both philosophical schools pushed sixth-century debates to new levels of sophistication, but by 450 B.C. philosophers in Athens and Syracuse had started asking different kinds of questions: How could philosophy help men succeed in the democratic societies that rationalism helped create? Athenians called the intellectuals who flocked to their city **sophists** *(sophistai)*, "wise men," really teachers whose instruction could improve a citizen's chance of influencing the *polis*. These sophists did not constitute a philosophical school but shared a dedication to practical affairs. They claimed that they could teach *aretê* (**ar**-e-tē), "virtue" or "excellence." They were skeptical about traditional explanations, and noting that conflicting claims about the nature of reality were irresolvable, they questioned whether anyone could know anything for sure. We know through our senses, yet they are untrustworthy. The object of our knowledge is the world, yet its nature or even existence is open to debate. If "hot" and "cold" do not exist but result only from the accidental mixture and meeting of invisible atoms, as Democritus maintained, then "good" and "evil" may also be relative, conventional categories. The sophists' **moral relativism** shook Greek intellectual life to its foundations. Socrates and Plato, often confused with the sophists by contemporary Greeks, dedicated their life work to dispelling such skepticism and to affirming the moral basis of the world.

In Syracuse, where the return of exiles after the fall of the tyrants in the 460s B.C. generated thousands of lawsuits over property, philosophers began thinking about and teaching the art of rhetoric. How do you persuade someone of something? Fortunes hung on the ability to speak well. Democracies assumed that the best way to make decisions was to gather a large number of citizens in assemblies or law courts; but if nothing about the external world could be known for sure, and right and wrong were merely conventions, then the art of persuasion, not facts, was the basis for power in the democratic assembly. Rhetoric seemed the highest form of philosophy.

The first handbooks on persuasion, the art of making something seem true whether it was or not, appeared in Syracuse around 450 B.C. When the famous teacher of rhetoric Gorgias of Leontini (near Syracuse) first spoke at Athens in 427 B.C., he created a sensation and sparked a rash of imitators. He is especially remembered for saying that (1) nothing exists; (2) if it did exist, you could not know it; and (3) if you knew it, you could never tell anyone about it. When Aristophanes made fun of sophists in his play *The Clouds* (423 B.C.), he particularly mocked their claims to make false arguments seem stronger than true ones.

Hippias and Protagoras were the most famous sophists. Plato wrote dialogues now called by their names. The versatile **Protagoras** coined the phrase "Man is the measure of all things," meaning that one man views the world in one way, another in another way, and that neither is right. Truth is relative and so are the moral categories of good and bad, although Protagoras insisted that some forms of behavior are more practical than others.

Protagoras pushed human-centered secularism to its limits. In Babylon, Egypt, and Israel, laws, rules for behavior, were justified as coming from the gods. By the late fifth century B.C., some Greeks concluded that laws were in fact merely conventions made by men and could thus be changed by men, just as decisions were made and unmade in the democratic assembly. Protagoras defined the secular social contract by which we live today: Laws exist to serve the social good; they do not reflect timeless values of right and wrong. If tradition, custom, and law are inconvenient, we can—in fact, should—sweep them aside.

**Socrates** (469–399 B.C.) vigorously opposed such moral relativism. Although he wrote nothing himself, he is the principal speaker in Plato's numerous dialogues. Scholars disagree about how far the opinions Plato ascribed to Socrates were really Socrates' own and how far they belonged to Plato, but most agree that Socrates maintained that "*aretê* is knowledge." The saying was directed against the sophists' assertions that they could teach *aretê*, which really means "efficiency at a particular task," while at the same time they held that nothing could really be known.

Socrates liked to speak in homely terms and would ask, "What is the *aretê* of a shoemaker?" Obviously, to make shoes. But in order to make shoes, you need to know the end in view, why you are making them, the facts that feet are soft, the ground is hard, and we are happier when well shod. Then you can proceed to the knowledge of how to make shoes. When the sophists claimed to teach *aretê* as a general concept, a quality that enriched a man's whole life, they implied that humans, too, must have an end, a purpose, an "efficiency for some task." But what is that task? What *is* the function of man?

Socrates never answered this question. The Socratic method meant convincing his interlocutors that when they thought they had an answer, they really did not. It is easy to see why Athenians disliked Socrates and confused him with the sophists. The sophists taught that nothing could be known; Socrates showed how no one knew anything, at least so long as their minds were cluttered with grand but ill-defined concepts like justice, love, and courage. When your mind is clear, then maybe you can acquire real knowledge. You simply must define your terms. If you know what justice is, you can act justly, but not before.

Hence Socrates' second famous dictum, that vice is the result of ignorance, is really a backhanded way of repeating that *aretê*, virtue, is knowledge. Socrates encouraged the inductive method for discovering general definitions. From a large body of acts that people consider "just," you should be able to distill an essence, the thing that all such acts have in common: "justice." Plato's most famous dialogue, *The Republic* (360 B.C.), is dedicated to discovering just such a definition.

## Conclusion

Serious speculation about the physical world began in the sixth century B.C. among Greeks under Lydian and then Persian rule. By the late sixth century, rival schools of thought were flourishing in Sicily and southern Italy, with a scattering of major thinkers across other Greek cities. By the late fifth century, the centers of gravity had shifted to Athens and, to a lesser extent, Syracuse. As wealth flowed into these cities, some people spent it to attract leading thinkers, and when the thinkers arrived, they made themselves useful to Athenians and Syracusans. The philosophers' debates affected both cities, but Athenian and Syracusan society, politics, and culture also affected philosophy.

Intellectuals turned to issues that mattered in their host cities: How to pursue truth and wisdom in a democracy and how to use truth and rhetoric to gain power and wealth. The evolution of philosophy into a system for persuasive thought gave Greek politics an intellectual dimension absent in other ancient civilizations. Where Assyrian or Egyptian kings could simply claim that they acted as the gods willed, Greek statesmen were obligated to defend their positions on philosophical grounds, as possessors of power in democracies must do today.

## MATERIAL CULTURE

A classic is something timeless that transcends the particular conditions of its moment of creation and attains a wider relevance for humanity. In the midst of their wars, personal hatreds, and sometimes crass pursuits of wealth and power, a few hundred men in Athens and Syracuse broke through the normal constraints of humdrum experience to change the world. In classical art, as in philosophy, innovation was increasingly centralized in these two cities, where the most important architects, sculptors, and painters gathered. Like philosophers, they responded to the issues of the day, including the Athenians' and Syracusans' sense of themselves as saviors of Hellenism from barbarian threats, and the tensions between this self-image and the crude realities of the power they exercised over other Greek cities. As they dealt with historically specific problems, they forged masterpieces that speak across the gulf of centuries.

## Sculpture

In the years after the great wars of 480 and 479 B.C. sculptors tried to bring out a new sense of idealized humankind. The Greeks had freed themselves from foreign threats, and artists struggled to express a sense of mastery over the world in the so-called **severe style** whose serenely calm facial expressions on statues contrast with the earlier frozen smiles of the Archaic Period (Figure 14.1) The most important Greek sculptors worked chiefly in bronze, but our knowledge comes mainly from marble statues because most of the bronze statues were long ago melted down for their metal. For bronze sculpture we have to rely on chance finds from shipwrecks, which saved the statues from being recycled.

**FIGURE 14.1**  Zeus (or Poseidon), found in the sea off Cape Artemision, ca. 460 B.C. Bronze, height 6 feet, 10 inches.

Sculptors cast these extraordinary bronze works by an ancient method called the **lost-wax technique.** First, the sculptor made a rough model of clay, then coated it with wax. He shaped the soft wax in detail, then coated it with a second layer of clay, leaving holes at the top and bottom of the outer clay layer. He poured molten bronze in the top hole. The heat of the bronze made the wax melt and as it ran out through the bottom hole, the bronze perfectly filled the space it had occupied. The sculptor then shattered the outer layer of clay, revealing (when he got it right) a beautiful hollow statue of thin bronze. He could leave the clay core inside the bronze statue, or chip it away through small openings.

Casting large lost-wax bronze statues required exceptional skill and cost a great deal of money. Bronze workers cast elaborate figures in several pieces, then soldered them together. Bronze was lighter than stone and gave sculptors more freedom. The statue in Figure 14.1 could not have been carved from marble; the stone is not strong enough to support the weight of outstretched arms. The sculptor would have to keep the arms down or add such unsightly supports as tree trunks to bear the load.

Larger than life-size, Figure 14.1 perfectly embodies the qualities of grace, restraint, dignity, self-control, and perfected manhood that fifth-century Greeks saw as ideal, a superb example of the severe style. The heel of the right foot is raised, the left hand extends to take aim, and the right hand is cocked to cast the thunderbolt (or trident). Fully bearded, the figure is naked, like the Archaic *kouroi,* its hair bound by a braid. The pubic hair is realistically portrayed. The Archaic smile is gone, replaced by a magisterial calm. The muscles of its beautiful body resonate with an inner intensity.

**FIGURE 14.2A**  Bronze statue of a warrior, perhaps by Phidias (ca. 460 B.C.). Two of these, larger than life-sized, were found in 1972 in the bay of Riace, Calabria, Italy The statues were probably taken from the sanctuary at Delphi.

One of the most extraordinary archaeological finds of the twentieth century was two bronze warriors in the severe style, probably thrown overboard to lighten a ship during a storm near the toe of Italy. Figure 14.2 shows one of them. These statues are not signed, but their date, style, and perfection lead many archaeologists and art historians to think that they were early works of the great **Phidias**, the most famous Athenian sculptor. As we will see in Chapter 24, "The Coming of Rome, 220–30 B.C.," in the second and first centuries B.C. the Romans carried many of Greece's art treasures off to Italy, perhaps including these sculptures. Restored after eight years of painstaking labor, the statues hint at the enormity of our loss of classical sculpture. They once held shields attached to their left arms and spears or swords in their right. The eyes are made of ivory and glass paste, the lips and nipples of copper, and the teeth of one statue of silver plate. The sculptor combined stylization of the hair and beard with exceptional naturalism in rendering the veins in the groin, inner elbows, and calves and feet. In a casual, relaxed poise, the weight shifted to the right foot, pelvis raised correspondingly on one side, their bodies in gentle S-curves, they stand among art's greatest achievements.

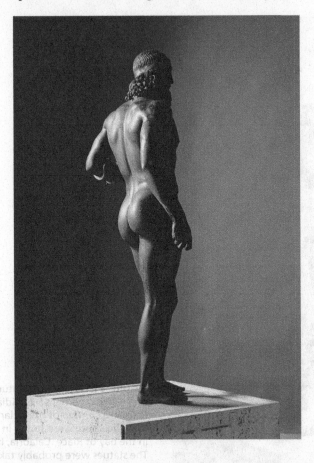

**FIGURE 14.2B** Bronze statue of a warrior, perhaps by Phidias (ca. 460 B.C.). Two of these, larger than life-sized, were found in 1972 in the bay of Riace, Calabria, Italy The statues were probably taken from the sanctuary at Delphi.

By the 450s B.C. sculptors were congregating in Athens, but not all did so. There was enough money in other *poleis* to support independent schools, some excellent. The museums of Syracuse are full of fragments of fine fifth-century statues, but Figure 14.3 shows a panel of the so-called Ludovisi Throne, a well-preserved example from a Greek city in southern Italy. It may represent Aphrodite's birth from the sea, assisted by two female figures. The sheer garments that enclose Aphrodite, known as *wet drapery*, reveal her body beneath, a device found in fifth-century sculpture to show women's forms without representing them as naked. To an Athenian eye, this panel would have seemed provincial and erratic: It combined the latest style of drapery on the central figure with old-fashioned hairstyles and much stiffer drapery on the two attendants.

We can make stylistic comments like these because sculpture developed very rapidly in the fifth century B.C. By 450 B.C. artists in Athens were already softening the severity of early fifth-century faces, loosening the poses, refining anatomy, and imbuing statues with a greater unity and sense of purpose. Archaeologists call the style of the mid-fifth century **high classical**, and to many tastes it is the zenith of ancient art. Beautiful and moving examples survive, but the best known come from buildings on the Athenian Acropolis.

After Xerxes destroyed the Archaic temples atop the Acropolis in 480 and 479 B.C., the Athenians vowed not to replace them until they had exacted revenge; but after 449 B.C., perhaps because a peace treaty had now been signed with Persia, they rebuilt their holy places on a massive scale. Their patron goddess Athena received a spectacular new temple, the

**FIGURE 14.3**   The birth of Aphrodite from the Ludovisi Throne, ca. 460 B.C., marble, width 56 inches.

**Parthenon,** whose architecture we examine in the next section. Inside was a forty-foot-high statue of Athena Parthenos, "the virgin" (Figure 14.4). It had a wooden frame with ivory-coated flesh parts and gold-plated clothing. The statue survived for over a 1,000 years, although it was stripped of its valuable coverings. Eventually, it was taken to Constantinople, where it was lost in the Middle Ages, and we know of it only from Roman copies.

The Parthenon had a secondary sculptural program on a series of high-relief carved panels. They decorated the pediments (the triangular openings at front and back) and the top of the high cella walls, some forty feet above the ground, hard to see (Figure 14.5). Because the Parthenon remained in use from the fifth century B.C. to modern times (becoming a church to Mary Mother of God in the Byzantine Empire, then a mosque under the Turks from the fifteenth century A.D. through the nineteenth), these sculptures were never broken up for reuse. They were damaged during the Venetian siege of Athens in 1687 A.D. when a mortar shell blew up gunpowder the Turks had stored in the mosque, but they were still more or less intact in the late eighteenth century when western Europeans first became interested in ancient Greek sculpture. In 1799 Lord Elgin (**el-ghīn**), a British diplomat in Constantinople, received permission to dig on the Acropolis and remove finds. He tore down every piece of sculpture he could find and shipped it back to London, hoping to sell the statues and make his fortune. English aesthetes, more familiar with Roman copies than Greek originals, did not know what to make of the treasures. The British Museum curators argued for years over whether the nation wanted such things, and Elgin died bankrupt. Eventually, the British Museum bought the statues, and the **Elgin Marbles** became world-famous (the Greek government has been demanding the return of these national treasures from Britain for many years and they have become a source of international tensions).

**FIGURE 14.4** One possible reconstruction of Phidias' gold-and-ivory statue of Athena in the Parthenon, ca. 439–432 B.C.

The Elgin Marbles were carved around 435 B.C., reaching unsurpassed levels of technical skill and artistic power. Figure 14.6 shows a marvel of stone cutting, the surviving part of a figure of Iris, messenger of the gods, from the west pediment of the Parthenon (see Figure 14.11). The sculptor used innovations to make Iris' form more naturalistic. Artificially high ridges on the folds of the drapery create an effect of transparency where it clings to the body. When real drapery folds over a limb, it does so in straight lines, but the Parthenon sculptor deliberately curved the lines of the folds, which paradoxically makes them look more real than straight lines would. The great Phidias oversaw the sculptural program but did not himself carve the statues. By chance, inscriptions survive that record payments for the carving and inform us that skilled slaves worked alongside free men at every stage.

## Architecture

By 500 B.C. Greek architects rivaled the builders of Egypt and the Near East in sophisticated constructions. Some sixth-century Greek temples in Sicily are bigger than anything built in the fifth century, but the craftsmanship, beauty, and expense of fifth-century temples surpassed anything done before. Through their buildings, architects expressed the ideal of the city-state as a community of citizens, equal in balance and harmony, honoring the gods while proudly displaying mastery over nature. Like fifth-century B.C.

**FIGURE 14.5** Water-carriers on the inner frieze of the Parthenon. Probably they were part of the Panathenaic festival that took place every fourth year, when Athena's statue received a new robe. Aristocratic girls played special parts in the procession (as in the story of the assassination of the Pisistratid Hippias, Chapter 10, "A Tale of Two Archaic Cities: Sparta and Athens, 700–800 B.C."). Parthenon, north side, slab VI, height 43 inches.

philosophy and sculpture, architecture reflected the new social force of democracy and the new wealth of great states. Syracuse was famous for its fifth-century temples, but like Syracusan sculpture, these are poorly preserved. The best-known monuments are once again clustered on the Athenian Acropolis (Figure 14.7a, 14.7b).

Plutarch explains that these buildings were very much part of Pericles' political program. He was writing 600 years after the event and we cannot be sure what evidence he used, but many historians think he had good sources for Pericles' intentions:

Pericles . . . wished that the rude masses, untrained in military tactics, be able to share in the city's income but not by lying around and doing nothing. He proposed to the *dêmos* huge building projects and complex plans requiring constant labor. His intention was to enable those kept at home to enjoy as large a share of the public good fortune as those sailing on the ships, serving guard duty, or going on campaign.

The materials would consist of stone, bronze, ivory, gold, ebony, and cypress wood. The arts to work up these materials belonged to the carpenter, modeler, bronze-smith, stone-mason, dyer, worker in gold and ivory, painter, embroiderer, embosser. There were those to transport and furnish

**FIGURE 14.6** The body of Iris, from the Parthenon west pediment, Acropolis, Athens, ca. 435 B.C.

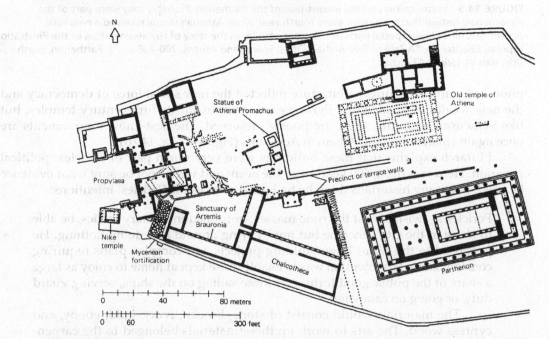

**FIGURE 14.7A** Plan of the Athenian Acropolis, ca. 400 B.C., showing the Parthenon (lower right), Erechtheum (upper right), and Propylaea (left), and outlines of the old temple destroyed by the Persians (faded lines, center).

**FIGURE 14.7B** Aerial view of the Athenian Acropolis. In the left foreground are the ruins of the theater of Dionysus. Portions of the circuit walls date back to the Bronze Age. The Erechtheum can be seen right of the Parthenon, and the Propylaea can be seen slightly on the left-hand promontory. The small theater visible in the left center (still used for modern performances) was built by Herodes Atticus in Roman times. The modern city spreads over the plain in all directions.

> the material: merchants, sailors and pilots by sea, and, by land, wagon makers, trainers of yoked beasts, and drivers. There would also be rope makers, weavers, leatherworkers, road-builders, and miners. And because each individual art, like a general with an army under his separate command, kept under its own direction a corps of unskilled and untrained laborers, as the hand holds a tool or the soul holds the body, he dispersed and spread the city's wealth to every age-group and to citizens of every capacity.

The new temples symbolized fifth-century Athens' power but were also shaped by that same power. No city had ever had the wealth or self-confidence to pursue such a coherent and striking architectural vision:

> And so the buildings rose, as amazing for their size as they were inimitable in their outline and grace, for the workers competed with one another in producing the finest public monument. The most amazing thing of all was the speed by which they were constructed. Most thought that it would take generations to construct each one, but they were all raised during the pinnacle of a single man's career . . .
>
> More than anything we wonder that works of such lasting value were created within so short a span. In beauty they seemed venerable from the moment they were made, but in their youthful vigor they seem still today as if newly built. Thus a freshness blooms from these monuments, forever untouched by time, as if an unfailing spirit and deathless soul were somehow breathed into them.

Plutarch, *Life of Pericles* 12–13

The program began with the Parthenon in 447 B.C. (Figure 14.8). Pericles worked closely with the architects and with Phidias. The temple was dedicated in 438 B.C. and the sculpture finished in 432. Meanwhile, work had begun on the great gate called the **Propylaea** (pro-pi-lē-a, "fore-gates") in 437 B.C. (Figure 14.9); it too was finished in 432 B.C.. The building of the strange but wonderful temple called the **Erechtheum** (e-rek-thē-um) was also begun in the 430s B.C. The financial stress of the Peloponnesian War, which broke out in 431 B.C., slowed construction; most of the work was done between 409 and 406 B.C. Finally, a beautiful little temple to **Athena Nikê** ("victory") (Figure 14.10a) was built in the 420s B.C., with a celebrated figure of Nikê (victory personified) adjusting her sandal added later (Figure 14.10b). This figure, with its transparent drapery and complex pose, shows high classical art at its best. Although it is the smallest building on the Acropolis, the temple of Athena Nikê is a compact masterpiece whose graceful Ionic columns perfectly balance the stern Doric of the Propylaea.

Following no overall design, Pericles' team reused the foundations of earlier buildings on the Acropolis, giving a chaotic appearance to the complex. Entering through the Propylaea (Figures 14.7a, 14.9), the visitor first encountered an enormous statue of Athena, which Phidias cast from the bronze of captured Persian armor (Figure 14.7a, just left of center). Behind this, to the visitor's left and at a higher level, was the oddly shaped Erechtheum, "house of Erechtheus," named after a legendary early king of Athens (Figure 14.12). Opposite

**FIGURE 14.8** The majestic ruins of the northwest corner of the Parthenon tower over loose blocks and broken columns strewn around its base. Acropolis, Athens.

**FIGURE 14.9** The west end of the Athenian Acropolis. The building in the upper left was an art gallery, part of the Propylaea, "gateway" to the Athenian Acropolis. Its Doric columns rise in the center. In the upper right is the small temple to Athena Nikê, "Athena, goddess of victory."

the Erechtheum, on the south, was the Parthenon. The Athena Nikê temple stood south of the Propylaea, on an outcropping (Figure 14.9).

The Parthenon was made entirely of a beautiful translucent marble from nearby Mount Pentelicus near Athens. In general pattern it was a Doric temple with eight columns on the short sides and seventeen on the long (Figure 14.11). Designed with astonishing

**FIGURE 14.10A** The Ionic temple of Athena Nikê, ca. 425 B.C. The blocks were later used as fill, and the temple was reconstructed in modern times. Notice the continuous frieze above the columns, characteristic of Ionic architecture (in Doric temples, the frieze is interrupted by blocks imitating beam-ends called *metopês*).

**FIGURE 14.10B** Nikê adjusting her sandal, ca. 410–405 B.C., from the Nikê temple.

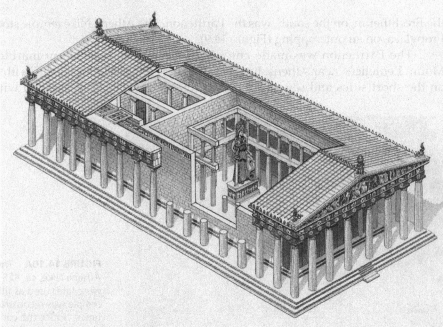

**FIGURE 14.11** Sectioned plan of the Parthenon, with wall and roof cutaway to depict internal structure, the *cella* with the gold-and-ivory statue of Athena, and behind the *cella,* separated by a solid wall, the "treasury" or *opisthodomos* ("house behind").

**FIGURE 14.12**   The Erechtheum, with its famous caryatid porch. The modern olive tree on the left stands where the ancient olive grew, sacred to Athena, miraculously regenerated after the Persian sack.

subtlety, the Parthenon has no straight lines. The stylobate ("column platform") swells in the middle, the columns lean inward, and the upper works lean slightly out. The columns at the ends are slightly closer together than in the middle. These adjustments compensated for the optical illusion that makes truly straight lines appear to sag and give to the Parthenon a lightness and liveliness not found in any other Greek temple. It seems to grow organically from the rock.

The Parthenon raised architectural beauty to new heights, but the Erechtheum (Figure 14.12) was a very unusual structure, consisting of three rooms. Some scholars think this was to venerate three deities: Athena, Poseidon, and the hero Erechtheus. Others suggest that its shape preserves the outlines of a Mycenaean palace that once stood on the Acropolis, which Classical Athenians believed to have been Erechtheus' home.

The Erechtheum is in an elaborate Ionic style, and in later centuries Romans often imitated the elegant carving around its doorways. The building's most famous feature is its south porch, where statues called **caryatids** (kar-i-**a**-tidz, named after priestesses of Artemis at Karuai, a village near Sparta) replace the normal fluted columns. The caryatids carry the weight of the porch as if they were carrying baskets or water (Figure 14.12). Much copied by later architects, the women probably held offering cups in extended hands and may represent girls who served the cult of Athena.

Outside Athens, Greeks built hundreds of other remarkable temples in the fifth century B.C. Even remote hilltops were beautified in the gods' honor. Figure 14.13, for example, shows the temple of Apollo at Bassae in Arcadia, the wild central portion of the

**FIGURE 14.13** The temple of Bassae in Arcadia, ca. 420 B.C. Ictinus, architect of the Parthenon, designed it. Today an ugly canvas tent protects the temple. Its friezes, now in the British Museum, preserve important sculpture.

Peloponnesus, so far from centers of population that, although it survives almost intact, no one but local shepherds knew it existed until a French adventurer stumbled on it in 1765 A.D. In the fifth century B.C. new temples like this, in perfect Classical proportions, arose in every part of the Greek world. Travelers in Sicily and southern Italy today can see many of them, in far better condition than most Aegean examples, in great avenues at Poseidonia (Paestum, in southern Italy), Selinus (western Sicily), and Akragas (south-central Sicily). At Segesta, the non-Greek Elymians of western Sicily built a perfect high classical temple in the 430s B.C.; many art historians think that the Elymians hired the same architects who designed the Parthenon.

Temples were not the only monumental buildings from the fifth century B.C. The Greeks also built theaters, administrative centers, and mile after mile of fortifications. They revolutionized the physical appearance of great cities like Athens and Syracuse, sweeping away the simpler monuments of Archaic times and making them places fit for democratic citizens who felt they had no rivals on earth. The Greeks' reason, will, and bravery had transformed the world they lived in.

## Painting

Ancient literary sources describe numerous fifth-century wall paintings, but hardly any examples survive. According to Roman writers, the greatest fifth-century painter was Polygnotus (po-lig-nō-tus), born around 500 B.C. on the island of Thasos in the north Aegean. By 480 B.C. he had moved to Athens, where he did his best work. Polygnotus is

**FIGURE 14.14**  The Tomb of the Diver, in Paestum (Italy). Ceiling block from a sarcophagus, ca. 480 B.C. Height 40 inches.

said to have represented individual character (what the Greeks called *êthos*) in his paintings, unlike the stiff representations in ancient Near Eastern and earlier Greek art. Polygnotus struggled to express depth and realism. The discovery of true perspective in painting did not come for another 1,800 years, but Polygnotus took the revolutionary steps of raising figures off the baseline and adding scenery.

We get some sense of painting from this period from tombs at the Greek city of Poseidonia in Italy (modern Paestum). Here, Greeks buried some of their dead in large stone boxes with painted scenes on the interior walls and ceilings. Figure 14.14 shows an elegantly arched diver caught in midair, hinting at the vitality and energy of painting in this period. Stark trees stand on either side of the pool, the one on the right growing above the base line out of the picture's border, suggesting depth, as does the curving pool.

Contemporary vases are a far richer source of evidence for fifth-century painting. In Chapter 9 we noted the connections between vase painting and other arts and the concentration of the best vase painters in Athens. Vase painters rushed to exploit Polygnotus' innovations. In Figure 14.15, for example, Odysseus and his companions, scattered on different base lines, prepare the stake they will use to blind the Cyclops. At the right, a satyr fills a wine cup, alluding to Polyphemus' drunkenness. Vase painters also imitated sculptors, trying (sometimes clumsily) to draw flimsy, semitransparent drapery as on the Parthenon sculpture.

Constantly innovating to stay ahead in a competitive market, Athenian vase painters developed a **white-ground style,** perhaps to imitate vases made of ivory but certainly better suited than red figure for mimicking the effects of wall painting. Artisans covered the surface of the vase with a chalky white pigment, then drew in the figures with fine black lines and filled them with thin washes of red, yellow, blue, and

**FIGURE 14.15** South Italian scene of the blinding of Polyphemus, by the Cyclops Painter, ca. 420–410 B.C. Height 18 inches.

other colors. The best examples, produced expressly to accompany the dead, are very beautiful. In Figure 14.16 a servant presents a jewelry box to the dead woman with whom the vase was buried.

## Conclusion

The concentration of resources and talents in Syracuse and above all Athens in the fifth century fueled feverish cultural experiments. Both were democratic, expanding cities; both saw themselves as the saviors of Greece. In their different ways, dramatists, historians, philosophers, sculptors, painters, and architects tried to represent a new vision that put triumphant humanity at the center of the universe. They asked how Greeks should exercise power justly; how they could know right from wrong; and how great and talented men should fit into triumphant, egalitarian, male-citizen communities. Although 2,500 years have passed and the world has changed beyond recognition, the achievements of the Greek Classical Period continue to speak directly to some of humanity's central concerns.

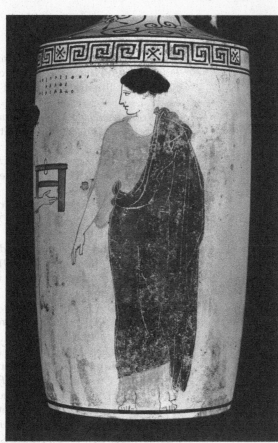

**FIGURE 14.16** A white-ground oil flask (*lekythos*) by the Achilles Painter, ca. 420 B.C., showing a servant bringing a box to the deceased.

# Key Terms

Heraclitus, *294*

*logos*, *294*

Anaxagoras, *295*

*nous*, *295*

Parmenides, *295*

Zeno, *296*

paradoxes of Zeno, *296*

pluralists, *296*

Empedocles, *296*

Democritus, *297*

atomic theory, *297*

sophists, *297*

*aretê*, *297*

moral relativism, *297*

Protagoras, *298*

Socrates, *298*

inductive method, *299*

lost-wax technique, *308*

severe style, *299*

Phidias, *301*

high classical, *302*

Parthenon, *303*

Elgin Marbles, *303*

Propylaea, *308*

Erechtheum, *308*

Athena Nikê, *308*

caryatids, *311*

white-ground style, *313*

## Further Reading

### PHILOSOPHY: GENERAL

Buxton, R., ed., *From Myth to Reason? Studies in the Development of Greek Thought* (Oxford, 1999). Engaging discussion of classical Greek thought.

Guthrie, W. K. C., *The Greek Philosophers: From Thales to Aristotle* (London, 1950). Now rather dated, but this remains a superb short review by one of the great scholars.

### PRESOCRATICS, SOPHISTS, ORATORY

Barnes, J., *The Presocratic Philosophers*, 2nd ed. (London, 1979). Barnes relies on modern analytic philosophy to discuss ancient philosophers.

de Romilly, J., *The Great Sophists in Periclean Athens* (Oxford, 1992). Astute assessment, originally in French.

Kennedy, G. A., *The Art of Persuasion in Greece* (Oxford, 1961). The classic study, never surpassed.

Kerferd, G. B., *The Sophistic Movement* (Cambridge, UK, 1981). Shows the seriousness of sophistic thought.

Lloyd, G. E. R., *Early Greek Science: Thales to Aristotle* (London, 1970). Excellent introduction to sixth- and fifth-century speculative thought by one of the leading scholars of ancient philosophy.

### ART

Boardman, John, *Greek Art*, rev. ed. (New York, 1985). Masterful overview by one of the world's leading ancient art historians.

Boardman, John, *The Diffusion of Classical Art in Antiquity* (Princeton, 1994). Shows how Greek styles of representation replaced earlier conventions, even influencing Buddhist art.

Hurwit, Jeffrey M., *The Athenian Acropolis: History, Mythology, and Archaeology from the Neolithic Era to the Present* (Cambridge, UK, 2000). The best book about the Athenian Acropolis.

Neils, Jenifer, ed. *Goddess and Polis: The Panathenaic Festival in Ancient Athens* (Princeton, 1992). Beautifully illustrated study of this central festival.

Osborne, Robin, *Archaic and Classical Greek Art* (Cambridge, UK, 1998). Penetrating analysis with good photos.

Pedley, John Griffiths, *Greek Art and Archaeology*, 2nd ed. (New York, 1998). The best textbook overview.

Pollitt, Jerome Jordan, *Art and Experience in Classical Greece* (Cambridge, UK, 1972). Discussion of ancient texts about art.

Rasmussen, Tom, and Nigel Spivey, eds. *Looking at Greek Vases* (Cambridge, UK, 1991). Walks the reader through the major issues in our study of illustrated pots.

Robertson, Martin, *A History of Greek Art*, 2nd vol. (Cambridge, UK, 1975). Comprehensive scholarly treatment.

———, *A Shorter History of Greek Art*, (Cambridge, UK, 1981). Summary of Robertson's 2 vols.

Stewart, Andrew, *Greek Sculpture: An Exploration*, 2 vols. (New Haven, CT, 1990). One of the most illuminating surveys of Greek statuary.

———, *Art, Desire, and the Body in Ancient Greece* (Cambridge, UK, 1998). Addresses the social context of Greek art and its focus on the human body.

### ANCIENT TEXTS

Kirk, G. S., Raven, J. E. and M. Schofield, eds., *The Presocratic Philosophers*, 2nd ed. (Cambridge, UK, 1983). The Greek text and good translations and explanations for the fifth-century B.C. philosophers.

## CHAPTER 15

# Fifth-Century Drama

In Chapter 14, "Art and Thought in the Fifth century B.C.," we reviewed art and thought in fifth-century Greece. In this chapter, we focus on fifth-century drama, the artistic form that many scholars see as Classical Greece's greatest achievement. Drama ("things done" in Greek) is so familiar to us that it is hard to imagine that it might not exist, yet all earlier societies lacked drama as we understand it: public presentations in which performers, pretending to be other people, speak in the first person, engage in conflict, and follow stories from beginning to end. The Greeks invented drama at the end of the sixth century B.C. It became one of antiquity's major art forms and, of course, continues vigorously to this day; but many scholars think that no one has ever surpassed the dramas of the fifth century B.C., when Athenians created a flexible and powerful artistic medium for reflecting on individuality, freedom, responsibility, and the burden of historical events.

The Greeks divided drama into two broad categories, tragedy and comedy. The Athenians invented tragedy, but by 400 B.C. tragedy was becoming a Panhellenic art form. Still, the three great Athenian tragedians—Aeschylus, Sophocles, and Euripides—formed an unchallenged canon. Athens was the main center for comedy also, but had several challengers, above all in Sicily.

## TRAGEDY

The genre's origins are highly obscure, but Athens and Syracuse were the major centers for its production. All thirty-three surviving tragedies are Athenian: seven plays by **Aeschylus** (ē-ski-lus, 525–456 B.C.), seven more by Sophocles (**sof**-o-klēz, 496–406 B.C.), and nineteen by Euripides (yu-**rip**-i-dēz, 485–406 B.C.). The titles of twelve of the surviving plays of Euripides begin with the letters A through K and probably represent part of an alphabetically arranged edition of his works. Each of these men wrote eighty or ninety plays, and, all told, more than a thousand tragedies were performed between about 530 and 400 B.C. Most ancient drama is lost. This miniscule sample from so large an original corpus puts us in an awkward position in understanding the nature of tragedy, but, as usual, we do the best we can.

## General Features of Tragedy

In Greek, *tragoidia* seems to mean "goat song." Because goats were associated with Dionysus, at whose spring festivals in Athens tragedies were staged, the name may derive from songs performed while goats were sacrificed in the god's honor.

The script of a tragic play was in some ways like a modern screenplay. It was not meant to be read but to serve as a prompt book for a live performance. After performance, copies of some scripts circulated and were even studied in schools and quoted in symposia to impress one's companions. The comic poet Aristophanes liked to quote verses from plays performed years before and expected his audiences to recognize the source. But Greek literature was always meant to be heard, not read as you are reading this book.

Tragedy was popular entertainment, directed to the concerns of Athenian citizens, including their tastes for patriotic propaganda, horror, violence, and vicious conflict between the sexes: themes that still draw a big audience. In studying the Greek tragedians we are studying the origins of modern entertainment. Aeschylus is the earliest tragedian whose works survive. He loved long, elaborate descriptions, especially of foreign lands, and high-flown metaphors containing words of his own invention (the despair of modern students of Greek!). He was the most old fashioned of the three tragedians. He used myth to explore grand moral issues like the conflict between individual will and divine destiny, but his language can be very difficult and abstruse. There is little action and his plays are not often performed in modern times. His characters tend to be types, embodying principles.

Aeschylus lived through Athens' rise to greatness, and his epitaph (which he himself composed) mentions that he fought at Marathon but not his literary achievements. His play *The Persians* (472 B.C.) is the only surviving tragedy that does not have a mythical theme (though others did exist). Setting tragedies in the heroic age allowed tragedians to experiment with stories that were already known to their audiences and to fill them with colorful kings, queens, and gods. By staging the core moral issues that faced democratic society against the backdrop of grand palaces and the ancient Trojan War poets could make their points more starkly than if they told stories set in their own world. Furthermore, Greek education in Homer and other epic poets created for the Greeks an imaginative world already at hand, in which they could explore contemporary literary goals.

**Sophocles'** career exactly coincides with the highpoint of Athens' political power. Born six years before the battle of Marathon, he died two years before Athens' defeat in the Peloponnesian War. His vivid characters are typically locked in bitter conflict. He liked to show the dignity of noble individuals caught in overwhelming crises with superior—often divine—forces. His heroes are lonely and unbending. They learn too late how to behave. He was deeply influenced by folklore: In all his plays, a prophecy or oracle predicts an unexpected outcome, as often in folktales. He wrote in the middle of the Peloponnesian War, and we are constantly tempted to see in his plays reflections on actual events. For example, in *Oedipus the King* a great plague has fallen on the city, and the story is a quest to find out why. In fact a great plague did fall on Athens in 430 B.C., probably one year before the play was performed, killing one Athenian in four including Pericles, architect of Athenian greatness. Still, such historical events are seen distantly and problematically through the complexity of the tale.

More survives of **Euripides'** work than of Aeschylus' and Sophocles' combined. Euripides subjected traditional myths to rigorous scrutiny and sometimes severe criticism or even ridicule. His characters are often deflated heroes, mere mortals caught up in all-too-human squabbles. His famous play *Medea* is about divorce in a monogamous society. Aristotle remarked that Sophocles showed men as they ought to be, but Euripides showed them as they really are. Euripides reflected contemporary Athenian rhetoric more than did Sophocles or Aeschylus; most of his plays focus on a long debate, reflecting Athenian experience of law courts and assemblies. He liked to celebrate emotion's power over reason.

In Aeschylus, inherited curses and divine will motivate action; in Sophocles, fate stands behind events; in Euripides, passionate, often erotic, and especially female emotion drives the action. He is the most modern tragedian. His plays were often revived later in antiquity and are commonly performed today. The plots of later comedies, and of modern sitcoms, derive directly from his bold innovations in the construction of plot and the depiction of character.

## The Origins of Tragedy

According to the fourth-century B.C. philosopher Aristotle, whose *Poetics* is the earliest surviving work of literary criticism, tragedy developed in the late sixth century B.C. out of **dithyrambs**, hymns to Dionysus danced and sung (presumably to accompany goat sacrifices) by choruses of fifteen or so members, with a chorus leader. Dithyrambs continued to be performed in the fifth century B.C., and the poem given below, from about 470 B.C., is a good example. It tells of the hero Theseus' arrival in Attica, and was a script for an actual public performance. The chorus sings and dances, and the chorus leader, taking the part of Theseus' father Aegeus (ē-jūs), responds to them:

> **Chorus of Athenians**
> King of holy Athens, lord of the lavish Ionians,°
> why do brass-belled trumpets scream new songs of war?
> Does an enemy warrior thrust at our borders,
> or do hostile raiders with violent hands
> drive off the sheep of protesting herdsmen?
> What harasses your heart? Speak, for of all men
> you have the bravest defenders and soldiers.
> Tell me, O son of Creusa and Pandion.°
>
> **Aegeus**
> Newly come is a messenger whose flying feet
> have run the long road that traverses Isthmus,°
> telling wonderful works of a man of great might.
> Proud Sinis° he slew, of all mortal men
> the strongest by far, son of Cronus' child,
> earthshaking Lytaeus.° Far off in the wood
> he slew the man-slaying wild sow of Crommyon.
> Arrogant Sciron died by his sword.
> The wrestling of Cercyon he ended forever.

°*Ionians:* The Athenians claimed to be ancestors to the Greeks living in Ionia and their dialect was Ionian.    °*Creusa and Pandion:* Parents of Aegeus.    °*Isthmus:* The narrow neck of land joining mainland Greece to the Peloponnesus.    °*Sinis:* We now get a list of the deeds of Theseus, parallel to the Labors of Heracles. These bandits are little known outside this story.    °*Lytaeus:* son of Poseidon.

Procoptes° has met the menace of a far better man
and abandoned the mallet of Polypemon.°
I dread where such exploits will finally finish.

**Chorus**
Who is this man? and whence does he come?
What following force do they say that he brings?
Does he lead a great army, in hostile array,
or advance alone, with a few attendants,
like a traveler seeking an unknown country?
Who is as strong, courageous, yes, rash,
as he who puts down from their seats the mighty?
A god must impel him to make law for the lawless.
One as busy as he must at times meet misfortune,
yet over the years the gods' will comes to pass

**Aegeus**
The messengers tell me only two stand beside him.
From his brawny shoulders, they say, hangs a sword.
In his hands are a pair of well-polished lances,
on his flaming hair a Laconian cap.
A sea-blue tunic wraps over his chest,
over all a Thessalian tunic of wool.
From his eye there flashes red Lemnian fire.°
He looks like a boy just entering manhood,
yet he seems to delight in bronze-ringing war,
as forward he strides to our glorious Athens.

Bacchylides, *Dithyramb* 18

°*Procoptes* ("shortener"): Another name for Procrustes, "stretcher," a brigand.   °*Polypemon:* Another name for Procoptes.   °*Lemnian fire:* The island of Lemnos was home to an ancient fire cult.

Bacchylides has created a situation by means of written verse. The chorus of ten or fifteen memorizes his words and dance to a complex rhythm even as they sing these words. They pretend to be Athenian citizens, while one of them, the chorus leader, pretends to be a figure from heroic myth, Aegeus, father of the Athenian hero Theseus. Actors and chorus have similar roles in tragedy. The chorus is inquiring and speculative, whereas the voice of Aegeus is explanatory and authoritative. Something is happening: A stranger is coming to town; he is Aegeus' son, whom Aegeus has not seen from birth and does not yet recognize. In describing Theseus' glory, Aegeus unknowingly describes his own son and heir, so there is tension between what Aegeus knows and what the audience knows. This too is common in Greek tragedy. If this dithyramb resembles earlier dithyrambs, we can perhaps see how tragedy developed from it. Homer sang in the third person, saying that "Aegeus did such and such," but now a man pretends to be Aegeus and speaks as him. Some Greeks ascribed this radical innovation to one Arion, a great sixth-century Corinthian singer. Arion visited Sicily and Italy (according to one story, unscrupulous sailors threw him overboard, but a dolphin heard his beautiful song and carried him safely home). Most commentators, however, attributed the crucial innovations to an Athenian named **Thespis** (hence the word "thespian," for actor), active in the 530s B.C. while Pisistratus was tyrant. Nothing of what he may have written has survived.

**FIGURE 15.1** Women followers dance and play flutes around an image of Dionysus consisting of a mask on a stake draped with robes; on a red-figured wine cup, ca. 450 B.C.

We might guess that Thespis (if it really was he) stepped forth from the chorus, put on a mask, and pretended to be a mythical character. The use of masks in both tragedy and in the cult of Dionysus (Figure 15.1) is striking and may support Aristotle's statement that tragedy grew out of Dionysiac celebrations. Be that as it may, the mask also met a practical need. The original sole actor selected a moment of choice in a hero's career, providing an opportunity for internal conflict. Shall I do this, or shall I do that? By changing the mask, the sole actor could become a second figure in the story, also speaking in the first person. Now conflict between individuals is possible (although they cannot meet face to face!). The "hero in conflict" is the basic plot of Greek tragedies, and Thespis appears to have found some way of presenting it. In the dithyramb quoted above, there is no choice and conflict and hence no drama.

For decades, tragedies remained highly stylized performances in which a single masked actor responded to the chorus's songs. Aristotle says that Aeschylus transformed the genre in the 470s B.C. by adding a second actor and reducing the chorus's role. The **protagonist** (literally, "first actor") could now come into direct face-to-face conflict with another hero (the **antagonist**), instead of interacting just with the chorus. Aeschylus' surviving plays present dialogues between one actor and the chorus or the chorus leader, while in his most famous works, a group of three plays (trilogy) called the *Oresteia* ("Story of Orestes," performed in 458 B.C.), he uses a third actor, an innovation that Aristotle attributed to Sophocles. Strikingly, there never were more than three actors in a Greek tragedy, although in one tragedy of Euripides (*Suppliants*) there are twelve speaking roles! The mask made such versatility possible.

Most tragedies were performed at the festival of the **City Dionysia**, a festival that Pisistratus, who controlled Athens in the 530s B.C., reformed from an older ceremony.

The City Dionysia, honoring the god of wine, was a gigantic public symposium for the whole *dêmos* from which the tyrant Pisistratus drew his political support. As poetry decorated the intimate aristocratic symposium, so tragedy and other poetry decorated the symposium of the *dêmos*. As the aristocrats had formed and sealed political alliances in the intimacy of the "men's room," so now did the City Dionysia bring together the whole *dêmos* as a single political force under Pisistratus' leadership.

If Thespis did invent the new genre of tragedy, Pisistratus exploited Thespis' invention for patriotic purposes. When the tyrants fell in 510 B.C., the popular tragic performances continued and spread, eventually, all across the Greek world. In Athens, tragedy became the quintessential democratic art form, while in Syracuse the tyrants sponsored tragedies too, just as Pisistratus had done. Hiero hired Aeschylus to write a play in 476 B.C. to celebrate his foundation of a new colony and had *The Persians* performed in Syracuse. Aeschylus returned to Sicily at the end of his life, when the tyrants had been overthrown, and died in Gela, Sicily, in 456 B.C.

## The Forms of Tragedy

The masked actors, never more than three, were always men. Early masks were not exaggerated, like the "comic" and "tragic" masks with up- and down-turned mouths familiar since Roman times, but realistic. They were probably made of molded linen. There were stock character types: the old man, the young girl, the young man, the king, the slave. Masked actors could communicate emotion only through words and gestures, not facial expressions.

Choral song remained an essential element in fifth-century tragedy. The dancers were accompanied by double pipes called *auloi* (a kind of oboe with a hollow vibrating reed). Music was as vital to ancient plays as it is to contemporary cinema but is of course not represented in surviving texts. Most tragedies have five choral songs called *stasima* (singular, *stasimon*), "songs sung in place," interspersed with portions of dialogue called **episodes**, "side-songs" (the origin of the word "episode"). The action takes place in the dialogue, while choral song offers reflections, not always close, on events in the plot. The presence of a choral song often indicates the passage of time.

The meters of the choral passages are complex, reflecting ancient dance steps, now completely unknown. Choral songs are abstract, impressionistic, and filled with invented words that do not occur elsewhere. Modern scholars do not so much *read* Greek choruses as interpret them and form theories on their possible meaning (as a comparison of different translations of Aeschylus' *Oresteia* will quickly reveal!).

The *episodes* of *tragoidia* are in simple meters, starkly different from choral song. The dialogue is often formalized, as when each speaker speaks in turn exactly one line (called *stichomythia*, "speaking line by line": see below), and reminiscent of ritual, as when two speakers sing a lament or a hymn of victory. Still, tragedy was not ritual, but entertainment.

## THE CITY DIONYSIA

An archon ("ruler") presided over this major tragic festival, which came to reflect the aspirations of the Athenian democracy. Each year, the archon chose three tragic and five comic poets and granted each a chorus. The Assembly imposed liturgies on eight rich men, requiring each to pay for costuming and training the actors for one of the poets, an expensive undertaking (see Chapter 13, "Democracy and Empire: athens and Syracuse, 479–431 B.C."). If the man paying for the play had political ambitions, he might spend heavily on lavish effects to impress the *dêmos*.

The City Dionysia lasted for five days in late March, at the time of the spring harvest, and was the civic highlight of the year. Two days before the festival, the poets presented a public summary of the plays and introduced the actors. On the day before the festival, the statue of Dionysus was removed from his small shrine near the theater, taken to the country-side, then brought back to the city and set up in the theater to oversee the play. On the first day of the festival a magnificent procession took place. Some participants carried large models of erect penises, tributes to Dionysus' life-giving power. At the end of the parade, bulls were killed, the meat eaten, and much wine drunk. Then came choral performances in which men and boys danced while singing. The second day began with another sacrifice, followed by awards to those who had benefited the state. Young men whose fathers died fighting for the *polis* paraded in new armor provided by the state. Then the plays began.

The only surviving complete set of three tragedies is Aeschylus' *Oresteia*, performed in a single day in 458 B.C. The trilogy tells of Agamemnon's murder by his wife and his son Orestes' revenge and fate. Trilogies by other poets, however, seem to have been related only loosely by theme, if at all. On the fifth day, five comedies were staged. Two days after the festival, the assembly met in the theater to review its conduct.

As a competition among poets and their patrons, entertainment at the City Dionysia had a lot in common with athletic contests (see Chapter 8, "Archaic Greece, 700–800 B.C.: Economy, Society, Politics"). In both, contests between the rich entertained the *dêmos;* in both, the winners received symbolic prizes, special wreaths, but never money. The real competition was for honor and glory, not wealth. Ten men drawn by lot from the ten Athenian tribes acted as judges. Certainly their judgments do not always agree with ours: Euripides took first prize only four times in his long career, while Sophocles' *Oedipus the King* (429 B.C.), which many think to be the finest story ever crafted and was for Aristotle the model tragedy, took second prize.

## THE THEATER OF DIONYSUS

The earliest tragedies were performed on the south slope of the Acropolis. In the late sixth century B.C. there was no theater, but only an *orchêstra*, a circular "dancing place" outside a small shrine to Dionysus (the origin of "orchestra"). At the center of the *orchêstra* was a round altar. The audience sat at first on the slopes of the hill, then later in permanent stone seats in the *theatron* ("viewing area," the origin of "theater").

A changing hut or *skênê* ("tent," hence the word "scene"), probably made of wood, was added behind the orchestra. There the actors could change their masks. The *skênê* had a single door facing the audience, through which actors entered and left, and a platform that could be rolled out into the *orchêstra*. This device was probably used for a famous scene in Aeschylus' *Agamemnon* (the first play in the *Oresteia*) in which Clytemnestra murders her husband Agamemnon offstage, inside the *skênê*, then suddenly appears, exulting over his body "I have killed him!"

There was probably no stage during the sixth and fifth centuries B.C., but there were special effects. A crane called a *mêchanê* ("device," hence our "machine") was attached to the top of the *skênê*, but we are not sure how it was used. By means of it, in Euripides' *Medea* the murderess was somehow whisked away on a chariot "drawn by dragons." Some tragedies ended when the *mêchanê* lowered an actor playing a god down to the earth to resolve a complicated plot. The familiar Latin phrase **deus ex machina**, "god from the machine," comes from this technique and refers to any abrupt or contrived ending to a story. In Sophocles' *Philoctetes*, for example, the Greeks must

**FIGURE 15.2** The Theater of Dionysus today, looking southwest. The horseshoe-shaped *orchêstra* is Roman, but the seating is fifth century B.C. The ancient sanctuary to Dionysus lay where the trees are in the center left of the picture.

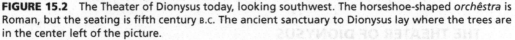

possess Philoctetes' bow in order to take Troy, but he hates them too much to give it up. The hero Heracles, who had once possessed the bow, suddenly appears from the *mêchanê* and settles the dispute.

At first, there was no scenery of any kind. Aristotle credited Sophocles with inventing painted scenery, presumably wooden panels attached to the front of the *skênê*. But scenery was never important in tragedy.

Surviving ruins of the Theater of Dionysus give us some idea of what it might have looked like in the fifth century B.C., although most of the theater was rebuilt in Roman times. In Figure 15.2, the once round *orchêstra* has taken on a horseshoe shape, according to Roman preference. Ruins of the fourth-century B.C. *skênê* are visible in the background.

## NARRATIVE STRUCTURE

In Chapter 6, "Homer," we explained that the *Iliad* and *Odyssey* have plots with three parts. They begin with a setup, explaining the situation, leading to the first plot point in which something happens to create conflict. Conflict dominates the middle of the story, until a second plot point opens the final stage, or resolution. We find the same basic structure (or *muthos*, "plot") repeated endlessly in modern novels and films: girl meets boy (beginning), girl loses boy (middle), girl regains boy (end). For all their sophistication, tragedies worked the same way.

For example, in the setup of Sophocles' *Antigonê* (an-**tig**-o-nē, ca. 441 B.C.), King Creon has issued a stern decree: It is a capital crime to bury Polynices (pol-i-nī-sēz), who attacked his own city of Thebes with a foreign army and was killed in a duel with his loyal brother Eteocles, who also died. Antigonê buries her brother Polynices anyway. She is caught, arrested, and brought before Creon (the first plot point).

In the middle portion, Sophocles generates conflict at many levels. Antigonê is young; her antagonist Creon is middle-aged. She is female; he is male. He is the king; she is a subject. He invokes the power of the state; she invokes the power of the family and its obligations. They have one thing in common: Neither will yield. Further conflict appears between son and father when Creon's son Haemon, engaged to Antigonê, pleads for his fiancée. The prophet Tiresias reveals unfavorable omens, but Creon thinks he is taking bribes: Thus religion conflicts with the state.

Creon condemns Antigonê to death. She enters the cave where she will die, the second plot point. Conflict can have one of two outcomes. Either a deal is struck between the contenders and the conflict resolved or one party to the conflict is removed or destroyed. In tragedy we find both outcomes, although the second is more common (hence the word "tragic"). In *Antigonê*, Creon, a late learner, now realizes his error and attempts to forestall the consequences of his actions. He reaches the cave too late to save Antigonê, who has killed herself; so ends her conflict with Creon. Haemon has come to the cave and in a fury attempts to kill his own father, then kills himself; so ends the conflict between Creon and Haemon. Creon returns to the palace to discover that his wife has hanged herself, almost an afterthought, as if Sophocles were trying to exaggerate Creon's suffering. In any event, the resolution of conflict leaves Creon a broken man. The End.

Euripides' *Bacchae* (404 B.C.) provides a more complex example. This time we learn the background to the setup in a prologue, a device invented or elaborated by Euripides, when a god comes on stage to tell us what has happened before the story begins—the "story thus far." In this case Dionysus, disguised as a stranger, explains how after a long journey in the East he has returned to his hometown of Thebes to take revenge on his mother's sisters, who slandered his mother by denying that her lover and bedmate was none other than Zeus. This, then, is to be a revenge play.

The citizens, including the ancient king Cadmus and the prophet Tiresias (who behave ludicrously in their religious devotion), go into the mountains to revel and adore the power of Dionysus. The stranger (Dionysus in disguise) is arrested and brought before Pentheus, the first plot point: The action turns to the conflict between Pentheus and Dionysus, who face off in a long *agôn*, or "contest," a formal debate common in the middle of Greek tragedies. The *agôn* rhetorically parallels debates in the Assembly and law courts, where each side had a chance to speak. They debate in *stichomythia*, "line-by-line talk":

PENTHEUS: First question: Just who are you? What's your family?

DIONYSUS: No need to shout; you want a simple answer.

         No doubt you've heard of Tmolus'° flowery hills?

PENTHEUS: Yes, it encloses the great city of Sardis.

DIONYSUS: That's where I come from. Lydia is my home.

PENTHEUS: And where did you get these rites you bring to Greece?

DIONYSUS: Dionysus, Zeus' son, passed through our land.

PENTHEUS: You have some sort of Zeus, who breeds new gods?

DIONYSUS: No, the same one who wedded Semelê here.

°*Tmolus:* A mountain that rises behind Sardis in Lydia.

PENTHEUS: Did he recruit in a dream or face to face?

DIONYSUS: We viewed each other when he gave his rites.

PENTHEUS: Tell me the form of these mysterious rites.

DIONYSUS: To uninitiates they may not be told.

PENTHEUS: What value do they have for worshipers?

DIONYSUS: Their worth is priceless—but *you* may not hear.

PENTHEUS: Hocus-pocus, to rouse my interest!

DIONYSUS: Your cynicism makes you mock our rites.

PENTHEUS: You saw the god so clearly. Just how did he look?

DIONYSUS: However he pleased. I didn't make his choice.

PENTHEUS: You ducked that nicely, making no real reply.

DIONYSUS: Speak sense to a fool, he thinks it's only nonsense.

PENTHEUS: Is Thebes the first place where you brought this god?

DIONYSUS: All other lands already dance in his rites.

PENTHEUS: Their wits are feebler far than those of Greeks.

DIONYSUS: In this, far stronger. All laws are not the same.

PENTHEUS: Do you worship him by night or in the day?

DIONYSUS: Mostly by night, for darkness fosters awe.

PENTHEUS: But night seduces women into vice.

DIONYSUS: If one should seek by day, she'd find it then.

PENTHEUS: You deserve punishment for your clever speech.

DIONYSUS: And you for your ignorant slander of the god.

PENTHEUS: This Bacchic priest speaks rash and slippery words.

DIONYSUS: What dreadful torture, then, do you propose?

PENTHEUS: First, to cut off your pretty curling hair.

DIONYSUS: My locks are sacred; I tend them for the god.

*(Pentheus cuts off the prisoner's hair)*

PENTHEUS: Hand over that thyrsus° you've got in your hands.

DIONYSUS: *You* take it from me. It belongs to the god.

*(Pentheus snatches it)*

PENTHEUS: We'll chain your body up in a cell, inside.

DIONYSUS: The god himself will free me when I ask.

PENTHEUS: Only when all your Bacchae° join your prayer.

DIONYSUS: No, he is close at hand and sees me suffer.

PENTHEUS: Indeed? just where? My eyes don't see a thing.

DIONYSUS: Right here with me. Your folly makes you blind.

PENTHEUS: (TO JAILER) Take him away for mocking Thebes and me.

DIONYSUS: I warn you triflers, trifle not with me!

°*thyrsus:* A phallic staff carried by the followers of Dionysus (see Figure 15.1).  °*Bacchae:* The female followers of Bacchus (Dionysus).

PENTHEUS: I warn you that I will, for I am the stronger.

DIONYSUS: What gives you power? What are you doing? Who are you?

PENTHEUS: Pentheus, Agavê's son, fathered by Echion.

DIONYSUS: A name of evil omen; it fits you well.°

Euripides, *Bacchae* 460–510

° . . . *fits you well:* The king's name Pentheus sounds like the Greek word *penthos,* "sorrow."

The *agôn* rehearses the play's central conflicts: traditional religion (Pentheus) against religious innovation (Dionysus); cousin against cousin (Pentheus' mother Agavê is the sister of Dionysus' mother Semelê); the ignorant (Pentheus) against the knowing (Dionysus); Greeks (Pentheus) against barbarians (Dionysus); day (Pentheus) against night (Dionysus); state (Pentheus) against religion (Dionysus); masculine (Pentheus) against effeminate (Dionysus); visible (Pentheus) against invisible (Dionysus); the sane/insane (Pentheus) against the insane/sane (Dionysus); the strong/weak (Pentheus) against the weak/strong (Dionysus). Such calculated oppositions were the stuff of sophistic thought and Athenian intellectualism. Dionysus is implicitly compared to the destructive sophists in his cleverness with words and his relativistic stance that different peoples value different things: In the eyes of people like Pentheus, who know nothing about themselves, these were the men who were destroying the state. It was fashionable at this time to question traditional accounts of the gods—how could their immorality be true?—but Euripides brutally mocks a rational removal of mystery from the world. He wrote this play at the end of the Peloponnesian War, around 403 B.C., and in it we may prefer to see a tribute spoken to the irrational forces in the world, which brought defeat to Athens.

Pentheus imprisons Dionysus. The god escapes and in a second *agôn* entrances Pentheus, tempting him to spy on the Bacchae abroad in the woodland. The deluded Pentheus agrees (plot point two), which leads to resolution of the plot in Pentheus' dismemberment at the hands of his own mother and aunts and his mother's triumphant return to the city, cradling the bloody head of her own son in her arms.

## CHARACTER AND OTHER DIMENSIONS OF TRAGEDY

Tragedies have plots, but they also have *characters,* from a Greek word meaning "imprint." We might think of character as the sum of the choices that someone makes. Tragedians rarely invented characters from whole cloth; they borrowed them from tradition. Odysseus was the clever man who relied on intelligence, not force, to achieve his aims; Agamemnon was the braggart who set self-importance above the interests of his people; Hector, the family man doomed to a frightful end along with the family he cannot save; and Achilles, the warrior-intellectual who will not compromise ideals for self-interest. Yet within these boundaries the poet was free to invent. For Euripides, as for everyone else, Helen was the lovely seductress, self-pitying but charming, who abandoned husband, family, and reputation out of desire for another man. In his *Trojan Women* (415 B.C.), he makes her refuse to accept responsibility for her choice. She blames Aphrodite (i.e., sexual attraction) for what happened. But in Euripides' *Helen,* the seductress never went to Troy at all—the whole war was fought over a phantom! Helen's character includes both representations.

In myths, characters are divine beings, mortals, or even talking animals, but tragic characters are nearly always humans (Aeschylus' Prometheus is an exception). Most are kings and queens. So far as we know, not one of the thousand tragedies performed between about 530 and 400 B.C. focused exclusively on the doings of gods and goddesses. In earlier Near Eastern (nondramatic) literature, by contrast, the principals are usually gods and goddesses (except for the human king Gilgamesh). The tragic characters' high social standing gave their choices gravity and consequence. Hence, Antigonê's choice to bury her brother against King Creon's mandate became a matter of state, not just a family dispute. Pentheus' choice to deny the new god destroyed his dynasty.

Aristotle took a keen interest in the structure and nature of tragedy. He notes in his essay the *Poetics* that

> Tragedy is the *mimesis* ["representation"] of a serious action that is complete and having a certain magnitude, using pleasing language separately suited to the various parts of the play. It represents action and does not move ahead through narrative. Through pity and fear it provides a *katharsis* ("relief") of such and similar emotions . . .
>
> Every tragedy has six parts, which determine its quality. These are *muthos* ["plot"], character, diction, thought, spectacle, and song . . . This list is exhaustive, and most poets use these elements, for every drama includes spectacle and character and plot and diction and song and thought.
>
> The most important of these is the arrangement of the incidents [i.e., the plot]. For tragedy is the *mimesis* not of human beings, but of action, of life, and of happiness and unhappiness. It is about action and not about qualities of character. Character makes men what they are, but their actions make them happy or unhappy . . . The first principle and, as it were, the soul of tragedy is *muthos* ["plot"]; character comes second.

Aristotle, *Poetics* 1449b–1450a

Aristotle's concept of **mimesis** ("representation" or "imitation") is probably the most discussed term in literary criticism. By "*mimesis* of a serious action that is complete and having a certain magnitude" Aristotle means that "action"—*drama*, as we noted earlier, means "things done"— is central to this form of poetry. Other kinds of poetry represent a point of view or a state of mind, not action. Because of the characters' high status, "what happens" is heroic and has consequences, unlike in some forms of modern literature that focus on people who do not possess power, whose acts lack consequences beyond their personal lives. The *mimesis* is "complete" because the issues raised in the middle portion of the plot, where conflict rages, are resolved in the third portion of the plot.

Modern film, to which we have compared tragedy's structure, is a story told in pictures within a dramatic context, with dialogue, but the stories of Greek tragedy, as they have come to us, are told in words. In this respect, tragedy and film are very different. Aristotle distinguishes between the spoken words of the *episodes* within which the action takes place and the choral songs, which are danced. The story is "acted out," we might say, unlike in epic (which tells the story in the third person) or in film (which tells the story in pictures accompanied by dialogue).

When the audience watches the *mimesis* of an action, the members feel pity for what the characters suffer, and they fear that the same fate might befall them. Tragedy allowed the audience to feel intense, sometimes disturbing emotions that cannot be experienced in real life without terrible cost. This may be what Aristotle meant by **katharsis**, "relief," a cleansing that audiences feel after experiencing the powerful emotions that a strong drama brings forth. People go to movies to experience tension and release. Dramatic art that does not generate tension is poor dramatic art. Tragedy, therefore, painlessly expands one's experience as a human being. No more effective answer has ever been offered to the self-righteous censors who, throughout history, have policed entertainment to make it conform to preconceived notions of what is proper.

To Aristotle's penetrating observations, we might add several more. Driving the plot is the protagonist's **dramatic need**, something he or she wants. Without dramatic need, there is no action, hence no plot and no drama. Oedipus' dramatic need in *Oedipus the King* is to find the truth about the death of King Laius, the cause of the plague. Antigonê's dramatic need is to bury her brother. Pentheus' dramatic need is to stop the new religion. The tragedians took their technique of storytelling from Homer. Achilles' dramatic need in the *Iliad* is to avenge an insult; Odysseus' dramatic need is to return home. In the third part of the plot, the resolution, the dramatic need is either met or not met, which concludes the action. Oedipus learns who killed Laius; Antigonê buries her brother and pays the price; Pentheus fails to stop the new religion.

## TRAGIC PLOTS

It is striking how rarely tragedians actually drew on the *Iliad* and *Odyssey* for their stories. Instead, they borrowed tales from the more manageable, lost epic poems called the Cyclic Poems, which told the rest of the story of the Trojan War. Tragic plots fall into several types. The theme of *Revenge* drives Aeschylus' *Oresteia* (the trilogy consisting of *Agamemnon*, *Libation Bearers*, and *Eumenides*). Clytemnestra kills her husband Agamemnon because he killed their daughter. Orestes kills his mother Clytemnestra to avenge his father Agamemnon's death. To avenge the matricide, the Furies persecute Orestes. Only an enlightened decision by an Athenian law court in the third play can resolve the conflict. In Euripides' *Bacchae*, Dionysus takes revenge on his aunts for slandering his mother. Revenge is a primitive form of justice and appeals to the audience's moral instincts, then as now. A good revenge story will always get the audience riled up and give them what they want, tension and release.

Another common theme is the *suppliant*, where an exile is thrown on the mercy of a foreign potentate, the story of Sophocles' *Oedipus at Colonus*. Oedipus comes as an old man to Theseus of Athens, seeking refuge from his own sons. In Aeschylus' *Suppliants*, the fifty daughters of Danaüs, who murdered their husbands, beg protection from the king of Argos.

A recurring plot element in Greek tragedy is the *foundling*. Oedipus was exposed as an infant, found, raised in a foreign land, then discovered. Foundling stories can reveal the horrors of self-discovery. In Euripides' *Ion*, Ion is exposed as an infant, survives, then as an adult is nearly put to death by his own mother. *Human sacrifice*, a form of horror, has high entertainment value and can form an essential plot element. In Euripides' *Iphigenia at Aulis*, Agamemnon prepares to kill his daughter Iphigenia, a fate that she accepts, while in his *Iphigenia among the Taurians*, Iphigenia (saved from sacrifice at Aulis by Artemis) seeks to sacrifice her own brother. Corollary to human sacrifice is the *bride of death*, where a virginal female victim laments her lot, complaining that death is the only husband she will ever know. Antigonê makes such a complaint as she enters the cave to die, though she has herself chosen to take this course.

Such themes and elements motivate the action of which the play is a *mimesis*, as the protagonist works through beginning and middle to the end. Aristotle analyzed the shape this trajectory might take. Tragedy's aristocratic and royal characters rise to high fortune, then in a "turning around," *peripeteia*, accompanied by a "recognition," **anagnorisis**, they come to a "down-turning," *katastrophê* (hence our "catastrophe"), a reversal of fortune. Aristotle speculates on what leads to *katastrophê*, emphasizing the role of something he calls **hamartia**, "missing of the mark" or "mistake":

The structure of the best tragedy should be complex, not simple, and should represent incidents that arouse fear and pity. For that is the nature of this kind of representation. First of all it is obvious that one should not represent a worthy man passing from happiness to unhappiness. That does not arouse fear or pity but simply shocks. Nor do we wish to see the wicked pass from misfortune to good. That is the most untragic of all, for it does not satisfy our feelings or arouse the emotions of pity or fear.

There remains the mean between these. There is such a man who is not outstanding in virtue or justice, who falls from fortune through no crime or villainy but through some *hamartia* ["mistake"], one of those men of high station such as Oedipus or Thyestes° and the famous men of such families. The best plots *[muthoi]* will have single, not double outcomes, as some maintain, and will represent the passage not from misfortune to happiness, but the opposite, from happiness to misfortune, and not through any villainy but through some great *hamartia* ["mistake"] in such a man as we have described, or in one still better, not worse. You can see this from actual practice. At first poets took stories from just anywhere, but now they concentrate on a few families to whose lot terrible suffering fell, or who committed atrocious deeds.

Aristotle, *Poetics* 1452b–1453a

°*Thyestes:* Brother to Atreus, who fed to Thyestes his own children.

Early scholars mistranslated *hamartia* as "flaw," leading to theories of the "tragic flaw" still mentioned in some handbooks today. But by *hamartia* Aristotle probably meant "misidentification," as when Iphigenia mistook her brother Orestes for a stranger and potential sacrificial victim. Many interpreters, however, think the word *hamartia* implies a broader intellectual or moral fault, and they seek these in studying tragic characters. In any event, in Aristotle's view protagonists do not deserve their misfortune but bring it on themselves through an error of judgment. So Oedipus mistook the man who struck him on the road for a brigand, not realizing it was his own father. His hastiness exaggerated the consequences of this mistake, but he was not morally responsible for the disasters that befell him. Oedipus did not mean to kill his father. Still, had he been less inclined to violence, he might not have done so, and in this sense his *hamartia* has led him to make a wrong decision at a moment of crisis. Agamemnon wreaked violence on Troy but did not deserve to be murdered by his wife in a bathtub. He missed the mark when he saw her as loving and devoted, when really she was a homicidal adulteress. Herodotus, writing during the heyday of Athenian tragedy, and surely a witness of tragic performances, shared a similar understanding of the structure of what we would call historical events. Hence Darius and Xerxes suffered *peripeteia* in their failed campaigns against Greece, as did Croesus when he marched against Persia. The Persian kings were not bad men, but they badly missed the mark when they imagined that the weak, insignificant Greeks would never stand against the greatest army the world had seen.

The plots in tragedy are a web of family histories. Tragedians showed little interest in great mythic cycles of creation, battles of Titans and Olympians, or the births and loves of gods. The focus was on the passions and horrors of family life. No possibility is omitted: sons kill mothers; wives kill husbands; sons kill fathers; mothers kill children; a father kills his daughter, or son, or all his children; a daughter kills her father; brothers kill each other; sons kill their stepmothers; mothers expose their infants to die; men and women kill themselves. Sexual trespass is as varied as violence: a son sleeps with his mother; a father rapes his daughter; adultery is rampant; lustful women seduce honorable men (never the reverse); husbands desert their wives and mistresses. Complementing such extreme dishonesty are intense love and devotion between brother and sister, brother and brother, father and son, husband and wife, and father and daughter.

## CONCLUSION

Two-and-a-half thousand years have passed since Arion or Thespis put on a mask and addressed his chorus. Greek tragedy can seem alien and stiff to modern audiences, but those familiar with its conventions can still experience the powerful *katharsis* that Aristotle described. It seems like an unlikely art form for a democratic *polis:* Its characters are royal, aristocratic, and often female, expressing and acting on extreme emotions, and consistently rejecting the cooperative values of the egalitarian city-state. But the tragedians took characters from the heroic age, like Agamemnon and Antigonê, and recreated their lives against the background of contemporary values, which the choruses regularly celebrate. The tragedies asked how great individuals like Odysseus could fit into real, everyday society. Not very well, it turns out.

## THE ORIGINS OF COMEDY

We normally think of "comedy" as something that makes us laugh—stand-up comics or TV sitcoms, a new one every season. But as we explained in Chapter 6, "Homer," literary critics use the word in a more technical sense, to mean a story that ends happily, whether it is funny or not. In this sense, the *Odyssey* (unlike the *Iliad*) is a comedy, although it is rarely funny. But the Greek word *kômoidia*, "song of the *kômos*," referred to something more specific.

Aristotle's analysis of comedy is unfortunately lost, except for his observation that comedy came "from those leading off phallic songs" (*Poetics* 1449a), just as he claimed that tragedy began "from those leading off the dithyramb." Phallic songs certainly were sung in processions for Dionysus where participants could also carry large artificial penises, and comic choruses often had large phalluses as part of their costumes. One of the curious features of comedy, the *parabasis* ("stepping forth"), where the action stops while the chorus sometimes comes forward to insult audience members, may conceivably derive from similar behavior during phallic processions. The evidence for the origins of comedy, however, is even less clear than that of tragedy. Scattered accounts suggest that in the late-sixth century B.C. in Athens, Syracuse, and several other cities, performers began turning *kômoi* (drunken revels shown on vases), into true dramas. However, we know no details. Western Greeks may have taken the lead in the evolution of this literary form. By 500 B.C. or soon after, one Epicharmus was active at Syracuse in crafting *kômoidia*. According to reports, his characters were mythical, and he produced burlesques about Odysseus and Heracles, but only fragments survive. Some ancient scholars thought the small city of Megara southwest of Athens was the home of comedy. Still, all surviving examples are Athenian, and for all practical purposes we can treat Athens as the home of comedy.

The first comic victor at the City Dionysia was recorded in 486 B.C., but nothing survives from before 450 B.C. The first complete comedy is the *Acharnians*, produced in 425 B.C. by **Aristophanes** (ar-is-**tof**-a-nēz; ca. 460–386 B.C.), one of the funniest men who ever lived. Eleven of Aristophanes' comedies survive complete. We know the names of another thirty-one of Aristophanes' works, but only fragments survive from the dozens of other fifth-century Athenian writers of comedy. Scholars call fifth-century Athenian comedy **Old Comedy** to distinguish it from New Comedy, the late fourth-century plays we will discuss in Chapter 23, "Hellenistic Culture, 323–30 B.C." Some scholars think there was also an intermediate form that they call "Middle Comedy," but we know little of it.

## THE PLOTS OF OLD COMEDY

Tragedy drew its plots from heroic myth, and Epicharmus of Syracuse apparently did the same in some of his early comedies. Aristophanes, though, more like a modern playwright, always produced original (albeit rudimentary) plots, set in the present. Aristophanes usually took an absurd situation in which an ordinary citizen stands in opposition to the mad, mad world around him and then, through some completely crazy scheme, gets the better of everyone.

In the *Acharnians* (425 B.C.), a protagonist weary of Athens' war with Sparta makes a private peace treaty. He sets out stones to mark the territory now at peace and goes about his business as if there were no war, as for him there is not. He declares a free market and makes a lot of money. In the *Clouds* (423 B.C.), an Athenian impoverished by his son's extravagant addiction to horseracing sends him to Socrates' sophisticated "Thinkshop" to learn debating skills. Then he can argue his way out of his debts! In the *Peace* (421 B.C.), the hero flies to heaven on a dung beetle, releasing "Peace," a naked woman, from imprisonment in a cave. In the *Birds* (414 B.C.), two disaffected Athenians flee the chaotic city to Cloudcuckooland, the idyllic home of the birds, where they plan a utopian new world. The Olympian gods are brought to their knees when the birds stop the smoke of sacrifice from reaching them. Thus the birds, with their Athenian advisors, become masters of the world. In *Lysistrata* (411 B.C.), we find another harebrained scheme: Athens' women deny sex to their (absent!) husbands in order to end the Peloponnesian War. In the *Frogs* (405 B.C.), the god Dionysus, anxious about the decline of tragedy, goes to the underworld to bring back Euripides, who died the year before. After a contest, Dionysus brings back Aeschylus instead, much to Euripides' chagrin.

In all cases, comic plots assume that the world has gone insane. The protagonist is normally a man (occasionally a woman) of common sense and traditional civic values, but because the world is topsy-turvy, he or she has to do something equally insane to put it straight. In both the *Lysistrata* (411 B.C.) and the *Assemblywomen* (392 B.C.), women take control of Athens, hysterically funny to the all-male Athenian audience. They institute a sex strike in the first play and introduce communal property (including sexual partners) in the second.

As such stories unfold, the characters and chorus indulge in brutal personal abuse against well-known political figures, no doubt sitting in the audience only a few feet away. In the lost play the *Babylonians* (426 B.C.), Aristophanes attacked the prominent politician Cleon (see Chapter 16, "The Peloponnesian War and Its Aftermath, 431–399 B.C.") so savagely that Cleon sued the playwright. Aristophanes' *Knights* of 424 B.C. represents Cleon as a pampered slave who robs and cheats his good-natured but lazy master Dêmos ("the people"). Cleon is worsted by a sausage seller who proves to be even more vulgar—and entertaining to Dêmos—than the repulsive Cleon himself.

Aristophanes made fun of pretentious Athenians who wanted to be thought special and also of overzealous democrats. Stupid and clever, rich and poor, young and old, all were targets of his ferocious wit. His protagonists mean well, but they are full of vanities and foolishness. Aristophanes harks back to an idealized image of Athens in the "good old days" before the Peloponnesian War, law courts, the sophists, and other contemporary evils ruined absolutely everything.

## THE STRUCTURES OF OLD COMEDY

Whereas the structure of tragedy is simple, consisting of alternating spoken portions (*episodes*) and choral song (*stasima*), the structure of Old Comedy is strikingly complex. In tragedy, the chorus rarely interacts with the actors or takes part in the action, but in comedy, the chorus regularly participates in the action. Conversations take place between the actors and the chorus leader (*chorêgos*). The metrical patterns of the different portions of the play are highly formalized and bewilderingly complex, and of course lost in translation.

The first part of the play is the *prologos* ("speech in front"), in which a leading actor warms up the audience and makes clear the general situation. Then the chorus comes in. In tragedy, there were twelve or fifteen members of the chorus, but in comedy, twenty-four. The chorus members introduce themselves by singing a song and by interacting, sometimes violently, with actors already on stage.

Then comes the *agôn*, which like the *agôn* in tragedy is a spirited debate. The victory of one speaker resolves the conflict raised in the first part of the play and, in a way, the plot of the comedy ends here, in the middle of the play. The protagonist has already satisfied his dramatic need.

Next comes the *parabasis*, sung either by the chorus leader or the whole chorus, a kind of first-person rant. In the *parabasis*, the playwright speaks in the first person on his own behalf and delivers a sermon on contemporary political or social issues utterly unconnected to the plot, shattering the illusion of dramatic time and setting. It is a political speech. You need to know a good deal about contemporary politics and life to understand what Aristophanes is talking about during the *parabasis*, and for this reason his plays are valuable sources for historians. After the *parabasis* comes the sequence of *episodes* that explores the consequences of the protagonist's success, interspersed with choral songs that abuse individually named members of the audience.

Here is a typical comic *episode*, the first after the *parabasis* in the *Acharnians*. Having won his point about making a separate peace, the protagonist Dicaeopolis (di-ē-o-po-lis, "justice of the city") conducts his free market. A man arrives from Megara, a city near the Isthmus that suffered greatly when Athens closed its ports to trade, one of the incidents that triggered the Peloponnesian War (see Chapter 13, "Democracy and Empire: Athens and Syracuse, 479–431 B.C."). Hard political reality stands behind his plight, but in the comedy the specter of starvation is a topic of hilarity. So driven to hardship is the Megarian that he attempts to sell his daughters in Dicaeopolis' marketplace by pretending they are pigs. The politically incorrect humor depends on the dual meaning of the Greek word *choiros* (plural *choiroi*), which means either "piglet" or "female genitals," especially the hairless genitals of a young girl. Its raunchy obscenity, and casual misogyny, is entirely characteristic of Old Comedy:

DICAEOPOLIS: These stones will mark the boundary of my market, which is open for trade to all the Peloponnesians, even Megarians and Boeotians° . . .

*Dicaeopolis goes offstage. An impoverished Megarian comes in with his two daughters.*

MEGARIAN: Greetings, O Athenian market! Sweet to Megara! By all that is dear, I need you, I need you like I need my mommy. Hey, you dirty little brats, go get me something to eat, if you can find it. And listen up: Turn your bellies *this* way, please. Would you rather be sold or die of starvation?

°*Boeotians too:* The Athenians had excluded Megarians and Boeotians from their markets as a means of political retaliation.

| GIRLS: | Sell, sell! |
|---|---|
| MEGARIAN: | My opinion exactly. But who would be so stupid to pay a thing for worthless trash like you? But I've cooked up a Megarian Device!° I'll fix you up like piggies and put you out for sale. Now put on these piggy hooves and look like you come from a fine breed. By Hermes, if you return home unsold, I'll starve you myself! Put on these snouts too, and crawl into this sack. Grunt and oink around in there, just like piggies at the mysteries.° I'll call out Dicaeopolis. |

O Dicaeopolis, do you want to buy some piggies?

| DICAEOPOLIS: | What's this? A Megarian? |
|---|---|
| MEGARIAN: | We have come to trade. |
| DICAEOPOLIS: | How goes it there? |
| MEGARIAN: | We are ever before the fire, fasting.° |
| DICAEOPOLIS: | That's pretty nice . . . if you've got a live band for entertainment! But, what are you offering, O Megarian? . . . |
| MEGARIAN: | Well, I got some pretty nice mystic piggies. |
| DICAEOPOLIS: | Sounds good. Let's have a look. |
| MEGARIAN: | Oh, they are very nice. You can touch them if you want. Fat and very nice. |
| DICAEOPOLIS: | What is this? |
| MEGARIAN: | A piggy, by Zeus. |
| DICAEOPOLIS: | What are you talking about? Where's this piggy from? |
| MEGARIAN: | From Megara. Why, you think this ain't no piggy? |
| DICAEOPOLIS: | Not as far as I can see. |
| MEGARIAN: | Can this man be real? He doesn't believe a thing. He says this ain't no piggy. So come on then, I bet you a pound of salt that *this* [pointing between her legs] is what the Greeks call a piggy! |
| DICAEOPOLIS: | But it belongs to a human! |
| MEGARIAN: | Well it belongs to *me*. Whose else do you think? Wanna hear it squeal? |
| DICAEOPOLIS: | Sure. |
| MEGARIAN: | Do a little squealing right now! What's the matter? Can't get it out you little wretch? I'm taking you home right now. |
| GIRL: | Oink, oink. |
| MEGARIAN: | Now, is that a piggy? |
| DICAEOPOLIS: | It may be a piggy now, but when it grows up it will be a pokey-pie! |
| MEGARIAN: | Ah, give it five years, she'll be just like her Mama. |
| DICAEOPOLIS: | But this one is not ready for sacrifice. |
| MEGARIAN: | How so? What do you mean? |

°*Device:* The Megarians were known for their underhanded ways.    °*Mysteries:* Pigs were sacrificed to Demeter and Persephonê at the mysteries of Eleusis.    °*fasting:* Because they have no food.

DICAEOPOLIS: It has no tail.°

MEGARIAN: Well, she's young. But when she's pigged out a bit, she'll get a big, fat, red one. So if you want to rear her, here's another one. [pointing to the other girl].

DICAEOPOLIS: Both their piggies look the same!

MEGARIAN: Well sure, they have the same Mom and Dad. Once it fattens up a bit, and blossoms out with some hair, it will be perfect to sacrifice to Aphrodite.°

DICAEOPOLIS: But piggies aren't sacrificed to Aphrodite.

MEGARIAN: No piggies to Aphrodite? To her alone, I think! And the flesh of these piggies, when skewered on a spit, is Oh so yummy delicious.

DICAEOPOLIS: But can they suck without their mother?

MEGARIAN: By Poseidon, and without their father too!

DICAEOPOLIS: Well, what do they like to suck on?

MEGARIAN: Anything you give them. Ask them.

DICAEOPOLIS: Piggy, piggy . . .

GIRL: Oink oink!

DICAEOPOLIS: You like to chew on "chickpea"?°

GIRL: Oink oink.

DICAEOPOLIS: Or maybe a fig stick?°

GIRL: Oink oink!

DICAEOPOLIS: And how about you? Which is it you want?

OTHER GIRL: Oink oink!

DICAEOPOLIS: They oink pretty loud when they hear "fig stick"!

Aristophanes, *Acharnians* 729–804

°*tail:* A sacrificial victim could not be deformed, with a pun on "tail" and "penis." °*Aphrodite:* There were several deities to whom pigs were not sacrificed, including Aphrodite, the goddess of sex and love. °*"chickpeas":* One of many Greek slang words for penis. °*fig stick:* In Greek, another slang word for penis.

The slapstick scene is typical of Aristophanic *episodes,* supported by the dramatic pretense of showing how the protagonist has taken advantage of his successful ploy, in this case to create an open market in the midst of war and to rescind the decree against Megara.

## CONCLUSION

Drama evolved rapidly, from choral songs in the sixth century B.C. to highly formalized, powerful, and sophisticated performances in the fifth century. It was not obvious to Aristotle why this had happened; 2,300 years later, the matter is still more obscure. Philosophers tried to make sense of nature and of how debate might generate truth. Dramatists explored the same issues by looking at extreme cases, where reason and order have broken down. The tragedians presented the spectacle of powerful individuals trapped in impossible situations; the comedians envisioned the consequences of ludicrous responses to the absurdities of the real world, while addressing contemporary political issues. Drama, like ritual, helped create feelings of solidarity in the democratic community. Drama was not ritual, however, but a powerful tool for reflection on the human condition.

## Key Terms

| | | |
|---|---|---|
| Aeschylus, *317* | *Oresteia, 321* | *peripeteia, 329* |
| *tragoidia, 318* | City Dionysia, *321* | *anagnorisis, 329* |
| Sophocles, *318* | *episodes, 322* | *katastrophê, 329* |
| Euripides, *318* | *deus ex machina, 323* | *hamartia, 329* |
| dithyrambs, *319* | *agôn, 325* | Aristophanes, *331* |
| Thespis, *320* | *mimesis, 328* | Old Comedy, *332* |
| protagonist, *321* | *katharsis, 328* | |
| antagonist, *321* | dramatic need, *329* | |

## Further Reading

### GENERAL

Csapo, Eric, and W. J. Slater, *The Context of Ancient Drama* (Ann Arbor, MI, 1995).

Easterling, Pat, *Greek and Roman Actors: Aspects of an Ancient Profession* (Cambridge, UK, 2002). Superior modern study of many aspects of ancient drama.

### TRAGEDY

Easterling, Pat, ed., *The Cambridge Companion to Greek Tragedy* (Cambridge, UK, 1997). Excellent essays on tragedy as an institution, literary features of the plays, and reception since antiquity.

Else, Gerald F., *The Origin and Early Form of Greek Tragedy* (New York, 1972). Presents Thespis as the inventor of Greek tragedy.

Goldhill, Simon, *Reading Greek Tragedy* (Cambridge, UK, 1986). No-nonsense introduction to tragedy, aimed at students more familiar with English literature.

Pickard-Cambridge, Arthur W., *Dithyramb, Tragedy, and Comedy,* ed. T. B. L. Webster, 2nd ed. (Oxford, 1962). Thorough treatment of the evidence; indispensable to the study of the subject.

West, M. L., *Ancient Greek Music* (Oxford, 1992). The definitive study, but tough to read.

Winkler, John J. and Froma I. Zeitlin, eds., *Nothing to Do with Dionysus? Athenian Drama in Its Social Context* (Princeton, 1990). Collection of modern essays addressing the ritual and sociological settings of Athenian drama.

### COMEDY

Bowie, A. M., *Aristophanes: Myth, Ritual, and Comedy* (Cambridge, UK, 1993).

Cartledge, P. A., *Aristophanes and His Theatre of the Absurd* (Bristol, UK, 1990).

Dover, K. J., *Aristophanic Comedy* (Berkeley, 1972). Pathbreaking analysis of the structures of Old Comedy.

Ehrenberg, V., *The People of Aristophanes,* 2nd ed. (Oxford, 1951). Readable survey looking at Aristophanes' characters as evidence for everyday life in Athens.

### ANCIENT TEXTS

Aeschylus, *Prometheus Bound and Other Plays,* tr. Philip Vellacott (Harmondsworth, UK, 1961) and *The Oresteia,* tr. Robert Fagles (New York, 1966).

Aristophanes, *The Frogs and Other Plays,* tr. David Barrett (New York, 1964), *Lysistrata and Other Plays,* tr. Alan Sommerstein (New York, 1973), and *The Birds and Other Plays,* tr. David Barrett and Alan Sommerstein (New York, 1978).

Euripides, *The Bacchae and Other Plays,* tr. Philip Vellacott (Harmondsworth, UK, 1954) and *Alcestis and Other Plays,* tr. John Davie (New York, 1996).

Sophocles, *The Three Theban Plays,* tr. R. Fagles (Harmondsworth, UK, 1947) and *Electra and Other Plays,* tr. E. F. Watling (Harmondsworth, UK, 1982).

## CHAPTER 16

# The Peloponnesian War and its Aftermath, 431–399 B.C.

The Peloponnesian War was an unmitigated disaster, destroying hundreds of thousands of lives and the accumulated wealth of decades. Athens' evolution toward a unified Aegean state collapsed; Greece would never become a nation-state. It was an unmitigated catastrophe for the Greek people; the very ideals of freedom and responsibility that made Greece great also destroyed her. Persia reentered the Aegean. Much of Sicily ended up paying tribute to Carthage, while Syracuse chafed under the strongest tyrant Greece ever saw. None of the politicians who led their states to war wanted or expected these outcomes.

Yet Thucydides says that even in 431 B.C., when the war began, the calamitous nature of the coming conflict was clear:

> Thucydides the Athenian wrote up the war between the Peloponnesians and the Athenians, how they fought against one another. He began his account almost immediately when the war broke out, for he foresaw that it would be a great war, one more worthy of remark than any fought before. His reasons for thinking this is that both parties were at the peak of their powers and elaborately prepared, and the other Greek states had either thrown in their lot with one side or the other or were preparing to do so. It was the greatest disturbance ever among the Hellenes and as great as you may find in any foreign land, or even in the whole world.
>
> Thucydides 1.1

Thucydides wrote or revised his account after the war's end in 404 B.C.; perhaps he credited himself with more foresight than he really had. But some Athenians and Spartans definitely opposed the war from the beginning, and debate was fierce.

In 431 B.C. Athens dominated the sea; Sparta, the land. The challenge was to convert control of one element into victory on the other. The twenty-seven-year struggle that followed was bewilderingly complicated but consisted of efforts by each side to do just this.

This famous war had three successive phases. The first (431–421 B.C.) is called the *Archidamian War*, after Archidamus, the Spartan king who invaded Attica each summer. The second phase (421–413 B.C.), known as the *Peace of Nicias*, begins with a treaty negotiated by the Athenian aristocratic leader **Nicias** (nis- ē-as) and ends with Athens' defeat at Syracuse. The final phase, called the *Ionian War* because most action took place off the Ionian coast, dragged on from 412 to 404 B.C. After Athens' defeat in 404–, civil war broke out in Athens, bringing in its train the execution in 399 B.C. of Socrates, one of Greece's most original thinkers. Four hundred miles away, in 409 B.C., Carthage invaded an exhausted Sicily, triggering wars that raged throughout the next century. It was an exciting but terrible time to be alive, and nothing was the same after the Peloponnesian War.

## THE ARCHIDAMIAN WAR, 431–421 B.C.

Pericles led Athens to war, but to do so he had to persuade the Assembly he could win it. As he saw things, the **Archidamian War** broke out because Sparta saw that Athens, left alone, would keep centralizing power until she became irresistibly strong (Map 16.1). For Athens, "winning" simply meant avoiding defeat; stalemate would leave Athens free to resume centralization and would mean certain ruin for Sparta.

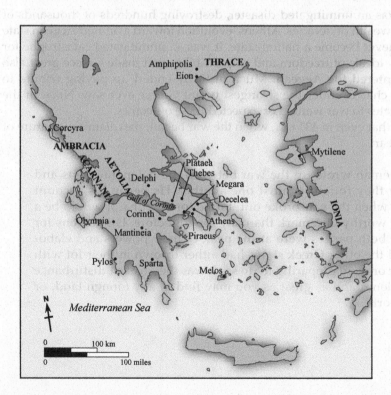

**MAP 16.1** The Archidamian War and the Peace of Nicias. Aegean sites mentioned in this chapter.

Pericles proposed a simple, two-part plan. First, stay behind the walls, keep the subject cities paying for the fleet, and use the fleet to protect the grain supply. Second, harass the enemy's coasts, seize offshore islands as bases, and keep up the military pressure. The Persian Wars consisted of a few key battles, but this would be a war of attrition. Eventually, Sparta would tire, back off, and Athens could resume her inexorable expansion, Pericles thought.

## First Struggles

In summer 431 B.C., as its first act of aggression, the Spartan army invaded Attica, burned and plundered, then halted outside the city's walls. Sparta's strategy was to provoke Athens into a pitched battle. Sparta's superior hoplites would then triumph, and Sparta could command the empire's dissolution. But the Athenians stayed behind the city walls and the Long Walls, secure in their access to the sea. The Spartans burned and plundered the countryside, then marched home. What else could they do? They returned in 430 B.C., and again in 429, and every year, but (as in the Greek siege of Troy) they made no headway against the fortifications. So long as the grain ships kept coming from the Black Sea and landing in PIRAEUS, and the supplies were transported to the city through the Long Walls, Sparta could not defeat Athens

In traditional Greek warfare, one hoplite army invaded enemy territory and another marched out to stop it. The Athenians (like Odysseus) suppressed their anger as the Spartans burned crops and farmhouses, seeing the further purpose. However, the crowding of refugees from the countryside into the space between the Long Walls created highly unsanitary conditions, and in the heat of summer in 430 B.C., plague broke out. One in four Athenians died. The Athenians turned on Pericles. Morale sank and Athens sued for peace in 430 B.C., just one year after the war began. Receiving no reply from Sparta, the Assembly dismissed Pericles as general and fined him. Even so, they kept pursuing his strategy, then voted him back into office. But Pericles himself died of the plague in 429 B.C. In understanding Thucydides' penetrating account, we might call this the law, in history, of unforeseen consequences. Pericles had planned everything out, but something happened that he did not foresee—his own death when he was most needed. Some critics have seen in Sophocles' *Oedipus the King*, probably performed soon after Pericles' death, a direct reflection of this subject. Oedipus was a wise and great leader, but a plague fell on the city and something unforeseen happened that brought destruction: He murdered his own father and married his own mother.

Thucydides saw the seeds of Athens' defeat in Pericles' unforeseen death:

> His successors did exactly the opposite [of Pericles' policy]. In matters unrelated to the war they conducted policy in a way friendly to their own interests and to their own profit, but with harmful effects upon the Athenians and upon the allies. When such schemes went well, they enhanced their own station and wealth, but when they went badly they harmed the overall war-effort.

As in tragedy, defeat followed from *hamartia*, a great mistake:

> His successors were more on a par with one another, and each strove constantly to become number one. In so doing they gave into demagoguery and lost control of affairs. From this situation arose many mistakes [*hêmartêthê*], but above all the expedition to Sicily [in 415–413 B.C.]. It was not so much a mistake [*hamartêma*]

about the character of the enemy against whom they sailed, as it was the mistaken failure of the city to support the troops properly once they had been sent abroad. Through constant striving to gain position within the state, the politicians allowed the campaign to lose its impetus and confusion to reign in state policy. Yet, after losing everything in Sicily, including most of the fleet, and with revolution breaking out in the city, the Athenians held out for eight more years against their original enemies, now joined by the Sicilians, with most of their allies in revolt, and with Cyrus, son of the Persian king, now providing money to build a Peloponnesian fleet. In the end it was because of their own internal strife that the Athenians fell.

Thucydides 2.65

After Pericles died, his quarreling successors abandoned his limited war aims. Instead of just trying to outlast Sparta, they pursued high-risk strategies aiming actually to destroy Sparta and the Peloponnesian League.

The Spartans also explored new strategies in the 420s B.C. Invading Attica by land was not winning the war, so Sparta looked to her ally Corinth to provide the nucleus of a fleet to defeat Athens at sea. In 429 B.C., the year that Pericles died, the Corinthians engaged the Athenian fleet in the Gulf of Corinth. Fearing the Athenians' famous skill, the Corinthians formed a circle, rams facing out. The Athenians responded by sailing round and round the circle, occasionally darting in to threaten a ship. One after another, the Corinthian ships backed water to avoid being rammed until they backed into each other, entangling their sterns and losing all order. The Athenians then wiped them out.

After this, Sparta avoided naval engagements. When Athens' important ally Mytilenê (the main city on the island of Lesbos just off the coast of Asia Minor, opposite ancient Troy), revolted in 427 B.C., Sparta offered support but was too afraid of Athens' fleet to deliver any. Pericles' successors became more aggressive, hoping to find allies among the warlike peoples in the western parts of mainland Greece (Acarnania, Aetolia, Ambracia: Map 16.1) who could provide enough troops to defeat Sparta in battle. The imaginative Athenian general **Demosthenes** (not the same as the famous orator Demosthenes, whom we will discuss in Chapter 19, "The Warrior-Kings of Macedon, 359–323 B.C.") apparently hoped to use these new allies to force Boeotia and then Corinth onto Athens' side and then defeat Sparta. His plan seemed to be working until 424 B.C., when the Boeotians shattered Athens' new alliance with the western Greeks in a pitched battle.

Thwarted in western mainland Greece, the Athenians looked still further west, to Sicily (see Map 16.2). As we saw in Chapter 13, "Democracy and Empire: Athens and Syracuse, 479–431 B.C.," Syracuse was reviving as a major power in the 430s B.C., and in 427 a general Sicilian war broke out. The Dorian cities sided with Syracuse (founded by Dorian Corinth) against the Ionian cities. Ionian Leontini north of Syracuse, a victim of Syracusan aggression, invoked its treaty of 433 B.C. with Athens, inviting an Aegean power for the first time to intervene in western struggles. By 424 B.C. Athens had sixty ships and as many as 10,000 men in Sicily. Alarmed by Athens' imperial intentions, both Ionian and Dorian Sicilians called a secret congress, where, Thucydides says, Hermocrates of Syracuse (about whom we hear more later) delivered this warning:

We should remember, if we are sensible, that we are meeting not about the affairs of individual cities, as it seems to me, but about whether we can save all of Sicily, on which the Athenians have fixed their sights. We ought to

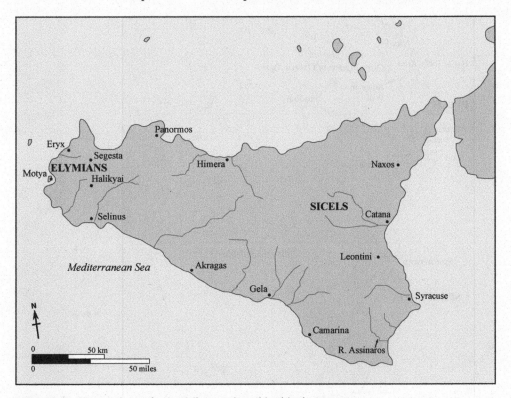

**MAP 16.2**  Sites and peoples in Sicily mentioned in this chapter.

consider the Athenians themselves to be far more forceful arguments for peace than anything I might say. They are the greatest power in Greece, and now they are here with but a few ships, watching to see if we make a mistake, and although we are by nature their enemy, under the guise of a lawful alliance they hope to turn things to their own advantage. If we war against one another and invite them in, who are happy to interfere militarily even when they are not summoned; and if we weaken ourselves at our own expense and do the preliminary work of empire on their behalf—when they see that we are weakened they will return with a larger force and endeavor to place us all under their control.

Thucydides 4.60

The Sicilian cities concluded a general peace and sent the Athenians away. When Athens' generals got home, the Assembly prosecuted them for taking bribes because the democratic Assembly wondered: Why else did they fail to conquer Sicily and bring back its hoplites to turn against Sparta? Confident as ever, Athens tried to raise another anti-Syracusan alliance in 422 B.C., but this too failed. Even Athens' vast wealth could not support strategic initiatives on this scale, although in 427 B.C. Athens had introduced new taxes and in 425 tripled the tribute from the subject cities. But despite all these efforts, Athens still gained no advantage over Sparta.

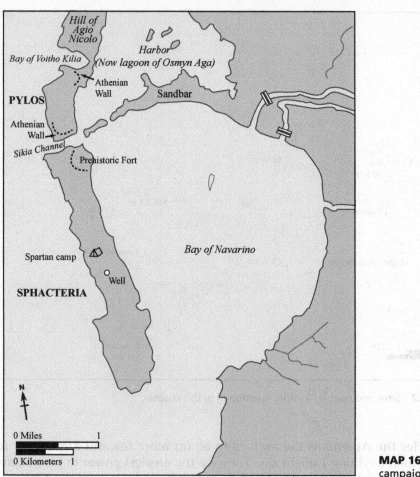

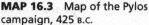

**MAP 16.3** Map of the Pylos campaign, 425 B.C.

## Pylos

In the end, it was a stroke of luck that gave Athens the upper hand in the Archidamian War. During a routine mission harassing the coast of the Peloponnesus in 425 B.C., Demosthenes noticed that the northern headland on the bay of **Pylos** (present-day Bay of Navarino), near the famous Bronze Age palace of Homer's Nestor, would make a good base for raiding Sparta and encouraging the helots to revolt. Demosthenes landed a small force and hastily fortified the headland with a wall of driftwood (Map 16.3). When the Spartans heard about this, they cut short that summer's invasion of Attica and rushed back to the Peloponnesus. Terrified that the Athenian base would inspire an uprising of helots, the Spartans

> made a proclamation that the helots should choose from among their number those who, in their view, had done the most for Sparta in war, as if the Spartans were going to set them free. It was a test conducted under Spartan conviction that those who thought they should first be set free were the very ones most

likely to revolt. The helots chose two thousand men. Crowned with garlands, they marched around the temples, thinking they were being set free. But the Spartans soon got rid of every one of them, though no one knew how they died.

Thucydides 4.80

The Spartans sailed their own small fleet into the Bay of Navarino, whose outlet is blocked by the long narrow island of **Sphacteria**, except for passageways at either end of the island. They landed 420 hoplites on the island, hoping to barricade the channels at either end so that Athenian ships could not sail into the bay. The Spartans then sailed up to the Athenian fort on the mainland opposite the northern tip of the island (on the modern Sikia Channel) and tried to force a landing. The Spartan general **Brasidas**, who commanded one ship, was wounded several times trying to establish a bridgehead. Thucydides noted the peculiarity of this fight,, in which Athenians were fighting on land, and Spartan land at that, while the Spartans attacked their own land, now hostile to them, from the sea!

After three days of inconclusive fighting, the Athenian fleet, which had sailed farther north after leaving Demosthenes on the headland, returned. The Spartans had not got around to barricading the entrances to the bay. The Athenian ships sailed in, destroyed the Spartan ships, and by encircling the island with their ships, trapped the 420 hoplites on Sphacteria.

The besiegers had become the besieged. The 420 Spartiates trapped on Sphacteria made up about 10 percent of the entire Spartan citizen body, and their loss would be a tremendous blow. Sparta immediately requested a truce. In Athens, the demagogue **Cleon**, a popular speaker at the height of his influence, persuaded the Assembly to reject the offer, certain that once Athens held the Spartiates hostage, she would get much better terms. Capturing them, however, would not be easy. The Athenians' position at Pylos was almost as difficult as the Spartans' position. Pro-Spartan helots dived beneath the encircling Athenian ships to bring food and water onto Sphacteria, while the Athenian besiegers grew short of both. As the crisis dragged on, the Assembly turned on Cleon, who had opposed the initial Spartan offer of peace. A heated Assembly debate rapidly spun out of control:

Cleon pointed to Nicias, son of Niceratus, who was general at the time and whom he hated and blamed for the situation. He said it would be easy to sail with a force to the island and capture those who were on it, if the generals were real men, and that if he had been in charge, he would have done just that.

The Athenians murmured against Cleon, saying that if he thought it was so easy, then he should sail there himself. Nicias, seeing that he was the object of attack, said that as far as the generals were concerned, Cleon should take whatever force he wished and try his own hand. At first Cleon thought that he was just saying this and so was ready to accept the offer, but when he realized that Nicias was serious in giving him the command, he tried to back out of it, and said that Nicias, not he, was the general. He was now thoroughly frightened, for he never thought that Nicias would go so far as to give up his post. Again Nicias repeated his offer and stood down from his command at Pylos, taking the Athenians as witness.

The more Cleon tried to get out of sailing to Pylos, the more he tried to take back his words, the more the crowd, in typical fashion, shouted to Nicias to give up his command and to Cleon to sail. Because he was unable to take back his words, Cleon at last agreed to undertake the voyage.

Thucydides 4.27–28

Just before Cleon arrived at Sphacteria, a fire broke out on the island, driving the Spartans to the cliffs on the northern tip. Cut off from water and food, with no prospect of resupply, to Greece's astonishment, the 120 surviving Spartiates surrendered to the demagogue Cleon. No Spartiate had ever surrendered before.

## Brasidas in Thrace

Invasions of Attica were fruitless, and since 429 B.C. Sparta had avoided challenging Athens at sea. By 424 B.C., she had approached Persia to finance a fleet against Athens, but was rebuffed. In 424 B.C., the ingenious Brasidas, who had attacked Demosthenes' fortifications at Pylos, had a bright idea. Realizing that some of Athens' richest subjects were on the mainland of northern Greece, not protected by the sea, he proposed that the Spartan army should attack them . Dubious of his strategy, fearful of his personality, and depressed by the Pylos incident, the Ephors refused to let Brasidas take any Spartiates north. Undeterred, he set off anyway with just 700 helots and a 1,000 mercenaries. Passing undiscovered through pro-Athenian territories, he suddenly showed up outside Amphipolis, the most important city in the northern region (Map 16.1), and offered generous terms for its surrender.

Athens sent Thucydides (author of the famous *History*) with ships and men to relieve the city, but hours before he arrived Amphipolis went over to Sparta. Thucydides (4.106) reports dispassionately that "thus was the city surrendered, and late that day Thucydides sailed into Eion with his ships [at the mouth of the Strymon River, which flows into the Aegean from the interior of Thrace three miles downriver from Amphipolis]. As for Amphipolis, Brasidas had just taken it, and would on the next night have taken Eion too. If the ships had not arrived so quickly to relieve it, Eion would have been in his hands by dawn." For his failure at Amphipolis, the Athenian Assembly exiled Thucydides for twenty years. He used this time to write his path-breaking *History,* one of the great intellectual achievements of the classical cultural revolution.

The fall of Amphipolis shocked the Athenians, who sent Cleon with a large force to regain it. In a great battle outside Amphipolis in 422 B.C., both Cleon and Brasidas were killed. As Aristophanes put it in one of his comedies (*Peace*), "the two pestles that mixed up the war were broken," and the struggle in the north Aegean fizzled out.

Athens and Sparta were exhausted. Despite ten years of bloody sacrifice, neither had found a strategy that delivered victory. In 421 B.C. the aristocratic Nicias, formerly the bitter enemy of the now-dead Cleon, negotiated a settlement and the return of the 120 Spartiates captured at Pylos several years before. The settlement is called the Peace of Nicias. On Pericles' terms, Athens had won: Sparta had failed to break up the empire. The ten years of the Archidamian War, though, had created such deep divisions that few Greeks seriously thought the struggle was over.

## Toward Total War

As Athens and Sparta had pursued their ineffective strategies, they had grown increasingly desperate and ruthless, a deterioration that Thucydides understood as a natural and inevitable consequence of all-out war. When the island of Mytilenê near the Ionian coast had revolted against Athens in 427 B.C., the Athenians had quickly crushed the rebellion, but it had shocked and unnerved them. They could not afford to fight many uprisings like this. To set an example, the Assembly angrily voted to kill all the men in Mytilenê and sell the women and children into slavery: They deserved it for their treachery! The Assembly dispatched a squadron to carry out the order.

Then, on the next day, stricken with remorse, the Council of 500 called a second Assembly meeting. Cleon defended the original decision, but a certain Diodotos, otherwise unknown, spoke vigorously against it. If rebels knew they would die whatever they did, he pointed out, there would be no incentive for them to surrender, and they would fight to the death. Such behavior is not good for empire. Also, with everyone dead, there would be no one to pay taxes.

The Athenians relented, rescinded the order, and sent out a fast ship to overtake the earlier one. The second ship reached Mytilenê just as the executions were about to begin. According to the new order, they were now to slaughter only 1,000 of the leading citizens, and, through the generosity of the Athenian people, the others would be spared. It is striking that Cleon and Diodotos both argued in terms of expediency—what would help Athens win the war—not in terms of right and wrong or what would please the gods. The *Realpolitik* in Thucydides gives his story an arresting modernity.

Immediately after describing the cold-blooded debate over Mytilenê, Thucydides turns to Spartan crimes at Plataea, the only community that had helped Athens at the battle of Marathon in 490 B.C. In 427 B.C. Sparta captured Plataea, now allied with Athens. The Spartans put the Plataeans on trial, asking each man one question: "What have you done to help the Spartans and their allies in the present war?" Of course they had done nothing. The Spartans executed the 225 captured men and sold the women and children into slavery. Neither side in this war had a moral edge.

The war's mounting brutality inflamed the conflicts within elites and between rich and poor that had divided *poleis* since archaic times. In 427 B.C. a pro-Athenian democratic faction on the island of Corcyra off the northwest coast of Greece (modern Corfu) defeated its aristocratic rivals in street fighting, then slaughtered everyone they could get their hands on. In one of his most vivid passages, Thucydides describes the breakdown of traditional values in the midst of civil war:

> The Corcyraeans went on killing those of their own citizens whom they considered to be enemies. The cause, they said, was their hostility to the *dêmos,* but in reality many died because of personal hatred or because they owed someone money. There was death in every form. And as usually happens in such cases, people went to every extreme and even beyond. Fathers killed sons. Some were dragged from the temples or slaughtered within. Some were walled up in the temple of Dionysus and died there.
>
> Such was the savagery of this civil strife, and it seemed all the worse because it was among the first. Later, of course, such disturbances appeared everywhere in Greece. There were rival parties in every state. The democrats

strove to bring in the Athenians, while the oligarchs tried to enlist the Spartans. In time of peace there would have been no pretext for doing this, nor would any one want to, but in time of war each party sought through forming alliances to harm its opponents and aggrandize its own power. For those hoping to establish a new government, it became a natural course to bring in help from the outside.

Civil strife caused these and many other calamities in many cities, such as always happens and always will happen so long as human nature remains what it is, though of course some evils were worse than others, and evil took on many forms in accordance with ever-shifting circumstance. In times of peace and prosperity both cities and individuals act in accordance with higher standards, when they are not in a position of having to do what they do not want to do. For war is a stern teacher. By depriving one of daily necessities, war brings one's mind down to a contemplation of what is actually there.

And so revolution broke out in many cities. In places where it broke out late, knowledge of what had gone before exaggerated revolutionary zeal and introduced fresh methods for seizing power and intensified the cruelties inflicted to take revenge.

Words changed their meaning to suit with changed events. What was once thought to be a thoughtless act of aggression became the courage one expects in a party member. To give careful thought for the future now was nothing but cowardice. To be moderate was to be unmanly. The ability to examine a question from all sides was proof that one was unfit for action. Wild fanaticism was the portion of a real man. To plot against someone in secret was a legitimate means of defense . . .

The cause and origin of all these evils was greed and a striving for status. Once strife broke out, a violent fanaticism came into play. Leaders of the parties in the cities placed forth programs that sounded fine—equality for the masses, on one side, and reasonable governance by the aristocracy, on the other—but while they professed to be working for the public good, in reality they struggled to win the prizes for themselves. They committed the most heinous acts and in taking revenge did things still worse. They cared nothing for justice or for the advantage of the city. They cared only for what brought pleasure to their own faction. Either by condemning the allies through an illegal vote, or asserting power over them through violence, they were ready to fulfill the hatred of the moment. They had no use for conscientious motives but were rather more interested in the man who through clever speech could justify some outrageous act. Those with moderate views were destroyed by both extremes, either because they wanted them to participate, or from envy that they might somehow survive.

In this way came a general deterioration of character throughout the Greek world because of civil strife [stasis]. The simple way of seeing things, which is the mark of nobility, was laughed at and ceased to exist. The world was divided into two mutually hostile camps.

Thucydides 3.81–83

Only victory mattered. Massacres, enslavements, and betrayals were simply tools. He who did not use them in pursuit of his own interests was a fool.

## THE PEACE OF NICIAS AND THE SICILIAN EXPEDITION, 421–413 B.C.

The **Peace of Nicias**, concluded in 421 B.C., stopped the fighting between Athens and Sparta but left too many things unsettled to bring real peace to Greece. The terms required Sparta to return Amphipolis to Athens, but Amphipolis refused to accept Athens' control, so Athens responded by keeping its fortress at Pylos. The treaty ignored Sparta's allies Corinth, Thebes, and Megara, who refused to sign. War smoldered on in some areas. Spartan allies spoke of breaking from Sparta and even joining Athens.

Within Athens, a young man in his late twenties named **Alcibiades** (al-si-bī-a-dēz), an Alcmaeonid, felt personally insulted by the treaty that Nicias had negotiated with Sparta. His family once represented Spartan interests in Athens, and Alcibiades thought that he, not Nicias, should have negotiated the peace. His family also gave him strong connections with leading men in other cities, and he set about undermining the fragile peace. Alcibiades was one of the extraordinary personalities of this period.

Working independently of the Assembly, Alcibiades put together an alliance between Athens, Argos, and other Peloponnesian cities. He achieved by diplomacy what Athens had failed to do in the Archidamian War, assembling such a threatening army that in 418 B.C. Sparta felt compelled to risk her very survival on a single hoplite battle against the allied army at Mantineia in the Peloponnesus. Athens, by contrast, risked very little: only 1,300 of the hoplites in the allied army were Athenians.

The battle of Mantineia showed Sparta's strengths and weaknesses. As at Plataea in 479 B.C., stubborn officers ignored orders they did not like, and when the armies clashed, the Spartan line was already in fragments. Nonetheless the ferocious Spartans stood their ground and cut down all who came against them. Alcibiades' alliance might have broken the power of Sparta, but by winning the hoplite battle at Mantineia, Sparta in fact restored much of the prestige and influence she had lost at Pylos.

### The Massacre at Melos

Still jockeying for position against Sparta, in 416 B.C. Athens decided to force the small independent Cycladic island of **Melos** to join the empire and pay tribute (Map 16.1). The Melians had done nothing against Athens, but the Athenians worried that the mere existence of an independent island implied Athenian weakness. Athens gave Melos an ultimatum: Join the Athenian league or be destroyed. The Melians replied that they had a defensive alliance with Sparta, who would protect them, and that because they had done no wrong, they would trust in the gods. In a portion of his *History* known as the "Melian Dialogue," Thucydides has the Athenian embassy reply with a chilling statement of the way things are in the world of secular power:

> We have no reason to think that we are any less in the gods' esteem than you are. We neither intend nor do we behave in a way inconsistent with the beliefs men hold about the gods, nor do we act differently than they do toward themselves. For we believe that both in the view of the gods and in the view of men the necessity of nature insures that one rules over what he controls. We did not devise this law, nor are we the first to act upon it when it was made. We found it already in existence. Leaving it to be true in the future, we act upon it now, knowing that you and others, were they in the same position of power, would do just the same.

They gave the Melians some advice:

> We advise you to take what you can from the situation, in view of what we both really think about it. For in dealing with practical people, we both know that justice in human affairs depends on the balance of power, and that the strong do what they can, while the weak do what they must.
>
> Thucydides 5.105, 89

The Melians nonetheless rejected Athens' terms. There was a siege, betrayal from within, and a brutal outcome: "The Athenians put to death all the men of military age whom they took and sold the women and children as slaves. They took over Melos for themselves, sending out a colony of 500 men" (Thucydides 5.115). Sparta did nothing.

## The Decision to Attack Sicily, 415 B.C.

In 415 B.C., the Athenians decided on a new gamble to win the Peloponnesian War. Despite her setbacks in Sicily in the 420s B.C., Athens had in 418 or 417 B.C. made new alliances with the non-Greek Elymian cities of Segesta and Halikyai in western Sicily (Map 16.2). The powerful Greek city Selinus—formerly friendly with Carthage but now allied to Syracuse—was constantly trying to expand into Elymian territory, and in 416 B.C. the Elymians asked their old ally Carthage for help. The Carthaginians, seeing that intervention would lead to war with Syracuse, refused. Segesta then approached her new ally Athens, saying that if Athens pushed Selinus out of Elymian lands, Segesta would pay all the costs. An Athenian embassy went to Sicily to investigate Segestan resources, to see if they could really afford to fund such a war. Every night, the Athenian ambassadors dined off gold and silver plates in a different nobleman's house. The Athenians were so impressed that they not notice that there was only one set of plates, passed from house to house. Next, the Segestans showed the Athenians chests of gold and silver in the mountaintop sanctuary of Eryx. Under the top layer of riches there were just rocks, but the Athenians did not look beneath the surface.

The embassy's favorable report set Athens abuzz. The cautious Nicias opposed wild adventures in Sicily, but Alcibiades, undeterred by the defeat of his earlier schemes at the battle of Mantineia, saw in the Elymian appeal a way to conquer all of Sicily and then defeat Sparta. By 415 B.C., Alcibiades was young, rich, handsome, talented, and impossible to deal with:

> Alcibiades strongly supported the expedition, because he wished to oppose Nicias, with whom he differed in political matters, and he was mindful of a personal attack in a speech that Nicias gave. He wished very much to command the expedition, and he hoped that he would have the good fortune to conquer Sicily and Carthage and thus increase his stature through wealth and fame. For he was much in the public eye, and his expenditures from raising horses and other extravagances far exceeded his means. This personal situation had much to do with the downfall of Athens.

Many feared Alcibiades because of a quality in him that went beyond the normal, testified by the manner of his private life and the spirit he showed in everything he undertook. Thinking he wished to become a tyrant, they became his enemies. Although his public conduct of the war was excellent, the circumstances of his private life offended everyone. Thus the Assembly turned affairs over to other men and quickly ruined the city.

Thucydides 6.15

Nicias and Alcibiades had a furious argument in the Assembly, but Alcibiades convinced the Athenians to launch the grandest expedition in their history. Thucydides implies that the Athenians, like Xerxes before them, had lost all sense of the limits of their power. With Sparta bloodied but unbowed, Persia waiting in the wings, and Syracuse the third-greatest city in Greece, Alcibiades was talking about conquering all of Sicily, south Italy, and Carthage! But according to Thucydides, the Athenians were poorly informed about the size of the island, the numbers of its inhabitants, both Greek and native, and hardly suspected that they were taking on a war of almost the same magnitude as their unfinished war against Sparta.

Nicias tried to dissuade the Assembly by emphasizing what huge forces the expedition would require, but this only succeeded in fueling the Athenians' imperial desires:

A passion for the expedition seized everyone. The older men thought that they would either conquer their objective or at least that being so great a force they could come to no harm. The young longed to see the distant sights and places and had good hopes of returning safely. The masses and the common soldiers looked forward to being paid for the present and, in the future, after acquiring new territories, the promise of permanent employment.

Thucydides 6.24

The Assembly was uncomfortable with having either Nicias or Alcibiades as sole commander, but the pair could not work together, so the Assembly appointed *three* commanders: Nicias, Alcibiades, and one Lamachus, a grizzled veteran. The Athenians hoped that each man would compensate for the others' limitations, but instead, each came up with a different plan. Nicias said they should go to Segesta, quickly settle its war with Selinus, and come home. Alcibiades said they should send heralds to all Sicilian cities except Selinus and Syracuse, raise a general anti-Syracusan league, and conquer the whole island. Lamachus said they should go straight to Syracuse, take it by surprise, and storm it. Eventually, they agreed to Alcibiades' plan.

This expedition that first set sail was the most expensive and the most resplendent that ever, in all of Greece, set forth from a single city up until that time . . . To the rest of Greece it seemed more a demonstration of the power and wealth of Athens than a campaign against an enemy . . . And the expedition became famous not so much for its astonishing daring and its brilliant show as in the magnitude of its power when compared with that of its enemy, as well as the fact that it was the largest expedition ever to depart from Athens and that it was undertaken with the hope of things to come greater than what was at hand.

Thucydides 6.31

One morning just before the fleet was to sail, the Athenians woke up to a shocking sight. Outside Athenian houses were small statues called **herms**, which turned away evil. A herm (somehow related to the god Hermes) was a block of stone with a face and an erect penis (Figure 16.1). During the night, someone had taken chisels and mutilated the herms. The Athenians feared a plot against the democracy, because the herms symbolized the freedom, manhood, and equality of each Athenian citizen at the head of his household. The Assembly rounded up suspects and tortured slaves to gain evidence. They learned nothing about the mutilation but discovered that a group of young aristocrats had been parodying the rituals of Demeter at Eleusis ("the Eleusinian Mysteries") in drunken parties in their homes. Alcibiades belonged to this group.

Alcibiades' rivals waited until the fleet had sailed, then persuaded the Assembly to recall him to stand trial for his impious behavior. Most of Alcibiades' supporters were with the fleet and would not be able to help him. About to be arrested in southern Italy, Alcibiades jumped ship and fled to Sparta, where he received a warm welcome, with disastrous consequences for all.

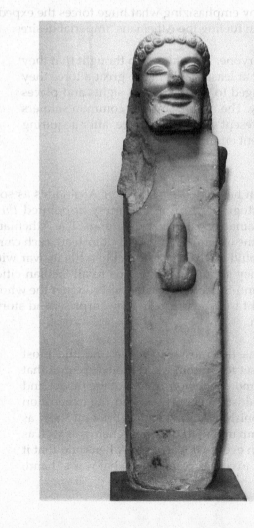

**FIGURE 16.1** Herm from Athens, ca. 520 B.C. This example was a hundred years old at the time of the Sicilian expedition.

## The Siege of Syracuse, 415–413 B.C.

Nicias and Lamachus persevered with Alcibiades' strategy. They hoped that the Sicilian cities would join Athens and that Syracuse would give up without a fight. Naxos, an Ionian city in eastern Sicily, welcomed the Athenians as saviors, but until some Athenians burst in through a badly closed gate, neighboring Catana refused them entrance, even though it was also Ionian. Segesta paid only half the money promised; in return, Athens did nothing to stop Selinus' war with Segesta. Everyone else turned the Athenians away. Sicilian Greeks feared Syracusan aggression, but they feared the Athenians even more.

Lamachus' strategy was probably the correct one. Many Syracusans did not believe the Athenians would attack, and a sudden assault might have broken through the dilapidated walls. Instead, Nicias wasted precious months sailing along the coast trying unsuccessfully to forge alliances. Not until winter did the Athenians assault Syracuse. They landed near the city and won a hoplite battle, but the city's walls were by now too strong to storm.

Winter passed. Sparta, on the advice of the vengeful Alcibiades, sent an energetic general named **Gylippus** (jī-**lip**-us) to assist the Syracusans. Also on Alcibiades' advice, Sparta fortified the hill of **Decelea** (de-se-**lē**-a) just a dozen miles north of Athens and garrisoned it year round (Map 16.1), forcing thousands of Athenian peasants to move permanently inside Athens' walls.

In Sicily, Nicias and Lamachus decided to invest Syracuse with a siege wall while the fleet cut off the city by sea (Map 16.4). Syracuse was as large as Athens, with 40,000 residents, and a tight siege would lead to starvation. The city occupied a small island, Ortygia, bridged to the mainland. To the south of the land bridge was the Great Harbor, spacious enough to receive a large fleet. Sea and seawalls surrounded the city, and just before the Athenians arrived, the Syracusans built walls on the land side and an attached looped double wall that ran along the foot of a steep hill north of the city called EPIPOLAI ("land above the city"): Whoever controlled Epipolai would control the city (Figure 16.2). The Athenians built a circle fort at the edge of Epipolai overlooking the city, then began constructing walls that extended out from the fort on both sides toward the sea, cutting the city off.

The Athenian walls quickly progressed. The Syracusans twice tried to build counterwalls cutting across the enemy's construction line at right angles (the standard defensive measure) but the Athenians stormed and destroyed them. Lamachus was killed in this fighting, but by now the Athenian siege wall was nearly complete. Only portions of the line proceeding north from the circle fort across Epipolai were incomplete. Syracuse seemed doomed.

But Nicias was not well, and without Lamachus to urge him on he allowed progress on the last stretch of the wall across Epipolai to slow to a crawl. When Gylippus, the Spartan commander, approached the city, he learned that the wall was still not complete. Rather than going straight to Syracuse, he sailed to Himera in northwestern Sicily, raised troops, then raced back to Syracuse and attacked from behind, breaking through the unfinished Athenian line and entering the city. The defenders now threw up a new counterwall onto Epipolai, and this time cut the Athenian line, preventing the city's envelopment (Map 16.5). A dozen Corinthian ships evaded the Athenian blockade and sailed into Syracuse's Great Harbor, where on the city side of the harbor the Syracusans were building new ships to challenge the Athenians at sea. The Athenians, meanwhile, had no good beach to bring their own ships ashore, and their waterlogged hulls were starting to decay.

At the close of summer 414 B.C., Nicias realized the siege was failing. He sent a letter to Athens with an ultimatum: Either send out another force as great as the original, he

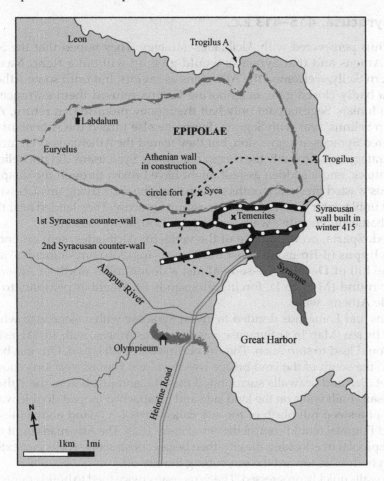

**MAP 16.4** The first phase of the siege of Syracuse, 415 B.C. The Athenian wall progresses, and Syracusan counterwalls fail.

said, or let him withdraw. Either way, he would resign the command because of ill health. The Assembly voted to send Demosthenes with a new force, but Nicias, they insisted, must remain in command.

Gylippus tightened his grip, capturing Nicias' forts guarding the south end of the Great Harbor. He seized large Athenian stores there, and newly built Syracusan ships intercepted and destroyed a convoy bringing timber for the Athenian fleet. Most of the non-Greek peoples of Sicily, who had suffered at the hands of Syracuse and Selinus, now supported Athens, but all the Greek cities on Sicily except Akragas supported Syracuse.

Gylippus no longer aimed just at saving Syracuse; he wanted to destroy the whole Athenian expeditionary force. He worked with feverish energy, inspiring the Syracusans. Recognizing that maneuverability was not very important for ships fighting in the narrow spaces of the Great Harbor, Gylippus added heavy timbers to the prows of the Syracusan ships, and in a fierce battle the heavy Syracusan ships smashed the bows of the Athenian ships, sank many, and forced the Athenian fighters to take refuge within their defenses on land.

At this crucial moment, Demosthenes sailed into the Great Harbor with 73 new Athenian ships, 5,000 fresh hoplites, and many light infantry. Nicias' men rejoiced as the

**FIGURE 16.2** Syracuse as seen from Epipolai. Ortygia, covered by houses, can be seen on the left of the photo; in the center is the Great Harbor.

Syracusans, dismayed by the Athenian reinforcements, pulled back. But Demosthenes soon realized that the Athenian position remained critical: Their only chance for victory, in fact, was to break through the Syracusan counterwall on Epipolai and finish the encirclement. He gambled on a night attack. At first, all went well, but at the vital moment the Athenians fell into confusion and were driven off with heavy losses.

It was now impossible for Athens to take Syracuse. They must get away as quickly as possible, but Nicias, who at first deferred to Demosthenes, reasserted his authority. He insisted that traitors were about to betray Syracuse, and in any case he preferred an honorable death in Sicily to execution in Athens on charges of treason.

Vital days slipped away. Sickness spread and morale plummeted before Nicias finally conceded that Syracuse would not be betrayed to him. He agreed to retreat, but on the evening of August 27, 413 B.C., as the army was packing to pull out, there was an eclipse of the moon, "and Nicias," says Thucydides (7.50), "who was too much given to divination and such things, said that until they had waited the thrice nine days recommended by the soothsayers he would not even join in further discussion how the move should be made."

Twenty-seven days is a long time in any war. While Nicias indulged his superstition, Gylippus threw a pontoon bridge across the mouth of the Great Harbor, trapping the Athenian ships inside. The Athenians launched a final, desperate attack on the pontoons, as the two armies watched:

> While the two navies battled it out, neither gaining the advantage, great stress and anguish of soul befell the foot soldiers on either side, watching from the shore . . . for the Athenians, everything depended on the navy, and their fear for

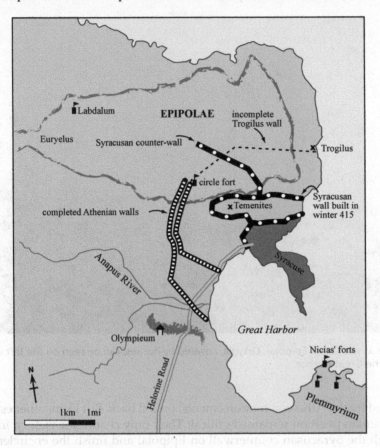

Labdalum
EPIPOLAE
incomplete Trogilus wall
Euryelus
Syracusan counter-wall
circle fort
X Trogilus
completed Athenian walls →
x Temenites
Syracusan wall built in winter 415
Anapus River
Syracuse
Olympieum
Great Harbor
Helorine Road
Nicias' forts
N
1km   1mi
Plemmyrium

**MAP 16.5** The second phase of the siege of Syracuse, 414 B.C. The Syracusan counterwall succeeds.

the future was unlike any they had ever known . . . So long as the naval battle remained in doubt, you could hear from the Athenian forces on land shouts of lamentation, "We are losing," then the chortling of victory, "We are winning," all mixed up and at the same time, and other such exclamations as are to be expected when a great army is in peril. The feelings of the men on the ships were much the same; until after the battle had lasted a long time the Syracusans and their allies broke the Athenian line and, laying hard upon them, with much shouting and abuse, drove them to the land.

Now the ships driven to land went some this way, some that, except for those captured on the water. The men leapt out and ran toward the camp. For the men on shore, the outcome had become certain, and with a single groan they bemoaned what had happened. Some ran down to help the men coming from the ships, while others took refuge behind the wall, while most contemplated what they might do to escape the situation alive. Never before had they experienced such a panic.

Thucydides 7.71

In the panic some 40,000 survivors in the Athenian force, stationed along the wall on the Epipolai and on the shore of the Great Harbor, abandoned the siege and marched north, hoping to fight their way through to CATANA, friendly to Athens (see Map 16.2). But the Syracusans had garrisoned the road, and after two days the Athenians turned back, now heading southwest for friendly CAMARINA on the south coast. Everywhere they went, Syracusan cavalry harassed them. Short of food and water under the baking September sun, they struggled as far as the swift-flowing River Assinaros (Map 16.2):

> The Athenians pressed on toward the river River Assinaros, being pressed hard on all sides by cavalry and a mass of troops on foot, thinking that it would go easier with them if they could cross the river. Also, they were exhausted and desired water.
>
> When they got there, they jumped in a chaotic mass. Each man wanted to get across first, but the enemy, lying in wait, made it hard for them to get across. Forced to crowd together, they fell in a mass upon one another and trampled one another underfoot. Some were entangled in their own equipment and died on their own spears, while others were caught up in the baggage and swept downstream. The Syracusans were stationed on the opposite bank, which was steep, and they hurled down weapons on the Athenians, most of whom in complete disorder were greedily drinking in the deep river bed. The Peloponnesians came down and killed them, especially those in the river. The water was soon polluted, mixed with mud and blood, but they drank it nonetheless. In fact most of them fought one another to get at it.
>
> Thucydides 7.84

More men died in the retreat than in the whole of the rest of the Sicilian campaign. The Syracusans captured Nicias and Demosthenes and put them to the sword on the spot. They herded the 7,000 or so survivors into deep stone quarries outside Syracuse (Figure 16.3):

> There were many of them crowded together into a narrow hole. First the sun and then the closeness of the air afflicted them, for there was no roof. With autumn came cold nights that from the change of temperature plunged them into disease. There was no space, so they had to do everything in one place, and then there were the heaps of bodies all around them, of those who had died of their wounds or from the change in temperature or something else. The stench was unbearable. At the same time they suffered from hunger and thirst. For eight months they received one half small jar of water per day and a small jar of grain. Every evil happened that you can imagine might happen to men in such a situation . . .
>
> This was the greatest event of the war or of any action that ever took place among the Greeks, as far as we know. To the victors it was the most brilliant success, and to the vanquished the most bitter defeat. They were utterly defeated, in every way, and their suffering immense, a complete catastrophe: soldiers and ships, all perished. From many, few returned.
>
> So much for the affairs in Sicily.
>
> Thucydides 7.87

**FIGURE 16.3**   The quarries at Syracuse where the Athenian prisoners were held captive.

## SICILY AND THE CARTHAGINIAN WAR, 412–404 B.C.

If the powerful Syracusan fleet that crushed the Athenians in the Great Harbor had attacked Athens in full force in 412 B.C., it might have cut off the Athenian grain supply and ended the Peloponnesian War right then. Hermocrates, the veteran general who dominated the Syracusan democracy since the 420s B.C., was eager to do so. But the city was exhausted. Syracuse's democracy was as divided as Athens', and her leaders squandered their brilliant success by fighting among themselves. A powerful speaker named Diocles, who had distinguished himself during the siege, became the leading man in the Assembly and in 410 B.C. removed Hermocrates from the generalship. Most important of all, though, Syracuse failed to intervene in the Aegean Sea because war threatened from Carthage. As we have seen, Syracuse's war with Athens had begun in western Sicily in 416 B.C. when Selinus attacked the Elymian city of Segesta. Segesta had asked Carthage to help, but when Carthage refused, it appealed to Athens, who used the request as a pretext for attacking Syracuse. Now in 410 B.C. Selinus renewed its attack on Segesta, and this time Carthage agreed to help the Elymians.

   Unlike Athens, Carthage had no regular system of military funding. She paid for wars by selling treasure and raising loans, then hiring as many mercenaries as possible for as brief a time as possible. It took Carthage a year to prepare a force under these conditions, while recruiters traveled into Spain, Italy, and Libya. In 409 B.C., Carthage was ready to attack Selinus. The Greek cities, either complacent or bankrupt after defeating Athens, made no preparations. Carthage's general **Hannibal** (meaning "the god Baal has given me grace," a distant ancestor of the Hannibal who fought Rome between 218 and 201 B.C.) shipped perhaps 100,000 men and advanced siege machines to Sicily. In just nine days, he smashed through Selinus' defenses. Diodorus of Sicily gives a harrowing description of what happened then:

> Those of the Selinuntians who fled into the marketplace died fighting there. The barbarians scattered throughout the city and plundered the houses of their wealth. Some houses they burned with the occupants still in them, others they drove into the streets where they put them to sword without distinction to sex or age—children, infants, women, old men. They showed no compassion. They mutilated the bodies in accordance with the traditional practice of these people, and some went around with bunches of hands tied to their bodies. Others carried heads stuck on javelins and spears . . .
>
> The savagery of the barbarians did not spare freeborn youths or women, but imposed on these unlucky people hideous suffering. As the women contemplated their impending slavery in Carthage and foresaw themselves and their children without status and forced to endure the abuse of their masters, whose speech was unknown and whose nature was brutish, then they mourned for their living children as if they were dead.

Diodorus of Sicily 13.57–58

The Syracusans gathered their ships, and Diocles rushed troops to Akragas to oppose the Carthaginian advance. But Hannibal was eager to destroy Himera in the north, in vengeance for his grandfather Hamilcar's defeat there seventy-one years before, and as he advanced, 20,000 of the indigenous population joined him. The Sicilian natives had joined Athens against Syracuse in 415 B.C. too, and now Carthage seemed preferable to the Syracusan yoke. Hannibal won a fierce battle outside Himera's walls, and Diocles, worried that Hannibal would make a sudden raid on Syracuse, returned to Syracuse with half the Himerans, all he could get on his ships. Before he could return for the others, Hannibal took the city. He sacrificed 3,000 prisoners on the spot where Hamilcar had been killed in 480 B.C. Then:

> After Hannibal embarked his troops on warships and merchant ships, leaving behind sufficient troops to meet the needs of his allies, he set sail from Sicily. When he sailed into Carthage with much booty, they all came out to greet him and they praised him as one who had accomplished more than any general before him.

Diodorus of Sicily 13.62

The Carthaginian War might have ended there, leaving Syracuse free to seek revenge against Athens, but in 407 B.C. Hermocrates, the general who had led Syracuse's resistance against Athens and then been chased out by Diocles in 410 B.C., returned from exile. Backed by Persian gold, he hired 1,000 mercenaries, assembled refugees from Himera, and tried to force his way back into Syracuse. When he failed, he seized the ruins of Selinus. His ranks swollen by returning Seliuntians, he soon had 6,000 warriors. To raise money, he raided the Phoenician cities at MOTYA on the west coast and PANORMOS (modern Palermo) on the northwest (see Map 16.2). In a brilliant propaganda move he next collected the Syracusan corpses that still lay on the battlefield at Himera and brought them back to Syracuse for proper burial, upstaging his rival in the city Diocles. The Syracusans voted to exile Diocles, just as Hermocrates had hoped, but they still refused to recall Hermocrates himself. Desperate, Hermocrates launched a coup in Syracuse, but was killed in the fighting that followed.

Hermocrates' wild ambition had scared the Syracusans but it had alarmed Carthage even more. Hannibal decided that only complete victory over Sicily's Greeks could stabilize the situation. With Himilco, probably his cousin, he raised another 100,000 mercenaries and in 406 B.C. attacked Akragas, perhaps the richest of all the Greek cities. Akragas had stayed out of recent wars, and its landowners had profited immensely from selling wine and olive oil to Carthage.

Akragas fell after an eight-month siege. Panic spread through Greek Sicily. Some of the richer Greeks fled to south Italy, while the Syracusans blamed each other for the disasters. Early in 405 B.C., a former follower of Hermocrates named **Dionysius** (aged just twenty-five) harnessed popular anger against the generals and persuaded the Assembly to recall its exiles, who were then under obligation to Dionysius personally. The democratic Assembly appointed Dionysius as the sole general with complete authority and a bodyguard of 600 (always sign of an approaching tyranny).

After destroying Akragas, Himilco now put Gela under siege and defeated Dionysius when he came to its relief. Dionysius told the people of Gela and Camarina that he could not save them; their only option was to fall back on Syracuse. With each Greek city that Carthage destroyed, refugees fled to Syracuse, and Syracuse became ever stronger. Dionysius was playing a cunning double game: If Syracuse could survive the impending Carthaginian attack, he would be left as the sole ruler of the only major Greek city in Sicily.

For the second time in a decade, Syracuse was besieged, but Himilco found the location as difficult as had Nicias. Plague broke out in the Carthaginian camp, and late in 405 B.C. or early in 404 Himilco made peace with Syracuse. Greek refugees could return to Selinus, Himera, Akragas, Gela, and Camarina, but they could not have fortifications and they had to pay tribute to Carthage. The other Greek cities and the native Sicels were to be autonomous.

The Carthaginian War of 409-404 B.C. left Dionysius dominant in Syracuse and left Syracuse dominant in Greek Sicily. It also, though, prevented Syracuse from finishing off Athens, giving the Athenians one last chance to win the Peloponnesian War.

## THE IONIAN WAR, 412–404 B.C.

The scale of Athens' losses in the Sicilian expedition of 415 to 413 B.C. was gigantic. In 412 B.C., Athens had barely a handful of hoplites, no ships in the docks, no crews to man them, and no money to pay for more. If Sparta could cut off the grain from the Black Sea, Athens would starve. If the grain kept coming, Athens might yet fight Sparta to a standstill. The strategic crux was the narrow Hellespont straits, linking the Black Sea to the Aegean (Map 16.6; Figure 16.4).

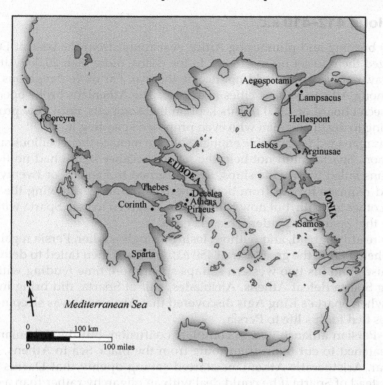

**MAP 16.6**  The Ionian War.
Sites mentioned in this chapter.

**FIGURE 16.4**  The Dardanelles (the modern strait of Canakkale). The European shore and the narrow entrance to the straits are clearly visible from the Asian shore.

## Athens' Dark Hour, 412–410 B.C.

The Spartans were burning and plundering Attica year round from the base at Decelea that Alcibiades urged them to set up in 415 B.C. In the chaos, more than 20,000 Athenian slaves had run away. But Decelea would not decide the war. Far more dangerous was a wave of revolts among Athens' subject cities in 412 B.C. The Athenians broke open their "Iron Reserve," a secret hoard of 1,000 talents kept on the Acropolis, until now protected by a law condemning to death any man who even proposed spending it.

The Athenians managed to assemble enough ships to menace the rebellious subjects back into submission. Sparta could not help the rebels, because it still had no fleet; so when the Syracusans failed to provide ships, Sparta turned to Persia. For twenty years Persia had ignored requests for aid from both Athens and Sparta, allowing the Greek cities to bleed each other to death, but now King Darius II agreed to help Sparta with gold on one condition—that Sparta surrender Ionia to Persia.

The Spartans readily agreed, and without losing a single soldier, Persia regained in 412 the position it held before the great war of 480 B.C. Darius II then failed to deliver the gold that he promised and his two western satraps spent more time feuding with each other than helping Sparta defeat Athens. Alcibiades, still in Sparta, did bring in some Persian gold, but when Sparta's King Agis discovered that Alcibiades was sleeping with his wife, Alcibiades fled for his life to Persia.

The Spartan–Persian alliance was in complete confusion, but the Athenians saw clearly that it threatened to cut their grain route from the Black Sea to Athens, which would end the war. Aristocratic Athenians started saying openly that Darius might support Athens instead of Sparta if he could deal with an oligarchy rather than a stupid and unruly mob. Alcibiades, too, hoped that an oligarchy would recall him to Athens. All the elements were in place for an oligarchic coup against the democracy.

In 411 B.C. a commander in the Athenian fleet named Pisander sailed from Samos, where the fleet was stationed, to Athens in order to organize just such an uprising. Pisander's supporters ran through the streets murdering democratic leaders, and in early summer 411 oligarchic plotters called a meeting of the Assembly *outside* the city walls, knowing that anti-Spartan democrats would be afraid to attend. The rump Assembly voted itself out of existence and authorized a commission of 400 men to run the city, ending nearly a hundred years of democratic government in Athens.

The oligarchy of **The Four Hundred** (411 B.C.), as they came to be known, said that it was going to draw up a list of 5,000 men of property—perhaps 20 percent of the citizen body—who would form the new government of Athens, but the conspirators were in no hurry. Instead, they relentlessly and mercilessly executed their enemies and confiscated their land while simultaneously negotiating with Sparta. The Four Hundred assumed that Sparta would offer favorable peace terms to a friendly Athenian oligarchy. But times had changed, and Sparta now wanted total victory. The sailors at Samos rebelled against the new Athenian oligarchy and declared themselves a democratic state in exile. The sailors wanted to return to Athens and restore the democracy, but if they did, Sparta, with its small but growing fleet financed by Persia, would surely cut off the grain supply and win the war. Alcibiades, still playing his own complicated game of betrayal and self-promotion, returned from Persia to Samos, stood before the fleet, and persuaded the sailors to stay where they were (and to elect him one of their generals!).

With the trickle of Persian gold that actually reached her in 411 B.C., Sparta built a second fleet in addition to the fleet in Ionia. This new fleet now sailed to the island of Euboea near Athens and raised a revolt. While Sparta's Ionian fleet threatened the Hellespont the new fleet now threatened to sail around the southern coast of Attica and blockade Piraeus. Victory lay within reach; yet the Spartans did not sail against either target! An amazed Thucydides remarked that on this occasion, as on so many others, the Spartans were the most helpful enemies that the Athenians could have had.

While Sparta dithered, the democrats in Athens quietly overthrew The Four Hundred and officially recalled the resourceful Alcibiades. The Spartan fleet off the coast of Ionia finally moved to block the Hellespont, but the Athenians at Samos defeated them in a savage battle. Shocked and dismayed, the Spartans consolidated their two fleets into one and abandoned the threat to Piraeus. Against all probability, by autumn of 411 B.C. Athens had regained the initiative in the war.

## Athenian Recovery, 410–406 B.C.

At this point, Thucydides' account of the war breaks off in the middle of a sentence; we will never know why. **Xenophon**, an essayist and friend of Socrates writing around 360 B.C., began his own *Greek History* where Thucydides stops, but does not match his detail or understanding. The war centered on a struggle for the Hellespont, he tells us. In 410 B.C. Sparta sent a new fleet to close it, but after wild adventures (including being captured by the Persian satrap and a dramatic escape from his castle), Alcibiades led the Athenians in destroying the new Spartan fleet. Sparta's admiral sent a desperate message home: "Ships lost. Mindaros [the previous Spartan admiral] dead. Men starving. Don't know what to do."

Sparta had no strategy except to wait for Persian intervention. A small but effective Syracusan fleet served alongside the Spartans, but the Carthaginian invasion of Sicily in 409 B.C. left Sparta to face the Athenians alone. Athens slowly won back her rebellious subjects, and in 407 B.C. Alcibiades dared to show his face again in Athens, the city that he had betrayed and that had betrayed him. The remarkable man got a hero's welcome:

> He set sail for home, the triremes decked out all around with the shields and booty of war. They towed behind them the prizes they had taken, and even more figureheads taken from the ships that Alcibiades had overcome and sunk. Taken together there were no less than 200 of these . . .
>
> When he landed the people seemed not even to see the other generals when they encountered them, but they ran to Alcibiades and crowded around him and shouted and embraced him. And those who were able to come in close placed garlands on his head, while the others watched from a distance and the elderly pointed him out to the young. Many tears were mixed with the city's joy when in their present good fortune they remembered the sufferings of the past, and they thought that they never would have suffered defeat in Sicily or in any of their other undertakings if only they had left Alcibiades in charge of the expedition and in charge of affairs. He found the city nearly expelled from the sea and possessing nothing more on land than its own suburbs, riven by civil strife, yet he raised her up from the low and miserable remnants of her glory to give her victory at sea and on land, victory over her enemies everywhere.

Plutarch, *Life of Alcibiades* 32

Even then, ominous events continued to unfold. Darius II of Persia, tired of the feuds between his two western satraps, sent his son Cyrus to replace them. Cyrus, like so many ambitious men in these years, had his own agenda: he was not Darius' eldest son, but saw that he could manipulate Sparta's war against Athens to push his elder brother aside and win the Persian throne for himself. His arrival in western Asia Minor coincided with the election of **Lysander** (lī-**san**-der) as admiral in Sparta. Charismatic and talented, Lysander forged a friendship with Agesilaus (a-jes-i-**lā**-us), the half brother of King Agis of Sparta, and when Lysander met the Persian Cyrus, he charmed him. Cyrus wanted Greek soldiers to back him in his coming bid for the kingship in Persia; Lysander wanted Persian money to defeat Athens. The two men had a lot in common.

At last with real financial support, Lysander resumed efforts to win over Athens' subject cities. In 406 B.C., while Alcibiades was away extorting money to pay his sailors, Lysander scored a minor victory over the Athenian fleet. This was not enough to change the military balance but it was enough to make Alicibiades look bad; and, deciding that returning to Athens was too dangerous, Alcibiades fled to a stronghold he had built near the Hellespont.

Because of Persian gold, Sparta could now offer higher pay to rowers than Athens could afford, and many of Athens' hired sailors deserted. By spring 406 B.C., the Athenians had a hundred ships, but crews only for seventy, while the Spartan fleet had swelled to 140 ships. Once again, it looked like Athens was doomed, but once again the personal agendas of the generals complicated the situation. Spartan admirals served nonrenewable twelve-month terms, and Lysander's term had now ended and Cyrus, wanting to keep his close ally Lysander in a position of power, refused to deal with the new Spartan admiral. The Spartan fleet had now grown to 170 ships and had the Athenians bottled up in a harbor on the island of Lesbos. The Hellespont was wide open, and it should have been easy for Sparta to cut off Athens' grain supply and win the war, but the confusion between the Spartan and Persian leaders gave Athens yet another chance. Desperate, the Athenians melted down their gold statues of the gods to raise cash, and in thirty days built 110 new ships. They offered freedom to any slave who would row (an unprecedented act), and in July 406 B.C. they engaged the Spartans at the Arginusae (ar-jin-**ou**-sē) Islands near the Hellespont, between Lesbos and the mainland. It was the biggest naval battle in Greek history and Athens' greatest naval victory. The Athenians destroyed two thirds of Sparta's fleet and killed the commander.

The Athenians pursued the remnants of the Spartan fleet, but in so doing they left over 1,000 of their own sailors to drown. A storm arose, and they were unable to recover the bodies of the dead. In Athens, people were overjoyed at the victory but appalled at the treatment of the dead. The Assembly condemned to death the victorious generals on charges of impiety, and after an illegal trial, executed six of them (including Pericles' only surviving son). Such was their reward for saving Athens from destruction.

## The End, 405–404 B.C.

Sparta despaired of victory and offered peace, but the Athenians, making yet another poor decision, rashly refused, assuming that Sparta could not replace its devastating losses. Sparta restored Lysander, and Cyrus not only came up with money for a new fleet but also put Lysander in charge of Persia's western provinces. With full Persian support, Sparta could now replace any fleet the Athenians could destroy. Without Persian support, a single defeat would be fatal for Athens.

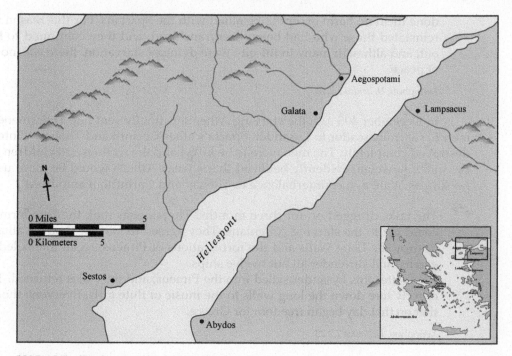

**MAP 16.7**  The Aegospotami campaign.

Late in 405 B.C., Lysander sailed for the Hellespont, where he captured a good base at the town of LAMPSACUS on the eastern side of the straits. He waited. To reopen the straits, Athens had to give battle, but the nearest secure harbor with water and food was 12 miles from Lampsacus, too far to be useful. The Athenians therefore decided to beach their ships at AEGOSPOTAMI (ē-jus-**pot**-a-mē, "goat river"), directly across the Hellespont from Lampsacus but lacking food and water (Map 16.7).

By a curious twist, Alcibiades' stronghold was also near Aegospotami. He rode over to the Athenian fleet and warned the generals that they were exposed. They arrogantly replied, "We are in command now, not you," and sent him away. For four days, the Athenians tried to lure Lysander out to battle. On the fifth day, Lysander's patience paid off. Short of food and water, the Athenian sailors scattered in foraging parties. Lysander stormed the Athenian camp, capturing 171 ships on the beach and rounding up 3,000 Athenians as they drifted back with supplies. Sparta's allies insisted on killing them all. Remembering what happened to Athens' victorious generals the year before, all the surviving Athenian generals fled in terror, most to Persia.

Xenophon, who was probably in Athens at the time, says (*Hellenica*, 2.2.9) that "as the news of the disaster was told, one man passed it to another, and a wailing arose and extended first from Piraeus, then along the Long Walls until it came to the city. No one slept that night." Lysander sailed to Athens and clamped the city under a firm siege. Disease and starvation set in.

Besieged by land and sea, the Athenians did not know what to do. They had no ships, no allies, and no food. They expected that they would now be treated as they had, through the arrogance of power, harmed others, small cities who had done them no harm except to be allied with the Spartans. For this reason they reinstated those who had been disenfranchised, and they continued to hold out, and although many in the city were dying of starvation, there was no talk of peace.

Xenophon, *Hellenica* 2.2.10

In December 405 B.C., the starving Athenians finally sent one Theramenes (ther-a-me-nēz) as ambassador to Lysander. Sparta's allies Corinth and Thebes wanted Athens destroyed completely. The men were to be killed and the women and children enslaved. Lysander, however, evidently believed that a weak Athens would be more useful than no Athens at all, as a counterbalance to Theban and Corinthian ambitions.

The talks dragged on for three months. Theramenes took the best terms he could get to the starving Athenians. They agreed to join the Spartan alliance, destroy the Long Walls and the fortifications of Piraeus, recall the exiled oligarchs, and surrender all but twelve ships.

After this Lysander sailed into the Piraeus, and the exiles returned. They eagerly tore down the long walls to the music of flute girls. Everyone thought that on that day began freedom for Greece.

Xenophon, *Hellenica* 2.2.23

## AFTERMATH, 404–399 B.C.

### The Thirty Tyrants and Athens' Civil War, 404–403 B.C.

As winter approached in 404 B.C., the struggle with Sparta ended. To rule Athens, Lysander established a council of thirty oligarchs and ordered them to restore Athens' "ancestral constitution." He wanted the city to survive and be loyal to him personally. He did not care that **The Thirty**, as the Athenians called them, had no interest in the rule of law. They were Lysander's allies, even if they were ready to sate their anger against the democrats in rivers of blood. The Thirty slaughtered their personal enemies, confiscated land, and owed allegiance directly to Lysander. Within a few months, The Thirty had murdered 1,500 Athenians (more than one in twenty of the citizens who had survived the war).

The Thirty's behavior generated strong resistance, and they therefore asked Lysander to install a Spartan governor and a Spartan garrison, for protection. Splits grew within their ranks. Critias (krit-i-as), a hardliner, once an associate of Socrates, relied increasingly on force, while Theramenes, at the other extreme, wanted to compromise. Theramenes persuaded The Thirty to make a list of 3,000 well-off men (10 percent of the citizens) who would have full rights. Critias then claimed that anyone not on the list could be killed or tortured at will. He prosecuted Theramenes, and when Theramenes gave a powerful speech defending himself, Critias had his name struck off the list. Theramenes was dragged away and poisoned.

By the end of 404 B.C., thousands of Athenians had fled the city. Even Thebes, Athens' bitter enemy, offered asylum; three months earlier they had wanted to extirpate Athens. In January 403 B.C., a group of Athenian democrats set up a small fort near the border with Theban territory. Their numbers swelled to 700, and they seized another hill overlooking the harbor of Piraeus where many poor, prodemocratic citizens lived. Critias stormed the hill with the few who would actually fight for The Thirty, but was killed. The surviving members of The Thirty now asked Lysander to save them from the uprising, but the Spartan kings, worried that Lysander was becoming more powerful than they, brokered a treaty with the Athenian rebels, restoring democracy (against every expectation) and removing Lysander's influence. In yet another unexpected twist, Sparta's internal conflicts had saved Athenian democracy.

## The Restored Democracy and the Trial of Socrates, 403–399 B.C.

Since the eve of the Peloponnesian War, Athens had lost a third of her population. Her agriculture and trade were ruined. Those Athenians who survived war, disease, and famine had taken up arms against each other, and even though The Thirty left Athens in 403 B.C., many of the Athenians who helped them stayed behind. To avoid revenge killings like those on Corcyra in 427 B.C., the Athenians proclaimed an *amnêsteia*, literally a "not remembering"—the first amnesty in world history. No one except The Thirty themselves and a couple of dozen senior officials could be prosecuted for crimes committed under the oligarchy. Athenians who wanted to pursue vengeance would be forced to cloak their intentions.

The great philosopher Socrates was one who fell victim to the raw hatreds in the city. Aged about seventy, he was well known around town and widely disliked. Because he never wrote anything, we have to rely on others' impressions, but his pupil Plato (427–337 B.C.) tells us that one of Socrates' friends visited the oracle at Delphi and asked whether anyone was wiser than Socrates. The oracle said no. Socrates was surprised. He did not think the god would lie, yet he felt anything but wise. He began interviewing men reputed to be wise, to find out what the god had meant. But each time,

> I got the impression that although many thought this man to be wise, and especially himself, in fact he was not. When I attempted to explain to the man that although he thought he was wise, he was not really wise, he only hated me for it, and so did many of those present. I went away thinking that I was wiser than this man. It may be that none of us knows much of anything, but this man at least thinks he knows something, when he does not. I too know nothing, but I don't think that I do. In that respect I am a tiny bit wiser than he, because I do not think I know something that I don't.
>
> Plato, *Apology* 21C–D

You do not have to look very hard to see that Socrates' philosophical arguments were also political claims. Democracy assumed that every citizen had political wisdom and that the way to maximize wisdom was for as many citizens as possible to debate questions and participate directly in public affairs. But if no one knows anything, democracy only maximizes ignorance and stupidity, as its enemies have always claimed. Plato explained this in another dialogue, set on the eve of Socrates' execution:

> SOCRATES: But my dear Crito, why should we pay attention to what "most people" think? Those whose opinions matter most will understand that things happened just as they did.

CRITO:   But I think you see now that sometimes it *is* necessary to take account of the view of the masses. I think the present circumstances make it clear that the masses are capable not just of petty annoyances but of inflicting the greatest harm°, if one falls foul of them.

SOCRATES:   I only wish that the masses were in fact capable of committing the greatest harm, because then they would be capable of doing the greatest good, which would be a splendid thing. But they can do neither. They cannot make a man wise or stupid. They simply act at random.

Plato, *Crito* 44C–D

°*harm:* They have just condemned Socrates to death.

Back in 423 B.C., Aristophanes had made Socrates the main character in his comedy *The Clouds,* representing him as a slippery, eccentric sophist who made regular citizens into laughing stocks and persuaded young men to mock traditional ways. This was funny when the Peloponnesian War was going well, but by 399 B.C., in the wake of defeat and a bloody oligarchic coup, it was no longer a laughing matter. To make matters worse, Socrates had also associated with the wrong people. Alcibiades was prominent in Socrates' circle, and some of The Thirty, including Critias, were admirers or hangers-on: No matter that Socrates (according to Plato) considered oligarchy to be as flawed as democracy or that he defied orders from The Thirty and was condemned to death for it (only the fall of The Thirty saved him). Charges of "corrupting the young" and of "introducing false gods" were now brought against him, the intellectual hero of democracy's arrogant, overeducated enemies.

In Athenian democratic courts of law there were no lawyers or judges. Instead, all citizens aged over thirty could serve as jurors. Each day, those who wanted to serve put their names into a lottery. If they were selected, a machine assigned them to a court. Depending on the crimes being tried, juries ranged from 201 to 501 members. The jurors took their seats; the charges were read; the citizen bringing the charges spoke and called witnesses; the defendant spoke and called witnesses; then the citizens voted, guilty or innocent. It was up to the speakers to cite relevant laws, and there was no cross-examination of witnesses. Witnesses testified to the defendant's and accuser's general way of life as well as to what we would consider the facts of the case. Jurors regularly interrupted proceedings with booing, clapping, and abuse. If they found the defendant guilty, some crimes carried fixed penalties. For other crimes, the prosecutor and the defendant each proposed a penalty, and the jury voted which to impose. All trials were over in a single day. The law courts were like tragedy in their love of debate and concern with moral issues.

In his dialogue the *Apology,* Plato presents Socrates as giving a sophisticated speech explaining his philosophy and mocking Athens' legal system for relying on superficial forms of knowledge. The vote was close, probably about 265 guilty to 235 not guilty. The prosecutors asked for the death penalty, harsh for these charges but reflecting the high feelings in the city. Socrates, instead of proposing a fine or exile, mockingly proposed that as "punishment" he should receive free dinners for life, like an Olympic athlete, as a reward for his forcing the citizens to think about how to live their lives. Some of Socrates' friends offered to pay a big fine on his behalf instead, but the irritated jurors approved the death sentence. About thirty days later, refusing to escape, Socrates drank a cup of poisonous hemlock, democracy's crime against philosophy.

## CONCLUSION

In both the east and the west, the great wars of 480 B.C. had given a few city-states chances to gain greater power than others and to challenge the entire system of autonomous *poleis*. But the resistance to any one city becoming the capital of a larger Greek state remained strong. In the west, Syracuse's power depended on its tyrants' ability to hold the population down, and by the mid-460s B.C. that power collapsed. In the east, Athens exploited the other Greeks' fear of Persia to centralize unheard-of resources, develop a sophisticated tax system, and assemble a huge military force. Athens' direct challenge to Sparta in the 450s B.C. failed, but the process of centralization continued so that by 431 B.C. many Spartans feared that if they did not stop Athens, it would be too late. The following 27 years of war destabilized the whole Mediterranean, consuming countless lives and vast stores of wealth.

Athens fell, her empire was dissolved, and with it ended the only opportunity that history offered for one *polis* to become the capital of a larger Greek state. No *polis* ever matched the wealth, power, and organization of Athens before 413 B.C. But Athens' bid for power drove the Greeks to exhaustion. Carthage and Persia nursed their wounds after 479 B.C., then after 410 B.C. reimposed their inexorable wills on the Greek city-states. Seventy years later, Macedon overthrew the Greek city-states of the Aegean, and another seventy years after that, Rome did the same in the West. The fall of Athens was the beginning of the end of an age.

## Key Terms

Nicias, *338*

Archidamian War, *338*

Demosthenes, *340*

Pylos, *342*

Sphacteria, *343*

Brasidas, *343*

Cleon, *343*

Peace of Nicias, *347*

Alcibiades, *347*

Melos, *347*

herms, *350*

Gylippus, *351*

Decelea, *351*

Hannibal, *357*

Dionysius, *358*

The Four Hundred, *360*

Xenophon, *361*

Lysander, *362*

The Thirty, *364*

## Further Reading

Connor, W. Robert, *The New Politicians of Fifth-Century Athens* (Princeton, 1971). Excellent account of the evolution of politics in democratic Athens.

Connor, W. Robert, *Thucydides* (Princeton, 1984). Careful reading of this major text, with great sensitivity to nuance.

Finley, Moses, *Ancient Sicily* (New York, 1968). Still the only narrative survey of Sicilian history. Tells the main story well.

Green, Peter, *Armada from Athens* (London, 1970). Dramatic retelling of the story of the Sicilian Expedition.

Hanson, Victor, *Warfare and Agriculture in Classical Greece* (Pisa, 1983; reissued Berkeley, 1999). Excellent study showing the limits of the damage Spartan armies could do to the Athenian countryside in the early stages of the war.

Hanson, Victor, *A War Like No Other: How the Athenians and Spartans Fought the Peloponnesian War* (New York 2005). Vivid account of the war from the soldiers' and sailors' points of view.

Kagan, Donald, *The Archidamian War* (Ithaca, NY, 1974), *The Peace of Nicias and the Sicilian Expedition* (Ithaca, NY, 1981), *The Fall of the Athenian Empire*

(Ithaca, NY, 1987). The second, third, and fourth books in a four-volume series, covering the period 431 through 404 B.C. A detailed account of the events of the Peloponnesian War.

Kagan, Donald, *The Peloponnesian War* (New York 2003). The best one-volume survey of the conflict, by the master of military and diplomatic history.

Lancel, Serge, *Carthage* (Oxford, UK, 1995). A survey of this city's history, including its relations with the Greeks of Sicily.

Lewis, David, John Boardman, John Davies, and Martin Ostwald, eds., *The Cambridge Ancient History*, 2nd ed., vol. 5: *The Fifth Century* B.C. (Cambridge, 1992). Essays by specialists covering 478 through 404 in the Aegean and western Greece.

## ANCIENT TEXTS

Aristophanes, *The Clouds*. In *Lysistrata and Other Plays*, tr. Alan Sommerstein (New York, 1973). Important negative view of Socrates, first performed in 423 B.C.

Diodorus of Sicily, *The History*, Books 12 and 13. In *The Library of History V*, tr. C. H. Oldfather (Cambridge, MA: Loeb Classical Library, 1946). Parallel Greek and English texts describing Sicilian history.

Plato, *The Last Days of Socrates*, tr. Hugh Treddenick (Harmondsworth, UK, 1954). Includes the *Apology* and *Crito*, important texts for Socrates' trial and postwar Athenian society.

Plutarch, Lives of Nicias, Alcibiades, and Lysander. In *The Rise and Fall of Athens*, tr. Ian Scott-Kilvert (Harmondsworth, UK, 1960). These biographies contain information on the end of the Peloponnesian War.

Thucydides, *The Peloponnesian War*, tr. Rex Warner (Harmondsworth, UK, 1954). Book 1 describes the years down to 431 B.C.

*The Landmark Thucydides*, ed. Robert Strassler (New York, 1996). Not such a good translation as the Penguin, but the abundant maps and excellent endnotes make it much easier to follow Thucydides' account.

Xenophon, *A History of My Times*, tr. George Cawkwell (Harmondsworth, UK, 1966). Translation of Xenophon's *Hellenica*, the main narrative source for the period 411 to 399 B.C., after Thucydides ends.

Xenophon, *Socrates' Defense*. In *Conversations of Socrates*, tr. Hugh Treddenick and Robin Waterfield (New York, 1988). A different version from Plato's of what Socrates said at his trial in 399 B.C.

## CHAPTER 17

# The Greeks between Persia and Carthage, 399–360 B.C.

A single story dominated the fifth century B.C.: Athens' and Syracuse's attempts to control their neighbors and the cultural revolutions that their new wealth supported. Their defeats, Sparta's triumph, and the return of Persia and Carthage begin a more complicated period. Once the Athenian empire fell, no one could recreate it. The forty years from 399 through 360 B.C. were filled with bloody, unproductive struggles between Sparta (with Persian backing), Thebes, and a revived Athens in the Aegean, and between Syracuse and Carthage in the west. No *polis* could reproduce fifth-century Athens' financial power, and to pay for these increasingly costly wars, *poleis* turned more toward their richest citizens. For four centuries, since 800 B.C., power had steadily shifted toward the mass of ordinary male citizens, so that by 400 B.C. democracy was a common form of government in Greek lands. But in the fourth century, as the rich started to shoulder more of the costs of the state's survival, aristocrats gained new confidence.

Another major change was also under way. During the Peloponnesian War, Thessaly, Macedon, and other large but loosely organized northern and western regions had provided men and materials for Athens and Sparta. In return, they learned the city-states' methods of organization and techniques of war. In the fourth century B.C., they applied these Greek techniques to their own reserves of manpower and wealth, eventually reaching the point that a northern king would turn tables on the *poleis* and bring their political independence to an end.

## SPARTA'S EMPIRE, 404–360 B.C.

The Peloponnesian War ended with singing and dancing as Athens' former subjects celebrated the destruction of the Long Walls as the beginning of liberty. These dancers were to be bitterly disappointed.

### Lysander, Agesilaos, and the Return of the Persian Empire, 404–387 B.C.

Athens' power was broken, but Sparta had no intention of setting the Greek cities free, as Plutarch explains:

> Lysander dissolved the democracies and other forms of government [in Ionia], and he placed a single Spartan governor over each city and beneath him ten magistrates chosen from the political associations Lysander had founded. Lysander behaved the same way both toward those who had been the enemy and those who had been allies. He sailed leisurely up and down the coast. In a way he had taken to himself all power over Greece. He did not base his choice of governors on birth or wealth but took them from partisans and supporters. He placed them in charge of deciding who would be punished and who rewarded. He was present at many massacres. He expelled the enemies of his friends, providing an unseemly example of what it meant to be under Spartan rule. The comic poet Theopompos seems to slip when he says that the Spartans were like barmaids, because first they give you the sweet draft of freedom, then mix in the vinegar. In fact the taste was bitter and harsh from the beginning, because Lysander would not allow the different cities to be masters of their own affairs, but turned them over to the most aggressive and fanatical of the oligarchic faction.
>
> Plutarch, *Life of Lysander* 13.3–5

Sparta had defeated Athens by making a deal with Persia, and in 404 B.C., both Sparta and Persia got what they bargained for. Sparta took Athens' empire, while Persia recovered Ionia and secured her northwest frontier. Many Greeks felt that Sparta had sold out Ionia, as, in fact, she had. Within Sparta and Persia too, the main players seemed to have got what they had bargained for in 404 B.C.

In Sparta, Lysander had made himself a great man. By installing oligarchies answering directly to him in Athens' former subject cities, Lysander took control of enormous revenues. He apparently took 1,500 talents in cash back to Sparta, kept more than 400 for himself, and instituted annual tribute of another 1,000 talents. No individual Athenian had ever controlled such wealth. His power seemed more than human, and some cities indeed set up altars to him as if he were a god—the first time Greeks so honored a living man. The centuries-old framework of Greek life, which held that all men were roughly equal and none had access to superhuman forces, could not easily accommodate someone as rich and powerful as Lysander. Within a few years, Lysander was campaigning to make Spartan kingship elective, presumably to win it for himself. The kings worried that Lysander was stronger than they were and that his followers' brutality would destabilize the new order. Hence the surprising events in Athens in 403 B.C. when the Spartans restored the democracy there: As the kings saw it, Lysander was more dangerous than the Athenian democracy!

In Persia, Lysander's close friend Cyrus also got the opportunity to fulfill all his plans. Within weeks of the end of the Peloponnesian War, his father Darius II died. As expected, Darius' elder son (and Cyrus' elder brother) **Artaxerxes** inherited the Persian throne, but Egypt immediately rebelled and Cyrus exploited the crisis to challenge Artaxerxes for the crown. Cyrus asked for Spartan help, and Sparta, welcoming the prospect of a grateful Cyrus on the throne, organized 13,000 Greek mercenaries to support him. Cyrus cut through Artaxerxes' defenses, and in the final battle, near Babylon, Cyrus' hoplites were victorious; but in a bitter twist of fate Cyrus himself was killed. His death left 10,000 Greeks marooned in hostile territory 1,000 miles from friendly lands. The Athenian Xenophon (ca. 428–357 B.C.), a friend of Socrates, was one of the Greek officers. He took command and led the army all the way back to the Black Sea (Map 17.1).

Xenophon wrote a famous (albeit self-serving) account of their escape, called the *Anabasis*, or "The March Up Country." Few Greeks lived more than a day's walk from the sea; now, after walking for months to reach it, fighting every inch of the way, the battle-hardened Greek veterans rushed into the water of the Black Sea, shouting "*Thalatta! Thalatta!*" ("The sea! The sea!"). Xenophon's triumph came at the same time that the Athenians were putting to death his teacher Socrates for "corrupting the youth" and "introducing false gods." Repelled by this horrible crime, Xenophon enrolled as a mercenary for Sparta, becoming fast friends with its young king **Agesilaos**.

The "March of the Ten Thousand," as it came to be known, proved that no Persian army could withstand Greek hoplites in battle. Why, then, should Sparta honor treaties giving Ionia to Persia? Lysander saw no reason, and in 398 B.C., after he had maneuvered

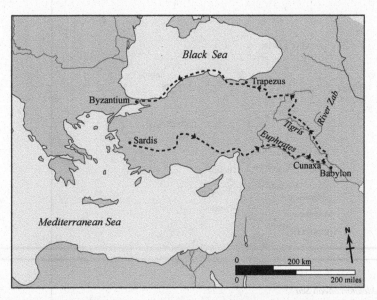

**MAP 17.1** The March of the 10,000. Cyrus' mercenaries left Sardis in spring 401 B.C. They won a battle at Cunaxa, but Cyrus was killed, and the Greek mercenaries withdrew. The satrap Tissaphernes treacherously captured the Greek commanders at the River Zab, and Xenophon took command of the remaining troops. He led them back to the Black Sea at Trapezus (modern Trebizond), finally returning to Byzantium in early 399 B.C.

his friend (and, according to rumor, his lover) Agesilaos onto the Spartan throne, freedom for Ionia became official Spartan policy.

Setting up Agesilaos as king should have stabilized Lysander's unparalleled power, but in fact the cunning admiral met his match in a now resentful Agesilaos. Agesilaos ignored Lysander's advice, passed him over for commands, and ruined his friends. In spite of Lysander's early support, Agesilaos was determined to break Lysander's power and save Sparta's traditional institutions. Eventually Agesilaos banished Lysander to a minor theater of war, where he died in 395 B.C.

Agesilaos made Ionian freedom his own cause, and, in 396 B.C., he advanced to Sardis, routing every Persian force in his path. Persia's King Artaxerxes, who at this time needed to reconquer rebellious Egypt, was thoroughly alarmed. Artaxerxes came up with a new strategy: Instead of fighting Sparta, he sent agents to Greece bearing gold. Several Greek cities, disillusioned with Sparta, took Persian money to finance an uprising. The Ephors called Agesilaos back from his campaigns in Asia to fight in Greece. Thus Artaxerxes achieved his goal without losing a single man.

The ensuing Corinthian War (394–387 B.C.), so called because most of the action took place around that city (Map 17.2), pitted Sparta against rebellious Thebes and Corinth (its two closest allies in the Peloponnesian War), a reviving Athens, and Persia. In a strange reversal, Athens rebuilt the Long Walls and an Athenian admiral commanding a Persian fleet defeated Sparta's fleet then ravaged Greece's coasts! The Corinthian War dragged on in a bloody stalemate. Spartan hoplites could win battles, evidently, but only Persian gold could win wars.

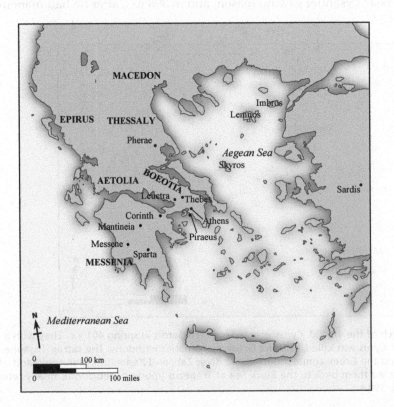

**MAP 17.2** Aegean sites mentioned in this chapter.

## The King's Peace, 387–371 B.C.

In 387 B.C, the Spartan king Agesilaos conceded this bitter fact. Confessing his failure to free the Ionian Greeks (whom Sparta had herself earlier betrayed to Persia), he sought an accommodation with Persia. Xenophon records Artaxerxes' terms:

> I, Artaxerxes, find the following conditions to be just: that the cities in Asia and the islands Clazomenae and Cyprus belong to me, and all other Greek cities, both great and small, are to be autonomous except for Lemnos and Imbros and Skyros. These, as in the past, are to belong to the Athenians. If either of the two parties° does not accept this peace, I and those who agree to it shall make war against them on land and on sea, with ships and with money.

Xenophon, *Hellenica* 5.1.31

°*two parties*: That is, Sparta or the alliance against her.

This **King's Peace** (387 B.C.) gave most parties what they wanted. Persia again controlled Ionia and protected its western borders by banning multicity alliances ("cities . . . to be autonomous"), except Sparta's Peloponnesian League. This left Artaxerxes free to launch a major (but unsuccessful) invasion of Egypt. Banning alliances also guaranteed Sparta's power within Greece. Athens kept its rebuilt walls and fleet. The Ionians, the losers, were too weak to protest, and no one on the mainland cared enough to restart the war. Thebes, by now Greece's second power, was the other main loser. She had controlled the other cities in Boeotia since before 500 B.C., but Thebes' Boeotian League was now dissolved under the King's Peace. Thebes would make Sparta regret this insult.

The King's Peace was full of ironies. Sparta had the job of making sure that all cities were free, when it was in fact to free themselves from Spartan tyranny that the Greek cities had fought the Corinthian War. In any event, Agesilaos interpreted the treaty as carte blanche to help his friends and hurt his enemies, above all his enemy Thebes. In 382 B.C., a Spartan officer named Phoebidas (fē-bi-das) was marching troops past Thebes when a pro-Spartan faction in the city offered him a chance to seize the city. Phoebidas did so, in flagrant violation of the King's Peace. Even his colleagues in Sparta were shocked. The Spartans put Phoebidas on trial, but King Agesilaos defended him, saying that he had only acted in Sparta's best interests. Phoebidas got off with a fine, which Agesilaos paid. Agesilaos kept the Spartan garrison in Thebes and the pro-Spartan faction in Thebes executed the leader of the anti-Spartan group for conspiring with Persia—a deeply hypocritical murder, given Sparta's cooperation with Persia under the King's Peace.

In 379 B.C., seven crossdressing conspirators disguised as *hetairai* stopped by a party that Thebes' pro-Spartan governors were throwing and stabbed them all to death. Just twenty-five years before, Thebes had urged Sparta to kill all Athenian citizens at the end of the Peloponnesian War; now, in a reversal typical of ancient Greece, Athenian volunteers arrived to expel the Spartan garrison in Thebes!

In retaliation, in 378 B.C. another Spartan officer, named Sphodrias (sfod-ri-as), decided to repeat Phoebidas' outrageous behavior by launching a night-time attack on Piraeus. Sphodrias, however, underestimated the distances involved, and the sun rose to find his band of adventurers in a field several miles from Piraeus. Humiliated, they withdrew. Like Phoebidas, Sphodrias was put on trial; again like Phoebidas, he was acquitted. So far, the Greeks endured Sparta's arrogance because opposition would (in theory) trigger Persian intervention, but Sphodrias' attempted coup was too much. Later in 378 B.C. the Athenians organized a new naval league. Between sixty and seventy states joined. The Athenians went to great lengths not to upset Persia, specifying that the league was not an alliance, as its fifth-century league had been, but an "association" to help members govern themselves, of course with the goal of keeping the King's Peace in force for all time. They insisted that, unlike in their fifth-century empire, no Athenian could own property in an allied state and that there would be no garrisons or tribute.

Artaxerxes took no action against Athens, no doubt because he was still concerned with reconquering Egypt. Even without formal tribute, the new Athenian league financed a fleet that destroyed Sparta's navy in an engagement in 376 B.C. For nearly thirty years, since 404 B.C., Spartan and Persian fleets had controlled the Aegean, and Athens had had to bow to these powers to preserve its grain supply. Finally, the grain route appeared to be secure. Full of confidence, the Athenians decided they did not need Thebes any more. Betraying their recent allies, in 375 B.C. the Athenians helped push through a **Common Peace** that committed all Greeks to the King's Peace, again dissolving Thebes' Boeotian League.

Four years later, in 371 B.C., Athens called a general congress to reaffirm the Common Peace. Every Greek state signed, but when it was Thebes' turn, her representative **Epaminondas** (e-pam-i-**non**-das) walked out in protest because Sparta insisted that he could sign only for Thebes, not for the whole of Boeotia as head of any league: According to the Common Peace (and the King's Peace before it), the Boeotian League did not exist. Agesilaos was sick, so his fellow-king Cleombrotus led a Spartan army into Boeotia to force Thebes to agree to the Common Peace and to abandon all thought of a Boeotian League. Epaminondas rushed back to Thebes to prepare a defense.

## ECONOMY, SOCIETY, AND WAR

The dramatic events of summer 371 B.C. took added significance from long-term social and economic processes. A hundred years earlier, economic changes had begun making the old style of Greek warfare obsolete. No matter how good Spartan hoplites were, they could not have beaten Persia in 480 to 479 B.C. without the Athenian fleet, which required large amounts of money. Athens could maintain this fleet and build the latest types of fortifications only by creating a multicity state in which many cities paid tribute. Relatively light taxes paid for a powerful fleet and cheap security, which made trade easier, increased overall wealth, and made Piraeus a major market.

In the Peloponnesian War, military spending exploded. Athens tightened its financial organization but constantly needed new income. Generals extorted money from the peoples among whom they campaigned and there was talk of extracting "loans" from the temple treasuries at Olympia and Delphi. Most cities turned to rich citizens for special contributions, yet archaeology shows that at just this time, around 425 B.C., rich Greeks also started spending more on expressions of personal status. The homes of the rich, simple and plain through most of the fifth century, now acquired elaborate colonnaded courtyards, mosaic floors, and painted walls. Expensive new tombs and a whole array of other elite monuments also appeared (Figure 17.1). As the state grew more dependent on the rich to pay for security, the rich asserted greater independence.

Generals experimented feverishly, looking for ways to fight wars more cheaply or, if they had money, to convert cash into victory. Some turned toward inexpensive light infantry (Figure 17.2), and the campaigns in mountainous western Greece in the 420s B.C.

**FIGURE 17.1** Grave stele of Ktesileos and his wife Theano; Athens, ca. 400 B.C. The husband stands in a relaxed pose, leaning on a staff before a pediment. His seated wife looks up while languidly holding the edge of her dress. Their names are written below the pediment. Marble, 5 feet high.

showed that javelin throwers (*peltasts*), archers, and slingers could damage a phalanx on the right terrain. In 390 B.C., Athenian light infantry, working in rough terrain, cut a Spartan regiment to pieces during the Corinthian War.

Other *poleis* tried to exploit the greater prosperity and assertiveness of the rich by recruiting more cavalry. In the sixth and earlier fifth centuries B.C., few *poleis* could muster more than a few hundred (or just a few dozen) horsemen, but by the early fourth century, it was not unusual to put 1,000 cavalry in the field. Once cavalry reached such numbers, they could use their speed to outmaneuver a phalanx. In another experiment, as early as 424 B.C., Thebes tried massing hoplites on a narrow front twenty-five ranks deep instead of the usual eight, aiming to crash through the opposing ranks before the enemy had time to encircle them. However, such tactics were effective only as part of a combined-arms operation using clouds of cavalry and skirmishers to hold back the enemy's wings.

All these innovations drove the costs of war higher, but advances in fortifications increased expenses even more. Athens had pioneered advanced fortifications with its Long Walls in the 450s B.C., and in the 380s B.C. tried an even more expensive innovation, ringing its whole territory with forts. Greek citizen armies avoided assaulting fortifications because they were unwilling to accept high casualties and, being tied to seasonal campaigns, could rarely stay in the field for long sieges. In the fourth century B.C., *poleis* responded by hiring

**FIGURE 17.2** A Thracian peltast, named after the *peltê*, a light wicker shield often shaped like a half- moon, on a red-figure wine cup, ca. 460 B.C. Peltasts wore no armor, but carried several javelins for harassing slow-moving hoplites. Peltasts became important in fourth-century warfare.

mercenaries, who would do things citizens would not, but these hired warriors raised the cost of war still further. As citizens' military contributions declined, so did their power within their cities relative to the aristocracy, who provided the funds for war.

Such economic and social changes shaped the struggles among Sparta, Athens, and Thebes. As the costs of war spiraled upward, no one *polis* could concentrate enough wealth to overwhelm the others without Persian gold. Their indecisive wars bankrupted everyone and gave further power to the rich.

Power also shifted away from the *poleis* toward the large, loose federations around the northern and western fringes of mainland Greece. Thessaly, Aetolia, Macedon, and Epirus had been second-rate powers in the fifth century B.C. These *ethnê* (**eth-nā**, meaning "peoples" or "nations"; singular, *ethnos*) had large populations, rich natural resources, and powerful aristocracies, but lacked the organization and civic traditions that would allow them to put hoplites in the field and fleets upon the seas. As the Peloponnesian War expanded, and these societies were drawn into the conflict, a transfer of institutions and techniques began. Through charisma, trickery, and ruthless efficiency, a man named **Jason of Pherae** (**fer-ē**) got control of most of Thessaly in the late 370s B.C. He seemed to come from nowhere, suddenly emerging as a major player:

> When Jason returned to Thessaly, he was a great man, legally appointed lord of Thessaly and having at his disposal large numbers of mercenaries, both foot soldiers and cavalry, and these trained to the height of excellence. His power was further enhanced by his many allies and those who wished to become his allies. Through the fact that no one dared disregard him, you might say that he was the greatest man of his time . . . the Greeks were seriously frightened that he might become the tyrant over all.

Xenophon, *Hellenica* 6.4.28, 33

Jason's power, however, was fragile, depending on his own skill and charisma rather than firmly grounded institutions, and when he was murdered in 370 B.C. Thessaly broke apart as his brothers fought and killed each other. But his rise showed the shape of things to come.

## SPARTA'S COLLAPSE, 371 B.C.

Sparta was becoming an anachronism. Lysander had wanted to modernize around 400 B.C., but King Agesilaos had defeated his plans, and by the 370s B.C. Sparta was obsessed with its past and its traditions. One consequence of this was that while the population of Greece was growing, the number of Spartiates was falling. A man could be a Spartiate only if he could afford to contribute to his dining group, but Spartan inheritance laws concentrated land in ever fewer hands, meaning that fewer men could afford to be full citizens; and despite the dangers this clearly posed, Sparta's reactionary leaders refused to countenance any change in the city's institutions. There had been 9,000 Spartiates in 479 B.C.; by 371 B.C., there were just 1,400. For all their ferocity, this tiny band could not keep their enemies and allies in line without both Persian support and a widespread belief in Spartan invincibility. Every time Sparta went to war in the fourth century, she risked everything, but the ruling elite refused to broaden the bases for Spartiate citizenship.

As we have seen, Cleombrotus marched against Thebes in 371 B.C. with 700 Spartiates and thousands of allies, trusting that his hoplites' morale and skill would make up for their tiny numbers. That turned out to be a mistake.

In previous years, the Thebans had hidden behind their walls whenever the Spartans approached, but this summer their leader Epaminondas decided to give battle. He knew that if he did not, the other Boeotian cities would desert Thebes and its claims to leadership. The armies met on level ground at a village called **Leuctra** (loik-tra).

Most cities now had strong cavalry, but not Sparta. The expert Theban cavalry drove back the weak Spartan cavalry, whose flight disrupted the Spartan phalanx. Epaminondas had drawn up his hoplites to an unprecedented fifty-ranks deep, a kind of human battering ram. Their spearhead was the **Sacred Band**, an elite corps reputed to consist of 150 pairs of lovers who would rather die than act shamefully before each other. Like the Spartiates, the Sacred Band were full-time warriors supported at public expense. As always, the Spartans showed astonishing ferocity and bravery, but the Thebans battered them until they fell back to camp, leaving behind over 400 dead Spartiates—more than a quarter of the whole Spartiate population, including not only Sphodrias, whose failed raid on Athens had caused so much trouble, but also King Cleombrotus.

Sparta was shattered. Her allies immediately defected to Thebes. Worse still, civil war seemed imminent. According to Spartan law, men who retreated in battle forfeited their citizenship and could not marry Spartiate women, and Agesilaos was terrified that if he followed the law and disenfranchised the 300 survivors of Leuctra—practically a third of the surviving Spartiates—they would rebel. Rather than change the laws and undermine his own authority, as Plutarch explains it (*Agesilaos* 31), Agesilaos "came into the Assembly and announced that the laws must be allowed to sleep on that one day, but that after that they must resume their force."

Epaminondas descended on Sparta with 40,000 hoplites, the first time an enemy ever ravaged Spartan territory. Only winter floods swelling the River Eurotas kept Epaminondas from sacking the city. Instead, Epaminondas headed west across the mountains to liberate the helots of Messenia and set up an independent city-state there.

When Agesilaos ascended the throne in 398 B.C., Sparta was at the height of her power. She had humbled Athens and threatened the Persian Empire itself. Twenty-seven years later, Sparta had lost everything. Agesilaos used to boast that no Spartan women had ever seen the smoke from enemy campfires; after 371 B.C., they knew them well.

## ANARCHY IN THE AEGEAN, 371–360 B.C.

The battle of Leuctra ruined Sparta, but it was not enough to make Thebes a major power. Epaminondas was a fine commander, but he had no strategic vision of what to do next. He headed off a Spartan attempt to get Persian aid in 367 B.C., but his anti-Spartan alliance quickly broke up, and petty wars followed everywhere. Thebes fought to keep Thessaly divided after Jason's murder; Athens fought to extend her power over her allies in the Second Athenian League; and Athens and Thebes fought each other. Cities changed sides with bewildering frequency. With no great struggle against Persia or Sparta to galvanize citizens, their participation declined steadily. Bands of marauding mercenaries, unemployed between jobs, soon posed a threat to public safety.

Agesilaos refused to acknowledge the loss of Messenia with all its helots and remained in a state of war with Thebes, and in 362 B.C., it seemed that he might actually win Messenia back. The city of MANTINEIA, Epaminondas' major ally in the Peloponnesus, broke away from Thebes and asked for Spartan support. Agesilaos, now aged eighty-two, took the small Spartan army to its aid. Epaminondas marched against undefended Sparta while her troops were away. Agesilaos raced back, saving the city only after desperate hand-to-hand fighting in the streets. Plutarch tells us that:

> Isidas, the son of Phoebidas,° must, I think, have presented an astounding sight not only to his fellow-citizens, but to the enemy. He was superbly handsome and large, at the age when human beauty flowers, when a boy becomes a man. He came from his house where he had just oiled his skin, holding a spear in one hand and a sword and in the other, naked, without clothes or armor, and so he pushed into the center of the fight and ranging up and down killed one Theban after the other. He was never hit, whether because a god protected him for his valor, or because the enemy thought that he was taller and more powerful than any mere man. For his achievement the Ephors crowned him with a garland, then fined him 1,000 drachmas for endangering his life by fighting without armor.

Plutarch, *Life of Agesilaos* 34

°*Phoebidas:* The same Phoebidas who had captured Thebes in 382 B.C.

But no amount of bravery or derring-do hid the fact that Sparta was now a second-rate power. The main armies clashed at Mantineia a few days later, and the Thebans again broke the Spartan phalanx. As the Spartans turned to run, one of them struck down Epaminondas. Legend had it that with his dying breath he urged Thebes to abandon conquest and make peace.

This was good advice. The Greeks were exhausted. Thebes could not take Sparta; Sparta could not recover Messenia; and Athens could not recreate its fifth-century empire. Persia, which might now have intervened decisively in Greek affairs, was still bogged down trying to recover Egypt and to suppress revolts among the western satraps. The fall of Sparta had brought on anarchy. As Xenophon concluded:

> The result of the battle [of Mantineia] was just opposite of what everyone thought it would be. The whole of Greece was there arranged against each other, and everyone expected that, if a battle took place, the victors would rule and that the vanquished would be ruled. But the god brought it about that both sides set up the victor's trophy, and neither side objected. Both sides, as if victorious, gave up the dead under truce, and both sides received their dead under truce, as if they had lost. Both sides claimed to have won, but as for territory, or cities, or power each side appeared to be the same after the battle as before. There was more uncertainty and confusion in Greece after the battle than before it.
>
> Xenophon, *Hellenica* 7.5.26–27

## CARTHAGE AND SYRACUSE, 404–360 B.C.

### Dionysius I of Syracuse Renews the Struggle against Carthage, 399–393 B.C.

On the face of it, Syracuse was in a much weaker position in 404 B.C. than Sparta (Map 17.3). Carthage had humbled Syracuse, while Sparta had overthrown Athens. But while Sparta faced challenges from Thebes and Athens as well as from Persia, Syracuse had no real Greek rivals. Syracuse had signed a humiliating treaty with Carthage in 405 B.C., but the

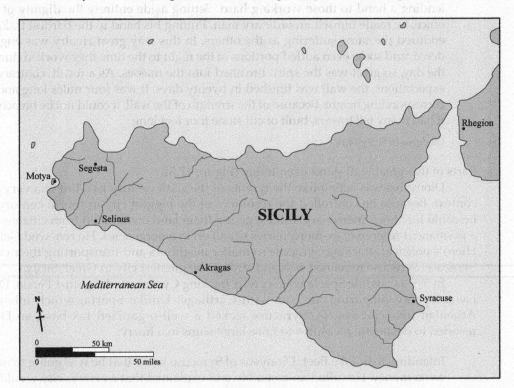

**MAP 17.3** Sites in western Greece mentioned in this chapter.

Syracusan strongman Dionysius had reasons to feel pleased. He had survived; the other Greek cities had been weakened even more than Syracuse; and within Syracuse, he was the sole ruler. He set about reviving Syracuse's fortunes.

Dionysius (whom we will now call **Dionysius I**, because he had a successor of the same name) needed to secure Syracuse against external attacks and secure himself against internal threats, such as the cavalry revolt that had almost toppled him in 405 B.C. He walled off the old city of Syracuse, the small island of Ortygia separated from the mainland by a narrow channel. There Dionysus could take refuge with his closest supporters and his mercenaries. In the Great Harbor, he built dockyards for a new fleet and fortified Epipolai, the high tableland behind the city, so that Syracuse could not be threatened as easily as it was in 415 and 405 B.C. He provided pay on a massive scale to the poor and showed a common touch:

> Wishing to build the walls quickly, Dionysius gathered a mass of peasants from the countryside, and from these chose 60,000 able men, to whom he parceled out the portions of the wall to be built. For each 200 yards he appointed a master-builder, and for each 100 feet a mason. He assigned 200 laborers from the common folk to each 100 feet. Beside these a great number of workmen cut the raw stone. Six thousand yoke of oxen brought the stone to its appointed place. The sight of so many workers astonished all who saw it, for each man worked eagerly to accomplish his task. In order to excite the enthusiasm of the masses Dionysus promised valuable gifts to those who finished first, special gifts for the master-builders, and still others for the masons and the common laborers. He himself, with his friends, oversaw the work every single day, inspecting each portion of the wall and always lending a hand to those working hard. Setting aside entirely the dignity of his office, he made himself an ordinary man. Putting his hand to the hardest task, he endured the same suffering as the others. In this way great rivalry was engendered, and some even added portions of the night to the time they worked during the day, so great was the spirit breathed into the masses. As a result, contrary to expectations, the wall was finished in twenty days. It was four miles long and of corresponding height. Because of the strength of the wall, it could not be breached. It had many tall towers, built of cut stone four feet long.

Diodorus of Sicily 14.18

Parts of this great wall stand even today (Figure 17.3).

Dionysius was acting like the tyrants of the sixth century B.C., but in a very different context. Because he controlled the resources of the biggest city in fourth-century Greece, he could hire huge mercenary armies, giving them land confiscated from citizens to create a permanent reserve of ex-mercenaries to call on in emergencies. He renewed Gelon's and Hiero's policies, attacking Syracuse's smaller neighbors and transporting their citizens to Syracuse. Syracuse remained rich and strong, the greatest city in Greek Sicily.

In 399 B.C., while Sparta was secretly backing Cyrus' revolt against Persia, Dionysius I was openly preparing for war with Carthage. Unlike Sparta, which inherited the Athenian financial system, Syracuse lacked a well-organized tax base, so Dionysius resorted to desperate measures to raise large sums in a hurry:

> Intending to build a fleet, Dionysus of Syracuse knew that he was going to need some money. He called an assembly and explained that a certain city would be betrayed to him, but for this he needed funds. He suggested that each citizen

**FIGURE 17.3**  The walls outside Syracuse, ca. 402 B.C., constructed by Dionysius I of Syracuse.

donate two staters.° This they did. After two or three days, pretending that the plot had failed, Dionysus thanked the citizens and returned to each what he had paid. In this way he gained their confidence. When he again asked for money, they gave it, expecting to receive it back. But this time he kept it for building the fleet.

. . . When he again needed money, he requested contributions. When the citizens declared that they had none to give, he removed all the furnishings from his palace and put them up for sale, pretending that he was driven to do this through lack of funds. At the sale he made a record of who bought what and for how much, and once he had the money, he ordered each man to return what he had bought.

Pseudo-Aristotle, *Economics* 2.1349a

°*staters:* Persian gold coins worth about twenty drachmas each (enough to feed a family of four for three weeks).

Dionysius made extraordinary efforts:

Gathering together a mass of workmen, he divided them up according to their abilities. He set over them the leading citizens and promised large rewards to those who could come up with a supply of armor. He distributed models of every type of armor, for he had gathered mercenaries from many nations. He wished that each of his soldiers use native armor, for he thought that in battle they would make a strong impression and that each man would fight best with armor to which he was accustomed. Because the Syracusans were much in favor of the plan, everybody worked as hard as possible to manufacture weaponry. Workmen filled not only the forecourts and back rooms of the temples, but the gymnasia and stoas in the agora. Apart from the public spaces, the most distinguished houses were filled with weaponry.

Diodorus of Sicily 14.41

As in his wall-building project, Dionysius ate, slept, and worked with the ordinary people, raising morale. He spent heavily on inventions, including the first effective war catapults, new siege towers, and special ships. He scoured Italy for the best timber and soon had 350 warships, and his metalworkers produced 140,000 shields, helmets, and daggers, and 14,000 breastplates. He offered high rates to attract the best mercenaries, including men from Sparta.

War fever ran high. In the fifth century B.C., Greeks and Phoenicians had coexisted in Sicily for a long time, trading and living together, but the bloody struggle of 409 to 405 B.C. changed that. In 398 B.C., Syracusans ransacked the homes of rich Carthaginians in their city, and the historian Diodorus of Sicily says that even though the Greeks hated the tyranny of Dionysius, they hated Carthaginians even more, murdering and torturing them wherever they found them.

In 397 B.C., Dionysius invaded Punic western Sicily (Punic is a Roman form of "Phoenician," used to describe the Carthaginians). He ravaged the country around Segesta, Carthage's strongest native ally (who had played a major role in the Athenian Sicilian expedition), and besieged Motya, a fortified island off the western tip of Sicily. His new catapults and siege towers worked well, and, after a long siege, his men stormed the town. The massacre that followed was as horrific as Carthage's destruction of Selinus, Akragas, and other Greek cities a decade before.

Now running short of money, Dionysius could not follow up his victory, and in 396 B.C., when Dionysius' force had dissipated, a vengeful Himilco (the victorious Carthaginian general in the war of 409–405 B.C.) reoccupied western Sicily and put Syracuse under siege for the third time in twenty years. Dionysius' warmongering had been popular a year before, but now that Carthaginians were camped outside the walls, a popular uprising almost overthrew him. The situation looked bleak for Syracuse until a plague broke out in the Carthaginian army, who, like the Athenians in 415 to 413 B.C. and the earlier Carthaginian force in 405 B.C., had pitched their camp in an unhealthy swamp:

The plague began with a mucous congestion, then came a swelling in the throat followed by a burning sensation and pain in the nerves of the back and a heaviness of the limbs. After that, dysentery, and pustules appeared all over the body. For most, such was the course of the disease, but some went mad or forgot absolutely everything and wandered through the camp completely out of their minds, striking anyone who came their way. In general, doctors were of no help both because of the severity of the suffering and the swiftness of the death that followed. Usually the afflicted died on the fifth or sixth day, enduring such awful tortures that those were considered fortunate who had died in battle.

Diodorus of Sicily 14.41

Dionysius defeated Himilco's now disintegrating army and broke up the Carthaginian fleet. Himilco paid a huge bribe to be allowed to sneak away while leaving his mercenaries to die. Back in Carthage, dishonored by defeat, Himilco starved himself to death.

The war between Carthage and Syracuse dragged on for a few more years until, in 393 B.C., the two sides made peace. The King's Peace of 387 B.C. left Sparta in control of the Aegean as a kind of Persian client; the Sicilian peace of 393 B.C. acknowledged Carthaginian control of the west and confirmed Syracuse as the undisputed ruler of Greek Sicily.

## THE GOLDEN AGE OF SYRACUSE, 393–367 B.C.

Dionysius I had not won a resounding victory, but he did restore Syracuse's prestige as the only major Greek city in Sicily. He wanted to establish himself as the great man of his age. He contracted polygamous dynastic marriages and brought more western Greeks under his control. In 388 B.C., after a year-long siege, he captured Rhegion on the toe of Italy, Syracuse's rival for a hundred years. Dionysius now became protector of most of the Greek cities in southern Italy. Fifty years earlier, there may have been 40,000 people living at Athens; now Syracuse had between fifty and a 100,000 residents, the largest Greek city in the world.

In 385 B.C., emboldened by success, Dionysius intervened in wars between Greek cities far up the Adriatic coast, showed interest in events in Epirus in northwest mainland Greece, and also supported Sparta in enforcing the King's Peace. Just as Sparta used fear of Persia to bolster her position in the Aegean, Dionysius used fear of Carthage to keep the Sicilian Greeks in line. Actually fighting Carthage, however, was ruinously expensive, and when Dionysius miscalculated and was forced to go to war with Carthage again between 382 and 374 B.C., he had the worst of it.

Like Gelon and Hiero a century earlier, Dionysius wanted to impress Aegean Greece with his magnificence. In 388 B.C., he sent his brother with several finely decorated chariot teams to the Olympic games along with professional singers to perform Dionysius' own poetry. Alas, his chariots were not successful, and the Greeks openly mocked his verse; some even demanded that Dionysius be banned from the Olympics. Undeterred, Dionysius promoted theater and art in Syracuse, bringing Aegean thinkers to his court. Plato visited in 388 or 387 B.C. One story (probably invented) says that Plato's philosophizing so irritated Dionysius that he had him thrown in chains and put up for sale in the slave market, where Plato's friends bought his freedom.

Syracuse was big, rich, strong, and cosmopolitan in the 370s B.C. After a lifetime of adventure Dionysius had made himself a great man, and in 367 B.C. he finally won the recognition he craved as a man of letters when his tragedy, *The Ransoming of Hector*, won first prize in a festival at Athens. Dionysius was so thrilled that, according to one source, he went on a drinking binge that killed him.

## ANARCHY IN THE WEST, 367–345 B.C.

Dionysius' rule over Syracuse was personal, and the tyrant-state unraveled after his death. Dionysius I was not the leader of a community of citizens, but a kind of bandit chief using bribes, threats, and trickery to keep the Syracusans under control, and the violence of his mercenaries when those methods failed. His son and successor **Dionysius II** (born around 396 B.C.) shared the first Dionysius' taste for wine and poetry, but lacked his edge, drive, and political skills. He was jealous of one **Dion** (dī-on), Syracuse's main diplomat, who was tied to the royal family by marriage. Dion, a devoted follower of Plato, was always urging philosophical purity on Dionysius II, and Dion talked Dionysius into inviting Plato, now at the height of his fame, back to Syracuse in 367 B.C. Plato apparently hoped to make Dionysius II into the philosopher-king he described in his celebrated dialogue, *The Republic,* a politically powerful man with philosophical training who would create a perfect society.

Unfortunately for Plato and Dion, while Dionysius II liked the idea of being an ideal ruler, he liked sex and drinking even more. Dion and his friends relentlessly pushed Dionysius II to embrace Platonic theory and to renounce tyranny, but Dion's enemies criticized such absurd fantasies. In 366 B.C., Dionysius II learned that Dion was talking secretly with Carthaginians. This presented a tough problem: if Dionysius did nothing Dion might launch a Carthaginian-backed coup, but if Dionysius killed Dion, that would surely set off other palace intrigues. Dionysius could exile Dion, but then he would have a rich and well-connected critic plotting against him. He compromised by sending Dion away while allowing him to keep his property. Dionysius II meanwhile kept Plato in Syracuse, but Plato kept urging him to surrender his ill-gotten gains and concentrate on virtue. Bored and irritated, Dionysius finally expelled Plato from the palace and made him live in the barracks with the mercenaries. In 360 B.C. Plato returned to Athens in disgust, this time for good.

Dionysius II fought another bloody and inconclusive war with Carthage and continued his father's policy of intervening in southern Italy, the Adriatic, and the Aegean, but paying for these wars diminished his power. In 357 B.C., Dion launched the long-awaited coup, leading to a decade of civil war during which Syracuse lost her dominion over the other western Greek cities. Carthage's last war against Syracuse ended in 366 B.C., after which the Carthaginians (like Persia) found that they could more easily keep the Greeks weak by supporting one faction against another than by defeating them in the field. In city after city, citizens and mercenaries now fought bloody battles for land while bands of ex-mercenaries wandered the countryside, sacking and taking anything they wanted. The population declined as rival warlords devastated the land. Plutarch claims that many of Sicily's cities were abandoned at this time and that in Syracuse wild animals prowled the marketplace. Around 350 B.C., anarchy gripped the west as strongly as it did the Aegean.

## CONCLUSION

Greece was passing through tremendous social change, driven in large part by its frenzied wars. States increasingly relied on the rich to finance common security, and a few men of staggering wealth, like Lysander and Jason, challenged entire city-states. The main beneficiaries were Persia and Carthage. Yet despite this backdrop of war, disorder, and fear, most Greeks were better off than before. More of them lived in democracies and traders filled their markets with exotic goods. Greek explorers visited India and the British Isles, and as we see in Chapter 18, "Greek Culture in the fourth century B.C.," artists and thinkers pushed outward the limits of imagination and reason. For all their problems, the Greeks in the mid-fourth century were right to see themselves as the center of world civilization.

## Key Terms

Artaxerxes, *371*

Agesilaos, *371*

King's Peace, *373*

Common Peace, *374*

Epaminondas, *374*

*ethnê, 376*

Jason of Pherae, *376*

Leuctra, *377*

Sacred Band, *377*

Dionysius I, *380*

Dionysius II, *383*

Dion, *384*

## Further Reading

Buckler, John, *The Theban Hegemony* (Cambridge, MA, 1980). Covers the exploits of Epaminondas.

Cargill, Jack, *The Second Athenian League: Empire or Free Alliance?* (Berkeley, 1981).

Cartledge, Paul, *Agesilaos and the Crisis of Sparta* (Baltimore, 1987). Detailed biography of King Agesilaos and sociological analysis of Sparta's decline.

Caven, Brian, *Dionysius I: War-lord of Sicily* (New Haven, 1990). The first book in English devoted to this key figure.

Davies, John, K., *Democracy and Classical Greece*, 2nd ed. (Stanford, 1993). Excellent chapters on early fourth-century Greece.

Dillery, John, *Xenophon and the History of His Times* (London, 1995). A study of Xenophon as a thoughtful and disillusioned observer of his age.

Lancel, Serge, *Carthage* (Oxford 1995). Overview of Carthaginian history and archaeology.

Lewis, David M., John Boardman, Simon Hornblower, and Martin Ostwald, eds., *The Cambridge Ancient History VI: The Fourth Century B.C.*, 2nd ed. (Cambridge, 1994). Thorough essays reviewing all parts of the Greek world.

Strauss, Barry, *Athens After the Peloponnesian War* (Ithaca, NY, 1986). Excellent study of how the demographic disaster of the Peloponnesian War affected Athenian society.

### ANCIENT TEXTS

Diodorus of Sicily, *The History*, Book 14. In *The Library of History VI*, tr. C. H. Oldfather (Cambridge, MA: Loeb Classical Library, 1946). Parallel Greek and English texts describing Sicilian history.

Plutarch, *Lives of Agesilaos, Pelopidas, and Dion*. In *The Age of Alexander*, tr. Ian Scott-Kilvert (Harmondsworth, UK, 1973). These biographies contain much information on Sparta, Thebes, and Syracuse in the early fourth century B.C.

Xenophon, *A History of My Times*, tr. George Cawkwell (Harmondsworth, UK, 1966). Translation of Xenophon's *Hellenica*, the main narrative source for the years 399 to 362 B.C.

Xenophon, *The Persian Expedition*, tr. Rex Warner (Harmondsworth, UK, 1949). Translation of Xenophon's *Anabasis*, an eye-witness account of the Greek mercenaries' march through the Persian Empire in 399 B.C.

## CHAPTER 18

# Greek Culture in the Fourth Century B.C.

The social changes that we traced in Chapter 17, "The Greeks between Persia and Carthage, 399–360 B.C." drove momentous cultural changes. We begin with material culture, which became more complex in the fourth century. Most patrons and craftsmen still worked within the classical framework developed in the fifth century, but some experimented boldly, trying to make sense of a new world where aristocrats increasingly rose above the mass of ordinary citizens.

## MATERIAL CULTURE

### Sculpture

The high Classical sculpture of the fifth century B.C. had worked magnificently. Its canons of proportion, pose, and subject matter seemed almost perfect, and artists who had learned their skills under the old masters could not think of abandoning classicism. But the Peloponnesian War changed art as much as it did everything else. After 404 B.C., Athens and Syracuse no longer dominated artistic patronage (Map 18.1), and new centers sprang up, providing more room for innovation and diversity and the evolution of the versatile **late classical sculpture**. Some sculptors self-consciously turned back to what they knew worked, producingstatues that echoed early-fifth-century formalism and evoked a more secure age. Figure 18.1 shows one such rendering of the goddess Athena. Gone is the clinging drapery of the Peloponnesian War years; the formal folds of her dense, heavy robe and her serious expression look back to the early fifth century, making her seem distant and imposing. Yet the sculptor tilted her head to the right, adding lightness to the pose. No expert could mistake her for a fifth-century statue.

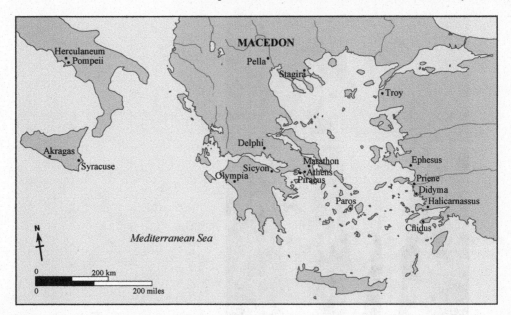

**MAP 18.1** Sites mentioned in this chapter.

**FIGURE 18.1** The Piraeus Athena, a bronze statue by an unknown sculptor, cast around 350 B.C. Height 8 feet.

**FIGURE 18.2** Hermes and Dionysus, probably by Praxiteles, ca. 340 B.C. Marble. Height 7 feet, 1 inch. *Piraeus Museum.*

Some fourth-century patrons wanted statues like this, which did not copy fifth-century masterpieces yet still spoke the same visual language of serenity and reliability. Others wanted the opposite, figures full of energy, verging on the lighthearted, as if celebrating their escape from the rigid social structures of the fifth century. Figure 18.2 shows a statue of the god Hermes with the baby Dionysus. The famous **Praxiteles** (prak-**sit**-e-lēz) probably carved it, the only statue by a classical master to survive antiquity. Praxiteles did not break with classical forms but used them to new ends, exaggerating the S-curve pose by having Hermes thrust out his right hip to balance the baby on his left arm. The statue looks unstable, implying movement, and gives a sense that we have caught a moment in a larger story. Praxiteles was famous for giving marble a kind of fluidity, almost a soft focus, as in the smooth junction of Hermes' torso and hips and soft modeling of his jaw. Praxiteles gave his statues long limbs and small heads, making them less realistic but more elegant.

Praxiteles' most famous achievement was to make female nudes acceptable. Since 700 B.C., Greek sculptors had always shown women clothed. Praxiteles' nude Aphrodite of Cnidus, carved around 350 B.C., created a sensation. The original is lost, but Roman copies survive (Figure 18.3). The statue stood in a circular open-air shrine in Cnidus in southwestern Asia Minor. It had the soft modeling and S-curves we have already seen, but whereas most statues were made to be seen frontally, Praxiteles carved this one to be seen from every angle. It quickly became the most famous statue in Greece. Lucian

**FIGURE 18.3** Roman copy of Praxiteles' Aphrodite of Cnidus. Marble. Height 6 feet, 8 inches. The original was carved around 350 B.C. Marble, H: 6 feet, 8 inches. *Olympia Museum.*

(or perhaps someone imitating his style), a Greek comic writer active under the Roman Empire around A.D. 100–120, described the impact it had on (male) visitors:

> After enjoying looking at the plants, we went into the temple [at Cnidus]. The goddess stands just in the center, a work of art made of Parian marble,° with a sublime smile, lips lightly parted in a laugh. All her glory is there to see. She wears nothing at all, but conceals her crotch nonchalantly with her hand. The artist's great skill has suited the hard, unyielding stone to every limb. Charicles,° as if quite mad, shouted out, "O lucky Ares who was bound to this goddess!°" He ran up to the statue and, stretching on his tippy toes, kissed the statue on her shining lips. But Callicratidas stood silent, his mind struck dumb.
>
> The temple had doors on either side so that you could get a good look at the goddess from the other side and every part of her could be wondered at. Those

°*Parian marble:* Marble from the island of Paros was the most expensive.   °*Charicles:* Charicles, Callicratidas, and "the Athenian" are fictional characters in the story.   °*this goddess:* Homer says that Ares (god of war) had an affair with Aphrodite, but her husband Hephaestus (the lame craftsman-god) trapped him in a net. Charicles says that Aphrodite is so beautiful that being thus humiliated was worth it.

entering at the opposite door got a good look at her from behind. We decided to see the whole of the goddess and so went around to the other side. When the key-keeper opened the doors, we were astounded at the beauty of the woman entrusted to us. Well, the Athenian, after he had regarded her quietly for a while, got a glimpse of her pudenda, and immediately began shouting, even more crazed than Charicles, "By Heracles! Check out the curve of that back! Great ass! Something to really grab on to! Check out the way he's carved that luscious bum, not too thin and hugging the bone, and not too fat. Her butt is smiling—and how sweetly! Nice turn of the thighs, and the shins, all the way down to the foot!" . . . Charicles was transfixed with amazement, and tears clouded his eyes . . .

Pseudo-Lucian, *The Lovers* 13–14

Others responded even more passionately. According to one story, a discoloration of the marble on the statue's buttocks marked the spot where one young man gave physical expression to his admiration!

Praxiteles' boldness no doubt shocked conservatives but was in tune with the times. Other sculptors experimented similarly with new subjects and a looser, more naturalistic form. Within twenty years, female nudes were common, and other sculptors (especially Skopas and Alexander the Great's personal sculptor Lysippos,) moved even further away from frontal views. To patrons and artists living in the rigidly egalitarian societies of the fifth century, it perhaps made sense that there should be just one way to see a statue and that the female form should be hidden. But in the brave, new, and very international world of the fourth century, the same figure might look entirely different, depending on the viewer's perspective. Assumptions that had guided life for 400 years were dissolving.

## Architecture

Architects too were caught between their fifth-century legacy and new demands. Just as some sculptors made statues more elegant by lengthening their limbs, some architects elongated columns to make taller, lighter, and airier temples. Ornate **Corinthian capitals**, wrapped in leaves and spirals, also lightened the effect (see Figure 9.6). The earliest known Corinthian column is a single example from the Temple to Apollo at Bassae from the mid-fifth century (Figure 14.13), but Corinthian capitals only really became popular around 350 B.C. Compared to the austere Doric and Ionic orders, Corinthian columns can seem frivolous and fussy—as, indeed, can much fourth-century art.

Architects experimented with other ways to enhance elegance. A gigantic new temple at Ephesus in Asia Minor, for instance, sat atop fourteen steps rather than on the two steps of the Archaic temple it replaced. Late in the fourth century, architects at Didyma, south of Ephesus, took even more chances: Thirteen steps led up to a forest of columns, beyond which was an elaborate inner doorway. Then, instead of entering a roofed *cella* as had been normal for 400 years, the visitor went down steep stairs into an open courtyard with a small *cella*, probably an ancient shrine, at the end (Figure 18.4). The open-air temple at Didyma cast aside conventional patterns of religious architecture, as did round buildings called *tholoi* (singular, *tholos*, Figure 18.5; *tholos* is also used to describe the round underground "beehive" tombs of the Bronze Age Greeks).

New forms for temples encouraged new uses, and some *tholoi* were used not to honor Olympian gods, but to worship underworld spirits, or even great men. Before the

**FIGURE 18.4** The inner court of the temple of Apollo at Didyma, begun in 313 B.C. The photo looks over the surprising open inner court toward the steps leading down from the magnificent entrance. The foundations of the *cella* are visible in the foreground. *Rome, Vatican Museum.*

century ended, the living royal family of Macedon honored themselves with a giant *tholos* in the sanctuary of Olympia itself.

Experiments with religious architecture and the erosion of longstanding boundaries between gods and mortals came together in such monuments as the **Mausoleum of Halicarnassus,** counted among the seven wonders of the ancient world. This city— Herodotus' birthplace—was under Persian control from 395 B.C. Around 370 B.C., the Persians appointed a non-Greek aristocrat named Mausolus as satrap for this part of the empire and Mausolus made Halicarnassus his capital. Before his death in 353 B.C., Mausolus hired Greek craftsmen to make him the grandest tomb the Aegean had ever seen. It was destroyed long ago, but Roman descriptions and surviving fragments make possible a rough reconstruction (Figure 18.6). The Mausoleum combined a massive base and over-life-sized sculptures with a temple-like second tier and steep roof with an enormous bronze four-horse chariot at the top. The monument stood 150 feet high, a hint of things to come as non-Greek kings from the edges of the Aegean appropriated the finest classical traditions but turned them to new uses. In the fifth century, great architecture was reserved for gods; no mortal was allowed such monuments. But by 350 B.C., if any doubts remained whether great men could challenge the *polis,* the new art styles dispelled them.

For 400 years, *poleis* had poured their greatest energy and wealth into religious architecture. But now Greeks started spending even more on non-religious civic buildings. The city of **Priene** (prī-ē-nē) on the west coast of Asia Minor, completely rebuilt between 350 and 325 B.C., is a good example. Priene's leaders built a beautiful but small Ionic

**FIGURE 18.5** The marble *tholos* at Delphi, ca. 360 B.C.

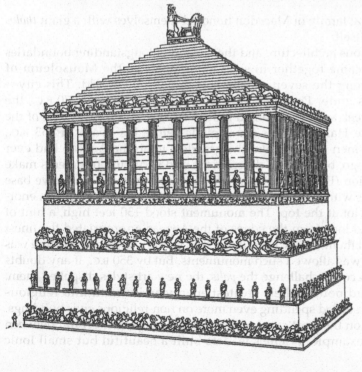

**FIGURE 18.6** Reconstruction of the Mausoleum at Halicarnassus, ca. 350–340 B.C. Only the lower walls and pieces of statuary survive. Height 150 feet.

temple (just 120 by 63 feet) at the top of the site but spent far more on enormous stoas around the agora, with a council chamber and other public offices along its upper side. A huge theater dominated the town, and an even larger gymnasium and stadium occupied its lowest area (Figure 18.7). The appearance of Greek cities was changing in the fourth century in line with changes in Greek society.

## Painting

We know more about painting in the fourth century than in earlier periods. As before, vase paintings hint at the lost techniques of wall painters, but after 400 B.C. mosaics of colored pebbles also reproduce the effects of painting, and after 350 B.C. we have actual wall paintings from Macedonian tombs. Dozens of wall paintings from Pompeii and Herculaneum in Italy, preserved when Mount Vesuvius erupted in A.D. 79, also appear to be copies, if sometimes remote, of fourth-century B.C. Greek works.

Two artists who worked at Athens during the Peloponnesian War made important technical advances in the early fourth century: Zeuxis (zūk-sis), famous for shadowing and delicate gradations of color, and Parrhasius (pa-rā-sē-us), known for subtle use of outlines. But Athens was now only one of several artistic centers. Artists traveled far and wide, adorning cities from Akragas to Ephesus. In the fifth century, the main employment for wall painters was on public monuments, but during the Peloponnesian War wealthy individuals began hiring these men. Alcibiades scandalized Athens by locking a famous painter in his house until he made it look as fine as the city's monuments. Fourth-century aristocrats went further still, marking themselves off from the mass of citizens by building bigger houses and adorning them with mosaic floors, tapestries, and statues. To keep up with fashion, they paid huge sums to hire top artists.

**FIGURE 18.7** Modern model of the city of Priene, ca. 325 B.C. The Ionic temple is at the top left. At the center is the agora, with stoas, surrounded by private housing; at the top, the theater; in the foreground, athletic facilities.

Such private money transformed the artists' status. Zeuxis and Parrhasius were famously arrogant. Parrhasius went around in a purple cloak and gold diadem, insulting everyone, while the wealthy Zeuxis claimed that his art was divine and priceless. Such men did not need to beg democratic assemblies for commissions, because they had private patrons. Increasingly, the best painters, sculptors, and architects felt that they had more to say to a narrow, highly educated elite who appreciated their work than they did to their fellow citizens.

Red-figured vases give a sense of the new developments, even though the genre declined in the fourth century as the rich shifted from painted pottery to metal plate—even silver and gold—for their dinner parties. Like sculptors, some vase painters clung to fifth-century traditions, while others pursued fluidity and elegance, adding more details, new colors, relief decoration, and gold leaf. To modern tastes, the effect often seems cluttered. Figure 18.8 shows an almost baroque example, made in southern Italy an to hold the ashes of a dead man. The main scene shows the deceased, standing beside his horse, as part of his own funerary monument. Above is a banquet scene. The other side shows a complex assembly of gods. The artist tries to give a sense of depth by overlapping the figures and packs every inch with curling tendrils of filling ornament.

Figure 18.9 suggests how fourth-century painters represented depth. It seems to show a scene from a play and reveals how elaborate stage scenery had become. An old man (out of the photo) talks to a young man, while a girl watches through an open door. We look up at the scene, seeing the porch ceiling. A column partly obscures the double doors.

**FIGURE 18.8** A south Italian volute krater (so-called because the handles look like volutes on an Ionic column) in an ornate style, ca. 310 B.C. This vase, set in its own stand, was used as a funerary urn in a Greek colony in south Italy. Height 48 inches.

**FIGURE 18.9** Fragment from a south Italian red-figure krater, ca. 350 B.C., with a scene from a tragedy, set in front of a palace. The painter is aware of foreshortening and illustrates sophisticated contemporary stage scenery. Height of fragment 10 inches.

The painter used foreshortening, making the girl in the door smaller than the man at the right, but did not use a vanishing point where the lines of the porch converge on some distant spot (the vanishing point in art was not discovered until the Italian Renaissance).

## Conclusion

Artists of all kinds simultaneously reflected and reinforced the new social structures emerging in the fourth century B.C. These artists were caught between the legacy of the fifth century, with its single way of seeing an idealized egalitarian *polis* set apart from the gods, and a new wish to express difference, change, and the power of great men.

## PLATO

As in earlier centuries, there were parallels between the creative struggles of visual artists and the achievements of Greek intellectuals. Fourth-century thinkers were also interested in defining a place within the egalitarian *polis* for outstanding individuals, balancing fifth-century traditions with new social forces. But while sculptors, architects, and painters needed rich patrons, philosophers were normally rich men themselves. And thanks largely to **Plato** (ca. 427–347 B.C.,) Athens' dominance over philosophy grew, rather than declined, in the fourth century.

Plato grew up in a wealthy Athenian family during the Peloponnesian War and, like many men of his background, was drawn to Socrates. After Socrates' shocking execution in 399 B.C., Plato devoted the next fifty years to systematizing and elaborating his master's thought, adding speculations of his own. Because Socrates wrote nothing down, we rarely know whether positions taken in Plato's literary texts belong to Socrates or Plato.

Plato wanted to pursue *aretê* (ar-e-**tā**), "virtue" or "excellence." Within the *polis* he saw two threats to *aretê*. The first was democracy, which (as Plato saw it) empowered ignorant people, like those who had condemned Socrates to death. Second was the false teaching of the sophists—that nothing is permanent, values are relative, and knowledge impossible. The structures of contemporary *poleis*, Plato felt, only encouraged nonsense like the sophists' claims; *poleis* should be placed in the hands of philosophers who understood the Socratic–Platonic way of seeing the world.

Plato's longest works explained how he thought society needed to change. The *Republic*, written probably in the 380s B.C., describes Plato's ideal state; the *Laws*, from around 355 B.C., describes the best that can be accomplished if *poleis* cannot reach that ideal. In either case, Plato insists, a small elite should rule, trained in philosophy, devoting their lives to the citizens' happiness, living without property or families.

Plato justified his arguments by developing the world's first coherent philosophical theory of knowledge. Like Socrates, he asked how we can know anything and how we can know that we know it. By 360 B.C., aristocrats all over Greece—like Dion, referred to in Chapter 17—were trying to put his theories into practice; and his theories remain at the center of philosophical discussion today.

## The Theory of the Forms

How can we measure the goodness of a life? It is not enough just to say that this or that act is just, or good, or beautiful. To live a good, just, and beautiful life, you must know what goodness, justice, and beauty are, not simply notice alleged examples. Socrates asked, how can we say something is just unless we know what justice is? "Justice," Plato reasoned, is a timeless, eternal thing. The everyday world of the senses is constantly changing, so the ultimate form of justice cannot exist in everyday life. According to Plato's **theory of Forms** (*eidea*, our word "idea"), there must be an unchanging world beyond the shifting world we live in. We cannot see the true forms of justice, goodness, and beauty because they exist in another and invisible realm, but they are more real than anything in our experience.

Plato's explanation combined Heraclitus' view that the world is in constant change with Parmenides' notion that reality is unchanging and knowable only through the mind. Objects in the changing everyday world depend on the world of Forms, of which they are dim and inadequate reflections. How can we say that a particular dinner "is a *good* meal" or that Bruce Springsteen "is a *good* songwriter," unless both—food and songwriting—share in an invisible and eternal quality of goodness?

We can grasp the Forms, Plato suggested, through mathematics. In Greek, *mathêmatika* means "things that are known," that is, through the mind. No one ever saw the square root of two, but it exists and will always exist, independent of the sensual world. Plato argued that the true Forms of goodness, justice, and beauty are equally independent of the world, as invisible as the square root of two.

Plato used stories to explain his sometimes very abstract thought. He rejected traditional myths because they lied about reality (saying that the gods were immoral and other absurdities) and invented his own myths to explain reality. He presents the relationship between the world of the eternal Forms and the everyday changing world in a famous dialogue between Socrates and his friend Glaucon, the **Parable of the Cave**, part of Plato's *Republic*. Socrates speaks first, and Glaucon gives brief replies:

> "I want you to think about human nature, whether it is enlightened or ignorant, as being similar to the following experience. Think of humans as living in an underground cave with a long entrance turned to the light all along its great

width. From childhood their legs and necks are bound so that they can only see ahead of them. They cannot turn their heads because of the bonds. From behind and above them, and at some distance, comes the light of a fire. Picture now between the fire and the bound humans a road, high, and along the road is built a low wall, very much as at puppet shows the puppet masters erect a wall between them and the audience, above which they show the puppets."

"I see it," he said.

"Imagine now that there are people walking along the wall, carrying animals made of stone and of wood and other substances. Some are speaking and some are silent."

"You speak of a strange place and of strange prisoners."

"Very much like ourselves," I said. "Now do you think that these prisoners can see anything of themselves or anything else except the shadows of the objects cast by the fire on the walls of the cave in front of them?"

"How could they see anything else if they spent their whole lives with their heads in bonds?"

"Would they see anything more of the objects carried along the road?"

"Of course not."

"If they were able to speak to one another, don't you think that they would think that the things they saw were real?"

"No doubt."

"What if there should be an echo from the wall of their prison opposite them? When one of those passing by behind them should speak, would they not think that it was the shadow passing before them on the wall?"

"Certainly."

"Consider," I said, "what would naturally happen to them if they were released from their bondage and their delusion? What if one of them were let go and compelled to stand up suddenly and to turn his head around and to walk and to turn his eyes upward toward the light? Wouldn't he feel pain, and because of the flashing and sparkling be unable to see the objects whose shadows he had seen formerly? And what if somebody said to him that what he saw before was illusion, and now that he was turned closer to reality he saw more correctly— what do you think he would say? And what if someone were to point out the objects that had been carried past and ask him what they were? Don't you think he would be a loss to say, and that he would think that what he used to see was more real than the objects now being pointed out to him?"

"Surely," he said.

"And if someone forced him to look at the light, don't you think he would be in pain, and would turn away and look at the things that he could see, and that he would think these things to be far clearer than the things pointed out to him?"

"Yes."

"And if someone should drag him by force out of there and up the rough and steep ascent, and he should not quit before dragging him into the light of the sun, don't you think that he would be in pain and would resent being dragged there? And when he came into the light, would not his eyes be so dazzled by the light that he could not see a single thing of what he was now told were real?"

Plato has Socrates imagine the freed prisoner's eyes adjusting to the light until he could at last see everything, whereupon he realizes that inside the cave he had mistaken illusions for reality. Socrates continues:

"When he thought of his former home and what passed for wisdom there, and of his fellow-prisoners, don't you think that he would congratulate himself on his good fortune, and take pity on them?"

"I think so."

"No doubt a certain amount of honor and respect was to be won among the prisoners, for whoever saw most keenly the shadows as they passed by and could remember in what order they were accustomed to come and go, so that he was best able to predict which would come next. Do you think that our released prisoner would want to have these honors or would envy those who, possessing them, exercised great power? Wouldn't he rather feel, as Homer puts it, that he would rather 'be a serf in the house of a landless peasant' or in fact anything else in the world, rather than think and live as they do?"

"Yes," replied Glaucon, "he would prefer anything to a life like theirs."

"Now think about this," I said. "Suppose this man were to return to his seat in the cave. Would he not be blinded by the darkness, after coming away from the sun?"

"Surely."

"If he were forced to distinguish the shadows in competition with the other prisoners, while he was still blinded, before his eyes got used to the darkness, a process that would take some time, don't you think he would make a fool of himself? Wouldn't they say that his trip up above had ruined his eyes, and for this reason there was no reason to attempt to go up out of the cave. And if anyone tried to release them and lead them upwards, would they not wish to seize him and kill him, and would they not do so if they could?"

"I very much agree."

"You won't go far wrong, my dear Glaucon," Socrates went on . . . "if you equate the upward assent and the viewing of the things there with the soul's ascent into the intelligible realm . . . and the final thing to discover there, and not easy to see, is the Form [*idea*] of the Good. Once seen, it is understood to be the cause of all that is right and beautiful, producing in the visible realm light and the source of light, and in the intelligible realm itself being the controlling source of truth and intelligence. Anyone who hopes to act rationally either in the public or private realm must perceive it."

"I agree, in as much as I can follow you."

"Well then, agree with this too, and don't be surprised if those who succeed in getting there have little interest in everyday affairs, but their souls constantly drive them upward . . . And don't be surprised if after contemplation of the divine, when returning to earthly affairs, that such men quite make the fool of themselves if, while they are still blinded and unaccustomed to the darkness, they are put on trial and forced to discuss the shadows and images of justice of men who have never seen absolute justice."

Plato, *Republic* 7.514a–517e

Plato's argument struck at the foundations of democracy. A democracy had executed Socrates because it could not accept his claim that he alone saw properly, in the intelligible realm. But Plato was not a simple oligarch: The rich and noble were as deluded as the poor. Only people who made the painful philosophical ascent to reality understood truth, and they could not explain this to the ignorant masses who had not. The sophists, who claimed to teach wisdom to anyone, were therefore charlatans. Socrates explains to Glaucon that if the Parable of the Cave makes sense, "we must reject the conception of education professed by those [sophists] who say that they can put into the mind knowledge that was not there before—rather as if they could put sight into blind eyes" (*Republic* 7.518c).

## Education, the Soul, and the State

Plato based his educational system on his understanding of the soul. Earlier notions of the *psychê*, the "breath-soul" or ghost, attributed to it a thin reality and an unhappy existence, but to Plato the soul is itself a Form, eternal and perfect. The modern vision of the eternal soul is Plato's formulation, as modified and refined by the early Christian fathers and later followers of Plato. When freed from the ever-changing body, the soul directly perceives the world of Forms. Each eternal soul occupies a series of mortal bodies. When the body dies, the soul is judged then sent for 1,000 years to tenfold rewards in heaven or tenfold punishments in the underworld. Then the soul enters a new body, but only after drinking from the River of Forgetfulness (*Lêthê*). Philosophy can break through the barrier of forgetfulness so that the soul remembers what it already knew, grasping once more the world of Forms.

Both the *polis* and the soul have three elements, Plato thought, and Justice is the product of their harmonious functioning. The ideal *polis* is like an individual writ large. In a *polis,* the first element is the *rulers*, embodying intelligence and reason. The second is the *warriors*, under the rulers' direction; and the third is the *workers*, in agriculture, commerce, and crafts. In an ideal *polis,* the rulers should live together communally, like the Spartiates (whom Plato admired), and own no property. They would then have no interest in profit, which, Plato thought, weighs down the soul and disguises its true nature. The justice of the *polis* consists of the three classes accepting their own obligations without coveting or resenting those of another.

Similarly, the individual soul has three parts: reason (like the rulers), desire (like the aggressive soldiers), and will (like the workers, who get things done). Hence we may desire to drink, but reason tells us the water is poisoned. *Will* decides the outcome of the conflict. Many sophists held that the world came from accidental, irrational forces, but the order and harmony of nature convinced Plato that intelligence came first—that very faculty which lives in the human soul and enables the individual to attune its harmonies with those of the greater world.

Plato never presented his philosophy as a system, leading from first principles to necessary conclusions. As he saw it, his task was to lead men toward remembering what their souls already knew. He taught through argument, or dialectic, as Socrates had done. He founded a school called the **Academy** in Athens' suburbs, and wealthy young men flocked there. Philosophy offered students a whole way of life. The process of arguing and reasoning was itself the education they received. Plato presented his theories in imaginary written debates between Socrates and other thinkers, often sophists. Most dialogues reach no conclusion about the problems they discuss. The dialogues of Plato were probably read aloud in this context, to serve as a basis for discussion. Philosophy is a work-in-progress where there are no simple answers, and sometimes no answers at all.

Few fourth-century Greeks liked the authoritarian worlds Plato described in the *Republic* and *Laws*, but the "Socratic method," using rigorous logic to examine the shortcomings of contemporary thought, became the central pillar of rational thought. It remains so today, regardless of cultural context.

## ARISTOTLE

The most famous of Plato's students was **Aristotle**, born in 384 B.C. in Stagira, a small town in the north Aegean. His father became court doctor at Pella, the capital of Macedon, and Aristotle grew up in a royal setting wholly different from the democratic city that shaped Plato's early experiences.

Aristotle moved to Athens when just seventeen. He distinguished himself at the Academy, but when Plato died in 347 B.C., the other members chose someone else to fill the master's shoes. Like many ambitious fourth-century intellectuals and artists, Aristotle attached himself to a minor king on the fringe of the Persian Empire. He settled near Troy, where he married a local king's niece. He did important biological research here, cataloguing over 2,000 species of animals and plants. His precise observations would not be equaled until the seventeenth century A.D., and in the 1850s Charles Darwin still found Aristotle one of the most reliable sources of information.

Aristotle seemed destined for a quiet life as a provincial professor until, in 342 B.C., he was summoned back to Macedon to tutor the king's fourteen-year-old son Alexander. When Alexander became king in 336 B.C., Aristotle returned to Athens and opened a new school, the **Lyceum** (lī-sē-um, named after a nearby shrine of Apollo Lykeios, "Apollo the wolf god"). The location of Aristotle's Lyceum was accidentally discovered during preparations for the 2004 Olympic games in Athens. Aristotle did his most important work here between 335 and 323 B.C., the year Alexander the Great died (Figure 18.10).

### Aristotle's Thought

Unlike his teacher, Aristotle systematized his philosophy. Of over 150 works that he wrote, 25 to 30 survive (the authorship of some is disputed); by contrast, all of Plato's writings survive. Aristotle's extant treatises are dry and dense. Several may be lecture notes, not finished compositions. They are comprehensive, analytical, and rigorous, but rarely entertaining. Scholars usually group them into three sets: (i) logic and metaphysics; (ii) nature, life, and mind (including biology, meteorology, physics, and a kind of psychology); and (iii) ethics, politics, and art.

Like Plato, Aristotle argued that true understanding must go beyond sense impressions: There must be first principles that underlie the variety and change in the world. Unlike Plato, however, Aristotle insisted that the sensual world is real, not illusory. To understand anything, he argued, we must still begin from sensory data. It might seem that experience provides no proper object for knowledge because everything is constantly changing, but by classifying data and organizing them into typologies, we can make sense of life's disorderliness and arrive at laws of nature, which are general principles that do not change.

Classifying observed data called for more rigorous **rules of logic**. Aristotle began from the principle that contradictory statements cannot be true: *A* cannot be *B* and not-*B* at the same time. People who maintain that contradictory statements *can* in fact be true refute themselves: "Contradictory statements can both be true" means that the contradiction to that very statement is also true, namely that "contradictory statements *cannot* both be true." Therefore any such contradictory statement is "illogical," that is, disordered, refuting itself.

**FIGURE 18.10** Portrait of Aristotle. Roman copy, ca. A.D. 100, of Greek original.

In Aristotle's view, we do not need to imagine invisible Forms existing outside time and space to explain what we see. For example, we can understand "dogs" by examining many of them, discovering what it is that leads us to classify them as dogs, why we think some animals (wolves, dingoes) are like dogs, and why others (spiders, birds) are not; but there is no ideal "dogness" of which all existing dogs are merely pale reflections. Aristotle could not see how Plato's Forms connected to the physical world or explained change in it. He also rejected the fifth-century atomist philosophers' theory that change was accidental, the result of random motion; the true cause or explanation of change, he insisted, lay in its *end*, its purpose (Greek *têlos*). Philosophers call this approach **teleology**, "the study of ends."

Aristotle's argument that change is always progress toward some end, and that the end *causes* the change, is called the **theory of potentiality** (Greek *dynamis*, our "dynamic"). An embryo, for example, is not a human but will potentially become one, like its parents. It is the *physis*, "nature," of an embryo to grow into an adult human. Humanness is the embryo's end, toward which it grows. That is why its development follows a certain course. The embryo is *potentially* an adult human, even if it died in the womb. Everything has an end, a *têlos*. The *têlos* of humans is to live together in communities; the *têlos* of communities is to maximize happiness; and the *polis* is the type of community that does that most efficiently.

But what causes movement toward the *têlos*? Here Aristotle abandoned observation and classification and moved toward a purely theoretical account. Nothing can be self-moved, self-caused, because all change is process, a growing toward a *têlos* that already exists somewhere outside the thing that is changing. To have a baby girl, you must first have an adult woman. Such must be true of the whole world and its operations. Just as there is an external cause for all change within the world, there must also be an external cause for the world itself, the **Prime Mover**, the ultimate "causeless cause" standing outside the universe, causing everything that happens within it. The Prime Mover is eternal and has always existed. It is the perfection toward which everything strives.

Motion is change from potential to actual, but the Prime Mover is perfect and without potential, containing no motion within itself. Its perfection led Christian thinkers to liken it to God, and the theologian St. Thomas Aquinas (A.D. 1225–1274) used Aristotle's argument as part of his proof of God's existence. But for Aristotle, the Prime Mover has no personality. It is pure mind, life itself, embracing through mind the entire universe for all eternity. The Prime Mover does not know about the things in the world, or even of the world's existence, because the world is characterized by motion and change, whereas the Prime Mover knows no motion or change.

Aristotle organized his account of the universe around the Prime Mover. The earth is at the center, surrounded by invisible spheres made of *aether,* the fifth substance (*quintessence*) after fire, air, water, and earth. The first sphere around the earth belongs to the moon and separates the realms of growth, change, and decay of this world from the celestial realms of eternally perfect, unchanging circular motion. The planets, sun, and moon are lights fixed each in its own sphere, and stars are fixed in the outermost sphere. The spheres rotate, but on different axes in a complex way (explaining the irregular motion of the planets). Beyond the sphere of stars is the Prime Mover, wrapped in eternal self-contemplation, toward which all the things of the world aspire through their *dynamis,* the urge of nature.

Virtually every Greek, Roman, Christian, and Muslim astronomer accepted Aristotle's model until Nicolaus Copernicus (A.D. 1473–1543) argued that the sun is the center of our system, and the physics and observations of Johannes Kepler (A.D. 1571–1630) and Galileo Galilei (A.D. 1564–1642) demonstrated the truth of these claims.

Some of Aristotle's differences from Plato seem not to have concerned Aristotle much, such as Plato's notion of immortal souls migrating from body to body, but their disagreement over the nature of virtue had to be faced. For Plato, proximity to the Forms explained what was just, good, and beautiful. Because Aristotle denied eternal, external standards, he had to think about right and wrong as purely practical matters. In this context, he made his famous remark that "man is a political animal": Humans are creatures designed to live in the *polis*. Behavior that favored life in the *polis* was "good," whereas behavior that interfered was "bad."

As a rule of thumb, "good" behavior follows the mean between extremes, which constitute "bad" behavior. This **doctrine of the mean** was the key to Aristotle's ethical thought. Courage lies between cowardice and recklessness. Temperance stands between self-indulgence and abstemiousness. Generosity comes between stinginess and extravagance. There is nothing absolutely "good" or "bad" about virtuous behavior, as there had been for Plato, but behaving "down the middle" favors harmony within the *polis*:

> First we must consider that moral qualities are so constituted as to be harmed by
> deficiency or excess as we see is the case with strength and health (for we must
> use the visible as witness to the invisible). Too much or too little exercise
> damages one's strength. Likewise too much or too little food and drink destroys
> the health, whereas just the right amount creates, increases, and preserves the

health. The same is true of temperance, courage, and the other virtues. He who runs away in fear all the time and never stands up to anything becomes a coward; he who never fears anything and takes everything on, becomes rash. He who indulges in every pleasure and abstains from none is a profligate; he who avoids every pleasure, like a bumpkin, becomes insensible. In short, temperance and courage are harmed by excess and deficiency, but preserved by observing the mean.

Aristotle, *Nicomachean Ethics* 1104a

For once agreeing with Plato, Aristotle linked individual virtue—ethics—with its communal pursuit—politics. As he saw it, personal ethics made sense only in the life of a *polis*:

From this it is clear that the *polis* belongs to a class that exists in nature and that the human is by nature a political animal [*politikon zoon*] . . . It is clear that the *polis* is by nature prior to the individual. For as the individual is not self-sufficient after separation, he will stand in the same relationship to the whole [i.e., the *polis*] as to the parts [i.e., the citizens]. Whatever cannot associate in a community with others, or through independence has no need of the *polis,* is either an animal or a god. The urge for such an association in all humans therefore comes from nature. Our greatest benefactor is he who first created such an association. As a man who has reached perfection is the greatest of animals, so he is the worst of all when separated from law and justice.

Aristotle, *Politics* 1253a

Aristotle divided the *polis* into component elements: individuals, households, villages, and the *polis* itself. Individuals combine into households, households into villages, and villages into *poleis* because otherwise they are incomplete. Individuals are not autonomous. Male and female, adult and child, and free and slave all need each other and can form appropriate relationships only within larger combinations. All such relationships are natural because the *polis* is humanity's *têlos* and must therefore be natural itself. Children need adults, because otherwise they cannot cope; adults need children, or there will be no more adults. Men and women need each other for reproduction; and the free need slaves because they are a specific and vital form of property:

It is natural that the free rule the slave, the male the female, and the man the child. But they are different. The slave has no portion of the deliberative faculty; the female does have it, but it is inoperative; the child has it, but it is undeveloped.

Aristotle, *Politics* 1260a

For Aristotle, society was a set of necessary hierarchies making it possible for some members—the male citizens—to pursue the good life. The superiority of men over women, old over young, and free over slave came not from culture, but from nature. A state has six needs: food, wealth, arts, defense, religion, and justice. Generating the first three of these requires "slave-like" behavior, so, Aristotle reasoned, agricultural laborers, traders, and artisans should be excluded from citizenship. Such men would be citizens in a democracy, of course, but to Aristotle democracy did not reflect nature.

## CONCLUSION

The Greek world in the mid-fourth century B.C. was wealthy and complex. It had more people, living at higher standards, than ever before; yet there was also a sense of decline. The power and financial efficiency of the Athenian Empire was gone, and mighty Sparta was humbled. After 404 B.C., increasingly expensive and meaningless wars killed thousands and squandered Greece's wealth. Sparta, Thebes, and Athens strained to dominate in the Aegean, while in Sicily tyrants turned their cities into armed camps. The endless fighting gave more room for Persia and Carthage to assert themselves within the Greek world. Persia funded Sparta and threatened to intervene against anyone who might unite the Aegean; Carthage directly attacked Syracuse and seized western Sicily. To pay for their wars without the benefits of Athenian-style taxation of subject cities, *poleis* surrendered ever more privileges to the rich citizens. By 350 B.C., houses and tombs of the elite were grander than ever. The new aristocrats filled their cities with monuments to their own glory.

Fourth-century artists struggled to express the specialness of the few without shattering the conventions of sixth- and fifth-century art, which had succeeded so magnificently, while philosophers addressed old puzzles head-on and displaced tragedians and historians as intellectual leaders, generating forms of expression that we still live with today. Fourth-century art, architecture, and painting impressed the Romans more than their fifth-century precursors had done, and Roman copies of fourth-century works inspired the eighteenth-century A.D. classical revival in western Europe and North America. The questions that Plato and Aristotle asked, the methods they developed, and the answers they offered similarly provided the foundations for modern philosophical thought. But despite its immense legacy, the creative and vibrant world of fourth-century Greece hovered on the brink of disaster. When Plato died in 347 B.C., the system of *poleis* that had flourished since the eighth century B.C. was still recognizable. When Aristotle died a quarter of a century later, that world was gone, gone forever.

---

## Key Terms

| | | |
|---|---|---|
| late classical sculpture, *386* | Plato, *395* | rules of logic, *400* |
| Praxiteles, *388* | *Republic, 396* | teleology, *401* |
| Corinthian capital, *390* | theory of Forms, *396* | theory of potentiality, *401* |
| *tholos, 390* | Parable of the Cave, *396* | Prime Mover, *402* |
| Mausoleum of Halicarnassus, *391* | Academy, *399* | doctrine of the mean, *402* |
| Priene, *391* | Aristotle, *400* | |
| | Lyceum, *400* | |

---

## Further Reading

**PLATO**

Guthrie, W. K. C., *A History of Greek Philosophy*, vol. 4, *Plato: The Man and His Dialogues: Earlier Period* (Cambridge, UK, 1975), and vol. 5, *The Later Plato and the Academy* (1978), have thorough reviews of his work, while vol. 3, *The Fifth-Century Enlightenment* (1969), contains a full account of what is known about Socrates.

Szlezák, T. A., *Reading Plato*, tr. G. Zanker (New York, 1999). Best short book on his thought.

Vlastos, Gregory, *Platonic Studies*, 2nd ed. (Princeton, 1981). Contains several classic papers.

## ARISTOTLE

Most scholarship on Aristotle is found in articles in professional journals, but there are several good introductions to Aristotle's thought:

Barnes, Jonathan, *Aristotle* (Oxford, 1982). Excellent general survey.

Barnes, Jonathan, Malcolm Schofield, and Richard Sorabji, eds., *Articles on Aristotle*, 4 vols. (London, 1975–79). The proceedings of the triennial *Symposium Aristotelicum*; contains some pathbreaking work.

Jaeger, Werner, *Aristotle: Fundamentals of the History of His Development*, 2nd ed. (Oxford, 1948, reissued 1962; originally published in German, 1923). Advances a theory of the development of Aristotle's thought.

Lloyd, G. E. R., *Aristotle: The Growth and Structure of His Thought* (Cambridge, UK, 1968). The best short survey.

## ANCIENT TEXTS

Aristotle, *Ethics*, tr. J. A. K. Thomson (Harmondsworth, UK, 1955), *The Politics*, tr. T. A. Sinclair (Harmondsworth, UK, 1962), *Rhetoric*, tr. P. J. Rhodes (New York, 1984), *The Athenian Constitution*, tr. P. J. Rhodes (New York, 1984), and *De Anima (On the Soul)*, tr. Hugh Lawson-Tancred (New York, 1986).

*Lucian*, tr. K. Kilburn ( Cambridge, MA: Loeb Classical Library, 1982).

Plato, *The Symposium*, tr. W. Hamilton (Harmondsworth, UK, 1951), *The Last Days of Socrates*, tr. Hugh Treddenick (Harmondsworth, UK, 1954), *The Republic*, tr. Desmond Lee (Harmondsworth, UK, 1955), *Protagoras and Meno*, tr. W. K. C. Guthrie (Harmondsworth, UK, 1956), *The Laws*, tr. T. J. Saunders (Harmondsworth, UK, 1970), and *Timaeus and Critias*, tr. Desmond Lee (Harmondsworth, UK, 1971).

## CHAPTER 19

# The Warlords of Macedon I: Philip II and Alexander The King

By the 350s B.C., *poleis* from Sicily to Ionia were bankrupt and exhausted and Persia and Carthage were playing the warring Greeks against each other. Jason of Pherae had shown how a strong man might organize one of the larger, looser states around the edges of the Aegean and use its manpower and wealth to overwhelm the *poleis*; and **Philip II** of Macedon (Figure 19.1; Macedon = Macedonia) now succeeded where Jason had failed. Philip II was a towering figure, with prodigious appetites for alcohol, sex, power, and violence; and in speeches to the Athenian Assembly in the 340s B.C., his subtlest opponent, **Demosthenes** of Athens (384–322 B.C.; not to be confused with the much earlier general of the same name who fought in the Peloponnesian War and died at Syracuse in 413) portrayed him as the ultimate lying, murderous tyrant. Demosthenes was the greatest orator that Greece ever produced. When Cicero of Rome wanted to abuse his enemy Mark Antony some 300 years later, he called his attacks *Philippics,* after Demosthenes' masterful and savage attacks on Philip II; when Winston Churchill wanted to awaken Britain to the German threat in the 1930s, he styled himself "Demosthenes" and referred to Hitler as "Philip," invoking for his classically trained constituency these long-ago events.

Yet Philip was also brave, intelligent, and determined, in fact one of the most remarkable leaders of the ancient world. He did not shrink from violence, but rarely used it for its own sake. He broke oaths and tore up treaties, but so did his enemies. He was a hard-core realist, ruthlessly pursuing power. He brought unity to Aegean Greece for the first time and set the stage for overthrowing the Persian Empire. Although a Macedonian, and not viewed by the Greeks as a Greek, he spoke Greek and insistently claimed Greek descent. He tried to demonstrate his Greekness by being admitted to compete in the Olympic games and building a shrine to the

**FIGURE 19.1**   Miniature ivory head of a middle-aged man, found in Tomb II of the Macedonian Royal Cemetery at Vergina. It dates ca. 340–300 B.C. and probably represents Philip II. Height 1 inch.

royal house near the temple at Olympia. Ironically, his Macedonian son Alexander was to spread Greek culture far beyond the Mediterranean, and we will speak of the Macedonian generals as "Greeks," an appellation they would have gladly approved, though certainly not all Greeks would have agreed.

## MACEDONIA BEFORE PHILIP II

When Philip came to the throne in 359 B.C., Macedonia was a backwater. It covered a large area, divided into Upper (western) and Lower (eastern) Macedonia (Map 19.1). Lower Macedonia was a land of plains, watered by wide rivers, with towns and a prosperous peasantry. Upper Macedonia, by contrast, was mountainous and wild. Its weather was cooler, and rain fell year-round. In matters of culture, its tribal chiefs looked north and west to mountain peoples as much as to the lowlanders. They were shepherds, not agriculturalists like the Greeks, and moved their herds to the lowlands in the winter, then retreated to the mountains during the summer. Macedonia and its rugged inhabitants provided the Greek cities' bulwark against dangerous movements of peoples in the uplands, but the warlords of Upper Macedonia would fight on both sides, resisting mountain raiders or joining them, as the occasion demanded.

Persia overran Macedonia in the 490s B.C., then, after 479, its excellent timber for shipbuilding made it strategically important to Athenians, who dominated Macedonia's

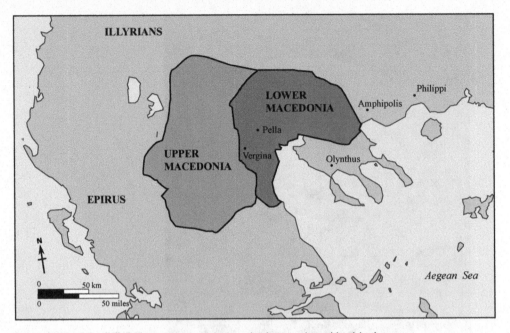

ILLYRIANS

LOWER
MACEDONIA

Philippi

Amphipolis

• Pella

UPPER
MACEDONIA

Vergina

Olynthus

EPIRUS

N

Aegean Sea

0        50 km

0        50 miles

**MAP 19.1**  Sites in northern Greece and Macedonia mentioned in this chapter.

weak kings. Whenever a king died there was an expectation that his oldest son would succeed him, but it was not a hard-and-fast rule. In fact, the kings hardly differed from the nobles who surrounded them: They dressed, ate, and lived like them and depended on personal ties and persuasion to mobilize them for war. A new king had to be acclaimed by the army, which the nobles dominated. Unlike the *poleis*, Macedonia had little civic solidarity, few civic institutions, and fewer farmer hoplites. Most farmers were serfs, better off than Sparta's helots, but the makings of poor infantry. The military striking force was the elite cavalry made up of the horse-owning Macedonian upper class.

Royal silver mines brought in one talent per day by 500 B.C., giving the king about half the revenue of the fifth-century Athenian empire, but not enough to win independence by hiring mercenaries, like Sicilian tyrants could do. Consequently, despite ruling a population of half a million, kings depended on a few hundred noble horsemen, called the **King's Companions**, who often preferred fighting each other to following royal orders. Only a king with talent and luck could tame such anarchy. The fifth-century Alexander I (498–454 B.C.) was such a man. He became a Persian client-king around 492 and gained some control over his feuding barons. After Persia withdrew in 479 B.C., he strengthened the army and got a better grip on Upper Macedonia. Alexander encouraged the aristocracy to speak Greek and act like Greeks, insisting (perhaps rightly) that the Macedonian royal family originally came from Argos. In a celebrated episode, probably in 476 B.C., Alexander I entered the Olympic games, where only Greeks could compete. When after an argument the Olympic officials allowed him to race, he claimed this as "proof" that he really was Greek. (He tied for first place.) But as late as the 420s B.C., Macedonia still struck Thucydides as wild and backward, and scholars today disagree about whether or not to consider the ancient Macedonians as "Greek."

Athens wanted to control Macedonian resources, and when Athens founded **AMPHIPOLIS** in 436 B.C. (the city that Thucydides failed to save from Brasidas in 424 during the

Peloponnesian War), Athenian pressure on Macedonia increased. During the Peloponnesian War, Macedonian kings tried to preserve their independence by switching alliances so often that no one knew which side they were on. The Macedonian King Archelaos (413–399 B.C.) resumed Alexander I's program of Hellenization by building a new Greek-style capital at PELLA, something like a real city, and bringing artists and thinkers there, including Euripides. Archelaos expanded the kingdom, but in the 370s B.C. his successor, King Amyntas (a-**min**-tas, 392–369 B.C.), fell under the influence of the Thessalian strongman, Jason. Amyntas made concessions to Thebes and Athens, covetous of Macedonia's wealth in timber and metals, and lost much of Upper Macedonia to a hill-people called the ILLYRIANS. Amyntas paid annual tribute to the wild Illyrians in order to avoid further raids.

Amyntas needed male heirs and took a young wife, Eurydicê (yu-**rid**-i-sē). She gave him three sons when he was in his sixties; our Philip II, a man of destiny, was the youngest, born after Alexander II and one Perdiccas. Then, according to the story, Eurydicê began an affair with a noble youth named Ptolemy (**tol**-e-mē). She arranged for Ptolemy to marry her daughter Eurynoê (yu-**rin**-o-ē, appropriately = "broad-minded") so she herself could continue sleeping with Ptolemy without raising suspicion. Emboldened with their success in the sexual intrigue, Eurydicê and Ptolemy now plotted murder. They would kill King Amyntas and take over the throne. But the plot then took a twist: Eurynoê got wind of it and told her father. From the shock, he fell down dead! Amyntas' oldest legitimate son, Alexander II, now took the throne, in 369 B.C. The army acclaimed him, as was the custom, but the adulterous and ambitious Ptolemy prepared a coup. To avoid a civil war, uncommitted aristocrats asked Thebes to arbitrate, Greece's greatest power after the battle of Leuctra in 371 B.C. The ambassadors favored Alexander II over Ptolemy.

Alexander II sent his youngest brother Philip II, aged thirteen, to Thebes as a hostage. This was a typical arrangement in ancient times; if Alexander misbehaved, the Thebans could execute Philip as revenge, while if Alexander kept the peace, Philip would form attachments to Thebes and the Thebans and serve as their ally. The Theban plan, however, did not make allowance for the cunning Ptolemy, who pretended to submit to the Theban arbitration, only to have Alexander II murdered at a folk dance as soon as the Thebans were gone from Macedon. Ptolemy now married the queen Eurydicê (we hear no more of the unhappy daughter Eurynoê) and announced that he would serve as regent for Alexander II's brother Perdiccas.

While this soap-opera-like drama was unfolding, Philip II spent two years in Thebes, living with a top general and moving among the most advanced military thinkers in Greece. His official tutor was a Pythagorean who advocated vegetarianism, pacifism, and sexual abstinence, but Philip was apparently unimpressed. In 367 B.C., Thebes sent him back to Macedonia. Now that Philip's brother Alexander was dead, keeping Philip as hostage would hardly restrain the unrelated Ptolemy.

In an unusual display of family sentiment, Queen Eurydicê and the regent Ptolemy spared the life of Philip's older brother Perdiccas, but when Perdiccas reached eighteen in 365 B.C. and actually succeeded to the throne, Perdiccas did not make the same mistake. Perdiccas quickly murdered the murderer Ptolemy and appointed Philip as a provincial governor. In Thebes, Philip had learned the importance of good hoplites, and he now developed an infantry corps for his older brother Perdiccas. Modifying Theban tactics, Philip trained his men to use spears eighteen feet long and small shields. The long spears held by men in the back ranks protruded ahead of the front ranks, so that the enemy faced a forest of spear points. They fought twenty-four ranks or more deep, rather than the traditional eight or twelve.

In 360 B.C., relying on this newly trained army, Perdiccas decided to stop paying protection money to the Illyrians who lived to the northwest of Macedon. He attacked the Balkan tribesmen but in a catastrophic battle, and a failure of the new tactics, Perdiccas and 4,000 of his men lay dead, leaving Macedon exposed to the angry Illyrians.

## PHILIP'S STRUGGLE FOR SURVIVAL, 359–357 B.C.

Perdiccas left one son, but because he was a child, his brother Philip, now twenty-two or twenty-three years old, was the logical heir. Initially, he may have served as regent for Perdiccas' son, but the army soon acclaimed him as king.

Philip faced problems everywhere. Several rivals made claims on the throne; the Illyrians and other neighboring peoples were massing to invade the weakened kingdom; and Perdiccas' defeat left Macedon without an army. But Philip responded coldly and carefully. First, he murdered all the rivals for the throne within the new city of PELLA; and then, recognizing that the threatening tribes wanted money more than power, he renewed the tribute to Illyria and agreed to a dynastic marriage with an Illyrian princess.

Philip used the time these steps had bought him to start rebuilding the army. The Thebans probably assumed that Philip, as their former "guest," would favor them, but Philip saw that Athens was stronger in the north than Thebes, and Athens wanted his timber. During Athens' and Thebes' complicated struggle for influence in the north in the 360s B.C., the Macedonians had garrisoned Athens' former colony at AMPHIPOLIS, and Philip realized that this city could be a crucial bargaining chip in a complicated game of diplomatic double-cross.

In 359 B.C. Athens sent 3,000 hoplites to Macedonia to support one of Philip's rivals for the throne and also began negotiating with the powerful northern Greek city of OLYNTHUS (see Map 19.1), which offered to help Athens recover Amphipolis from Macedon. Philip successfully disposed of this rival claimant to the throne but carefully avoided harming the Athenians who had come to Macedonia to assist him. In fact, he generously sent home the Athenians he captured, even giving money for the journey. Accordingly, the Athenians offered peace with Philip if he would return Amphipolis to them. Philip agreed, but sneakily pulled his garrison out of Amphipolis before signing the treaty. When the Athenians demanded that he honor his word and hand over the city, he pointed out—perfectly truthfully—that he did not actually hold Amphipolis, so unfortunately he could not give it back to Athens. Instead, he pledged, he would help Athens recover the city. In fact, Athens never did get Amphipolis back.

Having temporarily secured his position against Athens, Philip now raised a new army of 10,000 infantry and 600 cavalry. He trained hard, always refining the superior Theban tactics. He wanted a strong phalanx that would smash gaps in enemy lines, which the superior Macedonian cavalry could then exploit. Philip tried his new tactics against the hill-tribes, and for the first time the Macedonian tactics worked. Early in 358 B.C., Philip defeated the Illyrians and recovered Upper Macedonia. In a brilliant eighteen months after inheriting a kingdom in ruins, Philip's alliance with Athens and victory over Illyria made him secure (for now) from external threats.

Philip had strategic vision. In 359 B.C., the real issue had been survival, which Philip had achieved by offering Athens and Illyria what they wanted. In 357 B.C., Philip seized the metal-rich area of Pangaion in western Thrace, installed up-to-date mining technology, and soon was extracting 1,000 talents a year, as much as the revenue of the Athenian empire at its height. He founded a new city in Thrace, called PHILIPPI after himself, to protect the mines (much later St. Paul would be imprisoned here). Also in 357 B.C., Philip contracted two new marriages, his third and fourth, all perfectly legal according to Macedonian customs of polygamy. So far, his marriages had not given him a viable heir, but his fourth wife **Olympias** of EPIRUS from across the mountains would soon bear a remarkable one.

## PHILIP CONSOLIDATES HIS POSITION, 357–352 B.C.

Philip had managed matters cleverly. By 357 B.C. the main threat to his security was the powerful *polis* of Olynthus, but he knew that if Olynthus attacked him Athens would come to his help, because he was the only person who could help Athens recover Amphipolis against them. But in 357 B.C. the situation began to change again.

When Athens set up her Second League in 378 B.C., she promised not to exploit her allies, but constant wars with Sparta and Thebes forced her to break her word. In 357 B.C., three of the most important allies—Rhodes, Cos, and Chios—seceded, initiating a war that historians call the Social War (357–355 B.C.,) from the Latin *socius* meaning "ally." Being so preoccupied, Athens could no longer neutralize Olynthus, making useless Athens' friendship to Philip. As winter 357 B.C. closed in, Philip had no reason not to retake Amphipolis. Using the new siege engines that Dionysius I of Syracuse had developed forty years earlier and which Philip had perfected, Philip assaulted and captured the city. Times had changed: In the fifth century, walled cities were invulnerable unless traitors opened their gates.

In the next year, 356 B.C., Olympias delivered a healthy boy, Alexander III; Philip's chariot team won at Olympia; and he defeated Illyria again. The angry Athenians declared war on Philip for taking Amphipolis, but (as Philip foresaw) they were too busy fighting the Social War to do anything about it.

Complicated wars still raged between the *poleis*. The **Amphictyonic League** (*amphictyon* = "neighbor") was made up of various *poleis* neighboring the sanctuary of Apollo at Delphi (Map 19.2). Their purpose was originally to protect the shrine, but over time the League had become highly politicized. In 356 B.C., at Thebes' urging, the League

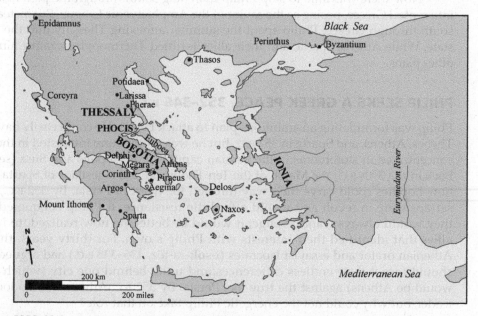

**MAP 19.2**   Aegean sites mentioned in this chapter during Philip's reign, 359–336 B.C.

imposed impossibly high fines on leaders of the backwoods territory of **PHOCIS**, which surrounds **DELPHI**, on trumped-up charges of sacrilege. Thebes, standing behind the plot, hoped to force the anti-Theban leaders in Phocis into exile, thereby increasing the influence of the pro-Theban faction. But Phocis rallied to the men's defense, seized Delphi, took "loans" from its treasures to hire mercenaries, and prepared to resist. Athens and Sparta, looking for ways to damage Thebes, came in on the side of the territory of Phocis.

Meanwhile, in summer 355 B.C. Athens conceded defeat in the Social War, let her "allies" go, and allowed the Second Athenian League to dissolve. The Thebans saw that Athens was now too weak to help Phocis and persuaded the Amphictyonic League to declare war against the Phocians, because "they had desecrated Delphi." But with the sanctuary's wealth in their hands, the Phocians offered wages 50 percent above the norm for mercenaries, expanded their army, and drove back the Theban citizen army.

Because bewilderingly complex alliances linked fourth-century *poleis*, various states now lined up either behind Thebes or Phocis. The situation is highly complex, but seems to have been something like the following. Larissa in Thessaly, home to Philip's third wife, was an ally of Thebes and had been fighting the nearby city of Pherae on and off ever since Jason was tyrant fifteen years before. Pherae was allied with Phocis in the dispute over Delphi. When Larissa asked Philip to help her against Pherae, Philip saw that if he defeated Pherae, she would probably ask Phocis for help; Philip could then pose as champion of the Amphictyonic League, the avenger of Phocian sacrilege, thereby enhancing his standing among the Greeks.

At first Philip's plan went well, but in spring 353 B.C. the Phocians defeated him in battle, the only serious military defeat in Philip's career. Many thought that Philip could not recover from this setback, and the wealthy northern *polis* of Olynthus broke its recent alliance with him, joining Athens instead. But in 352 B.C. Philip raised a new army, captured Pherae, and crushed a Phocian army then in Thessaly. Philip drowned 3,000 Phocian prisoners on charges of sacrilege (!) and crucified their dead leader's body.

Now there was little to stop Philip marching south through the pass of Thermopylae into central Greece, posing as the savior of the Amphictyonic League. But instead of rushing south through Greece, Philip spent the summer annexing Thessaly into the Macedonian state. While Athens, Sparta, and their allies fortified Thermopylae against him, Philip had other plans.

## PHILIP SEEKS A GREEK PEACE, 352–346 B.C.

Philip was formulating an ambitious plan to attack Persia. He could easily have conquered Thebes, Athens, and Sparta in 352 B.C., but he was rather more interested in the vast wealth concentrated in storerooms in the Persian capitals of Persepolis and Susa (see Map 19.3). Back in the 390s B.C., the March of the Ten Thousand and Agesilaos of Sparta had showed how hoplites could carve their way through the heart of Persia. By 352 B.C., the western satraps were in revolt and would offer little resistance. If Philip conquered the Greeks, they would always want revenge; it would be better, he now realized, to have them as allies that identified their interests with Philip's own. For thirty years, the influential Athenian orator and essayist Isocrates (ī-**sok**-ra-tēz, 436–338 B.C.) had argued that Greeks should forget their endless differences and unite behind one city (which he assumed would be Athens) against the true foe, Persia. By 352 B.C. Athens was no longer a viable leader, but why could not the energetic Philip take on that role?

The war between the Amphictyonic League and the Phocians dragged on, splitting Greece into two camps, pro-Theban (against the Phocians) and pro-Athenian (for the Phocians). Neither Athens nor Thebes could hurt Philip separately, but together they would be formidable. Philip therefore attempted to win influence in Athens, but the orator Demosthenes violently opposed him. Demosthenes delivered his first *Philippic* in 351 B.C., rousing his fellow countrymen to action by claiming that it was their own inaction that had created this monster from the barbarian north:

> Could anything more extraordinary ever happen? A *Macedonian* overcoming in war the Athenians and governing the affairs of all the Greeks? "Philip is dead," someone says. "No, he is only ill," says another. What difference does it make? If something should happen to this man you would swiftly make for yourselves another Philip, if you continue to govern affairs as you have. It is not so much from his own strength that Philip has prospered, as from your indifference.

Demosthenes, *Philippic 1*, 10–11

Demosthenes thought that Athens could be great again if she only acted resolutely, but Athens could no longer generate the revenues to compete with states like Macedonia. In 349 B.C., Philip moved against Athens' ally Olynthus, perhaps to show that resistance was futile. Demosthenes' rhetoric now reached a peak in three speeches called the *Olynthiacs*, claiming that Philip would soon be destroyed by his own evil:

> There is not a single state that he has not deceived, when they tried to make use of him. He has taken advantage of the foolishness of those who did not understand him to increase his own power. Thanks to such men, he has grown great, when they thought that they were going to use him for their own advantage. He will owe his destruction to the same forces, now that he has demonstrated his constant self-interest. Yes, citizens of Athens, the situation has now come to a head . . .
>
> When through greed and evil a man such as this has gained power, he falls to ruin through the slightest misstep. Never, gentlemen, never can a lasting power be founded on injustice, lies, and deceit. Such power lasts but a moment. They may blossom with fair hope, if they are lucky, but soon they are found out and brought low. As in a house, or a ship, or anything like that, where it is a strong foundation that counts, so it is with the actions of men's lives—they must be founded on truth and on justice. Such is hardly the case with the doings of Philip!

Demosthenes, *Olynthiacs* 2.7–10

Demosthenes urged Athens to find the money somehow and to sail to Olynthus' rescue. Other politicians, however, claimed that although Philip was a tyrant, Athens could work with him; and the Athenians, unable to decide, did nothing. In the meanwhile, Philip moved his engines against the walls of Olynthus. The democratic Athenians finally voted to send troops to war—but instead of attacking Philip, they decided to intervene closer to home, on the neighboring long island of Euboea. Then Philip's supporters betrayed Olynthus from within. He imprisoned the Athenians found there, sold the Olynthians into slavery, and burned the city to the ground, never to rise again—a boon to American archaeologists who excavated the ruins in the 1920s and 1930s to discover our clearest snapshot of classical Greek urban life.

Philip hoped to negotiate a general peace in Greece, leaving Athens dominant but dependent on his support. However, the "Sacred War" (as it came to be called) against Phocis was still dragging on, made a general peace difficult because most *poleis* had sided either with Thebes or with Athens. Demosthenes' attempt to create a broad anti-Macedonian alliance failed because other *poleis* mistrusted Athens. Pro-Macedonians in Athens undermined Demosthenes in 346 B.C. by pushing through their own treaty with Philip. Philip released the Athenian prisoners he took at Olynthus, then persuaded the Amphictyonic League to invite him to finish up the war with Phocis. The Phocians had looted 10,000 talents from the sanctuary at Delphi, a gigantic sum of money, but by 346 B.C. the cash was spent and they collapsed before Philip's attack.

Philip, still anxious to bring peace to Greece so he would be free to attack Persia, hoped to please Thebes (who opposed Phocis) by ending the war and avoid offending Athens (who supported Phocis) by dissolving Phocis' towns into villages rather than killing them all. His compromise satisfied no one. The Amphictyonic League invited Philip to preside over the Pythian Games at Delphi, which should have been his crowning moment; but Athens, swayed by Demosthenes' fiery rhetoric, refused to send delegates to the games, a bitter snub from the city of Pericles and Plato against the Macedonian monster.

## THE STRUGGLE FOR A GREEK PEACE, 346–338 B.C.

Athens' treaty with Philip divided the city. Anti-Macedonian feelings ran high. In 348 B.C., Aristotle, who had lived in the Macedonian court, felt it wise to leave Athens, and many pro-Macedonian politicians followed his example. Isocrates (now an old man of seventy), who had spent thirty years urging Athens to lead a Greek crusade against Persia, stayed and wrote a new booklet asking Philip to lead the crusade. Philip should build an army from the thousands of landless men and former mercenaries now in Greece, Isocrates suggested, and after defeating Persia, should settle these mercenaries on Persian lands, ridding Greece of the growing social problem of unemployed ex-mercenary gangs ravaging the countryside.

In 345 B.C., western Greece provided a striking example of the kind of thing Isocrates had in mind. Syracuse had been in chaos for some years, racked by civil wars and declining population, and now, in 345, the Syracusans asked their mother-city, Corinth, to send new colonists to replenish their ranks. The Corinthians only responded halfheartedly, sending a disgraced politician named Timoleon (tim-ō-le-on) with just 700 mercenaries. But Timoleon astonished everyone. He raised cash in Sicily and by 338 B.C. had deposed all the Greek tyrants and driven Carthage back into western Sicily. It was touch-and-go for a while; in a decisive battle, Timoleon was saved by a thunderstorm that drove hail and sleet into the Carthaginians' faces. Within a few years, though, Timoleon showed again that for an ambitious man with money to hire mercenaries, anything was possible, at least in Sicily:

> Timoleon had accomplished what were universally acknowledged to be the greatest achievements of his time. He was the only man who actually performed the kinds of deeds repeatedly praised in the national assemblies of Greece, which orators° urged their fellow countrymen to attempt . . . He displayed courage and justice toward barbarians and tyrants, and to his fellow Greeks and toward his

° . . . *orators*: For example, Demosthenes.

friends he was just and behaved with moderation. He set up his many trophies without causing tears to flow or mourning to be worn by the citizens of Syracuse or Corinth. In a mere eight years he gave Sicily back to its inhabitants and put an end to the strife and disorder that had for long plagued the island.

Plutarch, *Life of Timoleon* 37

Timoleon did what Isocrates preached, leading tens of thousands of Greeks from the Aegean to new land overseas, to begin a new life.

Despite Timoleon's successes in the west, though, Philip's own chance to act in the east was slipping away in the late 340s B.C. He made little progress in uniting the Greeks to back him. In city after city, feuds raged between "friends of Philip" and would-be patriots, that is, friends of the city. Meanwhile, in Persia, the King Artaxerxes III (359–338 B.C.) put down the troublesome rebel western satraps and improved the empire's ability to defend itself. Philip tightened his control of Upper Macedonia, Thrace, and Thessaly; transplanted populations into new cities; and organized them to raise troops more effectively.

We have few contemporary sources for Philip's reforms, and have to rely heavily on books written over 400 years later. These later writers often had sources going back to Philip's own time, but modern historians argue heatedly over how much we should believe them. According to one of these sources, the *Campaigns of Alexander* by one Arrian (A.D. 86-after 146), Philip's son Alexander III gave the following speech to the Macedonians, summing up Philip's achievements:

> Philip took you over when you were helpless vagabonds, most of you wearing skins and herding miserable flocks in the mountains and always getting the worst of it in battles against the Illyrians and the Triballians and your Thracian neighbors. He gave you cloaks to wear instead of skins and brought you down from the mountains into the plains. He made you a match for the barbarians who live near your borders so that you trusted more in your own valor for security than in the remoteness of where you lived. He made you city-dwellers and imposed order based on laws and useful custom. Instead of being slaves and subservient to the barbarians, he made you masters over them, who used to carry off your persons and your property. He added most of Thrace to Macedonia, and he took possession of the most favorable places on the sea as emporia for trade. He made it possible to work the mines without fear of attack.

Arrian, *Campaigns of Alexander* 7.9

Philip strengthened Macedon greatly, but Greek resistance forced him to abandon temporarily his strategy of uniting Greece behind a great campaign against Persia. Instead, Philip moved in 340 B.C. against BYZANTIUM and PERINTHUS, cities that controlled crossings into the Persian Empire. Byzantium and Perinthus also controlled the grain route from the Black Sea to Athens, so attacking them meant certain war with Athens. Macedonian siegecraft employed mobile towers one-hundred feet tall, rapid-fire catapults, and sophisticated tunnels to undermine walls, but Philip also skillfully exploited more traditional techniques: As he once remarked, no one had built a wall so high that gold (i.e., bribes) could not scale it. Neither bombardment nor bribery worked at Byzantium and Perinthus, however, which had state-of-the-art fortifications and superb natural positions. Athens duly declared war against Macedon, as Philip had predicted, while King Artaxerxes of Persia poured mercenaries and money into the defense of Perinthus and Byzantium against Philip's assaults.

By autumn 340 B.C., it was becoming clear that Philip could not take the two cities. But perhaps, he realized, he did not need to. Athens was now the big problem, and if Philip took Perinthus and Byzantium, he would still have to face Athens. However, if he defeated Athens, Perinthus and Byzantium would surrender soon enough. He therefore raised the sieges and intercepted a huge grain fleet bound for Athens, causing supreme hardship in the city. In 339 B.C., he persuaded the Amphictyonic League to declare war on Athens too, since Athens had been an ally of Phocis. Only when he could claim to be acting as the League's agent did he attack Athens directly.

Swinging inland to avoid Thermopylae, in spring 338 B.C., Philip suddenly showed up two days' march from Thebes, demanding that Thebes join the Amphictyonic League and help him punish Athens, but Demosthenes persuaded the Thebans to stand up with Athens. In August 338 B.C., Philip threw his highly trained army against well-prepared Athenian–Theban positions at **Chaeronea** (kī-ro-nē-a), a village near Thebes. We know little of the battle, except that the eighteen-year-old Alexander charged at the head of the King's Companion cavalry and smashed the legendary Theban Sacred Band, slaughtered almost to the last man (Figure 19.2). In the Athenian line, the great orator and persuasive politician Demosthenes was said to have disgraced himself by throwing down his shield and fleeing. Plutarch (who was born at Chaeronea) says that when Demosthenes caught his cloak on a thorn bush as he ran, he fell to his knees and begged the bush to take him alive before realizing his mistake. These stories may have been propaganda to discredit Demosthenes, but we do know that a thousand Athenian hoplites died at Chaeronea.

Philip had beaten the finest force the Greeks could assemble. According to one story, he drank himself into a stupor after the battle and danced on the piles of Theban dead; another

**FIGURE 19.2** The lion at Chaeronea. The Thebans erected this enormous lion, about 20 feet tall, to guard the common tomb in which the Theban Sacred Band was buried after Philip's victory in 338 B.C. The statue has been reconstructed in modern times and placed on a modern pedestal. Excavation in 1879 of a nearby grave revealed 254 skeletons laid out in seven rows (authors' photo).

story, though, has him weeping on seeing the corpses of the Sacred Band. He sent back the 1,000 Athenian dead for honorable burial and offered to free without ransom the 2,000 prisoners he had taken. Because Athens still had her fleet and long walls, a siege would be difficult and expensive. The desperate Athenians were in the middle of freeing their slaves to fight, reinforcing their walls, and preparing for a last stand when a messenger arrived to announce Philip's generous terms in the Assembly. The *dêmos* accepted them without debate, conferred Athenian citizenship on Philip and Alexander, and put up a statue of Philip in the marketplace.

Thebes, on the other hand, ransomed her prisoners at a high price. Her leaders were banished or executed, a Macedonian puppet government established, and a garrison stationed atop the acropolis. Athens, Philip reasoned, would now surely secure the Aegean and cover his back while he marched against Persia. Thebes was reduced to a second-rank power.

## Philip's End, 338–336 B.C.

Philip wanted to be seen as a legitimate leader of the Greeks he so admired. He had been careful to act in 338 B.C. as head of the Amphictyonic League, and in 337 he called a conference at Corinth to discuss the future of Greece. Only the now-irrelevant Sparta refused to attend. Philip proposed a Common Peace, like that of 371 B.C., with the *poleis* swearing not to act against Macedon. Macedonian garrisons, however, later known as "the fetters of Greece," occupied a few strategic spots to back up the fine phrases with brute force. Philip also promoted Isocrates' Panhellenism and explained his plans to avenge Persia's destruction of Greek temples nearly 150 years before. Lured by the promise of plunder in Persia, the conference appointed Philip and his heirs as commanders-in-chief.

By 338 B.C. King Artaxerxes of Persia had repaired the weaknesses that had made his empire so tempting a target in the early 340s, but just as Philip was cutting down the Thebans and Athenians at Chaeronea, Artaxerxes' grand vizier—a eunuch named Bagoas—murdered the king. For two months Persia was in virtual anarchy as Bagoas hunted down and killed claimants to the throne, until the only survivor was Artaxerxes' youngest son Arses, whom Bagoas favored. Bagoas restored order by November 338 B.C., but left Persia badly weakened.

As Philip foresaw, Byzantium and Perinthus yielded as soon as he defeated Athens, and in spring 336 a vanguard of 10,000 Macedonians crossed into Asia, meeting little resistance. The Ionians, once again, rose up against their Persian overlords, and in June 336 B.C. the eunuch Bagoas murdered Persia's King Arses too, and elevated a minor member of the royal family to the throne as **Darius III**. Darius' first act was to force Bagoas to drink the same poison he had administered to others. Persia had fallen into chaos.

Philip sent a man to Delphi to ask the god whether he would conquer Persia. The oracle answered: "The bull is garlanded. All is done. The sacrificer is ready." Philip took "the bull" to be Darius and "the sacrificer" to be himself. Like many visitors to Delphi, he appears to have missed the oracle's meaning, as events proved.

To clear up one last family dispute before he began the invasion of Persia, Philip arranged a wedding between his daughter and the brother of his fourth wife Olympias (confusingly also named Alexander!). All the dignitaries of Greece came. At the festival's climax, twelve huge statues of the Olympian gods were carried into the arena followed by a thirteenth statue, on the same scale, of Philip himself. Then came Philip in the flesh, flanked by Alexander his son and Alexander his brother-in-law, all dressed in white. Philip had ordered his bodyguards to stay a few yards back so everyone could get a good view of their entrance. Without warning, a bodyguard named Pausanias stepped in front of Philip and drove a short sword into his heart, killing him instantly. He was just forty-six years old.

## Who Killed the King?

Philip's bodyguards cut Pausanias down on the spot, so no one was able to interrogate him. Ever since that day, arguments have swirled over just why Pausanias killed Philip. The simplest theory is that Pausanias killed Philip for his own reasons, which we can never recover, but much more lurid theories also circulated. The historian Diodorus of Sicily, writing in the first century B.C., said that Pausanias had once been Philip's lover, but the king had abandoned him for a new boyfriend who had ties to one Attalus, a powerful nobleman from Lower Macedonia and the uncle of Philip's fifth wife (named Cleopatra). Pausanias caused a public scene and so embarrassed Philip's new lover (also named Pausanias!) that the new lover took his own life. The furious Attalus invited Pausanias to dinner, got him drunk, led the rest of the guests in gang-raping him, then turned over Pausanias to the stable boys, who raped him again. The much-abused Pausanias appealed to Philip for redress, but the king did not want a feud with Attalus. Pausanias then took matters into his own hands.

It is hard to know what to make of such stories. Another explanation places blame on Philip's fourth wife Olympias (Alexander III's mother). According to this story, Olympias suspected that Philip's union with Attalus' niece Cleopatra was part of a plan to repudiate Alexander and father a new heir. At Philip and Cleopatra's wedding, the proud uncle Attalus gave a speech praying for a *legitimate* heir for Philip, implying that Alexander was illegitimate. A drunken Alexander threw his wine cup at Attalus, and Attalus threw his back. Philip, drunker than anyone, pulled out his sword and lunged—not at Attalus, but at his own son Alexander! When Cleopatra bore Philip a son in summer 336 B.C. (earlier she had borne a daughter), the danger to Alexander III's succession seemed imminent. Did Olympias (and perhaps Alexander himself) plan Philip's death, persuade the angry Pausanias to do their dirty work, and then kill him to keep his mouth shut? As usual in stories surrounding the Macedonian family, there are many theories, but few facts.

## ALEXANDER THE KING

When news of Philip's death reached Greece, the *poleis* revolted. Athens proclaimed a public holiday. Everyone assumed that pretenders would emerge and that civil war would drive Macedonia back into obscurity. Like Philip in 359 B.C., Alexander III—just twenty years old—faced rivals for the throne, hostile Greeks, and threats from the Balkans. The greatest threats to his power were in fact his relative Attalus (the uncle of Philip's wife Cleopatra) and Philip's top general **Parmenio** (par-**men**-i-ō). Fortunately for Alexander, though, both men were away in Ionia with the advance guard. Alexander moved quickly: He persuaded the army in Macedonia to proclaim him king and he murdered all potential rivals within reach. His mother Olympias killed the two babies that Cleopatra had borne Philip, allegedly by pressing them face-down into red-hot coals. The unfortunate Cleopatra hanged herself.

Veteran soldiers around the twenty-year-old Alexander advised him that he could not meet all the remaining threats at once. He should abandon Greece and defend Macedonia against the Balkans, they said. But Alexander feared that Parmenio would claim that in this crisis Macedonia needed experience, not youth, and nominate Alexander's older cousin as king. Alexander realized that he needed to prove his excellence as a general right away, before Parmenio could start scheming. He therefore raced south against the Greek rebels.

Troops guarded the passes into Thessaly, but Alexander cut steps up the face of towering Mount Ossa and dropped down behind them. Thessaly promptly surrendered and the Thebans awoke to find Alexander camped outside their walls. They too surrendered, remembering Chaeronea. A week earlier, Demosthenes had been assuring Athens that Alexander was "a mere boy," but now the famous city capitulated without struggle.

Alexander called a meeting of the Greek *poleis* at Corinth, which named him general against Persia in place of his murdered father. In six weeks, Alexander had won back Greece without a single casualty. Parmenio recognized Alexander's leadership but insisted on filling top offices in the army with his own relatives. Alexander agreed—for now.

Early in 335 B.C., while the snow still lay deep in the mountains, Alexander struck north, pursuing hostile tribes into the interior and across the Danube River. He was gone for months; according to rumor he was dead. Thebes and Athens contacted Persia and revolted from Macedonian control once again. But Alexander was not dead. Concluding his northern campaign, he raced back to Thebes. The first the Thebans knew of it was when Alexander was just a day's march away. For a few hours, they refused to believe it was him. Then Alexander was upon them, offering generous terms that the Thebans rejected, calling him a tyrant. In a desperate battle, Alexander forced his way into the city. He cut down 6,000 Theban men, sold another 30,000 Thebans into slavery, and burned every house in the city except the home of Pindar, whose poetry Alexander admired. When persuasion fails, turn to terror—this was to be Alexander's policy. Thebes would never recover from the sack. Athens surrendered again (for the third time since 338 B.C.). The butcher of Thebes, though universally hated, need no longer fear revolt in his rear.

## Alexander's Strategy

The league of Greek *poleis* at Corinth proclaimed Alexander its avenger. By 335 B.C. Alexander had probably decided to replace Darius and rule the entire Persian Empire himself. This was a formidable challenge: Persians held that the god Ahuramazda had chosen the Achaemenid family to fight for the light against the darkness, saving the world, and to rule the empire, Alexander would need to fulfill the same role. He would have to kill or capture Darius, marry one of his daughters or his widow, and win over the Magi, the powerful priesthood. The war would be personal, a duel fought through vast armies.

Alexander would also have to defeat his own generals, particularly his rival Parmenio, Philip's right-hand man, whose appointees dominated the officer corps. Alexander needed to show that he *personally* made the difference between victory and defeat. He must lead from the front and make brilliant decisions. Throughout his campaigns, Alexander was recklessly courageous. He was to become the greatest field commander in the history of warfare.

Alexander also needed money to reward his men. Wages would cost 3,000 talents per year (three times the annual income of the fifth-century Athenian empire), and Alexander's only inheritance from Philip was a 500-talent debt. He had to borrow from his richest subjects, using royal land as collateral. In effect, he mortgaged the kingdom. After paying off his debts, Alexander set off for Asia with just eighty talents and thirty days' worth of supplies.

## Darius' Strategy

Darius had to choose how to resist. He might try to defeat Alexander in battle; or to use money to raise Greek revolts against Macedonia; or he could try to assassinate Alexander. He had one outstanding general, a Greek mercenary named Memnon, who spent 335 B.C. winning back some of the Ionian cities that had gone over to Parmenio the previous year. But

Darius did not follow up on Memnon's gains or try to to intercept Alexander's crossing. Most likely, Darius did not take Macedonia seriously and thought that his western satraps would crush Alexander easily. When Alexander proved him wrong, Darius hesitated, committing neither to Aegean revolts in Alexander's rear nor to a decisive battle. He seems to have misunderstood the war that Alexander brought him, and in return for his clumsy understanding he lost absolutely everything.

## THE CONQUEST OF PERSIA, 334–330 B.C.

### The Opening Moves, 334 B.C.

Alexander claimed that he was avenging the Persian invasion of Greece in 480 B.C., and made a point of following Xerxes' route in reverse. He was the first man ashore in Asia, at the head of the expeditionary force, casting his spear into the beach to claim the land by conquest. The earlier force under Attalus and Parmenio, consisting of 10,000 men, joined with Alexander's forces and marched to the site of ancient Troy. Here, Alexander and his closest friend (and perhaps lover) Hephaestion laid wreaths at mounds believed to be the tombs of Achilles and Patroclus, then raced naked around them. Alexander seems to have thought of his friendship with Hephaestion as like that between Achilles, on whom he modeled himself, and Patroclus. He dedicated his armor to Athena at the temple built on the ancient ruins of Troy and took another suit from the temple, said to be a relic from the Trojan War itself. Alexander liked to think of himself as the new Achilles and he carried a copy of the *Iliad* with him wherever he went.

Desperate for money, Alexander extorted cash from the Ionians, but he needed to fight a battle and capture plunder. Understanding this, Darius' general Memnon urged the western satraps to avoid battle, retreating ahead of Alexander and devastating the country, but the satraps did not want to tell King Darius that they had run from Alexander and burned their own territory. Therefore, the Persians massed their forces near where Alexander had crossed from Europe, at the small **Granicus** (**gran**-i-kus) **River** that flows into the Sea of Marmara (see Map 19.3).

Thousands of Persian cavalry (outnumbering Macedonians three or four to one), stiffened by Greek mercenaries, stood behind the fast-flowing river. The satraps threw back Alexander's efforts to force his way across the river. In a maneuver he would repeat many times, Alexander slipped away by night and crossed the river upstream. Next morning, the armies clashed head-on between the river and the foothills a mile away (the exact site of this battlefield is unknown).

Alexander took a post on the right, wearing the spectacular armor that he had taken from Troy, according to the story. He wanted the Persians to see him and send in their best cavalry against him. He would then be at the heart of the struggle while Parmenio, on the left, would merely anchor the Macedonian line. The Persians charged. Diodorus of Sicily (first century B.C.) describes the encounter as follows:

> Fortune had brought together in one place the best fighters to decide who would win the victory. The satrap of Ionia, Spithrobates, a son-in-law of the king, a Persian by birth and a man of high courage, attacked the Macedonians with a large force of cavalry ... Because the force of the attack appeared very great, Alexander turned his horse toward the satrap and rode to the attack.

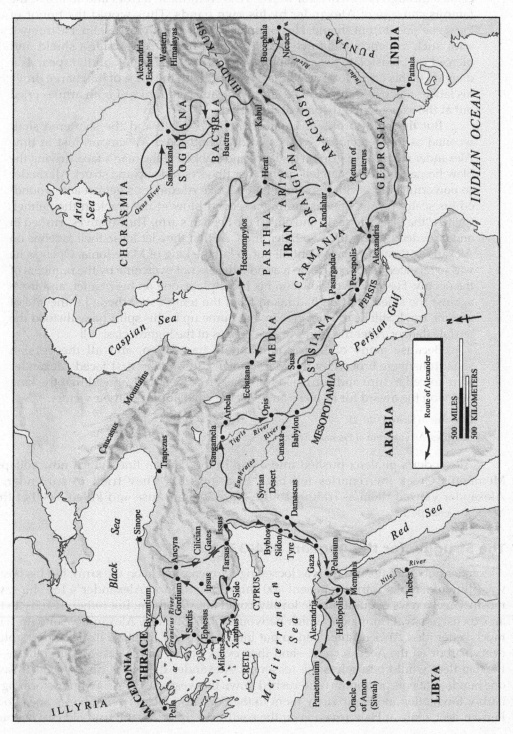

**MAP 19.3**  Alexander's invasion of the Persian Empire.

To the Persian the chance for single combat seemed a gift from the gods, a chance through his own valor to free Asia from these terrors and to arrest the famous courage of Alexander by his own hands. Thus would the honor of Persia be saved from shame. He got in the first shot with his javelin. He threw it with such violence and force that it went through Alexander's shield and pierced his breastplate near the shoulder. But the king shook off the spear as it dangled by his arm. He spurred his horse and with the force of his charge drove his lance smack into the satrap's chest. The adjacent ranks of both armies cried out at the exaggerated display of manhood.

But the point broke off against the breastplate and the shattered shaft recoiled as the Persian drew his sword and attacked Alexander. Just in time Alexander recovered a grip on his lance and stabbed at the man's face, driving the blow home. As the Persian fell, his brother Rhoaces rode up and struck Alexander so powerful a blow with his sword that it broke Alexander's helmet and wounded his scalp. Just as he was aiming a second blow at the crack in the helmet, Cleitus "the Black" rode up and cut off the Persian's arm. The Relatives° rushed in and crowded around the two fallen men. At first they let loose their javelins on Alexander, then in a mass went all out to kill the king of Macedonia. Open as he was to repeated fierce attack, he was nonetheless not overcome by the numbers of the enemy. He took two blows on his breastplate, one on his helmet, and three against the shield that he had taken from the temple of Athena [at the site of ancient Troy]. Still he did not give in, but borne up by his spirit he withstood the terrible danger. After this, three other Persians of the highest class fell . . .

Because many of their commanders had fallen, and all the Persian squadrons were broken by the Macedonians, those who first faced Alexander were forced to turn and run, then the others too. Everyone agreed that the king had won the award for bravery and was the chief author of their victory.

Diodorus of Sicily 17.20–21

°*Relatives:* An elite core of Persian cavalry.

Alexander's phalanx pushed into a gap in the Persian line, which now collapsed. Memnon's Greek mercenaries fell back to a low hill. They tried to surrender, but Alexander viewed them as traitors to the Macedonian cause and killed 3,000 of them. Memnon escaped.

## The Struggle for the Aegean, 334–333 B.C.

Alexander now had money and was loosening Parmenio's grip on the army, but his position was still vulnerable. Darius had sent 400 ships to Ionia, and Alexander's 160 ships, with mostly Greek crews of questionable loyalty, could not stop them. But rather than try to fight an expensive naval campaign, which he would probably lose, Alexander came up with a much better idea. Ancient ships had to put into shore every night; so if Alexander captured every harbor on the Aegean coast—and then every harbor in the east Mediterranean—the Persian fleet would be useless, he reasoned. Alexander dissolved his own fleet (saving one hundred talents per month) and rushed down the west coast of Asia Minor, storming one harbor town after another to deny them to the Persians, often arriving hours ahead of the Persian fleet. Only at Halicarnassus on the southwest tip of Anatolia, an old city famous as

Herodotus' birthplace and for its huge Mausoleum, did Memnon and the Persian fleet arrive first. For weeks, Alexander's siege engines pounded the walls of the city. Eventually the Macedonian attackers broke through. Memnon and his Greek mercenaries escaped by the skin of their teeth, but all cities on the Aegean coast were now in Alexander's hands.

The Greek Memnon pressed Darius to appoint him commander in the west, with money to take the war into Greece. The native Persian generals, however, urged staking everything on another land battle. While an indecisive Darius massed troops at far-off Susa, Memnon in the west hired new mercenaries. That winter (334–333 B.C.) one Ionian city after another went back to Persia. Memnon planned to sail to mainland Greece with 300 ships. Athens and Sparta were ready to rise against Macedonia.

Should Alexander turn back to defend Greece, or press ahead, gambling everything on a swift victory? While he pondered this vital decision, Alexander led his men from the southern coast of Anatolia across high mountains inland across the Anatolian plain to winter at Gordium, where supplies were better and the ancient Persian royal road ran west to Sardis and the Aegean coast 200 miles away. Alexander might need to return to the coast and reclaim the Ionian cities who had revolted to Memnon. In the middle of the town was an old ox-cart, said to have been dedicated to Zeus by the Great King Midas (a real man, who lived in the late eighth century B.C.). Arrian tells the story, a kind of folktale about "the impossible task":

> There was another story about this wagon, namely that whoever could untie its knot would become lord of Asia. The knot was made of the bark of the cornel tree and you could not see where it began or where it ended. Alexander was unable to loosen the knot, but he did not wish it to remain untied, in case that might lead to a disturbance among the people. Accounts differ about what happened. Some say that he sliced it with his sword, then said he had undone it. But Aristoboulos° says that he pulled out a pin that went straight through the knot into the pole, thereby releasing the yoke from the pole.

Arrian, *Campaigns of Alexander* 2.3

°*Aristobulos:* Aristobulos took part in Alexander's campaign and wrote a history of it after 301 B.C. Only fragments of his book survive.

From the story comes our saying, "to cut the Gordian (=from Gordium) knot," that is, to solve an impossible problem through decisive action.

Alexander decided that he had to cut his strategic Gordian knot just as decisively. He gambled that the Aegean would hold against the Persian threat. Even if Greece did rebel and even if the rebels invaded Macedonia, it did not matter as long as Alexander captured Persia. In spring 333 B.C., Alexander marched southeast across the Anatolian plain and through the towering Taurus Mountains to the broad plain of Cilicia (Figure 19.3).

Alexander's luck held. In mid-July, as Alexander neared Syria, Memnon died of disease. Darius' advisors in Babylon were split, the Persians urging him to abandon the west and his remaining Greek mercenary general insisting that Darius should take Alexander in the flank by attacking Macedon. The Greek general became so agitated about Persian military incompetence that Darius flew into a rage and had the man summarily executed. Having lost his two best commanders, Darius now blundered again, recalling his mercenaries from the Aegean to join the land army he was assembling. Darius had given up the Aegean.

**FIGURE 19.3** The high rugged Taurus Mountains separating the high inland plateau of Anatolia from the lowland plain of Cilicia in southeastern Anatolia. The mountains rise to 12,000 feet and in their eastern extension are the source of the Tigris and Euphrates rivers. Alexander crossed these mountains in 333 B.C.

## The Struggle for the East Mediterranean, 333–332 B.C.

Alexander pressed ahead, and Darius, panicking, offered 1,000 talents to anyone who could murder Alexander. When Alexander dived one day into an icy pool to escape the heat and went into convulsions from shock, no doctor dared treat him, for fear of being accused of treason if the king died. Only an old Greek friend named Philip came forward:

> Philip the Acarnanian saw that things were going badly with Alexander. He considered it a shameful thing that he not share in the utmost danger as he did his best to help Alexander and as he plumbed the resources of his art. He mixed up a medicine and persuaded Alexander to prepare to drink it down, if he wished to regain his strength for war. Just then Parmenio sent in a letter from the camp warning that "Darius has bribed Philip with the promise of valuable gifts and marriage to his daughter, if he kills Alexander." Alexander read the letter and placed it under his pillow without showing it to any of his friends. When at the appointed time Philip came in carrying the medicine in a cup, Alexander gave him the letter while he took the medicine eagerly and without suspicion.
>
> It was an amazing sight, worthy of the theater. As Philip read the letter, Alexander downed the potion, then both together turned their eyes at one another, but with dissimilar expressions. While Alexander looked at Philip with

cheerful and open disposition, showing his good faith and trust, Philip was beside himself at the accusation, raising his hands to heaven and calling to the gods as witness to his innocence, then falling onto Alexander's bed and urging him to be of good cheer and to obey his doctor's orders. At first the medicine utterly overcame him, driving the power of his body outward and downward into the depths so that he fainted utterly and lost all consciousness. Philip, however, soon brought him around, he regained his strength, and he showed himself to the Macedonians. They would not be comforted until they had seen Alexander.

Plutarch, *Life of Alexander* 19

When Alexander had recovered, Parmenio advised him to wait for Darius at a place called **Issus**, near the modern border between Turkey and Syria (Map 19.3). From Issus Alexander could watch all three passes by which Darius might come through the mountains between Syria and the sea in his march westward from Babylon. Alexander, however, was convinced that Darius would come through the southernmost pass. Alexander blocked its entrance, only for Darius to come through a pass further north, cutting Alexander's line of retreat and capturing injured troops whom Alexander had left back at Issus. To intimidate the Macedonians, Darius chopped off the prisoners' hands and sealed the wounds with boiling tar!

Alexander was now trapped between Darius to the north and hostile Phoenician cities to the south. The passes inland were closed. All Darius needed was to hold his position, starve out Alexander, and win the war. Instead, he bravely but rashly offered battle, forming up his troops along a two-mile front behind a small local river. Alexander moved to meet him. Parmenio, on the Macedonian left, would again anchor the position. The phalanx would advance in the center to pin the Persians down, while Alexander would lead the Companions in a diagonal charge into the heart of the Persian position.

Darius massed his best cavalry on his right. As the Macedonians advanced to within bowshot of the river, he launched them against Parmenio, hoping to break through and roll up Alexander's line. At the same moment, Alexander charged with his Companion Cavalry. The light-armed Persian infantry collapsed before the onslaught, while on the other wing the excellent Persian horsemen drove Parmenio back. In the center, the Macedonian phalanx and Darius' Greek mercenaries slaughtered each other in a classic hoplite battle:

The blood really flowed. The two ranks were so closely arrayed that they were striking their weapons together and jabbing their blades into one another's faces. There was no escape for the timid or the cowardly. Foot to foot, they fought as in single combat in which neither would yield, until one died and the other took his place. They only made progress forward by killing their opponent, only then, being exhausted, forced to meet a fresh enemy. Nor could the wounded withdraw as in other battles because the enemy pressed them from the front and their own troops pushed forward from behind.

Quintus Curtius, *Life of Alexander* 3.11

As Alexander's cavalry pressed ahead, a gap opened between them and the Macedonian phalanx, locked in combat with Darius' Greek mercenaries. Darius sent troops charging into this gap, taking the Macedonian infantry in their unprotected flank and killing many. He probably hoped that Alexander would abandon his cavalry charge

**FIGURE 19.4** The Alexander Mosaic, about 15 feet long, from a house in Pompeii, destroyed in A.D. 79 by the eruption of Mount Vesuvius. Based on a Hellenistic painting of the Battle of Issus, this mosaic consists entirely of small, cut colored stones. Alexander in his chariot on the left portion of the picture makes straight for Darius right of center, whose eyes seem to meet Alexander's.

and rush back to help his phalanx, but instead of going to the rescue, Alexander and his horsemen kept charging forward, making straight for Darius (see Figure 19.4):

> Alexander was as much a soldier as a commander. He sought the trophy of killing the king. Riding high in his chariot, Darius stood out, providing an incentive for his own men to protect him and a target for the Macedonians.
>
> Oxathres, Darius' brother, saw Alexander bearing down on the king and moved the cavalry under his command directly in front of the chariot. Oxathres surpassed his companions in the splendor of his arms and in his raw strength. Few could match his devotion to Darius. He distinguished himself in that battle by killing many who rashly attacked him and by putting others to flight. But the Macedonians fighting beside Alexander, encouraged by mutual sympathy, burst together with Alexander into the line of Persian cavalry. The carnage was phenomenal. Around the king's chariot lay dead his best generals, face down in the dirt where they fell fighting gloriously for their king, their wounds on the front of their bodies . . . The Macedonian dead were few, but among them were some of the best fighters, and Alexander had taken a sword cut on his right thigh.
>
> By now Darius' horses were pierced with lances and suffered from agonizing pain. They had begun to toss the yoke and were about to throw the king from his car. Fearing he might be taken alive, Darius leaped onto a horse kept behind the chariot for just this purpose. He even stooped to discard his royal insignia so they would not betray his flight. The rest of his men scattered in fear, breaking from the fighting wherever they could find an opening. They threw down the weapons that just before they had taken up in order to defend themselves. So does panic create fear even of the things that might help.

Quintus Curtius, *History of Alexander* 3.11

By chasing Darius off the battlefield, Alexander had won a major propaganda victory, showing himself to be the greater of the two men. He also scooped more than 3,000 talents in gold from the Persian camp, bathed in the Great King's jeweled tub, and put on his purple silk robes (even though Darius was much taller than Alexander). Most important, Alexander captured Darius' mother, wife, and daughters, who were traveling with the army. Alexander's triumph seemed to show that Darius could not protect his own women, let alone the Persian Empire. Alexander treated them courteously. Once he killed Darius, he could marry his widow and in this way make a legitimate claim to the throne.

Darius now made Alexander an unprecedented offer: In return for his family and peace, he would surrender to him most of Anatolia. Supposedly, Alexander hid Darius' letter, substituting for it a forged, arrogant note offering merely the ransom. Naturally, the Macedonians were furious, and Alexander wrote back to Darius:

> I am master of your country, which the gods have given me ... Come to me, then, as the lord of all Asia. If you fear by coming to suffer something unseemly from me, then send your friend to take pledge-tokens. Come to me and ask me for your wife, your daughter, your children, and you will have them and whatever else you persuade me to grant. But in the future when you send to me, address me as the King of Asia. Do not regard me as an equal, but tell me, as lord of all your possessions, what you need. If you will not do this, I shall set plans to treat you as a criminal. If you wish to dispute me for your throne, stand and fight for it. Do not flee, for I will pursue you no matter where you go.
>
> Arrian, *Campaigns of Alexander* 2.14

Alexander continued south, securing the Mediterranean coast. His main target was **Tyre**, the great Phoenician city that had founded Carthage (in present-day Tunisia) 400 years earlier. Tyre had the best harbor in the eastern Mediterranean. From here, Persian fleets could still threaten Alexander's rear, so he needed to capture it. Unfortunately, the city was built on an island half a mile offshore, and Alexander had no ships. The Phoenician Tyrians mocked his demands for surrender and laughed at him. In February 332 B.C., he started building an artificial land bridge 200-yards wide out to the city. The Macedonians dumped thousands of tons of rock, dirt, and timber into the sea, and the bridge crept out toward the island.

The Tyrians tried every device to prevent completion of the mole. They invented special ships able to mount the land bridge and set the Macedonian siege machinery on fire and wooden towers that tipped burning tar onto the besiegers. Alexander's engineers designed floating battering rams, but the Tyrians dumped debris into the sea to keep them away from the walls. The Macedonians then built floating cranes to clear the way. Finally, in July, the mole reached the island. After the most ferocious catapult barrage in ancient history, Alexander's 150-foot-tall siege towers moved against the walls. He led the assault in person and took the city. After a terrible slaughter he sold 30,000 survivors into slavery. Tyre would never be important again. Alexander's mole still survives today, making a peninsula of the ancient island.

Darius had lost the western empire. He now had no way to strike at the Aegean, and Alexander's road to Egypt was open. Now Darius offered Alexander everything west of the Euphrates, legitimate marriage to his eldest daughter, and 10,000 talents:

> When these things were reported in the council of the Companions, Parmenio is reported to have said that if he were Alexander he would be glad to stop the

war on these terms and be released from further risk. "So would I, if I were Parmenio," he said, "but because I am Alexander, I will send Darius a different answer." And so he did. He said that he had no need of money and saw no reason to accept part of the country when he could take it all. For all the money and all the country belonged to him. If he wanted to marry Darius' daughter, he would do so whether Darius liked it or not. Darius would have to come to him, if he hoped to be treated with respect. When Darius heard these things, he gave up all hope of making a deal with Alexander and once again prepared for war.

Arrian, *Campaigns of Alexander* 2.25

Alexander entered Egypt in October 332 B.C. and over the next twelve months disposed of Egyptian affairs as if the war were already won. He marked out a new city called ALEXANDRIA to replace Tyre as the east Mediterranean's principal harbor. Alexandria was destined to be one of the greatest cities of the ancient world. His governors would rule from here.

Persia had reconquered Egypt after a rebellion only eleven years before, and the Egyptian aristocracy now welcomed Alexander as a liberator. They crowned him pharaoh in the ancient city of Memphis. Alexander was proclaimed the son of Ra and incarnation of Horus. By proclaiming Alexander a god, Egyptians handed him a potent propaganda weapon; As we will see in the next chapter, Alexander may soon have begun to believe his own propaganda!

In January 331 B.C., Alexander tested his divine status with a 750-mile round trip trek to an oracle of Amun far out in the desert at Siwa (Figure 19.5). Greeks identified Amun

**FIGURE 19.5** The Siwa Oasis from the Mountain of the Dead. The salt lake Birket Siwa backed by distinctive high bluffs is visible in the distance.

with Zeus. According to the biographer Plutarch, writing over 400 years later, the high priest of Amun wanted to ingratiate himself with Alexander and decided to address the conquering king in Greek. However, because his Greek was not very good, he made a grammatical slip—which dramatically changed the meaning of his words; instead of saying "Welcome, my son," he actually said, "Welcome, Son of Zeus"!

After this episode, Alexander began claiming that the oracle had confirmed his divinity. A new phase of Greek history was beginning.

## Key Terms

Philip II, *406*

Demosthenes, *406*

King's Companions, *408*

Amphipolis, *408*

Pella, *409*

Olynthus, *410*

Olympias, *411*

Amphictyonic League, *411*

Phocis, *412*

Chaeronea, *416*

Darius III, *417*

Parmenio, *418*

Granicus River, *420*

Issus, *425*

Tyre, *427*

## Further Reading

Borza, Eugene, *In the Shadow of Olympus: The Emergence of Macedonia* (Princeton, 1990). Archaeological and historical study of Iron Age Macedonia.

Ellis, J. R., *Philip II and Macedonian Imperialism* (Princeton, 1976). Argues that Philip was always more interested in conquering Persia than in dominating Greece.

Lewis, D. M., John Boardman, Simon Hornblower, and Martin Ostwald, eds., *The Cambridge Ancient History VI: The Fourth Century* B.C., 2nd ed. (Cambridge, UK, 1994), chapters 14–18.

Roisman, Joseph, ed., *Brill's Companion to Alexander the Great* (Leiden, 2003). Scholarly essays on numerous aspects of Alexander's career.

### ANCIENT TEXTS

*Greek Political Oratory*, tr. A. N. W. Saunders (Harmondsworth, UK, 1970). Speeches by Demosthenes and pamphlets by Isocrates dealing with Athens' reaction to the growth of Philip's power.

Arrian, *The Campaigns of Alexander*, tr. Aubrey de Selincourt (Harmondsworth, UK, 1958). Roman-era history, but drawing on primary sources now lost.

Diodorus of Sicily, *History*, Books 16 and 17. In *The Library of History VIII*, tr. C.B. Welles (Cambridge, MA, 1963). Parallel Greek and English texts of Diodorus' accounts of Timoleon, Philip, and Alexander.

Plutarch, *Lives of Demosthenes and Alexander*. In *The Age of Alexander*, tr. Ian Scott-Kilvert (Harmondsworth, UK, 1973).

Quintus Curtius Rufus, *The History of Alexander*, tr. John Yardley (New York, 1984). Another Roman-era history, also drawing on primary sources now lost.

## CHAPTER 20

# The Warlords of Macedon II: Alexander the God

Alexander had defeated Darius in battle and overrun half his empire. Now, in April 331 B.C., he left Egypt and headed into the heart of the Persian Empire. At Babylon, Darius had assembled the largest army ever seen in antiquity—we do not know its exact numbers, though it may have had as many as 250,000 men. For the showdown, Darius chose the plain of **Gaugamela** (gau-ga-mē-la), in what is today Kurdish territory in northern Iraq. It was to be the greatest battle of ancient times.

## THE FALL OF THE GREAT KING DARIUS, 331–330 B.C.

When Alexander arrived at Gaugamela, Darius' army outnumbered his own about five to one. Darius had as many cavalry as Alexander had cavalry and infantry combined, and thousands of the Persians wore heavy armor. The Persian line was a mile longer than the Macedonian. Whatever Alexander did, he would be outflanked.

Parmenio suggested a night attack, but Alexander supposedly replied with scorn, "I will not steal my victory." He needed to defeat Darius in open battle to demonstrate his personal superiority over the Persian king. But how was he going to accomplish this? On the night of September 30, while his army slept, Alexander lay awake. Was there any way to offset the fearful odds? When he finally settled on a plan, Plutarch's colorful account reports,

it is said that Alexander retired to his tent and passed the rest of the night in a deep unaccustomed sleep. When his generals came to him in the early morning, they were astonished to find him still asleep. On their own authority they ordered the common soldiers to breakfast before they did. Parmenio is said to have come and, because of the urgency of the situation, to have stood at the bedside and called out Alexander's name two or three times. When he aroused him, Parmenio asked how Alexander could sleep as if he was already victorious when in fact he was about to fight the greatest battle of his life. "Why not?" Alexander said smiling. "We have already won the battle, I think, now that we have stopped racing around these endless ruined plains, chasing Darius who would not stand and fight." Both before the fight and at its height Alexander displayed the control and steadfastness of a man who knows just what he is doing.

Plutarch, *Life of Alexander* 32

Alexander invented a battle plan that 2,000 years later became a favorite of Napoleon. He angled both flanks backward in a kind of V-shape, making them look even weaker than they were, to entice Darius into attack. As the Persians found the flanks stronger than they had expected, they would (Alexander hoped) commit more and more men to these fights, thinking that they would crush the Macedonian wings. As the Persians moved their troops toward the flanks, they would eventually open a gap in their own center, through which Alexander would strike.

The plan depended on judgment and timing. From the moment Darius ordered his right wing forward, Parmenio on the Macedonian left was under intense pressure. Soon he was holding off ten times his own numbers. On the other wing, some Persian cavalry broke clear through the Macedonian line and started plundering Alexander's camp. But Alexander held on, waiting for the moment.

As Darius sent more and more cavalry against Alexander's straining right wing, the ranks in front of the Great King thinned, as Alexander had anticipated. Forming his men in a wedge, with himself and the Companions at the point, Alexander now charged. A quarter of a million men crowded the battlefield, but a few thousand would decide the fate of the Persian Empire.

The Companions hacked through the Persian guard, causing Darius to bolt and flee. Alexander wheeled around in time to save Parmenio's overwhelmed men. The Persians still vastly outnumbered the Macedonians, but with Darius gone from the field and many commanders dead, they began to lose order. The day was Alexander's. Alexander pursued Darius for seventy-five miles to Arbela (Map 19.3), where Darius tried to rally resistance. Failing, Darius then fled east into the Zagros Mountains separating Mesopotamia from the upland Persian plateau.

Darius was Ahuramazda's representative, protecting the Truth from the Lie, but he had become a refugee with a few wagonloads of gold and some mercenaries. Babylon, on the mid-Euphrates, surrendered to Alexander along with Susa, a Persian capital far to the east on the plain between the Persian Gulf and the Zagros Mountains (in today's Iranian oilfields). Was the war over? Alexander had avenged the invasion of Greece 150 years earlier and taken massive plunder: At Susa alone he captured 40,000 talents in coin! He appointed his friends as governors of some of the richest provinces in the world, and the army proclaimed him Lord of Asia.

Yet the Persian elite had not accepted Alexander as Darius' legitimate replacement. To them he was a western barbarian, a savage, even a madman. Replacing Darius was going to be more difficult than overthrowing him. Alexander advanced southeast to Persepolis, Persia's most sacred city, where he hoped its priests would recognize him as their master (Map 19.3). As he approached, though, he met 4,000 Greeks whom the Persians had afflicted with various kinds of torture. Some had their feet cut off, others their hands and ears. The Persians had branded them with their bizarre letter forms, keeping them for a long time as the subject for ridicule and amusement ... They seemed more unreal phantoms than men. Only their human voices remained. They caused more tears to flow than they themselves had shed.

Quintus Curtius, *History of Alexander* 5.5

Enraged at the mutilations, Alexander gave the order to loot Persepolis and kill everyone, although the city had surrendered. Then he burned the city, including its magnificent palaces (Figure 20.1). The soldiers might have thought that burning Persepolis meant that the war was over and they could now go home. They had marched 7,000 miles and acquired more plunder than any army in history. The war, though, was far from over. Alexander still had to kill or capture Darius to confirm his victory. He set out to march 500 miles northwest through the rugged Zagros Mountains to Ecbatana, ancient capital of the Medes, where Darius was reported to be gathering forces.

Darius fled again. Alexander sent Parmenio to seize Ecbatana while he pursued Darius with his best troops. Darius hoped to reach the rich eastern satrapies of Bactria and Soghdiana (roughly present-day Uzbekistan). He had never visited these places before, and their satraps, though nominally under the authority of the Persian king, were in reality virtually independent. **Bessus**, Darius' cavalry commander at Gaugamela and one of these eastern satraps, suggested that Darius temporarily hand over command to him so he could win over the other satraps. When Darius refused, Bessus threw him in chains and proclaimed himself king. As Alexander closed in, Darius' little band disintegrated. Bessus ordered Darius murdered, then fled east. Plutarch tells the story:

**FIGURE 20.1** The ruins of the audience hall of Darius and Xerxes in Persepolis, Iran. Built between 518 and 460 B.C., Alexander destroyed it in 330 B.C.

The pursuit became long and arduous. They rode for eleven days over a distance of 400 miles until most of the horsemen had given out, mostly from lack of water. Then he met up with some Macedonians leading mules with skins of water that they were bringing from the river. It was midday. When they saw Alexander suffering badly from dehydration, they quickly filled a helmet with water and brought it to him. When he asked them whom they were bringing the water to, they said, "To our own sons. But so long as you live, we can always get other sons, if they should perish." Alexander took the helmet, but when he looked around and saw that all the cavalry around him were craning their necks to get a look at the water, he gave it back without drinking. He praised the men for their efforts. "But if I alone drink, these men will lose heart," he said.

When his cavalry saw Alexander's self-control and his greatness of heart, they cried out that he should lead them forth boldly, and they goaded their mounts. They said they would not weary nor grow thirsty, nor even think of themselves as wholly mortal, so long as they had such a leader.

Thus were all eager to continue the pursuit; but only sixty remained when at last Alexander burst into the enemy camp.° They rode past quantities of gold and silver plate that had been thrown away and through wagons filled with women and children without drivers. They bore down on those foremost in flight, thinking that Darius must be among them. At last they found him lying in a wagon, pierced by javelins, at the point of death. Nonetheless, he asked for water, and when he had drunk some cool water, he said to the man who gave it to him, named Polystratos, "My man, this is the final stroke of misfortune, that I cannot return a favor given. But Alexander will return you the favor, and may the gods reward him for the kindness he shows to my wife and mother. Through you I extend to him my right hand." So speaking, he took the hand of Polystratos and died.

When Alexander came up, he was clearly in distress. He unloosened his cloak and spread it over the body. Later, when he captured Bessus who had killed the king, he had him ripped apart. He bent down two straight trees until they touched, then bound Bessus to both trees. When he cut the trees lose, they sprang back, ripping off the part of the body bound to it. But the body of Darius Alexander laid out as appropriate to a king and sent it to his mother for burial. He enrolled Darius' brother Exathres into the King's Companions.

Plutarch, *Life of Alexander* 42–43

°*enemy camp:* Near Hekatompylos ("the Hundred Gates") in northern Iran; see Map 19.3.

## ALEXANDER IN THE EAST, 330–324 B.C.

By giving Darius a proper funeral and accepting his brother into the Companions, Alexander treated the late king as his predecessor, thereby presenting himself as a legitimate ruler of Persia. Further, by punishing Bessus in a very Persian way, he acted as any Achaemenid would toward a regicide. With Darius dead and a story circulating that he had blessed Alexander's succession, Alexander needed only to present himself as a Persian king to win over the empire. Eventually, he hoped, the Magi and others would follow. The only problem was that if Alexander acted too much like a Persian, he would offend the Macedonians, who might rebel or even murder him.

Alexander therefore proceeded cautiously. He started wearing the Persian royal diadem, but not the tiara that went with it; he wore the Persian white robe and sash, but not Asiatic pants; he took over Darius' harem of 365 beautiful women (one for each night of the year), but ostentatiously refused to sleep with them. He used a Macedonian signet ring to seal documents going back to Europe and a Persian one for imperial affairs.

The Persians were not impressed. They expected a king to act like one. Nor were the Macedonians pleased; they despised what they saw as effete orientalism. Alexander appears to have decided to change the army from a national force into one loyal to him personally. He disbanded all non-Macedonians, giving each cavalryman one talent as a bonus and each infantryman 1,000 drachmas (equivalent to eight and three years' pay, respectively) then offered everyone the chance to reenlist for a further bonus of three talents! Every soldier was now a rich man and was obligated directly to Alexander for his fortune. Alexander's policy cost him 12,000 talents, a vast sum by Greek standards, but since he had captured about 180,000 talents, Alexander could afford it. He was by far the richest man in the world.

Alexander dealt with his old rival Parmenio by "promoting" him to the governorship of Ecbatana, thereby removing him from the centers of power. Alexander also put Parmenio's arrogant son Philotas under close surveillance, and when Philotas failed to report rumors of a plot, Alexander arrested him in a midnight raid. The "proof" of his guilt was a letter from Parmenio to Philotas, saying, "First of all take care of yourselves and then of your people—that is how we shall accomplish our purpose." Under torture, Philotas said that his father Parmenio was behind a conspiracy. Alexander sent assassins through the desert on racing camels to reach Ecbatana before Parmenio heard about his son's confession. The assassins handed Parmenio two letters, one from Philotas, the other his own death warrant. Parmenio tore open his son's letter, and, as he did so, the assassins stabbed the great general through the throat. They kept hacking at Parmenio long after he was dead. It was hard for Macedonians to decide which was the worse possibility—that Alexander had murdered his old friend Parmenio, or that Parmenio had conspired against his old friend the king. As one general put it, "If Parmenio plotted against Alexander, who can be trusted? And if he didn't, what's to be done?"

Alexander pushed deeper into central Asia to crush its still independent satraps. Early in 329 B.C., he marched through what is now Afghanistan, taking Kandahar and Kabul. No foreign army would repeat this feat until the American-led invasion of A.D. 2002. When they reached the River Oxus (today on Afghanistan's northern border) in June 329 B.C., in 100-degree heat, the troops mutinied and refused to go further. Alexander paid off the oldest veterans and sent them home, then enrolled local troops who had no qualms about the campaign and pushed on, leaving behind many of his mercenaries as garrisons in remote new towns (many of them called Alexandria).

Alexander was growing more distant from his Macedonian troops. Tensions erupted in Samarkand (in modern Uzbekistan) in autumn 328 B.C. That day had been a festival of Dionysus, the god of wine:

> The Macedonians keep one day sacred to Dionysus, and Alexander each year performed rites on this day. This year for some reason he did not sacrifice to Dionysus, but to the Dioscuri, Castor and Pollux°; something or other made him think of doing this. The drinking had gone on a good while—and Alexander had found new and rather barbaric methods for getting drunk—when the conversation turned to the Dioscuri and how Tyndareus had been robbed of their paternity, which was given to Zeus. Some of those present (such men have

°*Dioscuri, Castor and Pollux:* Brothers of Helen of Troy. According to the usual story, their mother Leda produced Castor through a union with her mortal husband Tyndareus and Pollux from an affair with Zeus. They were honored as heroes.

always been and will always be harmful to the interests of kings), trying to flatter Alexander, said that the deeds of the Dioscuri could never be compared favorably with those of Alexander. Others, deep in their cups, did not leave Heracles out of it. It was only because of envy that living men were not accorded the honor that they deserved at the hands of contemporaries, they said.

It was clear enough that Cleitus° was irked by Alexander's adoption of barbarian ways and by the flatteries of such men. Under the sharpening effects of the wine Cleitus was unwilling to allow such slights against the divine or the demeaning of the deeds of the ancient heroes in order to do a favor to Alexander that was no favor. Also, he did not believe that Alexander's deeds were so remarkable or wondrous as claimed. Nor had he accomplished them by himself, Cleitus said, but to a large part, they were the achievement of all the Macedonians.

These words stung Alexander to the quick. Nor do I approve of them, because it seems to me that in a drink-fest one ought to keep his views to himself without, of course, stooping to the flattery performed by others. But when others who also wished to curry Alexander's favor then took on the deeds of Philip, unjustly alleging that they were neither great nor wonderful, Cleitus lost all self-control and praised the accomplishments of Philip, saying that they were greater than those of Alexander. He was quite thoroughly drunk, and he went on abusing Alexander, reminding him that it was he who had saved his life at the battle on the Granicus River against the Persians.

"This is the hand," he said raising his right hand obscenely, "that saved you on that day!"

Alexander could no longer put up with the drunkenness and the abuse. He leapt angrily to his feet as if to strike Cleitus, but his fellow-drinkers held him back. Still, Cleitus went on insulting him so that Alexander called out for the guards. But no one answered.

"What? Am I to be like Darius, king in name only, dragged about in chains by Bessus and his friends?"

With that, they were unable to stop Alexander from leaping to his feet, seizing a spear from one of the bodyguards, and striking Cleitus a fatal blow.

Arrian, *Campaigns of Alexander* 4.8–9

°*Cleitus:* Cleitus "the Black," who had saved Alexander's life at the battle of the Granicus.

When the drunken Alexander realized what he had done, he tried to impale himself on the same spear. He fled weeping to his tent, where he refused food and water for three days (just as Achilles pouted in his tent when shamed by Agamemnon). Eventually, a Greek soothsayer drew Alexander out by telling him that he stood above normal law and morality. "Do you not know that Zeus has Justice and Law seated by his side to prove that everything that is done by the ruler of the world is lawful and just?" he said. Perhaps Alexander believed him.

Fighting dragged on for two more years against fierce tribesmen in rugged mountain fortresses, but one by one, the chiefs surrendered. In spring 327 B.C., Alexander married Roxane, daughter of one of these chiefs. She was said to be the second most beautiful woman in Asia, after the widow of Darius, with whom, according to rumor, Alexander had had sexual relations, and who died giving birth to a stillborn child on the eve of Gaugamela.

Alexander was deliberately merging the Macedonian, Greek, and Persian elites under his own personal rule. Since Darius' death, he had forced 3,000 Macedonians to marry Persians, and by marrying Roxane he showed the world that his heir would have central Asian blood. He also enrolled 30,000 Asian youths in a unit called "the Successors," who were taught Greek and learned Macedonian tactics.

Aggressive egalitarianism marked Macedonian and Greek societies. Persia, by contrast, was rigidly class-stratified (like most advanced societies) with an elaborate system for expressing deference. Equals greeted each other with a kiss on the lips; a superior gave a slight subordinate a kiss on the cheek; while a man entering the presence of a greatly superior being threw himself to the ground, with different degrees of groveling, depending on the disparity in ranks. In the Aegean, such prostration (in Greek *proskynêsis* [pros-ki-nē-sis]) was appropriate only before gods, and even then sparingly.

When Alexander admitted Persians to his officer corps, the Persians assumed that they should prostrate themselves before him, but the Macedonians thought such behavior unbecoming to a real man. Alexander favored *proskynêsis* because the Persians thought it was a Great King's due. If the Macedonians performed it too, Alexander would look more kingly in Persian eyes, but Macedonians would not accept the custom. Callisthenes, Aristotle's nephew and the official campaign historian, openly mocked orders to prostrate himself. According to one source, Alexander locked him in a cage and dragged behind the army until he died. Alexander, like his father Zeus/Amun, stood above all laws.

Many Macedonians thought he had gone completely insane.

## WAR IN INDIA, 327–326 B.C.

A hundred and twenty years earlier, Cyrus the Great, founder of the Persian Empire, had campaigned in what is now Pakistan, and Alexander was determined to do the same. The Persians called this area Hindush, and the Greeks called it India, but they were all vague about what lay there. According to rumor, there were tribes with dogs' heads and tails, man-eating monsters, and pygmies with penises as long as their legs (sixteenth-century Europeans brought home similar reports about America). The biggest error, though, was the belief that the great river Ocean, thought to flow around the world, lay just past the Indus River. In spring 327 B.C., Alexander thought that a month's march would take him to the edge of the world. A year earlier, he had told people that he planned to march to the river Ocean and return to Greece presumably by sailing on the river, which surrounded the world, then begin new campaigns around the Black Sea.

In 327 B.C., the Macedonians struggled across the Khyber Pass in the Hindu Kush Mountains (in present-day Afghanistan) and descended into the valley (see Map 19.3). In hard fighting, Alexander was wounded yet again, taking an arrow through the shoulder. He gave further displays of terrible rage: When 7,000 Indian troops surrendered but refused to sign up as mercenaries, he killed them all, along with their wives and children. In Indian history books today, the savage and perhaps unbalanced Alexander is chiefly remembered for this massacre.

In April 326 B.C., he entered the kingdom of **Porus** (his proper name was probably Parvataku), the strongest king in the region. Porus brought a large army to the River Jhelum, including 200 elephants (Figure 20.2).

As Alexander headed south to meet Porus, the monsoon broke. The downpour rotted the Macedonians' equipment and flooded every stream. Disease carried off men left and right. When the army reached the Jhelum in June, it found a raging torrent a mile wide with Porus on the other side, blocking the only ford. Still, Alexander's engineers managed to get half his army across the river by night during a violent thunderstorm.

**FIGURE 20.2**   A worn Macedonian coin from the eastern provinces, bronze, ca. 200 B.C., showing Alexander on a horse attacking two men with spears, mounted on an elephant.

Although the battle that followed was one of Alexander's greatest triumphs, even Alexander had to recognize after it that his army was coming to pieces. He had lost some of his best men, and the survivors refused to face elephants again. His beloved horse Bucephalas ("ox-head," from a mark on the horse), the most famous horse of the ancient world, was wounded and died. Alexander had ridden him throughout his wars, and he named a city after him (which still exists in present-day Pakistan; he named another city after his dog!).

Still, in early July 326 B.C., Alexander cajoled his men into advancing again. But they still did not find the river Ocean. Instead they reached the River Hyphasis in the Punjab (the present-day River Beas), a tributary of the Indus. Not even Persia's armies had gone further. Beyond lay the great Ganges plain:

> Alexander saw that his men were worn out by nearly eight years of campaigning in the midst of toils and danger, and that if he were to muster them for a campaign against the Gandaridae° he would need to rouse their spirits through an effective appeal. The losses had been great, and there was no end in sight. The hooves of the horses were worn thin through constant marching. Their weapons and their armor were worn out, and their clothes quite gone. They had no choice but to cut new clothes out of Indian garments. As luck would have it, this was the season of heaviest rain, and for seventy days it had rained, accompanied by continuous thunder and lightning.
>
> Diodorus of Sicily 17.94
>
> °*Gandaridae:* The inhabitants of the Ganges plain.

According to another ancient author, "Alexander's ambition prevailed over reason." He called an assembly, and in a driving rain by the mud-filled Hyphasis River, gave an impassioned speech about glory and honor, still insisting that they were near the river Ocean:

> After Alexander had spoken words such as these, silence prevailed. No one was willing to speak on the spur of the moment and no one was willing to agree with him either. Several times Alexander encouraged any to speak who might entertain contrary views. Nonetheless, no one spoke for a good while. At last, Coenus,° son of Polemocrates, plucked up his courage to speak.

°*Coenus:* A daring cavalry commander who had distinguished himself at the Jhelum River.

Coenus described the men's exhaustion. He closed:

> "My king, a fine thing in the height of good fortune is self-restraint. With you as leader, and we as army, we have nothing to fear from the enemy. But when something unexpected happens, as if sent by a god, then because it is unforeseen, we cannot prepare against it."

Just as he had done after killing Cleitus, Alexander withdrew in a sulk to his tent:

> After these words he withdrew into his tent and would not permit any of the Companions to come in until the third day. He waited, hoping that the Macedonians and the allies would have a change of heart, as often happens in the midst of military affairs, that would make them easier to persuade. Dead silence reigned throughout the camp. It was clear that the men were angry at Alexander's outburst and by no means persuaded by it to change their views. All the while Alexander went on taking omens for the crossing of the river (according to the account of Ptolemy° son of Lagos), but the omens were unfavorable. He assembled the oldest of the Companions and those most devoted to him. Because everything pointed to a withdrawal, he proclaimed openly to the army that he had decided to turn back.
>
> The mixed host shouted with joy. Most wept. They came to Alexander's tent and called down all good things upon him because he endured defeat at their hands alone.

Arrian, *The Campaigns of Alexander* 5.27–29

°*Ptolemy:* Ptolemy was one of Alexander's generals, who wrote an account of the campaigns. After Alexander's death, this Ptolemy made himself king of Egypt and founded a famous dynasty.

## THE LONG MARCH HOME, 326–324 B.C.

Even now, Alexander would not simply turn around. He built a fleet to sail down the Indus, intending to return to Mesopotamia along what we call the Persian Gulf, partly by fleet and partly by marching overland (see Map 19.3). Just as the fleet was about to sail, 30,000 infantry and 6,000 cavalry arrived as reinforcements, bringing medical supplies and 25,000 new suits of armor. After marching 7,000 miles, the men learned they were going home again. If the reinforcements had hoped for excitement, though, they were not disappointed. As they sailed down the Indus, they encountered storms, floods, and one hostile tribe after another. The Brahmins stirred up a holy war, calling Alexander a barbarous infidel. Day after day, the Macedonians fought skirmishes and stormed fortresses. The men grew even more exhausted and finally refused to climb the siege ladders. Only when Alexander himself, a kind of indefatigable superman, started up walls did they follow. Morale was near collapse. One day, as they faced yet another castle,

a seer announced that Alexander should postpone the siege, because his life was in danger. Alexander looked at Demophon (the seer's name) and said, "Demophon, I suppose that you would find it very annoying if someone interrupted you while you practiced your craft and examined the entrails." Demophon replied that would certainly be the case. "Well, then, I have my mind on weighty matters, not the guts of animals, and I don't enjoy the advice of a superstitious seer."

Hesitating only to give this reply, he ordered the ladders to be mounted against the walls. As the others hesitated, he scaled the wall himself. Instead of having the usual crenellations, the wall was a continuous parapet with a narrow cornice. Alexander was not standing on it, but hanging from it as he parried blow after blow with his shield. He was the unique target of long-range missiles flying from the towers along the wall. His men could not get to him because of the shower of missiles raining from above, but at last, shame gave them courage when they realized that by hesitating they were delivering Alexander to the enemy. But their haste only got in the way of their aid, because while they all scrambled to mount the ladders they overloaded them and came crashing to the ground, depriving their commander of his only hope. Alexander stood alone in the face of a huge army.

By now his left arm grew weary from constantly swinging his shield to deflect missiles. His friends urged him to jump down and prepared to catch him.

Alexander did jump, but against all reason he jumped *inside* the city walls, where he took up a position with his back to a giant oak tree, whose branches shielded him from missiles. Supporting the king in the fight was, first, the glory of his name. Second, desperation made keen his desire to die a glorious death. The enemy poured upon him, raining down missiles on his shield and smashing his helmet with rocks. His knees gave way from the strain. The Indians standing nearest to him incautiously rushed in and he killed two of them with his sword.

Then an arrow drove through Alexander's breastbone and lodged next to his heart.

When he was hit, a thick jet of blood shot out. He dropped his weapons and appeared to be dying. The man who had wounded him ran up to strip the body of its armor, eager and exultant. When Alexander felt his hands on his body he must have come around, indignant at the final insult. Bringing back his failing spirit, he brought his sword from up beneath and stabbed the man in his unprotected side.

Three bodies now lay at the king's feet, and the other Indians held back, not sure what to do … At last Peucestes, having dislodged the defenders in another part of the city, followed in Alexander's footsteps. When Alexander saw him he thought Peucestes has brought him consolation in death rather than hope in life. He fell exhausted on Peucestes' shield. Immediately after, Timaeus came up, and shortly after him Leonnatus, and then Aristonos.

The Indians, dropping everything else when they learned the king was within the city, now arrived at the spot and attacked Alexander's defenders. Timaeus fell with many wounds in his chest after a glorious fight. Peucestes, too, took three javelin wounds, but ignoring his own safety continued to protect the king with his shield. Leonnatus was wounded in the neck and fell half-dead at the king's feet. Alexander's last hope lay with Aristonos, but he was wounded too and unable to resist further the ferocious onslaught of the enemy.

A rumor reached the Macedonians outside that the king had fallen. What would have discouraged others only drove the Macedonians to action. Ignoring the risk, with axes they chopped down one of the gates and poured in through the breach. They killed the Indians wherever they found them—more ran away than dared to resist. They killed them all—old men, women, children. They blamed every one of them for the king's wounds. Finally, after mass carnage, their temper abated.

Quintus Curtius, *History of Alexander* 9.4–5

An emergency operation removed the arrow, but Alexander hemorrhaged. For a week, he seemed likely to die. The Macedonians were in a panic, thinking that without Alexander they would never get through. Then when

news arrived that Alexander was still alive, they hardly believed it. Nor was it clear that Alexander would go on living. When a letter arrived saying that he would soon come to the camp, most through fear would not believe it, but supposed that it had been forged by his bodyguards or generals.

When Alexander understood this, wishing to prevent a disturbance in the camp, he had himself carried as soon as he was able to the banks of the Hydraotes River. There he sailed downriver, for the camp was pitched at the confluence of the Hydraotes and the Acesines rivers, where Hephaestion was in charge of the land army and Nearchos of the fleet. When the boat carrying Alexander neared the camp, he ordered that the awning be taken down from the prow so that everyone could see him. Even then they did not believe it, thinking that this was the corpse of Alexander. But when the boat put into shore, he extended his hand to the crowd. A great shout arose as some raised their hands to heaven and others to Alexander. So unexpected was the event that many could not help themselves from weeping.

As he left the ship, a unit of his guards brought him a stretcher, but he called out for his horse. When he was seen mounted on the horse, the crowed clapped and clapped so that an echo rebounded from the banks and the nearby valleys. When he reached his tent he dismounted so that they could see him walking too. They crowded around him on every side, touching his hands, his knees, his clothing. Some just enjoyed being near to him, then turned away with a prayer on their lips. Some cast wreathes upon him, or such flowers as were then in bloom in India.

Arrian, *The Campaigns of Alexander* 6.12–13

Now progress down the Indus became a string of massacres as the Macedonians destroyed everything in their path. The army was degenerating into a pathological mob. The Indus tribes folded as stories of Alexander's invulnerability spread, and they handed over the Brahmins ("naked philosophers," as the Greeks called them) who had led the resistance. According to Plutarch, Alexander questioned them, ending by asking, "How can a man become a god?" The answer came: "By doing something a man cannot do." Their answer must have struck a chord with Alexander: He had overthrown Persia, invaded India, and, he believed, he would soon sail on the Ocean—did this not mean that he really had achieved divinity?

Some very real-world problems remained for Alexander, though. Only one-third of his army could fit on the ships he had, so to get home again the others would have to cross the fearsome Gedrosian desert that runs along the Persian Gulf. According to the plan, Alexander would set off walking with most of the men, with camels carrying food. His general Craterus would follow with the ships, bringing more food, and catch up with them when the monsoons stopped. Each night, Alexander would dig wells, which the fleet would use as they followed. The ships would reach them just before Alexander's food ran out, at the point where mountains blocked the coastal path, according to inquiries about the local geography. The army would then load up with a week's worth of food and swing inland, through the worst of the desert, and west over the mountains into the plains around Susa, where the living was good (see Map 19.3).

However, the monsoon did not stop when expected, so that the ships set off late and missed the rendezvous. Alexander waited for them as long as he dared, then headed inland without the extra supplies. He sent racing camels ahead ordering the local satraps to meet him with food and water, but none came. During the day the sun blazed, at night the desert froze. The only plants along the way were poisonous. Men died from heatstroke and dehydration, and hundreds more drowned when a flash thunderstorm flooded a dried-up streambed. Hundreds more perished when a sandstorm obliterated all landmarks, leaving them wandering in circles. Of 85,000 who entered the desert (mostly noncombatants), just 25,000 reached the other side.

More than a year had passed since the mutiny at the River Hyphasis. Few of the veterans who wept with joy when Alexander announced the omens against a further advance were still alive at the end of 325 B.C. Those who did survive now had different reasons to weep.

## THE LAST DAYS, 324–323 B.C.

Alexander's men straggled back into Susa in February 324 B.C. The king needed swiftly to organize his conquests and stabilize his authority. While he had spent six years campaigning in the east, his governors had run wild, embezzling huge funds, hiring their own mercenaries, and acting like independent kings. Alexander executed many of them, beginning with those who failed to supply him in Gedrosia, then ordered the survivors to dismiss their mercenaries. Desperadoes filled the countryside. To get rid of them, in summer 324 B.C. Alexander ordered all Greek ex-mercenaries to return home and all Greek cities to receive them. This created huge new problems: Many of the mercenaries were Greek outlaws who had been banished from their homes and their property divided.

Back in Babylon, Alexander continued "Persianizing" his army. The Hyphasis mutiny showed how dependence on Macedonian veterans left Alexander vulnerable. He put Persians into the highest staff positions and brought more into the Companion cavalry. He assembled the Macedonians at Opis just outside Babylon and announced that he was demobilizing the senior veterans. He offered huge bonuses all around, but the veterans took it badly:

> The men felt that Alexander did not value their services and considered them useless in war. Not unreasonably they were aggrieved by his speech. They had many causes for complaint during the expedition—his Persian dress offended them, which amounted to the same lack of respect, as did his issuing of Macedonian equipment to the "Successors"° and his incorporation of foreign cavalry into units of the Companions. They did not therefore endure in silence but called out for their dismissal from the army. They said that he could go on fighting with the help of his father, mockingly referring, apparently, to Amun.
>
> Alexander was furious. He was much quicker to take offence and, accustomed to oriental customs of subservience, he was less open-hearted to the Macedonians.

°*Successors:* The 30,000 Persians whom Alexander enrolled in 327 B.C. to learn Greek and use Macedonian tactics.

Just as he had done after the mutiny on the River Hyphasis in 326 B.C., Alexander retired to his tent, refusing food and drink. On the third day, he came forth and started putting Persians in charge of the army:

> When the Macedonians learned about the Persians and the Medes—the power to command being given to Persians, the barbarian forces being integrated into Macedonian units, a Persian corps called by a Macedonian name, Persian infantry units given the coveted title of "Companions," Persian "Silver Shields,"° and Persian mounted Companions being formed, and even a new Royal Squadron— they completely lost control. All together they ran to the palace, threw down their arms before the doors as signs of supplication to the king. They stood there shouting, begging to be let in. They said they would give up the instigators of the recent disturbance and those who had led off the clamor. They said they would not leave their place either day or night until Alexander took pity on them.

Arrian, *The Campaigns of Alexander* 7.8, 11

°*Silver Shields:* An elite corps

Alexander made up with his men but nonetheless sent 11,000 Macedonians home, giving one talent to each (enough to buy a farm and some slaves and retire). He drafted more Persians to replace them and persuaded the departing Greeks and Macedonians to leave behind the Persian wives he had given them along with the children the women had borne. In twenty years' time, he hoped, the boys would form the nucleus of a new army, loyal solely to their one and only king—himself.

Alexander's thoughts turned to further conquest. Early in 324 B.C., he spoke of attacking Italy, Spain, Sicily, and Carthage. He had 700 ships built on the Euphrates to explore India and circumnavigate Africa, and he ordered a fleet built on the Caspian Sea to repeat Darius I's campaign against the Scythians 200 years earlier. He also wanted to conquer Arabia. He had Phoenician ships dismantled and carried overland from the Mediterranean to the Persian Gulf to explore its coasts. In spring 323 B.C., he assembled an army at Babylon, determined to occupy the rich kingdoms in the Persian Gulf, who monopolized the spice trade with the Arabian Desert.

**FIGURE 20.3**  Greek coin representing Alexander as Heracles, wearing the skin of the Nemean Lion as a helmet, ca. 250 B.C.

At the Olympic Festival in 324 B.C., Alexander had proclaimed that the Greeks should now worship him as a god. For 500 years, Greeks had insisted that no man had such privileged attachments. The Greeks' response was as shocking as Alexander's claim. There were no revolts or violent protests. One Spartan simply said, "Since Alexander desires to be a god, let him be a god." "All right," Demosthenes said, "make him the son of Zeus—and of Poseidon too, if that's what he wants." The Greeks were beaten down, and after Alexander had overthrown the Persian Empire and marched to the ends of the known world, it no longer seemed so crazy to think that he really was divine. Alexander also likened himself to Heracles, the legendary wandering hero, who (like Alexander) was a son of Zeus, and artists regularly represented him as Heracles (Figure 20.3). When in India, he imagined he saw the descendants of Heracles in skin-wearing, club-toting native tribesmen.

Preparations for the god-king's Arabian campaign were well advanced by May 29, 323 B.C., when, as he often did, Alexander went to a drinking party. He wanted to go home early, but cronies talked him into staying and going to still another party. There he drank at one go an extra-large cup of unmixed wine. Suddenly he cried out in pain and was carried home. Next day, he was ill, but eventually got up, bathed, and drank more. After a few days, he discussed the Arabian campaign with his generals, but his fever returned. He went to bed and on the next day, June 6, feeling himself slipping away, gave his general Perdiccas control over the administration. Rumors flew that he was already dead. His generals had to knock a second door into his room so that men could file through to see him one last time. Asked to whom he left his empire, Alexander whispered, "To the strongest."

## CONCLUSION

Alexander passed through the Near East like a terrible dream. He left a trail of devastation from Thebes to the Indus Valley. Adding up the cities he sacked and casualties in battle, perhaps a million people died in his thirteen years of war. The famines and chaos that followed probably brought the total near two million, in a Persian Empire that numbered around 25 to 35 million before he came—the equivalent of an invasion of the United States today leaving twenty million dead. Alexander came, destroyed, and was gone. Alexander left no heir, just an unborn child in Roxane's belly. The legacy of war would be more war.

However, Alexander was not only a destroyer. In 340 B.C., the Aegean Sea was the center of the Greek world. By 320 B.C., it was a backwater. What Athens, Thebes, or Sparta did no longer mattered much. The Near East, where civilization first appeared, the center of wealth and learning since 3000 B.C., was now open to Greek exploration and exploitation. Between 330 and 250 B.C., tens of thousands of Greeks emigrated to make their fortunes in Egypt, Anatolia, and Syria. Standards of living rose, science and learning flourished, and population soared. The Greek-speaking city of Alexandria in Egypt became the cultural center of the Mediterranean and the Near East. In many ways, the period 300–250 B.C., not the fifth century B.C., was the Greeks' true Golden Age. Without Alexander, the shape of Greek history would have been very different.

Alexander was the greatest field commander in history, leading his heterogeneous army through foreign lands year after year, holding their loyalty and through audacious and brilliant generalship giving them victory after victory. He destroyed the greatest empire the world had yet seen, the Persian, and flooded the Greek world with its wealth. His victories made him seem to be more than mortal, and for the first time in half a millennium, many Greeks began to suspect that a living man really might be the son of a god. Stories about his miraculous powers grew more and more elaborate, until five centuries after his death the hugely popular tales known as the *Alexander Romance* turned him into a complete Superman. The *Alexander Romance* was retold in every language of the ancient Mediterranean and Near East and circulated widely in medieval times. A new version in Arabic was discovered recently. Even in early modern times, many European travelers fully believed the stories of the *Alexander Romance*, that in the wilds of central Asia they might yet encounter the immortal, unaging Alexander, still laying his plans to conquer the world.

## Key Terms

Gaugamela, 430                          *proskynêsis*, 436
Bessus, 432                             Porus, 432

## Further Reading

Bosworth, Brian, *Conquest and Empire* (Cambridge, UK, 1988). The best scholarly account of Alexander's campaigns.

Green, Peter, *Alexander of Macedon, 356–323 B.C.* (Berkeley, 1973). Probably the best single book on Alexander's career. A gripping read. Highly recommended.

Heckel, Waldemar, and J. C. Yardley, *Alexander the Great* (Oxford, 2004). Collection of the key ancient texts about Alexander.

Manfredi, Valerio Massimo, *Alexander: Child of a Dream* (London, 2001); *Alexander: The Sands of Ammon*

(London, 2001). Entertaining novels, telling the story well and sticking close to the facts, though unlikely to win prizes as literature.

Wood, Michael, *In the Footsteps of Alexander the Great* (Berkeley, 1997). Written to accompany a television series; excellent photos.

### ANCIENT TEXTS

*The Greek Alexander Romance,* tr. Richard Stoneman (New York, 1991). Translation of fascinating stories about Alexander the Superman.

## CHAPTER 21

# The Greek Kingdoms in the Hellenistic Century, 323–220 B.C.

For centuries Greeks had lived around the Mediterranean's shores, but now Macedon had cast down the Persian Empire. Tens of thousands of Greeks headed east, forging a new world. Since the nineteenth century, historians have used the term "Hellenistic" to describe the period from Alexander's death in 323 B.C. to the suicide of the famous Cleopatra VII, the last major Greek ruler (in 30 B.C.). "Hellenistic" has carried a double meaning—first, that Greeks who settled in the Near East brought Greek culture with them, changing native ways; and second, that the new culture was inferior to Classical Greek civilization. As classicists saw it, Hellenistic culture lacked the spark of brilliance and vitality that made Archaic and Classical Greece so special. But this view nowadays strikes most historians as misleading. The Hellenistic Period was not an age of decline. During this period, the Greeks (led by the Greek-speaking Macedonians) dominated a huge empire, invented new cultural forms, made remarkable scientific discoveries, and often lived better than ever before. In most ways, the messy, complicated Hellenistic world feels more familiar to us than the certainties and sharp divisions of Classical Greece, but its complexity also makes it hard to understand.

Great regional differences emerged. In this chapter, we examine the new centers of Greek wealth that sprang up in Egypt, Syria, and Mesopotamia, and in Chapter 22, "The Greek *Poleis* in the Hellenistic Century, 323–220 B.C.," we will look at the old Greek heartlands in the Aegean and Sicily. In the third century B.C., the great powers of classical times—Athens, Sparta, Thebes—were little pawns in the big games of mighty kings. In many ways, these kings behaved like Near Eastern rulers had since the Bronze Age; instead of the Hellenization of the Persian Empire, we might equally well speak of the orientalization of Greek politics.

But in other ways Greek traditions were stronger than ever. As we shall see in Chapter 23, "Hellenistic Culture, 323–30 B.C.," poetry, history writing, philosophy, science, engineering, sculpture, architecture, and painting all flourished, but now in the service of royal courts.

## THE WARS OF THE SUCCESSORS, 323–301 B.C.

### Phase I, 323–320 B.C.

Alexander's battle-hardened followers had little time to decide what to do when the great man died. Never had one man created such an empire so quickly, and there was no way to know what might happen now that he had died without viable heirs. A new king might take over the empire; a group of kings might divide it among themselves; or there might be a free-for-all. Alexander's closest male relative was a half-witted half-brother, Philip III, the son of Philip II and a dancing girl, born a year before Alexander,. However, Alexander's widow Roxane was pregnant, and later in 323 B.C. she bore a son, Alexander IV. It would be years, though, before he could take power. Right now, neither Philip III nor Alexander IV was a plausible successor.

Attempting to avoid civil war or division of the empire, the generals agreed that Perdiccas, commander of the Macedonian cavalry, would be "guardian of the kingdom." Shortly before his death, Alexander had sent his general Craterus back to Macedon to depose the regent there, one Antipater, but the other generals now appointed Craterus as guardian for the mentally defective Philip III and the unborn Alexander IV and ordered him to leave Antipater alone.

Perdiccas, Craterus, and Antipater decided to control the empire as a Gang of Three, but other generals felt that the empire was too large to hold together and that they should divide it up now. The general **Ptolemy** (**tol**-e-mē) insisted that Alexander had wanted *him* to govern Egypt, so he raced there and murdered the sitting governor. With the 8,000 talents he found in the treasury (fifty-seven pounds of gold!), Ptolemy hired mercenaries. In a propaganda coup, he intercepted the procession carrying Alexander's corpse back to Macedonia and brought it to Alexandria, embalmed in honey in a glass-topped coffin, where it was a major tourist attraction for generations to come. After giving Alexander a traditional pharaoh's funeral and placing his body on permanent display, Ptolemy started ruling Egypt like a king. It was to be the most successful of the successor kingdoms.

At the same time, the general **Antigonus**, known as "One-Eyed" from a war injury, took over much of ANATOLIA, and **Lysimachus** (lī-**sim**-a-kus) took THRACE, roughly present-day Bulgaria (Map 21.1). The key players, then, in the first phase of the struggle over Alexander's empire (Table 21.1) were *Ptolemy* in Egypt, *Antigonus* in Anatolia, *Lysimachus* in Thrace, and the *Gang of Three* (Antipater, who controlled Macedonia, plus Perdiccas and Craterus).

Perdiccas, Craterus, and Antipater were in theory supposed to be preserving the whole empire as a political unity, but according to Arrian, "everyone was suspicious of Perdiccas, and he was suspicious of them." When Perdiccas sent a governor to fight a mercenaries' revolt, the governor was tempted to join it; and by September 323 B.C., when Athens led an uprising against Antipater, it had become difficult to tell which side anyone was fighting on. Lysimachus in Thrace and Craterus (the regent of Philip III and Alexander IV) in Macedonia were conveniently too busy to help Antipater when Greek rebels besieged him in the Thessalian city of Lamia. Only after one of Craterus'

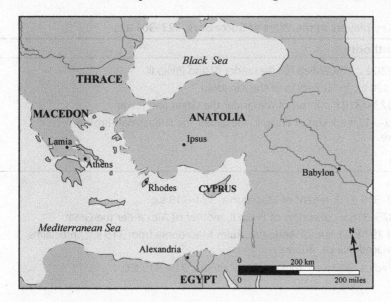

**MAP 21.1** Main kingdoms and locations from the Wars of the Successors, 320–301 B.C., mentioned in the text.

subordinates defeated the Athenian fleet in spring 322 B.C. did Craterus actually send support to Antipater.

Athens surrendered in August 322 B.C. The revolt had been a disaster. Many rich Athenians preferred peace under Macedonia to democratic freedom, and Antipater now executed Athens' democratic politicians. The great orator Demosthenes escaped only by committing suicide. Athens had been a democracy since 508 B.C., with only brief interruptions in 411 and 404/3, but Antipater now installed a garrison in Piraeus, set up a junta, and deprived 12,000 of the roughly 21,000 citizens of their votes. Athens remained a center for philosophy and produced some notable artists, but Athenian political greatness had come to an end forever.

The Greeks were not Antipater's only problem. Alexander's mother Olympias wanted her infant grandson Alexander IV, son of Roxane, to be king of Macedon, but Antipater, who hated Olympias, did not. To build up her power base, Olympias brokered a marriage between her daughter Cleopatra (Alexander the Great's sister) and Perdiccas, although Perdiccas was already married to Antipater's daughter! The naked ambition of Olympias and Perdiccas alarmed the other generals, but before the generals could act, Perdiccas murdered Craterus in spring 320 B.C. Perdiccas then overreached by sailing to Egypt and attacking Ptolemy. When 2,000 of Perdiccas' men drowned crossing the Nile and crocodiles ate hundreds more, his officers murdered him. They asked Ptolemy to take Perdiccas' place as guardian of the kingdom, but Ptolemy refused the honor: He wanted the empire to dissolve, leaving him in charge of Egypt.

## Phase II, 320–301 B.C.

The surviving generals convened in July 320 B.C., allegedly to decide who would replace Perdiccas in overseeing the empire, but in reality Antigonus (who ruled Anatolia), Antipater (who ruled Macedonia), Lysimachus (who ruled Thrace), and particularly Ptolemy (who ruled Egypt) simply wanted to secure their own positions. They now put Antipater in charge

**TABLE 21.1** Key players in the Wars of Successors, 323–301 B.C.

**Empire-wide Authority**

**Craterus** (died 320 B.C.): guardian for Alexander IV and Philip III.

**Perdiccas** (died 320 B.C.): "Guardian of the Kingdom."

**Alexander IV** (323–?310 B.C.): son of Alexander the Great and Roxane.

**Philip III** (ca. 357–317 B.C.): son of Philip II; Alexander the Great's half-brother; mentally defective.

**Local authority**

*Macedonia*

**Antipater** (?397–319 B.C.): regent of Macedonia, 334–319 B.C.

**Olympias** (ca. 375–316 B.C.): widow of Philip II, mother of Alexander the Great.

**Cassander** (died 297 B.C.): son of Antipater. Rules Macedonia from 315 B.C.; proclaims himself king of Macedonia ca. 305 B.C.

**Polyperchon** (died ca. 300 B.C.): regent of Macedonia, 319–315 B.C.

*Egypt*

**Ptolemy I** (367/6–282 B.C.): one of Alexander's generals, governor of Egypt 323–305 B.C.; proclaims himself pharaoh in 305 B.C.

*Thrace*

**Lysimachus** (ca. 355–281 B.C.): Alexander's bodyguard; governor of Thrace and sometimes parts of Anatolia, 323–305 B.C.; proclaims himself king in 305 B.C.

*Western Asia*

**Antigonus I the One-Eyed** (ca. 382–301 B.C.): one of Alexander's generals; based in Anatolia, but controls most of Alexander's empire in Asia, 319–301 B.C.; proclaims himself king in 306 B.C.

**Demetrius I the Besieger** (336–283 B.C.): son of Antigonus I the One-Eyed; proclaims himself king in 306 B.C., loses kingdom in 301 B.C., becomes king of Macedonia 294–287 B.C., and dies in Seleucus' prison.

**Seleucus I** (ca. 358–281 B.C.): one of Alexander's generals, satrap of Babylon 321–316 B.C., then again after 312; proclaims himself king ca. 305 B.C. and takes over most of Antigonus' kingdom after 301 B.C.

of the mentally defective Philip III and the three-year-old Alexander IV (to replace the murdered Craterus). Antipater, Lysimachus, and Ptolemy also wanted to neutralize Antigonus (based in Anatolia), so they arranged to put another of Alexander's prominent generals, **Seleucus** (se-lū-kus), in charge of Babylon and the lands to the east, as yet unclaimed.

In theory, nothing had changed since Alexander died in 323 B.C. The empire was united under Alexander IV (or perhaps Philip III) as presumptive king, with a former general, currently Antipater, acting as guardian for the future king. But in reality, the empire was breaking apart. Antipater (Macedonia), Lysimachus (Thrace), Antigonus (Anatolia), and Ptolemy (Egypt)—each had his own power base. The problem was that Antigonus believed he could reunite the empire by force of arms.

Antipater, aged nearly eighty, died of natural causes in 319 B.C. His final disastrous act was to name as his successor a fellow officer, Polyperchon (pol-i-**per**-kon), passing over his own son **Cassander.** Understandably angry, Cassander challenged the succession, and Ptolemy, Antigonus, and Lysimachus supported him. Polyperchon found his own allies as chaotic fighting broke out all over the empire. Antigonus spent three years defeating Polyperchon's allies, scattered from Anatolia to central Asia, and along the way expelled Seleucus from Babylon.

Back in Macedonia the slow-witted Philip III had stayed out of politics, but in early 317 B.C., his wife Eurydicê publicly announced that Philip III favored Cassander, Antipater's son. This upset not only Polyperchon but also Alexander the Great's mother Olympias, who still hoped that her grandson, the now five-year-old Alexander IV, would one day rule the whole of Alexander's empire. Olympias allied herself with Polyperchon and raised an army in the northwestern Greek province of Epirus. Attempting to unseat Cassander, she attacked Macedon. Philip III's wife Eurydicê put on armor and led her own troops into battle—only for them to betray her. When Olympias captured Eurydicê, she gave free rein to her refined cruelty:

> First Olympias placed Eurydicê and her husband Philip [III] under guard and began to maltreat them. She enclosed them in a small space where there was a slot through which things could be passed. This went on for several days until Olympias realized that she was losing support among the Macedonians, who took pity on the sufferers. She therefore commissioned some Thracians to stab Philip to death. He had been king for six years and four months.° Eurydicê, who was carrying on without restraint and claiming that the kingdom belonged to her, not Olympias, deserved a harsher fate. She sent her a sword, a noose, and some hemlock and ordered her to pick her manner of death. She showed no respect for the dignity of the person she was treating unlawfully, or pity for the lot that affects us all. When she herself met with a similar reversal, she experienced a death that was worthy of her cruelty. In fact, Eurydicê, in the presence of an attendant, had prayed for as much. Eurydicê laid out the body of her husband, cleaning the wounds as much as was possible under the circumstances, then hung herself using her own girdle, neither weeping for her fate nor broken by the misfortune that had befallen her.

Diodorus of Sicily 19.11

°*four months*: Diodorus is writing as if Philip had become king when Alexander died in June 323 B.C.

Few holds were barred in the gruesome, complicated struggle, but Olympias' cruelty went too far, turning former supporters against her. Cassander now attacked Macedon with his own army, promising to pardon Olympias if she surrendered. When she did, he stoned her to death.

Polyperchon and his allies were defeated everywhere except in Greece itself, where Cassander and Polyperchon each tried to persuade the *poleis* to support him. In 318 B.C., the Athenians overthrew their Macedonian-supported oligarchy (supported by Cassander), but the very next year Cassander starved Athens into submission and, disgusted with the constant squabbling, set up a philosopher named Demetrius of Phaleron as dictator. Demetrius of Phaleron's behavior was extraordinary: He revived property requirements for political activity and passed strict rules about upper-class behavior, then dyed his own hair blond, started wearing make-up, and engaged in prodigious sexual escapades with prostitutes of both sexes. Demetrius of Phaleron was evidently no Platonic philosopher-king. He did, however, keep Athens out of war and he did repair the city's shattered finances.

By 314 B.C., it seemed like the game was up for Polyperchon. His last significant ally, Seleucus, expelled from Babylon by Antigonus in 312 B.C., fled to Egypt. There he told Ptolemy (probably accurately) that Antigonus, who ruled Anatolia, wanted to be the sole king of Alexander's empire. Lysimachus and Cassander joined Ptolemy in commanding Antigonus to stop his efforts at expansion. Resenting the interference, Antigonus promptly dropped his alliance with Cassander and started backing Polyperchon in Greece. Antigonus promptly followed Polyperchon's example and offered to free the Greek *poleis*, withdrawing Macedonian garrisons from them and restoring self-rule all around in return for their support. Ptolemy immediately announced that he also wanted to free the Greek *poleis* from external control. For the next 150 years, "freedom for the Greeks" would be a recurring rallying cry and the cause of continuing catastrophes in the Greek-speaking world.

No sooner did the war in Greece wind down than a new front opened in Judea, where Ptolemy defeated Antigonus' son **Demetrius the Besieger** in 312 B.C. Exhausted by this baffling, constantly shifting set of wars, the major players drew up a treaty in 311 B.C.:

> Cassander, Lysimachus, and Ptolemy made peace with Antigonus and signed a treaty according to which Cassander would keep Europe until Alexander [IV], son of Roxane, should come of age; Lysimachus would keep Thrace; and Ptolemy would keep Egypt and the cities bordering Egypt in Africa and Arabia; Antigonus would take Asia [Minor]; and the Greek cities would live according to their own laws.
>
> This contract did not last long, as each tried to augment his own territories, putting forth plausible excuses. Cassander saw that Roxane's son Alexander was growing up,° and he knew that some were beginning to say that Alexander [IV] should be released from custody and given his father's kingdom. Fearing for his own safety, Cassander instructed Glaucias, who was in charge of the boy's safekeeping, to assassinate Roxane and then Alexander [IV] and conceal their bodies and not to tell anyone. Glaucias did what he was told, and this released Cassander, Lysimachus, Ptolemy, and even Antigonus from worries about what was going to happen in the situation with the king [i.e., Alexander IV]. Now that there was no one to take over the empire, each who controlled peoples or cities could entertain the notion that they could themselves be kings, controlling their territory as if it were a kingdom taken in war.

Diodorus of Sicily 19.105

°*growing up*: In 311, when the treaty was signed, Alexander IV was eleven years old.

Thus ended the glorious line of Philip II and Alexander the Great, undone in secret murders and buried in unmarked graves. Cassander had slaughtered a woman and a boy, but by this point no one cared.

None of the combatants took the treaty of 311 B.C. very seriously. Antigonus apparently decided that the best way to further his plan of uniting the empire under his own control was to move into the Aegean, still disputed between Cassander and Polyperchon, and get control of Macedon itself. To deter Antigonus, Cassander arranged with Ptolemy for an Egyptian fleet to sail to Athens. In 307 B.C., the Athenians woke up to see 250 ships sailing into the Piraeus harbor. Assuming they were Egyptian and that they belonged to Cassander's ally Ptolemy, they welcomed them; in fact, they belonged to Demetrius the Besieger, Antigonus' son. Demetrius thereby captured the city. He and his father Antigonus were poised to take over the whole Aegean. In the next year, they defeated Ptolemy's fleet near Cyprus:

After this victory the multitude for the first time greeted Antigonus and Demetrius as kings. His friends straightaway crowned him king, and Antigonus sent a crown and a letter to his son Demetrius in which he addressed him as "king." Ptolemy's followers in Egypt, when they heard of this, also addressed him as "king," in this way appearing not to have lost heart because of their naval defeat. This activity led to a spirit of emulation among the successors to Alexander whereby Lysimachus began to wear a crown and Seleucus behaved as a king in his dealings with the Greeks, as in fact he had done earlier with the barbarians. Cassander, however, although those around him addressed him as "king" in both letters and speech, continued to sign his correspondence with his simple untitled name.

This change of title did not amount merely to the addition of a name or a change of clothes. The new titles stirred the men's spirits, exalted their points of view, and injected into their daily lives and their dealings with others a pomposity and gravity. In the same way, a tragic actor suits to his costume his manner of walking, his voice, and his habits of speech. Hence, they became harsher in their judicial dealings. They set aside the dissemblance of power that before had made them gentler and kinder to their subjects.

Plutarch, *Life of Demetrius* 18

In sum, Alexander's successors were now independent kings, not loyal servants protecting the empire for Alexander's heir. Only Antigonus still thought it possible to reunite the empire by force of arms.

In 305 B.C., Antigonus' son Demetrius besieged the island of RHODES off the southwestern tip of Asia Minor, a fortified city that had become the key for dominating the Aegean. Demetrius earned his nickname "the Besieger" here, personally designing armored siege-towers a hundred feet tall that rolled forward on wheels sixteen feet across. Each tower held 3,400 men who could fire in all directions. Demetrius himself wore a suit of iron armor weighing forty pounds. According to Plutarch (in his biography of Demetrius), "to demonstrate the armor's strength and power to resist, Zoilus, the armor maker, shot a bolt from a catapult from a range of twenty paces. The armor remained unbroken at the point of impact and there was nothing on its surface except a small scratch such as an engraver might have made."

However, despite Demetrius' efforts, defensive technology had advanced even faster than offensive, and after a brutal year-long struggle, Rhodes' walls still stood. The siege drained both sides, and in 304 B.C, Rhodes agreed to be Demetrius' ally.

The Rhodians celebrated their survival by erecting the tallest statue ever made in antiquity, the 107-foot-high bronze Colossus of Rhodes, one of the Seven Wonders of the World. For fifty years it stood at the entrance to their main harbor; after an earthquake toppled it, the huge statue, too big to move, lay on the ground for another eight centuries until in A.D. 654 the Arab ruler of the island sold the remaining fragments for scrap.

Antigonus and his ferocious son pressed ahead from Rhodes to subdue the Aegean and capture Macedon. In 302 B.C., Antigonus formed a new league of Greek *poleis* explicitly modeled on Philip II's alliance of 338 B.C., signaling his intention to unite the Greeks against Cassander in Macedon. Matters had come to a head. Cassander, Lysimachus, and Seleucus banded together to stop Antigonus, and, in 301 B.C., the two sides clashed near **Ipsus** in central Anatolia (Map 21.1). It was one of the greatest battles fought in the ancient world. Each side fielded 75,000 troops, and Seleucus brought 400 Indian war elephants. Antigonus put his son Demetrius in charge of the cavalry. Demetrius led a great charge and broke through the enemy lines, then pursued too far, leaving Antigonus exposed to Seleucus' elephants. They trampled Antigonus' personal guard and the eighty-year-old Antigonus died at last, almost alone, in a hail of javelins. With him died Alexander's dream of a single empire from the Adriatic to India.

## THE HELLENISTIC WORLD AFTER IPSUS

The battle of Ipsus ended twenty years of nonstop, brutal, complicated wars. Ptolemy, Lysimachus, and Seleucus carved up Antigonus' empire "like the carcass of some great slaughtered beast," as Plutarch put it, and although another generation would live and die before the Aegean settled down, the Hellenistic world was taking on its basic configuration (Map 21.2). There were four great kingdoms: *Ptolemy* ruled in Egypt; *Seleucus* in Anatolia, Syria, and Mesopotamia; *Lysimachus* in Thrace and parts of Asia Minor; and *Cassander* in Macedonia. *Demetrius the Besieger* had become a king in 306 B.C., but the battle of Ipsus left him a king without a kingdom. He had vast wealth, with which he hired his own army and fleet, but no territory. He lived like a pirate on the high seas until in 276 B.C. yet more treachery and murder ended Cassander's line and enabled Demetrius the Besieger's son to move in to take the Macedonian throne. In 281 B.C., Seleucus killed Lysimachus in battle, extinguishing his kingdom in Thrace. By 275 B.C., the political history of the Hellenistic world had become the story of three families—the *Ptolemies* in Egypt, the *Seleucids* in Asia, and the *Antigonids* (Demetrius the Besieger and his descendants) in Macedonia (Table 21.2). Let us look at each in turn.

## THE SELEUCID EMPIRE

Seleucus in Asia ended up with the biggest territory by far, with a population of twenty-five to thirty million and immense geographical variety. It was, however, too large to govern easily. In 303 B.C., Seleucus traded eastern territory with Chandragupta, Porus' successor in the Indus Valley, for the elephants who won him the battle of Ipsus, but otherwise he tried to hold onto the old Persian Empire (except Egypt).

The Persians had ruled this huge region in Asia by interfering as little as possible in its internal workings. They picked their satraps carefully, then left them to administer their

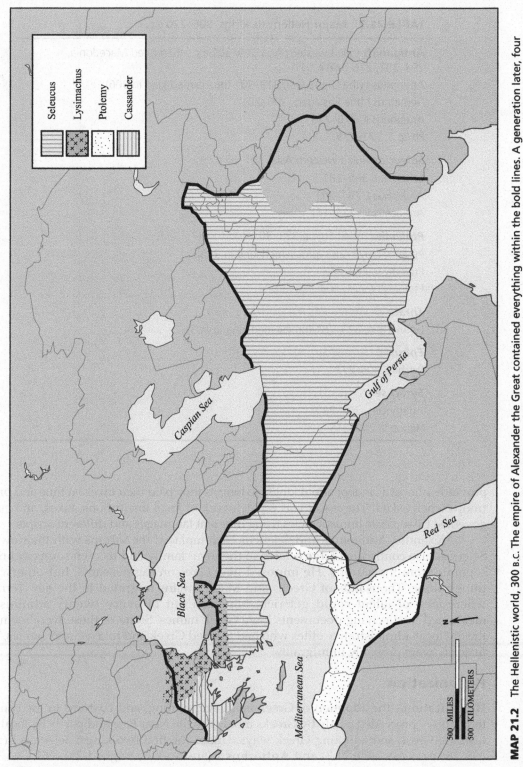

**MAP 21.2** The Hellenistic world, 300 B.C. The empire of Alexander the Great contained everything within the bold lines. A generation later, four of his generals ruled parts of it: Ptolemy, Seleucus, Lysimachus, and Cassander.

**TABLE 21.2** Major Hellenistic kings, 306–220 B.C.

*Antigonids* (ruled western Asia 319–301 B.C.; then ruled Macedonia, 294–287, 276–168 B.C.)

Antigonus I (the One-Eyed), 319–301 (proclaimed king in 306)

Demetrius I (the Besieger), 306–287

Antigonus II, 276–239

Philip V, 221–179

*Seleucids* (ruled western Asia, 301–63 B.C.)

Seleucus I, 305–281

Antiochus I, 281–261

Antiochus III, 223–187

*Ptolemies* (ruled Egypt, 323–30 B.C.)

Ptolemy I, 323–283 (proclaimed king in 305)

Ptolemy II, 283–246

Ptolemy IV, 221–204

*Thrace*

Lysimachus, 323–281 (proclaimed king in 305)

*Epirus*

Pyrrhus, 306–272

*Syracuse*

Agathocles, 304–289

Hieron II, 269–215

provinces almost as independent kings, so long as they paid their taxes on time and provided troops when asked. The result was a patchwork of local institutions, taxes, and customs, governed by separate bureaucracies using different languages and different scripts.

Alexander, Antigonus, and Seleucus each replaced the satraps with their own men. Seleucus also confiscated large estates so the royal family had its own sources of revenue separate from the satraps. He imposed new taxes on the peasants, but otherwise left things alone. Thousands of Greeks and Macedonians migrated to the new territories, where men of talent could get rich. Nineteen out of every twenty administrators mentioned in surviving documents have Greek names. Some of these were members of the old local administrative elites who had learned Greek and taken Greek names, but the majority were probably immigrants.

## Hellenization

**Hellenization**—the adoption of Greek language, writing, and customs in the conquered territories—proceeded partly by Greeks moving to the Near East and partly by local people learning Greek and adopting Greek ways. Under the first two kings, Seleucus I (reigned 305–281 B.C.; see Table 21.2) and **Antiochus I** (an-tī-o-kus; reigned 281–261 B.C.), tens of thousands of young Greek and Macedonian men came east as mercenary soldiers. Some died young or made their fortunes and went home, but most received land and citizenship in a new city in Syria, Mesopotamia, or even farther east. The Seleucids needed such settlements to control the sparsely settled countryside. Gymnasia and agoras were erected in the most unlikely places. A *polis* flourished on what is now the island of BAHRAIN in the Persian Gulf (Map 21.3), and a rich Greek kingdom grew up in BACTRIA, in present-day Afghanistan. A city at AÏ KHANOUM in present-day Uzbekistan (north of Afghanistan) not only had the standard gymnasium and theater, but also a column base in its agora inscribed with maxims copied from the sanctuary at Delphi 2,500 miles to the west! In Bactria cultural influences flowed in both directions. Around 258 B.C., the famous Indian king Asoka, a Buddhist, set up in the Indus River Valley (present-day Pakistan) an inscription in Greek and Aramaic, a language and script widely used for administration already in the Seleucid Empire, while around 100 B.C. a man with the thoroughly Greek name Heliodorus set up an inscription in Afghanistan to the Hindu god Vishnu.

Seleucus and Antiochus founded much larger cities at the core of the new kingdom. Imitating Alexander, they named the greatest cities after themselves: SELEUCEIA on the Tigris River near present-day Baghdad, and ANTIOCH near the Mediterranean in Syria (there were numerous of these Seleuceias and these Antiochs). Each of these cities swelled to over a 100,000 people, quickly surpassing Athens and Syracuse. From Antioch and Seleuceia-on-the-Tigris, the Seleucids administered rich lands, drawing in money as tax and rent and spending it on palaces, servants, and urban amenities. A dozen other cities with tens of thousands of residents sprang up around them, so by the late third century  B.C. new urban cores had developed in coastal Syria, western Anatolia, and Mesopotamia. Greeks and Macedonians settled predominantly in such cities rather than in the countryside.

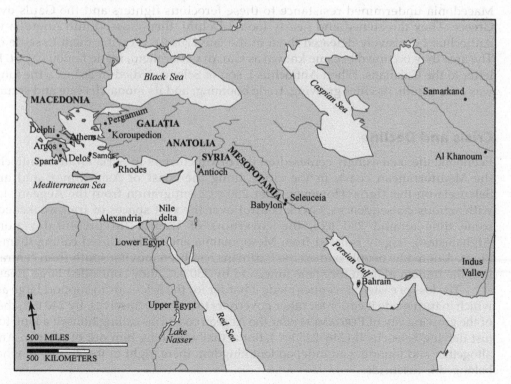

**MAP 21.3**   Third-century-B.C. sites mentioned in this chapter.

Educated Greeks could now travel from Syracuse to SAMARKAND in central Asia speaking the same language, discussing the same philosophers, looking at similar statues, and drinking the same wine all the way. They could even leave Greek lands altogether and still find people in India and Carthage able to discuss Plato in Greek. However, if they headed just ten miles into the countryside outside Seleuceia-on-the-Tigris or Antioch on the Mediterranean, they would find a world barely touched by the Greeks. Assyrian, Babylonian, Median, and Persian rulers had come and gone, speaking different languages and living in wholly different ways from their subjects; to most people in western Asia the Greeks were just the newest conquerors, doomed one day to go away. As in fact they did.

## The Seleucid Zenith: Seleucus I and Antiochus I

The growth of Seleucus' cities filled his coffers with gold and filled him with confidence—in fact, with too much confidence. Like Antigonus before him, he believed he could use western Asia as a base for reuniting Alexander's empire. In 281 B.C. he had killed Lysimachus, destroyed his army, and taken over his kingdom; but just when absolute power seemed within reach, Seleucus' allies betrayed and murdered him. His son and successor Antiochus I (reigned 281–261 B.C.) quickly dropped all claims to Macedonia; Anatolia, Mesopotamia, and Persia were enough.

For centuries, Macedonia had served as buffer between Greece and dangerous population movements in central Europe. Philip II and his predecessors worried as much about Illyrian invasions from the Balkans as about Athens or Sparta, and in the 270s B.C. new invaders from the northwest, the Gauls, burst upon Macedonia. Political divisions in Macedonia undermined resistance to these ferocious fighters and the Gauls overran Greece. They threatened and nearly looted Delphi, then crossed into Anatolia where Antiochus I decisively defeated them in the late 270s B.C., forcing them to settle down. The area they occupied became known as GALATIA after them, made famous by St. Paul's letter to the Galatians. When Antiochus I, son of Seleucus, died in 261 B.C., the kingdom was at its zenith, its cities growing, trade booming, and its monarchs safe and secure.

## Crisis and Decline

Economic life increasingly centered on the urban clusters in Syria around Antioch near the Mediterranean coast, in the cities along the coast of Asia Minor, and around Seleuceia-on-the-Tigris. However, after 250 B.C., emigration from the Aegean slowed, with serious consequences. Greek control over the vast spaces of Iran weakened, and some time around 250 B.C., the governors of Bactria (in present-day northern Afghanistan), largely isolated from Mesopotamia and Syria, started calling themselves kings. A nomadic people named the Parthians had been moving south from central Asia into the Iranian plateau for some time, and by 230 B.C., they controlled large areas of it.

The loss of eastern revenues made it harder for the Seleucids to support large armies, which in turn made it easier for other governors to assert themselves. By 240 B.C., the ruler of the growing city of PERGAMUM near the Aegean coast was calling himself a king too, not just defying Seleucus II (246–225 B.C.), but actually pushing him out of western Anatolia altogether and founding an independent kingdom there, right in the middle of what had belonged to Seleucids.

## PTOLEMAIC EGYPT

The country that Ptolemy seized in 323 B.C. was very different from Seleucus' sprawling realm. Ptolemy's Egypt stretched from the flat and marshy Nile Delta for a thousand miles up the river valley but was nowhere more than ten to fifteen miles wide, with forbidding deserts on either side (Figure 21.1).

There were always important cultural differences between Upper Egypt (south, whence the Nile flows), where indigenous traditions died hard, and Lower Egypt (north, the Nile Delta), but the river imposed an enviable unity. The Ptolemies' seven to ten million subjects were squeezed into the most densely populated land on earth, where they could be controlled and taxed and where a unique geography enabled two or even three harvests a year.

On his arrival in 323 B.C. Ptolemy I presented himself as the new pharaoh, claiming the ancient prerogatives of Egyptian kingship (though he did not dare use the title "king" among the Greeks until 305 B.C.). Like Seleucus, he kept the old local administrative structures largely intact, especially the complex systems of taxation developed by the great temples scattered up and down the Nile. Greek immigrants took many of the top positions in these temples and generated royal documents in Greek. Native-born Egyptian scribes, however, continued recording village activities in the Egyptian demotic ("people's") script. Such scribes often took Greek names. We know more about local administration in Ptolemaic Egypt than in any other ancient land because the dry Egyptian climate has preserved millions of fragments of papyrus from ancient archives (Figure 21.2).

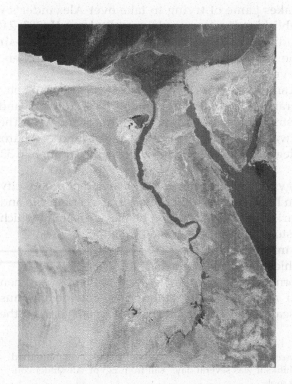

**FIGURE 21.1** Satellite photo of Egypt. Surrounded by deserts, the Nile makes its valley an oasis of agriculture and abundant life. The valley snakes in a line from modern Lake Nasser behind the Aswan high dam in southern Egypt to the Mediterranean Sea, where it widens into a fertile delta.

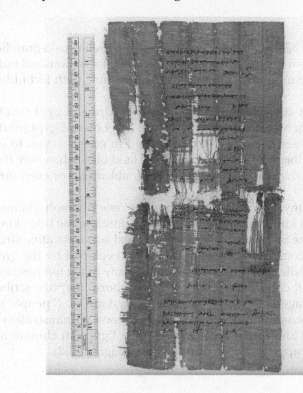

**FIGURE 21.2** Papyrus business letter in the demotic script, ca. 100 B.C. Tens of thousands of documents in Egyptian and Greek have been recovered from the sands of Egypt, many of them used to wrap mummified crocodiles.

Ptolemy rejected the high-stakes game of trying to take over Alexander's whole empire and worked instead on establishing local power. His son **Ptolemy II** (283–246 B.C.) adopted an ancient Egyptian tradition and married his sister Arsinoë (ar-**sin**-ō-ē; Figure 21.3), earning the nickname "sister-lover." Under the Ptolemies, brother–sister marriage became commoner than ever before.

As in Asia, Greek immigrants came to the cities, above all to Alexandria, built on a strip of land that separates the Mediterranean from the large inland Lake Mareotis and on a T-shaped peninsula attached to the strip that forms harbors on both east and west. The stem of the "T" was originally a breakwater leading out to the small island of Pharos, the crosspiece of the "T." According to legend, Alexander himself picked its location in 333 B.C.:

> After Alexander conquered Egypt he wished to build a great and populous city there, named after himself. On his architects' advice he chose a certain site and was about to measure and mark it out, but that night he had a dream in which a venerable gray-haired man stood by him and quoted from the *Odyssey*:
>
> > There is an island in the much-dashing sea
> > that stands off Egypt, which men call Pharos.°
>
> Alexander got up the next morning and straightaway went to Pharos . . . When he saw its superior natural advantages—for there was a wide isthmus here that stretched from the sea to a broad lagoon [Lake Mareotis] and on the

° . . . *Pharos:* Plutarch is quoting *Odyssey* 4.354–55. Pharos was a small island several hundred yards off the coast, though Homer thinks it was several days' sail from Egypt. Alexander connected Pharos to the mainland with a mole.

**FIGURE 21.3**  Ptolemy II and Arsinoë. Ptolemy is shown as pharaoh, with the traditional Egyptian double crown and scepter. In his upraised left hand, he holds a symbol of a thunderbolt, like Zeus. Arsinoë also combines Greek and Egyptian conventions of artistic representation. Their names are written above them in hieroglyphs. Painted limestone, ca. 250 B.C.

isthmus a wonderful harbor—he declared that Homer, in addition to his other qualities, was also a brilliant architect. He ordered that the city be laid out so as to conform to its geography. They had no chalk to mark out the ground line, so they used barley dribbled onto the black soil to make a semicircle, which they divided into segments by drawing lines from the inner arc to the outer circumference . . . While the king was enjoying the harmony of the design, suddenly from the river and the lagoon appeared large flocks of birds that descended and devoured every grain of the barley. The omen greatly disturbed Alexander, but when his seers encouraged him by saying it meant that the city would have much produce and would be a nurse to the diverse races of men, he ordered the men in charge to proceed with the work.

Plutarch, *Life of Alexander* 26

Alexandria soon became the greatest city in the ancient world. Before 200 B.C., its population approached 300,000. One Greek visitor wrote that

There are three sorts of men there: First, the native Egyptians, who are testy and always up to something; the mercenaries, who are crude, numerous, and overbearing (for the Egyptians were long accustomed to keep foreign troops there: Because of the weakness of the kings, they were more used to giving orders than being ordered around); third, was the Alexandrians themselves, not especially civilized (for the same reasons), but still superior to the mercenaries; for though they were of mixed race, nonetheless, they were ultimately of Greek stock and had not forgotten Greek ways of doing things.

Polybius 34.14

Greek Alexandrians looked down on the native Egyptians. Theocritus, a Sicilian poet who moved to Alexandria in the 270s B.C., described a Greek woman pushing her way through the crowded city, complaining thus:

> Whoa, what a crowd! how and when are we supposed to get through this terrible place? Ants, without number and uncounted! Many are the things, and great, that you've accomplished, O Ptolemy [II], since your father joined the immortals.° No one is up to mischief creeping toward you in the Egyptian style as we go by, rattling with deceit, playing games, all of them just the same, with their nasty tricks, every one of them cursed.

Theocritus, *Idyll 15*, 44–50

°*immortals:* Since his father Ptolemy I died in 283 B.C.

Alexandria was a place of urban unrest and ethnic tensions. The largest number of Jews outside Judea lived here, and, in many ways, Alexandria was the center of Jewish culture. In Alexandria, the Hebrew scriptures were translated from Hebrew into the Greek version called the *Septuagint*, "the product of seventy," because seventy scholars were said to have worked on it. These scriptures were a collection of manuscripts from different times and of different genres that Hebrew scholars had roughly organized and edited in the sixth century B.C. while exiled in Babylon. The *Septuagint*, probably prepared under Ptolemy II, was more widely used than the Hebrew versions in the Jewish diaspora and in Judea itself; its texts are considerably older than the oldest surviving Hebrew texts.

Alexandria's vistas were spectacular. Only in the late 1990s did underwater archaeologists begin exploring ruins of parts of the city, now submerged by the rising sea. Sailors entering its harbor first saw the famous lighthouse, built of white stone, then behind it tiers of multicolored palaces (Figure 21.4). The lighthouse, remains of which have recently

**FIGURE 21.4** The modern monumental lighthouse at Al-Montazah (probably never used as a real lighthouse) stands near the foundations of the great lighthouse of Ptolemy II, one of the Seven Wonders of the ancient world. Portions of the statuary and other fragments from the original lighthouse were recently found in the harbor. Pharos is no longer an island, but attached to the mainland.

been found, was the third-tallest building ever built in the ancient world, after two pyramids at Giza, and was more or less intact until the fourteenth century A.D. It marked the otherwise featureless coastline with reflected sunlight in the day and at night the reflected light of a fire, visible thirty-five miles out to sea.

Some of Alexandria's boulevards were a hundred feet wide. Here, all the Old World's goods were for sale, silk from China, spices from Arabia, wines and olive oil from Greece, and the wheat and barley of Egypt. You could listen to philosophers on street corners and visit Ptolemy II's great Museum (Greek *Mouseion*, "home of the Muses"), a combination of library, university, and center for artists. The Museum attracted intellectuals from all over the world, including native Egyptians, Jews, and Carthaginians as well as Greeks. The Museum established Greek as the international language of learning and its librarians set out to obtain a copy of every book ever written in Greek and huge collections in other languages too. Like an ancient version of Google, the library's million volumes provided the world's first comprehensive store of written knowledge. Virtually, all ancient Greek texts that have survived to modern times passed through the library at Alexandria, including those quoted in this book. There they were studied, inventoried, copied, and corrected. All surviving ancient Greek tragedies appear to descend from a complete set compiled in Athens, which Ptolemy II borrowed from the Athenians and then kept! The Museum gave Alexandria a cultural dominance beyond that of fifth-century B.C. Athens itself, and its influence is still felt strongly today.

The Ptolemies also engaged in massive land-reclamation projects, thereby increasing state revenues and providing land where they could settle ex-mercenaries without dispossessing too many of the natives. Records from one large estate of the 250s B.C. show that its manager experimented with figs, walnuts, peaches, plums, and apricots for sale in Alexandria. His letters reveal a modern-looking enterprise, maximizing profits in competitive markets.

Although the Ptolemies never tried to rebuild Alexander's empire, they did commonly intervene overseas to preserve a favorable balance of power, for example in Cyprus and Athens. Their five "Syrian Wars" against the Seleucids were ruinously expensive, though, and Ptolemy III also had to fight native revolts in Upper Egypt. When Ptolemy IV, aged about twenty-three, came to the throne in 221 B.C., his kingdom looked strong, but the decline in Greek immigration had ended its expansion. Revenues began to fall, a callow youth sat on the throne, and, despite Alexandria's splendor, state power was weakening.

## THE ANTIGONIDS: MACEDONIA

For the Seleucids and Ptolemies, the first half of the third century B.C. was a golden age, but not for Macedon. The people who created Alexander's empire got the least from it. Macedon was always poorer than her eastern rivals.

The main cause of Macedonia's troubles was Demetrius the Besieger, son of Antigonus the One-Eyed, who after the battle of Ipsus in 301 B.C. lost his kingdom but survived as a pirate king. Demetrius was able to exploit civil wars to recapture Athens in 297 B.C., and in 294 he added the throne of Macedon. Looking at Demetrius' checkered career, it is easy to see why Hellenistic writers personified **Tychê** (tī-kē), "Luck," as the greatest goddess of their age (Figure 21.5).

**FIGURE 21.5** The goddess Tychê, "luck," here probably representing the city of Antioch on the Syrian coast. Tychê sits atop a male swimmer, probably personifying the Orontes River, which flowed past Antioch. Tychê wears a crown of city walls, because she protects the city, and holds a sheaf of grain, because she brings abundance. Roman copy of a Greek marble statue by Eutychides.

Demetrius' victories so alarmed Seleucus and the other kings that, in 287 B.C., they joined together and drove him out of Macedonia. Demetrius' wife despaired and committed suicide, but Demetrius himself, never giving up hope, raised a new army and attacked Seleucus. After dramatic adventures, his army disintegrated, and in 285 B.C. Demetrius finally surrendered to Seleucus. After two years of luxurious house arrest, he died of alcohol poisoning in 283 B.C. Seleucus met his own violent end when in 281 B.C. an estranged son of Ptolemy I cut him down and seized the Macedonian throne for himself, only to fall in his turn to the marauding Gauls in 279 B.C. Demetrius the Besieger's son, Antigonus II (276–239 B.C., grandson of Antigonus I the One-Eyed), defeated the Gauls in 276 B.C., and when the Gauls retreated to Anatolia and settled in Galatia, Antigonus II took the Macedonian throne.

The Antigonids once again controlled Macedon, but it remained the weakest kingdom. Its most ambitious young men had emigrated to the east, and by the third century B.C. Macedon's tax base was just one-fifth the size it had been under Alexander the Great's father Philip II. In 221 B.C., the Antigonid *Philip V* (221–179 B.C.) took the Macedonian throne. At seventeen he was even younger than *Antiochus III* (now the Seleucid king, twenty years of age) and *Ptolemy IV* (the Egyptian king, twenty-three years old). These three kings—young, inexperienced, and new to their thrones—would soon be called upon to defend Hellenistic civilization against the Roman whirlwind.

## CONCLUSION

Alexander, who destroyed the ancient Persian Empire and made of it a personal possession, was a conqueror without equal. Nevertheless, this huge territory could not be held together by one man unsupported by a powerful ideology, as Zoroastrianism had supported the Persian kings. Collapse and dissolution were inevitable and, in practical terms, perhaps desirable. The Macedonian generals who fought over the conquered territories pursued their own self-interest with shocking cynicism and brutality. Yet as their wars slowed down in the early third century, it became clear that a whole new world was taking shape in which the little city-states that had dominated Greek life for so long were no longer the centers of power and influence.

## Key Terms

Ptolemy I, *446*

Antigonus, *446*

Lysimachus, *446*

Seleucus, *448*

Cassander, *449*

Demetrius the Besieger, *450*

Ipsus, *452*

Hellenization, *454*

Antiochus I, *454*

Pergamum, *456*

Ptolemy II, *458*

Tychê, *461*

## Further Reading

Aperghis, G. G., *The Seleukid Royal Economy* (Oxford, 2005). Pioneering study of the largest of the Hellenistic kingdoms.

Bugh, Glenn, ed., *The Cambridge Companion to the Hellenistic World* (Cambridge, UK, 2006). Expert essays on all major topics.

Chamoux, F., *Hellenistic Civilization* (Oxford, 2002). Good modern survey.

Carney, Elizabeth, *Olympias: Mother of Alexander the Great* (London, 2006). An examination of powerful Macedonian women.

Hölbl, G., *A History of the Ptolemaic Empire*, tr. T. Saavedra (London, 2000). He writes as an authority on both the demotic texts and the Greek sources.

Manning, Joseph, *Land and Power in Ptolemaic Egypt* (Cambridge, 2003). Shows how economic power shaped the development of the Ptolemaic kingdom.

Rostovtzeff, Mikhail, *The Social and Economic History of the Hellenistic World* (reprint, Oxford, 1993). Classic study by a major scholar.

Scheidel, Walter, Ian Morris, and Richard Saller, eds., *The Cambridge Economic History of the Greco-Roman World* (Cambridge, UK, 2007). Chapters 15–17 cover the Hellenistic period.

Sherwin-White, Susan, and Amélie Kuhrt, *From Samarkand to Sardis: A New Approach to the Seleucid Empire* (London, 1993). The first substantial treatment of Seleucid history to appear for fifty years.

Walbank, F. W., *The Hellenistic World* (Boston, 1993). Enormously informative, comprehensive, and concise.

### ANCIENT TEXTS

Austin, M. M., *The Hellenistic World from Alexander to the Roman Conquest* (Cambridge, UK, 1981). Indispensable selection of ancient sources in translation.

Diodorus of Sicily, *History*, Books 18–20. In *The Library of History IX*, tr. Russel Geer (Cambridge, MA).

## CHAPTER 22

# The Greek *poleis* in the Hellenistic Century, 323–220 B.C.

When Alexander died in 323 B.C., many Greeks thought that the *poleis* would now regain their former glory, but the *poleis* were in fact too small to compete with the new kingdoms. Since 314 B.C., all Hellenistic kings had preached that the *poleis* should be free, but any king who really allowed Greek freedom would immediately find some *poleis* actively helping his rivals. The real money and power now lay in great cities like Alexandria and Antioch. Adjusting to this new reality proved hard for many ancient city-states.

## IMPOVERISHMENT AND DEPOPULATION IN MAINLAND GREECE

Emigration from the Aegean had fueled the growth of the new kingdoms in the east. When emigration slowed after 250 B.C., it was because population in the Aegean had stagnated and by 150 B.C. was declining. The historian Polybius (203–120 B.C.) commented:

> In our times, a childlessness has fall upon the Greeks, so that there is a lack of population; the cities are deserted and agricultural production has declined, although not caused by continuous warfare or disease . . . the cause of the situation was clear enough and the means to correct it is in our power. The evil came upon us suddenly, and we never saw it coming. Through quack ambition, the love of money, and an inclination to idleness men no longer wished to marry, or if they did, to raise the children that were born; or out of many they would raise one or two so that they would have the advantages of wealth to squander.°

° . . . *squander:* Unwanted children were exposed in the wild to die.

It is obvious that where there are two children and one dies in war and the other of disease, that the house is left empty. Just as happens with beehives, in this way, the city loses its resources and its viability.

Polybius 36.17

From 800 through 300 B.C., population growth had drawn traders to the Aegean. Now, with population declining, merchants looked to Alexandria and Antioch, not Athens and Corinth. Rhodes, conveniently located between the Aegean and the east, flourished, and the ancient sacred island of Delos at the center of the Cyclades became an international slave market, capable of processing 10,000 slaves a day. The enormous numbers of slaves imported into Greece further altered the character of the dwindling population. The old centers of economic power shrank and decayed. A third-century B.C. guidebook paints a sad picture of Athens, now reduced to a kind of theme park, a backwater university town:

The city is dry, with no good water supply. The streets are narrow and winding, as they were built long ago. Most houses are jerrybuilt, and few reach a higher standard. At first, a stranger could not easily believe that this was the great city of Athens, though he may later come to believe this. There you will find the most beautiful sights on earth: A beautiful theater and above it the temple to Athena, called the Parthenon, which always makes a great impression, extraordinary and wonderful to see. There is the Olympieion.° Although only half completed, it has a wonderful design; if finished, it would be magnificent. There are three gymnasiums: The Academy, the Lyceum, and Cynosarges. All are planted with trees and decorated with gardens. They have festivals of all kinds where philosophers come from all over to pull the wool over your eyes and provide some entertainment. There is much to do for leisure and constant spectacles of all sorts. The local produce is wonderful to taste, though in short supply. However, the presence of foreigners, long common in Athens and to which they are accustomed, makes them forget about their stomachs and to divert themselves with other pleasant things. Because of the spectacles and the entertainments, the common people do not feel hunger because they are made to forget about food. For those with money, you will find no end of pleasures in this city.

Heraclides of Crete 1.1–2

°*Olympieion*: A huge temple to Zeus that Pisistratus began around 530 B.C. No one could afford to complete the work until the Roman emperor Hadrian intervened, around A.D. 130.

As the *poleis* weakened and could no longer patrol the seas, pirates flourished; and as trade declined, merchants could not afford to hire protection against the pirates. The line between piracy and war blurred as *poleis* preyed on each other, and, for a while in the 290s B.C., *poleis* also had to compete with Demetrius the Besieger when he turned pirate king.

The cities' impoverishment made them more than ever dependent on the goodwill of a few rich men. When so much depended on the whims of kings, men who knew them personally often mattered more than official embassies, and *poleis* depended on cash infusions from the rich. The Greeks called these rich local benefactors **euergetists** (yū-**erg**-e-tists), "doers of good deeds." Many Hellenistic cities have yielded public inscriptions celebrating euergetists' contributions to the community's well-being. One example from Samos records how a certain wealthy Boulagoras intervened with Antiochus I, fixed the gymnasium, sent envoys to Ptolemy I, and funded the food supply. Boulagoras doubtlessly acted out of concern for his fellow citizens, but euergetism, nevertheless, shifted political functions away from the citizens' collective hands into those of private individuals. With more power, the rich accumulated still more wealth, and so the impoverished *poleis* needed them still more.

The new super-rich did not, however, overthrow the democracies. Men like Boulagoras accepted that citizens should rule their *poleis* collectively, and more cities called themselves "democracies" in the third century B.C. than ever before. Nonetheless, the super-rich could deal, like lobbyists, directly with kings and perhaps did not care much what the assemblies said. The cities' inability to compete with the Hellenistic kings in wealth and military power drove these developments and inspired the formation of larger political units. In the fourth century B.C., the Aetolian (ē-tō-lē-an) and Achaean (a-kē-an) peoples formed loose federal leagues, the Aetolian League and the **Achaean League**. These had assemblies and councils, just like *poleis,* to which *poleis* sent representatives, who elected generals and other officers. The leagues were a kind of federal organization (Map 22.1).

In the 280s B.C., the Achaeans realized that by acting together the Achaean League could stand up to Macedonia. They agreed on common weights, measures, coinage, and laws, and in 245 B.C. elected the daring, young, and rich Aratos (a-rā-tus) as their general. He set about expelling Macedonian garrisons from all over Greece. The Aetolians followed suit, even gaining control of Delphi. More leagues now formed in Crete, the islands, Boeotia, Phocis, Thessaly, Ionia, and Thrace as it became clear that to survive *poleis* must either submit to the

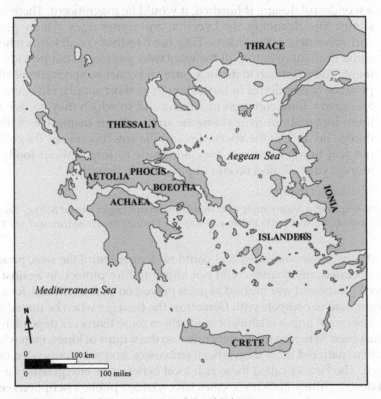

**MAP 22.1**  The federal leagues of the third century B.C.

great kingdoms or form competing multi-city organizations. Athens and Sparta, however, perhaps because both had such glorious histories, resisted absorption into federal leagues. Athenians learned to live with the kings and persuaded the poor to go along with them, but Sparta went through a fundamentalist revolt that sought to revive past glories—with disastrous results.

## ATHENS IN DECLINE

During the Wars of the Successors, Athens went through bewildering constitutional changes—oligarchy from 322 to 318 B.C., then democracy in 318–317, then another oligarchy under Demetrius of Phaleron from 317 to 307. Demetrius the Besieger claimed to reestablish democracy in 307 B.C., though in reality he directly controlled politics. A tyrant seized power between 301 and 295, then Demetrius the Besieger returned. Athens was democratic again in the 270s B.C., but a narrow clique paid for and directed her festivals and defense, bought grain, and talked Ptolemy II into generous gifts. A secret junta of big property owners dependent on Ptolemy's goodwill ran the city, while a Macedonian garrison held Piraeus.

The cost of dependence on Ptolemy was that he pushed Athens, Sparta, and the Achaean League into war against Macedonia in 268 B.C. Athens bore the brunt of the fighting and surrendered to Antigonus II in 262 B.C. after a terrible siege. Antigonus expelled Ptolemy's friends and put in a new dictator—by a cruel irony, the grandson and namesake of Demetrius of Phaleron, who had ruled the city fifty years before! An assembly met regularly but did little beyond pray for the health of Antigonus and his family.

In 229 B.C., a group of Athenian euergetists paid off the Macedonian garrison and freed the city. Two wealthy brothers, Euryclides and Micion, dominated the Assembly for the next thirty years. They understood that Athens was no longer a great power. They avoided depending on any one king and skillfully negotiated a neutral course. They scrapped the fleet and the Long Walls to save money and to avoid provoking attacks. They recognized that Athens could not compete with Macedonia or the Achaean and Aetolian Leagues and that being attached to any one power would ruin the city. The Athenians retreated into obscurity. Faraway Alexandria easily eclipsed little Athens. By 200 B.C. the city of Pericles was living off its past, a tourist attraction where something once had happened.

## SPARTA'S COUNTERREVOLUTION

When the Spartans conquered Messenia in the eighth century B.C., their need to control the helots led them to develop ritualized education, public dining, and the other odd customs we described in Chapter 10, "A Tale of Two Archaic Cities: Sparta and Athens, 800–480 B.C." The loss of Messenia in 371 B.C. after defeat at the hands of Thebes under Epaminondas removed the rationale for such institutions, but since the Spartans unrealistically expected to recover Messenia at any moment, they tried to preserve their ancestral ways. They sat out Athens' and Thebes' final stand against Macedonia at Chaeronea in 338 B.C., only to launch their own uprising in 331, which was quickly suppressed. Sparta's martial traditions survived, but her young men increasingly fought overseas as mercenaries.

Some Spartans welcomed such changes. A wealthy upper class had emerged since the fifth century B.C., concentrating land in its own hands through strategic marriages and pushing many former citizens out of the Spartiate class. By the third century B.C., these rich families occupied a position rather like the euergetists in other *poleis*. However, poorer and more patriotic Spartans kept asking what had gone wrong. In the 370s B.C., Sparta had dominated Greece; now she was merely a local power. The Spartans did not understand the demographic and economic changes that had undermined their system or the shift of power toward larger political units. As they saw it, the cause of decline must be that Sparta had abandoned Lycurgus' ancient and noble teachings. They wanted to restore the ancestral constitution, redistribute land to a large Spartiate class, and reinstate ancient simplicity and virtue. Such demands paralleled the wishes of the poor in other *poleis* but had a unique millenarian quality: If we only return to the original covenant that Lycurgus gave us, they fancied, Sparta will rule Greece again.

The tensions between rich Spartans happy with the way things were and those who sought a Lycurgan renewal broke into the open during the short reign of a king named **Agis III** (ā-jis; 244–241 B.C.):

> Swiftly the wealth of the city flowed into the hands of the few, and poverty gripped the city. There was no more time for refined pursuits or those worthy of a free man, but envy and hatred were directed against the wealthy. No more than 700 Spartiates remained, and of these about one hundred had any land in addition to their ancestral allotments. The great mass were without resources or standing within the city, forced to sit idly by, without zeal or energy to resist foreign wars but always on the lookout for revolution or a revision of the present arrangement.
>
> Understanding what was happening, Agis thought it to be a fine thing, as in fact it was, to restore equality to the citizens and to fill out their numbers. He therefore sounded out the people. The young, contrary to expectation, gave him their ear and stripped themselves for a contest with virtue and in a striving for liberty cast aside their earlier way of doing things like so many old clothes. The older men, by contrast, were tainted by corruption and feared and trembled at the name of Lycurgus, as if they were runaway slaves returned to their master, and they upbraided Agis for speaking ill of the present way of doing things and for wanting to recover Sparta's ancient renown.

Agis began his campaign by persuading his mother and female friends to divide their estates among the Spartiates:

> The women were so changed in their purpose by the young man's ambition, and so possessed by a desire to do the right thing, that they urged Agis on and told him to go faster, and they sent off to their friends among the men and urged them to help and to consult with the other women, knowing that among the Spartans the man is obedient to the woman, who has more say in public affairs than he does in private ones.
>
> At this time most of the wealth of Sparta was in the hands of women, and this made Agis' task difficult and grievous. The women opposed him not only because they would be deprived of the luxury that alone, because of their lack of refinement, made them happy, but because they saw being taken away the honor and power that came to them through their wealth.

Agis thought he was restoring ancestral virtue and bringing Sparta back to Lycurgus' true path. His opponents—including his fellow king Leonidas (whose famous namesake had led the 300 at Thermopylae in 480 B.C.)—saw the matter quite differently:

> Leonidas wished to help the rich, but he feared the people, who were eager for revolution. Therefore he did nothing openly in opposition, but in secret he did what he could to ruin and destroy the project, speaking with the magistrates and accusing Agis of having received a tyranny for which the payment was to hand over to the poor the wealth of the rich. By the distribution of land and the remission of debts he was purchasing bodyguards for himself, but he was not winning new citizens for Sparta.

Agis proposed dividing the land near Sparta into 4,500 equal lots to be distributed among the Spartiates and the land farther from the city into another 15,000 equal lots to be given to *perioikoi*. When Leonidas persuaded the Elders to block the proposal, Agis overthrew him. The Ephors struck back, saying that the cancellation of debts and the redistribution of land were illegal, but Agis declared that the Ephors' opinion mattered only if the two kings disagreed—and because he had deposed Leonidas, that was of course not the case. Backed by an armed gang, Agis threw the Ephors out of their official chairs in the agora and replaced them with his own supporters:

> But just as things were going well and no one was opposing or trying to derail the undertaking, one man, Agesilaos,° overturned and destroyed everything, allowing the most shameful avarice to wreck a noble and very Spartan plan. He was a great landowner but owed enormous sums of money. Not being able to pay his debts, and not being willing to give up his lands, he persuaded Agis that if he put through two major reforms at the same time, there would be great convulsion in the state. But if the men of property were first won over by the remission of debts, then afterwards they would willingly accept the redistribution of land . . . So they brought into the agora all the debtors' documents, made one big pile of them, and set it aflame. Once the flames rose up, all the rich and all those who had loaned money walked away with a heavy heart. But Agesilaos, as in mockery, said he had never seen a brighter light or a more brilliant flame.
>
> When the crowd demanded that the land be divided up at once, the kings agreed, but Agesilaos kept citing pressures from his other business and kept making excuses until so much time passed that Agis was called to military duty. The Achaeans, their allies, had sent to Sparta for aid.

°*Agesilaos:* Not to be confused with the classical King Agesilaos (400–359 B.C.).

When the poorer Spartans saw the redistribution of land being postponed so that Agis could go on campaign, they felt cheated and Agis' political alliance collapsed. Now persecuted, Agis took refuge in the sanctuary of Athena, but one day he left the sanctuary to go swimming. His enemies seized him, threw him into prison, and strangled him there. Hoping to root out such fundamentalism once and for all, they also strangled his mother and grandmother:

When the sad event was reported and the three bodies borne in, their terror was not so great as to prevent the people from showing their pain at what had happened, and their hatred for Leonidas and Amphares,° thinking that nothing more terrible or more unholy had happened since the days that the Dorians first settled in the Peloponnesus° . . . Agis was the first Spartan king to be put to death by the Ephors. Yet he had chosen a course that was noble and worthy of Sparta.

Plutarch, *Life of Agis* 5–21 (excerpts)

°*Amphares:* The man who performed the murders.    °*Peloponnesus:* That is, since the beginning of Spartan history.

So ended Agis' bid to revive Lycurgan Sparta. But assassinations could not crush fundamentalism:

Leonidas now forcibly removed Agis' wife, and her newborn son, from the house and married her to his son Cleomenes, although Cleomenes was too young for marriage; but Leonidas did not want her to marry anyone else. She was heiress to the great estate of her father Gylippus and she surpassed other Greek women in her youthful beauty, and she was of a pleasant disposition. She begged that she not be forced into the match, but once it was concluded she went on hating Leonidas while making a good and affectionate wife to Cleomenes. For his part, once they were married, Cleomenes became devoted to her and in a way sympathetic to her devotion to the memory of Agis. He listened with attention when she spoke about what had happened and about what Agis had hoped to accomplish,

**Cleomenes'** (klē-o-me-nēz) tutor was a Stoic philosopher (see Chapter 23) who had written a pamphlet *On the Spartan Constitution*. Influenced by the pamphlet and by his new wife, Cleomenes decided that Agis' policy was a better response to what had gone wrong in Sparta than his father Leonidas' support of the status quo. When Cleomenes himself ascended the Spartan throne in 235 B.C., he was ready to act. He decided that victories over the Achaean League, now Sparta's bitter enemy, might give him leverage against the conservative Ephors and win the poor in the Achaean cities over to his side.

Cleomenes defeated the Achaeans in battle in 228 B.C., then launched a coup. He assassinated four of the five Ephors and ten of their supporters. On the next morning, while the city was reeling from the news, he exiled eighty of the richest men, including many of Agis' enemies. He removed the Ephors' seats from the agora, leaving just one for himself, thus overthrowing Sparta's ancient traditions in the interests of restoring them! Aided by his wife's and mother's rich female friends, he divided his own family's land and that of the eighty fresh exiles among 4,000 new Spartiates and trained them to fight in the Macedonian style, with eighteen-foot-long spears. He went out of his way to play the part of a traditional Spartan king. He dressed simply and did not affect the pomp or display of eastern kings. In this way, he set an example to all.

Cleomenes' new army, stiffened with mercenaries, swept through the Peloponnesus. The new Spartiates fought enthusiastically, and the poor in other *poleis* welcomed them. It was starting to look like Sparta might, after all, revive her ancient glories. The members of the Achaean League were in turmoil and their cities on the verge of insurrection, with the people hoping for a division of land and the cancellation of debts. In 226 B.C. Cleomenes captured Sparta's ancient enemy Argos, and the entire Peloponnesus seemed to be on the verge of revolution. According to Plutarch, people admired the swiftness and intelligence of Cleomenes. Those who before had mocked him for feebly imitating the Athenian Solon and the Spartan Lycurgus through his abolishing debts and equalizing the wealth now were persuaded that his policies were the cause of the transformation of the Spartiates' conduct . . . Not much time had passed and the Spartans already had resumed their traditional customs and their famous education. Yet, as if Lycurgus himself were among them and conducting policy, they already offered evidence of their bravery and discipline and through their victories in the Peloponnesus were winning back Sparta's leadership of Greece.

Plutarch, *Life of Cleomenes* 1–18 (excerpts)

Yet the reality of great power politics had not changed. Sparta had won many battles but still had nothing like the wealth and manpower of the big kingdoms. When Antigonus III finally sent Macedonian troops to the Peloponnesus in 224 B.C., Sparta's only chance was for Ptolemy III of Egypt to intervene on her side. Ptolemy duly sent money to help Cleomenes, and the showdown between Sparta and Macedon came in summer 222 B.C. at a place called Sellasia (sel-a-**sē**-a), north of Sparta. The Achaean League in alliance with the Macedonians slaughtered the Spartans: All but 200 of Cleomenes' new Spartiates fell to the sword. So much for Cleomenes' reforms. Cleomenes chose not to emulate the valor of Sparta's ancient kings by dying with his men but fled to Alexandria, hoping that Ptolemy III would help him win back Sparta. But Ptolemy soon died and his successor, the ineffective Ptolemy IV, refused to help. Furious, Cleomenes tried to topple Ptolemy himself in 219 B.C. but was wounded and bled to death in chaotic street fighting. Antigonus, in the meanwhile, captured Sparta itself, something not even Thebes had done in 371 B.C. Antigonus reversed Cleomenes' innovations, enrolled Sparta in a pro-Macedonian league, then marched home. Sparta's great gamble had failed.

Sparta's fundamentalism was out of step with the times. Even if Cleomenes had defeated the Achaean League and redistributed property throughout the Peloponnesus, the great powers were only waiting to intervene, as they did in fact. The ancient ideal of the *polis* as a community of roughly equal men had simply ceased to work.

## THE WESTERN GREEKS: AGATHOCLES OF SYRACUSE (361–289/8 B.C.)

Miles of sea protected western Greece from the Hellenistic kings, and in Sicily the familiar old conflicts dragged on as if nothing had changed—Carthage against Syracuse; Syracuse against the other Greeks; tyrants against citizens; rich against poor; natives against Carthage, the Greeks, and each other (Map 22.2). It took a man named **Agathocles** (a-**gath**-ō-klēz), born in 361 B.C. in the western (Carthaginian) part of the island, to rearrange the balance of power. Moving to Syracuse, he gained influence there by championing the poor, exploiting fear of Carthage and the Sicels, and by exploiting hatred of the rich to whip Syracuse's poor into a frenzy. In 316 B.C., they slaughtered 4,000 wealthy citizens, while another 6,000 of the rich fled west to Akragas. The Assembly elected Agathocles commander-in-chief. He canceled debts, redistributed land, and lived in an ostentatiously simple style.

Agathocles' growing power was so alarming that Carthage sent troops to help the Greek exiles. In a great battle in 311 B.C., Carthage shattered Agathocles' army, killing 7,000 men and put Syracuse under siege. In a bold stroke, Agathocles slipped past the Carthaginian naval blockade with just 13,500 men, most of them mercenaries, set out to sea, and made straight for the city of Carthage itself, reasoning that

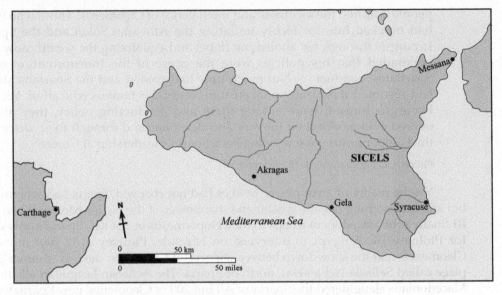

**MAP 22.2** Sites in the western Mediterranean mentioned in this chapter.

if he did this, those living in Carthage for a long time in peace and luxury and unpracticed in the arts of war would easily succumb to those schooled in danger; the Libyan° allies of the Carthaginians, resenting having to pay taxes to Carthage, would revolt and come over to his side; most important of all, by appearing unexpectedly he would be able to plunder the rich land of the Carthaginians, so long unspoiled by war, which because of Carthaginian prosperity abounded with good things; and in general he would be leading the barbarian away from his native city and away from Sicily and transferring the whole war to Libya.

Diodorus of Sicily 20.3.3

°*Libyan:* Greeks used "Libya" to refer to northwest Africa.

No one had ever attacked Carthage. When Agathocles wiped out a Carthaginian army that came against him, the Carthaginians recalled their best troops from Syracuse and raised the land siege of the city, though their fleet still blockaded the Great Harbor. In Carthage, Diodorus says, the desperate Carthaginians revived horrific religious practices to keep away disaster:

The Carthaginians alleged that Cronus° had turned against them because in earlier times they had sacrificed their noblest children to this god, but in recent times had secretly purchased other children, raised them up, and sent them to be sacrificed instead. An investigation revealed that substitutes had in fact been sent to be sacrificed. Realizing this, they fell into a superstitious panic when they saw the enemy camped before their walls, thinking that they had neglected the honors to the gods that their forefathers established. In their zeal to make up for their omission, they selected two hundred of the noblest children in the city and sacrificed them in a

°*Cronus:* In Greek myth, Zeus' father. Diodorus equates Cronus with the Phoenician storm-god Baal, to whom Semitic peoples performed human and infant sacrifice from the earliest times.

public ceremony. Others, who had fallen under suspicion, sacrificed themselves, totaling no less than three hundred. There was a bronze statue of Cronus in the city whose palms were turned upward and his arms slanted downward so that each child placed on the arms slipped downward and into a gaping pit of fire.

Diodorus of Sicily 20.14.4–7

The discovery at Carthage and other Phoenician sites of cemeteries of cremated children, many with inscriptions "offering to Baal," supports this lurid account.

Taking Carthage would have shot Agathocles into the same league of great kings as Ptolemy, Antigonus, and Cassander, but, back in Sicily, Akragas now entered the war on Carthage's side and renewed the siege of Syracuse. Late in 307 B.C., as the war turned against him, Agathocles abandoned his entire army and his two sons in Africa and sneaked through the blockade with only his close advisors. The forsaken mercenaries murdered Agathocles' sons and then signed up with Carthage.

After many adventures, Agathocles made peace with Carthage and in 304 B.C. took the title of king, imitating the Hellenistic monarchs. Once again, he confirmed that neither Syracuse nor Carthage was strong enough to destroy the other. Agathocles lived another fifteen years. If he could only bring the south Italian Greeks under his dominion, he might finish off Carthage, he now thought. He battered many south Italian *poleis* into submission, but his only lasting accomplishment was to weaken the Italian Greeks on the eve of their approaching struggle against Rome. He died in agony in 289 B.C., apparently from cancer of the jaw. Before dying, he abdicated, freeing Syracuse from tyranny and breaking up the kingdom he had worked so hard to create. The west would remain a world of independent *poleis*. In the end, Agathocles had had more in common with Dionysius I than with Demetrius the Besieger.

## PYRRHUS OF EPIRUS

Epirus, in rugged and remote northwest mainland Greece, had been a second-rank power in the fourth century B.C., slower than Macedon to adopt Greek warfare and organization, but in the 280s B.C. a king of Epirus named **Pyrrhus** played a major role on the Greek stage. Pyrrhus was a strange and aggressive man. Like Alexander, he loved war for its own sake, sought out enemy commanders for single combat, and made other people's quarrels his own. By 281 B.C., the rising Italian power of Rome was threatening TARAS (present-day Taranto; Map 22.3), a rich Greek city in southern Italy, and when the Tarentines asked him for help against the Romans, Pyrrhus apparently saw a chance to do in the west what Alexander had done in the east.

After nearly drowning during the crossing to Italy, Pyrrhus entered Italy in May 280 B.C. The Greeks of Taras struck him as lazy and incompetent, but their Roman enemies were neither. He won a difficult battle against the Romans, helped by a corps of twenty elephants that panicked the Roman cavalry (Figure 22.1). The Romans left 7,000 dead on the field to Pyrrhus' 4,000 dead, and many Italian tribes defected to him. Pyrrhus advanced to within forty miles from Rome, assuming that his enemies would now seek peace. He even freed his Roman prisoners as an incentive to Rome to strike a treaty. The stern oligarchs in the Roman Senate, however, whose iron will would one day conquer the Mediterranean, refused to negotiate. They actually sent back the prisoners whom Pyrrhus had released, decreeing that any who refused to return would be put to death. Rome then raised a new army.

When the armies clashed again, the battle lasted two days. Pyrrhus' elephants were again decisive. This time, 6,000 Romans fell to Pyrrhus' 3,500 dead.

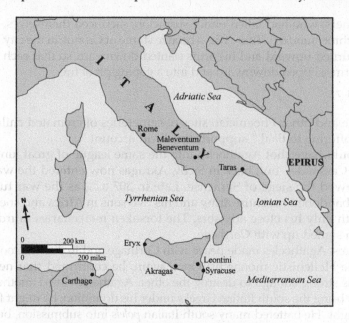

**MAP 22.3** Pyrrhus' campaigns in Italy and Sicily.

**FIGURE 22.1** A third-century-B.C. bowl from central Italy showing a war elephant and calf. The design of the tower on the mother elephant's back makes it likely that it represents one of Pyrrhus' elephants.

The story goes that when someone congratulated him after the victory, Pyrrhus said, "If we are victorious in one more battle with the Romans, we are ruined!" For he had lost a great part of the force with which he came, and all his friends and generals except for a few were dead. There were no replacements that he could summon from home and he saw that the allies were losing their enthusiasm. The Romans, by contrast, as from a spring welling up inside a house, were able to replace their losses easily and quickly from a constant stream of recruits.

Plutarch, *Life of Pyrrhus* 21

Hence our expression "Pyrrhic victory," when the cost of winning amounts to a defeat.

At this crucial moment two messengers reached Pyrrhus. Macedonia was in chaos, he learned, which offered a chance for him to seize its throne; also, the Sicilian *poleis* of Syracuse, Akragas, and Leontini were willing to submit to him if he would save them from Carthage. Making a difficult decision, in 278 B.C. he quit Italy (where things were going badly against Rome) for Sicily, defeated the Carthaginians there, and stormed the seemingly impregnable fortress of Eryx in the far west (Figure 22.2). Imitating Alexander, he was the first to scale its walls and jump down alone inside, standing alone amid a heap of corpses until his horrified troops hacked their way through to him.

In 277 B.C., Carthage offered generous terms, but Pyrrhus rejected them. He started conscripting Greeks for a great fleet to invade Africa, but his arrogance so alienated the Sicilian Greeks that they opened their own secret negotiations with Carthage to get rid of Pyrrhus. As his position deteriorated, in 276 B.C. Pyrrhus conveniently remembered his obligations to Taras, a plausible excuse to sail away so that his departure should not appear to be a flight. In fact he had failed to master Sicily.

To escape his predicament, Pyrrhus fought a tough rearguard action, at one point accepting single combat with a giant Sicilian, even though wounded. Pyrrhus split the man's body from skull to groin with one blow. Making his way to Italy and racing to intercept the Romans, Pyrrhus finally blundered into defeat at Maleventum (Latin for "bad wind") north of Naples. The Romans had learned to send light-armed skirmishers against Pyrrhus' elephants, tormenting them with javelins until they panicked and ran back through Pyrrhus' own troops, causing chaos. The Romans renamed the local town Beneventum, "good wind."

Undismayed by losing Italy as well as Sicily, Pyrrhus sailed back to Epirus in 275 B.C. He immediately invaded Macedonia, proclaimed himself king, then rushed south to the Peloponnesus, allowing Antigonus to recapture Macedonia. Hacking his way into Argos in 272 B.C., Pyrrhus engaged a young man in single combat. The man's mother, hiding on the roof, threw down a roof tile that stunned Pyrrhus, whereupon another Argive ran up and hacked off his head. And so the great man died. About Pyrrhus, Plutarch says:

**FIGURE 22.2**  The summit of Eryx, which Pyrrhus assaulted in 278 B.C. The walls in the photo are medieval.

Men think that in military experience, personal prowess, and daring Pyrrhus was greatest of the kings of his day but that what he won by his deeds he lost through his vain hopes. Through lust for things he did not have he failed to do what was required to secure what he did have. For this reason, Antigonus [II] likened him to a dice-player who makes many excellent throws but does not know how to exploit them.

Plutarch, *Life of Pyrrhus* 26
°*Antigonus:* The Macedonian king Antigonus II.

Pyrrhus had attempted to create a new Hellenistic kingdom in the west. Greek fear of Rome and Carthage gave him an entry, but he was unable to control the unruly *poleis* while fighting off two great powers. Perhaps he could have saved Taras if he had fought only Rome; perhaps he could have united Sicily if he had fought only Carthage. But he could not fight both Rome *and* Carthage. When Pyrrhus left Sicily, he is reported to have sighed, "My friends, what a wrestling ground we are leaving behind for the Romans and Carthaginians."

## HELLENISTIC SOCIETY: THE WEAKENING OF EGALITARIANISM

Since the eighth century B.C., the *poleis* had consisted of groups of roughly equal men. In the fifth and fourth centuries B.C., they could govern themselves as democracies or as oligarchies, but their leaders always belonged to a group in which no man was so superior to others that he need not answer to them, and no man so inferior that his voice could be ignored. Wealth, talent, education, or descent should not create barriers within the male community, nor should claims to special intimacy with the gods. Women were treated almost as a separate race, and, regardless of wealth or influence, could never directly exercise political power. Foreigners and slaves were permanent outsiders; it was almost impossible for either of them to become citizens.

This ideology suffered during and after the Peloponnesian War as the cities' incessant demands for money placed ordinary citizens in the debt of the rich. Then, as the Macedonian conquests brought previously unimagined wealth to the Greek world, the egalitarian ideology began to dissolve. By the third century B.C., the old claim that all men were basically equal within their own *poleis* was very hard to believe, and *poleis* mattered less within the huge new kingdoms. The Hellenistic world, spread from Sicily to central Asia, was vast and varied. As rigid Archaic-Classical notions of male citizenship softened, the power of the free poor declined; the rich pulled away from the rest of society; and the super-rich pronounced themselves the equals of gods.

### Male and Female

In Classical times, Greek women had little political or economic power, but in the Hellenistic period some women, especially queens and members of aristocratic families, began to enjoy wider horizons. We have already seen ferocious warrior-queens like Olympias and Eurydicê, murdering their way to the top and even leading armies, and also the influence of the royal women around Agis and Cleomenes in Sparta. Arsinoë of Egypt, who married her brother Ptolemy II around 275 B.C., actually ruled jointly with him until her death in 268. She appeared on Egypt's coins and built up Egypt's navy. Her authority was recognized across the Greek world. Royal women's power was greatest when weak men occupied the throne; under strong kings they were more likely to act as diplomatic tools, strengthening political alliances through marriage, just as women had probably done in the Bronze Age.

Thousands of wealthy but nonroyal women also enjoyed new opportunities. In Sparta, where (unlike in Athens) women could own land, in the 320s B.C. women controlled two-fifths of this vital resource; a century later, the proportion was higher. Already in the early fourth century B.C., a Spartan woman's chariot team won a crown at Olympia, and in the third century B.C. rich women all over Greece entered teams. As power shifted toward the upper classes, some women accumulated massive resources. Like male euergetists, they paid for public buildings and made loans to their communities, and their cities honored them in return. Women's names are prominent in private loan documents surviving from Egypt, and, in one case, a husband had to get his wife's permission before taking a loan. Increased economic power brought political influence and in third-century B.C. *poleis* some women had a voice in political decisions. In fifth-century B.C. Athens, no woman had had a voice.

## Human and Divine

In Classical times, a vast gulf separated mortals from the gods. If a man did something exceptional, like founding a new city, perhaps after his death—never before—he might be elevated to the status of *hêros*, not so much a god as a glorified ghost. Not even great leaders like Themistocles or Pericles could afford to be seen as more than mortal; it would undermine the proposition that all men are equally well qualified for public life. Philip and Alexander posed the first serious threat to conventional distinctions between mortal and the divine. Both claimed descent from gods. When Alexander ordered all Greeks to worship him as a god in 324 B.C., most went along out of fear but dropped the cult immediately after his death. Similarly, when Egyptians crowned Ptolemy I as pharaoh of Egypt son of the sun-god Ra, he remained just a general to most Greeks. Then in 311 B.C., an Ionian Greek city set up a statue of Antigonus I (the One-Eyed) and offered it the same honors as cult images of the gods. Such cults quickly proliferated, and Plutarch gives a telling example. In 307 B.C., Antigonus' son Demetrius the Besieger sailed into Piraeus and announced that he had come to throw out Cassander's puppet ruler, Demetrius of Phaleron:

> When these things were announced, most people threw their shields at their feet and began to clap, shouting that Demetrius [the Besieger] should sail on in, hailing him as their savior and benefactor . . . The gifts that Demetrius lavished on the Athenians made him great and famous, but he was just as well hated and abhorred because of the lavish honors that the Athenians voted him . . . They were the only people to call Antigonus and Demetrius "savior-gods," and they even voted to get rid of the eponymous archon, after whom each year had been named from time immemorial, in order to appoint a "priest of the saviors," whose name they wrote as a prefix to pubic edicts and private contracts. They voted to include images of Antigonus and Demetrius along with the gods in the weaving of the sacred robe given every four years to the statue of Athena on the Acropolis. They consecrated the spot where Demetrius first descended from his chariot and built an altar of "Demetrius who comes down" on that very spot . . .
>
> But the most monstrous brainchild of Stratocles, the man behind these clever and accomplished flatteries, was that whenever by public order and at public expense envoys were sent to Antigonus or Demetrius, they not be called ambassadors but "sacred deputies," just as when during the great festivals the various cities send men to Delphi or Olympia to perform the traditional offerings . . .

Another man, surpassing even Stratocles, in his love of servility, proposed that whenever Demetrius should come to town they should receive him with the ceremonies reserved for Demeter and Dionysus, and that to the man who surpassed others in the splendor and expense of his arrangements for the festival be given a sum of money from the public treasury so that he could purchase a dedication. Finally they changed the name of the month Mounychion to "Demetrion," and called the odd day that comes after the end of one month and before the beginning of the new "Demetrias," and to the festival called Dionysia they gave the name "Demetria."

. . . But of all the honors accorded Demetrius, none was more strange and monstrous than one suggested by Dromoclides of Sphettos. When the city was about to send off shields to be dedicated at Delphi, he suggested that they seek an oracle from Demetrius himself. I put down the actual words of the proposal he put to a vote:

"May it be for the best. Decreed that the people shall select one man of the Athenians who will go to the savior-god and after the omens have proved propitious he shall ask him what is the most reverent, decorous, and speedy manner of restoring the intended offerings to their proper places. Whatever he shall answer, that the people will do."

With such mockery they quite destroyed Demetrius' mind, which had been none too healthy to begin with.

Plutarch, *Life of Demetrius* 9–13 (excerpts)

To such depths had sunk the once egalitarian culture of mighty Athens!

When Demetrius fell from power in 287 B.C., the Athenians conveniently forgot their adoration. By then, though, there had been a sea change in Greek attitudes, and most kings now claimed divine honors, although some ruler cults were mere propaganda and Greek collaboration was often cynical. In 302 B.C., Athens honored three of Demetrius' lieutenants as *heroes,* the old category of semidivinity used only for the glorified dead. By the late third century B.C., hundreds of living men (and some women) were calling themselves *heroes* in inscriptions.

As new ideas developed about godlike kings and semidivine aristocrats, the old gods received fewer new temples in the third century B.C. Different gods, sometimes new ones, attracted attention instead. **Asclepius**, the healer-god, was one of the most popular. His devotees claimed miraculous cures and commemorated them with inscriptions:

Ambrosia from Athens, blind in one eye. She came as suppliant to the god, and as she walked about the sanctuary she ridiculed some of the cures as being incredible and impossible, that persons who were lame and blind should be restored to health merely by having a dream. But when she went to sleep she saw a vision. She thought the god was standing next to her. He said that he would restore her to health, but she must dedicate a silver pig in the sanctuary as a memorial of her stupidity. Having said this he sliced open her diseased eye and poured in a medicine. At dawn she went away, cured.

Syll.[3] 1168, lines 34–41

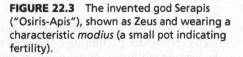

**FIGURE 22.3**   The invented god Serapis ("Osiris-Apis"), shown as Zeus and wearing a characteristic *modius* (a small pot indicating fertility).

The Ptolemies even created a new god called **Serapis**, a combination of the ancient Egyptian god of resurrection Osiris and the bull god of fertility Apis, but represented like Zeus to appeal both to Greek and Egyptian devotees (Figure 22.3). Cults of Egyptian gods, especially Serapis, spread rapidly outside Egypt. Like Asclepius, Serapis came to believers in dreams and provided miraculous cures. Worshipers were initiated into his cult through secret rites that ignored the distinctions of status so important in ordinary life. Serapis spread as far as central Asia before 261 B.C.

Great conquerors showed by their deeds that they walked with the gods; even normal aristocrats could describe themselves as semidivine *heroes*; and thousands of men and women initiated into the cult of Serapis believed that they too had privileged access to a supernatural world. Much had changed.

## CONCLUSION

The changes in the Greek world between 323 and 220 B.C. were as great as those between 750 and 650 B.C. In the earlier period, the complex of institutions, practices, and ideals that we call the *polis* took shape. In the third century B.C., these institutions crumbled. Traditionalists still resisted god-kings and powerful women, but vast inflows of wealth, a shift in power from poor to rich, and accelerating cultural interactions shattered ancient certainties.

Yet in a way, the third century B.C. was the high-water mark of Greek achievement. Alexander had destroyed Greece's ancient enemy Persia, and down to about 250 B.C. emigration from the Aegean drove expansion in the east. There, standards of living remained high while they stagnated or declined in the Aegean and the west. The Hellenistic kingdoms were the greatest military powers on earth with nothing to fear except each other. Their royal families lived in astonishing luxury. That, too, would change.

## Key Terms

euergetists, 465

Achaean
  League, 466

Agis III, 468

Cleomenes, 470

Agathocles, 471

Pyrrhus, 473

Asclepius, 478

Serapis, 479

## Further Reading

Cartledge, Paul, and Tony Spawforth, *Hellenistic and Roman Sparta* (London, 2001). An authoritative overview by leading scholars on ancient Sparta.

Habicht, Christian, *Athens from Alexander to Antony*, tr. D. L. Schneider (Cambridge, MA, 1997). By the leading authority on the political history of Athens in the centuries between the fall of the Athenian Empire, in 404 B.C., and the establishment of the Roman Empire.

Momigliano, Arnaldo, *Alien Wisdom: The Limits of Hellenization* (Cambridge, UK, 1975). Entertaining book arguing that in the Hellenistic period the Greeks, Romans, and Jews enjoyed a special relationship that guaranteed their lasting dominance of Western civilization.

Oliver, Graham, *War, Food, and Politics in Early Hellenistic Athens* (Oxford, 2007). Excellent new study of the economic basis of Athenian history in the third century B.C.

### ANCIENT TEXTS

Diodorus of Sicily, *History*, Books 18–20, tr. Russel Geer, In *The Library of History IX* (Cambridge, MA).

Plutarch, *Lives of Demetrius the Besieger, Pyrrhus, Agis, and Cleomenes*. In *The Age of Alexander*, tr. Ian Scott-Kilvert (Penguin, 1973) and *Plutarch on Sparta*, tr. Richard Talbert (Penguin, 1986).

## CHAPTER 23

# Hellenistic Culture, 323–30 B.C.

As large kingdoms, godlike monarchs, and super-rich euergetists came to characterize the new world of the third century B.C. and the *poleis* turned into backwaters, artists and thinkers responded to the new circumstances. The Hellenistic period saw the highest development of Greek mathematics and science and new forms of philosophy, poetry, and representational art. Greek culture became more complex and in many ways richer than before, reaching from Afghanistan to the Atlantic coast. The legacy of fifth-century B.C. classical thought and art remained strong, but creative Greeks pushed their culture in new directions.

It is easy to pinpoint the beginning of Hellenistic culture, because changes were rapid after Alexander's death in 323 B.C., but difficult to define its end. When the Romans gradually took over the East Mediterranean in the last two centuries B.C. they absorbed Hellenistic culture along with their conquests. We, therefore, take the story in this chapter down to 30 B.C., when Rome overthrew the last Hellenistic ruler, Cleopatra VII of Egypt; and on occasion we look further ahead, even to the second century A.D., when the final fusion of Hellenistic and Roman civilizations took place. We begin with Hellenistic literature then look at material culture, before turning to philosophy and science, where Hellenistic Greeks made their greatest contributions.

## HELLENISTIC HISTORIANS

One ancient Roman scholar commented that the day was not long enough to recite the names of all the historians from the Hellenistic period. Historians proliferated because Greeks felt a need to explain why their world had changed so much. They developed new genres of history to understand the times they lived in; we have already quoted them numerous times. Some scholars wrote local histories, rejecting all the attention given to the great kingdoms, but most celebrated the new Hellenistic world, writing for royal courts or the increasingly powerful aristocrats in Rome. Such scholars did not write for general audiences, like Herodotus, or for critical, rigorous thinkers, like Thucydides, but for the leisured rich. Historians developed type scenes, with emotional descriptions of battles, speeches, plagues, or other moments of emotion, then recycled them regardless of what actually happened, aiming more at moral lessons than at telling the truth about the past. They picked great men from history, selecting (and embellishing or even inventing) episodes from their lives to provide moral examples to the reader. Plutarch, writing around A.D. 100, one of the authors whose writings we have quoted repeatedly, explains this tradition well:

> We do not write history but biographies. For it is often not so much in the most celebrated deeds that one finds a demonstration of excellence or wickedness, but a small matter reveals one's character, even an offhand remark or joke ... Just as painters get their likeness from the face and from the expression around the eyes, in which character makes itself clear, paying much less attention to the other parts of the body, even so you must allow me to devote myself more to the signs of the soul and through these to sketch the character of a life, leaving to others a description of their mighty deeds.

Plutarch, *Life of Alexander* 1

The biographers' emphasis on great individuals fitted the Hellenistic world of kings and euergetists, but the rise of universal history was the most important development. Astonished at how Alexander (and later, Rome) drew together previously separate regions through conquest, universal historians sought to understand the entire Mediterranean world. The most important was **Polybius** (ca. 200–118 B.C.), who spent many years as a hostage in Rome and wrote a universal history in forty rolls to explain to Greeks how Rome had come to dominate the world. He based his history on documents, great men's memoirs, and travel, and scorned the so-called historians who wrote about places they had never seen. To Polybius, writing history was an analytical craft like medicine, and therefore fundamentally different from literature:

> The goals of tragedy and of history are not the same, but the opposite. The tragic poet hopes through his persuasive words to thrill and excite the audience for the moment, but the historian hopes through an account of things that really happened and were really said to educate and persuade the serious student, and the effect of his account will be permanent. The goal of the tragedian is to present what is *probable*, even if untrue, in order to beguile the audience, while the historian wishes to present the *truth*, the purpose being to benefit the serious student.

Polybius 2.56

Few Hellenistic historians reached this level of seriousness. **Diodorus of Sicily**, whom we have also quoted often, was more typical. Writing in the first century B.C. in Egypt and Rome, Diodorus also produced a forty-book universal history, but he uncritically copied from earlier writers, often confusing their accounts. He added his own tragic speeches and a strong moralizing tone, praising kings and leaders who seemed to him to act rightly.

**MAP 23.1** Sites mentioned in this chapter.

In their time, Hellenistic historians were hugely influential. By 200 B.C., indigenous historians (writing in Greek) appeared in Persia, Babylon, Judea, Egypt, Carthage, and Rome (Map 23.1). Yet, just five books of Polybius and fifteen of Diodorus survive from this ocean of historical writing. Despite the historians' success in their own time, their books were lost as people stopped reading them.

## POETRY

The rise of new centers of patronage transformed poetry. Gifted poets flocked to royal libraries and museums, where they earned good pay writing for a small elite of educated aficionados. Alexandria was by far the major center. Following the advice of the Athenian tyrant and Macedonian agent Demetrius of Phaleron, Ptolemy I endowed a *Mouseion*, or "Temple to the Muses," soon after 300 B.C., which we described earlier (Chapter 21, "The Greek Kingdoms in the Hellenistic Century, 323–220 B.C."). There he assembled copies of all Greek literature and spent lavishly to attract top men of letters from all over the Greek world. Some of these produced an official text of Homer, superseding the earlier texts, which had often varied. Translated into modern languages, the texts of Homer read in classrooms today go back directly to the Alexandrian edition.

Ptolemy's scholars were sometimes important poets in their own right. **Apollonius of Rhodes**, who directed the Museum (ca. 270–245 B.C.), wrote an epic called the *Argonautica* about Jason and the Argonauts' search for the Golden Fleece, the only ancient epic to survive from the period between Homer (eighth century B.C.) and Vergil (first century B.C.). While Homer was an oral poet whose verse was recorded by dictation, Apollonius self-consciously created his poem in writing, borrowing Homer's archaic language but combining it with contemporary, almost avant-garde, literary experiments. He liked to interrupt the action to show off arcane knowledge about rituals or geography or address readers directly about the difficulty of writing an epic. Only the well-educated elite would understand his allusions and subtle wordplays.

Other poets favored brief, intensely crafted works, but wrote for the same well-read urban elite. **Callimachus**, the greatest third-century B.C. poet, from Cyrenê in Libya, was to influence the Roman poets enormously, and through them has influenced our own poetry. Reputedly he engaged in scholarly feuds with Apollonius of Rhodes and famously said, "Big book, big evil"—that is, epic was no longer an appropriate vehicle for literary expression (unless he was complaining about the bother of a very long papyrus roll, as some scholars think!). Alexandrian poets invented anagrams to amuse and flatter their patrons. For example, the phrase *apo melitas,* "from honey," rearranged the letters of *Ptolemaios,* as Ptolemy's name was spelled in Greek; and *ion Eras,* "Hera's violet," rearranged *Arsinoë,* Ptolemy II's sister-wife. Riddle-poems were popular, in which the riddle's answer was revealed by the poem's shape when the words were written down (poets produced examples shaped like wings, an ax, an altar, and an egg). Sometimes the first letters of the poem's lines were an acrostic that spelled out a name when read downward.

Such poems appealed to the intellect, but some poems worked to move the heart, with short verses in which every word was carefully chosen. Such poems are always hard to translate well, but here is one example that Callimachus wrote about the death of a fellow poet:

> Someone told me, O Heraclitus, that you had died,
> and the tears welled in me when I thought of all those times
> that you and I, talking, talking, had put the sun to bed.
> And now, my friend from Halicarnassus,° you are
> for a long, long while nothing but ash. But your nightingales°
> live on, which Hades, snatcher of all, can never seize.

Callimachus, *Palatine Anthology* 7.80 9

°Halicarnassus: In southwest Anatolia, Herodotus' hometown.    °*nightingales:* That is, his poems (perhaps the little-known Heraclitus' book of poetry was called *The Nightingales*)

Callimachus was a towering scholar and compiler of information (he wrote a *Catalogue of Persons Conspicuous in Every Branch of Learning and a List of their Compositions* filling 120 rolls!), but he is most famous for his *Hymn to Zeus.* Like Apollonius with his epic, Callimachus revived an archaic poetic form to display learning, pose verbal puzzles, and delight educated readers who could identify his puns and allusions.

Although written in Alexandria, the *Hymn to Zeus* evoked the simpler world of Archaic Greece. Theocritus (whom we quoted earlier), a third-century B.C. emigrant from Syracuse, went further still, inventing bucolic (Greek for "concerning cowherds"), poetry filled with nostalgic images of a simple rustic paradise in Sicily and south Italy that never existed. He called his poems *Idylls* (Greek, "little pictures"). The poems idealized the countryside for urban elites who had rarely seen the real thing. "Back to the earth" movements in recent times share the same inspiration as this tremendously influential literary genre. The *Idylls* were the product of Ptolemy's Museum; but in one of them, Theocritus abruptly abandoned the countryside to write a court poem praising Ptolemy II, the man who subsidized his artistry and made this kind of poetry possible:

> Alone of men of former days, and of those who still
> impress their warm footprints in dust as they go,
> Ptolemy to his mother and father has set up

incense-scented altars and idols of gold and ivory,
now helpers to all mankind. Many are the thighbones
of fat oxen he burns on reddened altars, as the
seasons turn, and she° partners him in filial sacrifice.

Theocritus, *Idyll* 17.121–28

°*she*: Arsinoë, Ptolemy's sister, wife, and queen.

Another new genre was the "novel." Extended prose narrative fiction is not an obvious literary form, especially without the benefit of printing and in a context where all literature was read (or recited) aloud before a small audience. It remains unclear who enjoyed these stories, but the audience must have been less specialized than that of Apollonius or Theocritus. The earliest surviving example is a papyrus fragment of a story about an Assyrian king wooing a fourteen-year-old bride, probably from the first century B.C. Most examples were written by Greeks who lived in the Roman Empire, but they are unmistakably Hellenistic in tone. The themes are romantic and lighthearted. A boy and girl fall in love. Before or soon after marriage, fate separates them. The characters endure disasters, including incarceration, seduction, rape, torture, and apparent death. In the end they are found to be alive, reunited, and they live happily ever after, rather like in many modern feature films.

Audiences all over the Mediterranean attended tragedies by Aeschylus, Sophocles, and especially Euripides, but these were now "classics," self-consciously performed as great works from the past, rather than a living cultural form. Comedy won a new lease on life, but the New Comedy of late-fourth and third-century B.C. Athens had more in common with the later Hellenistic novels than with Aristophanes' Old Comedy. Instead of savage political humor, which had no place in this modern world, New Comedy had romantic, lighthearted plots and domestic settings similar to modern television sitcoms, which descend directly via a circuitous route from the Greek tradition. Only a single Athenian New Comedy survives complete, the *Dyskolos* ("Grumpy Old Man") by **Menander** (ca. 342–291 B.C.). Menander wrote over a hundred plays. He was the most quoted of all ancient authors, except for Homer, and constantly reperformed over generations.

New Comedy used stock characters (braggart soldiers, greedy pimps, love-struck young men, lecherous fathers, tricky or faithful slaves) and humorous confusions over identity (Shakespeare's *Comedy of Errors* of ca. A.D. 1590 is based on these ancient comic devices). A typical plot might involve an aging father and young son competing for the same courtesan, who is owned by a heartless pimp. The courtesan escapes through her cleverness and the attentions of the father. An object of some kind, like a necklace placed on the girl as a child, eventually reveals her to be nobly born and therefore eligible for proper marriage. The play ends with her marrying the young man.

By 200 B.C., drama attracted no leading Greek poets but was enthusiastically adopted in other Mediterranean societies. Plautus (ca. 254–184 B.C.) and Terence (ca. 185–159 B.C.), writing in Latin, brought New Comedy to Roman audiences, and most of our knowledge of the genre comes from their adaptations. A Jewish writer named Ezekiel produced a tragedy about Moses and the Exodus in Euripidean style (probably in the second century B.C.); and in 53 B.C., the king of the central Asian Parthian nomads was watching a performance of Euripides' *Bacchae* when news came to him that his army had defeated the Romans (the lead actor used the head of the Roman general as a prop for the head of the murdered Pentheus in the last scene!). From Iran to Iberia, anyone with pretensions to culture needed to know Greek and the Greek authors.

As the *polis* lost importance, audiences had little interest in the dramatization of the tensions of citizenship. As the finest poets served royal courts and proud aristocrats from Sicily to Bactria studied their learned verse, popular literature—dramas and novels—grew lighter and increasingly divorced from real time and place. Modern readers often criticize Hellenistic histories, New Comedy, and novels for their frivolity and sometimes absurd posturing, but non-Greek peoples imitated them far more widely than they did the literature of the fifth or fourth century B.C. They were among the Greeks' most successful cultural exports, and their influence is strong today.

## MATERIAL CULTURE

Hellenistic artists perfected techniques that had been developing for half a millennium, and their technical skills were not equaled in the west until the Italian Renaissance, 2,000 years later. The sheer size of the Hellenistic world encouraged regional variations, as royal centers, old *poleis,* and new sanctuaries developed in their own way. Traditionalism, overstatement, playfulness, virtuosity, and sometimes downright bad taste all swirled together, fueled by vast wealth that made anything seem possible. The overall effect was to abandon classical restraint as Greek art served a new world.

### Sculpture

As generals transformed themselves into kings, then into gods, they wanted statues to express their new status. Such statues filled royal cities like Alexandria and Antioch; even the *poleis* commissioned statues of beloved or prominent citizens. Figure 23.1 is a superb

**FIGURE 23.1** Portrait statue of Demosthenes. Roman marble copy of a bronze original by Polyeuktos of Athens, ca. 280 B.C. Height 6 feet 7 inches.

statue of the great orator Demosthenes from Athens, commissioned around 280 B.C. when Athenians briefly expelled their Macedonian garrison. Demosthenes is shown as pensive, even gloomy, his brow furrowed, looking puny before the scale of the task facing Athens. His heroism is moral and intellectual, not physical. The statue's base is inscribed thus:

> O Demosthenes, if your strength were equal to your will,
> no Macedonian Ares° would have ever ruled the Greeks.

Plutarch, *Moralia* 847A

°*Ares:* The god of war, referring here to Philip II.

Between 250 and 150 B.C. (sometimes called the High Hellenistic Period) some sculptors sought emotional drama, like the historians and novelists. The finest examples come from Pergamum, a magnificent fortress-city towering 1,000 feet above the Ionian coast. Pergamum's King Attalus I (241–197 B.C.) broke away from the Seleucid empire and commissioned a seventy-foot-long group of bronze statues to commemorate his victory over Gallic raiders in 237 B.C., probably showing his cavalry riding them down. The group is lost, but Figure 23.2 shows a marble copy of one statue, known as the Dying Gallic Trumpeter. The fallen warrior, powerfully understated, props himself up on one arm, staring in pain at his broken sword and trumpet as his life ebbs away.

The original monument must have been astonishing, but King Eumenes II of Pergamum (197–159 B.C.) outdid it with his **Great Altar of Zeus**, whose sculptures are now housed in a museum in Berlin (Figure 23.3). Traditional altars were simple structures outside temples, but in this radical combination of architecture and sculpture the altar

**FIGURE 23.2** The Dying Gallic Trumpeter, a Roman marble copy of one statue from a large group of bronzes set up at Pergamum, ca. 220 B.C. On the warrior's right side is a fatal wound, blood gushing forth; his broken sword and trumpet lie by him. Around his neck is a gold torque, a characteristic ornament of the Gauls who invaded Greece from central Europe in the third century B.C.

**FIGURE 23.3** Great Altar at Pergamum. Marble. Begun by King Eumenes II (197–159 B.C.); his successor Attalus II (159–138 B.C.) probably completed it. Once thought to honor Zeus, the monument was probably to Telephus, a local hero. German archaeologists removed the entire altar to Berlin in the nineteenth century.

replaced the temple. A broad stairway led to an Ionic colonnade, with double doors opening on the actual altar. The friezes on temples were high up, barely visible from the ground, but the innovative architect here put the frieze right before the spectator's eyes.

The frieze narrates the mythical battle of gods and giants. Its unknown designer packed it with detail (art historians call the style "Hellenistic baroque"). Figure 23.4 shows just one panel. On the left, a bearded giant with snakes for legs faces Hecatê, goddess of darkness. The giant hefts a boulder in his right hand while one head of his snake-legs bites her shield. She wields a burning torch like a spear. Hecatê's dog bites one of the giant's legs. A second figure, whose left arm and profile are visible behind Hecatê, imparts a sense of depth. To her right another giant leaves himself uncovered, a target for the goddess Artemis (not shown in the photograph). The torso and snaky legs of a dying giant are visible beneath the giant's legs. The figures are carved almost in the round and their muscular bodies even fall out of the frame onto the steps. The composition as a whole and the individual figures within it exude excitement and the drama of cosmic war. The sculptors packed every imaginable device into the frieze, bombarding the viewer's senses with different finishes, draperies, and moods. Originally painted in bright colors (like all ancient statuary), the impression in ancient times would have been even stronger than it is today.

Sculptors everywhere strove for dramatic effects. Figure 23.5 shows the **Nikê ("Victory") of Samothrace**. Landing from flight, she once stood on a base shaped like a ship's prow, located in a reflecting pool in an open-air sanctuary on the remote northern Aegean is land of Samothrace. The statue combines classical features—the drapery recalls the Parthenon frieze—with the new baroque style, in its twisting pose and rich, almost fussy surface detail.

**FIGURE 23.4**    Battle of the gods and giants, from the Great Altar at Pergamum, second century B.C.

**FIGURE 23.5**    Nikê of Samothrace,
ca. 190 B.C., marble, height 8 feet.

**FIGURE 23.6** Sleeping satyr, ca. 230–200 B.C. Roman marble copy of a Greek original. The statue is known as the Barberini Faun after the family that used to own it. The legs and hanging left arm are restorations.

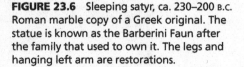

Other sculptors used similar techniques to create very different moods. Figure 23.6 shows a drunken satyr—he has pointy ears, invisible in the picture—caught as he sleeps. Super-rich Hellenistic aristocrats now decorated their homes with such whimsical statues; this one may have been an ornament in someone's garden. In search of novelty, sculptors turned to subjects that would have seemed undignified in Classical times: drunks, old people, dwarfs, even hermaphrodites, subject matter that parallels the domestic scenes and melodrama of New Comedy.

Other patrons, by contrast, rejected such whimsy and demanded a return to Classical seriousness. Figure 23.7, the celebrated **Venus de Milo** (Venus = the Roman Aphrodite), is an example of what art historians call "Neoclassicism." This Aphrodite strongly evokes Praxiteles' Aphrodite of Cnidus (see Chapter 18, "Greek Culture in the Fourth Century B.C.," Figure 18.3), with a gentle S-curve, and serene, late Classical face. The sculptor changed the proportions by moving her waist higher, and whereas Praxiteles' Aphrodite clutches her robe, the Hellenistic sculptor leaves it poised precariously, adding to the figure's eroticism.

Like so much of Hellenistic culture, Hellenistic sculpture profoundly influenced non-Greek peoples, and the Romans above all. Roman copies of Greek originals made possible the rediscovery of Greek art in the eighteenth century.

## Architecture

Far more expensive than sculpture, architecture was the medium for display *par excellence* of kings. We get the best idea of the splendor of a royal center from Pergamum. Its kings built on a spectacular, high, virtually impregnable peak (it is hard to imagine walking up

**FIGURE 23.7** The Venus de Milo, a marble statue of Aphrodite from the island of Melos, carved around 100 B.C. When this statue was displayed in Paris in 1820, it caused a sensation. Height 6 feet, 8 inches.

there from the fields every day). A huge theater dominated the upper city, and spectators at dramas and public meetings could look out over the fertile plans of Ionia (Figure 23.8). Everything about the city was designed for dramatic effect. Terraces immediately above the theater supported small but cleverly designed temples, the Great Altar of Zeus with its baroque frieze, and the large library, second only to Alexandria's (the word "parchment" is a corruption of the name Pergamum; parchment was invented there as an alternative to papyrus). Royal palaces and barracks for the king's guards occupied the summit. A huge, shady colonnaded porch, or **stoa**, below the theater provided a place to walk among shops, talk, and look out over the plain, giving architectural unity to the design. Stoas were typical elements of Hellenistic cities.

Old *poleis* like Athens lacked money to compete with the royal centers, but some kings paid for new buildings in Athens to advertise their own wealth and euergetism. Attalus II of Pergamum (159–138 B.C.) built a 126-yard-long, two-storied stoa in Athens containing forty-two shops (Figure 23.9).

## Painting

Just as we know most about New Comedy and sculpture from Roman imitations and adaptations, the best evidence for painting also comes from Italy and again attests to the impact of Greek art across cultural lines. In A.D. 79, Mount Vesuvius erupted, burying the

**FIGURE 23.8** The theater at Pergamum and its view across the Ionian plain.

**FIGURE 23.9** Reconstruction of the Stoa of Attalus in the Athenian agora by the American School of Classical Studies in Athens (1953–1956). Attalus II of Pergamum (159–138 B.C.) built it around 150 B.C. as a gift, thanking Athens for the education he received there. The stoa has a Doric colonnade on the ground floor and an Ionic upper colonnade with a balustrade. Shops ran along the back of the aisle; today it is a museum for finds from the American excavations in the agora.

**FIGURE 23.10** Wall painting from a house in Rome, ca. 50 B.C. one of a series of paintings of Odysseus' adventures. This scene shows the giant Laestrygonians hurling rocks at the fleet of Odysseus.

cities of Pompeii and Herculaneum in lava. Since A.D. 1738, archaeologists have recovered numerous Roman versions of Hellenistic paintings and mosaics there. Figure 23.10 shows one in a series of Roman wall paintings of Odysseus' journeys, dating around 50 B.C., representing his misadventures with the savage Laestrygonians. The landscape dwarfs the figures. You can just make out five boats in the harbor. Strong contrasts of light and shade emphasize nature's power over the puny mortals who crawl across the earth's surface. The painting probably copied a Greek original of the second century B.C.

Like dramatists and sculptors, painters now enjoyed domestic and even frivolous subjects. Scenes from New Comedy were popular. Figure 23.11, a mosaic of around 100 B.C. found at Pompeii, was signed by its Greek maker, Dioscurides of Samos. It too probably copied a second-century B.C. painting inspired by a scene in some New Comedy. The mosaicist imitated advanced painting techniques—shading, highlighting, and using multiple colors—for a lighthearted scene of masked actors playing street musicians on a narrow stage. He used the new technique of tessellated mosaic, building the scene from precut cubes of stone rather than pebbles. One man beats a tambourine, a second claps with small cymbals, and a third plays the double flute, while a boy wearing a cloak looks on.

Mosaics became an important art form in Hellenistic Greece. One craftsman, Sosus of Pergamum, was famous for illusionist scenes. A famous mosaic showed birds drinking from a basin of water, while another looked like an unswept floor with dinner scraps strewn across it. Sosus' mosaics do not survive, but Figure 23.12, a mosaic from the Roman emperor Hadrian's country estate (A.D. 120), probably imitates his drinking doves.

**FIGURE 23.11** Mosaic from Pompeii, signed by Dioscurides of Samos, ca. 100 B.C. Dioscurides probably copied the scene from a second-century B.C. painting. It shows street musicians from an unknown New Comedy.

**FIGURE 23.12** Tessellated mosaic from the Roman emperor Hadrian's villa at Tivoli, Italy (ca. A.D. 120). It probably copies a famous mosaic by the second-century B.C. artist Sosus of Pergamum. Length 3 feet, 3 inches.

We rely heavily on vase painting for information about Archaic and Classical wall painting, but in Hellenistic times painted pottery all but disappeared. The rich could now afford gold and silver plates, which rarely survive because later ages recycled precious metal; poorer people used mold-made black-glazed fine wares, which began as imitations of metal vessels. The black-glazed wares are attractive but of course tell us nothing about contemporary painting.

## HELLENISTIC PHILOSOPHY

### Skepticism and Cynicism

Aristotle had argued that man was a "creature of the *polis*" (*politikon zôon*), but now that men lived in a new world of great kingdoms, super-rich euergetists, and godlike rulers, philosophers began asking how to live a good life in such conditions. Some sought inner peace by showing how little the chaos of the world mattered; others sought to create alternative, better worlds by rejecting social conventions.

Athens remained a center for literature and sculpture until the 260s B.C., and it likewise dominated early Hellenistic philosophy. The Academy, Plato's philosophical school, gave birth to **Skepticism**, the conviction that nothing can be known about the world for sure. However, the Skeptics argued, it is nevertheless reasonable to form "plausible impressions" and act as if such impressions were true. In this way the skeptic might function adequately in society, while remaining tranquil within the chaos around him.

Diogenes (404–323 B.C.) of Sinopê, a town on the southern coast of the Black Sea, was an important exponent (and partial founder) of **Cynicism**, a kind of ancient counterculture (our word "cynicism" has a rather different meaning). Diogenes was called *kynikos* ("doglike") because he ignored social conventions and, as it were, lived like a dog. He owned no clothes, lived in a barrel, urinated and defecated where he pleased, and masturbated as the mood took him. He rejected private property and material things. According to a popular story, Alexander the Great made a special trip to Sinopê to meet Diogenes and offer him anything he wanted. The only thing the philosopher wanted from Alexander was that the king should step aside because he was blocking the sun!

Diogenes taught that wealth, status, and honor were empty and that one can pursue virtue, which brings happiness, even without them. Some Cynics made a living by traveling between *poleis*, mocking authority in a kind of oration called a *diatribe* (the origin of the word "diatribe").

### Epicureanism

Epicurus (341–270 B.C.; Figure 23.13) was born of Athenian parents on the island of Samos just off the coast of Ionia. He spent most of his life in Athens, where he studied with Platonists, then in 307 B.C. turned his home into a school known as "the Garden." There his followers—including women and slaves as well as the usual wealthy men—isolated themselves and followed the master's teachings.

We know a good deal about **Epicureanism**. Mount Vesuvius' eruption in A.D. 79 preserved a library of 1,785 papyrus scrolls on Epicurean philosophy in a villa that belonged to a relative of Julius Caesar (himself an Epicurean). Although carbonized, these scrolls can be read in part, and work on them continues to date. Our most important source of information about this philosophy, though, is a long poem in Latin, *On the*

**FIGURE 23.13** Roman copy of a marble portrait of Epicurus, originally carved around 270 B.C. The sculptor showed him with furrowed brows, expressing the strain of serious thought about the problems of the third century B.C.

*Nature of Things*, by a first-century-B.C. Roman named Lucretius. When the American Declaration of Independence declared that "We hold these Truths to be self-evident, that all Men are created equal, that they are endowed, by their CREATOR, with certain unalienable Rights, that among these are Life, Liberty, and the Pursuit of Happiness," it was echoing a principal tenet of Epicurus, who also insisted that happiness was the goal of life (as did the Cynics). And what is happiness if not pleasure? But Epicurus defined pleasure in very specific ways that followed from a larger theory of nature.

Accepting the atomism of Democritus (see Chapter 14, "Art and Thought in the Fifth Century B.C."), Epicurus argued that the universe consists of an infinite number of atoms drifting through space. The atoms have size, shape, and weight, and fall like an endless rain. Left alone, they would never touch, because they fall at the same rate, but (for unclear reasons) they sometimes swerve and strike each other. Because the swerve is unpredictable, Epicurus' universe is not wholly mechanical. His unexplained swerve lies behind what we call "free will" and was the first attempt to face the problem of free will in a mechanistic universe.

Epicurus' universe is infinite and comprises an indefinite number of *kosmoi*, "worlds," which come into being through the random collisions of atoms. Each *kosmos* eventually dissolves back into atoms, which continue falling until some swerve and recombine to form a new *kosmos*.

The mind, like everything else, is made of atoms, but finer ones than the body. We perceive objects when a thin film of atoms strikes the sense organs. Our thoughts are material too, made up of these films within our minds. Even the gods are material, but made up, like thought, of very fine atoms. They inhabit the spaces between the stars, and because they live in eternal, undisturbed happiness, they take no interest in our turbulent world and never interfere with its operation. For Epicurus, true happiness meant being undisturbed, like the gods (a state called *ataraxia*, "undisturbedness").

Because we are wholly material, when we die our atoms disperse and we cease to exist. It is therefore foolish to fear death: Because we cease to exist, nothing unpleasant can happen. Epicurus discussed the issue in a letter to a friend:

> The greatest anxiety that afflicts the human mind is the fear that the celestial bodies are divine and imperishable, yet they have desires, will, and can act to cause things. Furthermore, men cringe in fear as if they were doomed to experience an evil without end, no doubt because of all the fairy stories they have heard. They await in terror the unfeeling nothingness of death, as if that were the fate of all! They do not suffer in this way because they have thought things through, but rather they have fallen into a thoughtless panic. In fact, those who spend most time thinking about these things suffer as much as or more than those who take only a casual and occasional glance at the issue. Real peace of mind comes when you have freed yourself from these boogey-men, when you can keep always in mind constant and eternal truths . . .
>
> You must become accustomed to the thought that death does not concern us at all. Good and bad exist only by being perceived, but death removes all perception. Once we understand this truth, that death does not concern us, then even our mortality becomes a source of pleasure. We give up our attempts to add eternity to our span of life here and can abandon our foolish hope for eternal life. In life there is no terror when there is none in death! This worst of horrors, the fear of death, does not affect us. While we are, death is not; when death is, we are not.

Epicurus, *Letter*, quoted in Diogenes Laertius 10

We may wonder that the certainty of dissolution is supposed to bring comfort, but such was Epicurus' position. He denied religious accounts of the afterlife. Homer's *Odyssey* already related such terrors of the damned as Sisyphus rolling a stone forever up a mountain, Tityus crucified with a vulture devouring his liver, and Tantalus chained in a stream whose cool water he cannot reach. All this was nonsense, Epicurus maintained. The world one sees is all there is, and pleasure, which brings happiness, ultimately comes from the harmonious flow of the atoms that make us up.

There are two kinds of pleasure for Epicurus: The positive, such as enjoying food, sex, or music, and the negative, or absence of pain. The second is preferable to the first, because food, sex, and music provide only transitory pleasure, often followed by pain, while avoidance of pain is an appropriate end in itself.

New Comedy and some art turned away from the troubled world into a private sphere, and Skeptics escaped from Hellenistic upheavals by insisting that we can never know what is real anyway. *Ataraxia*, too, was at odds with the ideals of Archaic and Classical citizenship. Pursuing glory and power only stirs up the atoms and causes pain. Better to seek a quiet, secluded life, in a garden surrounded by flowers.

## Stoicism

Zeno (ca. 333–262 B.C.), from the Phoenician city of Citium on Cyprus (not to be confused with Zeno of Elea, who formulated the famous paradoxes in the fifth century B.C.), founded the most influential philosophical school of the Hellenistic Age. He studied with Cynic philosophers, taking several radical ideas from them, and then finished his training at the Academy in Athens. Late in the fourth century B.C., he opened his own school in the *stoa poikilê*, "painted stoa," on the edge of Athens' agora. American excavators uncovered its foundations in the 1980s beside the modern train tracks joining Athens with Piraeus. From this meeting place, his philosophy was called **Stoicism**.

Zeno's position was simple: To be happy, we must follow natural law. Those who follow natural law can be happy regardless of circumstance. Stoics ignored pleasure and suffering. Many Roman emperors proclaimed themselves Stoics, and one—Marcus Aurelius (reigned A.D. 161–180)—wrote a major Stoic treatise.

The divine *logos* ("reason, intelligence, God") permeates creation. *Logos* is the same as fate, an intelligent force that determines everything, that causes all things to happen as they do, and that gives all things their properties. Stoics therefore rejected Epicurus' theory that chance combinations of atoms explain the world's properties—hardness in a stone, coldness in ice, the smooth pelt of a Great Dane, or human personality. Although the *logos* determines everything, humans remain free and morally responsible. A favorite Stoic image for a human's relationship to moral choice was a dog tied to a moving cart. The dog can choose to run with the cart and do so happily, or he can choose to run the other way, or to the side, or sit down, and be dragged along by the neck. Yet the cart moves on unimpeded. You make your choice and you pay the price. Best to place oneself in harmony with natural law, with the *logos* that pervades and causes creation. By allowing *logos* to rule your life, you align yourself with the intelligence that rules the universe. That choice, made in agreement with reason, constitutes virtue (*aretê*), the very thing that sophists of the fifth century B.C. claimed they could teach (and that the Cynics taught you should desire). A virtuous life is a happy one because virtue is its own reward. Those who follow reason are few, of course, the philosophical elite, who form an international community of superior beings, while the suffering masses struggle against reason.

Stoicism justified the educated elites' acceptance of kings in the Hellenistic east and aristocrats in the Roman Empire. One of the most eloquent proponents of Stoicism was **Epictetus**, born into slavery around A.D. 50. After earning his freedom, he taught in Rome. He wrote nothing, but a follower named Flavius Arrian took notes and published them as the *Discourses*. The following selection explicates, by a political example, the Stoic teaching on necessity:

When the emperor Vespasian° sent word to Priscus Helvidius that he was not to attend the senate, Priscus replied, "You can prevent my being a senator, but so long as I am a senator I must attend the meetings."

"Very well, come, but do not speak."

"If you do not ask my opinion, I will be silent."

"But I have to ask for your opinion."

"And I must speak what seems right."

"If you do, I shall put you to death."

"Did I tell you that I was immortal? You will do your part, and I mine. It is yours to kill, mine to die without fear; yours to banish, mine to depart without complaint."

What good did Priscus do, one man against the emperor? What good does the red border do to the cloak? What else than to be distinguished as color, and a beautiful example to the rest?

Epictetus, *Discourses*, 1.2

°*Vespasian:* Reigned A.D. 69–79.

## Conclusion

Classical philosophers wondered about how they could explain change in the world and the relationship between substance and form, and how they could know the truth when they had found it. Their speculations often had political repercussions and were tied to the vigorous social life of the *polis*. Hellenistic philosophers asked how they could lead good lives in a world governed by kings who claimed to be more than human. Politics and the *polis* itself were no longer important subjects for philosophical investigation. The Cynics condemned political endeavor as worthless, while the Skeptics, Epicureans, and Stoics retreated into worlds of private knowledge and virtue. Stoicism, nonetheless, accommodated public lives lived by powerful men, whose destiny, decreed by fate, was to live in this fashion, and it soon became the most widespread and resilient of the Hellenistic philosophies. We still understand what it means to be stoical in the face of hardship.

## MEDICINE

Medicine and science advanced rapidly after Alexander, supported by the great wealth in royal centers. To understand Hellenistic doctors' achievements, we must look back to the Classical Period and **Hippocrates** of Cos, a fifth-century B.C. thinker and physician whom we met briefly in Chapter 2, "Country and People."

## The School of Hippocrates

Ancient societies had assumed that sickness came from possession by spirits or witchcraft, and that the physician's job was to drive out spirits or to break the sorcerer's spell. Such views remained common in Classical Greece (as they are in parts of the world today), but doctors of the Ionian Enlightenment rejected them. Hippocrates (ca. 460–370 B.C.) opposed such theories most vigorously. Sixty or seventy texts are attributed to him and his name was often attached to Hellenistic treatises that were actually by other doctors. A celebrated essay, *On the Sacred Disease* (probably epilepsy), describes the Hippocratic position on older views. When a person falls down, thrashes about, and afterward cannot remember what has happened, it is easy to conclude that spirits have possessed the victim, and the Greeks therefore called this illness "sacred." But Hippocrates says:

> In my opinion it is no more divine or sacred than any other disease, and its cause and origins are just the same. From ignorance and wonder men think its nature and origin are divine, because it is not like other diseases. The notion of its divinity is supported by the inability of men to understand it, and by the superficial methods used to treat it, for example, by purifications and incantations. If one considers it to be divine just because it is wonderful, then many other diseases are sacred too, not just this one. As I shall demonstrate, there are others no less wonderful and remarkable, which nobody wants to call "sacred" ...
>
> As I see it, the men who first called this disease "sacred" were the faith-healers, the mumbo-jumbo artists, and the phonies of our own day, who give themselves out as being so religious and as knowing more than anyone

else. Because they have no treatment of the slightest value, they have wrapped themselves in a cloud of superstitious gibberish rather than admit that they do not have a cure, calling the sickness "sacred" . . .

The disease called "sacred" arises from the same causes as other diseases, namely those things that enter and leave the body, cold weather, the sun, and changes in the climate.

Hippocrates, *On the Sacred Disease* 1.2.21

According to Hippocrates, the physician's main task was to establish a *prognôsis*, a "foretelling" of a disease's course by comparing it with the course of similar sicknesses. Afterward, there might someday be room for theoretical speculation about the causes of disease. We saw in Chapter 2, "Country and People," how Thucydides, who owed much to Hippocrates' thinking, applied a physician's eye to his description of the plague that struck Athens in 429 B.C. and to the "disease" of the Peloponnesian War, which afflicted the body politic of Greece. Thucydides' aim of establishing a prognosis of the course of the war paralleled Hippocrates' approach to disease. The following Hippocratic description is typical:

Apollonius of Abdera.° Although not feeling well for a long time, this man had not taken to his bed. His abdomen was swollen and for a long time he had a sharp pain in his liver. At this time he became jaundiced, had much gas, and his complexion turned pasty. After an unwise meal of beef accompanied by much wine, he felt hot and uncomfortable and went to bed. He then drank a quantity of milk, both sheep's and goat's, raw and boiled, an unwise act from which much harm resulted. His fever got worse and he excreted almost nothing of what he ate, only a little thin urine. He could not sleep and later developed a strong thirst. He fell into a coma. His belly was distended. There was a painful swelling on the right side just beneath the ribs. His extremities felt cold. He muttered a few things but was out of his mind and could not remember what he said.

Around the fourteenth day after he took to bed he had a chill followed by a fever, then he fell into a delirium. He shouted and thrashed his limbs and talked constantly. The sweating returned and he again fell into a coma. His meager urine was dark and thin. His bowels were much disturbed with foul, clumpy, and undigested excreta of different kinds, either black, thin, and reddish, or greasy, or raw and sharp. Sometimes the excreta were milky. By the twenty-fourth day he felt more comfortable. Though his symptoms were the same, he had partly regained his senses, but he could not remember anything that had happened since he took to bed. But soon he again went out of his mind and his condition rapidly got worse. Around the thirtieth day his excrement was thin and copious and he ran a high fever. He became delirious, lost his voice, and his limbs became cold. On the thirty-fourth day he died. From the time I first saw the patient, his bowels were constantly disordered. His urine was thin and dark. When not in a coma, he could not sleep. He was delirious all the time. His extremities were cold throughout this period.

Hippocrates, *Epidemics*, III, series 2, case 13

°*Abdera:* A city in north Greece.

Apollonius' unwise meal triggered his fatal illness, but the Hippocratic writer did not speculate on the sickness' ultimate cause. Instead of abstract and unprovable theorizing, he accumulated details, which might one day lead to secure knowledge of causes. Such inductive reasoning, proceeding from facts to theory, partly underlies modern experimental science, including medical science, and was a Greek invention.

## Galen

The Hippocratic writings were influential, but learned Hippocratic physicians worked alongside sorcerers, midwives, herb-gatherers, and priests of Asclepius, the god of healing (along with Apollo). There was no such thing as a medical degree or oversight of doctors. The famous Hippocratic Oath (see Chapter 2) was merely an effort at self-regulation. Hippocratic writers endorsed traditional practices like dream therapy, when patients slept in sanctuaries of Asclepius to receive the god's healing message.

We know little about Greek medicine in the four centuries between Hippocrates and the time of Christ. The Ptolemies supported human dissections in Alexandria in the third century B.C., allowing one Herophilus to distinguish between the sensory nerves. His technical terms for describing the eye are still used. He examined internal and sexual organs, distinguished between veins and arteries, and offered a plausible (but inaccurate) explanation of the functioning of the heart. His followers produced increasingly detailed explanations of bodily functions but were handicapped by the limits of the human eye. Without microscopes, they could see that blood flowed in both arteries and veins but could not understand how it got from one to the other.

Over the next three centuries, Herophilus' followers and rivals argued about physiology and, to some extent, divided into rival medical sects. Our best source of information is the later Roman writer **Galen** (A.D. 126–ca. 200), who collected all available medical knowledge in an encyclopedia that fills several feet of shelf space in modern libraries. Born in Pergamum, he studied philosophy, mathematics, and medicine. After working in Alexandria and as a doctor for gladiators in his native Asia Minor, he moved to Rome in A.D. 162 and served as a personal physician to several emperors.

Deeply influenced by Hippocrates, Plato, Aristotle, Stoicism, and Herophilus, Galen summarized 600 years of Greco-Roman thinking about health. He was more interested in diseases than patients and showed his debt to Aristotle by categorizing diseases. Like the Hippocratics, he aimed to elicit universals from particulars. He saw the need to build therapy on knowledge gained from dissection and on a theory of how the body worked. In these views, Galen was utterly modern, although many of his assumptions and conclusions were wrong.

Galen depended on Hippocrates, too, in his adoption of the theory of the four humors, or "liquids" (Latin *umor* = liquid), found in some Hippocratic writings. In these theories, health was the result of harmonious interaction between the humors, equated with the four qualities and the four elements of early philosophy: blood (hot, fire), phlegm (cold, earth), yellow bile (wet, water), black bile (dry, air). A predominance of a humor produces the four basic human character types: the *sanguine* ("bloody"), buoyant type; the *phlegmatic*, sluggish type (as when you get a cold and the nose fills with phlegm); the *choleric*, quick-tempered type (*choler*, "yellow bile"); and the *melancholic* ("black bile"), dejected type. Galen thought that disequilibrium among the humors in various organs caused diseases, and he was the first to localize diseases in specific organs.

Galen performed dissections, not of humans, which was no longer allowed, but of animals, then applied his results (sometimes wrongly) to humans. He presented a complex, consistent, philosophically and anatomically sophisticated description of how bodies work, what organs do, and how the heart functions. He was both practical and theoretical, and Galen's anatomy remained the standard textbook even in the nineteenth century A.D.

## QUANTITATIVE SCIENCE IN THE HELLENISTIC AGE

In ancient Greece, mathematics mostly meant geometry, working with proportions rather than numbers. In early Hellenistic times, **Euclid** (ca. 325–250 B.C.) gathered together all that was known about geometry. Some Greek writers said he lived in Alexandria, but we know nothing about his life. Around 300 B.C., he published the *Elements,* one of the most widely read books ever written. High-school geometry is virtually Euclid's *Elements* with examples and applications.

Unlike the inductive method that Hippocrates recommended, the *Elements* is a deductive system, arguing from first principles to conclusions. First come *definitions:*

- a point: "that which has no part"
- a line: "length without breadth"

and so on, applied to unproven statements about planes, right, acute, and obtuse angles, and so forth.

Second come *postulates*—for example,

- that a line can be drawn between any two points
- that a straight line can be extended from either end
- that all right angles are equal

After defining what he means by a geometric element, like a point, Euclid makes various unproven statements, the postulates, about features of these elements. Third come Euclid's *axioms,* or self-evident truths, which may justify statements he has made as postulates. For example, the Euclidean axiom that

two things equal to the same thing are equal to each other

justifies the postulate that all right angles are equal. If they were not, then if *a* equals *b* and *b* equals *c, c* would not necessarily equal *a,* which is absurd. Aristotle had shown long before that such contradictions are illogical and hence untrue.

In thirteen books following these preliminaries, Euclid presented his *propositions,* conclusions drawn from his definitions, postulates, and axioms. Propositions, which fell into the categories of plane and solid geometry, themselves generated further propositions, yielding further proofs. Euclid's argumentation remained standard for scientific demonstrations until the end of the seventeenth century.

Numerous exceptional mathematicians followed Euclid, but none was more important than **Archimedes** of Syracuse (287–212 B.C.). Educated in Alexandria, he spent most of his life at King Hiero II's court in Syracuse. Archimedes used deductions from axioms to make advances in plane and solid geometry, arithmetic, and mechanics. For example, he proved that the volume of a sphere is two-thirds the volume of a cylinder that circumscribes the sphere. He defined the principle of the lever and designed the first compound pulleys and hydraulic screws for raising water. His work on conic sections came close to integral calculus. He is best known for his discoveries in hydrostatics, the study of the equilibrium of liquids at rest and the forces exerted by them. His discovery of what is still called Archimedes' principle is a famous story:

> Archimedes discovered many ingenious things in many different fields, but of all, the one I am about to describe best illustrates his boundless cleverness.
>
> Because the affairs of King Hiero of Syracuse [275–216 B.C.] had so prospered, and his power increased, he decided to dedicate a crown of gold in a certain temple in thanks to the undying gods.
>
> He therefore contracted with a goldsmith to make the crown, giving him a fee and just enough gold to make the crown. After awhile, the goldsmith presented to Hiero a beautiful crown. Judging by the weight of the crown, the goldsmith appeared to have used all the gold given to him. But a little later Hiero heard a rumor that the smith had taken some of the gold and replaced it with an equal weight of silver. Hiero was furious at having been tricked, but he saw no way to prove what had happened. He asked Archimedes to give some thought to the problem.
>
> One day while Archimedes was thinking about the matter, he went to the city baths. He went into a small pool with an overflow pipe. While in the pool it occurred to him that a volume equal to that of the submerged part of his body overflowed out of the pool. He realized the principle on which the whole problem rested. In his delight he leaped from the pool and ran home naked, announcing in a loud voice that he had discovered what he was looking for. As he ran along he kept shouting in Greek, *"Eureka! Eureka!"*°
>
> The story continues that he took a slab of silver and another of gold, each weighing as much as the crown. He then filled a pot to the brim with water and dropped in the silver. As much water flowed out as the bulk of the bar. After removing the slab he measured how much water it took to refill the pot. In this way, he discovered what weight of silver corresponded to a known bulk of water.
>
> Next he dropped in the slab of gold, removed it, and measured how much water had overflowed. It was much less than had been the case with the silver, corresponding to the smaller bulk of gold when compared with the same weight of silver.
>
> Finally he lowered in the crown and found that it displaced more water than the bar of pure gold, although the weights were the same. From the difference in overflows between the crown and the bar Archimedes was able to calculate how much silver had been used in the alloy in the crown, and thus proved the deceit of the goldsmith.

Vitruvius, *On Architecture* 9.9–12

°*Eureka:* The motto of the state of California, because of the gold rush there in 1849.

## Astronomy

Astronomers occupied a middle ground between physicians' meticulous observations and mathematicians' deductions: They observed the positions and movements of stars and planets and reasoned toward theories explaining their observations. In some ways, astronomy was the most successful ancient science when weighed against modern achievements. The Pythagoreans and Aristarchus of Samos (third century B.C.) even calculated that the earth revolved around the sun, although most Greeks resisted this affront to common sense and to Aristotelian cosmology.

The need for reliable calendars drove much early astronomy. Near Eastern observers realized in the third millennium B.C. that the solar year was not an even multiple of cycles of the moon. Around 425 B.C., a Greek named Meton refined a nineteen-year calendar making solar and lunar cycles correspond closely, but not until the Gregorian calendar introduced by Pope Gregory XIII on February 24, 1582 (not accepted in America until 1752) was a calendar devised that corresponds to nature. The Gregorian calendar itself modified the Julian calendar introduced by Julius Caesar in 46 B.C., which in turn derived from the Egyptian civil calendar of 365 days (but no leap year).

The retrograde movement of planets—that is, when they appear to go backwards—was a problem for Plato's earth-centered cosmology. It stimulated increasingly complex attempts to reconcile observations with earth-centered models. The Alexandrian **Claudius Ptolemy** (ca. 87–150 A.D., not connected with the royal Macedonian dynasty of the Ptolemies) summarized earlier scholarship and added improvements. Ptolemy's book is known as the *Almagest*, a corruption of "the greatest" in Arabic, from the title of an Arabic translation rendered into Latin during the Middle Ages. His model held until A.D. 1543, when Nicolaus Copernicus showed that the sun must be the center of our system, later supported by Johannes Kepler (1571–1630), the first astronomer to understand that some force emanating from the sun holds the planets in orbit.

Ptolemy, however, argued that a spherical earth is the center of the universe and does not move. The sun, moon, and planets orbit the earth, not fixed on the surface of an invisible sphere, as Plato and Aristotle thought, but in perfect circles. The planets, while circling the earth, also move in smaller circles, called epicycles, centered on the planet's orbit; the planets' actual courses, therefore, are spirals. That is why planets sometimes appear to go backward, because their epicycle temporarily takes them in the opposite direction from their orbit around Earth (Figure 23.14).

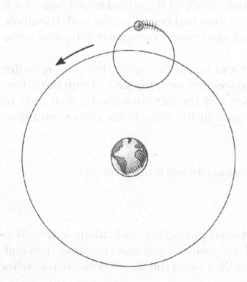

**FIGURE 23.14** Ptolemy's explanation of the retrograde movement of planets: A planet revolves around Earth, simultaneously performing a second orbit.

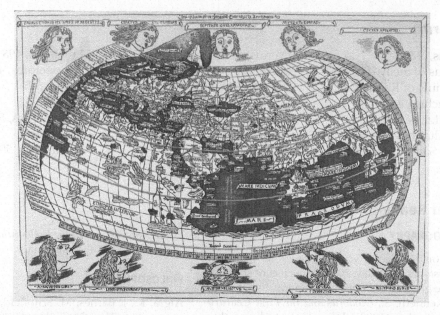

**FIGURE 23.15** Map of the world from the Latin edition of Ptolemy's *Geography,* published at Ulm, Germany, in A.D. 1482. Personifications of the winds surround the globe.

The *Almagest* contains a catalogue of 1,022 stars grouped into forty-eight constellations. Ptolemy believed in astrology, and his authority did much to give it credibility. He also studied the refraction of light. Finally, Ptolemy wrote on geography, producing a map of the world containing parts of Africa, Europe, and Asia (Figure 23.15).

He calculated the size of Ocean, the river that supposedly flowed around the continents (and which Alexander the Great thought he had found in 327 B.C.), but drastically underestimated it, a mistake that would have important results when Christopher Columbus set out to sail across the Ocean to India in A.D. 1492, depending on Ptolemy's calculations.

## CONCLUSION

The view of Hellenistic culture as decadent, declining after the Golden Age of Athens, is naïve. In medicine, science, and engineering, Hellenistic thinkers went far beyond those of classical times. In art, literature, and philosophy, they reworked their extraordinary classical heritage within a world utterly changed. Alexander and his Successors took Greek culture to Afghanistan and India and Greek became a *lingua franca* that served the educated in Carthage and Rome as well as in Athens. Non-Greek peoples adopted and adapted Greek culture enthusiastically, and its impact on the Jews and Romans had profound consequences. There is no way to draw a firm line between Hellenistic culture and what came later; through processes that we discuss in Chapter 24, "The Coming of Rome, 220–30 B.C.," the Roman aristocracy created its own version of Hellenistic culture. They and the Arabs who conquered most of the old Hellenistic world in and after the seventh century A.D. transmitted the Greek heritage to later ages. Hellenistic philosophy, science, and mathematics dominated European thought until the seventeenth century A.D.

## Key Terms

Polybius, *482*

Diodorus of Sicily, *482*

Apollonius of Rhodes, *483*

Callimachus, *484*

Menander, *485*

Great Altar of Zeus, *487*

Nikê of Samothrace, *488*

Venus de Milo, *490*

stoa, *491*

Skepticism, *495*

Cynicism, *495*

Epicureanism, *495*

Stoicism, *498*

*logos*, *498*

Epictetus, *498*

Hippocrates, *499*

Galen, *501*

Euclid, *502*

Archimedes, *502*

Claudius

  Ptolemy, *504*

## Further Reading

### HISTORIOGRAPHY

Champion, Craige, *Cultural Poetics in Polybius' Histories* (Berkeley, 2004). Most recent study of the greatest Hellenistic historian.

Sacks, Kenneth, S., *Diodorus and the First Century* (Princeton, 1990). Important study of this major source.

Walbank, F. W., *Polybius* (Berkeley, 1972). A classic review of this important historian.

### LITERATURE

Feeney, Denis, *The Gods in Epic* (Oxford, 1991). Influential and penetrating study of religion in the Hellenistic and Roman poets.

Gutzwiller, Kathryn, *Theocritus' Pastoral Analogies: The Formation of a Genre* (Madison, WI, 1991). Fine study of Hellenistic epigram and the culture it represents.

Hunter, Richard, *The Argonautica of Apollonius Rhodius: Literary Studies* (Cambridge, UK, 1991). Leads the reader through the most important surviving poem from the Hellenistic period.

MacKendrick, P., and Herbert M. Howe, *Classics in Translation*, vol. 1. (Madison, WI, 1952). Invaluable collection of primary sources with introductions and commentary.

Stephens, Susan, *Seeing Double: Intercultural Poetics in Ptolemaic Alexandria* (Berkeley, 2003). Study of the interplay of Greek and Egyptian traditions in Hellenistic poetry.

### ART AND ARCHITECTURE

Fowler, B., *The Hellenistic Aesthetic* (Madison, WI, 1990). How the Hellenistic Greeks saw art and what they enjoyed in art.

Pollitt, Jerome, *Art in the Hellenistic Age* (Cambridge, UK, 1986). Fine summary.

### PHILOSOPHY

Algra, K., J. Barnes, M. Schofield, and J. Mansfeld, eds., *The Cambridge History of Hellenistic Philosophy* (Cambridge, UK, 1999). Essays by various authorities on all the major philosophical schools.

Long, Anthony, and David Sedley, eds., *The Hellenistic Philosophers*, vol. 2. (Cambridge, UK, 1991). Thorough review clearly presented.

### MEDICINE

Sigerist, H. E., *A History of Medicine*, vol. 2. (Oxford, 1961). Good discussion of Hippocrates and his influence.

### MATHEMATICS AND ASTRONOMY

Feeney, Denis, *Caesar's Calendar: Ancient Time and the Beginnings of History* (Berkeley, 2008). Outstanding study of ancient calendars and thinking about time.

Lindbergh, David, *The Beginnings of Western Science* (Chicago, 1992). Exciting, lucid overview, stressing the haphazard, unsystematic progress of scientific discovery.

Lloyd, G. E. R., *Early Greek Science: From Thales to Aristotle* (London, 1970), Chap. 7. Lloyd traces the Greeks' indebtedness to the Near East.

Neugebauer, Oscar, *The Exact Sciences in Antiquity* (Oxford, 1957). Neugebauer was a pioneer in scholarship on ancient science; his books remain invaluable.

# The Coming of Rome, 220–30 B.C.

We saw in Chapter 19, "The Warlords of Macedonia I," how Macedonia, once despised as a backwater, became a major power in the fourth century B.C. In Italy, Rome likewise grew from a minor city to become the greatest imperial power the world has ever seen in the fourth century B.C. By 280 B.C. Rome so badly frightened the south Italian Greeks that they asked Pyrrhus to cross from Epirus and help them. Fifty years later, Rome had taken over western Greece; fifty years after that, Rome had humbled the Antigonids and Seleucids of Macedonia and Asia. The Greeks' story in the second and first centuries B.C. is one of responding to implacable Roman aggression, often—paradoxically—provoked by their own behavior.

Who were the Romans? Why did they expand so relentlessly? What did this mean for the Greeks? The Roman conquests meant massacres, enslavements, deportations, revolutions, and the collapse of a sophisticated, ancient civilization into anarchic impotence—much as the coming of the Macedonians and Greeks had meant for the Persian Empire in the fourth century B.C. Millions died and millions more were transported to labor in Italian fields or Spanish mines. But amidst this orgy of violence, Romans absorbed and modified Hellenistic Greek culture and transmitted it to later ages as the basis for modern Western civilization. They are our direct ancestors and, in many ways, our teachers.

## THE RISE OF ROME, 753–280 B.C.

Early legends say that Rome's story began with the Trojan War, when Aeneas, a member of Troy's royal family (and son of Aphrodite), fled west to Italy after the city's fall. Hundreds of years later, in 753 B.C. (although other legends gave other dates), his descendants Romulus and Remus founded the city of Rome (Map 24.1).

Archaeology shows that a village was indeed established at Rome in the eighth century B.C., though there may have been earlier occupation of the site. Traditions held that Rome had kings until aristocratic conspirators overthrew them in 509 B.C., establishing a **Republic** (Latin *res publica*, "public affair"). Violently opposed to monarchy, a **Senate** ("body of old men") of 300 aristocrats (serving for life) and a series of assemblies made key decisions. Each year, the assemblies elected two Senators as **consuls** ("deliberators"), who oversaw war, finance, and law. Replacing the consuls every year made it hard to formulate long-term policy, but

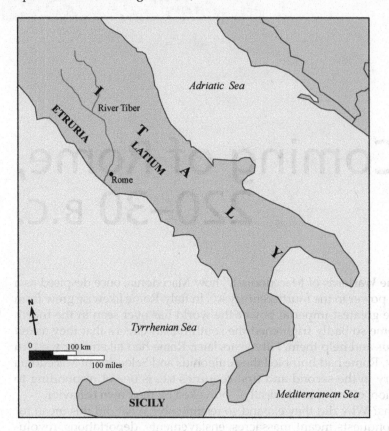

**MAP 24.1** Sites in Italy mentioned in this chapter.

the Romans were determined to avoid a return to monarchy. No man must be allowed to concentrate too much power in his own hands.

Roman government in the fifth century B.C. had, therefore, some similarities to Greek systems, notably its hostility to kings. But the rich aristocrats were stronger in Rome than in Greece. They monopolized the Senate, had more votes in the assemblies, and could often buy even more support through networks of patronage. The institution of citizenship was correspondingly weak, bringing fewer protections than in Greek cities. In such haphazard and sometimes self-contradictory political arrangements lay one secret of Roman power: By diffusing power among a sizable elite, it was much harder to overthrow the system merely by knocking off the top of the pyramid, as Alexander did in Persia when he replaced Darius. Rome lost general after general in her wars but the fight went on. The system lasted almost 500 years before one man finally did make himself an autocrat.

The Roman aristocracy's power came largely from its leadership in war. In the fifth century B.C. Rome crushed her central Italian neighbors through constant war. Plunder enriched the elite, but instead of ordering defeated enemies to pay tribute, as the Greeks generally did, the Senate required them to provide troops for further wars. New soldiers were part of the plunder. Rome took land from enemies and colonized it with poor Roman citizens, simultaneously garrisoning defeated states, exporting potential unrest, and blurring the boundaries between Romans and non-Romans.

By the time of the Peloponnesian War, Rome was already a major Italian power, but 338 B.C.—the year of the battle of Chaeronea—was as much of a turning point in Italy as in Greece. After smashing an Italian uprising, the Senate greatly extended Roman citizenship in 338 B.C., giving it to the defeated rebels. The Senate was always more pragmatic than the Greek *poleis*; by giving her neighbors a stake in the outcome, Rome made them partners rather than subjects. Former enemies henceforth fought for Rome, sharing the spoils of war, while giving Rome inexhaustible manpower. It was a brilliant policy.The city of Rome, meanwhile, grew to a 100,000 people, making it Europe's greatest metropolis, though it remained smaller than Hellenistic Greek cities like Alexandria in Egypt.

Over the next fifty years, Roman armies pushed inexorably into southern Italy, and in 282 B.C., the Greeks of Taras asked Pyrrhus of Epirus to help them. When he arrived in 280 B.C., he was astonished by Roman discipline. As we saw in Chapter 22, "The Greek *Poleis* in the Hellenistic Century, 323–220 B.C." Pyrrhus was able to defeat the Romans on the battlefield but was ultimately overwhelmed by their resources in manpower. The Greeks did not understand Rome; even 115 years later, when the Greek historian Polybius came to Rome as a hostage in 165 B.C., he was surprised by the Romans' obsession with war. He was particularly struck by the sharp contrast between Greek and Roman public funerals for the war dead. Greek funerals emphasized the community, treating the war dead as an anonymous crowd, while Roman funerals dwelled on the prowess of individual aristocratic leaders. Polybius concluded that

> the most important result of the ceremony is that it inspires young men to endure anything for the common good and for the sake of the good name that will come to the best men. You can recognize the truth of what I say from the following. Many are the Romans who have volunteered to engage in single combat to decide the whole battle. Not a few have chosen certain death, some to ensure in battle the safety of others, some in peace for the well being of the Republic. Some while in office have put to death their own sons, contrary to every custom and law, placing the interests of the group even above the closest ties of family. Many such stories are told about many such men in Roman history . . .
>
> Polybius 6.54

Roman aristocrats prided themselves on puritanical sternness and indifference to luxury, and their rituals emphasized martial virtues far more than did Greek ceremonies. In the third century B.C., Romans developed their famous game of violence, gladiatorial combat (Figure 24.1). Evidently, the game went back to an Etruscan custom, a form of human sacrifice performed at the funerals of great men, but the religious element had largely disappeared. The audience sat close enough to be splattered with blood and brains as men hacked each other to pieces for their entertainment. For variety, wild animals killed each other; men killed animals; or animals killed men. The only time a hippopotamus was seen in Europe before the eighteenth century was when one was killed in a Roman arena. The demand for wild animals to murder in public spectacle drove some species in North Africa to near extinction.

In the same years, Romans developed the **triumph**, one of the greatest spectacles of the ancient world. If a victorious general killed more than 5,000 in battle, the Senate might vote him a triumphal parade through Rome, in which he displayed his plunder and captives. The victorious general was allowed to ride in a chariot drawn by white horses, as

**FIGURE 24.1** Gladiators, from a first-century-A.D. Roman mosaic. In the center, a gladiator named Serpenius spears a lion or leopard. In the upper left, a gladiator lies dead; in the upper right, another fights a wild boar.

the gods were imagined to do, and, according to one source, a slave would stand behind him whispering in his ear "Remember, you are a mortal." The symbolism blurred the boundaries between great warriors and deities, but once the parade was over, the normal boundaries were reaffirmed. In Greece, the *poleis* of the fifth and fourth centuries B.C. had denied that anything could make a man like a god but the great conquerors of the Hellenistic period, following the example of Alexander, claimed to be gods. The Romans came up with a compromise: The greatest generals could be god for a day, but no more.

## ROME, CARTHAGE, AND THE WESTERN GREEKS, 280–200 B.C.

### The First Punic War, 264–241 B.C.

The endless wars between Syracuse and Carthage flared up once more in 265 B.C., when a civil war in Messana, at the northeast tip of Sicily, widened to draw in both great powers. What made this war special, though, was that the next year one faction in the Messanan civil war asked Rome to help them. From this dispute began the First Punic War (Romans called Carthaginians *Poeni*, "Phoenicians," which came into English as Punic). This war spelled the end of western Greek independence.

For fourteen years, fighting within a shifting and complex system of alliances, Roman and Carthaginian armies devastated Sicily. Many Greek cities were destroyed; Akragas never recovered from a Roman sack in 262 B.C. Only Syracuse flourished, under her cunning tyrant **Hiero II** (reigned 265–216 B.C.), who wisely joined the Roman side early on. Carthage and Syracuse had been fighting each other to an exhausting standstill for 150 years, but Rome now committed all the wealth and manpower of Italy to the struggle. This dwarfed the efforts Syracuse had previously made and drew a similarly massive response from Carthage. Eventually, though, after twenty-three years of war, Carthage sued for peace and abandoned all claims to Sicily. As Polybius explains:

> The war between the Romans and the Carthaginians went on without interruption for twenty-four years. It is the longest lasting and the most continuous and the greatest war of which we have knowledge. Apart from the other battles fought, and the preparations made that I described earlier, in one naval battle five hundred warships took part and seven hundred° in another. In the course of the war, counting those lost to shipwreck, the Romans lost seven hundred ships and the Carthaginians five hundred. One who is impressed by the naval battles and expeditions of an Antigonus, a Ptolemy, or a Demetrius would be astounded if he had to write an account of the size of these undertakings. And if we consider the size of these warships when compared with the triremes that the Persians used against the Greeks or the Athenians and Spartans against each other, we will have to conclude that never before in the history of the world were such mighty naval forces arrayed against each other. From these facts is clear the truth that I put forward at the beginning of my history, that the Romans did not achieve supremacy by chance or without knowing what they were doing, as certain Greek writers suppose. Rather, it is only natural that, schooled in such and similar enterprises, they should boldly aim at universal dominion, and that they should in fact have achieved it.

Polybius 1.63

° *seven hundred:* The first battle involved some 200,000 men; the second, probably 250,000.

## Greek Sicily under Roman Rule

The First Punic War finally united Sicily, but under Roman rule, not Syracusan or Carthaginian. The western Greeks' independent history was over. Only Syracuse remained free as Hiero II's reward for supporting Rome in the war. The Senate had to decide what to do with the Greeks, Carthaginians, and native Sicilians they now ruled. Rather than follow her normal pattern of enrolling the defeated enemies as troops for further wars, Rome changed policy and made Sicily her first *provincia* (a Latin word perhaps meaning "in return for conquest," from which the word "province" comes), a conquered territory governed directly by the Roman elite. The Senate extended to the whole island a system of taxation that King Hiero of Syracuse had copied from Ptolemaic Egypt and used for Syracusan territories. Unlike most *poleis*, Syracuse taxed crops and animals as well as goods coming through its harbors. Syracusan tax collectors were efficient and relentless, and those who now came to serve Rome, the ***publicani*** made so famous by the New Testament, followed the model that Hiero laid down.

While Hiero lived, Syracuse enjoyed a Golden Age. The city had shrunk since the fourth century B.C., but still numbered fifty thousand around 240 B.C. Hiero built the biggest theater in the world (Figure 24.2), with a beautiful stoa above it and an altar so big that a thousand cattle could be sacrificed on it simultaneously. The poet Theocritus and the

**FIGURE 24.2**   The Greek theater at Syracuse, ca. 225 B.C. A performance of Aristophanes' *The Clouds* is underway against modern scenery. Beyond lie the modern city and the Great Harbor, where the Athenian fleet was destroyed in 413 B.C.

great mathematician Archimedes frequented Hiero's court, creating hopes that Syracuse might rival Alexandria as Greece's cultural capital. Excavators have found rich gold and silver ornaments in tombs of these years.

But the First Punic War devastated western and southern Sicily. Akragas never recovered, and once-mighty Selinus, whose mighty ruins still astonish visitors, was abandoned forever after 250 B.C. The countryside changed too. As Rome grew, it needed food, and Italian investors bought up the conquered Sicilian countryside, drove off the peasants, and grew wheat on vast estates called *latifundia* ("broad acres") worked by the cheap and abundant slaves brought to market through Rome's wars. They then sold the wheat that the slaves had grown to markets in Rome. Many Greek aristocrats shared in the gains. Luxurious villas, paid for by trade with Rome, sprang up in the second century B.C. Yet, despite the brutality of the First Punic War and the expropriation of Sicilian land, the Roman conquest also brought the peace that the Greeks could never create for themselves. Rome ended the class conflicts that had torn Sicilian *poleis* apart since the fifth century B.C. These western Greeks now increasingly adopted Roman ways, while the Roman elite was imbued with sophisticated Greek culture.

## The Second Punic War, 218–201 B.C.

Despite its disastrous defeat in the First Punic War Carthage rebounded and carved out a new empire in Spain. Carthage's leading general, the famous **Hannibal** (Semitic "mercy of [the storm god] Baal," Figure 24.3) had learned from the First Punic War that manpower and

**FIGURE 24.3** Hannibal, from a Carthaginian coin, ca. 215 B.C.

money were decisive and came up with a daring strategy: If he cut off hated Rome from her allies, he reasoned, he could starve her of both these resources and so defeat her. In 218 B.C., he boldly led an army (including elephants) over the Alps, invading Italy from the north. The Romans were taken by surprise and, by 216 B.C., Hannibal had won three shattering victories. Most of Italy and Sicily defected to his side, as Hannibal had predicted. Victory over Rome appeared certain, and, in 215 B.C., Syracuse and Philip V of Macedonia joined Hannibal too. It looked like the western Greeks might soon be freed from the Roman yoke.

But the Roman Senate kept its nerve. The city was too big for Hannibal to attack and enough allies remained loyal to Rome that the Senate could continue the war in the field. Realizing that they could not beat Hannibal in open battle, the Romans adopted a new, ingenious strategy of avoiding battle and wearing Hannibal down with endless marching around Italy. In the meanwhile, Roman armies under senatorial commanders took the offensive against Hannibal's allies in Spain and Sicily. The result spelled disaster for those Greek cities that had rebelled against Rome, including the once great Syracuse. In a heroic last stand, Syracuse withstood a three-year siege by the Roman general **Marcellus**. The brilliant scientist and mathematician Archimedes helped Syracuse frustrate Marcellus with fiendishly clever defensive machines:

Enormous beams were extended from the walls over the ships. They would drop down huge boulders and sink the ships below, or giant iron claw-like beaks such as you find on cranes would drop down, seize the prow of a ship, and raise it up by means of counterweights until it stood on its stern. Then the Syracusans would release it to plunge to the bottom of the sea, or using a winding device from within the city they would spin the boat around and smash it against the steep cliffs and rocks that jutted out beneath the walls. Many sailors died. Often was a ship lifted completely out of the water and spun around until everyone within was thrown in every direction. Then the empty ship was smashed against the walls.

Plutarch, *Life of Marcellus* 15

Two hundred years earlier, the Syracusans had defeated a terrifying armada from Athens, but this time there was no salvation. Roman determination and manpower slowly prevailed. Syracuse fell in 212 B.C., permanently ending Greek freedom in the west. Amid horrific scenes of carnage, a Roman soldier killed the great Archimedes—too engrossed in his calculations to notice the soldier's presence in his room, according to a famous story. Marcellus, a new breed of Roman aristocrat who openly admired Greek culture, wept when he heard that his troops had killed Archimedes. Then he looted the city and carried Syracuse's greatest artworks off to Rome.

The major theater of war shifted to Spain after 212 B.C., where a dynamic young Roman named **Scipio** (**skip**-i-ō, 236–184 B.C., Figure 24.4) carved a path of blood. In ferocious battles, the Roman army developed ever-more efficient techniques of destruction. They made an art form of violence:

When Scipio judged that enough men had entered the city [a Carthaginian base], he let loose the majority of them against the inhabitants according to the Roman custom, ordering them to kill everything they came upon, sparing nothing. They

**FIGURE 24.4**  Scipio, marble bust, first century B.C.

should hold off from looting until the order was given. The purpose was to inspire terror. For this reason it is common to see in cities taken by the Romans not only the human dead, but animals too, dogs cut in half and other animals cut limb from limb. In this case, the carnage was especially horrific because of the large population.

Polybius 10.15

By 205 B.C. Scipio had driven Carthage out of Spain. In a brilliant stroke he carried the war to Africa itself, and in 202 B.C. defeated Hannibal, who had returned from Italy to defend Carthage, the only time this great general was beaten on the battlefield. For his victories Scipio was nicknamed Africanus, "the conqueror of Africa" (i.e., roughly present-day Tunisia). Carthage surrendered her fleet and her empire, leaving Rome mistress of the western Mediterranean.

## ROME BREAKS THE HELLENISTIC EMPIRES, 200–167 B.C.

Keeping multiple armies in the field year after year was difficult under Rome's old system of annual consulships, and during the Second Punic War Marcellus, Scipio Africanus, and a few other leaders emerged as "super-generals" who won wealth and power beyond anything Roman senators had seen before. Conservative Romans worried that these super-generals were moving beyond god-for-a-day generalships toward something like Hellenistic semi-divine kingship. Radicals wanted to become super-generals themselves by fighting yet more wars, and the obvious place to fight such wars was in Hellenistic Greece.

As we saw in Chapter 21, "The Greek Kingdoms in the Hellenistic Century, 323–220 B.C.," young kings had assumed all three major Hellenistic thrones in the late 220s B.C. (Table 24.1). Instead of preparing to meet Rome, these inexperienced rulers weakened themselves by fighting vicious wars against one another. Antiochus III attacked Egypt and Ptolemy IV drove him back only by enrolling indigenous Egyptians in his army. The native Egyptians, realizing their own strength, then rebelled, draining Ptolemaic power in a long civil war.

**TABLE 24.1** Principal Hellenistic rulers

*Macedonia*
Philip V 221–179
Perseus 179–168

*Syria*
Antiochus III 223–187

*Egypt*
Ptolemy IV 221–204
Ptolemy V 204–181
Cleopatra VII 51–30

Philip V of Macedon made an ill-judged alliance with Hannibal in 215 B.C. Antiochus III offered Philip support, hoping to drive the Ptolemies out of the Aegean, and a terrified Athens, which depended on Egyptian protection, sought Roman assistance against the Macedonian Philip in 200 B.C. Only a few months had passed since the Roman defeat of Carthage, but the Senate nonetheless voted for a new war against Philip, and in 197 B.C., Rome's General Flamininus shattered the Macedonian phalanx at **Cynoscephalae** (sĭ-nō-**sef**-a-lē, "heads of the dog") in Thessaly (Map 24.2). Polybius explains how Roman tactics proved superior to the formerly overpowering Macedonian army:

From a number of factors it is easy to understand that so long as the Macedonian phalanx maintained its characteristic form and strength, nothing could withstand it face-to-face or stop its charge. When the lines are closed up for action, the man with his weapons stands within a space of three feet square. The Macedonian spear [called a *sarissa*] is twenty-one feet long, and from that you must subtract the distance between where his hands hold it and the end of the spear, which serves to balance the weapon. This comes out to six feet, from which it is clear that fifteen feet of the pole will extend forward of the hoplite when he goes forward against the enemy holding the spear with both hands. This means that the spears of the second, third, and fourth ranks extend further in front of the fighter, while the spears of the fifth rank will still extend three feet in front of the formation, so long as the phalanx keeps its characteristic form . . . From this we can understand the nature and tremendous force of the Macedonian phalanx moving at full charge with its sixteen ranks of fighters . . .

With the Romans, each fighter with his armor also occupies a space three feet square, but according to Roman methods of fighting, each fighter makes his movements individually, turning his shield to block blows as they come and using his sword both to cut and to thrust. Because of this different style it is obvious that he will need some space around him in which to maneuver, that being three feet from the men in the same rank, if he is to do what is required. The result is that the Roman soldier has to face *two* men in the phalanx opposing him and ten spear points. Once the battle lines are engaged it is impossible for him to cut through so many points, nor is it easy to force the points away . . . It is easy to understand, as I said before, how no force can resist a Macedonian phalanx so long as they maintain their characteristic formation and power.

What then is the factor that enables the Roman to be victorious and the phalanx to fail? The answer is that whereas in war the times and places for actions are unlimited, the Macedonian phalanx is effective in but a single kind of terrain. If the enemy were compelled to fight according to the times and places favorable to the phalanx, the phalanx would always be victorious, for the reasons I have given. But if it is possible, or even easy, to avoid the charge of the phalanx, then how can you continue to regard the formation as being a formidable one?

Polybius 18.29–31

Many Senators had not wanted war with Macedonia. They preferred their traditional aristocratic way of life, taking turns to serve as consuls. They did not want Rome to become a superpower, because, they rightly foresaw, that would present dangers and temptations that would compromise traditional Roman values. After Cynoscephalae, their goal, therefore, became to avoid further entanglement in Greek politics. Flamininus made no attempt to annex Macedonia by making it into a province like Sicily; instead, he ordered its King Philip V to back off from controlling the Greek *poleis*, imposed a fine on him, and restated the principle of "freedom for the Greeks." But once Rome's armies had entered the quagmire of Greek rivalries, escape was impossible, and once Flaminius had shown the honor and wealth a general could win in Greece, it was inevitable that other Romans would want to copy his example. Flamininus brought home fine artworks for his triumph, and some *poleis* set up statues and cults in his honor, as they would to a Greek king.

The Hellenistic King Antiochus III in Syria now played into the hands of the Roman war party. He invited Hannibal (who had escaped after the battle with Scipio Africanus) to be his advisor, moved against the Greek *poleis* in Asia Minor, and, in 192 B.C., entered mainland Greece to support the Aetolian League in an anti-Roman alliance. Rome lost all patience and responded with overwhelming force, smashing Antiochus' army in the famous pass of Thermopylae in 191 B.C., then crossing to Anatolia to destroy another Seleucid army in 189 B.C. Hannibal fled, and, in 188, Antiochus sued for peace. Rome ordered him to evacuate Asia Minor, hand over his fleet and elephants, and pay 15,000 talents indemnity.

Ambitious young senators continued to push for military commands, and squabbling Greek *poleis* in the Aegean simultaneously sought Roman support against rivals. In the late 170s B.C., enemies of Philip V's son Perseus of Macedon (reigned 179–168 B.C.) convinced the Senate that Perseus was stockpiling weapons to attack Italy itself. Roman armies again quickly overran Macedonia. They found no vast stockpile of weapons, but the Romans extinguished the Macedonian monarchy anyway. Still eager to avoid annexations in the Balkan Peninsula, the Senate split Macedonia into four tiny republics in 168 B.C., governed by puppet kings.

In the same year, one of the interminable wars between Egypt and Syria spiraled out of control. The new Seleucid king, Antiochus IV, invaded Egypt and invested Alexandria. The Senate, impatient with Greek kings continuing to destabilize the east, drew up a decree ordering Antiochus to desist. They sent the Senator Gaius Popilius with a few officials to deliver the ultimatum:

> When Antiochus had advanced against Ptolemy [V] in order to take control of Pelusium,° the Roman commander Popilius met him there. Antiochus greeted him by voice and held out his right hand, but Popilius presented to him the wooden folding tablet he had in his hand, bearing the decree of the Senate.° He asked Antiochus to read it first. Evidently he did not want to show any mark of friendship before he found out what was the intention of Antiochus, whether he came as friend or foe. When the king had read the tablet, he said that he wished to consult with his advisors on these new developments, but Popilius did something that seems insolent and deeply arrogant. Holding a vine stick, he drew a circle around Antiochus and told him that he should give his reply to what was written before he left the circle. The king was astounded at such arrogance. Then, after hesitating for a moment, he said that he would do whatever the Romans wanted, and Popilius and his colleagues took him by the right hand and greeted him warmly.

Polybius 29.27

°*Pelusium:* One of the river's mouths, in the northeast Nile Delta.   °*Senate:* The letter would have been in Greek, the international language; Antiochus could not have read Latin.

Hence our expression "to draw a line in the sand." A Roman armed only with a stick had humiliated a great Hellenistic king. Although Rome had neither annexed nor garrisoned Greek territory, by 168 B.C. the Senators had in reality incorporated the Greeks into their empire.

## CONSEQUENCES OF THE WARS: THE GREEKS

Rome's wars against the Hellenistic kingdoms devastated Greece. More than a million people seem to have been killed or enslaved. In a single raid on Aetolia in central Greece in 187 B.C., Romans carried off golden crowns weighing 112 pounds; 83,000 pounds of silver; 243 pounds of gold; 130, 322 coins; 785 bronze statues; 230 marble statues; and a great amount of armor, weapons, and other enemy spoils, besides catapults and engines of every kind. In the most shocking episode, a Roman consul decided in 167 B.C. to punish Epirus in northwest mainland Greece:

> The consul summoned ten leading members of each community [in Epirus] and told them to bring out all their gold and silver and place it in a public place. The consul ten sent cohorts° to all the towns, sending out first those who had to go further, so that they should all arrive at their destinations at the same time. The tribunes and centurions° were informed of the plan. The silver and gold were collected in the morning and at the fourth hour the signal was given to plunder the towns. So great was the amount of plunder that each cavalryman received 400 *denarii* as his portion of the loot, and each infantryman 200,° and 150,000 captives were led off to be sold as slaves. The walls of the plundered cities, about 70 of them, the Romans razed to the ground.
>
> Livy 45.34
>
> °*cohorts:* Military units of about 500 men.   °*tribunes and centurions:* Different ranks of officers.
> °*200 denarii:* About twenty months' pay.

In one day, the Romans wiped Epirus, where mighty Pyrrhus once ruled, from the face of the earth.

The Aegean was suffering from depopulation, piracy, and the radical polarization of wealth. The Roman wars fed these evils. Indemnities bankrupted cities. Italian moneylenders helped the *poleis* pay their debts, only to extract still more assets by imposing exorbitant rates of interest. Rome was systematically plundering Greek lands and turning them into a desert. After an angry mob in Corinth almost tore Roman ambassadors limb from limb, the Senate decided to make an example of the ancient city. For two days in 146 B.C. Roman forces plundered and burned this famous, ancient city, dragging the survivors into slavery and destroying or capturing treasures of Greek art. Corinth would never recover.

In Roman eyes the Greeks were unrealistic, uncooperative, decadent, and a constant annoyance. When a pretender appeared in Macedonia in 148 B.C., claiming to be Perseus' son, Rome's Senate in disgust finally turned Macedonia into a province like Sicily, with a Roman governor, a member of the senatorial elite, supervising its affairs. The Greek *poleis* that cooperated, by contrast, did well under Roman rule. Athens had supported Rome since 200 B.C. and was rewarded in 167 B.C. with control of the lucrative slave markets on the tax-free island of

Delos. After Rome destroyed Corinth in 146 B.C., traders relocated to Piraeus, enriching Athens still further. Old political struggles between oligarchs and democrats melted away as if they had never existed. The Greek nobles, like the Roman elite, created *latifundia* worked by slaves, built beautiful villas, and commissioned lavish monuments in their own honor. Urban festivals and institutions continued, but citizen assemblies making real decisions were a memory.

There were more *latifundia* in Sicily than anywhere else, but the costs of exploitation could run high. This became clear in 134 B.C. when the largest slave revolt of ancient times broke out in Sicily:

> The Sicilians had grown rich and elegant in their style of life and they purchased many slaves. They imported them in masses from where they grew up, and as soon as they got them they branded them. The youngsters they used as shepherds and the others as need required . . . Oppressed by the hard labor and the beatings, abused for the most part beyond reason, at last the slaves could stand no more. They met together when they were able and they put together a plan . . .
>
> The revolt began in this way: There was in Enna° a man named Damophilos,° who used his wealth generously, but was exceedingly arrogant. He treated his slaves with ardent cruelty, and his wife Megallis strove to outdo him in vicious torture and inhumanity. Those so abused were like caged wild beasts and determined to rise up and kill their masters . . .
>
> They collected 400 other slaves and when the chance presented itself burst fully armed into Enna under the leadership of Eunus,° who performed tricks with flames of fire for them. They went into the houses and killed everyone. They spared not even suckling babes, which they ripped from the breast and dashed against the ground. One can never describe the outrages they committed against the women in the presence of their husbands. A large throng of slaves in the city joined them. After killing their masters, they joined in the general slaughter of anyone they could find.

Diodorus of Sicily 34

°*Enna:* A mountain town in the center of Sicily, where Hades raped Persephone, according to Sicilian legend.   °*Damophilos:* Ironically, his name means "friend to the people."   °*Eunus:* An enslaved Syrian priest.

The Romans finally crushed the revolt. They crucified thousands of men, women, and children, their broken bodies hanging on crosses for miles along Sicily's roads. Crucifixion seems originally to have been a Phoenician invention, taken over by the Persians, then the Romans as the ultimate punishment. It was reserved for bandits and rebels (Jesus was condemned as a rebel) and could not be inflicted on a Roman citizen.

Rome's armies had as yet scarcely set foot on Seleucid or Ptolemaic territory, but the Hellenistic monarchies were breaking down. The Seleucids lost Anatolia to Rome in 188 B.C., after the Romans crushed Philip V, and the Romans moved into Judea in 164 B.C. By 150 B.C., Parthian nomads from central Asia had overrun so much of Persia that their leaders started calling themselves Persian kings. The Parthians even captured one Seleucid ruler, and when they killed his successor on the battlefield in 129 B.C. the Seleucids gave up all claims to Mesopotamia and Persia. The Macedonian empire that once stretched from the Aegean to Afghanistan was reduced to parts of northern Syria, often with several men disputing the throne.

**FIGURE 24.5** The great temple in Kom Ombo in southern Egypt, not far from modern Lake Nasser, uniquely dedicated to two gods (Sebek the crocodile god and Horus the hawk god), built during the second and first centuries B.C. The best-preserved temples in Egypt today were built during the Ptolemaic period.

Since 170 B.C. two (sometimes three) Ptolemies had also been claiming the Egyptian throne at the same time, and their struggles grew increasingly brutal. In 131 B.C. Ptolemy VIII (nicknamed "Fatso") and his wife Cleopatra II were fighting for power within Egypt. Cleopatra stirred up riots in Alexandria and persuaded the mob to recognize as the true king the twelve-year-old son that she and Ptolemy VIII had produced. She did this because Ptolemy VIII and their son were in Cyprus at this time, so Cleopatra II would in effect be the sole ruler in Egypt. The angry Ptolemy VIII responded by having their own son torn into quarters and shipped back in pieces to his mother. Soon after, however, the loving father and mother were reconciled, let bygones be bygones, and ruled jointly for nine years! Despite the anarchy, the Seleucid and Ptolemaic economies still functioned, taxes were gathered, and temples built (Figure 24.5), but the Hellenistic kingdoms were tempting targets for Roman predation.

## CONSEQUENCES OF THE WARS: THE ROMANS

Wealth poured into the Roman aristocracy. Rome kept 150,000 men under arms; in any year in the two centuries after 225 B.C., one Italian farmer in eight was serving in the army. The average period of service was seven years, meaning that half of all Roman citizens must have served in the army at some time. The effect was equivalent to a massive migration out of Italy: Down to 146 B.C., roughly 100,000 conscripts were killed and twice this number settled overseas. Rich Romans bought up Italian farms weakened by the loss of these men, creating *latifundia* in Italy itself. Poor Italians left their farms and drifted to the city. By the first century B.C. Rome became the first city in history to have a million inhabitants. The urban market for food grown on the slave-run estates became enormous, and in an irresistible spiral, the rich got richer and many of the poor lost the little they had.

A whole class of Romans could now afford to live like Hellenistic kings, although they were private citizens. When the general Marcellus sacked Syracuse in 212 B.C. and "liberated" many of its statues and paintings, bringing them back to Rome, he set off a new fashion among Rome's super-rich:

> Before this time the Romans were unaware even of the existence of such elegant and fine things, and they had no taste for graceful and delicate art like this. Instead the city of Rome was filled with the bloodstained arms and spoils taken from barbarian peoples, crowned with monuments and trophies of victory. If you had no taste for war, or enjoyed beautiful things, you would find nothing to please your eye in the city . . .
>
> Marcellus greatly pleased the masses in Rome because he adorned the capital with Greek works that were graceful, charming, and imitated the forms of nature. By contrast Fabius the Delayer° earned the approbation of the older generation because when he took the city of Taras° he left things like that in their place and did not remove them. He carried away all the money and valuables of the city,° but allowed the statues to remain.

Plutarch, *Life of Marcellus* 21

°*Fabius the Delayer:* A conservative general, called the Delayer because he championed the strategy of avoiding pitched battles with Hannibal, instead wearing him down by guerilla tactics.   °*Taras:* Fabius recaptured the city from Hannibal in 209 B.C.   °*city:* He also sold 30,000 Tarentines into slavery.

Plutarch says that Marcellus thought that he had taught ignorant Romans to admire and honor the glories of Greek art, but traditionalists like Fabius the Delayer thought Marcellus had taught them to be lazy connoisseurs of art who idled away the day in "trivial chatter about aesthetics." What to do about Greek culture became *the* political issue of the second century B.C. Some of the aristocrats who admired Greeks sophistication also thought that men could be equal to gods—not just for a day, as in a triumph, but permanently. Some generals even hired Greek sculptors to represent them as Hellenistic kings (Figure 24.6).

Upper-class education became essentially Greek. Rhetoric, a thoroughly Greek topic, was coming to have very practical consequences for Senate debates, where persuasion was a key way to win votes. Conservative Romans, however, thought that the study of rhetoric, "the art of persuasion," would infect the ruling class with Greek weakness. The conservatives' champion, **Cato** (234–149 B.C.; Figure 24.7),

> feared that the younger generation might allow their ambitions to be turned in this direction so that they valued more highly a reputation built on feats of oratory than on feats of arms . . . He was opposed on principle to the study of philosophy, and his patriotic ardor caused him to view with contempt all Greek culture and its methods of education . . . he announced with solemnity, like a prophet, that if ever the Romans became infected with Greek literature, they would lose their empire.

Plutarch, *Life of Cato the Elder* 22-23

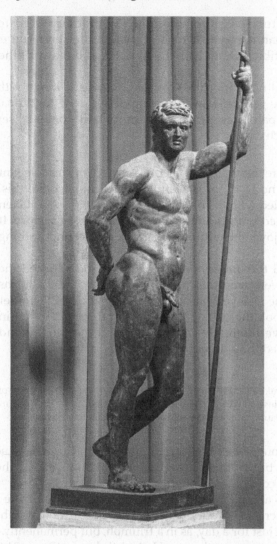

**FIGURE 24.6** Bronze statue representing a Roman general as a Hellenistic king, ca. 150 B.C. The workmanship is Greek, and the pose imitates a famous statue of Alexander the Great, but it seems to portray a Roman—the figure lacks the short cloak normal on Hellenistic royal statues and has a typically Roman stubbly beard and a Roman hairstyle. The heavy musculature follows a style popular at Pergamum. Height 7 feet, 9 inches.

Cato insisted (Plutarch, *Life of Cato the Elder* 24) that "Greek literature is only worth a glance, the Greeks are a wicked and stubborn race, their literature will ruin Rome, their doctors will bring Rome to her knees. The Greeks have sworn to kill all barbarians with their medicine, and they include Romans among the barbarians."

But despite his fierce language, the venerable Cato fought a losing battle. To compete against trained orators in Senate debates, Cato needed to speak effectively himself; in fact he had himself studied Greek literature closely in his youth, memorizing Thucydides and Demosthenes to improve his powers of persuasion, which were considerable! The only way for Romans Senators to fight Greek culture was to act more Greek than its champions.

By the 130s B.C., aristocratic Romans had thoroughly absorbed Hellenistic Greek culture. Paradoxically, this was one of the most important developments in Greek history. Roman tastes in art, literature, and philosophy largely determined what has

**FIGURE 24.7**   The Roman statesman Cato in a toga. Life-size, marble, first century B.C.

survived from ancient Greece because in culture and politics we are the heirs of the Romans. Ambitious Romans quoted Greek poetry (especially Homer), studied and promulgated Stoicism (which appeared to justify traditional values), and switched back and forth between Greek and Latin in everyday conversation. The last words of Julius Caesar, spoken to his friend and assassin **Brutus** were in Greek (*Kai su teknon?* "and you, my son?" It was Shakespeare who translated them into the Latin "*Et tu Brute?*"). As the Roman poet Horace (65–8 B.C.) put it (*Epistles*, II.i.156), "Captive Greece captured her wild captor and brought arts to the rustic Latin." We rightly speak of Greco-Roman culture.

## ROME'S MILITARY REVOLUTION

The forms of Roman government, designed to serve a city-state, were being strained to the utmost in the 130s B.C. by the need to govern a vast empire. Rome needed a large, standing army to preserve the peace, but traditionally the army had been a militia in which farmers served for the summer then went home again. As rich aristocrats bought up Italy's land in the second century B.C., though, the number of farmers declined, creating a manpower shortage for the army. Attempts by reformers to redistribute land in the 130s and 120s B.C. only led to bitter resistance and even political violence from conservatives. The pool of military recruits steadily shrank, and in 113 B.C., Germanic raiders swept past Rome's inadequate army and plundered northern Italy. The state was in crisis.

Because rich senators would not redistribute land to increase the number of recruits to maintain the army that would defend Italy and the empire, a previously obscure soldier named **Marius** (157–86 B.C.) persuaded the Roman assemblies to adopt a different solution to the manpower crisis: Simply abolish property qualifications for military service. This revolutionary policy hugely increased the pool of recruits and the expanded army quickly won its wars. The victories, though, laid the foundations for one hundred years of unparalleled civil violence. In earlier days, soldiers wanted to finish their service and get back to their farms, but most soldiers now had no farms to retire to. Instead, they looked to their commander to set them up with plunder and give them land they could retire on. To succeed, a general therefore needed to take care of his men, which meant seizing land for his troops; land owned by political enemies was hard to resist. The generals were becoming warlords, capable of defying the state if necessary with his landless, loyal, often highly experienced and heavily armed troops. For a man prepared to risk everything, anything was now possible.

## THE AGONY OF THE AEGEAN, 99–70 B.C.

As Roman politics grew increasingly brutal and exploitative, Rome's Italian allies revolted in 91 B.C., demanding better treatment from the ruling elite. They were defeated only after bitter fighting and extreme savagery on both sides. Resentment also burned in the Greek world, and new slave wars broke out in Sicily and Athens. The Hellenistic kings were too weak to exploit the chaos and Rome's weakness, but in 88 B.C. **Mithridates** (mith-ri-dā-tēz; 121–63 B.C.), the non-Greek ruler of the kingdom of Pontus on the Black Sea coast of Anatolia (see Map 24.2), hit Rome suddenly and very hard.

Mithridates had ruled Pontus for thirty years, sometimes as Rome's ally and sometimes by resisting Rome. Seeing Rome distracted by her struggles in Italy and the Greeks' anger toward the Romans he built up a powerful army and overran Bithynia, one of Rome's client kingdoms in Anatolia. He defeated two Roman armies sent against him, then captured, tortured, and executed a Roman general. The war then turned into ethnic cleansing. Mithridates told the Greeks that he would rid the world once and for all of the hated Italian race:

> [Mithridates] wrote in secret to all his satraps and the magistrates in the [Greek] cities [in Asia Minor], instructing them that on the thirtieth day they should rise up and kill all the Romans and Italians in their cities, including their wives and children and freedmen° of Italian origin. Then they should throw the bodies into the street and share their goods with King Mithridates. He would punish anyone who buried the dead or concealed the living. To slaves who killed their masters he offered freedom; to debtors who killed their creditors he offered the

°*freedmen:* Freed slaves who acted as assistants to the Italian *publicani.*

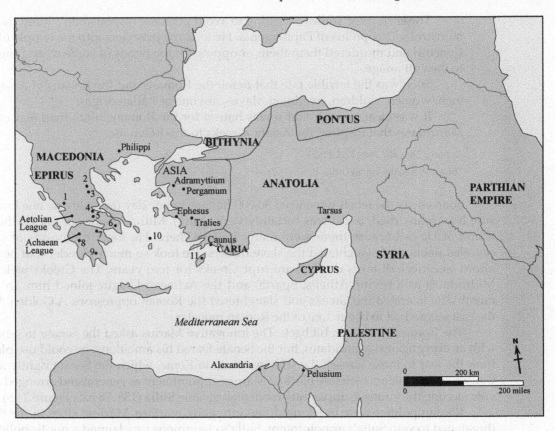

**MAP 24.2** Sites in the east Mediterranean mentioned in this chapter. Aegean cities: (1) Actium; (2) Cynoscephalae; (3) Pharsalus; (4) Thermopylae; (5) Delphi; (6) Athens; (7) Corinth; (8) Olympia; (9) Sparta; (10) Delos; (11) Rhodes. Kom Ombo lies 350 miles (off the south edge of the map) far up the Nile valley in southern Egypt.

remission of half the debt. Mithridates sent these secret letters to all the cities at the same time.

When the appointed day came, disasters of various kinds took place in Asia,° among which I might mention:

The residents of Ephesus tore away from the altar of Artemis° those who had taken refuge there, clasping the image of the goddess, and killed them.

The residents of Pergamum shot with arrows those who had taken refuge at the sanctuary to Asclepius, as they clung to the god's image.

The people of Adramyttium° followed into the sea those who tried to escape by swimming, killed them, then drowned their children.

The Caunians° . . . pursued the Italians into their senate house and, tore them away from the statue of Vesta there, then killed the children in front of their mothers, then killed the mothers, then killed the men.

°*Asia:* That is, western Asia Minor, which had been made a province in 133 B.C.   °*Artemis:* In her great temple at Ephesus, one of the Seven Wonders of the Ancient World.   °*Adramyttium:* On the Ionian coast opposite the island of Lesbos.   °*Caunians:* On the southern coast of Asia Minor opposite Rhodes.

The citizens of Tralles,° wishing to avoid personal responsibility, hired the monstrous Theophilus of Paphlagonia. He took the prisoners into the temple of Concord and murdered them there, chopping off the hands of some who clung to the cult image.

Such was the terrible fate that befell the Romans and the Italians of Asia, men, women, children, freedmen, slaves, anyone of Italian origin.

It was clear enough that it was hatred for the Romans more than fear of Mithridates that inspired the Asiatic Greeks to this behavior.

Appian, *The Civil Wars* 12.4.22–23

°*Tralles:* A wealthy city in Lydia.

Sources say the rebels massacred 80,000 Italians in one day (in reality no one knew for sure how many died, but it was certainly very many). Mithridates even raided the holy island of Delos because there were many Italians there. He freed thousands of slaves, canceled debts, and slaughtered the slave traders. He took so much plunder that he could afford to cancel all taxes on the bankrupt Greeks for five years. The Greeks welcomed Mithridates as a savior. Athens, Sparta, and the Achaean League joined him. In a few months, he liberated the Greeks and slaughtered the Roman oppressors. A Golden Age in the east seemed set to begin, free of the Roman monster.

The Romans, however, hit back. The innovative Marius asked the Senate to send him with an army against Mithridates, but the Senate feared his ambitions; he could use plunder from the war to make himself the strongest man in Rome, which the Senate rightly feared. Conservative senators therefore blocked Marius' appointment as general and arranged a new vote electing the younger, apparently more manageable **Sulla** (138–78 B.C.; Figure 24.8).

Roman politics were breaking down into gang warfare. Marius' allies in the Senate threatened to veto Sulla's appointment. Sulla's champions proclaimed a public holiday so no veto could be issued; Marius' allies declared the proclamation illegal, and—after their supporters won an armed battle outside the senate house—went ahead with their veto, then took a further vote rigged to reinstate Marius as the official commander of the army.

Sulla, however, ignored the Senate's vote and raced south to join the 50,000 troops waiting to sail to Greece against Mithridates. By proclaiming himself as general before the troops he was in reality turning outlaw, taking up arms against the state, and instead of leading the army to Greece, he marched back to Rome. Marius fled. The frightened Senate announced that Marius was now the outlaw, and Sulla the legitimate general. Without a trial, they declared Marius a criminal and murdered his many supporters in the streets. Law and order no longer counted for anything.

Sulla sailed for Greece, but in January 87 B.C., when Sulla was gone, Marius came back to Rome and forced the Senate to reverse itself again, declaring Marius to be a consul and Sulla a criminal! Meanwhile in Greece, because the Senate was not paying his army, Sulla looted everything he could find to raise money. He besieged Athens, plundered Olympia and Delphi, and on March 1, 86 B.C., when Athens fell, Sulla unleashed a frenzy of murder and plunder on Greece's most distinguished city:

Sulla himself entered the city after midnight, when the fortifications between the Dipylon Gate and the Sacred Gates had been thrown down. The moment was made terrible by the blasting of trumpets, the blaring of bugles, and

**FIGURE 24.8**  Lucius Cornelius Sulla, marble, first century B.C.

shouts of men as Sulla turned them loose to plunder the city. They poured down the narrow streets, swords drawn, bent on slaughter. There is no way to know how many died. Their number is estimated by the area that was drowned in blood. The blood shed in the agora alone, without counting that in the rest of the city, flowed so deep that it went all through the potters' quarter inside the Dipylon Gate and even under the gate and outside through the suburb. Many died in this way, but just as many died who through pity and love for their city took their own lives. They thought that their city was doomed to extinction, which made the best of them give up all hope. They even feared to survive, expecting from Sulla no generosity or even humanity.

Plutarch, *Life of Sulla* 14

Meanwhile, Mithridates needed increasing amounts of money to oppose Sulla, who was bearing down on him, so he too started squeezing the Greeks and deporting entire cities that would not pay. After two years of rape, murder, burning, and enslavement of local populations by both sides, Mithridates and Sulla—who had not yet even come to blows—made a private deal. Mithridates would give Sulla money to pay his soldiers, whom Mithridates would allow to punish the very Greeks who had supported him:

> Sulla distributed his army among the remaining places [in Asia Minor] and ordered that the slaves freed by Mithridates must return to their masters. Because many disobeyed his orders, and several cities went into revolt, massacres followed of both free men and slaves, on this or that pretext. He dismantled the walls of many towns. Many others he plundered and sold the inhabitants into slavery. He severely punished the pro-Mithridates faction, both individuals and cities, and especially the Ephesians who had treated with disrespect Roman offerings in their temples.

Sulla summoned the leaders of the Greek cities to Ephesus and collectively fined them 20,000 talents (twice the penalty Rome had imposed on Carthage in 201 B.C.):

> After he had spoken, Sulla apportioned the fine to the various cities and sent men to collect it. The cities were in financial straits and had no choice but to borrow the money at high interest rates, mortgaging, while the soldiers looked on, their theaters, gymnasia, walls, harbors, and public property of every kind. In this way was the money collected and brought to Sulla, and the province of Asia was filled with misery.

Appian, *The Civil Wars* 12.9.61, 63

Sulla returned to Italy in 83 B.C. He left the Aegean a wasteland. Cities went bankrupt and could no longer protect themselves. Pirates extorted protection money and enslaved still more people. In 69 B.C. pirates attacked the sacred island of Delos and left the ancient shrine in ruins, just twenty years after Mithridates had murdered every Italian there. The once-prosperous market never recovered. The only way for cities to protect themselves was to borrow still more money, often at extortionate rates, and to hire private armies. Adding insult to injury, *poleis* were sometimes compelled to honor as euergetists the Italian moneylenders!

By the time Sulla returned to Italy, the aged Marius had died a natural death, but his cronies remained in Rome, and Sulla technically remained an outlaw. His army, though illegal, was now invincible, and rich citizens, eager to be on the winning side, raised private armies (also illegal) to support him. Sulla again marched into the city of Rome and took it with little fighting. For three years, he ruled as *dictator*, previously a legal office for times of emergency but now a constitutional mask for an autocrat. He executed thousands of his enemies, took their land, and settled 120,000 of his veterans on it. He apparently sincerely believed that his outrages would save Rome, returning it to its roots before (as he saw it) populist demagogues like Marius had ruined everything. In 79 B.C. he announced that he had been successful and that the Republic was restored. He retired and died a year later.

Within months, Sulla's settlement came to pieces. Dynamic young generals, learning from Sulla's example, found wars of their own to fight, thereby creating armies loyal to themselves alone. The greatest of the new generation, Gnaeus Pompeius (known as **Pompey the Great**), went as general to Spain in 77 B.C. (Figure 24.9). Another, Lucullus, went to Anatolia in 74 B.C. to finish the war with Mithridates, still dragging on; and a third, the super-rich Crassus, received an army in 72 B.C. to suppress Spartacus' famous slave revolt. In 71 B.C. Pompey and Crassus won their wars, but rather than repeat

**FIGURE 24.9** Pompey the Great, marble, first century B.C.

Sulla's march on Rome or fight each other, they forced the Senate to elect them as consuls for 70 B.C. and demanded that the state give their veterans land. Pompey and Crassus were giving the orders now and the Senate was taking them.

## POMPEY'S GREEK SETTLEMENT, 70–62 B.C.

Sulla left such chaos in the Aegean that the Senate felt compelled to send yet more commanders there to contain the pirates who now controlled the seas. When they failed, in 67 B.C. the Senate gave Pompey an extraordinary command over the entire Mediterranean Sea and everything up to fifty miles inland, with instructions to destroy the pirates. Pompey fell on them with terrifying efficiency, dividing the Mediterranean into thirteen sections and systematically sweeping them from west to east. After just three months he stormed the pirates' principal lair in southwest Asia Minor and wiped them out.

The Senate wanted a Roman new world order. Rome's normal practice was to support local aristocracies who would govern in Roman interests, but Sulla had crushed the Greek upper classes with debt and little power remained to them. Debtors who could not pay, whether individuals or entire cities, fell into the power of their creditors, leaving many *poleis* virtual debt-slaves to private Roman financiers. Lucullus, who had been fighting Mithridates in Anatolia since 74 B.C., took aggressive action to ameliorate the terms under which Roman financiers lent money, and within four years most cities were debt free.

The influential moneymen hated Lucullus for this and lobbied the Senate to depose him. In 66 B.C. they got their way, and the Senate sent Pompey to replace Lucullus and finish off Mithridates. Cornered at last, Mithridates fled into exile. Dreaming of becoming an eastern Hannibal, he planned to cross the Black Sea to Ukraine, then work his way up the River Danube, enrolling central European tribes to murder still more Romans. When Roman agents closed in on him, Mithridates, now an old man, first tried poison, but it would not work because for many years he had taken small doses to make himself immune. He finally ordered one of his own soldiers to stab him to death.

The financiers welcomed Pompey in the east, but Pompey realized that Rome must annex what remained of the Seleucid kingdom if she ever wanted to end the financial and social chaos. He created four new provinces, restored dozens of cities, and swept away a mosaic of tax exemptions and unfair practices. He kept the Hellenistic distinction between privileged Greeks and native populations but made everyone pay taxes to Rome. He doubled Rome's tax revenue while lowering most Greeks' payments. He also marched into Palestine to end a Jewish civil war, but while there reportedly marched into the holy of holies in the Jewish temple, which only the high priest could enter on one day a year. The Jews never forgave Rome for this blasphemy.

The Greeks honored Lucullus and Pompey like gods. One *polis* named Pompey "savior and benefactor of the people of all Asia, guardian of land and sea, because of his excellence and goodwill toward them." When he returned to Rome in 62 B.C., the Senate voted Pompey a triumph "over the whole universe" and the unique title "the Great": He was a Roman Alexander. Pompey had restored order after the disaster of the 80s B.C., saved countless Greek cities from dissolution, and brought peace.

But even Pompey could not solve all the problems in Greece, and abuses continued. In 56 B.C. the prominent Senator Brutus (whom Shakespeare called "the noblest Roman of them all"), who was to assassinate Julius Caesar twelve years later, forced one Greek city in Cyprus to borrow from him at 48 percent interest (which meant that the size of the debt would double every eighteen months). When the Greeks complained, pointing out that Lucullus had passed a law capping interest at 12 percent, Brutus got an exemption from the Senate. When the city elders tried to pay off the loan, the noble Brutus used Roman troops to drive them away. The great orator and politician Cicero (106–43 B.C.) described the situation in a letter of 60 B.C. to his beloved brother, governor of the province of Asia:

> The big problem here is the moneymen. If we go up against them, we will alienate from ourselves and from the Republic a group that has brought us great benefits, which my own efforts° have brought into good relations with the Republic. If on the other hand we go along with them on every occasion, then we will harm the interests of those we are bound to protect,° not to mention threaten their very existence. This is the great difficulty in your entire government, if we wish to see things as they really are . . .
>
> After hearing the grievances of residents in Italy at *their* treatment by the tax-collectors, I can understand what those must suffer in distant lands. In order to satisfy the *publicani*, who have sometimes undertaken contracts wherein they lose money, but also to save the allies from ruin—this problem requires a virtue so exceptional as to be called divine, a virtue that you possess.

°*own efforts:* Cicero had been very active in reconciling the Senate and the financiers and *publicani*.
°*bound to protect:* That is, the Greeks of Asia.

Cicero goes on to justify Roman taxation of the Greeks:

> The Greeks question our right to tax them at all, their greatest grievance, but in fact they paid taxes before the Romans came, living under their own laws. Nor does it make sense for them to complain about the "financiers," when without them they could not pay at all the taxes assessed by Sulla . . . Let Asia think about this, that if it were not for Rome's protection there is no calamity of foreign war or of internal strife to which they would not be subject.
>
> Cicero, *Letters to Quintus* 1.1.11

Rome had brought peace by killing and enslaving Greeks, looting their cities, and extorting protection money, and they should be grateful. Cicero admired the Greeks and attributed his own success to training in Greek studies, but cautioned his brother

> not to get too friendly with the Greeks, except in exceptional cases with those who would be worthy of ancient Greece (if you can find any!). As it is, few of them can be trusted. They are false and they have learned, through long servitude, the arts of exaggerated adulation.
>
> Cicero, *Letters to Quintus* 1.1.5

## THE END OF HELLENISTIC EGYPT, 61–30 B.C.

The Senate never fully recovered control after Sulla's revolt, and from then on individual bigmen dominated Roman history. When Pompey returned from Greece in 62 B.C. he held a secret meeting with Crassus, the wealthy aristocrat who had defeated Spartacus' slave army, and with the young and daring **Julius Caesar**, whose military and political skills were the talk of Rome. Pompey, Crassus, and Caesar pooled their power and wealth to subvert what was left of the ancient constitution. People called them the *triumviri,* or "Gang of Three." Each gang member wanted something: Pompey, to settle his veterans and consolidate his position in Rome; Caesar and Crassus, to build their own armies. Caesar wanted a war in Gaul, roughly modern France, while to build his own glory Crassus looked east to the Parthian Empire that had replaced the Seleucids in Iran and Mesopotamia.

Caesar got his command in Gaul. He borrowed massively to pay his men and in 58 B.C. left Rome just one step ahead of his creditors. A brilliant and ruthless soldier (Figure 24.10), he was also a fine propagandist, sending back to Rome gripping accounts of his military experiences: In modern times school children used to learn Latin from reading his *Gallic Wars*, models of clarity and precise expression. Caesar overran Gaul and even raided Britain in 55 and 54 B.C. By the time he was done, a million natives, a third of Gaul's Celtic population, were dead or enslaved. Caesar was now a great conqueror and had a great army, loyal to him alone.

Crassus also got his command in the east but blundered into a trap in the Syrian desert in 53 B.C. In a catastrophic encounter, the Parthians killed him and most of his troops. With Crassus dead and Caesar still in Gaul, Pompey dominated the Senate. He eventually turned against Caesar, challenging the legality of the war in Gaul, which had gone on for many years. Caesar tried to negotiate, but Pompey refused, and in 50 B.C.,

**FIGURE 24.10** Bust of Julius Caesar, bronze, ca. 47–44 B.C.

the Senate recalled Caesar from Gaul to face trial. The Senate was terrified of Caesar's power, and was taking its stand. But Caesar knew that if he returned to Rome without his army, as the law required, his enemies would certainly kill him; yet if he refused, he would become an outlaw. Like Sulla before him, he chose to break the law and led his army against Rome. In a panic Pompey withdrew to Greece, taking 200 senators with him. In 48 B.C., Caesar defeated Pompey's army in a great battle near a village called Pharsalus in Thessaly. Caesar may have been genuinely pained by having to wage civil war: Surveying the mangled bodies of Rome's aristocracy, he sadly said, *hoc voluerunt*— "This is what they wanted."

Pompey fled across the Aegean to Alexandria, hoping to fight on from the last Greek kingdom, but agents of Ptolemy XIII cut him down on the beach, chopped off his head, and put it in a jar. A few days later, Caesar arrived with 4,000 troops to find Egypt in dynastic crisis once again. Three years earlier, in 51 B.C., the ten-year-old Ptolemy XIII and eighteen-year-old **Cleopatra VII** had become joint rulers, but court factions had shunted Cleopatra aside (Figure 24.11). Caesar said that he had come to Egypt only

**FIGURE 24.11**  Portrait of a Hellenistic queen, probably Cleopatra VII. No certain portraits of Cleopatra survive, but some think this is she because the shape of the nose is reminiscent of the queen's profile on coins. Marble, 30s B.C.

to punish Pompey's murderers and collect the 2,000 talents that Ptolemy owed him, but when Ptolemy was slow to pay, Caesar secretly summoned Cleopatra, thinking he might do better with her. Thus began one of the most famous romances in history:

> Taking only one man with her, Apollodorus the Sicilian, Cleopatra embarked in a small skiff and landed at the palace just as it was getting dark. Because there was no other way to escape detection, she stretched herself out full length inside a bed-sack, which Apollodorus bound with a cord, then carried inside to Caesar. It was this trick that first captivated Caesar, showing her to be a bold coquette. Charmed by his further company with her, Caesar arranged that she be reconciled to her brother Ptolemy and that the two of them rule in Egypt jointly.
>
> Plutarch, *Life of Caesar* 49

The amorous Caesar and the ambitious Cleopatra became lovers in the royal palace during the winter of 48 to 47 B.C. while street battles raged through Alexandria. Ptolemy XIII at first besieged them in the palace, and in a ferocious naval battle in the harbor, Caesar's ship was sunk beneath him. Caesar only escaped with his life by swimming across the huge harbor. Caesar finally outwitted Ptolemy, recovered his 2,000 talents, and left Cleopatra behind—pregnant with an unborn son—as sole ruler of Egypt. Their child would be named Caesarion (in Greek, "Little Caesar").

Caesar returned to Rome and with considerable wisdom attempted to reform the state's basic institutions. Among his innovations was the Julian calendar, which, with minor modifications, is the basis for the modern calendar. Enthusiastic supporters urged him to become Rome's king; twice he publicly rejected the honors pressed on him. Some Senators, though, believed that it was all an act and that Caesar did plan to become sole ruler. If they could only kill him, they thought naively, they could return happily to the days when the Senate had ruled the state.

Caesar magnanimously forgave his enemies and, expecting the same from them, refused to keep a bodyguard. On March 15, 44 B.C., the Ides of March in the Roman calendar, Brutus (the senator who had extorted money from the Cypriots) and **Cassius** led a gang of likeminded senators in murdering Caesar as he was preparing to address the Senate—ironically, in the Theater of Pompey. Their frenzied attack left Caesar bleeding to death from thirty wounds. Brutus and Cassius expected Rome to rise up after their brave deed and welcome the return of former times, but the conspirators' shouts of freedom echoed down empty streets.

Months of chaos ensued before **Mark Antony** (Caesar's right-hand-man), Lepidus (Caesar's cavalry chief), and **Octavian** (Caesar's nineteen-year-old great-nephew, whom Caesar adopted as son and heir in his will) formed a Second Gang of Three to govern the state. The Senate carried on meeting but the Republic effectively ceased to exist in 43 B.C., a year after Caesar's murder. The new *triumviri* pursued Brutus and Cassius into northern Greece, just five years after Caesar had pursued Pompey there. In an enormous battle near Philippi in thrace (where St. Paul later was imprisoned) they crushed Brutus and Cassius' army. The young and cunning Octavian soon forced Lepidus into retirement, and he and Mark Antony divided the Roman Empire between them. Octavian stayed in Rome, controlling the west, while Antony headed east to take over the Greek world and to punish Parthia for destroying Crassus' army a decade before.

Because Antony needed to pay his men, he ordered the dreaded *publicani* to raise money from the Greeks, washing away twenty years of slow recovery in weeks.

> Finally, when he imposed a second levy on the cities,° Hybreas,° speaking on behalf of all Asia, rhetorically and rather to Antony's taste dared to say, "If you are able to tax us twice in one year, then you should arrange for there to be two summers and two harvests." He then added, plainly and boldly, that Asia had already given him 200,000 talents.° "If you have not received this money, then you should ask about it from those who took it. If you have received this money, and no longer have it, then we are ruined." This speech made a strong impression on Antony. For he knew little of what was going on around him, and because he was easy-going he was simple enough to trust his subordinates.

°*on the cities:* His initial extractions had not raised enough money.   °*Hybreas:* Otherwise unknown.   °*200,000 talents:* An exaggeration, although huge sums were extracted.

As part of his fundraising campaign in 41 B.C. Antony summoned Cleopatra to meet him. At first, she ostentatiously ignored him, then

She sailed up the River Kydnos° in a barge with a gilded hut built on the stern, its purple sails spread wide. Its rowers urged it on with silver oars to the sound of the oboe blended with pan-pipes and the lyre. She herself lay beneath a gold-spangled canopy, adorned like Aphrodite in a painting. Boys dressed up to look like cupids° in a painting stood on either side and cooled her with a fan. Likewise her most beautiful attendants, arrayed like Nereids or Graces,° stood beside the rudders or the tackle of the sails. Wonderful scents came from many censers and floated to the river banks. Crowds of people accompanied the boat from the mouth of the river, along both banks, and others came down from the city of Tarsus to behold the spectacle. Gradually the crowds thinned out in the marketplace until Antony was left there alone, sitting on his throne. The word went abroad that Aphrodite had come to revel with Dionysus, for the benefit of Asia.

°*River Kydnos:* In southern Asia Minor.   °*cupids:* Aphrodite's boyish companions, who fired arrows of love.   °*Graces:* Greek mythical figures.

Cleopatra hosted a grand banquet for Antony that evening and

on the next day Antony hosted Cleopatra, hoping to surpass her in magnificence and elegance, but falling far short in both categories. Being bested, he was the first to rail against the meagerness and rough quality of his own arrangements. Cleopatra saw from Antony's jokes that he was much the soldier and no man of the court and she behaved toward him in the same way, not holding back and with great boldness. For, as we are told, her beauty was not in and of itself without compare, nor such as to strike one who saw her, but conversation with her had an irresistible charm. Her very presence, enlivened by a persuasiveness and a character that she somehow cast about all her relationships with others, was highly stimulating. There was a sweetness even in the sounds of her voice. Her tongue, like an instrument with many strings, she turned to the speaking of many languages . . .

Instead of attacking Parthia, Antony followed Cleopatra to Alexandria. While his moneymen ran amok in the Greek world, taking everything, he surrendered himself to pleasure, at least according to stories filtered through his enemy Octavian. So Plutarch writes:

Plato describes four types of flattery, but Cleopatra knew a thousand. No matter whether Antony was in a somber or happy mood, she could find some device to delight and charm him. She utterly occupied his attention and would not release him day or night. She diced, drank, and hunted with him, and when he practiced with weapons, she watched.

At night Antony liked to wander about in the city, standing at peoples' doors and windows and mocking those inside. She would accompany him, dressed as a maidservant, and would participate in his other madcap pranks, for he liked to go out dressed as a slave. On such occasions he was always roundly insulted and sometimes beaten up before he returned to the palace, though most guessed who he was. In fact the Alexandrians rather liked his buffoonery and enjoyed these amusements in a refined and elegant way. They liked him personally and used to say that Antony put on his tragic mask for the Romans and kept the comic mask for themselves.

Plutarch, *Life of Antony* 24–27 (excerpts)

While Antony played, Octavian plotted. Antony, Octavian told the people of Rome, planned to move the empire's capital from Rome to Alexandria and to deliver Roman power to the Greeks. The proud senators would have to fall to the ground and kiss the feet of an alien Macedonian/Egyptian queen!

When Antony finally got around to attacking Parthia, the campaign was a disaster, and the sham triumph he celebrated in Alexandria further offended public opinion back in Rome. In 40 B.C., Antony had married Octavian's sister Octavia in order to strengthen the two men's political alliance, but in 37 he bigamously married Cleopatra too; Antony might have argued that his Egyptian union was not valid under Roman law. In 34 B.C. he recognized Caesar's son Caesarion and his own daughter and two sons by Cleopatra as legitimate and announced that he was dividing the Greek world and Mesopotamia between the four children. In 32 B.C., he divorced Octavia.

The Senate back in Rome, under Octavian's control, declared Antony a public enemy. For the third time in seventeen years, a Roman civil war would be decided in Greece. Most former supporters of Julius Caesar backed Antony, and Cleopatra provided troops. Antony dared not take the war to Italy, where Octavian was so strong, but in 31 B.C. he advanced to Actium, a promontory on the coast of northwest Greece near the border with modern Albania, just across from Italy. Octavian crossed to meet him, bottled up Antony's fleet, and cut off his supplies.

Antony decided to fight his way out by sea, but much of his fleet, realizing that the tide had turned in Octavian's favor, ignored the order to attack. Panicking, Antony and Cleopatra fled with forty ships to Egypt, leaving the Egyptian/Roman army and many ships behind. Thus abandoned, Antony's men defected. Octavian sent word that he would give Cleopatra anything she wanted if she would only murder or banish Antony. She refused.

Octavian invaded Egypt. Antony challenged Octavian to single combat, but Octavian replied that Antony had other ways to end his life. As Antony prepared to defend Alexandria, his ships and cavalry deserted him. According to Plutarch's colorful account, Antony

> retreated into the city [of Alexandria], crying out that Cleopatra had betrayed him to those against whom he had fought for her sake. In terror at his anger and madness, Cleopatra fled to her tomb and let fall the drop-doors that were strengthened with bolts and bars. She sent messengers to tell Antony that she was dead. Antony believed them and said to himself, "Why do you hesitate? Tychê has taken away your sole remaining reason for wanting to stay alive . . . "
>
> Now Antony had a trusted slave whose name was Eros. Long before he had instructed Eros to kill him if the need arose, and now he asked him to do it. Eros unsheathed his sword and held it aloft as if he were about to kill him, then turned away his face and killed himself. He fell at Antony's feet. "Well done," Antony said, "you could not do it yourself but you have shown me what I must do." He stabbed himself in the belly with his own sword and fell onto the bed. But the wound did not kill him quickly . . .

While dying, Antony learned that Cleopatra was really still alive (Shakespeare uses this same motif of the falsely reported death in *Romeo and Juliet*, one of the best known stories in the world):

Antony ordered his slaves to lift him up. They carried him in their arms to the doors of Cleopatra's tomb. She would not open the doors, but showing herself at a window she let down cords and rope. The slaves attached the ropes to Antony, and Cleopatra drew him up, assisted by the only two women she allowed to accompany her into the tomb. Those who were there say there was never so pitiable a sight. Covered in blood, in his death throws, Antony reached out his hands toward Cleopatra as he dangled in the air. The task was not easy for women, and barely could Cleopatra draw him up, clinging with her hands and straining in her face, pulling at the cord. Those below shouted out encouragement and shared in her pain . . .

When she had got him up she lay him on a bed, tore off her dress and spread it over him, beat and scratched her breasts and spread the blood of his wounds on her face. She called him lord, and husband, and emperor, and nearly forgot her own suffering in her pity for his.

Antony . . . begged her to look past his shift in fortune and to remember the glories he had won and to remember that he had reached the highest fame and power of any man in the world, and that now it was not dishonorable to die as a Roman, conquered by a Roman.

Plutarch, *Life of Antony* 76–77

Antony's death, we are told, moved even the hardened Octavian. He allowed Cleopatra to prepare Antony's body for burial with her own hands. She attempted suicide, but when that failed she began a complicated negotiation with Octavian, hoping he would allow her and Caesarion to rule Egypt as his clients. When it became clear that Octavian would allow no such thing, she again shut herself in the tomb:

According to one account an asp° was brought in a basket filled with figs, hidden in the leaves, for she had desired that the snake should fall upon her without her knowing. But when she picked up some of the figs she saw it, so the story goes, and so bared her arm. Saying "Here it is," she extended her arm to be bitten. According to another account the asp was hidden in a pitcher and Cleopatra provoked it with a golden spindle until it leaped out and struck her arm. In fact nobody knows the truth. Another story reports that she carried poison with her concealed in a comb that she wore in her hair. However no inflammation or other symptom of poison ever appeared on her body. Nor was the asp ever found in the tomb, but some say that its trail was found in the beach on the side of the tomb where the windows faced the sea . . .

Octavian was unhappy about her death,° but he had to admit that she showed nobility of spirit. He ordered that she be buried with royal splendor and display, and that she be placed next to Antony.

Plutarch, *Life of Antony* 86

°*asp:* Apparently a cobra.   °*death:* Evidently he wanted to parade her in chains in a Roman triumph, then kill her at the end.

Octavian ordered that Caesarion, Caesar's son, be strangled. Caesarion was then seventeen years old and the last Ptolemy to rule in Egypt (with his mother). As Octavian put it: "Two Caesars is one too many." Cleopatra's other children were given to Octavia to raise. Cleopatra's daughter later married a North African king, but the two boys drop from history (the Roman emperor Caligula killed the daughter's son, ending the Ptolemaic line). Octavian annexed Egypt as his private possession and headed back to Rome.

## AFTERMATH

With a flourish, Octavian announced that the Republic was restored. Things would be as once they were, when Rome was Rome and everyone knew it. In reality everyone knew that things could never be the same, but pretence was preferable to further conflict. In gratitude for restoring the ancient order, the Senate voted Octavian a new name, **Augustus** ("most revered one"), and proclaimed him *princeps* (**prin**-keps)—not king, but "first citizen." Behind a screen of titles, he would rule the empire for forty-four peaceful, prosperous years. The Greek world slowly recovered from the civil wars Romans had fought across its soil. Rome founded new cities and encouraged development. The old Greek independence was gone, but a new, modern, more sedate, and prosperous urban society developed. Its aristocrats built fine theaters and its famous cities attracted gifts from rich Romans. Athens did particularly well (Figure 24.12). Roman forms of literature and art flourished, sophisticated adaptations of Greek models. The literary achievements of the poets Vergil (70–19 B.C.) and Horace (65–8 B.C.) have in some ways never been surpassed. Greece's stoic philosophers and professors of rhetoric earned good salaries in Rome, Gaul, and Britain. Emperors sported Greek hairstyles and beards and wrote treatises on Stoic philosophy.

**FIGURE 24.12** The temple to Olympian Zeus beneath the Athenian Acropolis, begun in the sixth century B.C. by the tyrant Pisistratus and finished 600 years later by the Roman emperor Hadrian (ruled A.D. 117–138).

# Chapter 24 • The Coming of Rome, 220–30 B.C.  **539**

The classical world was ending. Christianity grew from a tiny Hebrew sect to a major cultural force that reached right around the planet. As most Jews read scriptures in the Greek *Septuagint,* so were the founding documents of Christianity written in Greek. In A.D. 312 the emperor Constantine became Christian, and in A.D. 391 Christianity became the empire's official faith. Many early Christians claimed that God had revealed to them many of the same ethical precepts that Socrates and Plato reached through reason, but in the fourth century A.D., some Christian thinkers argued that revealed wisdom made philosophical learning unnecessary. Christianity was from the beginning a complicated mixture of Greek philosophy, Hebrew myth and ritual, the theology of Paul, and the teachings of Jesus.

The western Roman Empire began breaking up in the third century A.D. under the pressure of population movements from central Asia flooding over its frontiers, but the urbanized Greek east survived. In A.D. 330 the emperor Constantine founded a new city, Constantinople, to rule over the eastern parts of the Roman Empire. It stood on the site of Byzantium, an ancient Greek city guarding the passage from the Mediterranean to the Black Sea; once again the Greek world was the center of political power in western Eurasia. The western empire broke into Germanic kingdoms in the fifth century A.D., but the Greek-speaking eastern empire continued classical traditions for another thousand years. Ancient literary genres—history, philosophy, drama—declined after the sixth century A.D., and in the Balkans, the Byzantine Empire (as we call the Greek part of the old Roman Empire) was an utterly different world from Pericles' Athens. But while backward, impoverished, and depopulated western Europe turned its back on the ancient Greeks during its long Middle Ages, the Greek scholars of Byzantium, and the Arabs who now occupied the formerly Greek cities of western Asia Minor and Egypt, copied out, translated, and passed on the writings of Aristotle and Thucydides.

## Key Terms

Republic, 507
Senate, 507
consuls, 507
triumph, 509
Hiero II, 510
*publicani,* 511
Hannibal, 512

Marcellus, 513
Scipio, 514
Cynoscephalae, 516
Cato, 521
Brutus, 523
Marius, 524
Mithridates, 524

Sulla, 526
Pompey the Great, 528
Julius Caesar, 531
Cleopatra VII, 532
Cassius, 534
Mark Antony, 534
Octavian/Augustus, 538

## Further Reading

Alcock, Susan, *Graecia Capta* (Cambridge, UK, 1993). Pioneering study using archaeological evidence to understand social change in Hellenistic and Roman Greece.

Astin, A. E., *Cato the Censor* (Oxford, 1967). Classic account of Cato's life and struggles against Hellenism.

Badian, Ernst, *Roman Imperialism in the Late Republic* (Ithaca, NY, 1968). An attempt to understand the Romans' perspective on their imperial expansion.

_____, *Publicans and Sinners* (Ithaca, NY, 1972). Classic study of the *publicani* in the period covered by this chapter.

Beard, Mary, *The Roman Triumph* (London, 2008). Entertaining account of this distinctive Roman ritual.

Cornell, Timothy, *The Beginnings of Rome* (London, 1994). Detailed review of Roman history and archaeology from the earliest times through 264 B.C.

Eckstein, Arthur, *Mediterranean Anarchy, Interstate War, and the Rise of Rome* (Berkeley, 2007). Historical background to Rome's rise.

Gruen, Erich, *The Hellenistic East and the Coming of Rome,* 2 vols. (Berkeley, 1984). Detailed analysis of Rome and the Greek world, focusing on Polybius' account.

Harris, William V., *War and Imperialism in Republican Rome, 327–70 B.C.* (Oxford, 1979). Argues that greed drove Rome's expansion.

Hopkins, Keith, *Conquerors and Slaves* (Cambridge, UK, 1978). Outstanding sociological analysis of the interconnection of war, slavery, economics, and institutions in Rome between the Punic Wars and Augustus.

Kallet-Marx, Robert, *Hegemony to Empire: The Development of the Roman Imperium in the East from 148–62 B.C.* (Berkeley, 1995). Good survey of Rome's expansion into the Greek world.

Lancel, Serge, *Hannibal* (Oxford, 2003). Biography of the Carthaginian general.

Mayor, Adrienne, *The Poison King: The Life and Legend of Mithridates the Great* (Princeton, 2009). Fascinating account of the greatest threat Rome ever faced in the Greek world.

Meier, Christian, *Caesar* (New York, 1982). Excellent biography.

Strauss, Barry, *The Spartacus War* (New York, 2009). Gripping account of the great slave uprising against Rome.

Woolf, Greg, *Et Tu, Brute?* (Cambridge, MA, 2007). Excellent and entertaining study of what Caesar's murder tells us about politics.

**ANCIENT TEXTS**

Appian, *The Civil Wars,* tr. John Carter (New York, 1996). A vital but underappreciated source for history of the late Roman Republic.

Austin, Michel, *The Hellenistic World* (Cambridge, UK, 1981). Superb selection of ancient sources.

Livy, *Rome and the Mediterranean,* tr. Henry Bettenson (New York, 1976). Books 31–45 of Livy's history of Rome, covering the period 201–167 B.C.

Plutarch, *Lives of Marius, Sulla, Pompey and Caesar, The Fall of the Roman Republic,* tr. Rex Warner (Harmondsworth, UK, 1958), and of Fabius, Marcellus, Cato, and Mark Antony in *Makers of Rome,* tr. Ian Scott-Kilvert (Harmondsworth, UK, 1965). Biographies of the major Roman generals involved in the destruction of the Hellenistic world.

Polybius, *The Rise of the Roman Empire,* tr. Ian Scott-Kilvert (New York, 1979). The main surviving parts of Polybius' account of Rome and the Greeks.

Suetonius, *Lives of Julius Caesar and Augustus.* In *The Twelve Caesars,* tr. Robert Graves (Harmondsworth, UK, 1957). Highly entertaining biographies.

## CHAPTER 25

# Conclusion

We have come a long way, from the end of the last Ice Age to the Roman Empire. We have seen how in the first millennium B.C. the Greeks created a remarkable culture. We have described its expansion around the Mediterranean basin, its struggles with Persia and Carthage, and how in the fourth century B.C. the Greek-speaking Macedonians took over the Greek world, only to succumb to Rome. We close our book by summing up the major phases in the story of ancient Greece.

## THE BRONZE AGE (CA. 3000–1200 B.C.; Chapter 4)

The Bronze Age provides the prologue. Complex civilizations with large populations, grand monuments, beautiful art, and strong class divisions first developed on this planet in the Near East and Egypt around 3000 B.C. Literate elites with special access to divine power oversaw complex divisions of labor and networks of skilled craftsmen and literate officials. The rulers centralized power under palatial control, creating command economies that told people what to produce, where, and when, and then redistributed the produce among the population according to status and need. Similar systems organized around palaces, and temples spread east onto the Iranian plateau and west into the Aegean Sea by 2000 B.C. Minoan and Mycenaean society stood on the fringes of this Near Eastern world.

## THE DARK AGE (CA. 1200–800 B.C.; Chapter 5)

Around 1200 B.C., Bronze Age centers burned to the ground all round the east Mediterranean. Populations shrank and many advanced crafts disappeared. The collapse, whose causes remain unclear, was most severe in the Aegean. By 1000 B.C. small groups of Greeks huddled around Bronze Age ruins, largely cut off from the outside world. The art of writing was lost and complex social hierarchies dissolved. Greece was separated from the world of Bronze Age palaces that survived in modified forms in Egypt and the Near East. We know little about the Greek Dark Age, but in some way the Classical Period grew from it.

## THE ARCHAIC PERIOD (CA. 800–500 B.C.; Chapters 6–10)

All across the Mediterranean, population increased in the eighth century B.C. Trade boomed. Thousands of Greeks emigrated to Sicily, southern Italy, and points further west; thousands more moved to the Black Sea coasts. They tied the Aegean to other regions, and traders exploited the Mediterranean's economic and cultural diversity.

The new colonies and the older communities that dispatched them crystallized into hundreds of small city-states, governed very differently from the communities that had been ruled by the Bronze Age palaces. The principle of equality among male citizens was overriding. The Greek city-states enthusiastically rejected the notion that intimacy with divine power translated into political authority. People believed in gods, built temples, and offered sacrifice, but unlike in the ancient Near Eastern civilizations there was no priestly caste and there was no scribal class that served the state and religion.

In some ways, the Greek universe was bleak: Humanity stood alone, without any god's guidance. Greeks asked: How can we govern society if we are on our own? To answer this question Greeks developed increasingly rational forms of inquiry to determine their place in the cosmos. If there is no source of wisdom outside human deliberation, they concluded, then it made sense to involve as many men in government as possible, not just a privileged elite. The more Greeks moved toward democracy, breaking down barriers within the male community, the more they strengthened barriers between free citizen males and everyone else: women, foreigners, and slaves, who were imported in increasing numbers.

Through the long centuries between the rise of the Roman Empire and the European Enlightenment of the eighteenth century A.D. no one much cared about the political, moral, intellectual, and religious problems faced by the Archaic Greeks. When in the eighteenth century A.D. west Europeans also began to reject the claims of divine monarchy, struggling with similar questions about reason, citizenship, and equality, historians and politicians realized that others had faced parallel problems a long time ago, and once again turned to the literature of ancient Greece.

## THE CLASSICAL PERIOD (CA. 500–350 B.C.; Chapters 11–18)

As they became economic and military powers, the Greeks drew the attention of the mighty Persian Empire in the east and the rich city of Carthage in the west. Archaic culture had developed in a power vacuum, with few external threats. All that ended in 480 B.C. To resist Persian and Carthaginian attacks, Greeks in the Aegean and Sicily alike formed larger political units. If Greeks had not formed such larger units, they would soon have been forced into such units anyway, as subjects of the great empires that threatened them.

Many Greeks thought that the larger political units that emerged after 480 B.C. were temporary, but they were not. Athens and Syracuse created multi-city states that other *poleis* viewed as tyrannical empires. Money flowed into Athens and Syracuse, fueling one of history's greatest cultural explosions. In Athens, above all, artists, poets, and intellectuals wondered how a democratic city of equal men could justly rule over others and how great individuals could fit into a society of equals.

The *poleis* became more complex and diverse. The more they expanded their power, the more violent their wars became. The struggle of Athens against Sparta drew in Syracuse, then neighboring peoples in Sicily and Macedon, and finally Persia and

Carthage. The scale of war far outstripped the *poleis'* ability to pay, forcing them to turn outward for resources to their mighty imperial foes, and upward, to their own rich citizens. After 404 B.C., when the Athenian empire collapsed, no individual *polis* could compete in the enlarged world, and as the rich took more responsibility for paying for security, they chafed at restrictive fifth-century egalitarian ideals.

Classical thought and art captivated Europeans and Americans in the eighteenth, nineteenth, and twentieth centuries A.D. The sublime ideals of human potential that its poets, sculptors, and painters expressed struck responsive chords, while Thucydides laid bare the dark recesses of human nature that morally virtuous leaders must master if they wish to survive on the stage of power. Politicians, journalists, and artists saw the Greeks through the prism of their own times but also made sense of their own times by studying the Greeks' triumphs and disasters. In some European countries, educators concluded that training in Greek and Latin language, history, art, and philosophy was all that young people needed to lead the modern world, and that there was no true education without knowledge of classical Greece.

## THE MACEDONIAN TAKEOVER (CA. 350–323 B.C.; Chapters 19–21)

The Aegean *poleis*, hungry for manpower and resources, drew northern neighbors like Macedonia into their conflicts in the fifth and fourth centuries B.C. These large, loosely organized societies had previously counted for little in Greek affairs, but in the fourth century they learned to raise taxes, tame their noblemen, and organize armies. In the 370s B.C. Jason of Thessaly almost conquered the Aegean; after 350 B.C., Philip of Macedon actually did so. In the 330s B.C. Alexander the Great actually conquered the Persian Empire, and little *poleis* either combined into larger units, like the Aetolian and Achaean Leagues, or ceased to have any importance.

Alexander's rampage through the Near East brought into question a central Greek belief—that a gulf separates man from god. Alexander supposed that only a god could do what he had done, and many agreed. His death cut off his extreme vision, but, before 300 B.C., even democratic Athens honored some men as gods.

## THE HELLENISTIC PERIOD (CA. 323–30 B.C.; Chapters 22–24)

Third-century B.C. artists and thinkers wondered how they could combine Greece's ancient traditions with the realities of great kings ruling populations of millions, including many non-Greeks. In some ways, the third century B.C. was the highpoint of the history of the Greek cities, which spread all over western Asia, reached record sizes, and adorned themselves as never before. Within the cities, however, power shifted steadily toward rich euergetists, and the cities' security increasingly depended on kings in Macedonia, Syria, and Egypt.

The old *polis* was gone forever. Some cities openly sold citizenship to rich foreigners, and the old struggles between democrats and oligarchs became a thing of the past. Squabbles between little cities like Athens and Sparta had little importance. Stoic philosophers, complex Alexandrian poetry, and the Great Altar at Pergamum belonged to a world massively changed from the classical.

In the second and first centuries B.C., the unstoppable advance of Roman power turned upside down the sophisticated, wealthy Hellenistic kingdoms. Greek-speakers struggled to understand how this could happen, while their Roman conquerors struggled to make sense of the Greek world they had suddenly mastered. Roman aristocrats absorbed and reformulated Hellenistic culture within their new world order.

Through the nineteenth and twentieth centuries A.D., Hellenistic history was largely neglected. Its kings, empires, fussy buildings, and pedantic professors seemed the antithesis of what made classical Greece important. However, in the twenty-first century A.D., increasing globalization and enhanced mobility has made the Hellenistic world look rather familiar; and the world created by the Romans' conquest of the whole Mediterranean is in some ways even more like our own. In a world with only one superpower, how should that state use its power for good?

## CONCLUSION

We might think of Greek history as being something like the swing of a pendulum. The arc began in the Bronze Age with a society in which status was distributed along a continuum, from exalted king to humble palace servant tied to the land. In the fifth century B.C., the pendulum reached the opposite point of its arc in societies divided sharply between free male citizens and all the others. The free, equal male citizens ruled the *polis*, denying distinctions within their ranks and dominating those who were not male citizens. Around 400 B.C., the pendulum began swinging back to a world of god-kings and complex overlapping hierarchies based on wealth, gender, ethnicity, and religion.

The Greeks lived a remarkable story, an adventure in egalitarianism that has guided intellectuals, artists, and politicians for the last 250 years. The way we now tell the story is quite different from John Keats' idealization of Greece as the source of beauty and truth, which we quoted at the beginning of this book. The ancient Greeks, like us, were human, finding real solutions for real problems, to the best of their ability, in a dangerous and complex world. Their millennium-long experiment bequeathed a lasting legacy, and the Greeks remain good to think with as we go forward with our own adventure.

# PRONUNCIATION GUIDE

## ROMAN AND GREEK FORMS OF CLASSICAL NAMES: SPELLING AND PRONUNCIATION

In this book we will enter a forest of unfamiliar names and often be at a loss how to pronounce them. Unfortunately, even professionals can be unsure of how to pronounce many names, and, moreover, they are pronounced differently in, for example, England and the USA. Standard rules, however, govern the pronunciation of proper names from classical Greece as they were later transliterated into the Latin alphabet. In this process a few changes had to be made, and the Latin forms, therefore, are somewhat different from the Greek ones. Latin is presently broken up into the Romance languages (Italian, French, Spanish, and Portuguese), each of which has its own peculiarities of spelling and pronunciation. English is not a Romance language, but its speakers were members of the western Christian Church, which—in its Roman Catholic branch—used Latin for its liturgy and for almost all of its business down to the mid-twentieth century. In consequence, throughout all western Europe, Latin was a universal second language for the educated classes for about 1500 years. For this reason, the most familiar spellings of the proper names of ancient Greek historical and literary figures are Latinized forms of Greek names, sometimes further altered in standard English. Because of their familiarity, these are the forms used (mostly) in this book. About a hundred years ago, however, some scholars and translators urged a reform of this system and the use of the Greek forms of classical names rendered in the Roman alphabet, so that one may find tales about "Klytaimnestra," "Akhilleus," and others. We have occasionally allowed some of these Greek forms in this book, especially in quoted passages where the names appear only once or twice. To aid reference, because such Greek forms often appear in English translations, the following index gives the Greek forms in parentheses after the Latinized forms.

The principal differences between the Latinized and Greek forms are as follows:

Latin *j* = Greek *i*: Jason = Iason

Latin *c* = Greek *k*: Cimon = Kimon

Latin *ae* or *e* = Greek *ai*: Gaea = Gaia; Clytemnestra = Klytaimnestra

Latin *e* or *i* = Greek *ei*: Rhea = Rheia; Pisistratus = Peisistratus

Latin *i* = Greek *oi*: Delphi = Delphoi

Latin *oe* = Greek *oi*: Oedipus = Oidipous

Latin *u* = Greek *ou*: Creusa = Kreousa

Latin *y* = Greek *u* (sometimes): Clytemnestra = Klutaimnestra

Latin final *a* = Greek *e*: Athena = Athene

Latin final *um* = Greek *on*: stadium = stadion

Latin final *us* = Greek *os*: Asclepius = Asklepios

Finally, the Greek letter *chi* (χ) is rendered *ch* in Latin but either *ch* or *kh* in the Greek forms.

How ancient Greek names are pronounced today in English is a matter on which people agree to disagree; certainly an ancient Greek would be astonished at the ordinary English pronunciation of his or her name. There is little agreement on how to pronounce the vowels, so one hears the name of the Athenian playwright pronounced as *E*-schylus or *Ē*-schylus or sometimes *Ī*-schylus. Is the famous king of Thebes called *E*-dipus or *Ē*-dipus? With many names, however, there is a conventional pronunciation, which we give in parentheses in the index, as we do in the text. Consonants, which arouse less dispute, tend to follow the following rules in the anglicized forms of words Latinized from the original Greek:

The letters *c* and *g* are "soft" before *e* and *i* sounds (not necessarily letters) and "hard" before *a*, *o*, and *u* sounds in words and names of Greek or Latin origin: for example, *c*enter, *C*aesar, *c*ivic, *c*ycle; *g*entle, E*u*gene, a*g*ile, but *c*ategory, *c*ooperate, *c*uneiform; *g*arrulous, *g*onad, *g*usto. Notice the requirement "in words of Greek or Latin origin": "get" and "give" are of Germanic origin and do not follow the rule.

The Greek letter *chi* (χ), written *ch*, represented a sound like *k* but pronounced back in the throat; in English it is pronounced like the "hard" *c* in "card," not like the *ch* of "*ch*icken."

Final *e* must be pronounced as a separate syllable: Daph-*ñe*, Cir-*c̄e*. To remind the reader of this rule, we place a circumflex over the *e* in such syllables (except for the common Aphrodite): Daphn*ê*, Circ*ê* . Final *es* is also pronounced, as in Achill*ēs*.

Another problem is the accent—where to stress the word. Latin and Greek rely chiefly on pitch and quantity, whereas English depends on stress. Quantity is the length of time it takes to pronounce a syllable; pitch is the register of the voice. Because of the influence of Latin on Western culture, the English accent on proper names follows the rule that governs the pronunciation of Latin: If the next to last syllable is "long," it is accented; if it is not "long," the syllable before it is accented. How does one know whether a syllable is "long" or "short"? If the next-to-last syllable ends with two consonants, or if it contains a diphthong (-*ae*-, -*oe*-, -*au*-, -*ei*-), or if it contains a vowel "long" by nature, it must be accented. Otherwise, the accent goes on the third syllable from the end. But how does one know whether a vowel is long by nature? Unfortunately, only by knowing Latin well can you know whether a vowel is long by nature.

These rules are useful but complex. For many it will be easiest simply to consult the pronunciation given after each name in the text and in the index, where the syllable to be accented is printed in **bold** characters. Vowels should be pronounced according to this key:

ā = pay
ē = be
ī = wife
ō = no
ū = cute

# PHOTO CREDITS

**Chapter 1:** Barry B. Powell, 2; Scala, Art Resource, NY, 3; Barry B. Powell, 4, 8, and 10.

**Chapter 2:** Charlie Waite, Getty Images Inc.—Stone Allstock, 13; © Gian Berto Vanni/CORBIS, 13; Nick Nicholls © The British Museum, 22; Art Resource/The British Museum Great Court Ltd., © The Trustees of The British Museum, 23.

**Chapter 3:** Nick Nicholls © The British Museum, 29; The Granger Collection, NY, 30; Ashmolean Museum, Oxford, 31; Nick Nicholls © The British Museum, 33; Phintias (Painter), "Attic red-figure Kylix." The J. Paul Getty Museum, Villa Collection, California. Malibu 80. AE.31 © The J. Paul Getty Museum, 35; Schlossmuseum, Gotha, Germany, Stiftung Schloss Friedenstein, 36.

**Chapter 4:** Barry B. Powell, 42, 43, 44, and 47; Dorling Kindersley, Museum of Cycladic Art © Nicholas P. Goulandris Foundation—Museum of Cycladic Art, Athens. N.P. Goulandras Collection, no. 206, 48; The Art Archive/National Archaeological Museum Athens/Dagli Orti, 49; William Donahue © Dorling Kindersley, 50; Barry B. Powell, 51; Bull-leaping (Toreador Fresco), from the palace at Knossos, Minoan, c. 1450–1400 B.C. Greece. Courtesy of Nimatallah/Art Resource, NY, 52; R. Sheridan, The Ancient Art & Architecture Collection Ltd., 53; Dean Fox, SuperStock, Inc. 54; Hellenic Republic Ministry of Culture, Archaeological Receipts Funds, 55; Getty Images, Inc.—Photodisc./Royalty Free, 56; Knossos, Crete/Kurt Scholz/Superstock, 56; © Hugh Sackett; Reproduced with permission of the British School at Athens, 57; Patricia C. Rice, 58; Erich Lessing, Art Resource, NY, 58; Margot Granitsas, Photo Researchers, Inc., 59; Nimtallah, Art Resource, NY, 60; Alison Frantz Photographic Collection, American School of Classical Studies at Athens, 60; National Archaeological Museum, Hellenic Ministry of Culture—Archaeological Receipts Fund, 61; Deutsches Archäologisches Institut, Athens, German Archaeological Institute, Greece, Mykene 63, 63; Piet de Jong, The Throne Room of the Megaron. Courtesy of The Department of Classics, University of Cincinnati, 64.

**Chapter 5:** Barry B. Powell, 73 and 74; Plate 13 of "Lefkandi II: The Protogeometric Building at Toumba," ed. by M.R. Popham, P.G. Calligas, L.H. Sackett, Part 2, The Excavation, Architecture and Finds, with J. Coulton and H.W. Catling, The British School of Archaeology at Athens, 1993. Reproduced with permission of the British School at Athens, 76; Barry B. Powell, 77; Nick Nicholls © The British Museum, 81; Greek Vases VIII Century B.C. Attic Geometric Vase, Dipylon: colossal, with funeral scenes. H.40-1/2". The Metropolitan Museum of Art, Rogers Fund, 1914 (14.130.14). All rights reserved, The Metropolitan Museum of Art, 88; Original drawing by Barry B. Powell, 1986, 91.

**Chapter 6:** Bildarchiv Preussischer Kulturbesitz, Art Resource, NY, 94; Art Resource/The British Museum Great Court Ltd., © The Trustees of The British Museum, 96; The Milman Parry Collection of Oral Literature, Harvard University, 97; Corbis/Bettmann, 101; Circle of Antimenes Painter (Greek, Attic, active 530–510 B.C.). Dinos, c. 520–510 B.C. Black-figure terracotta, D. 50.8 cm. The Cleveland Museum of Art. John L. Severance Fund, 111; Barry B. Powell, 112; Archeological Museum, Eleusis, 546, Erich Lessing, Art Resource, NY, 115; Ivor Kerslake ©The British Museum, 116.

**Chapter 7:** Musée du Louvre/Reunion des Musées Nationaux, Paris, France. Art Resource, NY, 127; Delphi, Picture Desk, Inc./Kobal Collection, 128; Art Resource/The British Museum Great Court Ltd., © The British Museum, 129; Alinari, Art Resource, NY, 131; Hirmer Fotoarchiv, 133; Alinari, Art Resource, NY, 134; Erich Lessing, Art Resource, NY, 136; Herve Lewandowski, Art Resource, NY, 136; Staatliche Antikensammlungen und Glypthothek, Munich, Germany, 137; The Lykaon Painter, "Pelike (storage jar)," Greek, Classical Period, c. 440 B.C.; ceramic, red-figure; Height: 47.4 cm (18-11/16"); diameter: 34.3 cm (13-1/2")/ Museum of Fine Arts, Boston, William Amory Gardner Fund, 34.79. Photograph © 2004 Museum of Fine Arts, Boston, 141; Barry B. Powell, 144; Orpheus Painter (5th B.C.), "Orpheus among the Thracians," Red-figure crater from Gela, ca. 450 B.C.; H: 50.5 cm, view 1/2 INV. V.I. 3172. Photo: Johannes Laurentius. Antikensammlung, Staatliche Museen zu Berlin, Germany. Bildarchiv Preussischer Kulturbesitz, Art Resource, NY, 145; Art Resource/The British Museum Great Court Ltd., © The British Museum, 146.

**Chapter 8:** Barry B. Powell, 152; John Heseltine © Dorling Kindersley, 153; © Foto Marburg/Art Resource, NY, 155; Hirmer Fotoarchiv, Munich, Germany, 155; "Reproduced with the permission of the Masters and Fellows of Corpus Christi College and of the Fitzwilliam Museum Cambridge. © Fitzwilliam Museum Cambridge," 159; Scala, Art Resource, NY, 162; Barry B. Powell, 165; Art Resource/The British Museum Great Court Ltd., © The British Museum, 171.

**Chapter 9:** Barry B. Powell, 175; Erich Lessing, Art Resource, NY, 184; Scala, Art Resource, NY, 185; Greek, Attic, "Statue of a *kouros* (youth)," ca. 590–580 B.C. Marble. Naxian. Height without plinth: 76 5/8 (194.6 cm). The Metropolitan Museum of Art, Fletcher Fund, 1932. (32.11.1). Photograph © 1997 The Metropolitan Museum of Art, 186; Scala, Art Resource, NY, 187; Acropolis Museum, Studio Kontos Photostock, 188; Stokstad, Marilyn, "Art History Digital Image CD-ROM", 2002. Reprinted by permission of Pearson Education, Inc., Upper Saddle River, New Jersey, 189; Richard Bonson © Dorling Kindersley, 191; Art Resource/The British Museum Great Court Ltd., © The British Museum, 192; Scala, Art Resource, NY, 193; Alison Frantz Photographic Collection, American School of Classical Studies at Athens, 194; Scala, Art Resource, NY, 195; Chateau Museum, Boulogne-sur-Mer, France, 195; Johannes Laurentius, Art Resource, NY, 196.

**Chapter 10:** Barry B. Powell, 200; Roderick Chen, SuperStock, Inc., 201; Loraine Wilson, Robert Harding World Imagery, 202; Art Resource/The British Museum Great Court Ltd, © The British Museum, 205; Reinhard Saczewski, Art Resource, NY, and Nick Nicholls © The British Museum, 212; Barry B. Powell, 215; Art Resource/The British Museum Great Court Ltd, © The British Museum, 216; Art Resource, NY, 218; Barry B. Powell, 220; The Granger Collection, 221.

**Chapter 11:** Barry B. Powell, 226; Art Resource/The British Museum Great Court Ltd., © The British Museum, 227; Jehu, King of Israel, prostrating himself before King Shalmaneser III of Assur. Basalt bas-relief. Black stele of Shalmaneser III. British Museum, London, Great Britain. Erich Lessing, Art Resource, NY, 227; Relief, Israel, 10th-6th century: Judean exiles carrying provisions. Detail of the Assyrian conquest of the Jewish fortified town of Lachish (battle 701 B.C.). Part of a relief from the palace of

Sennacherib at Nineveh, Mesopotamia (Iraq). British Museum, London, Great Britain. © Erich Lessing Art Resource, NY, 228; Barry B. Powell, 231; SEF, Art Resource, NY, 232; Reunion des Musées Nationaux, Art Resource, NY, 234; Alan Hills and Barbara Winter © The British Museum, 236; Richard Ashworth, Robert Harding World Imagery, 238; Maynard Owen Williams/NGS Image Collection, 241; Susan Muhlhauser / Time Life Pictures / Getty Images, Inc., 245; Barry B. Powell, 247.

**Chapter 12:** Barry B. Powell, 255, 261, and 268; Greek. Vase, red-figure. Attic. ca. 480-470 B.C. Neck amphora, Nolan type. SIDE 1: "Greek warrior attacking a Persian." Said to be from Rhodes. Terracotta. H. 13-11/16 in. The Metropolitan Museum of Art, Rogers Fund, 1906. (06.1021.117) Photograph © 1986 The Metropolitan Museum of Art, 269.

**Chapter 13:** Wikemedia Commons, 274; Barry B. Powell, 275, 279, 280, 283, and 287. "A Bronze Foundry," red-figure decoration on a kylix from Vulci, Italy. 490-480 B.C. Ceramic, diameter of kylix 12" (31 cm). Staatliche Museen zu Berlin, Preussischer Kulturbesitz, Antikensammlung. Foto: Ingrid Geske. Bildarchiv Preussischer Kulturbesitz, Art Resource, NY, 288; Martin von Wagner Museum der Universität Wurzburg Photo: K. Oehrlein, 288.

**Chapter 14:** Barry B. Powell, 294; The striding god from Artemisium is a bronze statue dating from about 460 B.C. National Archaeological Museum, Athens, 300; Erich Lessing, Art Resource, NY, 301, 302, and 303; With permission of the Royal Ontario Museum © ROM, 304; Acropolis Restoration Service, 305; Werner Forman, Art Resource, NY, 306; Pearson Education/PH College, 306; Yann Arthus-Bertrand, Corbis/Bettmann, 307; Bill Bachmann, Stock Boston, 308; SuperStock, Inc., 309; Alison Frantz Photographic Collection, American School of Classical Studies at Athens, 309; Acropolis Restoration Service, 310; Stephen Conlin © Dorling Kindersley, 310; Guy Thouvenin, Robert Harding World Imagery, 311; Erich Lessing, Art Resource, NY, 312; Nick Nicholls © The British Museum, 313; Art Resource/The British Museum Great Court Ltd, © The British Museum, 314; "The Achilles Painter, lekythos (oil bottle)," Greek, high classical period, c 440 B.C. Ceramic, white ground. height: 38.4 cm (15-1/8 in.). Museum of Fine Arts, Boston. Francis Bartlett Donation of 1912, 13.201. Photograph © 2004 Museum of Fine Arts, Boston, 315.

**Chapter 15:** Staatliche Museen zu Berlin/Bildarchiv Preussischer Kulturbesitz, Berlin, Germany/Photo by Ingrid Geske-Heiden. Art Resource, NY, 321; Michael Holford Photographs, 324.

**Chapter 16:** Barry B. Powell, 338, 341, and 342; National Archaeological Museum, Athens/Hellenic Republic Ministry of Culture, Athens, Greece, 350; Barry B. Powell, 352, 353, and 354; Demetrio Carrasco © Dorling Kindersley, 356; European Tourists Services, 359; Barry B. Powell, 359 and 363.

**Chapter 17:** Barry B. Powell, 371 and 372; Hirmer Fotoarchiv, 375; Harvard Art Museum, Arthur M. Sackler Museum, Bequest of David M. Robinson, 1959.219 Photo: Imaging Department © President and Fellows of Harvard College, 376; Barry B. Powell, 379; Dagli Orti, Picture Desk, Inc./Kobal Collection, 381.

**Chapter 18:** Barry B. Powell, 387; Piraeus Museum, Bronze Statue of Athena, Hellenic Ministry of Culture, Rob Reichenfeld © Dorling Kindersley, 387; Praxiteles (c. 400-300 B.C.), "Hermes and Dionysius," c. 350-330 B.C. National Archeological Museum, Olympia. Scala, Art Resource, NY, 388; Aphrodite of Knidos. Roman copy after an original, c. 330 B.C. by Praxiteles. Marble. H.: 6 ft. 8 in. Vatican Museum. Alinari, Art Resource, NY, 389; Pawel Kumelowski, Omni-Photo Communications, Inc., 391; Dagli Orti, Picture Desk, Inc./Kobal Collection, 392; Yale University Press, 392; © Ruggero Vanni/CORBIS All Rights Reserved, 392; Bildarchiv Preussischer Kulturbesitz, Art Resource, NY, 393; Founders Society Purchase, Hill Memorial Fund, William H. Murphy Fund, Dr. and Mrs. Arthur R. Bloom Fund and Antiquaries Fund.The Detroit Institute of Arts/The Bridgeman Art Library, NY, 394; Martin von Wagner Museum, der Universität Wurzburg, Germany. Photo: K. Oehrlein, 395; Louvre, Dept. des Antiquités Grecques/Romaines, Paris, France. Photograph © Erich Lessing, Art Resource, NY, 401.

**Chapter 19:** Ephorate of Prehistoric and Classical Antiquities, 407; Barry B. Powell, 408, 411, 416, and 421; Wikemedia Commons, 424; David Lees/Corbis, 426; Peter Wilson © Dorling Kindersley, 428.

**Chapter 20:** Corbis/Bettmann, 432; Nick Nicholls © The British Museum, 437; Corbis/Bettmann, 443.

**Chapter 21:** Barry B. Powell, 447, 453, and 455; Jeff Schmaltz, MODIS Rapid Response Team, NASA Headquarters, 457; Digitally reproduced with the permission of the Papyrology Collection, Graduate Library, University of Michigan, 458; Alan Hills and Barbara Winter © The British Museum, 459; Alistair Duncan © Dorling Kindersley, 460; Art Resource, NY, 462.

**Chapter 22:** Barry B. Powell, 466, 472, and 474; Scala, Art Resource, NY, 474; Nigel Hicks © Dorling Kindersley, 475; Alinari, Art Resource, NY, 479.

**Chapter 23:** Barry B. Powell, 483; Scala, Art Resource, Art Resource, NY, 486; Corbis/Bettmann, 487; Johannes Laurentius, Art Resource, NY, 489; Reunion des Musées Nationaux, Art Resource, NY, 489; Vanni, Art Resource, NY, 490; John Serafin/SBG, 491; William Aylward - Classics Department University of Wisconsin —Madison, 492; American School of Classical Studies at Athens: Agora Excavations, 492; Vatican Museums and Galleries, Vatican City/SuperStock, 493; Museo Archeologico Nazionale, Naples/The Bridgeman Art Library, New York, 494; Scala, Art Resource, NY, 494; Erich Lessing, Art Resource, NY, 496; John Woodcock © Dorling Kindersley, 504; The Granger Collection, 505.

**Chapter 24:** Barry B. Powell, 508; Scala, Art Resource, NY, 510; Getty Images Inc.—Hulton Archive Photos, 512; © Dorling Kindersley, 513; Art Resource, NY, 514; Mich.Schwerberger/Das Fotoarchiv GmbH, Peter Arnold, Inc., 520; Scala, Art Resource, NY, 522; Roman. Cato. (Ancient sculpture.) Museo Lateranense, Rome. Alinari, Art Resource, 523; Barry B. Powell, 525; Art Resource, NY, 527; NY Carlsberg Glyptotek, Copenhagen, 529; Bildarchiv Preussischer Kulturbesitz, Art Resource, NY, 532; © Sandro Vannini/CORBIS, 533; Guy Thouvenin, Robert Harding World Imagery, 538.

# INDEX

Acarnania (a-kar-**nā**-ni-a), a region in northwestern Greece, 338, 340, 424

Achaean League, 466, 467, 470, 471, 526, 543

Achaeans (a-**kē**-ans. Akhaians), a division of the Greek people, Homer's word for the Greeks at Troy, 9, 65, 82, 83, 100–109, 127–129, 137, 142, 466, 469, 470

Achilles (a-**kil**-ēz. Akhilleus), greatest Greek warrior at Troy, 9, 95, 96, 101–110, 129, 137, 138, 141, 167, 181, 192, 193, 296, 315, 327, 329, 420, 435

Acropolis (a-**krop**-o-lis), hill in Athens on which the Parthenon is built, 168, 186, 187, 210, 211, 216, 222, 263, 284, 302–309, 323, 360, 477, 538

Aegean (ē-**jē**-an) Sea, between Greece and Turkey, 8, 12, 47, 57, 138, 152, 174, 200, 229, 237, 270, 279, 356, 372, 408, 444, 541

Aegeus (ē-**jūs**. Aigeus), father of Theseus, a king of Athens, 319, 320

aegis (ē-jis), "goat skin," a shield with serpent border used by Athena and Zeus, 121, 133, 137

Aegisthus (ē-**jis**-thus. Aigisthos), son of Thyestes, lover of Clytemnestra, murderer of Agamemnon, killed by Orestes, 113, 114, 117

Aeneas (ē-**nē**-as), son of Aphrodite and Anchises, ancestor of the Roman people, 507

Aeolians (ē-**ō**-li-ans), a division of the Greek people, 10, 230

Aeschylus (ē-ski-lus, **es**-ki-lus) (525–456 B.C.), Athenian playwright, 6, 17, 38, 39, 140, 250, 265, 272, 293, 317–323, 327, 329, 332, 336, 485

Aetolia (e-**tō**-li-a), district north of the Corinthian Gulf, 165, 340, 376, 518

Aetolian League, 466, 467, 517

Africa, 153, 260, 442, 450, 472, 473, 475, 505, 509, 515

Agamemnon (a-ga-**mem**-non), son of Atreus, brother of Menelaüs, leader of Greek forces at Troy, 60, 65, 102–109, 113–117, 119, 126, 128, 138–141, 167, 323, 327–331, 435

Agathocles (304–289 B.C.), Syracusan tyrant, 454, 471, 472, 473, 480

*agathoi*, "the good," members of the upper classes, 151, 158–161, 164, 167, 172, 180, 181, 211, 221

Agavê (a-**gā**-vē), daughter of Cadmus and Harmonia, mother of Pentheus, 327

Agis (**ā**-jis) (1) (fifth century B.C.), king of Sparta, 360, 362; (2) Agis III (244–241 B.C.), king of Sparta, 469, 480

Ajax (Aias), son of Telamôn, Achaean hero, 95, 105, 194, 195

Alcestis (al-**ses**-tis. Alkestis), wife of Admetus, who dies in her husband's place, 336

Alcinoüs (al-**sin**-ō-us. Alkinoos), "strong of mind," king of the Phaeacians, father of Nausicaä, who entertains Odysseus, 114

Alcmeon (alk-**mē**-on. Alkmeon), son of Amphiaraüs, who led the Epigoni against Thebes and killed his own mother Eriphylê, 166

Alexander the Great (356–323 B.C.), 6, 13, 36, 93, 218, 232, 252, 390, 400, 406–463, 473, 475, 477, 481–482, 495, 499, 505, 508, 510, 522, 530, 543

Alexander, another name for Paris (which see), 100

Alexandria, city in Egypt founded by Alexander the Great, 25, 120, 421, 428, 434, 444, 446, 447, 458–461, 464–467, 471, 483–486, 491, 501, 502, 509, 512, 517, 520, 525, 532–536

Alexandrian poetry, 543

Alexandrian scholars, 483, 484, 504, 543

alphabet, a writing that can be pronounced, 39, 61, 87, 89, 90, 91

Ammon, or Amun, Egyptian god equated with Zeus, 444

Amphictyonic League, 411, 412, 413, 414, 416, 417, 429

*amphidromia*, "running around," Roman ceremony acknowledging membership in a family, 38, 40

Amphipolis, city in northern Greece, 338, 344, 347, 408, 410, 411, 429

*anagnorisis*, "recognition," in plot, 329, 336

Analysis, an approach to Homer that wishes to divide his texts into constituent parts that once had an independent existence, 5, 38, 59, 98, 118, 149, 178, 180, 197, 224, 292, 331, 336, 385, 540

Analyst, a scholar who wishes to identify the small parts of which Homer's poems are made, a follower of F. A. Wolf, 95–100

Anatolia, "sunrise," the Asian part of modern Turkey, synonymous with Asia Minor, 50, 57, 66, 69, 72–74, 229, 230, 233, 422–427, 444–450, 452, 455, 456, 462, 484, 517, 519, 524, 528, 529

Anaximander (sixth century B.C.), Milesian philosopher, 175–179, 295, 296

Anaximenes (sixth century B.C.), Milesian philosopher, 176–179

*andrôn*, "men's room," where the symposium took place, 159, 172

antagonist, "second actor," in Athenian tragedy, 328, 321, 336

Antigonê (an-**tig**-o-nē), daughter of Oedipus, buries brother Polynices against state edict, 324, 328–331

*Antigonê*, a play by Sophocles, 324, 328–331

Antigonids, 461

Antigonus I, the One-Eyed (ca. 382–301 B.C.), general of Alexander, 446–454, 456, 461–463, 467, 471, 473, 475, 476, 477, 511

Antiochus (1) I (unknown–261 B.C.), a general of Alexander, 454–456; (2) III, a Hellenistic king, defeated by the Romans, 462, 515–517; (3) IV, a Hellenistic king, son of Antiochus II, 517

Antipater (ca. 397–319 B.C.), a general of Alexander, regent in Macedon 334-319 B.C., 446–449

*aoidos* (a-**oi**-dos, pl. *aoidoi*), Greek word for such oral poets as Homer and Hesiod (contrast with "rhapsode"), 99, 114, 132

Aphrodite, Greek goddess of sexual attraction, related to Inanna/Astartê/Ishtar, equated with Roman Venus, 30, 32, 36, 124, 133, 134, 138, 148, 302, 303, 327, 335, 388–389, 490, 491, 507, 535

Apollo, son of Zeus and Leto, god of music, medicine, reason, and prophecy and archery, 21, 78, 102, 126–129, 133–138, 142, 148, 162, 163, 218, 235, 274, 311, 390, 391, 400, 411, 501

Apollodorus (a-pol-o-**dor**-us) (second century A.D.), author of handbook on Greek myth, 533

Apollonius (a-pol-**lō**-ni-us) of Rhodes (third century B.C.), author of the *Argonautica*, 484, 506

Apsu, Mesopotamian god of the primordial waters, 176

Aramaic, a West Semitic dialect spoken in Aram (Damascus) and widely used by Near Eastern bureaucracies, employing a West Semitic script, 455

Arcadia (ar-**ka**-di-a), mountainous region in the central Peloponnesus, 15, 165, 311, 312

Archaic Period, ca. 800–480 B.C., 6, 151, 152, 158, 299

Archilochus (ar-**kil**-o-kus. Arkhilokhos) (seventh century B.C.), Greek lyric poet, 181, 182

Archimedes (287–212 B.C.), Sicilian mathematician, 5, 502, 503, 506, 512–514

Areopagus (ar-ē-**op**-a-gus), hill in Athens, where homicides were tried, 213, 224, 282

Ares (**ar**-ēz), Greek god of war, 107, 134, 181, 213, 389, 390, 487

*arete* (ar-e-**tā**), "virtue," 297–298, 315, 395

Argeïphontes (ar-jē-i-**fon**-tēz), "Argus-killer," epithet of Hermes, 113, 114

Argonauts (**ar**-go-notz), Jason and his companions on the *Argo*, 483

Argos, city in the Argive plain in the northern Peloponnesus, 78, 86, 102, 133, 135, 140, 165, 279, 282, 329, 347, 408, 411, 455, 470, 475

Argus (Argos), "swifty" (1) many-eyed monster killed by Hermes, 30–32, (2) Odysseus' dog, 113, 117

Arion (a-**rī**-on), legendary Corinthian poet, 320, 331

Aristarchus of Samothrace (ca. 217–145 B.C.), Alexandrian scholar, 504

Aristophanes (ar-is-**tof**-a-nēz) (448-380 B.C.), Athenian writer of comedies, 17, 36, 40, 251, 252, 291–293, 298, 318, 331–336, 344, 366, 368, 485, 512

Aristotle (384–322 B.C.), Greek philosopher, 5, 16, 17, 21, 25, 108, 109, 117, 175–177, 210, 213–215, 224, 286, 289, 316, 319–324, 328–331, 335, 400–405, 414, 436, 495, 501–506, 539

Artemis (**ar**-te-mis), daughter of Zeus and Leto, virgin goddess of the wild, equated with the Roman Diana, 127, 133, 134, 137, 138, 148, 190, 191, 207, 216, 294, 311, 329, 488, 525

Arthur, King, 52, 54, 56, 336, 540

Asclepius (as-**klēp**-i-us. Asklepios), son of Apollo and Coronis, Greek god of medicine, 21, 478–480, 501, 525

Aspasia (fifth century B.C.), mistress of Pericles, 35, 40, 291

Assyria, an area on the upper Tigris river, powerful in the Bronze and Iron Ages, 72, 84, 92, 175, 187, 225–229, 238

Assyrians, a warlike Semitic people of northern Mesopotamia, 225–229, 237, 252

Athena (Athene), virgin goddess of war and handicrafts, equated with the Roman Minerva, 30, 32, 66, 82, 99, 104, 105, 111, 114, 117, 133–137, 142, 148, 212, 216, 238, 252, 302–304, 308–311, 315, 386, 387, 420, 422, 465, 469, 477

Athens, main city in Attica, 2, 5–9, 15–20, 24, 26, 35–41, 60, 71, 75–80, 86, 88, 91, 95, 134, 137, 140, 143, 148, 152, 153, 158, 160, 163–173, 179, 187, 188, 192, 194, 198–224, 233, 244, 247–249, 264–299, 301–322, 327–333, 336–379, 383–387, 393, 395, 399, 400, 404–419, 423, 429, 444–451, 455, 456, 461, 465, 467, 477–480, 483–487, 491, 492, 495, 498, 500, 505, 514–519, 524–526, 538, 539, 542, 543

atomic theory, 297

Atreus (**ā**-trūs), legendary king of Mycenae, son of Pelops, 104, 113, 330

Attica (**at**-ti-ka), region in central Greece where Athens is located, 2, 148, 168, 186, 210–219, 249, 251, 257, 279–286, 290, 293, 319, 338–340, 342, 344, 360, 361

Augustus (aw-**gus**-tus) (63-B.C. – A.D. 14), originally called Octavian, first Roman emperor, 538–540

Aulis (**aw**-lis), port in Boeotia from which the Trojan expedition set sail, 329

Baal (**bā**-al), "lord," a Levantine storm god, 357, 473, 512

Babylon, major city on the middle Euphrates, 53, 94, 95, 135, 158, 226–229, 235–239, 241, 253, 298, 371, 423, 425, 430, 431, 441, 442, 447–450, 455, 460, 483

Babylonians, 174, 235, 236, 332

Bacchae (**bak**-kē. Bakkhai), female followers of Dionysus, a play by Euripides, 146–148, 325–329, 336, 485

Bacchus (**bak**-kus. Bakkhos), another name for Dionysus, 146, 148, 326

Bacchylides (ba-**kil**-i-dēz. Bakkhylides) (fifth century B.C.), Greek lyric poet, 320

*basileus* (ba-**sil**-us, plural *basileis*), "big man, chief," 75, 82–85, 92, 102, 103, 114, 117, 118, 150, 151

Black Sea, also called Pontus, 26, 50, 73, 77, 79, 92, 175, 215, 226, 231, 278, 283, 287, 339, 358, 360, 371, 411, 415, 436, 447, 453, 455, 483, 495, 524, 530, 542

black-figure, a style in Greek pottery decoration, 195

Boeotia (bē-**ō**-sha. Boiotia), region north of Attica, where Thebes was situated, 22, 133, 268, 282, 340, 374, 377, 466

Boreas (**bō**-re-as), the North Wind, 14, 15, 261

Brasidas (fifth century B.C.), Spartan general, 343, 344, 367, 408

Briseis (brī-**sē**-is), Achilles' war-captive, taken by Agamemnon, 105

Bronze Age, ca. 3000–1200 B.C., 3, 4, 46–53, 56, 57, 61–72, 75, 78, 80, 82, 87, 92, 100–102, 106, 130, 150, 157, 162, 183, 190, 199, 307, 342, 390, 445, 476, 541, 542, 544

Brutus, "stupid," Marcus Junius (85–42 B.C.), assassin of Caesar, 523, 530, 534, 539

Byron, Lord (1788–1824), British poet, 1–3, 7, 228

Byzantium, Greek colony at the entrance to the Bosporus (= later Constantinople), 93, 245, 274, 278, 279, 371, 411, 415–417, 539

Cadmus (**kad**-mus. Kadmos), father of Pentheus, king of Thebes, 75, 143, 258, 325

Caesar, Julius (100–44 B.C.), Roman general and politician, assassinated by his friends, 495, 504, 530–538, 540

Caesarion (47–30 B.C.), son of Julius Caesar and Cleopatra, 534–537

Calchas (**kal**-kas. Kalkhas), prophet of the Greek forces at Troy, 103

Callimachus (ka-**lim**-a-kus. Kallimakhos) (third century B.C.), Alexandrian poet, 484, 506

Calydon (**kal**-i-don. Kalydon), main city in Aetolia in western Greece, 175, 192

Calypso (ka-**lip**-sō. Kalypso), "concealer, burier," nymph who kept Odysseus for seven years on her island Ogygia at the navel of the sea, 114, 116

Cambyses (kam-**bī**-sēz) (ruled 530–522 B.C.), son of Cyrus the Great, second Achaemenid king of Persia, 237–242, 252, 271

Carthage, Phoenician city in modern Tunisia, enemy of Syracuse and Rome, 5, 9, 153, 225, 229, 237, 252, 254–260, 271–277, 337, 338, 348, 349, 356–358, 369–385, 404, 406, 414, 427, 442, 456, 471–476, 483, 505, 510–512, 515, 516, 528, 541–543

caryatids, 311

Cassander (unknown–297 B.C.), a general of Alexander, 448–453, 463, 473, 477

Cassius (first century B.C.), conspirator who killed Caesar, 534, 539

Castor, mortal son of Tyndareus and Leda, brother of the immortal Polydeuces (= Pollux), 165, 434

Cato (95 B.C.–46 B.C.), Roman statesman, enemy of Caesar, 521–523, 539

Caucasus Mountains, at the eastern end of the Black Sea, 231, 421

cella, where the cult statue was kept in a Greek temple, 189, 191, 303, 310, 390, 391

Cercyon (**ser**-si-on. Kerkyon), bandit wrestler killed by Theseus, 319

Chaeronea, in northern Boeotia, where Philip II defeated a Greek coalition in 338 B.C., 416–419, 429, 467, 509

Chaos (**kā**-os. Khaos), "chasm," the first thing that came into being, 122, 123, 148

Charybdis (ka-**rib**-dis. Kharybdis), dangerous whirlpool, with Scylla, said to be in the Straits of Messina, 112, 116

Chios (**kē**-os), Greek island near Asia Minor, often claimed as Homer's birthplace, 94, 152, 281, 411

choral lyric, 181

Christians, 100, 147, 539

Chryseïs (krī-sē-is), daughter of Chryses, given as booty to Agamemnon during the Trojan War, 128

chthonic cult, pertaining to powers that live beneath the earth, 132, 148

Cicero (106–43 B.C.), Roman politician and orator, 95, 406, 530, 531

Cilicia (si-**lish**-a), region in southeastern Asia Minor, 69, 423, 424

Cimon (**sē**-mōn, **kē**-mōn. Kimon) (510–450 B.C.), Athenian leader, son of Miltiades, 278–282, 289, 292

Circê (**sir-sē**. Kirke), "hawk," daughter of Helius, enchantress who entertained Odysseus for a year on her island, 115–117, 139

Cithaeron (si-**thē**-ron. Kithairon), mountain south of Thebes, where the Bacchae roamed and Oedipus was abandoned as an infant, 276

Claudius Ptolemy, see Ptolemy

Cleomenes (third century B.C.), Spartan reformer king, 219, 222, 254, 470, 471, 476, 480

Cleon (fifth century B.C.), Athenian demagogue, 332, 343–345, 367

Cleopatra (Kleopatra) (1) (69–30 B.C.), queen of Egypt, first century B.C., lover of Julius Caesar and Marc Antony, defeated by Augustus, 6, 447, 481, 515, 532–539; (2) Philip II's fifth wife, 418; (3) sister of Alexander the Great, 447; (4) wife of Ptolemy VIII, 520

Cleisthenes (**klī**-sthen-ēz. Kleisthenes) (sixth/fifth centuries B.C.), founder of Athenian democracy in 508 B.C., 165, 166, 215, 219–223

Clytemnestra (klī-tem-**nes**-tra. Klytemnestra), daughter of Zeus and Leda, wife of Agamemnon, whom she killed, then was herself killed by Orestes, 113, 117, 139–142, 323, 329

Cnidus, Greek city on southwest coast of Asia Minor, 387–389, 490

Cnossus (**knos**-sus. Knossos), principal Bronze Age settlement in Crete, where labyrinthine ruins have been found, 47, 50–55, 61–65, 70, 75, 77

consuls, in Rome, 518

Corcyra (cor-**sī**-ra. Kerkyra), modern Corfu, an island off the northwest coast of Greece, 112, 279, 290, 338, 345, 359, 363, 365, 411

Corinth (**kor**-inth. Korinth), city on isthmus between central Greece and the Peloponnesus, 35, 86, 128, 155, 160, 162, 166–172, 175, 191, 200, 209, 260, 268, 270, 282, 290, 338, 340, 347, 359, 363, 364, 372, 414–417, 419, 465, 518, 519, 525

Corinthian order, in architecture, 390, 404

Cos (kos), Greek island near Asia Minor, home of a cult to Asclepius, 21, 258, 411, 499

Craterus (unknown–320 B.C.), general of Alexander, 441, 446–448

Creon (**krē**-on. Kreon), "ruler," a king of Thebes, 324, 328

Crete, largest island in the Aegean, 46–59, 63, 70, 74, 77, 89, 91, 124, 167, 183, 184, 268, 465, 466

Creusa (kre-**ū**-sa. Kreousa), first wife of Aeneas, who perished in the flames of Troy, 319

Crimea (krī-**mē**-a), peninsula on the north coast of the Black Sea, 279

Croesus (**krē**-sus), king of Lydia, sixth century B.C., defeated by Persians under Cyrus the Great, 166, 230, 233–235, 252, 271, 330

Cronus (**krō**-nus), child of Uranus and Gaea, husband of Rhea, overthrown by Zeus, ruled in the days of the Race of Gold, 75, 122, 123, 132, 139, 148, 151, 275, 319, 472, 473

Cumae (**kū**-mē. Kymai), site of earliest Greek colony in Italy, north of the bay of Naples, where Aeneas descended to the underworld, 275, 276

Cybelê (**sib**-i-lē. Kybele), great mother goddess of Phrygia, 147

Cyclades (**sik**-la-dēz), "circle" islands, around Delos in the Aegean Sea, 49, 57, 62, 69, 71, 91, 270, 284, 465

Cycladic figurines, 48, 70

Cyclops (sī-**klō**-pēz. Kyklopes, sing., Cyclops), rude one-eyed giants, including Polyphemus, whom Odysseus blinded, 79, 115, 117, 192, 313, 314

Cynics, philosophers who denounced worldly value, 495–499

Cynoscephalae, "dog's heads," site in Greece where the Romans defeated the Macedonians in 197 B.C., 516, 517, 525, 539

Cyprus, large island in eastern Mediterranean, home of Aphrodite, 26, 69, 70, 74, 75, 138, 244, 278, 283–287, 373, 451, 461, 497, 520, 530

Cyrus (**sī**-rus. Kyros) the Great (590–529 B.C.), founder of the Persian empire, 436

dactylic hexameter, the meter of Homer, six feet per line, 96

daedalic style, in archaic sculpture, 184

Daedalus (**dē**-da-lus. Daidalos), Athenian craftsman who built the labyrinth, 183

Danaans (**dā**-na-anz. Danaoi), descendants of Danaüs, one of Homer's name for the Greeks, 9, 65, 69, 102, 126, 128

Danaüs (**dā**-na-us. Danaos), legendary e king of Argos, 102, 329

Danube River, 45, 242, 419, 530

Dardanelles (= Hellespont), straits between the Aegean Sea and the Propontis (= Sea of Marmora), 359

Darius (1) II (fifth century B.C.), a Persian king during the Peloponnesian War, 223, 232, 237, 240–249, 253, 257, 271, 330, 360, 362, 371; (III) (fourth century B.C.), Persian king defeated by Alexander, 417–427, 430–436, 442, 507

Dark Age, ca. 1150–800 B.C., 4, 6, 12, 17, 24, 25, 72–93, 150, 151, 175, 183, 188–190, 197, 199, 541

Darwin, Charles (1809–1882), British biologist, 296, 400

Decelea, outpost in Attica fortified by the Spartans, 338, 351, 359, 360, 363, 367

Delos (**dē**-los), "clear," tiny island in the center of the Cyclades, where Apollo and Artemis were born, center of the slave trade in Hellenistic times, 87, 247, 248, 270, 279, 284, 411, 455, 465, 483, 519, 525–528

Delphi (**del**-fī), sanctuary of Apollo at foot of Mount Parnassus, 78, 87, 128, 152, 162, 164, 219, 233, 235, 258, 261, 274, 275, 301, 302, 338, 365, 374, 387, 392, 411–414, 417, 455, 456, 466, 477, 478, 525, 526

Demeter (de-**mē**-ter), daughter of Cronus and Rhea, mother of Persephonê, goddess of the grain harvest (= Roman Ceres), 15, 16, 134, 135, 143, 144, 148, 269, 291, 334, 350, 478

Demetrius of Phaleron (fourth century B.C.), (1) philosopher/ strongman who ruled Athens 450; (2) his grandson (third century B.C.) by the same name, 467, 477, 483

democracy, 5, 7, 86, 158, 161, 219–223, 243, 254, 276, 282, 285, 286, 289, 292, 299, 305, 322, 350, 356, 360, 365, 366, 369, 370, 395, 399, 403, 447, 467, 542

Democritus (ca. 460–380 B.C.), pluralist philosopher, invented atomic theory, 296, 297, 315, 496

demography, the biological aspects of human societies, 16, 17, 26, 41

*dêmos*, "the people," 151, 167, 172, 210, 213, 219, 256, 289, 290, 305, 322, 323, 345, 417

Demosthenes (dem-**os**-the-nēz), (1) Athenian general (fifth century B.C.), 340–344, 352, 353, 355, 367, (2) Athenian orator (384–322 B.C.), 40, 406, 413–416, 419, 429, 443, 447, 486, 487, 522

Deucalion (dū-**kā**-li-on. Deukalion), husband of Pyrrha, survivor of the Flood, 8

*deus ex machina*, "god from the machine," a manipulated ending to a plot, 336

Diodorus of Sicily (first century B.C.), Greek historian, 254, 259, 260, 272, 277, 278, 281, 292, 357, 368, 380, 382, 385, 418, 420, 422, 437, 449, 450, 472, 473, 480, 482, 483, 506, 519

Diogenes (dī-**oj**-e-nēz) (ca. 412–323 B.C.), founder of Cynicism, 495, 497

Dion (fourth century B.C.), Syracusan diplomat, rival to Dionysius II, 384, 385, 396

Dionê (dī-**ō**-nē), feminine form of "Zeus," a consort of Zeus, 133, 138

Dionysius (1) Greek pirate, 245, 255, 256 (2) I (fifth century B.C.), tyrant of Syracuse, 358, 379–382, 411, 473; (3) II (fourth century B.C.), son of Dionysius I, 383, 384;

Dionysus (dī-ō-**nī**-sus. Dionysos), son of Zeus and Semelê, god of wine, see also Bacchus, 121, 134, 135, 146–148, 193, 307, 318–331, 336, 345, 380, 381, 388, 434, 478, 535

Dioscuri (dī-os-**kū**-rī. Dioskouroi), "sons of Zeus" and Leda, Castor and Polydeuces (= Roman Pollux), brothers of Helen, protectors of seafarers, 434, 435

dithyramb (**dith**-i-ram), a choral song, especially in honor of Dionysus, 319, 320, 331

divine myths, where divine beings are the principal characters, 121, 148

Dorians, a division of the Greek people, 9, 10, 70, 190, 199, 230, 470

Doric order, in Greek architecture, 189, 190, 308–309, 390, 492

dramatic need, 109, 329, 333, 336

Echion (**ek**-i-on), husband of Agavê, father of Pentheus, 327

Electra (Elektra), daughter of Agamemnon and Clytemnestra, 336

Eleusinian mysteries, in honor of Demeter, 145, 149

Eleusis, site of the mysteries to Demeter and Persephonê, west of Athens, 115, 143, 144, 158, 194, 220, 334, 350

Elgin (**el**-ghin) Marbles, sculptures from the Parthenon, 303, 315

Elis, territory in the northwest Peloponnesus, 166

Elpenor (el-**pē**-nor), companion of Odysseus who died after falling from Circê's roof, 141

Elymians, native people of western Sicily, 254, 255, 275, 276, 312, 348, 356

Empedocles (ca. 492–432 B.C.), pluralist Sicilian philosopher, 296, 297, 315

Eos (**ē**-os), the dawn goddess (= Roman Aurora), 133, 139

Ephesus (**ef**-e-sus. Ephesos), city in Asia Minor, site of a temple to Artemis, 175, 190, 191, 294, 387, 390, 393, 525, 528

Ephialtes (ef-i-**al**-tēz) (fifth century B.C.), an Athenian democratic political reformer, 262, 263, 281, 282, 292

epic, a long poem on a heroic topic, 23, 64, 94, 96, 100, 101, 110, 116, 118, 180, 318, 328, 483, 484

Epictetus (first century A.D.), Greek stoic philosopher, 498, 506

Epicureanism, a philosophical school that taught happiness as the end in life, 495, 506

Epidaurus (e-pi-**dow**-rus. Epidauros), city in the northeast Peloponnesus, site of a cult to Asclepius, 483

Epimetheus (e-pē-**mē**-thūs), "after-thinker," brother of Prometheus, who married Pandora, 31, 32, 221

episode, "song in place," in Athenian tragedy, 22, 98, 110, 322, 333, 408, 518

epithets, in epic poetry, 97, 103

Erebus (**er**-e-bus. Erebos), "darkness," a region of Tartarus, 140

Erechtheum (er-ek-**thē**-ūm), temple to Erechtheus on the Acropolis, 306–311, 315

Erechtheus (e-**rek**-thūs), an early king of Athens, 308, 311

Erinyes (e-**rin**-i-ēz), the Furies or Eumenides, 123

Eros (**er**-os), "desire," sprung from Chaos, or the child of Ares and Aphrodite (= Roman Cupid), 122, 123, 148, 536

Eryx, Phoenician city in western Sicily, 341, 348, 474, 475

Eteocles (e-**tē**-o-klēz. Eteokles), son of Oedipus, kills brother Polynices in attack of seven against Thebes, 325

Ethiopia, region in Africa, 18

Ethiopians, a dark-skinned people who dwell in the extreme south, where Poseidôn and Zeus sometimes visit, 113, 237

etiological myth, concerned with causes, 132, 148

Etruscans (ē-**trus**-kans), inhabitants of Etruria, north of Rome, 112, 275

Euboea (yū-**bē**-a. Euboia), long island east of Attica, site of vigorous Iron Age community where the alphabet may have been invented, 75–78, 86, 89, 92, 244, 248, 256, 261–262, 265, 279, 284, 361, 411, 413

Euclid (ca. 325–250 B.C.), Alexandrian mathematician, 502, 506

*Eumenides* (yū-**men**-i-dēz), "the kindly ones" = the Furies), the third play of Aeschylus' *Oresteia*, 329

Euripides (yū-**rip**-i-dēz) (480–406 B.C.), Athenian playwright, 6, 17, 37, 38, 146, 147, 317, 318, 321, 323–329, 332, 335, 336, 409, 485

Euryclea (yū-ri-**klē**-a. Euryklea), Odysseus' nurse, who recognized his scar, 66

Eurydicê (yū-**rid**-i-sē. Eurydike), (1) beloved of Orpheus, who tried to bring her back from the underworld, 146; (2) mother of Philip II, 409, 449, 476

Eurylochus (yū-**ril**-o-kus. Eurylokhos), one of Odysseus' men, 139

Evans, Sir Arthur (1851–1941), British archaeologist, 52, 54, 56

evolutionary religion, based on fear, 124, 125, 148

Exekias (ek-**sē**-ki-as) (sixth century B.C.), Greek painter of pots, 193–195

Fates, see also Moerae, 71, 131

Fertile Crescent, that band of fertile land arcing from southern Mesopotamia, through Palestine, to Egypt, 42, 43, 70

Flood, that destroyed the world, 70, 113

folktale, traditional tales that are neither myths nor legends, 113, 114, 117, 121, 148, 423

Fontenelle, Bernard (1657–1757), French author and critic (the nephew of Pierre Corneille), 120

formula, a building block in the formation of oral verse, 97, 119

Gaea (**jē**-a. Gaia), or Ge (jē), "earth," sprung from Chaos, consort of Uranus, mother of the Titans, 122–124, 133, 139, 148

Galen (A.D. 126–ca. 200), Greek physician, 38, 501, 502, 506

Gaugamela (gow-ga-**mē**-la), in north central Mesopotamia, where Alexander fought his last battle against Darius III in 331 B.C., 430, 432, 435, 444

Gaza, a territory in southern Palestine in which were built the five cities of the Philistines, 70

Genesis, biblical book of, 94

*genius* (**gen**-i-us), male creative power in Roman religion, 271

*geras*, "prize," the outward and visible representation of a hero's honor (*timê*), 102–105, 108

ghosts, 4, 17, 116, 132, 139–142, 144–148

Giants, "earth-born ones," sprung from the blood of Uranus that fell on Gaea, 124, 295

Gibraltar, Straits of, at entrance to the Mediterranean Sea from the Atlantic Ocean, 196

Gilgamesh, Mesopotamian hero, 110, 118, 328

Golden Age, 444, 505, 511, 526

Gorgons (**gor**-gonz), three hags whose look turned one to stone, 192

Graces (Charites), attendants of Aphrodite, imparters of feminine charm, 30, 535

Granicus River, near the Hellespont, where Alexander first fought the Persians, in 332 B.C., 420, 421, 429, 435

Grave Circle A, at Mycenae, 59, 60, 70

Great Altar of Zeus, in Pergamum, 487, 491, 506

Greek alphabet, invented ca. 800 B.C., 87–92, 180

Greek problem, how to decide value independently of religion, 5, 6, 119

guilt culture, where the sanctions of society are internal, 102, 106

*guslar* (plural *guslari*), a South Slavic oral poet, who sings to the *gusle*, a one-stringed bowed instrument, 98

Gyges (seventh century B.C.), king of Lydia, 182, 229, 230, 252

Gylippus (fifth century B.C.), Spartan general who assisted the Syracusans, 351–353, 367, 470

*gymnasium*, "naked place," where Greek males worked out, 36, 37, 163, 166, 191, 393, 455, 466

Hades (**hā**-dēz), "unseen," lord of the underworld, husband of Persephonê, 140, 142, 143, 484, 519

Haemon (**hē**-mon), son of Creon, fiancé of Antigonê, 325

*hamartia*, "mistake," in Athenian tragedy, 330, 336, 339

Hannibal (fifth century B.C., "mercy of Baal"), (1) Carthaginian general, 357, 358, 367; (2) (third century B.C.), descendant of Hannibal (1), who fought Rome, 512–517, 521, 530, 539, 540

Hebê (**hē**-bē), "youth," married to Heracles on Olympus, 133, 138

Hebrews, the descendants of Abraham and Isaac and Isaac's son Jacob, 89

Hector, greatest of the Trojan warriors, married to Andromachê, killed by Achilles, 96, 106–109, 114, 141, 327, 383

*hekatompeda*, "hundred-footers," a kind of temple from the Archaic Period, 86, 92, 170

Helen, daughter of Zeus and Leda, husband of Menelaüs, lover of Paris, 76, 100, 101, 110, 182, 199, 327, 434

Helicon (**hel**-i-kon), a mountain in Boeotia, where Hesiod had a vision, sacred to the Muses, 121, 132, 135

Helius (**hē**-li-us. Helios), sun god, son of Hyperion, father of Phaëthon, 133, 139

Hellas, "land of the Hellenes," 8, 9, 67, 293

Hellên (**hel**-ēn), son of Pyrrha and Deucalion, eponymous ancestor of the Hellenes, 8, 9

Hellenes (**hel**-ēnz), the Greeks, inhabitants of Hellas (at first southern Thessaly, then all of Greece), 7, 9, 156, 165, 215, 337

Hellenistic Period, 323–30 B.C., 6, 445, 487

Hellenistic, referring to Greek culture between Alexander's death in 323 B.C. and the ascendancy of Rome, 6, 7, 12, 17, 21, 25, 38, 332, 426, 445–463, 515, 517, 518, 519, 520, 521, 522, 524, 530, 533, 539, 540, 543, 544

Hellenization, 409, 445, 454, 463, 480

Hellespont, straits between the Aegean Sea and the Sea of Marmora (= the Dardanelles), 100, 225, 258, 261, 266, 358, 359, 361–363

helots, state-owned slaves in Sparta, 199–202, 214, 224, 269, 281, 282, 342–344, 377, 378, 408, 467

Hephaestus (he-**fē**-stus), Greek god of smiths (= Roman Vulcan), 29, 32, 134, 389

Hera (**hē**-ra), "mistress?" daughter of Cronus and Rhea, wife and sister of Zeus (= Roman Juno), 68, 133–139, 146, 148, 484

Heracles (**her**-a-klēz. Herakles), son of Zeus and Alcmena, greatest of Greek heroes, 9, 37, 39, 138, 319, 324, 331, 390, 435, 443

Heraclitus of Ephesus (535–475 B.C.), presocratic philosopher, 294, 295, 315, 396, 484

Hercules, Roman form of Heracles (which see), 9

Hermes, son of Zeus and Maia, Greek god of travel, tricks, commerce, and thievery (= Roman Mercury), 30–32, 67, 68, 107, 113, 114, 115, 135, 196, 222, 334, 350, 388

herms, apotropaic pillars with head of Hermes, erect phallus, 350, 367

Herodotus (her-**od**-o-tus) (ca. 484–425 B.C.), Greek historian, 6, 9, 17, 120, 152, 153, 156, 158, 164, 166, 168, 169, 179, 180, 197, 214–216, 218, 223, 229–236, 239–258, 262–267, 270–274, 282, 330, 391, 423, 482, 484

Hesiod, Greek poet, eighth century B.C., composer of *Works and Days* and *Theogony*, 6, 14–16, 26–29, 32, 34, 75–78, 81, 82, 85, 86, 121–124, 131–135, 138, 139, 150, 151, 159, 188, 210

Hestia (**hes**-ti-a), Greek goddess of the hearth (= Roman Vesta), 38, 40

*hetaira* (he-**tī**-ra), "companioness," Greek courtesan, 159

Hiero (1) I (unknown–467 B.C.), Sicilian tyrant 256, 275, 276, 322, 380, (2) II (269–215 B.C.), Sicilian tyrant, 385, 502, 503, 510–512

high classical, style in Greek art, 302, 308, 315

Hipparchus (hi-**par**-kus. Hipparkhos), Athenian leader, son of Pisistratus, sixth century B.C., brother of Hippias, 95, 217, 224

Hippias (**hip**-i-as), brother of Hipparchus, son of Pisistratus, 217–219, 223, 224, 248, 249, 298, 305

Hippocrates (fifth century B.C.), Greek physician, 21, 26, 27, 165, 255, 256, 499–502, 506

*historiê*, "inquiry," into the causes of human events, 179, 180

Hittites (**hit**-ītz), Indo-European Bronze Age warrior people in central Anatolia, whose capital was Hattusas near modern Ankara, 67, 69, 72, 135

Homer, composer of the *Iliad* and the *Odyssey*, eighth century B.C., 6, 9, 39, 48, 64–69, 75, 76, 79–86, 89–122, 126–130, 137–143, 147, 150, 156, 161, 179, 180, 192, 199, 318, 320, 324, 329, 331, 342, 389, 398, 458, 459, 483, 485, 523

Homeric Question, really "Homeric Investigation," into the origin of Homer's texts, 96

hoplites (**hop**-lītz), "shield-bearers," heavy-armed Greek warriors of Classical Period, 156, 157, 170, 209, 218, 229, 248–251, 254, 258, 260, 262, 268, 271, 281, 289, 339, 341, 343, 347, 352, 358, 371–377, 408–412, 416

Horus, the child of Isis and Osiris, 428, 520

human sacrifice, 75, 138, 329, 509

humor, in the human body, 501

Hygieia (hī-**jē**-a), "health," daughter of Asclepius, 21

Hyperion (hi-**per**-ion), "he who travels above," a Titan sun god, 111, 113, 116

Iapetus (ī-**ap**-e-tus. Iapetos), a Titan, 131, 133, 139

Icarus (**ik**-a-rus. Ikaros), drowned when he disobeyed his father Daedalus' instructions not to fly close to the sun, 183

Ilium (Ilion), another name for Troy, 100

Illyria, the northeast coast of the Ionian Sea (coast of Albania, Montenegro), 410, 411

Imbros, island in the northeast Aegean, 372, 373

Indians, 439, 440

Indo-European language, 45

Indo-Europeans, 44, 45, 50, 70, 71

inductive method, 299, 315, 502

Ion (ī-on), son of Apollo, eponymous ancestor of the Ionians, 9, 175, 329

Ionia, the west coast of Asia Minor, 5, 177, 179, 190, 196, 197, 229, 243–244, 272, 279, 294–297, 319, 360, 361, 370–372, 406, 418, 420, 422, 466, 491, 495

Ionian Enlightenment, 175, 177, 180, 499

Ionians, a division of the Greek people, 9, 10, 190, 230, 235, 243–247, 270, 271, 278, 279, 295, 296, 319, 320, 373, 417, 420

Ionic order, in Greek architecture, 189–190, 308, 309, 390–394, 488, 492

Iphigenia (if-i-jen-**ī**-a), daughter of Agamemnon and Clytemnestra, sacrificed by her father at Aulis (or transported to Tauris in the Crimea), 138, 329, 330

Ipsus, site in central Anatolia where Antigonus I was defeated and killed in 301 B.C., 447, 452, 461, 463

Iraq, 3, 7, 43, 72, 226, 228, 229, 236, 430

Iris (ī-ris), "rainbow," messenger of the gods, 304, 306

Ishtar, Akkadian fertility goddess, 227

Isis (ī-sis), Egyptian goddess, wife of Osiris, 121

Ismenus (is-**mē**-nus) River, near Thebes, 142

Issus, in northeastern Syria, where Alexander defeated Darius III in 333 B.C., 421, 425, 426, 429

Istanbul, formerly Byzantium, then Constantinople, 93, 245, 274

Italy, 26, 78, 111, 112, 163, 165, 175–177, 179, 252, 255, 257, 264, 277, 286, 287, 295, 299–302, 312–314, 320, 349, 350, 357, 358, 382–384, 393, 394, 442, 473–475, 484, 491, 494, 507–539, 520, 523, 524, 528, 530, 536, 542

Ithaca (Ithaka), off the northwest coast of Greece, home of Odysseus, one of the Ionian Islands, 82–85, 99, 111–114, 117, 118, 140, 150, 173, 292, 367, 385, 539

Jason of Pherae (fourth century B.C.), Thessalian strongman, 376–377, 385, 406, 446
Jason, husband of Medea, leader of the Argonauts, 483
Jesus of Nazareth (ca. 7 B.C.–A.D. 30), 1, 120, 125, 130, 519, 539
Julius Caesar, see Caesar, Julius

*kakoi*, "the bad," members of the lower classes, 151, 161, 164, 167, 168, 172, 211, 221
*katastrophê*, "turning downward," in plot, 329, 336
*katharsis*, "relief," said of Greek tragedy, 328, 329, 331, 336
Keats, John (1795–1821 A.D.), British poet, 2, 3, 544
Korê (**kō**-rē), "girl," an archaic female clothed statue, 186, 188
Kosovo, site of battle in 1389 between Turks and Serbs, celebrated in guslar song, 100
*kouros* (pl. *kouroi*), an archaic nude male statue, 185, 186

Labyrinth (**lab**-e-rinth), "house of the double-ax," home of the Minotaur, 51
Lacedaemon (las-e-**dē**-mon. Lakedaimon), another name for Sparta, or the territory around it, 201–203
Laconia (la-**kō**-ni-a), territory in the southern Peloponnesus surrounding Sparta, 199–203, 209, 224
Laestrygonians (les-tri-**gō**-ni-anz. Laistrygones), "gnashers," cannibal-giants who destroy all Odysseus' ships save one, 117, 494
Laius (**lā**-yus. Laios), father of Oedipus, killed at a cross road, 143, 329
Larissa, a town in Thessaly, 411, 412
Leda (**lē**-da), wife of Tyndareus, mother of Helen, 434
legend, "things that must be read," stories of famous early men and women, 58, 62, 163, 182, 192, 199, 458, 519
Lemnos, island in the northern Aegean, associated with Hephaestus, 18, 20, 320, 372, 373
Lerna, swamp in the Argolid where archaeological remains from the Early Bronze Age survive, 46–50, 70
Lesbos, island in the Aegean, near Troy, 29, 182, 230, 340, 362, 525
Leto (**lē**-tō), mother of Apollo and Artemis, 126, 127, 133, 138
Leuctra, site of Epaminondas' victory over Sparta in 371 B.C., 377, 378, 385, 409
Linear A writing, 91
Linear B writing, 70
Lion Gate at Mycenae, 63, 66
Livy (59 B.C.–A.D. 17), Roman historian, 518, 540
*logos*, "word," Stoic principal of divine intelligence, 294, 295, 315, 498, 506
Lord, Albert B. (1912–1991), student and assistant to Milman Parry, author of *The Singer of Tales*, 1, 68, 69, 97, 98, 228, 303, 431
lost-wax technique, in casting, 300, 315
Lotus Eaters, tempted Odysseus' crew with a drug that removes all longing to go home, 115
Lucretius (lu-**krē**-shus) (ca. 99–44 B.C.), Epicurean author of *De rerum natura*, "On the Nature of Things," 496
Lycurgus (lī-**kur**-gus) (seventh century B.C.), Spartan law-giver, 165, 199–207, 211, 215, 224, 468, 471
Lydia, a region in western Anatolia centered on Sardis, 26, 171, 182, 196, 223, 225, 229, 230, 233, 235, 252, 258, 325, 526
Lysander (fifth century B.C.), Spartan general, 362–372, 377, 384

Lysimachus (ca. 355–281 B.C.), a general of Alexander, 448–456, 463
Lysistrata (li-**sis**-tra-ta), "looser of armies," heroine in play by Aristophanes, leads a sex strike, 332, 336

magic, "art of the Magi," 17, 31, 121, 125–127, 142, 148, 229
Mantineia, site of Spartan defeat in 367 B.C., 338, 347, 348, 372, 378, 379
Marathon, plain near Athens where Persians were defeated in 490 B.C., 200, 217, 220, 243, 247–252, 259, 271, 318, 345, 387
March of the Ten Thousand, through Persia, in 399 B.C., 371, 412
Marduk (**mar**-dūk), Babylonian storm god, 135, 236, 237
Marius (157–86 B.C.), Roman general, enemy of Sulla, 524, 526, 528, 539, 540
Marmara (**mar**-mar-a), Sea of, between the Aegean and the Black Sea (= Propontis), 420
Medea (me-**dē**-a), witch from Colchis, wife of Jason, 38, 319, 323
Medes (mēdz), another name for the Persians, 229, 252, 262, 276, 432, 442
Mediterranean triad, bread, olives, wine, 23, 26, 45
Megara (**meg**-a-ra), city between Corinth and Athens, 168, 200, 210, 215, 255, 279, 282–284, 291, 331–335, 338, 347
megaron, "great hall," a large room in the center of which was a circular hearth and a smoke hole above, 63, 70
Mejedovich, Avdo (1875–1953), M. Parry's best guslar, 97
Melos (**mē**-los), one of the Cycladic islands, whose population the Athenians destroyed in 416 B.C., 338, 347, 367, 491
Memnon, king of Ethiopia, ally of the Trojans in postHomeric epic, 419–423
Menander (ca. 342–291 B.C.), Athenian comic playwright, wrote New Comedy, 15, 485, 506
Menelaüs (men-e-**lā**-us. Menelaos), son of Atreus, husband of Helen, brother of Agamemnon, 105, 110
Mercury, Roman god of commerce, equated with Greek Hermes, 32
Mesopotamia, "land between the rivers," the Euphrates and the Tigris, 3–6, 13, 47, 73, 119, 176, 196, 226, 228, 233, 235, 237, 241, 431, 438, 445, 452, 455, 456, 519, 531, 536
Messenia (mes-**sē**-ni-a), territory in the southwest Peloponnesus, 61, 79, 80, 92, 201, 209, 224, 285, 377, 378, 467
Messina, Straits of, between Sicily and the toe of Italy, 112, 277
*miasma* (mī-**as**-ma), "stench," the pollution that attends the shedding of blood, 143
Midas (**mī**-das), Phrygian king, in legend cursed by the golden touch, 229, 252, 423
Miletus, an important city in Ionia, 152, 168, 175, 177, 179, 242–247, 268, 294
Miltiades (mil-**tī**-a-dēz), Athenian commander at Marathon, 243, 249, 250, 252
*mimesis*, "representation," the essence of literary narrative according to Aristotle, 328–329, 336
Minoans, Bronze Age inhabitants of Crete, 55, 57, 62, 63, 80
Minos (**mī**-nos), Cretan king of Cnossus, son of Zeus and Europa, husband of Pasiphaë, judge in the underworld, 51, 52, 57, 70, 183
Minotaur (**mī**-no-tawr), "bull of Minos," half-man, half-bull offspring of Pasiphaë and a bull, 51, 70, 183
misogyny, "woman-hatred,", 29, 40, 333
Mithridates (134–63 B.C.), king of Pontus, enemy of Rome, 524–530, 539, 540
Moerae (**mē**-rē. Moirai), "portions," the Fates, 131
moral relativism, 297, 298, 315
motif, an element in folktale, 54, 63, 113, 116, 536
Motya, island off west coast of Sicily settled by Phoenicians, 254, 256, 260, 382, 382
Mouseion, "temple of the Muses," in Alexandria, Egypt, 461, 483

Muses, the inspirers of oral song, a personification of the oral tradition, 65, 67, 81, 121, 122, 133–135, 139, 148, 180, 181, 461, 483

Mycalê, peninsula in Asia Minor, site of Persian defeat in 479 B.C., 267, 278

Mycenae (mī-**sē**-nē. Mykenai), largest Bronze Age settlement in the Argive plain, home of the house of Atreus, 47, 59–61, 65, 70, 102, 162

Myrmidons (**mir**-mi-dons), "ants," followers of Achilles, 141

myth, "word, plot," a traditional tale with collective importance, 119–149, 316, 336

Mytilenê (mit-i-**lē**-nē), city on Lesbos, revolted from Athenian empire in 427 B.C., 340, 345

Naples, "new city," a Greek colony in southern Italy, 78, 111–113, 218, 275, 295, 475

Naucratis, Greek trading colony in the Egyptian delta, 175, 184

Nausicaä (na-**sik**-a-a), "ship-girl," Phaeacian princess who helped Odysseus, 114, 117, 137

Naxos, one of the Cycladic islands, 231, 244, 247, 248, 279, 280, 351

nectar (nektar), "deathless," drink of the gods, 138

Nemea (**nem**-e-a), village west of Mycenae, where Heracles killed the lion, 152, 163

Neolithic ("new stone age") Revolution, dependent on the first agriculture, 44–46, 50, 70, 71, 91

Neoptolemus (nē-op-**tol**-e-mus. Neoptolemos), "new-fighter," son of Achilles, 129

Nereids (**nē**-re-idz), "daughters of Nereus," nymphs of the sea, 535

Nestor, garrulous septuagenarian Greek at Troy, who owned a famous elaborate cup, 114, 342

Nicias (fifth century B.C.), Athenian general, 338, 343, 344, 347–355, 358, 367, 368

Nineveh (**nin**-e-va), capital of the Assyrians on the upper Tigris river, destroyed 612 B.C., 226–229

Noah, biblical survivor of the Flood, 139

nymphs, "young women," spirits of nature, 122, 125, 146

Oceanus (o-**sē**-a-nus, Okeanos), Ocean, a Titan, the river that encircles the earth, 133, 139

Octavian, see Augustus

Odysseus, son of Laertes, husband of Penelopê, 66, 81–85, 95, 97, 99, 105, 110–118, 128, 137–141, 150, 161, 162, 192, 313, 327–331, 339, 493

*Odyssey*, by Homer, 6, 22, 64, 66, 76, 78, 79, 82–85, 89, 93, 95, 99, 109–119, 139, 140, 324, 329, 331, 458, 497

Oedipus (**ē**-di-pus, or **ed**-i-pus. Oidipous), "swellfoot," son of Laius and Jocasta, married his mother, killed his father, 38, 76, 121, 128, 142, 143, 318, 323, 329, 330, 339

*Oedipus at Colonus*, a play by Sophocles, 329

*oikos*, "household", 28, 35, 40, 118

Old Testament, 237

oligarchy, "rule by the few," 151, 172, 257, 360, 365, 366, 449, 467

Olympia, sanctuary of Zeus in the western Peloponnesus, site of the Olympic games, 78, 86, 87, 92, 152, 161–163, 172, 175, 183, 278, 338, 374, 389, 390, 407, 411, 477, 525, 526

Olympians, Zeus and his cohorts and children, 132, 134, 147–149, 330

Olympias (ca. 376–317 B.C.), mother of Alexander the Great, 411, 417, 418, 429, 447–449, 463, 476

Olympic games, founded in 776 B.C., 162, 165, 168, 383, 400, 406, 408

Olympus, Mount, in north Greece between Thessaly and Macedonia, 13, 30, 47, 66, 83, 113, 121, 122, 132, 138, 260, 429

Orchomenus (or-**kom**-en-us. Orkhomenos), major Bronze Age site in northern Boeotia, 106

*Oresteia* (or-es-**tī**-a, "story of Orestes"), trilogy of plays by Aeschylus, 140, 322, 323, 329, 336

Orestes (or-**es**-tez), son of Agamemnon and Clytemnestra, who killed his mother and her lover Aegisthus to avenge his father, 38, 39, 113, 114, 139, 321, 323, 329, 330

Orpheus (**or**-fūs), son of Apollo, musician, tried to bring back his wife Eurydice from the dead, 144, 145

Orphism, teaching allegedly from Orpheus about human destiny, 125, 145

Ortygia (or-**tij**-a), "quail island," equated with Delos, birthplace of Apollo and Artemis, 351, 353, 380

Osiris (ō-**sī**-ris), Egyptian god of resurrection, husband of Isis, 121, 479

Ossa, mountain in northern Greece, 260, 418

ostracism, 169, 172, 220, 224, 277

Ottoman empire, 2

Palestine, the southern portion of the eastern end of the Mediterranean Sea, named after the Philistines, 70, 73, 87, 530

Pallas (**pal**-as), an epithet for Athena, 64, 66, 142, 163

Panathenaic Festival (pan-ath-en-**ē**-ic), annual festival to Athena at Athens, 131, 163, 217, 305

Pandora (pan-**dor**-a), "gift of all," or "all-giver," the first woman, who released evils into the world, 30–32

*pankration*, "all-in wrestling," permitting various techniques, 162, 172

papyrus, Egyptian "the thing of the royal house," because its sale was a royal monopoly, 30, 63, 93, 180, 183, 457, 484, 485, 491, 495

paradoxes of Zeno, 296, 315

parchment, a writing surface made from the skin of a sheep or goat, 491

Paris, son of Priam and Hecabê, lover of Helen, 100, 137, 199

Parmenio, general of Alexander, 418–434

Paros, one of the Cycladic islands, 387, 389

Parry, Milman (1902–1935), American classicist, creator of the oral-formulaic theory of Homeric composition, 96–98

Parthenon, "place of the Virgin," temple to Athena on the Acropolis in Athens, 6, 131, 134, 147, 213, 303–315, 465, 488

Patroclus (pa-**trok**-lus. Patroklos), Achilles' best friend, killed by Hector, 102, 106–109, 141, 161, 192, 420

Paul, St. (unknown–A.D. 65), founder of the Christian church, from Tarsus in Cilicia, 11, 125, 130, 224, 385, 410, 456, 480, 534, 539

pederasty, "love for boys," 36, 37, 40, 163

pediment, the triangular area at the front and back of Greek temples, 303, 304, 375

Pelasgians, "peoples of the sea," an unknown people or peoples who lived in Greece before the Greeks came, 9

Peleus (**pē**-lūs), husband of Thetis, father of Achilles, 101, 143

Peloponnesian War (431–404 B.C.), 9, 18, 27, 79, 273, 292, 308, 318, 327, 332–333, 337–368, 385, 386, 393, 395, 406, 409, 476, 500, 509

Peloponnesus (pel-o-po-**nē**-sus. Peloponnesos), "island of Pelops," the southern portion of mainland Greece linked to the north by the narrow Isthmus of Corinth, 26, 78, 131, 165, 171, 258, 260, 267, 269, 286, 312, 319, 342, 347, 378, 470, 471, 475

Pentateuch (**pen**-ta-tūk), "five rolls," the first five books of the Bible, 94

Pentheus (**pen**-thūs), Theban king who opposed Dionysus, 121, 147, 325–329, 485

Perdiccas (unknown–320 B.C.), a general of Alexander, 409, 410, 443, 446–448

Pergamum (**per**-ga-mum), city in Asia Minor, center of a Hellenistic kingdom, 455, 463, 483, 487–493, 501, 522, 525, 543

Pericles (**per**-i-klēz) (495–429 B.C.), Athenian statesman, 17, 18, 35, 38, 219, 282–285, 290–292, 295, 305, 307, 318, 338–340, 344, 362, 414, 467, 477, 539

*peripeteia*, a "turning around" in Athenian tragedy, 329, 330, 336

Persephonê (per-**sef**-o-nē), daughter of Demeter, wife of Hades, (= Roman Proserpina), 140

Perseus (**per**-sūs), (reigned 179–168 B.C.), of Macedon, 515–518

Persia, 5, 6, 9, 18, 21, 158, 180, 196, 209, 217–221, 225–252, 260, 269, 271, 274, 278–284, 302, 330, 337, 344, 349, 360–363, 369–385, 406–408, 412–419, 422, 423, 428–429, 433, 436, 441, 456, 480, 483, 508, 519, 541, 542

Phaeacia (fē-**ā**-sha. Phaiakia), the island of Scheria, where Nausicaä lives, 112, 114, 117, 161

phalanx, in the Classical Period a form of close-line fighting whose deep ranks were made up of heavily-armed hoplites, 155–158, 172, 250, 262, 375, 377, 378, 410, 422, 425, 426, 516

Phemius (fē-mi-us), "the famous one," an *aoidos* who sang for the suitors, 99

Pherae (**fer**-ē), a town in Thessaly, 372, 376, 411, 412

Phidias (ca. 480–430 B.C.), sculptor who worked on the Parthenon, 6, 17, 131, 291, 293, 301–304, 308, 309, 315

Philip II (382–336 B.C.), father of Alexander the Great, 406–429, 446–452, 456, 462, 487

Philoctetes (fi-lok-**tē**-tēz. Philoktetes), inherited bow of Heracles, abandoned on Lemnos, 323

Phocis (**fō**-sis. Phokis), region in central Greece, where Delphi is, 412–416, 429, 466

Phoebus (**fē**-bus. Phoibos), see Apollo, 129, 133, 134, 138

Phoenicia, the coast of the Eastern Mediterranean, modern Lebanon, 14, 73, 77, 87, 229, 283

Phoenicians, "red-men," from the dye that stained their hands, a Semitic seafaring people living on the coast of the northern Levant, 26, 77, 78, 87–90, 113, 138, 153, 180, 225, 229, 238, 254–259, 261, 265, 275, 276, 358, 382, 425, 427, 442, 472, 497, 510, 519

Phrygia (**frij**-a), region in Asia Minor, 147, 229

Phthia (**thī**-a), region in southern Thessaly, home of Achilles, 105

Pindar (ca. 522–423 B.C.), Greek poet, 163, 164, 172, 273–276, 419

Pindus (Pindos), range of mountains that forms the backbone of Greece, 13

Pisistratus (pi-**sis**-tra-tus) (sixth century B.C.–527 B.C.), tyrant of Athens, 95, 214–220, 224, 233, 248, 249, 320, 321, 465, 538

Plataea (pla-**tē**-a), site of battle in southern Boeotia against the Persians in 479 B.C., 247, 249, 267–278, 345, 347

Plato (428–348 B.C.), Greek philosopher, 5, 12, 17, 35, 37, 45, 62, 95, 145, 158, 204, 221, 224, 229, 293, 297–299, 365–368, 383, 384, 395–405, 414, 456, 495, 501, 504, 535, 539

Plautus (**plaw**-tus) (ca. 254–184 B.C.), Roman playwright, 485

plot, 35, 98, 108, 109, 117, 119, 202, 217, 239, 319–328, 332, 346, 350, 381, 409, 412, 434, 485

plot-point, separates the parts of a plot, 109, 114, 117

pluralists, Greek philosophers who sought more than one prime element, 296, 315

Plutarch (ca. A.D. 46–120), Greek essayist and historian, 16, 28, 199–208, 211, 214, 224, 282, 291–293, 305, 307, 361, 368, 370, 377, 378, 384, 415, 416, 425, 429–433, 441, 451, 452, 459, 470, 471, 474–482, 487, 514, 521, 522, 527, 533–537, 540

*polis*, "city state," the principal form of political and social organization during the Classical Period, 4, 5, 9, 28, 80, 106, 142, 150, 151, 157, 166–170, 190, 208, 209, 233, 241, 243, 276–279, 297, 323, 331, 367, 369, 376, 391, 395, 399–403, 411, 412, 455, 471, 479, 486, 495, 499, 530, 543, 544

pollution, see miasma

Pollux (= Polydeuces (pol-i-dū-sēz. Polydeukes), legendary brother of Castor, 165, 434, 434

Polybius (ca. 200–118 B.C.), Greek historian, 459, 464, 465, 482, 483, 506, 509, 511, 516–517, 540

Polynices (pol-i-**nī**-sēz. Polyneikes), son of Oedipus, buried by Antigonê, 324

Polypemon (pol-i-**pem**-on), "troubler," another name for Procrustes, enemy of Theseus, 319

Polyperchon (unknown–320 B.C.), regent of Macedonia, 448–451

Polyphemus (pol-i-**fē**-mus. Polyphemos), "much famed," the Cyclops blinded by Odysseus, 115, 313, 314

polytheistic, "believing in many gods," 124, 125, 147, 148, 172

Polyxena (po-**lik**-se-na), Trojan princess sacrificed over the grave of Achilles, 129

Pompey (**pom**-pē. Pompeius), the Great (106–48 B.C.), Roman statesman and general, enemy of Julius Caesar, 528–534, 539, 540

Pontus (Pontos), "sea," (1) offspring of Gaea, 123; (2) kingdom south of the Black Sea, ruled by Mithridates, 286, 525

Porus (fourth century B.C.), Indian leader who fought Alexander, 436, 444, 452

Poseidon (po-**sī**-don), Greek god of the sea, Zeus, 51, 67, 68, 113, 114, 117, 133–134, 138, 148, 259, 300, 311, 319, 335, 443

Priam (**prī**-am. Priamos), king of Troy, husband of Hekabê, father of Hector and Paris, 107, 108, 129

primary sources, 51, 52, 57, 67, 70, 94, 100

Procris (**prok**-ris), daughter of Erechtheus, wife of Cephalus who killed her accidentally, 148

Procrustes (pro-**krus**-tēz), "stretcher," killed by Theseus, 320

Prometheus (prō-**mē**-thūs), "forethinker," a Titan, maker and benefactor of humankind, 31, 32, 131, 222, 272, 327, 336

prophecy, 107, 138, 318

Propylaea, "fore-gate," to the Athenian Acropolis, 306–309, 315

*proskynêsis*, "bowing down to kiss the ground," before the emperor, 436, 444

protagonist, "first actor," in Athenian tragedy, 321, 329–332, 335

Protagoras (pro-**tag**-o-ras) (ca. 490–420 B.C.), Greek philosopher (a sophist), 221–224, 228, 315, 405

Protoattic, style in Greek pottery decoration, 192–194

Protogeometric, artistic style ca. 1025–900 B.C., 77, 92

proto-Indo-European, 45, 70

*psychê* (plural *psychai*), "breath, soul," the ghost that survives the death of the body, 139–141, 177, 399

Ptolemy (**to**-le mē), (fourth century B.C.), regent of Macedonia, 409; (1) Ptolemy I (367–282 B.C.), Alexander's general, occupied Egypt, 446, 448–454, 457, 458, 462, 466, 477, 483, 484, 511; (2) Ptolemy II (285–246 B.C.), son of Alexander's general, 458–461, 467, 473, 476, 484, 485; (3) Ptolemy III, 471; (4) Ptolemy IV, 462, 471, 515; (5) Ptolemy V, 517; (6) Ptolemy VIII, "Fatso," 520; (7) Ptolemy XII, killed Pompey, 532; (8) Ptolemy XIII, brother of Cleopatra VII, 532, 533; (9) Claudius Ptolemy (ca. 87–150 A.D.), Alexandrian astronomer, 504–506

*publicani*, Roman tax-collectors, 511, 524, 530, 534, 539

Punic (**pū**-nik) Wars, between Carthage and Rome, third-second centuries B.C., 382, 510–512, 515, 540

Pylos (**pī**-los), Bronze Age settlement in the southwest Peloponnesus where important archaeological remains have been found, 47, 61, 62, 64, 67–70, 114, 338, 342–344, 347, 367

Pyrrhus (**pir**-us. Pyrrhos) (third century B.C.), "red head," king of Epirus, 454, 473–476, 480, 507, 509, 518

Pythagoras (pith-**ag**-or-as) (sixth century B.C.), Greek philosopher, 177–179, 197, 295, 296 red-figure, a style in Greek pottery decoration, 30, 376, 394

Remus (rē-mus), twin founder of Rome, 507

Renaissance, period of cultural ferment mostly in Italy, in fourteenth-sixteenth centuries A.D., 78, 395, 486

*res publica* (rās **pub**-li-ka), "public matter," the oligarchic government at Rome before 30 B.C. when Augustus defeated Marc Antony and Cleopatra, 507

revealed religion, has a founder, 125, 147, 148

rhapsode, "staff-singer," performers who memorized written poetry, especially Homer, 95

Rhea (rē-a. Rheia), a Titaness, wife of Cronus, 122, 124

Rhodes (rōdz), Aegean island near southwestern tip of Asia Minor, 224, 405, 411, 447, 451, 452, 455, 465, 483, 525

Romulus (rom-u-lus), twin founder of Rome, 507

Roxane, Alexander's Asian wife, 435, 436, 444–450

sacrifice, "making separate," 51, 68, 124, 126–132, 138–143, 147, 148, 259, 271, 323, 329–332, 334, 344, 434, 473, 485, 542

Salamis (sal-a-mis), island near the port of Athens, site of Persian naval defeat in 480 B.C., 200, 211, 215, 261–268, 271, 272, 275, 276, 280

Samos (sā-mos), island in the east Aegean, 152, 171, 175, 177, 242, 246, 268, 270, 285, 294, 359–363, 455, 465, 493–495, 504

Samothrace, island in the north Aegean, 483, 488, 489, 506

Sanskrit, an ancient Indian language, 44

Sappho (sixth century B.C.), Greek poet, 29, 30, 40, 158, 182, 183, 229

Sardis, capital of Lydia, 223, 226, 230, 234, 235, 244, 246, 249, 253, 258, 261, 266, 325, 371, 372, 423

Scamander River, on the Trojan plain, 100, 107

Schliemann, Heinrich (1822–1890), German archaeologist, 59, 60, 100, 101

Scipio, Africanus (236–183 B.C.) Roman general during the second Punic War, 514–517, 539

Sciron (skī-ron), "limestone," brigand killed by Theseus, 319

Scylla (sil-la), "dog," many-headed monster who attacked Odysseus, 112, 116, 117

Second Palace Period, on Crete, ca. 1800–1400 B.C., 53, 70

secondary products revolution, 45, 91

secondary sources, 52, 70

Selenê (se-lē-nē), goddess of the moon, 133

Seleucus I (305–281 B.C.), (1) Alexander's general, the founder of a line of Hellenistic kings (several named Antiochus), 448–457, 462 (2) II (246–225 B.C.), son of the former, 456

Selinus, powerful Greek city in southwest Sicily, 175, 190, 254, 259, 271, 275, 277, 294, 312, 341, 348–352, 356–358, 379, 382, 512

Semelê (sem-e-lē), mother to Dionysus, destroyed by lightning, 325, 327

Semites, "descendants of Shem," a son of Noah, peoples of the Near East speaking a language with triconsonantal roots, including Assyrians, Babylonians, Hebrews, Phoenicians, 87–90, 473, 512

Senate, "body of old men," in ancient Rome, 498, 525, 526

Serapis, "Osiris-Apis [bull]," a god invented by the Ptolemies, 479, 480

Seven Wonders of the Ancient World, 525

severe style, in Greek art, 299, 300, 315

Shakespeare (1564–1616), English playwright, 110, 485, 523, 530, 536

shame culture, where social sanctions are external, 102, 106

Sicily, 5, 8, 9, 26, 66, 78–80, 111, 153, 169, 179, 190, 196, 209, 229, 254–260, 271–278, 285, 286, 291, 296–297, 299, 312, 317, 320, 322, 337–341, 348–358, 361, 367, 368, 380, 382–385, 404, 406, 414, 415, 442, 445, 471–476, 484, 486, 510–513, 517–519, 524, 542

Sicyon (sis-i-on), city in the northern Peloponnesus, 131, 152, 166, 268, 270, 387

Sinis (sī-nis), pinebender killed by Theseus, 319

Sirens, creatures who through the beauty of their song lured sailors to their deaths, 116, 117

Sisyphus (sis-i-fus. Sisyphos), punished in the underworld, 497

Skepticism, a philosophical school that doubted knowledge is possible, 495, 506

slavery, 25, 26, 172, 210, 211, 214, 246, 250, 275, 277, 286, 345, 357, 413, 419, 427, 498, 518, 521, 528, 540

Socrates (469–399 B.C.), Athenian philosopher, executed by the state, 17, 32–34, 221, 293, 297–299, 315, 332, 338, 361, 364–368, 371, 395–399, 405, 539

*Song of Roland*, medieval French epic, 100

sophists, 297–299, 315, 327, 332, 396, 399, 498

Sophocles (496–406 B.C.), Greek playwright, 6, 17, 45, 142, 293, 317–324, 325, 336, 339, 485

soul, 34, 69, 139, 145, 147, 158, 177, 178, 294, 297, 307, 328, 353, 398, 399, 482

Sparta, city in southern Peloponnesus, 5, 8, 9, 37, 40, 79, 80, 95, 110, 152, 154, 169, 198–224, 234, 235, 242, 244, 247, 249, 251, 254, 258–262, 268, 269, 271–285, 290–292, 305, 311, 332, 338–351, 358–385, 404, 408, 411, 412, 417, 423, 443, 445, 455, 456, 467–471, 476, 477, 480, 525, 526, 542, 543

Spartan mirage, 199, 224

Sphacteria, an island in the bay of Pylos, 343, 344, 367

stoa, 491, 492, 498, 506, 511

stoicism, Greek philosophy that taught submission to natural law, 470, 497–501, 506, 523, 538, 543

Sulla (138–78 B.C.), Roman general and statesman, 526–532, 539, 540

symbolism, 117, 126, 183, 510

symposium, "drinking party," 36, 37, 159–161, 172, 173, 180–182, 322

Syracuse, powerful city in eastern Sicily, 5, 24, 79, 254–258, 273–291, 297–299, 302, 305, 312, 314, 317, 322, 331, 333, 337–341, 348–358, 67, 369, 379–383, 404, 406, 411, 414, 415, 454–456, 471–475, 484, 502, 503, 510–514, 521, 542

Syria, the territory surrounding the upper Euphrates, 17, 43, 52, 57, 68, 69, 72, 73, 77, 87, 135, 187, 212, 423, 425, 444, 445, 452, 455, 456, 515, 517, 519, 543

tablets, for writing, 52, 64, 67–69, 160, 517

talent, a large unit of money, 408, 434, 442, 454, 476

Tantalus (tan-ta-lus. Tantalos), one of the damned in the underworld, 497

Tartarus (Tartaros), place for punishment in the underworld, 122

Telemachus (tel-em-a-kus. Telemakhos), "far-fighter," son of Odysseus and Penelopê, 66, 82–84, 99, 114, 118, 150

Telephus (tel-e-fus. Telephos), a son of Heracles, wounded and healed by Achilles, 488

Tenedos (ten-e-dos), an Aegean island near Troy, 126–128

Teshub (tesh-ūb), the Hittite storm god, 135

Thales, sixth century B.C., Milesian philosopher, 175–180, 316

theater, 128, 247, 307, 323, 324, 372, 383, 393, 424, 455, 465, 491, 492, 511, 512, 514

Thebes (thēbz), principal city in Boeotia, 75, 86, 106, 121, 142, 147, 200, 222, 249, 261, 271, 325–338, 347, 359, 363, 364, 369, 372–379, 404, 409–419, 443–445, 467, 471

Themis (them-is), "law," a Titan, 83

Themistocles (the-mis-to-klēz) (ca. 524–459 B.C.), Athenian statesman, 221, 257, 261–266, 271, 272, 278, 280, 292, 477

Theognis (sixth century B.C.), Greek aristocratic poet from Megara, 27, 160–164, 167, 168, 172

Thera (**thē**-ra), southernmost of the Cyclades (modern Santorini), 58, 71

Theseus (**thē**-sūs), son of Poseidon and Aethra, father of Hippolytus, killer of the Minotaur, 137, 319, 320, 329

Thespiae (**thes**-pi-ē), town in Boeotia, 262

Thespis (sixth century B.C.), inventor of tragedy, 320–322, 331, 336

Thessaly, region in Greece south of Mt. Olympus, 105, 132, 166, 218, 260, 266, 267, 372, 376–378, 412, 415, 418, 466, 516, 532, 543

Thetis (**the**-tis), mother of Achilles, 105, 133, 138

Thirty, The, an oligarchic cabal in Athens, 274, 467

tholos, (1) a kind of Bronze Age underground tomb on mainland Greece in the shape of a beehive, 61; (2) a circular temple from the Classical and Hellenistic Periods, 390, 393, 404

Thrace, region northeast of Greece, 145, 243, 266, 297, 344, 410, 415, 446–454, 466

Thucydides (thu-**sid**-i-dēz) (ca. 460–395 B.C.), Athenian historian, 6–9, 17–20, 26, 27, 51, 52, 55, 57, 58, 67, 112, 120, 168, 169, 210, 273, 281–286, 291, 293–295, 337–349, 353–355, 361, 367, 368, 408, 482, 500, 522, 539, 543

Thyestes (thī-**es**-tēz), father of Aegisthus, brother of Atreus, 330

thyrsus, phallic staff carried by followers of Dionysus, 147, 324, 325

Tiamat (**tē**-a-mat), Babylonian monster, 176

Tiber River, in Italy, 508

*Timaeus*, dialogue of Plato, 405, 440

*timê* (**tē**-mā), "value, worth," the honor for which a hero strives, 102–110

Tiresias (ti-**rē**-si-as), blind prophet of Thebes, 115, 139, 140, 325

Tiryns (**tir**-inz), Bronze Age city in Argive plain, 47, 50, 96

Titans (**tī**-tans), offspring of Uranus and Gaea, 122, 148, 330

Tityus (**tit**-i-us), tortured in the underworld by vultures, 497

Tmolus (**tmō**-lus), Mount, behind Sardis, 325

tragedy, "goat-song," a dramatization of legend in festivals at Athens, 38, 142, 147, 194, 247, 272, 320–333, 336, 339, 366, 383, 395, 482, 485

triumph, Roman military parade, 118, 122, 164, 274, 283, 339, 369, 371, 427, 509, 517, 521, 530, 536–537

Troezen (**trē**-zen), city in the Argolid, associated with Theseus, 268

Trojan War, 8, 9, 67, 70, 76, 100, 101, 110, 118, 121, 137, 180, 192, 193, 199, 329, 420, 507

*Trojan Women*, a play by Euripides, 327

Troy, in northwestern Asia Minor, 46, 59, 64–67, 76, 81–83, 89, 100–110, 114–116, 129, 138, 140, 161, 182, 199, 324, 327, 330, 339, 340, 387, 400, 420, 424, 434, 507

Tunis, in North Africa, 229

Turkey, 5, 8, 17, 43, 45, 57, 100, 136, 175, 223, 425

Tyndareus (tin-**dar**-e-us. Tyndareos), Spartan king, father of Leda, 434

tyranny, when one man ruled, 95, 166–173, 177, 182, 191, 209, 210, 211, 214, 215, 242–243, 256–258, 273–278, 289, 320, 322, 337, 349, 376, 404, 412, 413, 419, 469, 483, 510, 538

Tyre, Phoenician city in the Levant, 73, 77, 226, 427–428

Uranus (**yur**-a-nus. Ouranos), "sky," one of the first gods, consort of Gaea, castrated by his son Cronus, 122–124, 148

Vatican, one of the seven hills of Rome, 391

Ventris, Michael (1922–1956), British decipherer of Linear B, 61

Venus de Milo, 490, 491, 506

Venus, Roman equivalent to Greek Aphrodite, 32, 174, 490, 491, 506

Vergil (70–19 B.C.), Roman poet, 483, 538

Vesta, Roman goddess of the hearth (= Greek Hestia), 525

violated prohibition, 113, 116

Vulcan, Italian fire god (= Greek Hephaestus), 32

West Semitic writing, a family of scripts from ca. 1800 B.C., including Phoenician, Hebrew, and Arabic, 87–89, 92

white-ground style, in Greek art, 313, 315

Wolf, Frederick August (1759–1824), German classicist who formulated the modern Homeric Question, 94–96

*Works and Days*, poem by Hesiod, eighth century B.C., 14–16, 26, 27, 32, 76, 82, 85, 86, 151, 210

Writing, a system of marks with a conventional reference that communicates information, 2, 4, 7–9, 16, 26, 50, 54, 61, 62, 66, 67, 70, 73, 80, 87, 89, 90, 95–100, 108, 120, 121, 125, 158, 180, 199, 207, 267, 305, 330, 361, 418, 429, 446, 449, 454, 481–485, 539

*xenia* (ksen-**ē**-a), "guest friendship," the conventions that govern relationships between host and guest, 117

Xenophon (**ksen**-o-fon) (430–354 B.C.), philosopher and essayist, friend to Socrates, leader in the March of the Ten Thousand, 32, 34, 37, 38, 40, 199, 201, 207, 224, 361, 363, 364, 371, 373, 376, 379, 385

Xerxes, the Great King of Persia (reigned 485–465 B.C.), 253, 254, 257–268, 271–273, 280–281, 302, 330, 349, 420, 432

Zeno (**zē**-nō) (1) (fifth century B.C.), Eleatic philosopher (see *paradoxes of Zeno*), 295, 296; (2) (334–262 B.C.), founder of Stoicism, 497, 498

Zeus, "shining," son of Cronus and Rhea, Greek storm-god, 29–33, 67, 68, 75, 76, 81, 83, 84, 86, 102–106, 111–125, 131–149, 143, 144, 147–148, 151, 168, 170, 188, 222, 275, 300, 325, 334, 423, 429, 434–436, 459, 465, 472, 479, 484, 487, 488, 538

Zoroaster (zor-o-**as**-ter) (sixth century B.C.), Persian prophet, who founded a religion named after him, 125, 237